Chant of Saints

CHANT OF SAINTS

A Gathering of Afro-American Literature, Art, and Scholarship

Edited by
Michael S. Harper
and Robert B. Stepto

UNIVERSITY OF ILLINOIS PRESS
Urbana   Chicago   London

for Sterling A. Brown

"YOU DID WHAT YOU DID"

CONTENTS

Foreword *by John Hope Franklin*   ix

Preface   xiii

A Son's Return: "Oh, Didn't He Ramble" *by Sterling A. Brown*   3

"Uplift from a Dark Tower" and Other Poems
   by Michael S. Harper   23

The Historical Frequencies of Ralph Waldo Ellison
   by John F. Callahan   33

Paintings *by Richard Yarde*   53

Elegies for Paradise Valley *by Robert Hayden*   61

Covenant of Timelessness and Time: Symbolism and History
   in Robert Hayden's *Angle of Ascent by Wilburn Williams, Jr.*   66

Sculpture *by Richard Hunt*   85

A Sense of Story *by James Alan McPherson*   87

A Music of the Streets *by Frederick Turner*   105

Someone Sweet Angel Child *by Sherley A. Williams*   117

The Blues Roots of Contemporary Afro-American Poetry
   by Sherley A. Williams   123

Packwood's Sermon by Firelight *by Leon Forrest*   136

"If He Changed My Name": *An Interview with Leon Forrest*   146

The Art of Romare Bearden *by Ralph Ellison*   158
   The Odysseus Collages *by Romare Bearden*

The Schooner *Flight by Derek Walcott*   166

Toward a World Black Literature and Community
   by Melvin Dixon   175

I Thought I Knew These People: Richard Wright and the
   Afro-American Literary Tradition *by Robert B. Stepto*   195

From *Sula by Toni Morrison*   212

"Intimate Things in Place": *A Conversation with Toni Morrison*   213

Siras Bowens of Sunbury, Georgia: A Tidewater Artist in the
   Afro-American Visual Tradition *by Robert Farris Thompson*   230

Africa, Slavery, and the Roots of Contemporary Black Culture
by Mary F. Berry and John W. Blassingame   241

Shadows in the Moonlight *by John Stewart*   257

Photographs *by Lawrence Sykes*   278

The Star-Apple Kingdom *by Derek Walcott*   286

Reflections before and after Carnival: *An Interview with
Derek Walcott*   296

The Militance of a Photograph in the Passbook of a Bantu
under Detention *by Michael S. Harper*   310

An Image of Africa *by Chinua Achebe*   313

Poems *by Robert Hayden*   326

Four Poems *by Michael S. Harper*   333

In My Father's House *by Ernest J. Gaines*   339

Almeyda *by Gayl Jones*   349

Gayl Jones: An Interview   352

Deep Song *by Gayl Jones*   376

Looking for Zora *by Alice Walker*   377

Love's Dozen *by Jay Wright*   393

Three Poems *by Michael S. Harper*   408

Late Coltrane: A Re-membering of Orpheus
by Kimberly W. Benston   413

From Experience to Eloquence: Richard Wright's *Black Boy*
as Art *by Charles T. Davis*   425

Duke Ellington Vamps 'til Ready *by Albert Murray*   440

Backwacking, A Plea to the Senator *by Ralph Ellison*   445

Study and Experience: *An Interview with Ralph Ellison*   451

After Modernism, After Hibernation: Michael Harper, Robert
Hayden, and Jay Wright *by Robert B. Stepto*   470

American Journal *by Robert Hayden*   487

FOREWORD

John Hope Franklin

Throughout the history of this country there have been some Negro Americans who have worked at the cutting edge of literary and artistic creativity. The national experience as well as their own peculiar experiences often prompted them to extend themselves to artistic expression of one form or another. Their poetry and song celebrated the achievements of their heroes and bemoaned the fate of their common folk. Their prose registered vigorous protests against slavery and other forms of human degradation. Their graphic arts captured the mood of the moment as well as the meaning of life. Some of the more gifted were sensitive to the creative impulse, while others were not conscious of the talents they possessed. Every age produced its complement of what Benjamin Brawley called "The Negro genius," while a somewhat incredulous America had difficulty in reconciling these feats to its theories of the innate inferiority of blacks.

Some thought that the poetry of Phillis Wheatley was not so good, while others doubted that she wrote it anyway. To the men at the University of North Carolina, the poetry that they hired George Moses Horton to write was more than satisfactory if the women for whom the lines were intended were duly impressed. David Walker's indictment of the United States government for protecting slavery was regarded by many as the most dangerous document that circulated in the Old South. The eloquence of a Frederick Douglass oration must have caused some to wonder about the doctrine of white supremacy. The *History of the Negro Race* by George Washington Williams was convincing proof that a black man could engage in a scholarly enterprise of the highest order. The lectures and essays of Frances E. W. Harper gave evidence of the oratorical skill as well as the sensitive creativity of a gifted black woman.

Prior to the present century the problem of literary and artistic creativity among Negro Americans was the problem of impact, of persuading the larger community of the existence of a "Negro genius." At the end of the last century and early in this one, numerous Negro Americans made strenuous efforts to demonstrate the existence of talent among them. There was a veritable outpouring of works with such ambitious and optimistic titles as *The Progress of a Race, Twentieth Century*

Afro-American   Literature,   and   *Afro-American   Encyclopaedia;   or
Thoughts, Doings, and Sayings of the Race*. If they indicated with some
degree of accuracy the status of Negroes in American life, they failed to
persuade many that the status was something to cheer about. And there
remained no significant, generally impressive statement on the subject
until well into the twentieth century.

The first important statement on the subject appeared in 1925 with
the publication of *The New Negro: An Interpretation*, edited by Alain
Locke. In the first essay, Locke said that in the last decade "something
beyond the watch and guard of statistics" had happened in the life of
Negro Americans; and the three norms that had traditionally presided
over the Negro problem—the sociologist, the philanthropist, and the
race leader—now had "a changeling in their laps." The phenomenon
that he proceeded to describe was the "Negro Renaissance" that had
occurred since World War I. And the volume that he edited sought to
document that change: "the transformations of the inner and outer life
of the Negro in America that have so significantly taken place in the last
few years." It was a remarkable document, opening its pages to such vet-
erans as William Stanley Braithwaite and William E. B. Du Bois, and to
such promising young people as Langston Hughes and Zora Neale
Hurston. While not thoroughly encompassing or all embracing, these
pages came close to a complete canvass of the status of Negroes in the
United States at the time.

The present volume may well be regarded as a yardstick by which to
measure the evolution of Afro-American literature and culture, and as a
commentary on what has happened in these areas since the appearance
of *The New Negro* in 1925. Even when it appeared in two issues of the
Massachusetts Review in the fall and winter of 1977, *Chant of Saints*
elicited memories of and comparisons with *The New Negro*, especially
in that work's first incarnation in the *Survey Graphic* for March, 1925.
While some comparison is understandable and even inevitable, it is,
perhaps, not a very fruitful exercise. For if *The New Negro* was a land-
mark for its time, it was not an impossible achievement in view of the
limited range of Afro-American cultural and literary activity, as well as
the limited number of participants. By contrast, the editors of *Chant of
Saints* were confronted with the staggering task of selecting representa-
tive authors and works from the most productive period in the history
of Afro-American literature and culture. The years since 1925 have seen
an increase not only in the number of writers that could not have been
imagined a half-century ago, but also in the styles and forms by which
they could communicate what they had to say. If the representation is
not complete—and how could it be, within the limits of one volume?—
that very fact is an indication of the formidable nature of the task the
editors have undertaken.

There is an air of security, if not solidarity and self-esteem, if not chauvinism, that permeates this work. One sees it in the dedication to Sterling Brown, dean of Afro-American letters, whose early works constitute an important link between the Negro Renaissance and the present. One sees it in the interviews with several distinguished writers who explain in succinct and quite felicitous statements just what messages they seek to convey in their works. One sees it in the richly textured poetry of Robert Hayden, with its wise and timely observations on the problems of our society, and in the powerful, almost scientific prose of Chinua Achebe, with its incisive comments on the shallow posturing of Joseph Conrad, one of the high priests of European imperialism in Africa. They and all the others who fill these pages know whereof they speak, and this very knowledge gives *Chant of Saints* an authenticity that is the basis for much of its strength.

The real authenticity of this work derives from the fact that virtually all of its contributors are professionals. From day to day most of their time and energy are devoted to the kinds of performances that one sees here. They teach their art and craft at an impressive array of American colleges and universities, or they write, paint, or photograph full-time, or their daily preoccupations are in activities very germane to the creative efforts by which they are represented here. At no other period in the history of this country have so many Negro Americans been professionally involved in literary, artistic, and other cultural activities. That is why those who appear in *Chant of Saints* are in the enviable position of representing a very large number of their fellows in this significant work.

PREFACE

In my recent reading, I have come upon a number of provocative remarks about anthologies, or perhaps the idea of the anthology, and I would like to share two of them. The first is from Claudio Guillén's *Literature as System:*

> A history of anthologies—of *how* the canons of authors and authorities arose and coalesced through the centuries of late antiquity and the Middle Ages—would contribute a great deal to our understanding of systematics. It would probably begin with the consideration of the most elementary questions: What did the anthologists build upon? How coherent were the "classification[s] of genres" . . . ? What other orders or systems did they reflect? No doubt a certain kind of anthology offered a mere succession, a serial choice. In other cases, a process of selection was derived from orderly criteria, thus facilitating a restricted roster of "representative works," fragments of works, or . . . brief quotations.

The other is by Richard Wright and, rather curiously, is the second paragraph of "The Literature of the Negro in the United States":

> As we all know, anthologists are legion today; to make an anthology requires simply this: Get a big pile of books on a given subject together, a big pot of glue, and a pair of sharp scissors and start clipping and pasting.

I offer these remarks not only because they seem to represent the alpha and omega of opinion on the value of anthologies, but also because my response to them has helped me clarify what Michael Harper and I have tried to do in editing *Chant of Saints*. *Chant* was more than three years in the making and many of the items it collects—including the Ralph Ellison, Toni Morrison, and Gayl Jones interviews, the essay on Siras Bowens, and the study of *Angle of Ascent*—were prepared expressly for its pages. For these reasons, we must demur from (and probably even resent a little) any suggestion that a pile of books, a pot of glue, and a pair of scissors doth an anthology make. On the other hand, I must say very quickly that we never swung so far in the direction of Professor

Guillén's thinking that *Chant* became the kind of gathering that thoughtfully answers all the questions he raises. Nevertheless, we take a certain pleasure from the extent to which *Chant* is clearly an orchestrated and, if you will, a premeditated volume, and I would like to suggest some of the ways in which this is so.

In the first place, a primary goal of *Chant* is to present most of the contributing authors and artists in a substantial and varied way. Of the seven fiction writers in the volume (Ralph Ellison, Leon Forrest, Ernest Gaines, Gayl Jones, James Alan McPherson, Toni Morrison, and John Stewart), four are featured as the subjects of interviews. In the special case of Mr. Ellison, one of his essays also appears, and quite fittingly that essay studies the art of Romare Bearden—examples of which are prominent throughout these pages. Each of the five poets in *Chant* (Michael Harper, Robert Hayden, Derek Walcott, Sherley Williams, and Jay Wright) have graciously allowed us to include long poems or sequences of poems which, in our estimation, allow a full portrait of their talent. These selections could most certainly stand alone, but we have made an effort to seek out complementing statements that may be examined along with the poems themselves. Hence the inclusion of Wilburn Williams's essay on Mr. Hayden's verse, Sharon Ciccarelli's interview of Mr. Walcott, Sherley Williams's examination of blues and contemporary poetry, and my own essay on Harper, Hayden, and Wright. With the regrettable exceptions of Richard Powell and John Wilson, the six visual artists in *Chant* (Romare Bearden, Richard Hunt, Powell, Lawrence Sykes, Wilson, and Richard Yarde) are all represented by substantial folios. Complementing these are the aforementioned Ellison essay on Bearden and Robert Farris Thompson's statement of the transatlantic tradition in black art as exemplified by the resonant forms collected, rendered, and seen by the late Siras Bowens. To be sure, the Ellison and Thompson pieces appear to harmonize to a greater degree with the collages of Bearden, sculpture of Hunt, and photographs by Sykes, but Powell, Wilson, and Yarde are hardly removed from *Chant*'s grand machinery.

Most of the remaining essays discuss either prose (usually fiction), music, or cultural history, and while there are bound to be a few of *Chant*'s readers who will argue that an important category has been left out, we feel assured that as a group these essays are sufficiently broad in scope and interdisciplinary in approach and purpose to counter any charges of narrowness that are worth refuting. Here I must point out that, as paradoxical as it may seem to some, *Chant* is an Afro-American collection but emphatically not in intent or purpose a social scientific book. It takes its name from the Sterling Brown poem "When de Saints Go Ma'chin Home," and more specifically from the poem's opening lines:

He'd play, after the bawdy songs and blues
After the weary plaints
Of "Trouble, Trouble deep down in muh soul,"
Always one song in which he'd lose the role
Of entertainer to the boys. He'd say,
"My mother's favorite." And we knew
That what was coming was his chant of saints,
"When de saints go ma'chin home . . ."
And that would end his concert for the day.

While many things are suggested by this glimmering language, few if any of those matters may be presented successfully through data or demography. If Big Boy Davis's "chant of saints" is in some sense a listing of names and events, that list is much more of a "dripping" catalog, an extended conceit, a ritualized and requisite calling of the names than it is a statistical chart or print-out. My point here is that, generally speaking, the essays on prose, music, and history in *Chant* share an abiding interest in what I'm going to term a culture's effort (indeed, its human compulsion) to translate data and prosaic fact into metaphor. In pursuing this interest, the essays intuitively answer (or epilogue) the "chant" for which this collection is named.

The essays on prose all speak to one another in a wonderful way, but some special conversings within the group are apparent and worth noting. For example, John Callahan's study of Ralph Ellison's use of history and Wilburn Williams's piece on Robert Hayden as historian and symbolist are rather straightforward considerations of the rendering of data and fact as metaphor in specific and, I believe, seminal contexts. Melvin Dixon's essay on Claude McKay, René Maran, and Jacques Roumain and my essay on Richard Wright are as much or more about literary history—and the place of such ideas as tradition, transition, and intertextuality in the study of literary history—as they are about the authors so prominently cited. Chinua Achebe's remarks on Joseph Conrad's *Heart of Darkness* are a special addition to the group, not only because they join Melvin Dixon's in expanding the discussion to literatures and voices not tethered in some way to North American tropes, but also because they confront a text that unquestionably presents an influential vision of (to use the Invisible Man's phrase) "what other men call reality." Because Achebe is less concerned with how Conrad transforms data into metaphor and more concerned with the moral siting of those figures, his essay is probably the most controversial of the group—and for good reasons.

The essays on music and cultural history are only four in number, but each is a major statement of its kind that speaks in harmonious ways with other materials assembled in *Chant*. In thinking about

these essays, I am reminded of a remark Norman Granz made in
the early 1950s when he invited only one trumpeter, Charlie
Shavers, to a jam session that assembled about a half-dozen premier
alto and tenor saxophonists: "I used Charlie Shavers on trumpet
for the brass section. I say section because Charlie blew almost
as much as an entire section." As Granz felt about Shavers, so I
feel about the essays by Frederick Turner, Kimberly Benston, Al-
bert Murray, and Mary Berry and John Blassingame. In its way,
Turner's elegant memorial of Big Jim Robinson restates Big Boy
Davis's "chant" and begins the study of jazz which Ellison calls
for in the final remarks of his interview. I would like to suggest
as well that a modal link exists between Robinson's experiences
in the segregated army of the Great War and the Richard Yarde
watercolors entitled "Departure" and "The Return." The Benston
piece on John Coltrane's "Orphic spirit" complements the Robin-
son portrait and, in its remarks on jazz and poetry, complements
Sherley Williams's essay on blues and poetry as well. What we
could not foresee when *Chant* was begun years ago is the fortuitous
conversation between Benston's traceries and Michael Harper's
remarkable new sequence of Coltrane poems. The Berry/Blassin-
game collaboration on "Africa, Slavery, and the Roots of Con-
temporary Black Culture" figures as one of the linchpins of the
volume. Turner's remarks on New Orleans funerals, Thompson's
discussion of Siras Bowens, and Sherley Williams's study of blues
are all reinforced and in some instances revoiced by the Berry and
Blassingame essay.

  More than the other materials, the remaining entries in *Chant*
raise an issue that we have wrestled with from the beginning:
namely, to what extent *Chant* is designed to be an expression of
Afro-American art and culture in the 1970s. On the one hand,
there is no doubt that we wanted to "document," if you will, the
current resurgence of interest in Sterling Brown, Zora Neale Hurs-
ton, and Richard Wright, and to do so with materials that are in a
sense occasional. On the other hand, ever mindful of the false
sense of autonomy that too many anthologies attribute (wittingly
and unwittingly) to cultural events and periods, we strove to gather
selections that contextualize specific voices and events in such a way
that those voices and events are presented as being mobile in time.
As a result, Sterling Brown's address ("A Son's Return: Oh,
Didn't He Ramble") upon his "return" to Williams College as a
man of letters and an alumnus seemed a far more important state-
ment than any of the tributes which quite rightfully have come his
way in recent years. Similarly, we were drawn far more to Alice
Walker's compelling account, "Looking for Zora," in which Ms.

Walker hears Hurston's calling of her name in a nearly forgotten Florida graveyard, than to the recent scholarly studies of the Hurston canon that will soon deserve an estimable anthology of their own. Charles Davis's essay on *Black Boy* is the most scholarly statement of the three, but it is also an occasional piece in that it is the address delivered at the opening exhibition of the Richard Wright Papers in Yale's Beinecke Library. Professor Davis was a member of the team of scholars that negotiated the return of the Wright Papers to the United States, and for this reason it might be said that his essay reflects a "search" for Wright as well.

While one must be cautious about declaring that *Chant* documents a decade or even an era, one can be much more confident about suggesting that the volume records major moments in the careers of many of its contributors. To cite just a few examples, we are very pleased to have been afforded the opportunity to publish new verse by Robert Hayden that was completed during his tenure as consultant in poetry at the Library of Congress. Similarly, it is an honor to receive fiction in progress from Ralph Ellison and Gayl Jones. Romare Bearden's Odysseus collages are without question major works; Richard Hunt's folio presents, for the first time in a book, his new work with large forms; and the Yarde and Sykes folios might very well signal the beginning of a truly national stature for each of these deserving artists. The Gayl Jones interview is the first she granted after the publication of *Corregidora* and, interestingly enough, is conducted by the former teacher to whom she dedicated her second novel, *Eva's Man;* the Toni Morrison interview includes a fascinating exchange about the award-winning *Song of Solomon* while it was still in progress; and Derek Walcott's remarks about Carnival in his interview tell us much about his present views on ritual, drama, and the Caribbean. Furthermore, I must point out that two of the essays are from scholarly works in progress: the Berry/Blassingame article is excerpted from *Long Memory: The Black Experience in America,* and Robert Farris Thompson's study of Siras Bowens draws on research that will be presented in his eagerly awaited volume on the transatlantic tradition in black art.

Chant is a gathering that has grown from a few poems and essays in hand in 1975 to the kind of rich tapestry that appears to embrace and define a literal and figurative world. And so the question arises, is *Chant* a construction of the Afro-American canon in our time? Knowing full well that a few major voices do not appear in these pages, Michael Harper and I hesitate to issue a resounding "yes." But then the question can be asked in another way: which voices in *Chant* are extraneous to the canon? In our opinion, *none* are—and for the moment we are happy to leave the business of refining or embellishing the canonistic statement implied by *Chant* to others for whom that is a concern.

Chant expresses the Afro-American canon in only a rough (but diamond rough!) way, primarily because the editors' energies were directed to another concern. In truth, while preparing *Chant,* we were far more greatly motivated by the goal of selecting first-rate expressions of varying genres and disciplines that speak to one another, and thereby suggest an artistic continuum, than by the tempting but ultimately secondary (or tertiary) concern of announcing who and what is in and out of some small circle. For this reason, we are especially delighted when a reader of *Chant* makes a compelling link between, say, Toni Morrison's remarks on the Odysseus motif in Afro-American literature and what they *see* in Romare Bearden's collages, or quite rightly asks what we are attempting to express by having John Stewart's Caribbean-set short story followed by Larry Sykes's photographs, Derek Walcott's "Star-Apple Kingdom," Michael Harper's passbook poem, Achebe's consideration of Joseph Conrad, and Robert Hayden's poems about Phillis Wheatley and Matthew Henson. In sum, we want *Chant of Saints* to be *read;* at its best, it is an epic and familial poem—and, for those who need it, it is a place to begin.

—Robert B. Stepto

New Haven
1978

Chant of Saints

A SON'S RETURN:
"OH, DIDN'T HE RAMBLE"

STERLING A. BROWN

Thank you a great deal. Fifty-one years is a long time. I was happy to be invited. I'm somewhat melancholy now, which is not my usual state. I've seen briefly the campus. I've seen the changes. I've seen the Observatory that was way back, and it's right here now on the street. I've forgotten many of the street names. I've never been in Griffin Hall before. This was for government and history. I've been looking at a *Gulielmensian* and memories have come back, some bitter, some happy. I've thought about the return ever since I was invited back. When I heard the introduction, which was overgenerous, I thought this must be old folks' week, and you're good to gray hairs and bent-over people. I am grateful to you young people that you respect your elders, but I thought of the Playboy of the Western World who, in his coffin, hearing the eulogies about him, rose up and said, "Is it me?" and I always wonder is it me? At my age, these compliments, whether they are true or not, are awful damn good to hear. I talked to Robert Burns Stepto. It's no accident that Robert Burns is one of my favorite poets, and if Robert Burns Stepto keeps introducing me like this, he's one of my favorite people. These notes are not for the "Images and Reality" lecture. I gave that talk at Brown, and I will give it again elsewhere, and I will write an article about it, but I'm talking tonight on a son's return, not a prodigal son, though I'm certainly getting the fatted calf.

The subtitle comes from an old famous folksong that is well known on college campuses, and that is "Oh, Didn't He Ramble"—because I'm a ramblin' wreck, not from Georgia Tech, but I am going to ramble. I am 72 years old, and if I give three minutes to each year that is a long ramble. At Howard University I have been returned. I am the oldest person on the Howard University campus now in active duty. I am older than any maintenance man, any gardener. I am the oldest so and so at Howard, and I am unique in that I'm the only person at Howard who was hired, fired—and I was, I'm not ashamed of it, I'm proud of it, I'm not going to tell you why but the cause was good—but I was hired, I was fired, I was rehired, I was retired, I was again rehired. If I tell many lies tonight and you get them taped, I may be refired.

Professor Brown delivered this speech at Williams College on September 22, 1973.

Oddly enough there are a host of my students down at Amherst and at the University of Massachusetts. And you know Williams' attitude to Amherst. But there's a colony of Howard people at Amherst, and some of them are here, and I'm glad to see them. I don't think they heard my lecture which was a few years back—no, that was at Brown. I get all these Ivy Leagues mixed up, you see, in my rambling way.

I am doing my autobiography at Howard, and they're taping me. I think they have hours and hours, let us say sixty-some hours they have taped me, and I'm now at the fourth grade at Garnet-Patterson School. Frank Marshall Davis, a very good poet who has gone to Hawaii, came back, and we had him read some poems, and I told him about my auto-biography. His is finished, and I told him that I was at the fourth grade, and he said, "You must be a slow learner." I did not appreciate that. I am not a slow learner. I *am* a long talker. And I remember vividly, and I'm in two traditions. One is the tradition of Mark Twain. I remember vividly what happened and also a large number of things that did not happen, but sound good. I am the best yarnspinner at Howard University. I am the best liar at Howard University, in the Mark Twain tradition. I can outlie Ralph Bunche, who was a great liar. I'm not talking about the Nobel Peace Prize winner—oh no, oh no. Ralph could tell a wonderful story, but Ralph's political science experience stood in his way; he didn't have Mark Twain behind him. He had a Harvard Ph.D., but he told a good lie. E. Franklin Frazier was a great liar, and our President Mordecai Johnson was a tremendous liar. And these are meant as words of praise. The Mark Twain yarn, this is the anecdote with a point, with pith, sometimes with a little profanity. But of course I would not do that, not always. J. Saunders Redding stated that one quality of Negro folklore was that they had no dirty stories except in the dirty dozens. And I want to know what fraternity houses J. Saunders Redding did not go into. Now I am going to say something that may hurt your feelings, but the dirty story is important in American litera-ture, and I point to Mark Twain. But certainly in our tradition some of the finest dirty stories that I have heard from people—I'd better not say it, but they are close to the theological department at Howard. I am not going to tell you a dirty story. I'm trying to point to a tradition. Of course, I learned this at Williams. I did not read Mark Twain's "1601— A Social Conversation in the Time of the Tudors" under Sam Allen— "Straw Allen"—or under George Dutton, but I learned a great respect for Mark Twain, and I learned a great respect for the tradition of the anecdote.

But I'm going to be serious tonight for about five minutes of these sev-enty-two and talk about Williams. Why did I come to Williams? I came to Williams because I grew up on the Howard University campus, and my father knew that I was not going to do any studying there. I knew the

Howard University campus like the back of my hand. I was mascot at
Howard when I was seven. I would get up at five o'clock in the morning.
They had a great team in those days. They had a guy whose name, whose
nickname, was Bulldog. Bulldog was really a wonderful fullback. At
seven years old I would go out in the early morning and struggle under
all those sweaters and helmets and whatnot and carry the water bucket,
and I used to have to carry the water bucket to them, and in the football
games I carried the water bucket to them and also carried signals in.
And I'll never forget how red the water bucket was. The sponge of
course you know, but I saw all this gore and so forth But I would tell
'em go over left end, or the right end was laggin' or something. In those
days it was shock freelance football. A wedge, you know, like push for-
ward and then just pile over. It was rough and tough football. I was the
mascot. I grew up on the campus. I knew it inside out. My father said,
"Go to Williams." At Dunbar, they had the tradition of giving annual
scholarships to Williams and Amherst and Bowdoin and Bates and
Dartmouth, but chiefly Williams. Williams would give a scholarship to
Dunbar, and the top man got it. Generally he was the "greasy grind,"
and the athlete got into Amherst. I was the "greasy grind." I may have
been greasy, but I was not exactly a grind. But I had read a lot of books.
My house was full of teachers. Everybody in my house was a teacher.
Most of them had gone to Howard. I grew up with books. My mother
came from Fisk. She was valedictorian of her class. My father met her at
Fisk. They were there when Du Bois was there.

I met Du Bois, and Du Bois said, "Who are you?" I said, "I'm Sterling
Brown," and he said, "Who was your father?" and I said, "Sterling Nel-
son Brown." And then Du Bois grabbed me and hugged me. And that is
the only time I have known him to hug me. And I think it is the only time
I've known him to hug a man. But Du Bois certainly would hug the
ladies, for which I am very proud. I am very proud of Du Bois for his
great affection for people, including the ladies. I knew Du Bois quite
well. I love him, I admire him, and one of the things I admire is what I
mentioned.

I won the scholarship to Williams, and I came here to Williams. Now
I came here in the SATC. I am a veteran. I am an army veteran. I was
wounded on Cole Field. I was also wounded, I don't know which direc-
tion, but which is Vermont? There is a plateau on a mountain up there.
There is a mountain dome and a plateau, and they had a rifle range up
there. And you went straight, and this guy in front of me had his rifle
over his shoulder, and he poked me in the eye. And I should have a hash
mark. I was in the SATC, which is not to be confused with the ROTC. I
was in the Student Army Training Corps, and I got thirty dollars per
month. I put my age up to get in because my friend, named Axe Ellis,
was eighteen and he wanted to go; and the men that I respected—like

Rayford Logan, people of that sort—they were drafted, and they had gone into the Army Training Corps, so I wanted to fight for my country and beat the Kaiser and whip the Huns. But the main thing, I wanted to be with the guys who were going. I always went with older men, so I put my age up and got thirty dollars per month. And when my father found it out he wanted to shoot me or something, and he said that I did it for the thirty dollars. The thirty dollars went nowhere because the junior, Carter Marshall, would beat me and make me buy him soda pop and chocolates, and my thirty dollars went for nothing. I had a uniform. I was fed, and I started as a corporal, and was busted. I ended up as number four in the rear rank of the first squad of D Company, which I resented because I had been a major in the cadets at Dunbar. And I showed off, and we had a little man who didn't finish Williams but he had learned in some summer camp, and he came here and he threw his weight around. And he made wrong orders and I would say, "As you were." And he resented that and he busted me. And he said, "Mr. Brown, when Major General Pew was talking to the troops you were standing like this (*slumps*)," which I was, because Major General Pew was long-winded. Major General Pew used to sing us a song, "Only the Gamefish Swim Upstream," and he was a game fish if there ever was one. Pew was talking and I was loafing, but I was a corporal and the shavetail said, "Do you know, Corporal Brown, how you were standing when Major General Pew was talking? You were standing like this (*slumps*)." And I said, "Do you know how you were standing? You were standing like this (*slumps*)." So he busted me, and I was four in the rear rank . . . and Carter Marshall got to be corporal.

Now Carter Marshall was another one of the token Negroes. Carter was a junior. He had come here earlier, and he was accommodated. Henry Adam Brown was not old enough; he was the sophomore. And so you had a junior and a private, and of course he was number four in the front rank, and I was number four in the rear rank. As we marched to this hill to go to the Commons Club to eat, I would trip Carter Marshall. He would turn around and throw me down in the snow. We were in D company, that was the last company. All the others had gone in to eat, and Carter and I were back here cavorting, which shows the kind of military life I had. But I had bad eyes. I had to memorize the letters in order to get in. So I signed up for the artillery, because I couldn't make the rifle range and I was good in mathematics. I was shooting right-handed, and my right eye wasn't any good, and I didn't have glasses. And so the sergeant said to me, as I would shoot away, "Pull the trigger," and they would wave down there that I had missed the target completely. So he said, "Are you afraid to shoot?" I said, "No, my father's a great hunter; I shoot, but I just can't see it." So he said, "Try left-handed," and the bolt came over this way, you see, you couldn't shoot left-handed. So he put me down in the pit. And in the pit the boys were shooting craps to decide what numbers to put up there. And they would say, "Give him an eight, give him a ten." They were shooting dice. They had no money. It was a beautiful experience. It was freezing cold. That is where I got what nearly caused my early death. It was the coldest place. With raincoats—we had slickers, no overcoats. You climbed up this plateau, and then I went and got down in the pit. And of course I don't like to gamble, but I had to go along with my peers!

What was Williams? Was it just the joy? The SATC was good. It was democratic. A lot of the boys were brought in from North Adams and Williamstown. Carter Marshall and I lived in Williams Hall, and I can't remember whether we lived on the top floor or the first, because we had a roommate, a Jewish fellow named Victor Leo Jacobson. And Victor Leo Jacobson was not tall enough to be in our squad. He was short, but he was long on knowledge. He was from Cleveland. He was long on knowledge that I didn't know much about. And I don't know whether he was first floor or not, but he left the room, and we had to puff his pillow and things to make it seem that he was in the bed, because he was out with women from North Adams. I think he was on the first floor because I think we put the window up to let him in. I do not remember for sure. But he was not letting the army interfere with what he would call his "basic training." Victor Leo Jacobson did not return to Williams. But he was our roommate, he selected me and Carter as we had something of his kind of situation. He was in our squad; he could not drill. He didn't do anything except to go out with the women and never get caught. The SATC ended with Armistice Day. I was to go to artillery camp, and Carter Marshall was to go to infantry camp. Well, now I've already taken a whole lot of time on SATC.

The second year that I was here . . . I was looking at the *Gulielmensian*, and I noticed that everybody had "East Hall" or "West Hall" or "—Fraternity" except me and Ralph Winfield Scott, who was then a freshman. I was a sophomore, and beside our names was the expression —"Mrs. Hogan's." Beside Carter Marshall's was "East College" and beside Henry Brown's was "East College." But they lived at Mrs. Hogan's too. President Harry Garfield was not here, and I don't know who it was, but somebody said that Negroes at Williams would be happier together. So they put all four of us at Mrs. Hogan's. And Mrs. Hogan's was between the tailor shop on Spring Street and Jesup Hall. It was not an alley, but it also was not a street. Mrs. Hogan, I can't remember; I know she was delightful. But we paid our rent, and we were told that the reason we were there was that we had not paid our advance on the dormitory room. I know that was true of Carter because he was poorer than I, and Henry A. Brown was even poorer than he, but my father had put down some money on my room. Nevertheless we were all four there.

I had the largest room because, I think, my father had paid something for Berkshire Hall. Ralph Scott, the freshman, had a fairly small room, and Henry Brown and Carter had the double. We lived there for a year, and the statement was made that the college was looking out for our happiness. They thought we would be happier together. And I know, this is very arrogant for me to say it, but I was the spokesman even though I was the sophomore. And I said that we came to Williams for an education, and let Williams give us the education and we would look out for our own happiness. And I would still say that, except I might be a little more profane and state what kind of g.d. happiness I am going to look out for! But I looked at the pictures that I had taken then, and there was a great deal of bounce and resiliency. One picture that I'm going to show Robert Burns Stepto—but I couldn't bring it up—is a picture of me sitting in shirtsleeves in six feet of snow, fanning, and I sent it down to Washington, and all my schoolmates had it, and I'm fanning and I'm grinning. I was doing a lot of grinning then, and I had a lot of bounce. Now in my melodramatic moments, and having heard a lot of propaganda, much of which I agreed with, I've been told that Williams was a traumatic experience. And you know I had fallen for that and sometimes later spoke of how unhappy I was. I was not unhappy. My letters home were not unhappy. And I've been thinking about it. Why should I expect graduates of Andover, Exeter, and Groton to take me in and know me? They had never seen a Negro, and I had never seen a white man their age. Until I came to Williams, I had never spoken to a white boy except the little son of the drugstore man where we used to go to get sundaes for my family; and he and I were friends until Negroes came around with me or whites came around with him. Then we didn't know each other. But until that point we would speak. You know. So this was the separation that was strong.

So, when I came to Williams, I have mentioned, I met with (I think it's President Nixon who said it) "benign neglect." I did not meet with anything blatant. I did not meet with anything flagrant. Carter Marshall was called a "nigger" on Main Street, and he knocked the guy down. And I was right behind him to help on that. I was not a fighter, but I had my race to defend. And that's the only time I heard the word "nigger." I've talked to other people and Rayford Logan says that a professor from Louisiana teaching Kipling threw in the word "nigger" unnecessarily, and he told me that he thought that no Negroes should study under this man. I did, and I'll tell you about that a little later.

One of the big shots in my class from Louisiana would come to us (we wore knickerbockers in those days), and he would say "Look at the little 'knickers'?" but you didn't know whether it was *ck* or *gg*. And the last lie I want to tell is that they used to call me Brownie. But how the hell could

I object to them calling me Brownie? My name was Brown, but they never missed on Brownie. I was Brownie.

During the Depression, a man as seedy looking as I, as indigent as I and as much in need of relief as I, met me at Times Square and he said to me, "Brownie, are they doin' you all right?" This cat was one of the best artists at Williams; and for the *Purple Cow* he drew beautiful cartoons. He was in French class with me and a very nice guy, and I know that he knew during the Depression, if I needed any help, he would help. I think I could have helped him. I was not professor at Howard, I was assistant professor, making the glamorous amount of $1500 a year. This is not Depression time, this was before Depression. So I might have helped him, but the business of Brownie and the rest was there. Now, I have not been a good son of Williams in respect to contributions to the alumni fund. I have not done as well as I should. Nor has the Class of '22, according to the *Record*. I know that is wrong, every now and then I have sent my . . . my modicum. And I'm going to send a lot more now that I'm back here, because the place is very dear to me. Now why is the place dear to me? I owe this place more than this guy at Times Square could tell me. I learned how to read at Williams. I learned how to teach at Williams. I want to read what your new president has said. Your new president, in greeting the freshmen, has said:

These next four years will come to represent many things to you. Friendships that you will cherish for the rest of your life. The development and enjoyment of a variety of skills. Growth in social skills and self-confidence. Other skills—theatrical, athletic, and musical. But I hope you will perceive your stay at Williams, *principally*, as a unique opportunity for the development of a range of intellectual skills and habits that will stay with you for a lifetime and add to your enjoyment, stature and usefulness as a human being.

I did not store up this friendship, except for the nucleus of Negro students. I got to know Allison Davis very well. I got to know Carter Marshall and Henry Brown well. Allison Davis and Ralph Scott and I used to go for long walks, and we decided the race problem, we decided the problem of women, which was a serious thing here.

This was a monastic institution, and the opportunities for, let us say, for conversation with the fair sex were limited. The dirtiest thing I did at Williams was when I went over to be initiated into the Omega Phi Psi fraternity. I went to Boston, Massachusetts, and I had never seen so many beautiful women in my life. Of course, male Bostonians stated that they were not beautiful; I had just not seen women, period. But anything I saw was beautiful. I went over there and the fraternity guys said to be at the fraternity house at midnight, dressed up for this rough initiation. I came to the fraternity house at one o'clock in a blue coat and white flannel britches and was not bothered about the initiation. I had just fallen in love with six different women. I'm going to call up five of them on this trip—and their grandchildren, I'd like to send some of their grandchildren to Williams. Not out of any paternal relationship, but out of love of both Williams and these lovely things. So I went to this fraternity house late, and they nearly killed me. These were people from Lincoln University and Howard, and they resented my going to Williams anyway, you know, and me, Ivy League conceited egotist and wearing white flannel britches. They wore those britches out. They beat me up and down the Charles River. They beat me in South Boston, Somerville, North Cambridge, Arlington, Boston Common. I died on Boston Common, a death that Crispus Attucks never suffered. I still cannot sit down on my memories of the Boston Massacre. I had on my breast, or chest, or whatever a man has—I had Omega Phi Psi all over me. I went down later to Tuskegee, where the guys from B.U. were, and they had become great lawyers and doctors, but they nearly killed me.

I came back to Williams, and I had both consecutively cut and I had also overcut, and that was bad. We had to make chapel at seven forty-five every day God sent, including holidays. Not on Sunday, that was later and longer. But we had seven forty-five chapel, because of eight o'clock classes. Seven forty-five you went in there, you had to go in. Most guys went in pajamas and heavy coats. They bet. (I was not alienated: I participated.) They bet on what would be the length of the prayer—six minutes, seven minutes, eight minutes. They'd bet on anything. They were not very religious. Nor was I. So, you could not cut consecutively, you could not overcut . . . and I had overcut and consecutively, and Dean Howes said, "Mr. Brown, you have got to go. You have got to be suspended." I knew that as much beating as my fraternity brothers had given me that was nothing to what my father was going to give me. I committed one of the worst deeds of racism in my career. I said to Dean Howes, "You would not do this if I were not a Negro." It was the college law, he would have put out Nixon's son or daughter. He would have put out anybody—I had broken the law. I threw race at him and said he's picking on a poor little Negro. And it worked. He was the descendant of abolitionists. This man's grandfather had probably fought at Chickamauga or something, and he nearly cried. He said, "Mr. Brown, do you really feel that?" I said, "Yes, and the other fellows feel it too." From then on I not only consecutively cut, you know, I ain't thought about chapel. That's not true really, but it's a good lie.

So at Williams I made friends with people who have been good friends, good mentors, brothers. Allison Davis is now John Dewey

Professor at the University of Chicago. He's been there thirty years, almost, on the faculty. He's a great guy. A great teacher. Rayford Logan was before me. Rayford Logan is a professor emeritus at Howard. He's teaching courses at Howard. He's one of the oldest people. He's older than I, but not in length of service. Rayford has received from Williams an honorary degree. He's Ph.D. from Harvard. He got an A.B., an M.A., and a Litt.D. from Williams, and he is one of my best friends. We were close. He was not here with me, he was three or four years ahead of me. Allison was here, Carter Marshall became a noted doctor, taught at Yale, taught at Howard. Ralph Scott, first rate in government and history, was a principal at a school in Washington, and died untimely. Mortimer Weaver made Phi Beta Kappa here, taught at Howard. Made Delta Sigma Rho. I didn't make Delta Sigma Rho. I won one oratorical contest, was second once, and made alternate on the debating team. When they had the debate, I wore a full dress suit. I got a picture in the *Gulielmensian* of me in a full dress suit. I have on a white tie, and I'm sitting there conceited, posing unnaturally, and the full dress suit was green with age. It had been worn by Montgomery Gregory, who was on the Harvard debating team, about ninety years before. He was my Sunday School teacher, and he let me have it. It did not fit well, but you can't tell that in the picture.

And we had a great tennis team. There was this man named Chapin. I was number one on the Commons Club tennis team. I learned playground tennis in Washington, which was scrambling like Bobby Riggs tried to against that woman champion, you know, way back, that proved women's superiority. And I had the scrambling game, and then I learned to drive. I had a good forehand. And when I went back to Washington they said "You play like a fay boy"; I had learned to drive at Williams. I always had a weak backhand, and I ran around it; therefore I was vulnerable. But I was the best man on the Commons Club team. And Chapin was a great player, and there was a guy named Bullock who was the captain. He was a pretty good player. Allison Davis and I were the Commons Club's doubles team, and we were pretty good. I had to play for the Commons Club against the fraternity, and they brought in a guy whose service I have not seen until yet. And this guy was a great baseball player and was seldom on the courts, and so I thought I had something good. I have never seen the ball. He had all the stuff that is today known, you know that Ashe would have, that Smith would have, and what not, and I've never seen the ball. It was a shame. The ball would fly off my racket. We were playing in front of Williams Hall, and I was hitting the ball in the Grace Auditorium. But I was a good tennis player.

I was good in track in SATC. They thought I had to be a good runner because all Negroes can run. We got longer heels in the back. You know, that kind of nonsense. So I was fast and they put me in a race, but they put spikes on me and I'd never had spikes on. And get on your mark, get set, go . . . and I'm stuck in the heel with those spikes on me, and I've never had spikes on. And I came in last. I'll tell you one last lie about athletics and Du Bois's double consciousness. I rooted strongly for Williams all the time. Ben Boynton was one of the greatest athletes Williams ever had. He played professional football, and I saw him at the Griffith Stadium in Washington. He remembered me. So I was all for Williams until Amherst would come over with the track team and there were boys I had grown up with. So I wanted to cheer for purple Williams, but Amherst was also wearing purple and white, and they were my buddies at Dunbar High School. So I would be cheering for Percy Barnes, who became professor of chemistry at Howard—a great guy at Amherst, Phi Beta Kappa—Montague Cobb, and Bill Hastie, and Charlie Drew. I would cheer for them all when they ran against Williams. What happened was there was a man over there named Parker who ran a two-mile race and we're cheering for all the Negroes on the team, 'cause we wanted the race to be well represented. But in the two-mile race Parker came in about a mile and a half behind everybody, and we wanted to lynch him. He was the slowest man. I was not too fast. I was fast in the SATC. So athletically I did not achieve a great deal.

I learned how to read, however. And I want here to give my testimony to great teachers here at Williams, because the whole business of teaching is very important to me. I want to read what was said by ex-President Pusey of Harvard speaking of Colonel Williams's legacy. He says here:

> Teaching is a very demanding profession. If your college has spoken to you truly and deeply you have seen in your relationship with one or more of your teachers, what teaching can be, and what it can mean in life. It is no secret that the profession does not hold out promise of financial reward. [Amen.] There are very few places in American society where the results of selfish material greed have shown itself more hideous than in the relative depressed condition of the profession of teaching. Did we think clearly, this career would certainly be held to be one of the most deserving of all. These unfortunately are facts one cannot ignore.

He mentions then that

> All professions in the full range of calling make a legitimate claim on me and on you, but if you have the skill, personal gift, and love of the enterprise which might enable you to become a truly great teacher, may I urge you not to close your eyes to this road without giving it careful consideration. For if you can be a teacher, you are needed more, more than ever before.

At this stage in my life, it is a good thing to hear that kind of statement, when you find out your life has not been completely empty. My students have meant a great deal to me. Now, in my seventh decade, I hear from Kenya that "I am your son." An article says I have no sons—I have no children. I have an adopted son and this guy writes me from Kenya and tells me he is my son and I've got thousands of them. I don't know whether I got thousands, but I have plenty of them. Some of them are in here now. That's a very important reward and I'm glad to hear that from President Pusey. And we have here something about Ephraim Williams's remarks on Mark Hopkins and the little log:

> There was a rare simplicity in Hopkins's approach to his pupils. He sought to train them to think their way into the hearts of things and to think in such a fashion that life would have meaning, and they could use their powers to the best advantage.

Pusey continues:

> Our need today is to convert his age old persistence into a steady stream of able young people who with the spirited zeal of a pioneer like Colonel Williams will homestead our contemporary educational frontier and keep alive and extend the faith.

I want to pay tribute here to some of the English teachers. I cannot give you a list of the great teachers I had at Williams. I look at the *Gulielmensian* and I remember a man like Professor MacElfresh in physics. I remembered Professor Carl Whetmore. I met only recently a novelist, married to a poet in Washington. He heard that I was coming to Williams, and said he was Karl Weston's nephew. But I want to speak of four men in the English department. One of them is Carroll Maxcy, who had been dean of Williams, who taught me Chaucer, who taught me Rhetoric 7-8, he taught me the Lincoln-Douglas debates, he taught us argumentation and debating. He has a statement I was going to read later. There was one who was called "Straw" Allen. His name was Samuel S. Allen. They say he was a poor student who paid his way to Williams with a load of straw. He was a very democratic, excellent, rather dry teacher of American literature. He was an excellent friend who wrote me a beautiful letter when *Southern Road* came out. I didn't know he even knew about it. And the third was a man named Albert Licklider and Licklider was the man I was told never to study under. Licklider was a Princeton man. One of the lesser ambitions of Williams in those days was to be a second Princeton. Which I could never understand, because I didn't think much of the first Princeton, which of course never let a Negro in there unless he was waiting tables at a fra-

ternity, and they didn't have many of them. That has changed. I have
lectured at Princeton. Will Thorpe is one of my good friends. He went
to Hamilton; but he went to Hamilton, he didn't go to Princeton.
Princeton was one of the worst. Harvard, as far as my people are con-
cerned, was one of the best. Yale was one of the worst and Williams,
with its Haystack Monument, was one of the leaders.

But Williams fell down at a certain time, I think under President
Dennett, when it was said Negroes would be happier elsewhere, but
more than that, Williams should be democratic, and being democratic
it should get students from the South. And these students from the
South should be white and they may reject Negroes being here; there-
fore in the spirit of democracy let us leave Negroes out of here. For-
tunately, that did not prevail, that failed, according to one of the
trustees—he has told me much about this. But when we were staying
in Mrs. Hogan's, Harvard was keeping people out of its dormitory.
Princeton was not letting anybody in, nor was Vassar, and I taught at
Vassar when they didn't even have the token they had in my day here.
So there was this whole picture in American life. Rayford Logan said
he had no problems about living here because the law was you could
not live in a dormitory.

Now Williams has had the Haystack Monument tradition and it has
had these excellent men. This is a lead-up to Licklider. Licklider was
from the Deep South and would let you know it. I was told not to take
Licklider. I took him and I got "A" almost all the way with Licklider.
I heard nothing—there was nothing at all of disparagement or whatnot.
He treated me well and made no racial statement. I took a course in
creative writing and he said, "Mr. Brown, you have no sense of
rhythm." I was the only Negro in the class and everybody else was
rhythmical except me. Which was ridiculous. I have a marvelous sense
of rhythm, not because I am a Negro but because I am rhythmical.
Or, as Louis Armstrong says, "rhythmatical." I am a good dancer and
I know a whole lot of Negroes are not good dancers. And when you
start talking about all Negroes having a sense of rhythm, ask a lot of
girls they've been dancing with recently. Take a lot of Mississippi
fieldhands who just came from plowing that mule and put them in the
country dance and ask the girls, "Have they got rhythm?" This whole
nonsense about racial rhythm is ridiculous. But this man had said I had
no sense of rhythm for this reason. He was giving us French poems to
translate, and I was a first-rate student of Jean and Albert Cru and
Karl Weston, and I knew a lot about French and was giving a literal
translation, getting the meaning of the French. The boys—the other
guys in the class did not know French, and all they knew was beat, so

they had the iambs going but the French was bad. So he said you have
no sense of rhythm. So I gave him three poems I had just written to
three girls—one in Boston, one in Baltimore, and one in Washington.
Because I was a *true* Williams Man. I believe in spreading the blessings
around. I wrote a beautiful poem with a beautiful beat and he said,
"Mr. Brown this is much more like it."

My last problem with Licklider was that I could not meet a dead-
line. So I got an "incomplete" in my senior year in rhetoric, whatever
was the number, creative writing. There I saw the loyalty of my class-
mates, because they wanted to raise the devil because they said Lick-
lider, from the Deep South, is pressing this poor Negro, you know.
So they sided with me. Because they felt a kind of neglect from him,
they were still from the North. So they fought my battle. But I said
"nay, nay, my work is late." At 11:59 on the deadline date *I stuck it
under the door* of the faculty club over there off Spring Street and I got
my B with him. I didn't get an A. I took Shakespeare with him, Eliza-
bethan drama and creative writing. It was not my lack of rhythm that
got me the B; it was that the work came in late.

Now the important man is George Dutton. George Dutton was sar-
castic, sharp witted; he didn't suffer fools gladly, he was a tough guy.
He taught me English 5-6, he taught me the Romantic movement, he
taught me the modern novel. He was in bad at Williams because he had
written an article in the *Redbook* on modern fiction. And that was
too advanced. You must remember that this was in the twenties and
American literature was unpopular. He taught the English novel but he
made us read *Madame Bovary*, he made us read *Brothers Karamazov*,
he told us of Dostoevsky, Tolstoy, he told us about the new Sinclair
Lewis. He taught me critical realism. He was a tremendous influence.
I learned to read at Williams College. I could not stand the cold up
there. I was from the Deep South, Washington, D.C., and I could not
stand this weather. So I caught either the pleurisy, pneumonia, or
something, and was out of school but I could go to the library. So in
the library, right across from here, in about two days I read Thomas
Hardy's *Return of the Native*, George Meredith's *Diana of the Cross-
ways*, and Balzac's *Père Goriot*. I could not do it now. I could not read
Diana of the Crossways now in six months. Back there I was very bright
and I read. I learned then. I was a junior then. I learned then what read-
ing meant. Last anecdote about Dutton. Dutton was teaching Joseph
Conrad. He said Joseph Conrad was being lionized in England—
H. G. Wells and Galsworthy and all the ladies and lords and the rest
were making over Joseph Conrad and whatnot, and Conrad was sitting
over in the corner, quiet, not participating. Dutton said he was brood-

ing and probably thinking about his native Poland and the plight of
his people. He looked straight at me. I don't know what he meant, but
I think he meant, and this is symbolic to me, I think he meant don't
get fooled by any lionizing, don't get fooled by being here at Williams
with a selective clientele. There is business out there that you have to
take care of. Your people, too, are in a plight. I've never forgotten it.
He was a great man. He was a man who was forbidding until he knew
you. He was one of the warmest human beings I have ever met. I said
this once and his son heard it. His son, who graduated from Williams,
has written me a letter. I'm going to write him about my return. Dutton
taught me, he *taught* Allison Davis, he *taught* Mortimer Weaver. He
was a great teacher. He was not alone. Williams was full of great teach-
ers. One last thing. (I've taken up 72 years almost.) I want to read what
Carroll Maxcy wrote about another great teacher whom I had at Har-
vard. And this man's name is important in the history of Williams. This
is Bliss Perry. Bliss Perry was at Harvard and he also taught at Wil-
liams. (I studied at Harvard in '23 and then I went back in '31; I took
courses with Bliss Perry both times.) Carroll Maxcy said:

> Whatever fame Professor Perry may have attained in the field of litera-
> ture, to Williams men he is the teacher. In the amateur spirit he has writ-
> ten, "Your born teacher is as rare as a poet. Once in a while your college
> gets hold of one. It does not always know that it has him, and proceeds to
> ruin him by overdriving the moment he showed power; or let another
> college lure him away for a few hundred dollars more a year. But while
> he lasts—and sometimes, fortunately, he lasts until the end of a long life—
> he transforms a lecture hall by enchantment. Lucky is the alumnus who
> can call the roll of his old instructors, and among the martinets, and the
> pedants, and the piously insane can here and there come suddenly upon
> a man."

And that was Dutton and that was Bliss Perry. Upon a man, a man who
taught him to think or help him to feel and thrill to a new horizon. And
Maxcy said of Bliss Perry, "scholarly in his taste, clear in his thinking,
simple and direct in the expression of his thought and always human
in his personality. He taught us to *think* he helped us to *feel* and he
thrilled us to a new horizon. To us he seemed the ideal teacher. And
this teacher, and this man withal, he has won the loyalty of Harvard,
Princeton and Williams men alike." This was written by Carroll Lewis
Maxcy, class of '76 and appeared in a Williams anthology in 1921.

These men taught me to think. At Harvard, I went into careful study
of American poetry. I learned from Edwin Arlington Robinson's *Til-
bury Town,* where he took up the undistinguished, the failures, and
showed the extraordinary in ordinary lives. I learned Robert Frost.
I learned from my own; the man I was brought up on was Dunbar. I
learned from Claude McKay. I participated in what I called the New

Negro Renaissance. I wrote poetry. I went South. I taught at Virginia
Seminary, where I learned a great deal that I could not learn at Wil-
liams, I learned the strength of my people, I learned the fortitude. I
learned the humor. I learned the tragedy. I learned from a wandering
guitar player about John Henry, about Stagolee, about "The Ballad
of the Bollweevil." I learned folktales. I learned folkstuff. I was like a
sponge. I had a good eye. I had a good ear. I had a good mind trained
by people like Dutton. I learned how to read American literature and
found out how much stupid stereotyping of my people there was. I
read all the Jim Crow *additions* to the history of American literature.
I read nonsense from people who talked about *the Negro,* who prob-
ably knew their cook and would generalize from that. I read the non-
sense of people like Thomas Nelson Page. I saw the limitations of Joel
Chandler Harris, of whom the first historian of the Negro in literature
said that in sixteen lines of Brer Turtle you have the whole range of
Negro character. That kind of nonsense I read. I wrote *The Negro in
American Fiction.* I wrote many essays. I am still writing them. Howard
University is bringing out a book of mine. It is called *To a Different
Drummer* and I pay credit, of course, to Thoreau, whom I learned of
in "Straw" Allen's class and under George Dutton. *Southern Road* is
going to be reprinted. I'm bringing out a book of poems, *Thirty-six
Poems Thirty-six Years Later,* because friends of mine, like Stokely
Carmichael and the rest, think that I wrote the poems after discussing
these things with them.

I am an *old Negro* and I am proud of it. My students get angry be-
cause I do not use the word "black." I do use the word "black." If a per-
son wants to call himself black, fine. I am very glad the word "black" has
different connotations now than what it had. I am an old Negro, as
W. E. B. Du Bois is an old Negro, Paul Robeson is a Negro, James
Weldon Johnson is a Negro, Mordecai Johnson is a Negro, Jack John-
son is a Negro, and a whole lot of other Johnsons are Negroes. I am not
a worshipper of the bourgeoisie. I am not one who has piled up money
at the cost of my deprived brethren. There are a whole lot of people who
called me a "bourgeois Babbitt" whom I am going to meet on the shores
when they come to Africa, but I am not going back to Africa tomorrow
. . . I am going to Tipton, Mississippi. They need me over here and a
whole lot of Africans don't. I was taught Sunday School by an African.
Many of my best friends, this is an awful thing to say, I'll change that,
my best students, friends, teachers and the rest are Africans. I have had
a love for Africa since I was a child. But I know a whole lot of people
who are talking about going to Africa and are going to stop in Paris on
the way over. A lot of them are not going to stay over there because it is
tough and rough there, and many are copping out on what is tough and
rough here.

I am an integrationist, though that is an ugly word, because I know what segregation really was. And by integration, I do not mean assimilation. I believe what the word means—an integer is a whole number. I want to be in the best American traditions. I want to be accepted as a whole man. My standards are not white. My standards are not black. My standards are human. I love the blues. I love jazz and I'm not going to give them up. I love Negro folk speech and I think it is rich and wonderful. It is not *dis* and *dat* and a split verb. But it is "Been down so long that down don't worry me," or it is what spirituals had in one of the finest couplets in American literature: "I don't know what my mother wants to stay here for. This old world ain't been no friend to her." I'm teaching spirituals at Howard. You get a lot of nonsense about the spirituals talking about the good ole days, or when the Negro sings of wanting to be free he means freedom from sin. So when he says, "I've been rebuked and I've been scorned" that means, you know, that he hasn't been baptized yet or something. That kind of nonsense. Newman White, who was a great scholar on Shelley, says the Negro seldom contemplated his low condition. And I want him to ask . . . his mama where he heard that the Negro did not contemplate his low condition. Which Negro, which cook, said that to him and how much winking did the Negro do after he said what he did? The whole picture of the Negro I saw was flagrantly ridiculous. Sometimes the motive was not ignorance, but evil, and that I have fought and am continuing to fight.

Now I want to close this with a statement from another of the people about Williams. But I think the business of the teaching and the importance of Williams to me is there. I learned here to think, I try to make my students think. I learned, I say, critical realism. I want my students to be critically realistic. I want them to look at what is on the page, and think about it.

One last anecdote. I like to send out the audience laughing. I had a room in Berkshire Hall about as big as a telephone booth, but that was all my father could afford. My father had two jobs. He was professor of theology at Howard, and he was a minister; and he got no money for either job. My sisters taught school and put me through. I waited tables at Zeta Psi fraternity for one year. Then I ate on Spring St. and I lived on Western sandwiches, which I still love, and Lorna Doones and water. This is not *Black Boy* . . . I ate, as you can see I have an *embonpoint* (French for belly). I was skinny then, but I was eating enough. I was eating a kind of monotonous diet. But I still love Lorna Doones. They are better than ordinary crackers; they got a little butter or shortening or something in them. But I ate Westerns. I had Westerns, I had Easterns, and I had milkshakes. I spent most of my money across the street at Bemis's store, buying second-hand books that the Williams students had sold there. I have a beautiful library, and that was the nucleus of it—a lot of books—from Williams 1913, Williams 1919. Fine books, 'cause Williams made you buy good books. So I ate on Spring St. and starved. When I went to Boston to join the fraternity, I didn't eat for a while, but I made it. I made it down to the present until I have, you know, a "bay window."

Carter was even poorer. We went to a dance in Pittsfield one cold night. We did not have many clothes, and Carter did not have a full suit with long breeches. We were wearing knickerbockers which we got at Rudnick's; these were second-hand knickerbockers. Lots of people wore rough clothes then. This was after World War I. Carter Marshall comes to a dance—a full-dress dance at Pittsfield. Everybody else is there in full dress. I had on a suit. Henry had on a part suit. Carter came in with a long coat and nothing but golf stockings showing beneath. Looked very bad. And he says to me, in front of these people who were running the dance . . . they did not like us much, we were intruders. Carter has to explain why he comes there in a long coat and his skinny legs in golf stockings and his great big shoes. He says, "Sterling, the news of the dance came to me when I was on the links. And I could not go home and change." There was six feet of snow on the ground. Carter Marshall did not know which end of the golf stick to use. And this guy comes telling me that "I was out on the links." Good God Almighty!

The last lie is that I had a kind of literary group in this telephone booth in Berkshire. And a lot of the intellectuals and the mavericks— you know, the ones who didn't mind being known to associate with a Negro—the rebels—they would come in there. You can always find five or six of them. We were sitting in there one night and in comes Gyp Symonds with a hat on, a kind of Alpine hat, knickerbockers, and a cane. He comes in and he starts with the Latin: *Non sum qualis eram bonae sub regno Cynarae.*

All of us looked at him like he was crazy, which he was. He was a great guy. He was a fine poet and I looked for great things from him, but I think he went the other way. He intoned:

> Last night, ah, yesternight, betwixt her lips and mine
> There fell thy shadow, Cynara! thy breath was shed
> Upon my soul between the kisses and the wine;
> And I was desolate and sick of an old passion,
>   Yea, I was desolate and bowed my head:
> I have been faithful to thee, Cynara! in my fashion.

And then he went through the next two stanzas and closed with

> I cried for madder music and for stronger wine,
> But when the feast is finished and the lamps expire,

Then falls thy shadow, Cynara! the night is thine;
And I am desolate and sick of an old passion,
    Yea, hungry for the lips of my desire:
I have been faithful to thee, Cynara! in my fashion.

Oh, he was great. I learned the poem by heart. I quoted it all up and down the Atlantic seacoast. I won my wife by reciting it, "I have been faithful to thee, Cynara!—in my fashion."

It introduced me to Ernest Dowson. We had studied Swinburne. But here was a better Swinburne and he was something! So, Symonds broke up the meeting; we had never heard such things. That was the temper of the times. But when I went to Harvard, I learned about Edwin Arlington Robinson, Edgar Lee Masters, and that monstrosity written by Vachel Lindsay called "The Congo." When I read this poem to my classes they love it and I say, "think about it": and then they hate it. "Then I saw the Congo creeping through the black, cutting through the jungle with a golden track!" I tried to write a parody, with Severn cutting through the Anglo-Saxon, but I couldn't get a rhyme for "Anglo-Saxon" except "claxon" and "claxon" is a bad horn. So I had to give it up. But I do have a poem called *The New Congo*. And it is a killer.

Now I'm going to close this with a poem from a man who taught at Dartmouth. He comes from this neighborhood and he wrote about New Hampshire and north of Boston, a man who has meant a great deal to me. Langston Hughes has meant much to me, Richard Wright, Claude McKay, Ralph Ellison, and I have learned also from people like Robert Frost. And this is the end of my 72nd year to you. I swear I'm not going to say one word after I explain this poem. I must explain it. Because you will say, "Why does a man who studied T. S. Eliot and Ezra Pound give us this doggerel?" It is not doggerel. This, to me, says more than a whole lot of the *Cantos*, which I have read, and have not dug completely, as many critics haven't. I read T. S. Eliot's *Waste Land* when I was at Harvard. I bought a copy at the Harvard Co-op and I worked out at that time a good exegesis of it. And I knew a lot about those allusions. "And April is the cruelest month." I knew it almost by heart. So I had my Eliot period, and I've also had my falling out with the Anglican so forth and so forth and so on.

This poem is called "In Dives' Dive." I met Robert Frost once and quoted this to him and he said that I was the only person he knew that knew this poem and respected it. I loved it. He asked me did I play poker and I told him no and he said that he didn't play good poker either. We talked about poker and there were a whole slough of new poets there. He and I were the old poets talking about "Dives' Dive." Ladies and gentlemen, from an Old Book known as the Bible, there was a character named Dives. And in the spiritual it is:

> Rich man Dives he lived so well, don't you see
> Rich man Dives lived so well, don't you see
> Rich man Dives lived so well,
> When he died he found a home in hell
> He had a home in that Rock, don't you see.
>
> Po' boy Lazarus, po' as I, don't you see
> Po' boy Lazarus, po' as I, don't you see
> Po' boy Lazarus, po' as I,
> When he died he found a home on high
> I got a home in that Rock, don't you see.

So Frost takes Brother Dives. Ladies and gentlemen, the word "dive" means a low place. It means a haunt of iniquity. It means what you privileged children know nothing about. This is not worth going into. That is what a dive is. There is gambling there and many other things unmentionable in a mixed society. I am trying to give you now an exegesis in the manner of the New Critics. I want you to understand the language and then you get the meaning. And of course the structure of the poem is the important thing. The biography of the author has nothing to do with it. So you get your meaning, but I want you to know *what in the hell I'm talking about.* They're talking about a game named "poker." I've got to explain it afterwards, because if you don't like this poem my evening is ruined. And don't throw "Ash Wednesday" at me either. This is a poem for me. This is an autobiographic "sounding off."

> It is late at night and still I am losing,
> But still I am steady and unaccusing.
>
> As long as the Declaration guards
> My right to be equal in number of cards,
>
> It is nothing to me who runs the Dive
> Let's have a look at another five.

Now this means that Frost is gambling, and he has been a loser all of his life. As far as I am concerned, I have been a loser most of my life. But in the seventies, I've been a winner; you know like coming back to Williams, etc. "It is late at night": Frost was in his seventies or later, that's what "late at night" means. It is late at night and still I'm losing. But *still I* am steady and unaccusing. He is not laying any blame on anybody. If I lose I am not singing blues about anybody else causing it. I am steady and unaccusing. As long as the Declaration—*the Declaration of Inde-*

pendence as long as the Declaration guards—g-u-a-r-d-s. "As long as the Declaration *guards* my right to be *equal* in number of cards." You don't have any more cards than I have. I don't have any more than you have. We got the same number of cards. As long as the Declaration guards my right to be equal in number of cards, it does not matter to me who runs the dive. Now that's where a lot of my liberal friends disagree, and I too would agree with them somewhat. It matters who runs it. But he is saying it does not matter who runs the dive. I, Frost, an American individual, will take my chance. I'm not a good poker player, but I'm not complaining. It does not matter to me who runs the dive. Let's have a look at another five. That means he wants five more cards, his right in the game. I'm going to play my hand out with the cards that come. And that to me is a strong statement of a man's belief in America and in himself.

And that is the last of my 72 years speech to you.

UPLIFT FROM A DARK TOWER AND OTHER POEMS

MICHAEL S. HARPER

Those who profess to favor Freedom, and yet deprecate agitation, are men who want crops without plowing up the ground. . . . Power concedes nothing without a demand.
FREDERICK DOUGLASS

Because in a day when the human mind aspired to a science of human action, a history and psychology of the mighty effort of the mightiest century, we fell under the leadership of those who would compromise with truth in the past in order to make peace in the present and guide policy in the future. W. E. B. DU BOIS

The presentation of facts, on a high, dignified plane, is all the begging that most rich people care for. . . . It is easily possible that some of my former owners might be present to hear me speak. BOOKER T. WASHINGTON

I. THE BATTLE OF SARATOGA (Springs) REVISITED

Just when I think I've got you nailed
to your cross of uplift
I see your name in the private printing
of a history of *Yaddo,*
meaning *shadow* or *shimmering,*
its 500-acre testimonial to lakes
over gardens, trees
buried with *lost* children
whose memory donated this tower
studio to my writing of you.

Outside the door might lie *Etienne,*
the cannibal brought by missionaries
from Africa to be trained for service
in the experimental summer of 1881.
He would be St. Patrick to Yaddo's Ireland

handling snakes, woodland spiders,
as simple playthings, his station
outside this room, asleep at threshold,
his carving knife, guarding me safely from exit.
Such loyalty, devotion might lie in
pure strain of his cannibal ancestry:
"my body may be black but my soul is white."

He went back to Africa as a trader.

II. DINING FROM A TREED CONDITION, *An Historical Survey*

> *"in order to be successful in any kind of*
> *undertaking, I think the main thing is for*
> *one to grow to the point where he com-*
> *pletely forgets himself; that is, to lose*
> *himself in a great cause."*

At the dinner table where you sat with Peabody,
stirred by the shrewd handicap of scholars and savants,
you opened your certain ginger face
"I was born a slave," rolling jordanized,
accomplished in freedom of all pride,
of all bitterness of a handicapped race
made really safe from Democracy,
the *Trask* check slipped in loamed black
cloth in many dinner wallets of conversation.

I look out the Tower window over the sun-dial
of Etienne's savage memory carved in blue spruce
and the rainbowed cypress hearing Christmas prayers
of Barhyte's slaves, Thom Campbell, his wife, Nancy,
quartered in clear pieces of Bear Swampground
southeast of the Rose Garden, conjuring amused
comic tales of Tom Camel's unselfish episodes
of tree-climbing and masquerade.
Told to saw off a limb on Mr. White's place
he sat on the limb vigorously sawing the obstructing
branch; dazed after a loud crack, on the ground
Tom cried to Mr. White: "Oh, no Sah! I had the good
fortune to land on mah head";
dressed up in carriage, in woman's clothes,

Camel posed as Burr's Mistress in Stone's
"Reminiscences of Saratoga," as Madame Jumel on one of her
visits in 1849, in *criminal* intimacy, at US Hotel,
threatened, bribed, as she followed her counterfeit
double, Tom Camel, fanning himself, curtseying
to crowds on every side to the lakefront with Burr.
(Poor Hamilton never had a chance at masquerade;
Burgoyne, Benedict Arnold cavort on Saratoga field.)

Tales of remembrance, of master and slave,
of mistress, of American patriot in the French style,
take me through statuary, rock and rose gardens,
lakes named for children, concola, white pines
as "spiritual linguist," the shadow of Yaddo's
pine and rose on thresholds of cypress, the hanging tree
where Mohawks worshipped
and Camel's chained image swung to ground,
a head injury of coiffured masquerade.

The caned walking stick
I borrow from bicycle paths
in metaphor for your whipping to early death,
inviting Madame Jumel perhaps,
your huge clothesbasket full of checks,
the *exposition* address
marketed in cottonballs of fleeced gowns
in a dining hall
where the surprise party
was held on the burned ashes of this rainbow.

III. THE FOUNDING FATHERS IN PHILADELPHIA

*"some of the questions he asked about the
Negro church denominations were: the
number of communicants, the percentage
of male and female members, the seating
capacity of the churches, the value of the
parsonages, and the total collection of the
African Methodist Episcopal Missionary
Department from 1904 to 1908. Again,
there was no connection drawn between
any of the material offered in 1909 and the
data given in the earlier v's."*

Meeting in secret, with my great
grandfather AME bishop in Philadelphia,
just before his debarking the ship
from South Africa, I see the choices
for education and literacy of a *downtrodden* people
flushed down the outlet of the ocean
liner, where my earmarked greatgrand
fluxed precious diamonds from the Zulu
chiefs, before stolen by customs.

What tongues did the diamonds speak?
To be educated by black spiritual linguists
from runaway Canada
or the pontifs of paternity
in the plazas of Saratoga,
I remind myself with a visit to harnessed
racing, no single black jockey present,
for this is even betting handicapped
at fifty dollars and my best thoroughbred
in August, where the Indian spirits
praise a five-hundred-year-old tree
nourished by sacred sping water,
its radioactivity signs ignored,
the freed slave runaways
paddling down the Hudson to Catskill
to the dayline my grandfather ran
before the bridge to Kingston
took his house, his children, to Brooklyn.

IV. PSYCHOPHOTOS OF HAMPTON

> . . . *in all fairness to Washington we must
> recall that Armstrong, in effect, gave
> Washington his career.* ROBERT B. STEPTO

Dining at 8 and 6:30
with a lunchpail for noon,
I type out the echoes of artist
in the high studio of the tower,
blackened in the image of Etienne,
his cannibal ancestry sharpened
by the sloped Adirondacks toward Montreal

where French/Indian alliances of beaver pelts
end in burrows of buffalo on open plains,
another mountain range to cross, the salt lick
of lake claiming runaway bigamists,
and the great Sioux herds on the run to Cody,
named for the diseased man who died in Denver,
his widow offered forty grand to be buried near his name.

On a ride down 9W to Esopus, New York
where Wiltwyck boys from five boroughs
came to the Roosevelt mansion-estate, the volunteers
driving buses with Mennonite alms, to home visits
of abandoned projects, each welfare roll breaking
in fired windows, I take the granite sites
of General Armstrong into view, his great twin
burial rocks, Vermont granite, Sandwich lava
entrancing the mausoleum of the great divide
of history, of railroad lands, of the *Dakotah*,
Sandwich missions, the uplift of schoolmarms
tuning the pens of the Freedmen's Bureau toward
the thin line of traintrack near Emancipation Tree.

At $68/head, the great Dakotah nation went to college,
from Black Hills to mosquitoed swamp near Fort Monroe,
where the fevered zeal of the government
reimbursed each Indian with black suit,
haircut, and a class photograph:

I walk out over swampgrounds, campsites,
drumbeats of the great cemetery
surrounded by sane spirits of the great mansion
at Arlington where Robert E. Lee's doorstep
sprouted with Union graves terraced from his veranda:

For Daniel Fire-Cloud, Sioux, South Dakotah
died September 3 1886, 14 years
Armstrong Firecloud, Sioux, born Hampton
died August 6 1886, infant
Virginia Medicine-Bull, Sioux, South Dakotah
died January 30 1886
Simon Mazakutte, Sioux, South Dakotah
died March 26 1884, 18 years
Benjamin Bear-Bird, Sioux, South Dakotah

died August 4 1885, aged 2 years
Edith Yellow-Hair, Sioux, South Dakotah
died November 26 1885, aged 8 years
Emma Whips, Sioux, South Dakotah
died March 25 1885
Lora Bowed-Head Snow, Sioux, South Dakotah
died March 20 1885, aged 22 years
Mary Pretty-Hair, Sioux, South Dakotah
died January 6 1885, aged 14 years
Eva Good-Road, Sioux, South Dakotah
died January 4 1884, aged 17 years
Belany Sayon-Sululand, South Africa
died December 10 1884, aged 22 years
Edward Buck, Sioux, South Dakotah
died May 30 1884, aged 17 years
Croaking Wing, Mandan, North Dakotah
died April 21 1884, aged 17 years
Francesca Rios, Papago, Arizona
died August 21 1883, aged 15 years
Henry Kendall Acolehut, Yuma, Arizona
died August 13 1883, aged 22 years
Tasute White Back, Gros Ventre, North Dakotah
died January 24 1882, aged 15 years.
I leave out fully anglicized names,
some duplications among the Sioux (meaning dog)
for fear of repeat of the Dakotah.
Buried in graveyards of the great founding
academies, their souls finally saved
from highlands where they were born.
The great Lincoln train
winds into great centennial avenues
where each kneeled slave has the great veil
lifted from his eyes, his enlightened
face literate from heart to mind,
penciled in nightmare,
where the rainbow mansion,
tiered rose garden, Bearground Swamp
vessels the dark interior
of this book I write of the Shadow,
Unjungian and unsurveyed,

in the cleaning of your first bedroom,
over and over the coaldust you brought
under fingernails
as you scratched toward the caning
which would take your exhibition,
your address of the great ship,
its crew calling for water,
clear-watered-buckets-scooping-downward
in five equally broken fingers.

Separate as the limed hand
the five great Indian nations
disappear along the trail
of tears, the common man of Andrew
Jackson looking moonstruck in black regiments
for the Seminoles of Florida,
each Catholic outpost
St. Paul's reservation of Little Crow
waiting for rations,
the St. Louis Fair
where Geronimo breathed the gas
from the Ford caught in the mud
gatewayed in his western eyes,
to New Orleans, where the musicians
stomp all night to Buster's for breakfast,
the buildings boarded up with slave anklets,
the militia protecting the war ships
of Toussaint in Napoleon's gift to Jefferson.

Your simplest image was the crab-barrel,
each black hand pulling the escaping soul
back into the pit where the turpentine
gangs sang, cutting their way through each
wilderness, each Indian amulet dropping
in cross-fires of settlers,
your great dining hall opening:
"I was born a slave,"
countered by Aristotle's
"some men are natural born slaves,"
in the boards of Wall Street,
where Melville wrote the dark glimmerings
scrimshaw tales, attached by the whale,

his bludgeoned knife raised in combat,
his sweat in the oiled battle with self,
where the nation stormed in fish beds
as laughing men and women dove
in triangular trade winds.

The last view is the best,
from the terrace overhang,
with a toothbrush,
seeing rock gardens and roses
pool in cascading fountains:
the Renaissance built on slave trading,
Etienne proud of his lineage,
Booker T's bookings humbling his beginnings,
the abstract masks giving off power,
its conjured being dynamized in my skin,
reminiscing at the founder's table
where the talk was of politics,
rhetoric, and the literature of the great
rainbowed swamp from the vision of the black tower

GOING TO THE TERRITORY:
ICONS OF GEOGRAPHY OF THE WORD:
A MEDITATION ON THE LIFE AND TIMES
OF RALPH WALDO ELLISON

Ethical schizophrenia you called it:
come back to haunt the cattle-drive,
Indians coming into blacktown
because it's home; your father's will
lies uncontested, his blood welling up in oil;
'Deep Second' hones its marks in Jimmy Rushing;
Charlie Christian's father leads the blind.

Such instruments arrange themselves
at Gettysburg, at Chickamauga;
the whites in Tulsa apologize
in the separate library,
all the books you dreamed of,
fairy tales and Satchmo jesting
to the court of St. James,
infirmary is the saints already home.

The hip connected to the thigh
converges in tuberculosis; your mother's
knees spank the planks of rectory,
your father's image sanctified
in documents, in acts won out
on hallelujahs of "A" train,
nine Scottsboro Boys spun upward
over thresholds of Duke's dance.

Dance and mask collect their greasepaint,
idioms stand on bandstand, in stove-
pipe pants of riverman, gambling shoes,
gold-toothed venom vexing sundown,
the choir at sunrise-service cleansing
a life on a jim crow funeral car.

The first true phrase sings out in barnyard;
the hunt in books for quail.

THE HAWK TRADITION:
EMBROCHURES OF A PHOTO
NOT TAKEN OF COLEMAN HAWKINS

This is not a poem about flying
in the wrong direction;
into the sun no shadow
appears on the ground;
up in the clouds
a man in middle age
walks into the Missouri River
not far from St. Jo.

Why mention the Pony Express
as umbrella, a swift pinto horse
manacled in hurricanes of dance;
he rides in the eye of storm,
his echo glissing neither
nameless nor without displacement.

His arms around a Lady,
pressed trousers, 'round his armpits,
his roostered shirtfront perfect
before the band; her earthy toothbrush
sings up-front of Hawk's solo:
this photo's familial with information:

Remember the river; the pony express:
his relatives know each place where his songs
bristle, where his name dances on water,
the back of any swift horse.

THE HISTORICAL FREQUENCIES OF RALPH WALDO ELLISON

JOHN F. CALLAHAN

I

In recent years critics have shared with politicians a strange fixation with history, as if the word itself were an incantation. This may be simply a guise learned from public men. One of the tests on the stump these days is whether a presidential candidate has a sense of history. Once in office, a president's mere mention of American history seems to ward off criticism, like a charm keeping away evil spirits. Even Gerald Ford's bicentennial misquotation of Paul Revere—"one if by day and two if by night," I think he said—didn't offend people very much. Like presidents, writers, particularly novelists and critics of the novel, are often prepared to take advantage of the spell of history. Now there is an explanation, if not an excuse for this; after all, the novel emerged as a response to changing social and economic relationships in the eighteenth century, and its form has continued to change with society's changing patterns. Yet in our time a certain posturing often accompanies invocations of history. Mailer did it in *The Armies of the Night,* titling Book One "History as a Novel," Book Two "The Novel as History." Critics, in their aversion for declarations of self, frequently tend to mix abstraction with incantation.

Behind the use of history as incantation lies an understandable human desire to magnify the self through identification with larger forces and realities: the big picture. The danger is twofold. First is the mumbo-jumbo syndrome; i.e., everyone uses history and tacitly agrees not to question another's meaning. Second, true believers of all persuasions pin down history to such an extent that it's pinioned to ideology, its complexities reduced to formulas and stereotypes. I am afraid the handiest example of the merging of these dangers is Walter Cronkite's patented line: "That's the way it is, such and such a day, such and such a month, nineteen hundred and so and so." No matter what's happened, that's the way it is. Who knows what that means? All we know is that what we've watched during the last half-hour is supposed to cover all bets. With what's happened to point of view in this century, it's a wonder of the world that Walter keeps saying his line night after night, and greater wonder that for his pains he is regarded as the most trusted man in America.

The foregoing is by way of counterpoint to Ralph Ellison's use of history. Though deadly serious about the meaning and the use of history in his work, Ellison approaches the subject partly from a comic perspective. Like all incongruities, history, no less than posturings of history, is comic in the sense that it opens up the field of possibility. On one occasion, Ellison irreverently told the Southern Historical Association: "I don't think that history is Truth. I think it's another form of man trying to find himself, and to come to grips with his own complexity, but within the frame of chronology and time." [1] Earlier in his remarks he had claimed that American historiography and American fiction are "both artificial; both are forms of literature, and I would suggest further that American history grows primarily out of the same attitudes of mind, and attitudes toward chronology, which gave birth to our great tall stories" (p. 62). This is a comic clue to Ellison's quarrel with American history as written. A little later he narrows the focus to those "realities of American historical experience ruled out officially," that "stream of history which is still as tightly connected with folklore and the oral tradition as official history is connected with the tall tale" (p. 69). "Stream of history"—the words telegraph Ellison's sense that, taken in all its forms, this republic's history lives up to its motto, *e pluribus unum,* even as the Mississippi is composed of countless independent, related tributaries.

Alongside chaos, a name for raw, uncharted experience, is the making of history—the forms we come up with when consciousness goes to work on what's happened and what's happening. Ellison never loses sight of the elusive play between the past and attitudes and circumstances behind human attempts to order the past. Here are two illustrations of how Ellison works, the first involving Irving Howe, the second Imamu Baraka (then LeRoi Jones). In response to Howe's essay "Black Boys and Native Sons," Ellison wrote Part I of "The World and the Jug," to which Howe replied, and to which Ellison wrote Part II. The following exchanges are sad and funny and devastating insights into the frequencies of American consciousness.

ELLISON: Well, it all sounds quite familiar and I fear the social order which it forecasts more than I do that of Mississippi.[2]
HOWE: This sentence seems to me shocking, both as it links me with a cultural authoritarianism I have spent decades in opposing and as it declares the state of Ross Barnett more palatable than what I am alleged to represent.[3]
ELLISON: . . . Ross Barnett is not the whole state, . . . there is also a Negro Mississippi which is more varied than that which Wright depicted.[4]

Given America's peculiar fluidity and diversity, historical consciousness depends on a well-honed sense of nuance and complexity. To use a metaphor: Ellison threw Howe a round-house curve on a three-two pitch when the latter thought he had every right to expect a fastball. Howe, in the assurance that he knows Ellison's stuff inside and out, fails to realize that one's best pitch depends on the circumstances. Fooled and made a strikeout victim, Howe looks to the umpire and, finding none, appeals to the crowd. Ellison, however, is defiantly in control of his stuff, and when Howe hollers, he points out that the stereotype is in Howe's mind and not in the word "Mississippi."

Similar in what it reveals of the quality of Ellison's mind is his response to a statement made by Jones in *Blues People:*

"A slave," writes Jones, "cannot be a man." But what, one might ask, of those moments when he feels his metabolism aroused by the rising of the sap in spring? What of his identity among other slaves? With his wife? And isn't it closer to the truth that far from considering themselves only in terms of that abstraction, " a slave," the enslaved really thought of themselves as *men* who had been unjustly enslaved?[5]

It is one of Ellison's great strengths that his sense of everlasting relationship between chaos and possibility steels him against the superficialities of passing vogues. For him an individual is not wholly defined by history and ideology; always there is some act of will; always possibilities of an unforeseen, unpredictable nature intervene. Yet Ellison is finely scrupulous about his own point of view. After destroying Jones's absolute assertion, he writes that slavery was not a state of absolute repression. He does not say that no such state could exist, but calls attention to fluidities which for his purposes are even more important than the injustices and oppressions of slavery.

Over the years Ralph Waldo Ellison has become a preeminent American moral historian. In his essays as well as in his novel, he combines the myth-maker's imagination with the historian's instinct for specific acts of the past. While in Rome, he tells us in "Tell It Like It Is, Baby," [6] he dreamed of Lincoln's body defiled by the mob—Lincoln as coon, picked clean like poor Robin of folklore. Like Hawthorne's "My Kinsman, Major Molineux," it is a tale of fatherhood and nationhood, and Ellison is explicit about the role of his father, who died when he was three. The dream also resonates with images of democratic affirmation and denial as old as the republic—and as new. Specifically, Lincoln's stand for freedom and democracy and the mob's desecration of those principles is Ellison's working out of "the horror generated by the Civil War" and contained in the contemporary situation—explicitly, the Supreme Court's 1954 desegregation decision and the 1956 manifesto of southern congressmen against the court.

For Ellison the "moral predicament of the nation" is revealed everywhere in American life as essential baggage destined to accompany the "American experiment." His sense of American history involves a chronology, but the chronology's form follows the trajectory of a boomerang—"(Beware of those who speak of the *spiral* of history; they are preparing a boomerang)." [7] The words and promises hurled at the republic's beginning return over and over again to startle, injure, and, certainly, to challenge those who speak for the country and those who hold it accountable for its democratic promises and traditions. In the Epilogue to *Invisible Man* Ellison's character speaks of "the principle on which the country was built." He does not mention explicitly the Declaration of Independence, the Bill of Rights, Lincoln's Gettysburg Address or Second Inaugural, or any of the documents of state that Ellison builds his case on in his essays. Nevertheless, there emerges a notion of history as a name for the process by which man shapes his destiny out of the chaos of circumstances. Everywhere in Ellison's work chaos appears as the front man for possibility. It is, Ellison believes, man's fate to defy the formlessness of chaos and the abyss, and at the same time to recognize that possibility flows from chaos. Ellison's parable comes down to the myth of creation reworked by the historical mind in a battle royal of consciousness and circumstances. He doesn't crow about it—much—but Ellison plays out a defiant, richly independent variation on the romantic myth of Eden so often and so simplistically associated with America. His bent is historical, perhaps because his mind listens to what his experience is telling him: to ignore history ("To ignore," however, as he says of the racial issue, "is not to nullify") [8] is to miss out on the world of possibilities inherent in the interplay between the individual and society. In any case, Ellison's version of the beginnings of the American nation is secular, sacred too, but he uses that word with a twist. For him the responsibilities citizens have to each other and to society in a democracy are no less than sacred; that is, involving dedication and sacrifice, and charged with the ultimate concerns that were once reserved for religion and the gods.

Therefore, in his version of the beginning, Ellison concentrates on the shaping of the nation. Circumstances—grievances against the crown—provided an occasion to articulate fully and put to the test principles which hitherto had existed in men's minds. As Invisible Man puts it in the Epilogue—really a Bill of Rights (and responsibilities), just as the Prologue acts as a Declaration of Independence—this nation was an expression of the "principle, which they themselves had dreamed into being out of the darkness and chaos of the feudal past" (p. 433). Notice the mixing of history and myth. The feudal past is

alluded to as an almost primal state of formlessness; the founders'
dream is a dream of creation but not of Eden or any private Utopia.
Instead, they dream of government, of society, of the rights and duties
of individuals in society, and of the public happiness John Adams felt
would exist in such a state.

In "Society, Morality, and the Novel"—a 1956 essay critics neglect
at great peril—Ellison writes eloquently about what was set in motion
by those who founded the nation. "In the beginning was not only the
word but the contradiction of the word." [9] Affirming the novel, he
affirms also the country as a field of change and possibility—and
absurdity, another of Ellison's characteristic words. In the beginning
was the assertion of equality and the contradiction of slavery. In the
beginning was the declaration of the right to life, liberty, and the
pursuit of happiness and the contradiction of the right. But—and this is
Ellison's magnificent point—in the state of contradiction lay a world of
democratic possibilities. "For in no other country was change such a
given factor of existence; in no other country were the class lines so
fluid and change so swift and continuous *and intentional*. In no other
country were men so conscious of having defined their social aims or so
committed to working toward making that definition a reality"
(pp. 66–67). These possibilities of self Ellison grounds in public moral
and social commitments. "The major ideas of our society," he observes,
were "all grounded in a body of the most abstract and explicitly stated
conceptions of human society and one which in the form of the great
documents of state constitutes a body of assumptions about human
possibility which is shared by all Americans—even those who resist
most violently any attempt to embody them in social action" (p. 69).

Form is the heart of the matter. Like Frederick Douglass when he
broke with Garrison, does Ellison have in mind the Constitution whose
open form invites social and political change? Clearly, Ellison both
accepts and rejects contradictions of the early republic, "for man cannot
simply say, 'Let us have liberty and justice and equality for all,' and have
it; and a democracy more than any other system is always pregnant
with its contradiction" (p. 70). The central contradiction of course
involved slavery and democracy, a contradiction whose tensions
erupted in the Civil War eighty-five years after Americans had declared
themselves free. During the war years President Lincoln leavened his
sense of fated tragic necessity with a quality of leadership both stoical
and tender, and therefore was able to reconcile the inevitable with the
possible. For Lincoln the word was as sacred as the deed—an enabling
force. In the Gettysburg Address and Second Inaugural he com-
mitted the nation to resolve its contradiction in favor of freedom and
equality. What is uttered is the word and the fulfillment of the word.
Yet, as Ellison reminds us, and Lincoln warned, the Gettysburg

Address, once hallowed, became unhallowed (the contradiction again). But not entirely. Because how many Americans, reading and memorizing its words, like Ellison "pondered its themes of sectional reconciliation and national rebirth many times long since, as the awareness grew that there was little about it that was simple and that it was profoundly implicated both in my life and in the failure of my promised freedom."[10] In this case the destiny of the word was tied up with the destiny of the man: hallowed in death, Lincoln's memory and accomplishment were soon unhallowed by violations of the principles he gave his life for. In a judgment both measured and passionate, Ellison suggests that "all the material progress released after the war" made Americans "evasive and given to compromise on basic principles." As a result, in his words, " . . . we have the interruption of moral continuity symbolized in the failure of Reconstruction and the Hayes-Tilden Compromise."[11]

    Ellison develops this theme of the nation's exchange of "moral predicament" for "moral evasion" in a 1960 essay called "Stephen Crane and the Mainstream of American Fiction." "To put it drastically," he observes, "if war, as Clausewitz insisted, is the continuation of politics by other means, it requires little imagination to see American life since the abandonment of the Reconstruction as an abrupt reversal of that formula: a continuation of the Civil War by means other than arms." He writes of an "unceasing state of civil war," characterizing the "America into which Crane was born" as "one of mirrorlike reversals in which the victors were the defeated and the defeated the victors; with the South, its memory frozen at the fixed moment of its surrender, carrying its aggression to the North in the form of guerilla politics, and with the North, compromising as it went, retreating swiftly into the vast expanse of its new industrial development, eager to lose any memory traces of those values for which it had gone to war."[12] Given the submergence of these reversals in national consciousness, it is small wonder Ellison links official American history to the tall tale.

    I have called Ellison a moral historian. Unlike the conventional historian, whom he claims is dedicated to chronology, he explores a great issue which, because of its abiding human qualities and specific national circumstances, informs chronology and prevents official history from imposing too false an order on American life. To put it positively, the pursuit of history provides a form and a frame for self-discovery. For Ellison the crucial point is that time and chronology offer cover to the historian, whereas the novelist, as he sees the craft, has nowhere to hide from the requirements of the moral imagination. Even Hemingway, whose narrator in *A Farewell to Arms,* according to Ellison, "denied the very words in which the ideals were set down," "affirms the old American values by the eloquence of his denial; makes his moral point by stating explicitly that he does not believe in morality; achieves his eloquence through denying eloquence; and is most moral when he denies the validity of a national morality which the nation has not bothered to live up to since the Civil War." [13] For Hemingway too the boomerang is a metaphor for the inescapable presence of morality and history in a writer's craft. In the denials is the contradiction of denial; with the reversals comes a sharpened consideration of human values, not the least of which is history.

Diversity, fluidity, absurdity, complexity, chaos, swiftness of change —the words stand out in Ellison's mind like tablets "announcing" the conditions of American life. One cannot overestimate the extent to which he derives his point of view from the experience of growing up in Oklahoma, a state admitted to the Union as late as 1907, seven years before Ellison's birth. It was the place, as he is fond of pointing out (bragging a little), that Twain had in mind when Huck Finn talks about lighting out for the territory. Oklahoma—a dream world.

"Geography is fate," Ellison recently told those present at the dedication of the Ralph Ellison Branch Library in Oklahoma City.

> The outcome of that national tragedy the Civil War brought the parents of many of us, both black and white, to the Oklahoma territory, seeking a new beginning. This I see as their enactment of a strongly held American proposition that men make their own fate through the humanization of geography and by the concerted assertion of their human will. At any rate, our forefathers collected here, and strove anew to make manifest the American Dream. They came from many places, with many philosophies, and with conflicting interpretations of the democratic compact which our nation's founding fathers had made with history. [14]

During Ellison's youth Oklahoma was segregated and becoming more so under the thumb of the notorious Alfalfa Bill Murray. Yet there were openings. He writes movingly that "my father had many white friends who came to the house when I was quite small, so that any feelings of distrust I was to develop toward whites later on were modified by those with whom I had warm relations." [15] There was enough fluidity in race relations for Ellison and a half-dozen of his friends to project themselves as Renaissance Men. "Renaissance Men, indeed!" he writes in retrospect, thinking that he and his companions were "but two generations from that previous condition" of slavery. [16]

Behind the mask of irony and self-mockery Ellison is deadly serious. In reality, he has absorbed the qualities and the learning of the Renaissance Man and reinforced the concept with the style and traditions of black American experience. He is fiercely proud of his people; doubtless, this accounts for his refusal to let anything go that might deny or diminish the heroic scale of slavery. Here is his evocation of the indomitable past which lies behind his complex, independent imagination: "Any people who could endure all of that brutality and keep together, who could undergo such dismemberment and resuscitate itself, and endure until it could take the initiative in achieving its own freedom is obviously more than the sum of its brutalization. Seen in this perspective, theirs has been one of the great triumphs of the human spirit in modern times. In fact, in the history of the world." [17] There it stands: Ellison's heritage and his consciousness of its moral and historical meaning. He is a man who carries on the traditions of which he speaks and writes, a man who, in James McPherson's words, "doggedly affirms his identity as a Negro-American, a product of the blending of both cultures." [18]

"'I recognize,'" he told McPherson, "'no American culture which is not the partial creation of black people. I recognize no American style in literature, in dance, in music, even in assembly-line processes, which does not bear the mark of the American Negro.'" [19] It goes way back, this matter of race and personality in American society. One thinks of landmarks along the way, of Du Bois's assertion at the beginning of the century that "the problem of the twentieth century is the problem of the color line." [20] Bound up with this are his metaphors of double-consciousness and the veil, both of which Ellison picks up and tests in *Invisible Man* as he explores the dream of personality. Again, Du Bois: "The history of the American Negro is the history of this strife,—this longing to attain self-conscious manhood, to merge his double self into a better and truer self" (p. 17). Of course this is a universal longing, but the specific circumstances of race and their location at the center of the American experiment put the dream in the marrow of Ralph Ellison's experience and tradition. Maybe this is what he means when he says, "I don't think that history is Truth," and when he says that the craft of novelist in the United States "offers me the possibility of contributing not only to the growth of the literature but to the shaping of the culture as I should like it to be." [21] When all is said and done (and written), there remains the process of self-creation, that transforming passage to a "better and truer self." Because of democracy, this is, has been, and shall be for the individual and for the nation a matter of urgent, utmost craft.

II

Well, what is the use of history in *Invisible Man*? In the novel as well as in essays it is through form that Ellison reveals his approach to history. Obviously, there is both chronology and a reality beyond chronology. For Ellison, the historian and the historical method operate "within the frame of chronology and time," but, for the novelist, consciousness is all. The making of self, however, is linked to the making of history. Both processes are continuous, and so it is that in *Invisible Man* Ellison aims for a time frequency that I'll call the continuing present.

Consciousness and chronology is the paradox Ellison explores. Consider the form of *Invisible Man*. Formally, the Prologue comes before the narrative. Chronologically, it comes after. And in terms of consciousness the narrative follows the Prologue because, *as he writes,* Invisible Man's sense of himself and his story deepens and changes. The last piece, the Epilogue, follows the Prologue and the narrative in the sense of carrying forward both chronology and Invisible Man's consciousness. In the Epilogue chronology and consciousness come together in the word and act of the present moment.

Even if there were no Prologue or Epilogue, the novel would open alluding not to what has happened, but to what continues to happen. "It goes a long way back, some twenty years" (p. 13) is the first sentence of the narrative, and Ellison concludes the opening paragraph with Invisible Man's declaration "That I am nobody but myself. But first I had to discover that I am an invisible man!" *Invisible Man,* above all, is a novel about the process of consciousness, and about how the passage to one's root self is a passage through and beyond versions of self prepared by others. Invisible Man, the writer he becomes, is able to see himself three ways: as he was, as his present self sees that former self retrospectively, and, finally, as the person he is in the present. He rarely judges. Instead, he observes and reflects, recognizing that selfhood, like nationhood ("and the novel," Ellison has written, "is bound up with the notion of nationhood" [22]), is a continuing process, and that the game is kept open by a fluid and tolerant as well as a rigorous sensibility.

For a novelist like Ellison the relationship between history and imagination is necessarily complex, and it is no surprise that there are some principles fluidly yet scrupulously at work in *Invisible Man*. The Prologue makes chronology wholly a matter of consciousness, and it is not until the beginning of the narrative that Ellison begins to make clear the principle of his allusive/elusive, explicit/implicit approach to historical time and chronology. When, for example, Invisible Man speaks of "it" going back "some twenty years," he is signalling that this is his time, and that it depends on frequencies of consciousness. In the next breath he speaks of having been in the cards "about eighty-five years ago"—a veiled reference to the public chronology of the Civil War-Reconstruction era. Clearly, the intent is to link consciousness to a definite historical chronology, yet the reference is indefinite and inexplicit; Invisible Man deliberately does not particularize the situation.

Jefferson, Lincoln, Booker T. Washington, Garvey; the Civil War, Emancipation, Reconstruction, World War I—these are presences on Invisible Man's historical landscape. On the other hand, during his some twenty years' experience in the narrative, he avoids even implicit reference to matters of history. Concerning the twenty years in question, presumably from *about* 1930 to *about* 1950, all is veiled and metaphoric. It's as if Ellison holds Invisible Man to a distinction between historical and imaginative consciousness. And the principle is that history (factual matters of chronology and identity) is free to occupy space during the time previous to the fictional experience, but, at that point, imagination assumes full responsibility for the word (and the world).

It is a dilemma, this relationship between history and imagination. Ellison tries to unriddle it by explaining the differing traditions of history and fiction:

> The moment you say something explicit about history in a novel, everybody's going to rise up and knock the Hell out of you, because they suspect that you are trying to take advantage of a form of authority which is sacred. History is sacred, you see, and no matter how false to actual events it might be. But fiction is anything but sacred. By fact and by convention fiction is a projection from one man's mind, of one man's imagination.[23]

Having made the distinction, Ellison affirms the connection between historian and novelist, and suggests that each is responsible for keeping the other honest.

Throughout the narrative Ellison's strategy is one of connotation. He seeks to open up associations and extend significance. For example, although times are tough when Invisible Man, recently arrived in Harlem, accidentally (and fatefully) gets involved in a tenement eviction, there is no mention of the Great Depression. Needless to say, it was for some purpose that Ellison resisted the pull to get some explicit mileage from the thirties. He seems unwilling to restrict the Provos' condition to one point in time, perhaps because of the danger that, if he did so, what has been archetypal in black experience might be laid simply at the door of hard times. Likewise, despite the one-to-one associations critics have made between the Brotherhood and the Communist party, it seems obvious that Ellison invented the Brotherhood precisely in order *not* to limit his portrayal to the Communist party. Surely the Brotherhood derives a measure of significance from its similarity in *some* respects to the relation between American blacks and the Democratic and Republican parties, not to mention the Progressive party of 1948.[24] The same thing is true of the race riot near the end of the book. It bears some relation to the Harlem riot of August,

1943, as well as perhaps to the Harlem riot of March, 1935.[25] But the point is that the riot is Ellison's archetypal projection, in fiction, of the race riot as an American form of violence by no means limited to any particular time and place.

Keeping to his theory, Ellison puts as much distance as possible between events of history and the imagined situations in his novel. With historical figures it is the same. Ras the Exhorter partakes of but is not Marcus Garvey. As a fictional character, he is compelling and lasting in a different way, again because he evokes black nationalism as a power-ful archetype in American experience. As if to underscore this point, Ellison includes allusions to Marcus Garvey alongside the living fic-tional presence of Ras. Clearly, he is making distinctions in order to play out differences *and* associations between history and fiction.

The most complex historical presence in Ellison's novel is Booker T. Washington. From Invisible Man's speech in the South—"In these pre-invisible days I visualized myself as a potential Booker T. Washington" (p. 15)—to the Brotherhood's seductive question after his impromptu first speech in the North—" 'How would you like to be the new Booker T. Washington?' " (p. 231)—his public self is as haunted by Washington as his private self is by his grandfather. Yet, by emphasizing Washing-ton so explicitly and frequently, Ellison plays him off against other veiled but important presences in black American experience. For example, Invisible Man's speech after the battle royal recapitulates differing points of view. His memorized oration takes its form and content from Booker T. Washington's "Atlanta Exposition Address." The other aspect, the slip if you want, derives its form and substance from the improvising tradition represented by Douglass and count-less others, by the black preacher, the blues musician. At any rate, the two phrases—"social responsibility" and "social equality"—express both sides of an old debate in the black community. In the novel both the white men and Invisible Man are so shocked by his substitu-tion that they mutually write it off as wholly an accident having no significance. Yet a few months after Washington delivered his Atlanta Address, a young black scholar named John Hope said this in Nash-ville in public repudiation of Washington's stance: "Now, catch your breath, for I am going to use an adjective: I am going to say we demand social equality. In this republic, we shall be less than freemen, if we have a whit less than that which thrift, education, and honor afford other freemen." [26] Consciously, Invisible Man evokes one tradition, unconsciously another—between the lines of contradiction lie the pain and possibility of his passage to identity.

There is more to be said on Booker T. Washington. Despite Ellison's creation of an unnamed Founder of an unnamed Negro college, critics

perversely insist on one-to-one correspondences. The Founder, some
say, is Booker T. Washington; the college, Tuskegee Institute. Never
mind that Ellison knew the names and chose not to use them. Never
mind that the novel distinguishes—" 'You hear a lot of arguments about
Booker T. Washington, but few would argue about the Founder' "
(p. 232). But there is a larger question. Why should the Founder evoke
only Booker T. Washington? Why not other founders as well? Not
only the founders of Negro colleges, but also figures like George Wash-
ington, Frederick Douglass, and Abraham Lincoln are evoked by the
composite character of the Founder. Here as elsewhere in *Invisible
Man* Ellison creates an archetype that is national as well as racial. For in
these episodes he recapitulates in a tragicomic way the founding of a
social order after the Civil War. The reality is historical and mythic—
archetypal. The circumstance is that unspoken compact arrived at by
certain northern and southern interests. A compact institutionalized
in some of the Negro colleges founded in the South. Doubtless, the
college in the novel partakes of Tuskegee, but it is not contained by
the association. And that is purposeful. Ellison's elusive allusions
parallel the themes of his essays. Mr. Norton, proud of being one of the
original founders, is called a "trustee of consciousness." He evokes
those New Englanders who thought freedom and abolition tran-
scendent goals but who, caught up in Gilded Age materialism, offered
money in place of moral commitment and whose money often upheld
the new order of white supremacy.

   This fictional reversal of transcendent (transcendental) American
principles is climaxed by Mr. Norton's appearance at the Golden Day.
The name evokes a contemporary affirmation and repudiation similar
to the pattern of the nineteenth century. With World War I and Amer-
ica's promise to "make the world safe for democracy" came renewed
hopes that long-denied promises would be honored at home. Instead,
the parades were hardly over, the troops hardly home, before these
hopes were dashed by a decade of reaction epitomized by the resur-
gence of the Klan.
   Ellison's Golden Day is a raunchy sporting house which serves as a
weekly release for a bunch of black veterans who have been consigned
to a quasi insane asylum for transgressions of Jim Crow rules after
their return from France. Again, the interplay is between history and
consciousness. The heroism of black regiments is well known; perhaps
less well known are the humiliations and terrors these soldiers faced
back home, especially in the South. The power of consciousness is
such that Invisible Man tries, but cannot blot out the chaos and con-
tradictions these veterans represent. "Whenever I saw them I felt un-
comfortable. They were supposed to be members of the professions

toward which at various times I vaguely aspired myself; and even though they never seemed to see me I could never believe that they were really patients" (p. 57). Of course he is right; they are not patients but prisoners.

The key episode involves Invisible Man, Mr. Norton, and a vet who has been a brilliant surgeon, a man gifted enough to be only the second doctor able to diagnose Norton's condition—and this in a sporting-house room. Flabbergasted, Norton demands to know more:

> "Oh, yes, and how long were you in France?" Mr. Norton asked.
> "Long enough," he said. "Long enough to forget some fundamentals which I never should have forgotten." (p. 70)

The conversation drags on, Norton asking foolish questions, the vet giving cryptic answers which presuppose that to understand truly a person has to develop an authentic historical consciousness. A whore interrupts, distracting the vet from his strategy. Suddenly, he challenges Norton directly: " 'To some, you are the great white father, to others the lyncher of souls, but for all you are confusion and chaos come even into the Golden Day' " (p. 72). Partly through the complicity of the Mr. Nortons, a social order came into being which destroyed the vet's creative social potential. " 'Ten men in masks drove me out from the city at midnight and beat me with whips for saving a human life. And I was forced to the utmost degradation because I possessed skilled hands and the belief that my knowledge could bring me dignity—not wealth, only dignity—and other men health' " (p. 72). During the encounter Invisible Man experiences ambivalent feelings akin to those two contradictory phrases, *social responsibility* and *social equality*. He realizes the vet's performance may be spoiling his game at the college, yet he receives "a fearful satisfaction from hearing him talk as he had to a white man" (p. 71).

There is no question about who holds the power. Dr. Bledsoe, the amoral, cynical, complex, fascinating president of the college, has both the vet and Invisible Man out of the state the next day. But what of the power of consciousness? The power to keep the game of personality open? In a last encounter on the bus taking each away, the vet gives Invisible Man some curious advice. " 'Be your own father, young man,' " he tells him. " 'And remember, the world is possibility if only you'll discover it' " (p. 120). In the person of Invisible Man, Ellison plays out the psychological urgency of leaping back to one's grandparents in order to discover origins and therefore possibilities of identity. Because of his situation, Invisible Man has little choice but to be his own father in the sense of fathering (looking after, making) himself.

In New York City Brother Jack gives what looks like similar advice. Characteristically, the words are portentous—like a pronouncement by the voice of time in the old newsreels. " '*History* has been born in your brain,' " Jack tells Invisible Man, hoping to persuade him that individuals (" 'agrarian types, you know. Being ground up by industrial conditions' ") don't count (pp. 221, 220). Invisible Man, however, connects these old folks and their imagery to the power of the word. Strewn on the street, the Provos' belongings become a succession of images evoking ancestral kinship ties. Free papers/knocking bones/a curling iron/ nuggets of High John the Conqueror/a small Ethiopian flag/a tintype of Abraham Lincoln/lapsed life insurance policies/a newspaper photo captioned: "MARCUS GARVEY DEPORTED"—these fragments evoke the texture of a people's experience. Invisible Man suddenly feels so deeply part of these folks and his own grandparents that he has no need to contest Jack intellectually. His source of energy is not science but the blues. " '. . . seeing them like that made me feel bad,' " he tells Jack. " ' . . . they're folks just like me, except that I've been to school a few years.' " Listening to Jack's paradigm of rebirth, reminiscent of the company hospital's attempt to erase consciousness and make his brain blank, Invisible Man becomes, if Jack could see him, visibly angry. " ' . . . I made that speech,' " he insists, " 'because I was upset over seeing those old folks put out in the street, that's why. I don't care what *you* call it, I was angry' " (pp. 220-21). Here and elsewhere in *Invisible Man* there is a kinetic flow between experiencing what has been handed down for generations and the capability of action in the present. Acting for Invisible Man is of course speaking (" 'I *like* to make speeches' " [p. 222]), for it is Ellison's purpose to show how Invisible Man has the gift of speech but cannot shape the people's response beyond a formless, chaotic, futile response. Even so, Invisible Man's public consciousness is heightened by the past merging with present moments; his gift is tied to the oral tradition—where the act of improvisation attains force through the old themes, the familiar struggle.

The point is that while the Brotherhood works to instill a rational, scientific view of history in Invisible Man's brain, those powerful images he suppresses on his journey north come to consciousness. It's as if geographically he had to go north to feel the coherence of southern experience, and likewise, intellectually, he has to get involved with scientific politics to discover the power of feeling and intuition—the heart's territory. For a true sense of history he has to leave familiar environments and hear truly that " 'whole unrecorded history . . . spoken' " in " 'gin mills and the barber shops and the juke joints and the churches, Brother. Yes, and the beauty parlors on Saturdays when they're frying hair' " (p. 356). And on the deepest private level he has to hate Tod Clifton, regard him as an enemy, and see him die in the street before he knows the love he bears, before he can ask the question he (and his countrymen) have long repressed: "And could politics ever be an expression of love?" (p. 341) rather than of fear and guilt, of self-absorption, self-justification. We do not know, but we do know that in the world of Ellison's novel knowledge and the transformations that follow depend on some principle of reversal.

Perhaps Ellison holds his character to the same standard against which he tests American identity in the essays. Namely, he argues that "we are a people who, while desiring identity, have been reluctant to pay the cost of its achievement. We have been reluctant since we first suspected that we are fated to live up to our sacred commitments or die, and the Civil War was the form of that fateful knowledge." [27] Invisible Man himself is driven by internal and outside forces to seek his American identity in the riddle spoken by his grandfather in words he hears as a boy, words his father seems too surprised and frightened by to heed. " 'I never told you,' " the old man says on his deathbed, " 'but our life is a war and I have been a traitor all my born days, a spy in the enemy's country ever since I give up my gun back in the Reconstruction' " (p. 13).

This is the language of reversal, and Ellison makes Invisible Man look for the act preceding the shadow of metaphor. The act's the gun and its surrender. It's left to succeeding generations to dig out the history of Reconstruction, especially to those like Invisible Man whose dreams make them vulnerable to Dr. Bledsoe's question: " 'My God, boy! You're black and living in the South—did you forget how to lie?' " (p. 107). The grandfather's imperative is urgent enough today— how much more so a generation ago when, as a matter of course, school books wrote up Reconstruction along straight *Birth of a Nation* lines. Without stating it, he veils *and* reveals the opinion that he and other freedmen were damn fools to give up their guns. We know that some two hundred thousand Negroes fought for the Union Army. We know that President Lincoln in his Second Inaugural Address made freedom and justice for freedmen a sacred moral imperative. We know too of promises made and hopes raised high by the Thirteenth, Fourteenth, and Fifteenth Amendments, by the Freedmen's Bureau and the Freedman's Bank. Finally, we know of the betrayal orchestrated in the Hayes-Tilden Compromise of 1877 and formalized as the law of the land by the *Plessy* v. Ferguson decision of 1896. Again, Ellison's metaphor—life as an "unceasing state of civil war":

> What is the meaning of music?
> What is the meaning of war?
> What is the meaning of oppression? [28]

There is a world of history behind the assertion that " '. . . our life is a war' "; there is also a terrible question: how does a minority, having long since given up its guns, fight such a war? The strategy the old man hands down is based on the complexity of the minstrel tradition.

" '. . . overcome 'em with yeses, undermine 'em with grins, agree 'em to
death and destruction, let 'em swoller you till they vomit or bust wide
open' " (pp. 13-14). After Reconstruction was overthrown, the war
became a guerilla war fought with tactics of pretense, concealment,
masking, or, as Robert Toll calls it in his book on minstrel traditions,
blacking up. These tactics formalized certain ancient and complex folk
techniques of survival.

Invisible Man comes slowly to an understanding of his grand-
father's human complexity. Late in the novel he articulates the
essential role metaphor plays in the drama of historical conscious-
ness. His language goes underground and flows internally, unspoken,
as he begins to see how he has mirrored the Sambo image society
keeps flashing at him. He sees the Brotherhood version of history not
as an absolute but instead as one of many possible metaphors—and
not a very good one at that. "What if history was a gambler," he
muses, "instead of a force in a laboratory experiment. . . .?" Or a
"madman full of paranoid guile" instead of "a reasonable citizen"
(p. 333)? He spoofs the progressive, spiral conception of history, con-
jures up "grooves" of history, and suggests that any number of people
may pass their lives outside history, or at least outside official history.
As if to complement the reversals, he begins to see history in the form of
a boomerang. Best of all, while he meditates, some small boys run by
dropping looted candy bars, a man from the store in pursuit. Confused
by the sudden chaos, Invisible Man stifles an impulse to trip the man
"and was confused all the more when an old woman standing further
along threw out her leg and swung a heavy bag" (p. 335). Again, action
arises from some undeclared tradition of consciousness. During the
riot the same thing happens on an articulate level when Invisible Man
watches several men execute a long-held desire to burn down their
squalid tenement. "Capable of their own action . . ." (p. 414; Ellison's
ellipsis), he muses, meditating again as history gets made before him,
improvisationally, in variations going back to the profound double
meanings of the sorrow songs and the complex ruses of the under-
ground railroad.

Where is Invisible Man in all this? Escaping down a manhole, he
finds refuge in a coal cellar and dreams a nightmare of castration.
But in the dream his "generations" stand not for manhood but instead
for the illusions fed him by almost everyone he has encountered. Free
of these illusions, he nevertheless feels " *'painful and empty'* " (p.
430). Meanwhile, his testicles, thrown over a bridge, give the inani-
mate structure the mobility of a robot, and Invisible Man awakens
vowing action to stop the mechanical, man-created monster. Here,
raised one more time, is the fearful specter which haunts him. Over
and over he has been confronted with the likelihood that unless he

makes a stand in the world, he will be reduced to a "cog," an "automaton," a "mechanical man," a "walking zombie." Finally, by bringing the nightmare into the forefront of consciousness, he exorcizes the robot in him, and prepares to resist society's turn in that direction.

The novel stops at this point—the novel as narrative. What follows is an Epilogue on the process of self-realization in America. It is in the form of a memoir or fictional essay, and Ellison's strategy is similar to that employed in the narrative. There is no mention of historical persons, events, or dates, but unmistakably, the Epilogue bears the mark and resonance of the late forties and fifties—the continuing American present.

The novel's trajectory follows the path of a boomerang. A boomerang returns—that much we can say, predictably. But the precise point of return is unpredictable, erratic, uncyclical. From the Prologue through a careening ride out, and back to the Epilogue, Ellison takes his chances with open form. In the case of Invisible Man, the metaphor is trenchantly apt. Returning, he sees things from a different perspective because he has turned around. One starting point he boomerangs back toward I take to be his grandfather, whose image grows larger and clearer because now Invisible Man travels toward it. In the beginning his grandfather's words presented fearful dangers to his dream of individuality, whereas now he interprets those same words as a command of nationhood. "I" has become "we" in the testamental way of black experience.

> Could he have meant—hell, he *must* have meant the principle, that we were to affirm the principle on which the country was built and not the men, or at least not the men who did the violence. Did he mean say "yes" because he knew that the principle was greater than the men, greater than the numbers and the vicious power and all the methods used to corrupt its name? Did he mean to affirm the principle, which they themselves had dreamed into being out of the chaos and darkness of the feudal past, and which they had violated and compromised to the point of absurdity even in their own corrupt minds? Or did he mean that we had to take the responsibility for all of it, for the men as well as the principle, because we were the heirs who must use the principle because no other fitted our needs? (p. 433)

He (and we) are back at the beginning, back to democracy's form of diversity and oneness, its promise of equality. But not quite at the same point. The principle affirmed is other than that expressed by Invisible Man's former belief in the gospel of "hard work and progress and action" (p. 435), and different from his grandfather's strategy of "'agree 'em to death and destruction'" (p. 13). No, freed from the bondage of absolute idealism, absolute oppression, absolute ideology, all states of mind, Invisible Man affirms a reality of "infinite possibilities." For him, historical consciousness has come to stand for the endless range of complexity between chaos and possibility:

> —diversity is the word. . . .
> America is woven of man strands . . . .
> Our fate is to become one, and yet many—. (p. 435)

Like consciousness, the acts of personality are inclusive. "So I denounce and I defend and I hate and I love" (p. 438).

In the Epilogue, memoir becomes history as Invisible Man affirms America as a metaphor for possibilities that are democratic provided individuals take personal responsibility for the country's principles. Affirming his complex history, Invisible Man transforms his sense of himself from everybody's stereotype to an indivisible person. Perhaps most important, the man who began by asserting his invisibility ends by asserting his connection with every last American one of us. No, he does more than that. He suggests he is speaking for us: "Who knows but that, on the lower frequencies, I speak for you?" (p. 439). Who knows? We do, if we've tuned into the frequency of his life. Not to mention the other essential frequencies of American life, the lower frequencies—the bass line from which independent, individual melodies soar.

Of the great nineteenth-century American novels, Ellison has written: "The moral imperatives of American life that are implicit in the Declaration of Independence, the Constitution, and the Bill of Rights were a part of both the individual consciousness and the conscience of those writers who created what we consider our classic novels— Hawthorne, Melville, James, and Twain." [29] Aware of the novel as an experimental form with stress on both permanence and variation, he asks of the craft of his time: "How does one in the novel (the novel which is a work of art and not a disguised piece of sociology) persuade the American reader to identify that which is basic in man beyond all differences of class, race, wealth, or formal education?" He asks: "How give the reader that which we do have in abundance, all the countless untold and wonderful variations on the themes of identity and freedom and necessity, love and death, and with all the mystery of personality undergoing its endless metamorphosis?" [30] The questions are wonderful and profound, especially as they grant the possibility of making one culture out of many individuals, many peoples, many traditions, many idioms and styles—all the contradictions and possibilities of American life. If novelists and readers are faithful to first principles, we and those who follow will be able to repeat Invisible Man's transformations in endless variation.

Certainly Ralph Ellison could pose these questions, confident that he had met the test of a prose "flexible, and swift as American change is swift, confronting the inequalities and brutalities of our society forthrightly, but yet thrusting forth its images of hope, human fraternity and individual self-realization." [31] Certainly *Invisible Man* modulates history, self, and form to a frequency that is unique, complex, and accessible, a frequency embodying the high democratic standards Ellison sets for American fiction.

NOTES

[1] "The Uses of History in Fiction," *Southern Literary Journal*, 1, no. 2 (1969), 69. Additional remarks culled from this source appear parenthetically in the text.

[2] "The World and the Jug," *The New Leader*, 46 (9 Dec. 1963), 26.

[3] "A Reply to Ralph Ellison," *The New Leader*, 47 (3 Feb. 1964), 13.

[4] "A Rejoinder," *The New Leader*, 47 (3 Feb. 1964), 20. The two Ellison pieces are published as "The World and the Jug," in *Shadow and Act* (New York: Random House, 1964), pp. 107-43.

[5] "Blues People," in *Shadow and Act*, p. 254.

[6] *The Nation*, 201 (20 Sept. 1965), 129-35.

[7] *Invisible Man* (New York: Random House, 1952), p. 5. All further references to *Invisible Man* are contained in the text.

[8] "Beating That Boy," in *Shadow and Act*, p. 98.

[9] In *The Living Novel*, ed. Granville Hicks (New York: Macmillan, 1957), p. 62.

[10] "Tell It Like It Is, Baby," p. 135.

[11] "Society, Morality, and the Novel," pp. 70-71.

[12] "Stephen Crane and the Mainstream of American Fiction," in *Shadow and Act*, p. 67.

[13] "Society, Morality, and the Novel," pp. 72, 74.

[14] Quoted in Jervis Anderson's "Profile," *The New Yorker*, 52 (2 Nov. 1976), 94-96.

[15] "That Same Pain, That Same Pleasure," in *Shadow and Act*, p. 12.

[16] "Introduction," in *Shadow and Act*, p. xviii.

[17] Ellison quoted by Steve Cannon, Lennox Raphael, and James Thompson in their interview, "A Very Stern Discipline," *Harper's Magazine*, 234 (Mar. 1967), 84.

[18] "Indivisible Man," *The Atlantic*, 226 (Dec. 1970), 46.

[19] Ibid.

[20] *The Souls of Black Folk* (1903; rpt. New York: Fawcett, 1961), p. 23.

[21] "The Art of Fiction: An Interview," in *Shadow and Act*, p. 183.

[22] "Society, Morality, and the Novel," p. 61.

[23] "The Uses of History in Fiction," p. 64.

[24] James Baldwin's "Journey to Atlanta," rpt. in *Notes of a Native Son* (Boston: Beacon Press, 1955), is a powerful exposition of the contradiction between theory and practice in the Progressive party's relation to blacks.

[25] See Baldwin's "Notes of a Native Son," and Russell G. Fischer's "*Invisible Man* as History," *CLA Journal*, 17 (1974), 338-67.

[26] Quoted by Edgar A. Toppin in *A Biographical History of Blacks in America Since 1528* (New York: David McKay, 1971), p. 165.

[27] "Society, Morality, and the Novel," p. 72.

[28] Michael S. Harper, "*Bird Lives:* Charles Parker in St. Louis," in *History Is Your Own Heartbeat* (Urbana: University of Illinois Press, 1971), p. 80.

[29] "Society, Morality, and the Novel," p. 67.

[30] Ibid., p. 91.

[31] "Brave Words for a Startling Occasion," in *Shadow and Act*, p. 105.

PAINTINGS BY
RICHARD YARDE

SWEET DADDY GRACE   *oil on canvas   1976   116" x 73"*

ONE-MAN BAND   *watercolor on paper*   *1976*   *15" x 9½"*

DEPARTURE   *watercolor on paper*   1975   *15½" x 16¼"*

THE RETURN   *watercolor on paper   1976   15½" x 20".*   *Courtesy Museum of Fine Arts, Boston*

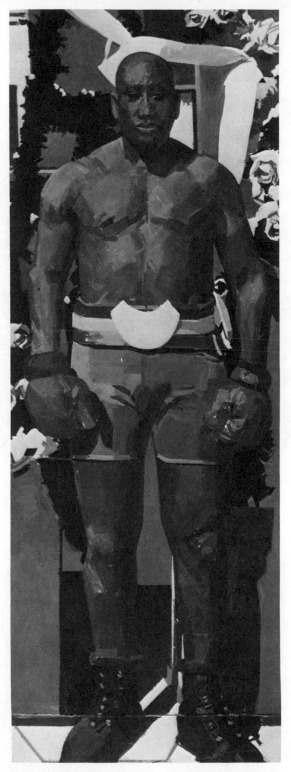

THE CHAMPION *oil on canvas   1975   81" x 36"*

GARVEY'S GHOST   *oil on canvas   72¼" x 24"*
Courtesy Fisk University Museum

THE FALLS *oil on canvas 1975 96″ x 84″*   *Courtesy Center of Afro-American Artists*

RICHARD YARDE

was born at Boston, Massachusetts, in 1939. He has studied at the School of the Museum of Fine Arts, Boston, and at Boston University, BFA, MFA. His work is included in the collection at the Springfield Museum of Fine Arts, the Museum of Fine Arts, Boston, and the museums of art at Smith and Wellesley colleges. In 1976 Mr. Yarde was the recipient of a National Endowment for the Arts fellowship in painting. He was recently artist-in-residence at Amherst College. The title page painting is The Emperor, *watercolor on paper, 1975, 16⅝″ x 20⅛″. These reproductions are made possible by a grant from the Commonwealth of Massachusetts Council on the Arts and Humanities.*

ELEGIES FOR PARADISE VALLEY

ROBERT HAYDEN

I

My shared bedroom's window
opened on alley stench.
A junkie died in maggots there.
I saw his body shoved into a van.
I saw the hatred for our kind
glistening like tears
in the policemen's eyes.

II

No place for Pestalozzi's
fiorelli. No time of starched
and ironed innocence. Godfearing
elders, even Godless grifters, tried
as best they could to shelter
us. Rats gnawing in their walls.

III

Waxwork Uncle Henry
(murdered Uncle Crip)
lay among floral pieces
in the front room where
the Christmas tree had stood.

Mister Hong of the
Chinese Lantern (there
Auntie as waitress queened it
nights) brought freesias, wept
beside the coffin.

Beautiful, our neighbors
murmured; he would be proud.
Is it mahogany?
Mahogany—I'd heard
the victrola voice of

dead Bert Williams
talk-sing that word as macabre
music played, chilling
me. Uncle Crip
had laughed and laughed.

IV

Whom now do you guide, Madam Artelia?
Who nowadays can summon you to speak
from the spirit place your ghostly home
of the oh-riental wonders there—
of the fate, luck, surprises, gifts

awaiting us out here? Oh, Madam,
part Seminole and confidante
("Born with a veil over my face")
of all our dead, how clearly you
materialize before the eye

of memory—your AfroIndian features,
Gypsy dress, your silver crucifix
and manycolored beads. I see
again your waitingroom, with its wax
bouquets, its plaster Jesus of the Sacred Heart.

I watch blue smoke of incense curl
from a Buddha's lap as I wait with Ma
and Auntie among your nervous clients.
You greet us, smiling, lay your hand
in blessing on my head, then lead

the others into a candlelit room
I may not enter. She went into a trance,
Auntie said afterward, and spirits
talked, changing her voice to suit
their own. And Crip came.

Happy yes I am happy here,
he told us; dying's not death. Do not grieve.
Remembering, Auntie began to cry
and poured herself a glass of gin.
Didn't sound a bit like Crip, Ma snapped.

V

And Belle the classy dresser, where is she,
who changed her frocks three times a day?
   Where's Nora, with her laugh, her comic flair,
   stagestruck Nora waiting for her chance?
Where's fast Iola, who so loved to dance
she left her sickbed one last time to whirl
in silver at The Palace till she fell?
   Where's mad Miss Alice, who ate from garbage cans?
   Where's snuffdipping Lucy, who played us 'chunes'
on her guitar? Where's Hattie? Where's Melissabelle?
   Let vanished rooms, let dead streets tell.

Where's Jim, Watusi prince and Good Old Boy,
who with a joke went off to fight in France?
   Where's Tump the defeated artist, for meals or booze
   daubing with quarrelsome reds, disconsolate blues?
Where's Les the huntsman? Tough Kid Chocolate, where
is he? Where's dapper Jess? Where's Stomp the shell-
shocked, clowning for us in parodies of war?
   Where's taunted Christopher, sad queen of night?
   And Ray, who cursing crossed the color line?
Where's gentle Brother Davis? Where's dopefiend Mel?
   Let vanished rooms, let dead streets tell.

VI

Of death. Of loving too:
Oh sweet sweet jellyroll:
so the sinful hymned it while
the churchfolk loured.

I scrounged for crumbs:
I yearned to touch
the choirlady's hair,
I wanted Uncle Crip

to kiss me, but he danced
with me instead;
we Balled-the-Jack
to Jellyroll

Morton's brimstone
piano on the phonograph,
laughing, shaking the gasolier
a later stillness dimmed.

VII

Our parents warned us: Gypsies
kidnap you. And we must never play
with Gypsy children: Gypsies
all got lice in their hair.

Their queen was dark as Cleopatra
in the Negro History Book. Their king's
sinister arrogance flashed fire
like the diamonds on his dirty hands.

Quite suddenly he was dead,
his tribe clamoring in grief.
They take on bad as Colored Folks,
Uncle Crip allowed. Die like us too.

Zingaros: Tzigeune: Gitanos: Gypsies:
pornographers of gaudy otherness:
aliens among the alien: thieves,
carriers of sickness: like us like us.

VIII

Of death, of loving,
of sin and hellfire too.
Unsaved, old Christians
gossiped; pitched

from the gamblingtable—
Lord have mercy on
his wicked soul—
face foremost into hell.

We'd dance there, Uncle
Crip and I,
for though I spoke
my pieces well in Sunday School,

I knew myself (precocious
in the ways of guilt
and secret pain)
the devil's own rag babydoll.

COVENANT OF TIMELESSNESS AND TIME

SYMBOLISM AND HISTORY IN ROBERT HAYDEN'S
ANGLE OF ASCENT

WILBURN WILLIAMS, JR.

I

The appearance of Robert Hayden's *Angle of Ascent* is something of a problematic event for students of the Afro-American tradition in poetry, for while it gives us occasion to review and pay homage to the best work of one of our finest poets, it insistently calls to mind the appalling tardiness of our recognition of his achievement. A meticulous craftsman whose exacting standards severely limit the amount of his published verse, Robert Hayden has steadily accumulated over the course of three decades a body of poetry so distinctive in character and harmonious in development that its very existence seems more fated than willed, the organic issue of a natural principle rather than the deliberate artifice of a human imagination.[1] But in spite of official honors—Hayden is now the poetry consultant at the Library of Congress and a Fellow of the Academy of American Poets—and a formidable reputation among critics, Hayden has received surprisingly little notice in print. Unless we suffer another of those sad fits of inattention that have so far limited Hayden's readership, *Angle of Ascent* should win for him the regard he has long deserved. With the exception of *Heart-Shape in the Dust,* the apprenticeship collection of 1940, poetry from every previous work of Hayden's is represented here, and we can see clearly the remarkable fertility of the symbolist's union with the historian, the bipolar extremes of Hayden's singular poetic genius.

Robert Hayden is a poet whose symbolistic imagination is intent on divining the shape of a transcendent order of spirit and grace that might redeem a world bent on its own destruction. His memory, assailed by the discontinuities created by its own fallibility, is equally determined to catch and preserve every shadow and echo of the actual human experience in which our terribleness stands revealed. In poem after poem Hayden deftly balances the conflicting claims of the ideal and the actual. Spiritual enlightenment in his poetry is never the reward of evasion of material fact. The realities of imagination and the actualities of history are bound together in an alliance that makes neither thinkable without the other. Robert Hayden's poetry proposes that if it is in the higher order of spirit that the gross actualities of life find their true meaning, it is also true that that transcendent realm is meaningful to man only as it is visibly incarnate on the plane of his experience.

Viewed as a theory of poetics, Hayden's characteristic method of composition will hardly strike anyone as unique. His preoccupation with the relationship between natural and spiritual facts puts him squarely in the American tradition emanating from Emerson; we are not at all amazed, therefore, when we find correspondences between his work and that of figures like Dickinson and Melville. The brief lyric "Snow," for instance (all page references in this essay are to *Angle of Ascent,* New York, 1975):

> Smooths and burdens,
> endangers, hardens.
>
> Erases, revises.
> Extemporizes
>
> Vistas of lunar solitude.
> Builds, embellishes a mood. (p. 84)

recalls the Dickinson of "It sifts from Leaden Sieves—." [2] But the brooding presence of death lurking behind the brave outward show of a playful wit that is common in Dickinson is uncharacteristic of Hayden, and a comparison with Melville casts more light on his habitual concerns. In "El-Hajj Malik El-Shabazz" Malcolm X is likened to Ahab—"Rejecting Ahab, he was of Ahab's tribe. / 'Strike through the mask!'" (p. 57)—and "The Diver" (pp. 75-76) closely parallels Chapter 92 of Melville's *White-Jacket.* To be sure, Hayden's speaker and Melville's narrator are impelled by distinctly different motives. The former's descent is a conscious act, a matter of deliberate choice, whereas White-Jacket's one-hundred-foot fall into a nighttime sea cannot be ascribed to his sensible will, however strong his subconscious longing for death might be. Yet the underlying pattern of each man's ordeal is the same. The approach to death is paradoxically felt as a profound intensification of life. Death takes, or at least seems to promise to take, both men to the very core of life. Thus White-Jacket in his precipitous drop "toward the infallible center of the terraqueous globe" finds all he has seen, read, heard, thought, and felt seemingly "intensified in one fixed idea in [his] soul." Yielding to the soft embrace of the sea, he is shocked into revulsion of death almost purely by chance—"of a sudden some fashionless form" brushes his side, tingling his nerves with the thrill of being alive.[3] In like manner, Hayden's diver's longing to be united with "those hidden ones" in a kind of well-being that lies so deep as to be beyond the reach of articulate speech, his passion to "have / done with self and / every dinning / vain complexity," can be satisfied only if he tears away the mask that sustains his life. The intricate contrapuntal development of the poem brings an overwhelming extremity of feeling to the critical moment that finds the diver poised between life and death. His going down is both easeful and swift, a plunge into water and a flight through air. The flower creatures of the deep flash and shimmer yet are at the same time mere "lost images / fadingly remembered." The dead ship, a lifeless hulk deceptively encrusted with the animate "moss of bryozoans," swarms with forms of life that are themselves voracious instruments of death. And what liberates the diver from this labyrinthine and potentially annihilating swirl of contradictory instincts and perceptions is never clear. As is the case with White-Jacket, he "somehow" begins the "measured rise," no nearer to winning the object of his quest but presumably possessed of a deeper, more disciplined capacity for experience. ("Measured" is decidedly meant to make us think of the poet's subordination to the rules of his craft.)

The most fruitful area of comparison between Hayden and Melville is to be found in their tellingly different attitudes toward the symbolistic enterprise itself. Committed to reconciling within the ambiguous flux of poetic language the warring oppositions created by the divisiveness of discursive logic, the symbolist finds himself necessarily presupposing the very terms of order—subject and object, mind and matter, spirit and nature—his method seeks to erase.[4] Because the symbolist's stance is such a difficult posture to keep, the idea of the artist as acrobat and the conception of his craft as a dance of language are conventional figures in modern literature and criticism. In Hayden, however, the drama of the symbolist's tightrope walk is objectified infrequently. The symbolist's striving for balance is not seen in what Hayden's speakers do but is heard in how they talk: tone assumes the burden that topic might bear. Hayden's characteristically soft-spoken and fluid voice derives much of its power from the evident contrast between the maelstrom of anguish out of which it originates and the quiet reflecting pool of talk into which it is inevitably channeled. Interestingly enough, when Hayden does write poetry in which the action is clearly analogous to the symbolist's task of wizarding a track through a jungle of contraries, the prevailing tone is not his customary seriousness. In "The Performers," the modesty of two high-rise window cleaners subtly mocks the speaker's misuse of their daring as a pretext for a kind of absurd metaphysical strutting that his own desk-bound timidity will not allow (p. 27). In "The Lions" an animal trainer whose mentality is a peculiar blend of Schopenhauerian wilfulness and transcendentalist vision breaks out into an ebullient speech that is at once divinely rapturous and somehow wildly funny:

> And in the kingdom-cage
> as I make my lions leap,
>   through nimbus-fire leap,
> oh, as I see them leap –
> unsparing beauty that
> creates and serves my will,
>   the savage real that clues
> my vision of the real—
>   my soul exults and Holy cries
> and Holy Holy cries, he said. (p. 64)

Yet whenever Robert Hayden loses his artistic balance, his fall is not likely to be in Melville's direction. The enormous gulf between the unified paradise of the symbolistic imagination and the outright hellishness of a world rife with division, the gulf which drew Ahab and Pierre to their deaths and drowned Melville the writer in silence, poses no threat to Hayden. Hayden's peril comes from a different quarter, and it comes disguised as his salvation. It is precisely Hayden's faith in the ultimate redemptiveness of the universal and timeless order of spirit that threatens to kill the life of his art. Insofar as his poetry is concerned, Hayden's God and Devil are one. The blinding light of faith can shrivel up the sensuous specificity of poetry just as surely as it can enkindle the life of the world of inert fact. Hayden's divergence from Melville here is nowhere more apparent than in "Theme and Variation." Readers of Hayden will recognize the voice of the Heraclitus-like stranger who delivers the poem's wisdom as the poet's own:

> I sense, he said, the lurking rush, the sly
> transience flickering at the edge of things.
> I've spied from the corner of my eye
> upon the striptease of reality.
>
> There is, there is, he said, an imminence
> that turns to curiosa all I know;
> that changes light to rainbow darkness
> wherein God waylays and empowers. (p. 115)

Set the above lines against this sentence from the famous last
paragraph of "The Whiteness of the Whale" in *Moby Dick:*

> And when we consider that other theory of the natural philosophers,
> that all other earthly hues—every stately or lovely emblazoning—
> the sweet tinges of sunset skies and woods; yea, and the gilded
> velvets of butterflies, and the butterfly cheeks of young girls; all
> these are but subtle deceits, not actually inherent in substances,
> but only laid on from without; so that all deified Nature absolutely
> paints like the harlot, whose allurements cover nothing but the
> charnel-house within; and when we proceed further, and consider
> that the mystical cosmetic which produces every one of her hues,
> the great principle of light, forever remains white or colourless in
> itself, and if operating without medium upon matter, would touch
> all objects, evaj tulips and roses, with its own blank tinge—
> pondering all this, the palsied universe lies before us a leper;
> and like wilful travellers in Lapland, who refuse to wear coloured
> and colouring glasses upon their eyes, so the wretched infidel
> gazes himself blind at the monumental white shroud that wraps
> all the prospect around him.

Hayden's stranger reverses Ishmael on every point. His percep-
tions nourish belief; Ishmael's skepticism and doubt. He is pious
and Ishmael is blasphemous. Melville's Nature dresses while Hay-
den's disrobes. The former's adornment is emblematic of a dia-
bolical deceitfulness; the latter's nudity points to a sanctuary of
grace. Where Melville's eye strips away delusory hues to gaze in
horror upon the "blank tinge" of a "palsied" and leprous universe,
Hayden's eye spies out an indwelling spirit that transforms an
undifferentiated light into a sacredly tinged darkness wherein man
discovers his hope and his blessing. But here Hayden can no more
be accused of a naive optimism than Melville can be charged with
blind cynicism. The ironic intimation of violent assault reverbera-
ting in "waylays" checks the stranger's rush into the plenitude of
divine imminence, maintaining the poem's complexity and integrity.

Nevertheless, the point remains that the beneficent banditry of
Hayden's divinity has far more in common with the onslaughts of
Donne's Three-Personed God than with anything ever done by the
maddeningly elusive Jehovah of Melville. Hayden's supreme high-
wayman is more apt to strip the poet of his facts than to rob him of
his faith, which might be heaven for religion but certainly hell for
poetry. As much is evident in the increasingly sparing detail and more
cryptic utterance that marks the poet's recent work. At his best

Hayden composes poetry that is paradoxically both rich in statement and ascetic in temperament. In "Stars" and the Akhenaten section of "Two Egyptian Portrait Masks," however, an abstract and unconvincing expression of acute religious belief shows only a marginal relation to the concrete particularities of human experience. The latter verse segment plainly suffers in contrast to the paean to Nefert-iti that precedes it. Meditating on the carving of a woman

> whose burntout
> loveliness alive in stone
> is like the fire of precious stones
>
> dynastic
> death (gold mask and vulture wings)
> charmed her with so she would never die (p. 16)

the poet tersely harmonizes a succession of discordant sensations. But in the Akhenaten companion piece, the poet's contemplativeness has no equivalent object on which it can focus—admittedly, it would take an extraordinary imagination to bridge the gap between the majesty of Akenaten's dream of human oneness and the fat hips and bloated abdomens of the Pharaoh's Karnak colossi—and consequently the poetry lacks force:

> Aten
> multi-single like the sun
> reflecting Him by Him
>
> reflected.
> Anubis howled. The royal prophet reeled
> under the dazzling weight
>
> of vision,
> exalted—maddened?—the spirit moving
> in his heart: Aten Jahveh Allah God. (p. 17)

Certainly there is nothing in this like the faultless description of death as "dynastic," a brilliant conceit whereby Hayden associates the idea of the unbroken hereditary transfer of power from generation to generation with the eternal dominion of death, thus finding death's very indomitability dependent upon the principle of generation, or life. What Emerson, the one indispensable figure in any discussion of American symbolism, once said about the poet's duty is patently applicable to Robert Hayden, and it can serve both as an accurate representation of what Hayden does in his best work and as a necessary corrective to the etherealizing proclivities of Hayden's symbolist genius:

> The poet, like the electric rod, must reach from a point nearer the sky than all surrounding objects, down to the earth, and into the dark wet soil, or neither is of use. The poet must not only converse with pure thought, but he must demonstrate it almost to the senses. His words must be pictures, his verses must be spheres and cubes, to be seen and smelled and handled.[5]

II

However much we might like to dwell on the manifold possibilities of Hayden's symbolism, particularly in relation to the practices of Yeats and Eliot (to whom he sometimes alludes) and to Auden (whom he has said was a key factor in his growth as a poet[6]), no discussion of his poetry can avoid the question of the place a sense of history occupies in his work. Every reader is quick to detect a pervasive sense of the past and a powerful elegiac strain in his work. In the most thorough examination of Hayden's poetry we have, Charles T. Davis has recounted the crucial contribution of Hayden's extensive research in the slave trade to "Middle Passage," and he has called attention to the importance of Hayden's grasp of the Afro-American folk tradition to "O Daedalus, Fly Away Home," "The Ballad of Nat Turner," and "Runagate Runagate."[7] Aware of the paradox, Hayden has referred to himself as a "romantic realist," a symbolist compelled to be realistic, and Michael Harper has called him a "symbolist poet struggling with the facts of history."[8] Now, nothing is perhaps more tempting or more mistaken than to infer from all this that the historian in Hayden is at odds with the symbolist. A close reading of the poetry will not support such a conclusion. Because of the popularity of "Middle Passage" and "Runagate Runagate"— poems unmistakably black in subject matter and sometimes identifiably black in use of language—the historical impulse in Hayden is understandably allied in the minds of many readers with the poet's pride in his own blackness. Since Hayden's recognition of his blackness is widely (and, we think, most aberrantly) perceived as a grudging one, the symbolist in Hayden is often viewed as the enemy of his essentially historical, and black, muse. If that Bob Hayden only knew better, the argument (it is hardly reasoning) goes, he would leave that symbolism stuff alone (the poetry of *The Night-Blooming Cereus,* for example) and get back to his roots. Certainly Hayden's insistence that he be judged as a poet and not as a Negro poet only exacerbates this misapprehension, and no appeal to the extensive exploitation of symbolism in the spirituals and the blues is likely to quiet the suspicion that Hayden's symbolist clings parasitically to the creativity of his black historian.[9]

But while it is easy to see that the symbolistic method is operative in poems as disparate as "Middle Passage" and "The Night-Blooming Cereus," it is not so evident that Hayden's historical sensibility is also at work in poems that have no obvious connection with historical incidents. To apprehend the unity of Hayden's entire body of work, it is necessary to understand that his fascination with history is but one part of a more comprehensive entrancement in the mystery of time. Robert Hayden is clearly more intrigued by the process of change, the paradoxes of permanence and evanescence, than the particular substances that undergo change. Here we are interested in the psychological and artistic implications of his dramatic re-creations of historical events, and not just in the nature of the events themselves. Throughout the poetry of Hayden we encounter a memory and an imagination pitted against the losses time's passage inevitably entails. We meet a consciousness struggling to retain the finest nuances of its own experience and seeking to enter into the experience of others from whom it is alienated by time and space. The fundamental source of Hayden's productivity, the wellspring of his poetic activity, lies in the ability of the human memory to negotiate the distance between time past and time present and the capacity of a profoundly sympathetic imagination to transcend the space between self and other. The complex interactions generated by the life of memory and imagination define the basic unity of Hayden's work.

But while we think that Hayden's obsession with time is, in a sense, larger than his deep involvement in the Afro-American past, it would be foolish to deny the special place black American history occupies in his development as a poet. The 1940s, the years in which Hayden patiently studied the annals of his black past, are also the years in which he matured as artist.[10] To simply live in a culture with a sense of the past as notoriously shallow as this one's is burden enough. A black like Hayden, the fierceness of whose need to know his history is matched only by the ponderousness of the mass of distortion and fabrication under which his past lies buried, finds that even the truthful accounts of the black American experience, which cannot really take him farther back than the eighteenth century anyway, give him the composite picture of a

collectivity, rather than detailed portraits of individuals. It can
hardly seem an accident to him that historians have until recently
slighted the value of the slave narratives, documents that shake
him with a revelation more awesome than any truth contained in
the most complete compilation of data seen even in the wildest
dreams of the maddest cliometrician. When he looks at his mental
picture of Representative Afro-American Man, he sees that it is
a mosaic formed of bits of the lives of many men, and there are
moments when he wonders whether the portrait typifies the truth of
art or the deceit of artifice. The face is formed of fragments them-
selves faceless; the sacred text of his people's experience an accretion
of footnotes culled from the profane texts of another's. His past is
pregnant with a significance that it is incapable of giving birth to.
It is a speechless past peopled with renowned personalities who
are ironically impersonal:

> Name in a footnote. Faceless name.
> Moot hero shrouded in Betsy Ross
> and Garvey flags—propped up
> by bayonets, forever falling. ("Crispus Attucks," p. 20)

Viewed in this somber light, the primary significance of Hayden's
famous poems of Cinquez, Turner, Tubman, and Douglass resides
in the poet's imaginative attempt to reforge his present's broken
links with the past. The past, Hayden says, need not be past at all.
His speakers confront their history as active participants in its mak-
ing, and not as distant onlookers bemoaning their isolation; the
past is carried into the present. Although the poet's mind ventures
backward in time, the poems themselves invariably close with a
statement or action that points forward to the reader's present.
The progress of "Middle Passage" is through death "to life upon
these shores," and the reader leaves the poem with his attention
riveted to *this* life on *these* shores just as much as it is fixed on the
historical reality of the slave trade. The man we leave at the con-
clusion of "The Ballad of Nat Turner" has his revolution still
before him. "Runagate Runagate" ends with an invitation, "Come
ride-a my train," whose rhythm subtly anticipates the action to be
undertaken, and the powerful assertion of yet another intention to
act—"Mean mean mean to be free" (p. 130). The accentual sonnet
to Frederick Douglass is poetry that moves like the beating of a
living heart. The poet emphasizes that the dead hero is still a vital
force. The first long periodic sentence seems to resist coming to an
end. The poem celebrates not a man who has been, but a man
still coming into being. Although commemorative in nature, it does

not so much elegize a past as prophesy a future. Frederick Douglass, the poet, and all enslaved humanity are united in one generative process:

> When it is finally ours, this freedom, this liberty, this beautiful
> and terrible thing, needful to man as air,
> usable as earth; when it belongs at last to all,
> when it is truly instinct, brain matter, diastole, systole,
> reflex action; when it is finally won; when it is more
> than the gaudy mumbo jumbo of politicians:
> this man, this Douglass, this former slave, this Negro
> beaten to his knees, exiled, visioning a world
> where none is lonely, none hunted, alien,
> this man, superb in love and logic, this man
> shall be remembered. Oh, not with statues' rhetoric,
> not with legends and poems and wreaths of bronze alone,
> but with the lives grown out of his life, the lives
> fleshing his dream of the beautiful, needful thing. (p. 131)

A great deal of Hayden's success in undoing the dislocations of time and space can be attributed to his poet-speakers' uncanny ability to give themselves over to the actuality they contemplate. They become what they behold; known object and knowing subject unite. Like psychic mediums, his speakers obliterate distinctions between self and other; the dead and distant take possession of their voices. Take for example these lines from "The Dream (1863)":

> That evening Sinda thought she heard the drums
> and hobbled from her cabin to the yard.
> The quarters now were lonely-still in willow dusk
> after the morning's ragged jubilo,
> when laughing crying singing the folks went off
> with Marse Lincum's soldier boys.
> But Sinda hiding would not follow them: those
> Buckras with their ornery
> funning, cussed commands, oh they were not were not
> the hosts the dream had promised her. (p. 36)

The poem is obviously a third-person narrative, but the space separating narrator and actor is frequently violated. The speaker's voice modulates effortlessly into the cadences of the slaves. "Marse Lincum," "Buckra," and "ornery" are words heard in the accents of the slaves. The pathos of the cry "oh they were not were not" is so extraordinary because, syntax notwithstanding, it is Sinda's own voice we hear, and not the poet's. In six lines in "The Rabbi" Hayden gives a virtuoso demonstration of the resources of his voice:

> And I learned schwartze too
>
> And schnapps, which schwartzes bought
> on credit from "Jew Baby."
> Tippling ironists laughed and said
> he'd soon be rich as Rothschild
>
> From their swinish Saturdays. (p. 81)

In the first two lines the poet's retrospective view of the blacks of his youth is clearly refracted through the cultural lens of the Jews he knew. By the end of the third line, however, his perspective has shifted, and it is now the Jews who are being looked upon from a black point of view. "Credit" is the pivotal term in this transition, for it not only allows the speaker to describe objectively the economic relationship of black to Jew but also lets him draw on the powerful connotations this word has in the Afro-American speech community. The last three lines of indirect quotation, framed by two jocularly incongruous phrases that are clearly of the poet's own making, indicate that the speaker finally assumes an amused posture independent of the viewpoint of either black or Jew, but remarkably sensitive to both. And there is a social morality implicit in this display of Hayden's multivocal talents. What might at first seem to be merely a technical device has enormous ethical implications. When the poet says in the last stanza,

> But the synagogue became
> New Calvary.
> The rabbi bore my friends off
> in his prayer shawl (p. 81)

he means for us to see that the loss of his childhood friends Hirschel and Molly is part of a wholesale separation of black and Jew, a separation that will brook no opposition from considerations as flimsy as one human being's love for another. "New Calvary," tellingly isolated in a single line, is not only the name of the black church that succeeds the synagogue. It represents too a place and an action. It is the hill where Christianity and Jewry part ways, the site where Hayden's ideal of human oneness is sacrificed, a modern reenactment of that old attempt at redemption that ironically, bitterly, only sped man in his fall out of unity into division.

But there is a sinister dimension to this intercourse between self and other, present and past. Robert Hayden knows, and this is a sign of his strength, that openness is also vulnerability, that the past in which one finds possibilities of inspiration and renewal can exert a malignant influence on the present. In "A Ballad of Remembrance" the poet is besieged by specters pressing upon him the value of their individual adaptations to American racism. The Zulu King urges accommodation, the gunmetal priestess preaches hate, and a motley contingent of saints, angels, and mermaids, blind to the realities of evil, chime out a song of naive love. These competing voices drive the poet to the brink of madness. In "Tour 5" an autumn ride into the country becomes a frightening excursion into a surreal world alive with ancient conflicts between black, white, and red men. In "Locus" the Southland lies wasted under the blight of its own history. The present abdicates to the superior force of the past. The redbuds are "like momentary trees / of an illusionist"; there is a "violent metamorphosis, / with every blossom turning / deadly and memorial soldiers." Life here is stunted, reality the bondsman of a dream of disaster. The past forecloses its mortgage on the future:

> Here spareness, rankness, harsh
> brilliances; beauty of what's hardbitten,
> knotted, stinted, flourishing
>   in despite, on thorny meagerness
> thriving, twisting into grace.
>   Here symbol houses
> where the brutal dream lives out its lengthy
> dying. Here the past, adored and
>   unforgiven. Here the past—
> soulscape, Old Testament battleground
> of warring shades whose weapons kill. (p. 45)

Closely related to Hayden's interest in the cunning ironies of history is his anxiety for the fate of myth and religion in the modern world. This concern provides the motivation of some of his best poetry. Take "Full Moon," for example, which we quote in full:

> No longer throne of a goddess to whom we pray,
> no longer the bubble house of childhood's
> tumbling Mother Goose man,

The emphatic moon ascends—
the brilliant challenger of rocket experts,
the white hope of communications men.

Some I love who are dead
were watchers of the moon and knew its lore;
planted seeds, trimmed their hair,

Pierced their ears for gold hoop earrings
as it waxed or waned.
It shines tonight upon their graves.

And burned in the garden of Gethsemane,
its light made holy by the dazzling tears
with which it mingled.

And spread its radiance on the exile's path
of Him who was the Glorious One,
its light made holy by His holiness.

Already a mooted goal and tomorrow perhaps
an arms base, a livid sector,
the full moon dominates the dark. (p. 79)

The world we encounter here is radically impoverished. The slow process by which the rise of positivistic science has emptied Nature of all religious significance is recapitulated in the fall of child-hood's illusions before the advance of adult skepticism. For contemporary man, the moon exists only as a means of flaunting the triumphs of his technological vanity. But the poet sees in this diminished moon an analogue to the deprivations death has exacted from him, and with this crucial recognition of a mutuality of fates begins the movement toward recovery. Like the breathtaking expansion of meaning we witness in Eliot's "Sweeney Among the Nightingales" when we leap from the nightingales "singing near / The Convent of the Sacred Heart" to those that "sang within the bloody wood / When Agamemnon cried aloud," [11] there is a startling intensification of feeling in the transition from a light that "shines tonight upon their graves" to the light that "burned in the garden of Gethsemane." But Hayden knows that this age looks upon Jesus Christ and the prophet Baha'u'llah (The Glorious One of the penultimate stanza and the founder of Hayden's Baha'i faith) with a cynical regard, and that any appeal to them to restore the significance of a degraded Nature would sound highly artificial and entirely unconvincing. Like Flannery O'Connor, who frequently discerns in overt denials of faith ironic avowals of the existence of God, Hayden subverts the materialism of technology to make a claim for the reality of spirit. The moon that is now meaningless will once again become all-meaningful, he says, not as the throne of a benign deity or as an object of harmless childish fancies, but as an arms base that can end all life. The meaning that has been lost to the achievement of science reasserts itself with a vengeance by means of that very same achievement. This ironic turn of events is itself fully in keeping with the traditional view of the moon as the symbol of eternal recurrence. The full weight of this paradox is felt in the critical word "livid," on which a whole world of ambiguities turns. As meaning ashen or pallid, livid is both a forth-right description of a full moon and suggestive of the moon's fearful retreat before the press of technology. As meaning black and blue, livid, in conjunction with the reference to the moon as "the white hope of communications men," suggests a moon bruised and discolored by the assaults of the Jack Johnsons of science. As a synonym for enraged or angry, livid further elaborates upon the implied meanings of this prize-fighting metaphor, and, by con-necting it to the ominous possibilities of the moon's use as an arms base, subtly transforms the earlier reference to the moon as victim into an image of the moon as aggressor. And when we finally consider livid as meaning red, that satellite's consequence as an object of martial reverence is fully revealed, for the red moon is the moon foreseen by John of Patmos, and its appearance an-nounces the coming of God in His wrath, the destruction of nations and the end of time.

III

When we review the entire course of Hayden's development, the importance of the poet as historian seems to lessen drastically over time. In his last two volumes of verse, only "Beginnings" immediately strikes us as aspiring to the largeness of historical vision of a "Full Moon" or the early explorations of the Afro-American past for which Hayden is chiefly known. What we feel is responsible for this change is not something so simple as the symbolist's displacement of the historian, but a growing preoccupa-tion in the historian with ever smaller units of time. Having ex-hausted his examination of the problematic interactions of present and past, Hayden's historian is free to chronicle the mystery of change itself. Instead of feeling obliged to overcome the effects of change, he is more and more fascinated by single moments of metamorphosis. This is clearly the case in the poetry of *The Night-Blooming Cereus*. Standing before the "Arachne" of the black sculptor Richard Hunt, the poet is transfixed by the impenetrable mystery of the total change of essence he witnesses. At the same time his language manages to evoke Arachne's terror, it confesses, by the violent juxtaposition of concepts of motion and stasis, the human and the animal, birth and death, the singular incapacity of rational terms to represent adequately such an event:

> In goggling terror fleeing powerless to flee
> Arachne not yet arachnid and no longer woman
> in the moment's centrifuge of dying
> becoming (p. 23)

The capacity of short-lived and seemingly trivial events to manifest truths of exceptional import is shown in "The Night-Blooming Cereus." The speaker initially anticipates the blooming of that flower with a casual disregard for the miracle it will actually be. He and his companion are, in effect, two decadent intellectuals whose interest in the "primitive" is really just a shallow trafficking in the exotic. For them the blossoming sanctions hedonistic indulgence: they will paint themselves and "dance / in honor of archaic mysteries." Yet so much more than they can possibly imagine depends on the appearance of that blossom. When the bud unfolds, the phenomenon of its transformation enlarges into the enigma of eternal recurrence, the riddle of the cyclical alternation of life and death. And the blasphemous are reduced to near speechlessness:

> Lunar presence
> foredoomed, already dying,
> it charged the room
> with plangency
>
> older than human
> cries, ancient as prayers
> invoking Osiris, Krishna,
> Tezcatlipoca.
>
> We spoke
> in whispers when
> we spoke
> at all . . . (p. 26)

Just as Hayden's historian's engrossment with the epochal modulates into an absorption with the momentary, there is a parallel shift of his focus away from the history of a people to the biographies of individuals, away from the public figures of the past to persons who are the poet's contemporaries. The boxer Tiger Flowers and the artist Betsy Graves Reyneau take the place of Nat Turner and Harriet Tubman. If the personages that engage him impress us as having little relation to the main currents of our history, they clearly arouse anxieties in him that nothing less than a total reconsideration of the nature of history itself can assuage. Just as Hayden's early historian is compelled to personalize the past he confronts, his later one is compelled to objectivize his own subjectivity. His private anguish never locks him into the sterile dead-end of solipsism; it impels him outward into the world. "The Peacock Room," Hayden tells us, grew out of an intense emotional experience. A visit to that room designed by Whistler excited painful recollections of his dead friend Betsy Graves Reyneau, who had been given a party in the same room on her twelfth birthday.[12] Contemplating the rival claims of art and life,

> Ars Longa   Which is crueller
> Vita Brevis   life or art?

the poet seeks shelter in Whistler's "lyric space," as he once did in the glow "of the lamp shaped like a rose" his "mother would light / . . . some nights to keep / Raw-Head-And-Bloody-Bones away." But he knows that the dreadful facts of the nightmare that is our history—"Hiroshima Watts My Lai"—scorn "the vision chambered in gold." The very title of the poem, however, has already hinted that his meditations will not issue into a simplistic espousal of art's advantages over life. The peacock is an ambiguous figure. The legendary incorruptibility of the bird's flesh has led to its adoption as a type of immortality and an image of the Resurrected Christ; but as the emblem of Pride, the root of all evil, the bird has always had ominous connotations in Christian culture. These intimations of evil remind the poet of the artist driven mad by Whistler's triumph, and the Peacock Room is transformed in his mind from sanctuary to chamber of horrors. The echoes of Stevens's "Domination of Black" and Poe's "Raven" heighten the poet's fears:

> With shadow cries

> the peacocks flutter down,
> their spread tails concealing her,

then folding, drooping to reveal
her eyeless, old—Med School
cadaver, flesh-object
pickled in formaldehyde,
who was artist, compassionate,
clear-eyed. Who was belovéd friend.
No more. No more.

The paradox of a lasting art that mocks man's fragility at the same time that it realizes his dream of immortality is resolved in the beatific, enigmatic smile of the Bodhisattva ("one whose being—sattva—is enlightenment—bodhi"):

. . . What is art?
What is life?
What the Peacock Room?
Rose-leaves and ashes drift
its portals, gently spinning toward
a bronze Bodhisattva's ancient smile. (pp. 28-29)

In a remarkable way, "Beginning," the first poem of *Angle of Ascent*, re-enacts the course of the fruitful collaboration of Hayden's historian and symbolist. The historian summons up the essential facts of the poet's ancestry, and the symbolist immediately translates them into the terms of art:

Plowdens, Finns,
Sheffeys, Haydens,
Westerfields.

Pennsylvania gothic,
Kentucky homespun,
Virginia baroque.

As the poem moves forward in time, the ancestors are particularized. Joe Finn appears "to join Abe Lincoln's men" and "disappears into his name." Greatgrandma Easter lingers longer before the poet's gaze, and she is remembered not for the role she took in an historic conflict, but for her individual qualities: "She was more than six feet tall. At ninety could / still chop and tote firewood." The progression toward individuation that accompanies the poem's movement to the present—the sharpness of focus of the portrait of an ancestor is a direct function of that ancestor's nearness to the poet's own present—is paralleled by a growth in the poet's awareness of the figurative possibilities of language. As the historian's field of view contracts, the symbolist's artfulness becomes increasingly apparent. As we move from summaries of the entire lives of Joe Finn and Greatgrandma Easter to select moments in the lives of the poet's aunts, the symbolist's reveling in words for the beauty of their sound and rhythm becomes more evident:

> Melissabelle and Sarah Jane
> oh they took all the prizes one Hallowe'en.
> And we'll let the calico curtain fall
> on Pocahontas and the Corncob Queen
> dancing the figures the callers call—
> Sashay, ladies, promenade, all.

But when the poet himself finally appears, a curious—but, for Robert Hayden, characteristic—change occurs. The historian reasserts his centrality (the concluding piece is called "The Crystal Cave Elegy"), and the poem's steady flow toward life and the present is momentarily reversed in commemoration of the death of the miner Floyd Collins. The symbolist's increasing involvement in the resources of his art does not end in an autistic preoccupation with the poet's inner life but finally turns outward in prayer for the liberation of Collins. The timeless paradise of the imagination is invoked to release humanity from the limitations of time:

> Poor game loner
> trapped in the rock
> of Crystal Cave, as
> once in Kentucky coal-
> mine dark (I taste the
> darkness yet)
> my greenhorn dream of
> life. Alive down there
> in his grave. Open
> for him, blue door. (p. 5)

The province of the poet is neither the realist's moonscape of inert matter nor the romantic's starfire of pure spirit, but the middle kingdom of actual earth that unites the two. Robert Hayden's symbolist and historian long ago joined hands to seize this fertile territory as their own. Together they have kept it up very well.

NOTES

[1] This meticulousness poses problems for the critic. Robert Hayden frequently revises his work, and a poem in one collection can appear in considerably altered form in a later collection. In general, Hayden's revisions involve deletions; he characteristically seeks greater economy of expression. His revisions could form the topic of a separate essay. To avoid confusion among variants, all our references are to poems as they appear in *Angle of Ascent* (New York, 1975). Page numbers after quotations pertain to this volume.

[2] Thomas H. Johnson, ed., *Final Harvest: Emily Dickinson's Poems* (Boston, 1962), p. 59. The Dickinson influence here might not be direct. It is quite possible, given the extraordinary likeness Hayden's "Witch Doctor" bears to Gwendolyn Brooks's well-known "The Sundays of Satin-Legs Smith," that the Dickinson influence is filtered through Brooks, particularly the Brooks of *Annie Allen* where one finds poems ("A light and diplomatic bird," for example) that are virtually indistinguishable from the work of Dickinson's own hand.

[3] Herman Melville, *White-Jacket: The World in a Man-of-War* (New York, 1952), p. 370.

[4] Charles Feidelson, Jr., *Symbolism and American Literature* (Chicago, 1953), p. 71.

[5] Quoted in F. O. Matthiessen, *American Renaissance* (New York, 1941), p. 54.

[6] John O'Brien, ed., *Interviews with Black Writers* (New York, 1973), p. 114.

[7] Charles T. Davis, "Robert Hayden's Use of History," in Donald Gibson, ed., *Modern Black Poets* (Englewood Cliffs, N.J., 1973), pp. 96-111.

[8] *New York Times Book Review*, February 22, 1976, p. 34.

[9] Hayden's insistence that he is a poet who happens to be Negro, made most dramatically at the Fisk University Centennial Writers' Conference in 1966, inevitably calls to mind the stance taken by Countee Cullen in the Foreword to *Caroling Dusk* (New York, 1927). Hayden was enamored of Cullen as an undergraduate, and the careful reader can detect significant correspondences between "The Ballad of Nat Turner" and "The Shroud of Color." Yet when Cullen rejected the idea of a black poetry in favor of a poetry written by blacks, his equation of a black movement in poetry with disease clearly indicated how much he underestimated the possibilities for poetry in black American culture and how much he was intimidated by the richness of the Anglo-American poetic tradition: "to say that the pulse beat of their [i.e., the blacks'] verse shows generally such a fever, or the symptoms of such an ague, will prove on closer examination merely the moment's exaggeration of a physician anxious to establish a new literary ailment." Hayden throughout his career has prized his independence, but he has never hesitated to exploit the possibilities for poetry in Afro-American culture. At any rate, Melvin B. Tolson, the magnificent and neglected black poet who rose in opposition to Hayden at Fisk to say that blackness is prior to poetry, has himself been accused of denying his own blackness. No issue in Afro-American letters has to date generated more heat or less light than the question of what "black poet" means.

[10] For the assertion that Hayden was especially concerned with Afro-American history during the 1940s, we refer the reader to Davis, "Hayden's Use of History," p. 97. Proof that Hayden reached his maturity during these years is to be found in the difference between the stiff poetry of *Heart-Shape in the Dust* and the elastic verse of *The Lion and the Archer* (New York, 1948).

[11] T. S. Eliot, *The Waste Land and Other Poems* (1922; rpt. New York: 1962), p. 26.

[12] O'Brien, *Interviews*, pp. 120-22.

SCULPTURE BY
RICHARD HUNT

RICHARD HUNT

*is one of the leading sculptors in America. His work is international-
ly known and honored. A native of Chicago, Hunt, 43, started his
interest in art at the age of thirteen. His works range across America
and Europe and constitute a towering body of artistic achievement.
In these photos by the talented Cal Kowal, we see images of one of
Hunt's recent works,* Jacob's Ladder. *The work was unveiled at the
Carter G. Woodson Public Library on Chicago's south side in
September, 1977. The permanent home of* Jacob's Ladder *is in the
Vivian Harsh Room of African-American Literature; according
to Dr. Donald Franklin Joyce, Curator, the Harsh Collection is
the largest in the Midwest.*

A SENSE OF STORY

JAMES ALAN McPHERSON

AT THE MURDER TRIAL THE DEFENDANT, ROBERT L. CHARLES, AFTER having sat four days in silence while his court-appointed lawyer pleaded for him, rose suddenly from his chair during his counsel's summation and faced the jurors. "It wasn't no accident," he told them in a calm voice. "I had me nine bullets and a no-good gun. Gentlemens, the *onliest* thing I regret is the gun broke before I could pump more than six slugs into the sonofabitch."

Thus ensuring his doom, the defendant sat down.

The entire courtroom hushed, except for defense counsel's condemnation of his client. The judge quickly ordered the jurors from the room and motioned both counsel, and the court reporter, to approach the bench. The defendant remained seated, ignoring the heated remonstrations of his lawyer. And while the others huddled before the judge—the assistant district attorney, a dapperly dressed student D.A., the court stenographer and, reluctantly, the defense attorney—Robert L. Charles remained impassive in his chair. He looked neither ahead nor behind him, neither to his right or left. His eyes were unfocused. He seemed to have accepted whatever fate he had assigned himself.

The judge was in a quandary. There was no rule covering such an outburst. There was no way it could be erased from the jurors' minds. There was no point in going on with the trial. The two lawyers and the judge agreed finally that, since the outburst had occurred during defense counsel's summation, the record of prior proceedings should be examined. In this way it could be determined whether a preponderance of the evidence had already tipped the scales of justice against the defendant, making his confession of insignificant weight. This unfortunate decision was to be left with the judge. A thoughtful, painstaking man, he recessed court, dismissed the jurors, and retired to his chambers with as much of the transcript of the trial's proceedings as his clerk could supply. He ordered the court stenographer to transcribe the most recent testimony as rapidly as possible. Then, in his book-lined, green-carpeted office, the judge browsed hurriedly over the record.

It was an open and shut case. The defendant, Robert Lee Charles, was accused of shooting his employer of thirteen years, Frank Johnson, on the afternoon of June 12, 197-. Though there was no witness to the actual shooting, a second Johnson employee, a mechanic named Jed Jones, had rushed into the office after hearing six shots and had seen the defendant, Charles, bending over the body of the deceased man. The smoking gun was still in his left hand. With his right hand, according to Jones, Charles was stuffing bullets into the deceased man's mouth. Charles had not resisted the arresting officers: he had waited quietly in the office for them to arrive. At the pre-trial hearing he had pleaded *nolo contendere* and remained silent, leaving it to his court-appointed attorney to plead mitigating circumstances in an effort to convince the jury that manslaughter, with life imprisonment, was all that was due the state. By presenting such evidence, the defense counsel had contrived to prevent Robert Lee Charles from being the first man condemned to death under the state's new, carefully drafted, capital punishment statute. But by his speech in the courtroom, whether inspired by madness or by over-confidence in his lawyer's case, the defendant had doomed himself to death.

The judge leafed through the record of three days before. He scanned part of the testimony by the arresting officer, Lloyd Scion:

MR. LINDENBERRY: Officer Scion, at the time of the arrest, what was the scene when you entered the deceased's office?

MR. SCION: Mr. Johnson was on the floor next to the desk in a pool of blood. The defendant—that man, Robert Charles seated over there—was sitting on the desk holding a gun. Mr. Jones there was standing by the door, possibly to prevent the defendant's escape.

MR. LINDENBERRY: What did the defendant do when you entered.

MR. SCION: Nothing. Well, I mean I had my own gun drawn, so there wasn't nothing much he could do. I ordered him to drop his gun. He did. I put the cuffs on him.

MR. LINDENBERRY: What did he say?

MR. SCION: Nothing. He didn't say anything. He threw the gun on the floor near the body of the deceased. There was no fight in him. I took him on down without a word, without a tussle.

MR. LINDENBERRY: Officer Scion, what was the condition of deceased's body at the time of defendant's arrest?

MR. SCION: He had six bullets in him, three in the belly, two in the chest, and one in his right arm. There was also . . .

MR. GRANT: Objection.

COURT: On what ground?

MR. GRANT: Counsel and Officer Scion have already established Mr. Johnson was dead. My client has not denied he shot the deceased.

MR. LINDENBERRY: Your honor, I think that what Officer Scion has to say may be of interest to the jury. I think it should be let in.

MR. GRANT: May my colleague and I approach the bench, your honor?

COURT: Proceed

. . .

MR. LINDENBERRY: Officer Scion, according to your records, was the defendant drunk at the time of his arrest?

MR. SCION: No, sir

. . .

MR. GRANT: I have no questions

Here was the testimony of Jed Jones, the employee who had been first in the office after the shooting:

MR. LINDENBERRY: How long have you worked at Rogers' Auto Service?

MR. JONES: Ten years.

MR. LINDENBERRY: Was the defendant an employee there when you were hired?

MR. JONES: Yes, sir.

MR. LINDENBERRY: How long had he been employed there?

MR. JONES: Before me?

MR. LINDENBERRY: Yes.

MR. JONES: Two or three years. Closer to three, I think.

MR. LINDENBERRY: Was he at the time of your arrival a difficult fellow?

MR. GRANT: Object.

COURT: Sustained.

MR. LINDENBERRY: Did you get along with Mr. Charles?

MR. JONES: We got along. But we never got to be friends.

MR. LINDENBERRY: Why was that?

MR. GRANT: Objection.

COURT: Does counsel have a line of questioning in mind?

MR. LINDENBERRY: Yes, your honor. I hope to establish something about the character of this witness relating to an ancillary issue involved here.

COURT: Proceed.

MR. LINDENBERRY: Was it Mr. Charles' race that prevented you from becoming friends?

MR. JONES: No. I get along with most everybody. I've drunk beer with several of the other colored . . . black guys that work up to Rogers'. We don't visit each other's homes or stuff like that, but we get along. But Bob was different.

MR. LINDENBERRY: You refer to the defendant, Mr. Robert L. Charles. How, in your opinion, was he different?

MR. JONES: Well, he never joshed around like the others do. It's a mite hard to explain. He was always off in a corner moping or

something. And it wasn't just me. Bob didn't have much truck
with the other colored fellows there either. It was like there wasn't
no funning in him. I know he made them colored fellows nervous.

MR. LINDENBERRY: How do you know this?

MR. GRANT: Object.

COURT: Sustained.

MR. LINDENBERRY: What recollections do you personally have of the
defendant's character?

MR. JONES: Like I say, he was always off in a corner sulking or some-
thing. Bob was a good worker, tops. But even when he was work-
ing it was automatic-like, like his mind was always on something
else. I tried once or twice to get friendly with him, but I didn't get
very far. So after awhile I quit trying. He never said nothing
harmful to me personally, but I will say that his manner was cold,
businesslike. I would say he was a loner

. . .

MR. LINDENBERRY: Would you give us your recollection of the trouble
between defendant and the deceased Mr. Frank Johnson?

MR. JONES: I first notice it about eight years ago, two years after
I had come there to Rogers'. This was back during the time when
them foreign cars was flooding the market. Every shop in town was
trying to switch over. There was few mechanics able to deal with
them Jap gas sippers. Most of our boys was raised on Detroit. But
Bob was one of the few in our shop that could ease right into the
newer models. I think he must of studied them at home or some-
thing. Anyway, he come in the shop one morning saying he had
put together a lube mixture that was going to add years to the
valves and pistons of them new models. He said the formula was
going to grease his way to a desk job over in the main office. He
wouldn't tell nobody the formula, but I know he talked to Mr.
Johnson in great detail about it.

MR. LINDENBERRY: How do you know this?

MR. JONES: Because about two weeks later old Johnson . . . Mr.
Johnson told me, "Bobby Lee has gone crazy. He thinks some
bathtub concoction is a miracle drug. He's sounding like a sarsa-
parilla drummer singing down a country road. I can't bother them
down to the main office with this kind of foolishness." I remember
he said that to me just as plain as day.

MR. LINDENBERRY: What else did Mr. Johnson tell you?

MR. JONES: About a month later he told me in the john, "Bobby Lee
has threaten me, Jed. His formula don't work, he lost it or some-
thing, and he thinks I am the cause."

MR. LINDENBERRY: Would you repeat Mr. Johnson's words to you so
the jurors can hear?

MR. JONES: Mr. Johnson told me that the main office had rejected
Bob's formula and Bob blamed him for it. He said, "Jed, Bob has

threaten me. His formula don't work, and he thinks I am the one that soured the main office on it."

MR. LINDENBERRY: Mr. Jones, in your opinion did the defendant take a hardened attitude toward Mr. Johnson after that?

MR. JONES: Yes, sir. In my opinion, he surely did.

MR. LINDENBERRY: In what ways did this attitude express itself?

. . .

MR. GRANT: No questions, your honor.

The judge rang for his secretary and ordered coffee and a cottage cheese sandwich. Then he continued poring through the transcript. It was shortly after noon, and there was a judges' conference scheduled for 3:00 p.m. When the secretary brought in his lunch and some additional transcripts he had reached in his reading the direct examination of Mr. Orion W. Rogers, owner of Rogers' Auto Service and Supply:

MR. LINDENBERRY: Now Mr. Rogers, how would you characterize your late employee, Mr. Frank Johnson?

MR. ROGERS: I would say he had love in his heart for everybody in the world.

MR. LINDENBERRY: How long had the deceased worked for you?

MR. ROGERS: Frank was one of my first employees. He was with me eighteen years ago, when I first started out. He was a very dedicated employee, and one of the few whose insights I trusted in matters of money as well as of morals.

MR. LINDENBERRY: What do you mean by morals, Mr. Rogers?

MR. ROGERS: It was Frank's suggestion, when I opened tnat shop on Guilford, to add a black or two to the crew there. I must confess that such a thought had never entered my mind. I say this in all candor, as an indication of the level of my social consciousness relative to Frank's. But he prodded and pushed until I agreed to bring a black or two into all three shops.

MR. LINDENBERRY: Would you please look at this defendant. Can you recall whether he is one of the blacks recommended to you by Mr. Johnson?

MR. ROGERS: I can't recall. You understand that a man in my position can't possibly keep such things in mind. But I do recall this man's face. He came up to the main office regularly to deliver invoices, pick up payrolls, a variety of things. He was always civil and soft-spoken. I remember this aspect of his personality distinctly because he reminded me of my favorite waiter at a resort my wife and I visit frequently on an island off the Carolina coast. As I said, he had those kinds of qualities that made me think of a loyal, gentle person. So you can understand how shocked—outraged, really—I was when this thing happened.

MR. LINDENBERRY: Mr. Rogers, do you recall an incident in which
Mr. Johnson spoke to you about the behavior of the defendant? I
mean with respect to an automotive lubricant compound sup-
posedly invented by Mr. Charles?

MR. ROGERS: No, sir. I cannot recall such a conversation. But I can
assure you that Frank would have been the first to extend his
every effort to give its highest recommendation to the company.

MR. LINDENBERRY: Then what, in your opinion, accounted for the
development of the animosity on the part of defendant toward
Mr. Frank Johnson?

MR. GRANT: Object. Witness is in no position to psychoanalyze the
defendant. These judgments are beyond his competence to make.

COURT: Mr. Lindenberry?

MR. LINDENBERRY: Your honor, I ask you again to consider my posi-
tion. I assure the court that this is not a fishing expedition. Since
I will have no opportunity to examine the defendant, his wife, his
children or anyone with an intimate sense of him, I have no choice
but to glean testimony shedding light on his possible motives
from whatever sources possible. Now it strikes me that this wit-
ness' insights are valid here, more so in light of the defendant's
silence. If this witness, as an employer with special insights into
the nature of typical employer-employee conflict, is ruled to be not
competent to make such judgments, then why not also strike the
testimony of Mr. Jed Jones? If this witness's testimony on this
important point cannot come in, I do not see how I can make the
best possible case for the state.

COURT: Mr. Lindenberry, I am still bothered by your expressed in-
tention to proceed from inferences about the defendant's person-
ality based not on direct observation of the defendant but on an
abstraction called the "typical employee" that exists only in this wit-
ness's head. Mr. Grant, is this the essence of your objection?

MR. GRANT: Yes, your honor. And I would add that anything said by
the witness about this particular employee would be doubly imma-
terial. One, for his lack of personal knowledge, and, two, because
even if his insights were valid with respect to the typical employee,
I submit that this defendant is not typical. He is in a class by him-
self. I submit that he is an illiterate southern black, socialized in
an environment of violence, who possesses a single skill. He is a
man who acted out of motives beyond the competence of this
witness, and of most white people, to know.

COURT: I have taken your point under advisement, Franklin. It goes
against my better judgment, and perhaps I am wrong, but my
intuition tells me there is a sense of story here. I am going to let
the testimony in. I remind you of our talk at the bench on yester-
day, and of the responsibility we have to hold this defendant to the

same standard as everyone else. The rules of society are made for all. His membership in the negro race . . .

The judge paused to fill his pipe and light it. Then he took a pencil from the green holder on his desk and underlined part of this exchange between himself and Franklin Grant. He leaned back in his chair, puffing his pipe and reflecting. Then he looked at his watch and resumed reading:

MR. LINDENBERRY: Now Mr. Rogers, I repeat, based on your own experience as an employer, in the typical rub of egos and elbows, what is the most likely source of conflict?

MR. ROGERS: Sometimes you get an employee whose talent does not match his ambition. This is a painful truth, one of which most fair employers have to be aware. The Good Lord did not distribute talents equally, that's in the Bible. But some employees find it hard to accept their lot. They agitate and see offense where none was intended. They blame others, even those with their best interest in mind, for their own personal failings. Such employees — prima donnas, we call them — usually fail to get along. If they have a sense of humor, the situation is bearable. If they do not—well, sometimes the consequences can be tragic.

MR. LINDENBERRY: Would you say that this profile fits the defendant here, Mr. Charles?

MR. GRANT: I object, your honor.

COURT: No. Since I've started this I am going to let it in.

MR. LINDENBERRY: In your opinion, Mr. Rogers, does the defendant here fit this profile?

MR. ROGERS: Since this tragic event I've checked our records. I know now that Mr. Charles came to us about thirteen years ago. I don't recall anything personal about him, except that three weeks ago one of my former secretaries called to tell me that he is the same man who, about nine years back, caused a bit of disturbance in my office. She recognized his picture in the papers. She said. . . .

MR. GRANT: Hearsay.

COURT: Sustained.

MR. LINDENBERRY: Your honor, since the time of the incident under exploration here, the secretary, Mrs. Ellen Claus, has been

· · ·

MR. ROGERS: . . . demanded to see me without stating the nature of his business. Well, Mrs. Claus, as you might imagine, was protective of my time. He would not state his business and she therefore could not let him through. That is all I can say about this man

· · ·

MR. GRANT: I have no questions.

The judge skipped a few pages and then resumed his reading. Here was part of the testimony of Mr. Otis Pinkett, another employee at Rogers' Auto Service and Supply:

MR. LINDENBERRY: Now during the incident you speak of, what in your opinion seemed to be the quality of the relationship between the deceased Mr. Johnson and the defendant?

MR. PINKETT: Like I say, I first become uneasy that time I was cleaning up round the office and Bobby Lee come in. This was about five or six years ago, as I recall. Mr. Johnson was at his desk eating his lunch. Bobby Lee walk right up to the desk and say, "Is it time?" And Mr. Johnson look up at him and smile and say, "No. No. Not yet." Then Bobby Lee turn and walk out.

MR. LINDENBERRY: How would you characterize Mr. Johnson's attitude during this exchange?

MR. PINKETT: I told you he smiled. That's all I can recollect to my mind.

MR. LINDENBERRY: And what about the defendant's attitude? How would you characterize that?

MR. PINKETT: He wasn't smiling and he wasn't mad. Truth is, I ain't never seen him look that way before. His face was set and his eyes was almost popping out of his head. But he didn't look mad. He walk like he had a board pressed up against his back. He didn't look at me. He just look down at Mr. Johnson and say, "Is it time?" And Mr. Johnson smile up to him and say, "No. No. Not yet." He said it real soft and easy like, the way you would talk to a woman. I remember it well, because it like to scare the . . . out of me. I mean to

. . .

MR. LINDENBERRY: And when did defendant communicate this threat?

MR. PINKETT: I didn't say...

MR. GRANT: Objection.

COURT: Sustained.

MR. LINDENBERRY: When did you hear the defendant remark that he had something against Mr. Johnson?

MR. PINKETT: I never said it was a threat. I myself would not call it a threat. You know how it is when people get mad. They say things they don't mean.

MR. LINDENBERRY: Mr. Pinkett, when did Mr. Charles communicate these words to you?

MR. PINKETT: It was about four years ago. See, I was just kidding around with him about a customer that gived me a hard time. I said something like, "I felt like laying out that so-and-so." Then Bobby Lee look toward the office and say, "I would like to do that very same thing, Otis."

MR. LINDENBERRY: Who was in the office at that time?

MR. PINKETT: Mr. Johnson was in there.

. . .

MR. GRANT: I have no further questions, your honor.

. . .

Testimony of Dr. Walter R. Thorne, resident psychiatrist at the state mental hospital.

MR. LINDENBERRY: Now Dr. Thorne, considering your examination of this defendant's psychological profile, how would you characterize his mental make-up?

MR. THORNE: One must begin by first noting the peculiarities of the area of the subject's earliest socialization for insights into his emotional background. According to records collected during my investigation, this man spent most of his formative years in the South, in the state of Virginia. As you will recall, during the period of his childhood the South practiced rather crude and often vicious methods of caste segregation. The effects of this on the human personality, especially the concomitant violence, are inestimable. Coupled with this were the traumata of an abrupt move, with a family of three, from an agricultural situation to one that is highly structured, competitive, mobile and impersonal. Such a transition is bound to cause a degree of dislocation. Some of this can be quite serious.

MR. LINDENBERRY: Dr. Thorne, in your opinion, was the defendant stable enough to appreciate the consequences of his act? Would the possible dislocation you describe distort his sense of reality to such an extent that he would not know right from wrong?

MR. THORNE: Not in my opinion. I say this for three specific reasons. First, the move from the South took place while the defendant was still a relatively young man, and I see no evidence that he has not made the necessary adjustment. Second, my examination of his family has convinced me that all of them, especially the oldest boy, show no signs of having been influenced by a maladjusted personality. They are perfectly normal, if one makes allowances for their economic and social status vis-à-vis the broader society. Third, the fact that the defendant never missed a day from work and functioned in the choir of his church demonstrates, for me at least, that he had settled into a structured way of life that was at least comfortable. Considering all this, I am forced to conclude that the defendant was indeed stable when he acted. Why he acted is a conclusion I must leave to you, or at least to these jurors who are better qualified than I am to apply the law.

MR. LINDENBERRY: Dr. Thorne, in your experience as a psychiatrist have you had occasion to observe a streak of paranoia in members of the negro race, specifically in negro males?

MR. THORNE: I recall having read some studies on the subject.

MR. LINDENBERRY: Can you summarize what you can remember of those studies?

MR. THORNE: There was one out of Michigan, by a man named Slovik, I believe, noting the frequency with which negro males instinctively grab their testicles when startled. Also, an old study out of New York presented data presuming to show that when confronted by obstacles which to them appear threatening, negro males tend more frequently than whites to assign blame not to themselves but to whomever happens to be most proximate in positions of authority. This reaction, the study concluded, can sometimes take on suicidal dimensions. And I recall a more recent study, done in Florida, purporting to show that males of that group are more frightened of dogs than are males of the white group. Well, as you might expect, I discount a great deal of this. I would say, in my considered judgment, that there is little scientific evidence for a disproportionate amount of paranoia among males of the black group than for males of the white group. Of course, statistics aside, one must always leave room for chance.

MR. LINDENBERRY: Dr. Thorne, in your opinion, could this defendant have acted out of a paranoid fear of his employer, Mr. Johnson?

MR. THORNE: Considering the evidence in this specific case, I would have to say no.

MR. LINDENBERRY: Your witness, sir.

MR. GRANT: No questions.

The judge sipped the last of his coffee and reflected over the transcript. It was 1:25 p.m. He was to meet with his clerk at 2:00 p.m. to prepare for the judges' conference. He cleaned his pipe, then began moving forward again in his reading. But for some reason he paused. He turned back a great number of pages he had already skimmed to a section he had skipped entirely. This was the cross-examination, and re-direct examination, of Otis Pinkett:

MR. GRANT: Why did you advise the defendant to give up his job and seek employment elsewhere?

MR. PINKETT: Well, see, I'm like this here. If I see where I ain't wanted in a place, I don't waste my time there. Me, I believes in moving on.

MR. GRANT: Mr. Pinkett, what is your present position at Rogers'

Auto Service and Supply?

MR. PINKETT: After Mr. Jones over there, I guess you could call me third in command. I been around a long time, so people usually ask for me when they come in.

MR. GRANT: And to what do you attribute your success?

MR. PINKETT: I guess I know how to deal with the public. There's just a certain way you handle people, certain things you do to get along with the public.

MR. GRANT: Was it the lack of this social grace in Mr. Charles that caused you to advise him to move on?

MR. PINKETT: Well, since you ask, I will have to say yes. Now I don't mean no dirt to nobody, especially Bobby Lee. But it look to me like, being from the South and all, he didn't have no common sense. Me, myself, I felt that I was as good as Mr. Johnson or anybody else. But Bobby Lee, look like he thought he was better than Mr. Johnson. It wasn't like he thought black was better than white. He act like he thought they was something better than black and white and he already had it in a jug with the stopper in his back pocket. Well, I'm smart enough to know you don't do that around the folks that's paying your salary. That's why I told him I thought it best for him to move along.

MR. GRANT: Could it be, Mr. Pinkett, that you were jealous of the defendant?

MR. PINKETT: No, it wasn't that way at all. I was making more than him at the time, my job was secure, so it wasn't no sweat off my back. I just felt sorry for him.

. . .

MR. GRANT: Mr. Pinkett, can you recall any instance when the deceased disclosed the existence of hostilities toward you because of your color?

MR. PINKETT: No, sir. I have told you that Mr. Johnson have always been kind to me. He liked black people. He always asked how we was doing, how our families was doing, whether we needed a credit reference down to a store.

COURT: Where is this leading, counsel?

MR. GRANT: Your honor, I hope through this witness to establish something about the personality of deceased that Mr. Pinkett here seems, for some reason, reluctant to disclose. I hope to establish that deceased was something less than a model employer.

COURT: Well, this is tedious for me because you seem to be fishing. But I'll let it go on, if you have no objection, Paul.

MR. LINDENBERRY: I have no objection so far.

COURT: Proceed.

. . .

MR. GRANT: You have testified that the deceased's treatment of you was gracious beyond question.

MR. PINKETT: No nevermind about it. He was a good man, a prince of a man.

MR. GRANT: Would you say that defendant shared your opinion of Mr. Johnson?

MR. LINDENBERRY: Object, your honor.

COURT: Sustained.

MR. GRANT: Mr. Pinkett, did the defendant ever express to you any jealousy of the superior treatment you were receiving?

MR. LINDENBERRY: Your honor, I object. Counsel is trying to elicit from the witness speculation about motives immaterial to the issue here. That issue is whether or not defendant showed suffi-cient hostility to support the inference of premeditation. What my colleague seems to be after is speculation. Or is it gossip?

. . .

MR. GRANT: Judge, I accept the ruling. But I feel I must make my position a matter of record. I remind the court that the defendant has not contributed in any way to his defense. His plea of *nolo,* his refusal to allow his family to testify on his behalf, and his refusal to even discuss this case with me—these things put me in a very awkward position. Since he has even refused to take the stand in his own defense, I am obliged to defend him as best I can without any clear sense of his motives having been communicated to me. I was from the beginning reluctant to take this case, but since I make a point of honoring my assignments I have tried to do my best. Now, if I am not allowed to introduce what my colleague calls speculation, I do not see how I am to continue.

. . .

MR. GRANT: Now Mr. Pinkett, please repeat, as clearly as you can recall, the defendant's words on that occasion.

MR. PINKETT: He said he had gived up on life. He said he didn't under-stand things he thought he understood. We were in the john at the time. I was taking a pee and he was in the stall. I couldn't see his face but I could hear him. He said, "Mr. Johnson has hurt me so bad, Otis, till I don't want to live." He said to me, "There ain't nothing more I want than to get out of life."

MR. GRANT: Did you ever see the defendant argue with or threaten the deceased?

MR. PINKETT: No. I have said before that I seen them together on many occasions, but they never did say nothing much. Only thing I ever heard was this time Bobby Lee and me was in the office on a Friday night picking up our pay. I had got a raise. I don't think Bobby Lee had got one. When Mr. Johnson go to pass the envelope to Bobby Lee, he smile and say, "I'm white."

MR. GRANT: What did the deceased say?

MR. PINKETT: He look at Bobby Lee and say, "I'm white."

MR. GRANT: That was all?

MR. PINKETT: Yeah.

MR. GRANT: Could there conceivably have been a dispute over something and deceased was saying, "I'm right."?

MR. PINKETT: That could of been. But it sound to me like he said "I'm white."

MR. GRANT: How did he look and act when he said that?

MR. PINKETT: He said it in a low voice, and when I look over at him his face change. It was real funny.

MR. GRANT: What do you mean?

MR. PINKETT: Well, he didn't look mad or nothing. But when I first look his eyes was all wide and blue and sparkling like he was drunk. But then when I look again, he look sort of sleepy, like he had just woke up and there was something he forgot.

MR. GRANT: Did his look change before or after you heard him say what he said?

MR. PINKETT: It was a little before and a little after.

MR. GRANT: Mr. Pinkett, please be specific.

MR. PINKETT: I don't know, it happened so fast. I don't know if he saw me watching him.

MR. GRANT: Can you remember whether his face changed after he saw you watching him?

MR. PINKETT: I don't know. I can't remember.

MR. GRANT: What color was Mr. Johnson?

MR. PINKETT: Why, he was a white man with light brown hair.

MR. GRANT: And what color is the defendant, Mr. Charles?

MR. PINKETT: As you can see, he is just about as black as the ace of spades.

MR. LINDENBERRY: Your honor, I must rise to

. . .

COURT: I remind you to remember who and where you are, Paul. I was not asleep. Ladies and gentlemen of the jury, at certain points, especially in a trial as complicated as this one, a judge must weight

. . .

MR. LINDENBERRY: Would you repeat that so the jury can hear.

MR. PINKETT: He lent me that money out of the goodness of his heart. Another time he let me off from work just so I could go to a ball game. Many a time he put in a kind word to people downtown so I could get some more credit. He gave me plenty grace. To me he was a man of his word. If he told me a chicken spit tobacco juice, I would never of looked under that chicken's wing for the snuff box. That's how close Mr. Johnson was to me. He was a prince, and I can't hold back from saying this much about him, even if I wanted to help Bobby Lee.

MR. LINDENBERRY: Now Mr. Pinkett, you have said that the defendant "went soft." Would you elaborate on this?

MR. GRANT: I object.

COURT: Overruled. I am going to let this in, Franklin. You had your chance, and now I want to see where this is going.

MR. LINDENBERRY: Would you elaborate, sir?

MR. PINKETT: What I mean is that Bobby Lee seem to put his self in positions that was bound to cause friction between him and Mr. Johnson. I myself notice that he wouldn't follow orders straight. Many a day he took his own sweet time on a repair job. I think he done that just to devil Mr. Johnson. Well, something bad was bound to happen. If you get in people's way too much, they going to knock you back in your place. I believe that's what happen to Bobby Lee toward the end there.

MR. GRANT: I have to object strenuously, your honor.

COURT: Sustained. Mr. Pinkett, I must warn you to refrain from making value judgments. By that I mean you are not being asked to assess whether the defendant in your opinion was a good or bad man, or whether he engineered his own failures. You must tell what you know that bears on the issue in contention here.

MR. PINKETT: Contention?

COURT: You must tell the truth about Mr. Charles' possible reasons for wanting to kill Mr. Johnson.

MR. PINKETT: But I'm just telling what I know, your honor, sir. I'm not trying to take sides.

COURT: I must remind you, Mr. Pinkett, that you have been re-called as a prosecution witness. You must refrain, sir, from voicing opinions not solicited by counsel. You may not be aware of this, but Mr. Lindenberry is responsible to the rules of evidence and not to you. You must answer directly the specific questions put to you by him. Do you understand, sir?

MR. PINKETT: Yes, sir, your honor.

COURT: Ladies and gentlemen, I feel I must apologize to you for these lengthy excursions. I have attempted to grant leeway to counsel for both sides because it seemed to me that my own decisions, based solely on the rules of evidence as I know them, would prevent your viewing the cross-light of competing views which I consider essential to the adversary process. But it seems now that I have made a mess of things. Still, in my mind law is an art, and my function here should ideally be no different than that of a literary critic. But, as I have said, I have probably. . . .

The intercom on the judge's desk buzzed. It was his clerk, reminding him of the conference in the common room at 3:00 p.m. It was now

2:05 p.m. The judge advised the clerk to buzz him again at 2:30 p.m. Then he rang for his secretary and instructed her to bring in the remaining transcripts as soon as they were typed. This done, he lit his pipe and puffed it almost into flame as he read faster through the thin pile of papers.

He read very fast.

The secretary rapped gently on the door, then entered and placed a note on the desk beside his coffee cup. The judge paused in his reading and glanced at it. The note was from his clerk. It said, "Sir, I must insist that you take time out to be briefed. Garson is up for re-election this year, and his clerk told me he is prepared to shine. It would be bad, considering the circumstances, if he caught the collective eye during this session. There won't be another until February. Call at 2:20 p.m.? Mills."

The judge glanced at his watch. It was already 2:13 p.m. He puffed his pipe and read hurriedly. He read quickly over the testimony of Reverend Lorenzo Blake, the minister of the church attended by defendant:

MR. GRANT: Sir, what can you tell the court about the character of Mr. Robert L. Charles?

MR. BLAKE: I always took him to be a gentle, God-fearing man. I'm sure there's not a soul in my church that would have a different opinion of him. It hurts me to say this, but what he has done reflects badly on them, and on the black folks of Roanoke.

MR. GRANT: What had Roanoke to do with this?

MR. BLAKE: Most of my congregants come from Roanoke, Robert Charles too. You'll find that people who come up here usually follow the trails of people from their home-towns who have come before. In every city you find settlements of people from Birmingham, Charleston, Macon, Durham, even the thousands of little towns. The Texans, I believe, go to California, along with those from Arkansas. But we are Virginians. We tend to look out for our own.

MR. GRANT: Considering this bond, did Mr. Charles ever come to you for advice of any sort? Did he ever confide in you about some difficulty he was having?

MR. BLAKE: As I told you before, I can recall no conversation about his job. But I remember one instance about another matter. You see, Robert was very, very concerned about his lack of formal education. He cannot read or write. But he does have a genius for cars, for repairing cars. He repaired cars on weekends at his home. But for some reason he was ashamed of this. He came to me

one Sunday and confided that he was losing the respect of his
oldest boy, Robert, Jr. It was my understanding that the boy was
moving with a fast crowd, was experimenting with drugs, and
Robert did not have the time to discipline him.

MR. GRANT: You are saying then, Reverend, that he was a concerned
parent?

MR. BLAKE: Yes, sir. He was very concerned. He wanted me to talk
with Robert, Jr. He wanted me to help him get the boy involved
with boys his own age who had more positive activities. He asked
me if I knew any boys who read books.

MR. LINDENBERRY: Your honor, with all due respect to the Reverend,
I must say that this is not getting us anywhere. The jails are full of
homocidal maniacs who like to read books.

MR. GRANT: I find intolerable this lapse on the part of my colleague.
I must object.

COURT: Paul, I agree with your conclusion, but I must say that I too
find your sentiment objectionable. Where do you hope to take us,
Franklin?

MR. GRANT: I am only trying to show the jurors that the defendant had
an interest in his son's education. I want to show that he placed
much value on his boy's progress. If I may, I would like to build
toward something.

COURT: Well, speed things up a bit.

MR. GRANT: Yes, your honor. Mr. Blake, would you call the defendant
a devout Christian?

MR. BLAKE: I am not prepared to make that judgment.

MR. GRANT: Well, did he attend church regularly?

MR. BLAKE: Yes.

MR. GRANT: Did he drink?

MR. BLAKE: I can't say.

MR. GRANT: I remind you, Reverend Blake, that you are under oath.
I also remind you of your statement in your pre-trial deposition.
Now I ask you again, sir, did this defendant drink?

MR. BLAKE: Yes, sir.

MR. GRANT: Heavily?

MR. BLAKE: At times, yes. But he was always gentle. Usually, his wife
told me, he went to sleep afterwards.

MR. LINDENBERRY: At this point it is really not in my interest to ob-
ject, but I will. Hearsay. Besides, the best witness is available
right in this courtroom.

COURT: Again I ask, Franklin, where is this going? How does the
fact of the defendant's drinking help the case you are trying to
make? How do his drinking habits detract from his possible
motives for killing Mr. Johnson?

MR. GRANT: Your honor, I remind you again that the defendant and his family have refused to testify on his behalf. I am doing what I can to plead the best possible case for him. I intend to tie things together shortly.

COURT: Well, be brief, Mr. Grant.

MR. GRANT: Reverend Blake, was the defendant known to get drunk at Christmas, Thanksgiving, Easter and on other special occasions? Is that not the custom in the South?

MR. BLAKE: All of us do that, I am sure. But yes, it is a custom.

MR. GRANT: I did not ask your assessment of the habits of mankind. I asked did this defendant have a reputation for getting drunk on special occasions, and does not this habit derive from a widespread custom in the South?

MR. BLAKE: Yes. There is a custom of drinking heavily in the South.

MR. GRANT: And is there not also a tradition of handling guns in the South? Specifically, don't people there sometimes shoot off their guns to celebrate special occasions?

MR. BLAKE: Yes, sir. That is true.

MR. GRANT: Then there are many customs, drinking and handling guns on special occasions among them, that blacks bring up from the South?

MR. BLAKE: I am not aware

. . .

MR. LINDENBERRY: I remind the jury that according to the testimony of Officer Scion, defendant was not drunk when arrested on the afternoon of June 12, 197-.

. . .

Again the secretary rapped lightly on the door. She entered and placed another note, and the last of the transcript, on the desk beside the judge's coffee cup. This note, also from the clerk, said, "It is 2:25 p.m. I will wait. But you are just hurting yourself. Mills." The judge scribbled "ten minutes" on the back of the note and handed it to his secretary. She walked out on tiptoes. The judge leaned back in his padded chair, stuffed his pipe and lit it. Then he rose from the chair and walked to the window and looked out. Down in the parking lot, against a backdrop of concrete driving ramps, dozens of cars shone in the sunlight like metal, multicolored animals. From this height they looked like toys. He puffed his pipe and looked up. The specially treated glass in the picture window made the sky seem more bright and blue than it really was. The judge straightened his tie. He flicked a spot of ash from the sleeve of his blue coat. Then he went into the bathroom and washed his face and hands. Refreshed, he returned to his desk and began gathering up the transcript. The last few pages he had not read. He skimmed quickly over the summation by Paul Lindenberry, the Assistant District Attorney. Then he wrote a short note to his secretary, listing things to be done before she went home. He also wrote a note to his clerk, directing how the verdict in this case should be entered: guilty as charged. He put his desk in order, collecting stray papers and laying the bulky transcript of the trial face down on the green mat. He walked toward the door. Then he turned slowly, and walked back to the desk. He turned over the last page of the transcript and read the last of defense attorney Franklin Grant's summation:

> . . . worth very little to the ideal of justice if you, ladies and gentle-men of the jury, as the conscience of the community, cannot en-vision in your minds, and find room in your hearts, for an illit-erate black. Here is a man, descended from slaves, who, on the day of his son's graduation from high-school did the habitual thing for the celebration of such a grand event. He had a drink. We all do it on the 4th of July. Why can't he? We shoot off firecrackers, cannons, sometimes our mouths. Look at this man's wife and family out there, look carefully at little Robert, Jr., and think to yourselves that, but for the grace of God, this could be your family, this could be your weeping wife. Or you could be this defendant, made passionate by the fact that his oldest child had achieved literacy. Here is the picture I want you to see clearly in your minds, while in that jury room. After attending the graduation ceremony, this defendant does the usual thing to celebrate. He had a nip. But linked in his mind with drinking is that other custom, that other part of the ritual of celebration so honored among blacks in the South. But he is in the city and feels restrained. So he puts the gun in his pocket. Then, a man of habit, he goes to work. There, knowing his boss takes an interest in the families of his employees, he goes into the office with the news. But he has had a nip. And in retelling this good news, there is a lapse of logic in his mind. Perhaps remembering past friction, but most likely in celebration of the event, the defendant takes the gun and acci-dentally . . .
> At this point the defendant interrupted.

The judge placed the page neatly, face down, on the top of the pile.

A MUSIC OF THE STREETS

FREDERICK TURNER

FOR THE PAST SEVERAL YEARS I HAD WANTED TO EXTRACT A PROMISE from Alan Jaffe. Jaffe is the young man who runs Preservation Hall in New Orleans where the city's traditional music can still be heard in something of its vibrant authenticity. Would he, I wondered, notify me in the event of the death of Jim Robinson, the old trombonist who plays regularly at the Hall and with Jaffe's touring group? Robinson was well into his eighties, and though apparently quite healthy, who could tell in this age?

I never asked Jaffe for this. It seemed ghoulish somehow, with Robinson going so strong, and it might easily be construed as a hanger-on's mean desire to be in at the death: long before rock, with its Beatles and Stones, jazz was afflicted by groupies, most of them white, middle-class non-performers whose reasons for their strange allegiance were both tangled and transparent, and I had no wish to be taken as one of these. So I never asked Jaffe and knew that notice would have to come in more accidental fashion—and well after the fact.

As it happened, when Robinson died, May 4, 1976, Jaffe in his considerate way did try to contact me. But it is left to a friend who knows of my relationship with Robinson to call my attention to the obituary in the day's newspaper. The funeral is scheduled for the morning following, and as I absorb this news the sun is already well spent in the hills of western Massachusetts, and I wonder whether I can possibly make it.

To verify these vital details I call Willie Humphrey, the clarinetist who had played alongside Robinson for many years. His voice is casual, acceptant, as if after these many years and at his age such things are matters of course. "Yeah, you could still get here," he says slowly. "They goin' to have two bands an' start at 10:30 in the mornin' from his house. 'Course you won't get much sleep."

At 9:00 the next morning I walk St. Philip Street up out of the French Quarter toward Jim Robinson's house. Already a crowd is gathered across the street from it. Behind them lies the unfinished park, a mess of dried mud, weeds, and boards with a vacant en-

closure just opposite the house where they plan to erect a statue of
Louis Armstrong. And behind that Congo Square with its great
Spanish oaks, brooding, writhing their long branches like black
snakes over that stretch of ground where so much of this music's his-
tory sank its roots into American soil. Many a time after the inter-
vening houses had been torn away Jim Robinson and I had sat in the
shade of his stoop and looked across to that bit of green where once
the transplanted Africans had danced and drummed their own his-
tory, the native sounds mingling over time with European modalities
and instruments in the fusion that produced jazz. I never knew how
much of this history Jim Robinson had ever known.

The day at this hour is already steaming up under a white sun.
Beneath this colors match the heat. Umbrellas of various shades are
unfurled above the crowd, not only black ones but red and blue
striped, flowered parasols, and particolored jobs that look as if they
might have been gotten up for just such occasions. The crowd's
clothing suggests more a fair, a ballgame, or a circus than a funeral.

Around the corner from the house St. Claude Street is packed too,
but these are neighborhood people who have merely stepped out of
doors. A festive air lends ephemeral brightness to a decaying com-
munity Jim Robinson had not seen much of in recent years. It had
become too rough for an old man who might be presumed to have
some money on him. As his wife Pearl had observed, "If you go away
without someone to watch, they liable to just run a truck right up
to your door an' take everythin'."

"They" must certainly be out this morning, the whole neighbor-
hood seemingly assembled in the street, along the walks, in doorways:
sleepy-eyed drinkers; clots of chattering women with children at their
knees; old men with hands clasped behind them, straw hats shading
their faces. At the door of the funeral home, I come upon a moun-
tainous man in a t-shirt leaning against a car fender, a pair of
crutches, their tops padded with torn sheets, arrayed against an ex-
panse of belly. It is Fats Houston, once grand marshal of these
parades, now clearly but a stranded witness. I shake his hand,
noticing its missing fingers. "They takin' us old timers out, one by
one."

The parlor of the Blandin Funeral Home is about the size of a
large hotel room. Before anything else, I am struck by the faces
ranked herein. Some look straight out of Africa or at least the West
Indies, while others seem colored Creole. An old man with a dignity,
burning, intense, sits near the door at the rear, his face molded as if
some ancient master craftsman had exhumed it out of purest mahog-
any; this set off by a starched white collar and neat, figured four-in-
hand. Beside him, same hue and deportment, a tiny woman in red

with stiff pigtails curving in crescents out from her head. A row of three women in flowered, close-wrapped turbans with almond eyes in cafe-au-lait faces; one speaks to a child in rapid Creole. A young woman, beautiful as whipped and molded chocolate, her face as serene as that confection heated to shimmering liquid then come to perfect rest, wears a denim hat that says, "Dy-no-mite."

Here as in the streets a festive air: laughter unstrung, visiting between and among the rows, watchers singly or in pairs moving forward to view the body casually and just as casually sauntering back to gossip and make plans while right in all our faces the coffin is propped on its formica catafalque. Under all this buzz, Jim Robinson lies squeezed into his box.

Too old to have living blood kin, Robinson is attended in this by relatives through marriage: a grand-niece, Tammy, and her father, Joe, who had for the past three years lived with Robinson and had taken on the household duties. And there is a cousin, George, a big square ex-trucker, now slowly dwindling back into what Big Jim himself became in time—a man whose frame spoke as with an echo of old power.

It is hard to tell whether Jim is the victim of a poor mortician's job or of the terrific, wasting disease that took him so quickly. But this clay-colored mummy in gabardine with a wilted rose on what had once been a chest looks like nothing I've ever known. Especially the lips, sealed and grim like an alien slash across the visage. No lips like these could ever have cradled and caressed the mouthpiece of a trombone.

The finishing touches are an American flag folded into a triangle and propped on the rough pillow at the coffin's head; a floral heap at the foot with a red ribbon spelling "Family"; a floral cross at the right; and another arrangement at the left in the shape of a trombone ("Preservation Hall"). Behind the coffin there is a large portrait of Jesus.

A salutary experience this, being from time to time the only white in the warm and humming room, witness to a way of life and a ritual of death that are surely American but just as surely not my own; as if even here—perhaps most especially here—one was fated to come up against the great cleavage, the chasm, of the national culture and be thus forced into the role of the strange intruder, the visiting ethnographer. Still, I feel no hostility now, only small wonder amidst unconcern in the rush of other ways. And after all, this is a role I have become accustomed to over the years, though it is not one I can ever feel comfortable in. Indeed, it was in this very role that I first made Jim Robinson's acquaintance in the spring of 1968.

At that time I had asked his permission to call on him at his home. There on a warm afternoon much like this one-in-the-making we had sat in the front room of his long, narrow house around the corner from this funeral home, the tape recorder picking up the sounds of glasses clinking and the casual noises of the street sifting through an open door. There was a bottle of whiskey and a mixing bowl full of ice cubes and talk of vanished bands and players, styles of music, and of his own style and musical philosophy.

At that time I had the intention of working up a tape-recorded autobiography of a traditional New Orleans musician, and Big Jim Robinson seemed a most likely subject: he was friendly and approachable; he was certainly old enough to have strong ties to the tradition; and his open, big-toned playing style spoke of one of the happiest aspects of the city's musical heritage. My feeling then was that these musicians' lives, the cultural significance of their dedication, the sacrifices entailed, were an absorbing and little understood part of our common history.

That is still my conviction, but Jim and I never completed the project. Over the next few years I got down to New Orleans whenever I could and interviewed him at some length. But over that same stretch it became clear that Jim wasn't interested in this work. It also became clear that we enjoyed each other's company, so that finally the visits came to be just that, and I never bothered anymore to bring the recorder or the camera.

In those days Jim's wife Pearl was still alive, and the three of us would sit in the close, immaculate living room with its heavy plastic covers for the chairs and davenport rustling when we moved, the walls dotted with brown, crisped photographs of musicians and bands with which Jim had played. Above the television set there was a large photo of a young, strikingly handsome Jim with his horn held easily aslant his chest, looking as if casually conscious of his youth, looks, talent: the artist in his prime. The photo served as a combination reference point and standard joke, useful to date something from, to measure aging by, or to suggest his ways with women.

Our talk was of such random things, but especially of the past—which I still tried to lead him into. He and I would sip our drinks, and Pearl would have an occasional beer. Sometimes she would disappear into the recesses of the house and emerge later to tell us she'd fixed a meal—beans, rice, and ham hocks, maybe. When properly warmed, Jim would play some of his favorite recordings which often had to compete with a seemingly eternal American Bandstand the grand-niece Tammy attended on t.v. He would point out particular passages he wanted me to listen to, especially his own ("Just listen to what I do here: some a these fellas, all they can play is melody!"), and after one of these that particularly roused him he would strike his knee with a long, limber hand and wag his head in affirmation, gold-capped teeth sparkling out of the Indian-wide face of the artist, satisfied just here with himself: justified, vindicated, and exalted.

Gradually, in this no longer systematic way, Jim's life details emerged, the rambling talk striking here and there against some fact of place, name, or time. In such a fashion I learned one evening that Jim's given name was Nathan and that "Jim" was a shortened version of a boyhood nickname, "Jim Crow," but he never told me how this came about; some old joke, maybe, that even he had forgotten.

That boyhood itself had been spent about thirty-five miles down river at Deer Range Plantation where Nathan Robinson was born on Christmas Day, 1892. I always planned to sometime rent a car and drive Jim down to his old home until one day he told me it wasn't there anymore: the big river had washed it all away.

His father had come down there from Richmond, Virginia, perhaps as early as the 1870's. There he met a Louisiana woman, married her, and stayed on to work as a teamster and breaker of horses and mules. Jim recalled trailing the dusty roads and paths behind his mother, using her long dresses as both handkerchief and security blanket; remembered too the omnipresence of the mules and horses and tack his father worked with; and, of course, the river the other kids would swim in. "I never could swim," he laughed. "Other boys, they'd say, 'Do this-a-way, Jim.' But I'd go right to the bottom like a stone." What schooling there was, he had here; and, though I have seen him sign his autograph in a slow, neat hand, I came to suspect that he was illiterate.

Another, more native sort of schooling was to be had here, however, and this was the music of the country bands. In those days bands made up of country boys, the children of the teamsters and cane workers and sharecroppers, were forming around the old plantation seats, their music teachers the Creole professors from the city who traveled the outlying parishes showing their pupils the correct way with instruments. What many of these same pupils made of this instruction, however, belongs to the history of jazz and not to that correct Creole tradition. Thus the Old Faithful of a spirited exchange with Jim was a passing reference to these country bands, forgotten, unrecorded, except in the memories of a few old men.

Deer Range was just up river from Magnolia Plantation where perhaps the most significant of these bands was formed, and on Saturdays Jim and his friends would go down there to hear them play a dance. Once he scoffed at me when I confused Louis Keppard's Magnolia Orchestra, a city group of around 1909, with this plantation outfit that had thrilled him in his youth: "Naw, naw, naw," flapping his hand at me. "This was a *country* band. Man, I'm tellin' you, them fellas was *tough*! *Hogs*!"

One of Jim's three brothers played valve trombone in such a band, and Jim told me he "used to fool" with that instrument sometimes, though on another occasion he remembered he'd first tried to produce music on a guitar. In either case, what is important is the strength and uniformity of the precedent: there was the music and there were immediate models for those who aspired to play it.

In 1910, like a lot of country kids, he came to the city. Here the music was in its brightest effulgence, dozens of bands, each with its great players, blasting away at each other from cabarets and dance halls on opposite corners, from wagons advertising dances, from the streets during parades. This was the time when the tradition took cognizance of itself, when the legends took shape, and the reputations were established. Yet in all this Jim Robinson had no part: in those days he was a longshoreman, and it is possible he would have remained one had he not entered the army in 1917.

In France, where his segregated unit worked at building and repairing the roads of war, "They was some fellas was gettin' up a jazz band, y'know. An' they need a trombone. Well, I had been foolin' with my brother's trombone—back in the country my brother had a trombone, but it was a valve trombone an' this here was a slide.

"Trombone is a tough instrument: it's a guess instrument. Anyway, he says to 'em, 'We'll take Bob here (he called me Bob), an' we'll teach 'im an' he can play the trombone parts.'" And so while the band practiced at a YMCA building, Jim would practice by himself on a slope behind it ("They didn't want me 'round playin' all them bad notes.") until he could get along in the ensemble unnoticed.

"Pretty soon, maybe two, maybe three weeks, I was doin' pretty good. Six weeks, why I could play right along with 'em. We'd have a special car, the back all fixed up, y'know, like a truck, with a Red Cross painted on the side, an' we'd play all over." Then, lowering his voice a bit, he winked at me: "Nurses travelin' with us, too."

In 1919 when Jim got back to New Orleans the great flowering of the music was just past, many of the major figures like Freddie Keppard, King Oliver, and Louis Armstrong having gone North; others, like Bunk Johnson, were drifting back into the country; the District which had provided so many jobs was closed; and the mythic originators like Buddy Bolden were memories. Still, it was a fine place for a musician and would have been called "great" were it not for the scale of comparison. Indeed, there were yet so many accomplished musicians in town that Jim once laughed at me when I asked him whether on his return he had started right in playing with some local group. As he subsequently explained, he was far from good enough to cut it in New Orleans, and so he went back to his former

job on the docks. But still the music called, not only from all around
him but now also from within. He had the taste of brass in his mouth,
and in the early days of our acquaintance he told me of a specific
call and of what must now seem an inevitable response—a kind of
autobiographical antiphony.

"I was livin' then down on Marais an' Iberville, an' I could hear
them fellas playin' trombone right next door. When I was on the day
shift I could come out at night an' sit on my porch an' just listen to
them fellas playin'—*dat-dat-dat*—in that hall. Sometimes I'd sit out
there all night long an' listen to 'em play, an' I'd think, 'Shucks!
I could do that! I could do what they doin'!' Sometimes they'd play
till six in the mornin'.

"Well, my sister—I was livin' with her then—, my sister, she got this
player piano. You ever seen a player piano? Got all them great big
rolls on it? Well, she got this player piano, an' when I'd be on the
night shift, then durin' the day I'd just sit there an' work them pedals
an' figure out the trombone. An' that's where I learned my stuff.

"I'd come home seven in the mornin', sleep a little, an' then get
up an' just *work* that piano an' figure out the trombone. Sometimes
my sister, if she was home, she would pedal for me."

His break came when the Kid Rena band needed a trombone to
advertise a dance. Jim's friend John Marrero, who played banjo with
them, brought Jim around so that Rena could audition him. The great
trumpet star was surprised and impressed, and when the band set up
later that day at a street corner, Jim remembered that someone had
gone to the house of the regular trombonist with some bad news. His
voice rising higher, verging on laughter, Jim reconstructed the mes-
sage: "He say, 'Morris! Morris, you better come out here. They's a
new trombone player, Morris, an' he sound *real* good!' Morris, he
come out to see who was playin' that way, an' if he thought he was
sick before, you should have seen 'im when he seen me!"

Thus when I first met Jim Robinson he had more than half a cen-
tury of playing behind him and an even more remarkable amount of
music and life within him. Some of these latter seemed to alter subtly
when Pearl died unexpectedly—though at her age of seventy-six what
can truly be unexpected? It was a different Jim I visited thereafter,
and I even fancied I could hear the older, chastened tones of this
change coming out of the bell of his horn. He was given sometimes to
dark moods where he seemed to huddle within himself and from
which not even a stiff glass or two of I. W. Harper could release him.
For some time after Pearl's death he continued to speak of her as an
active presence. "I get into bed at night," he said once, "an' I lie
right in the middle. I know Pearl, she around, an' this way, if I lie in
the middle, she have to squeeze in on one side or the other." And
sometimes when the mood struck he would kiss a heavily retouched

photograph of her as a young woman.

For a time Pearl's sister Viola came over often from Slidell to help
out and keep company, and once I had a magnificent fried fish
dinner she fixed and during the course of which I had to make two
beer runs to the corner market. But then she stopped coming, and
Jim was at home alone a good deal, though his relative Joe was
around when not working. Many nights he would sit alone behind
shuttered windows and bolted door, listening to his music, sipping a
glass of whiskey, and go to bed at first light. Occasionally neighbors
visited, especially children, and on warm days Jim, sitting on his stoop
beneath a green awning, would be like a great-grandfather to the
block, waving to the children, laughing at their roller-skating mis-
haps, pointing out to them a brightly painted mural of himself on the
wall of a building facing the vacant lot in which they played.

And of course the work at Preservation Hall took him out. Here
in the tiny, airless hall with its splintered floors and massed, sweating
tourists and on tours the band made throughout the states, he was
still the irrepressible crowd-pleaser, the clown, arms flapping, bony
butt stuck out, moving in his pigeon-toed circle dance to someone
else's solo.

The edge to this act, of course, was that he could still play, the
audience's delighted laughter to be followed in the preserved order
of things by its admiration as he followed his own dance routine with
some wide, swinging solo, deep, tremulous reworking of a hymn, or
spirited ensemble work, the long slide of the horn glinting out and
down, the face intent, wholly serious behind the mouthpiece. Now he
was beyond them, his talent and his dedication to it taking him as
much out of reach of laughter as of admiration, the artist here entirely
himself; so that whatever the white tourist crowd's response to him
and to his aged black colleagues, however much this might speak of
that original condition we have not moved too much beyond—the
blacks entertaining the whites with their happy routines—yet by this
inward movement, this allegiance to talent, Robinson and his fel-
lows were always secretly saved from even their most ardent fans; as
they were saved also in some measure from a culture and a history
that could but marginally include them.

Some of all this comes back now in the funeral parlor with its
central object no one seems much to notice, and these images and
words jumblingly assemble themselves as I gaze at that estranged
face or turn away to watch the plaster scallops climb the heavily
repainted walls. While we await our appointed time, folk keep filter-
ing in, and, whenever the doors at the rear are opened, noises of the
band and of the building crowd enter and mingle with the vivacious
chatter here within.

Then the floral tributes are taken up with the inescapable brutality of all such ceremonies by two ebony messengers with stiff hair and suits; two further messengers in smoked glasses flank the coffin; a minister emerges from a side room and reads something from a missal, his voice strong and steady but barely rising above the level within and the swell without. And then the lid comes down on Jim Robinson, lying now with a flag folded across his chest.

Outside the streets blaze, and as the coffin makes its careful, jerky descent to a hearse all but swallowed by the crowd, one of the bands, their instruments resplendent in the dented and scored glory of many parades, bellows above the street sounds, "Just a Closer Walk with Thee." As the last of those within enter this larger scene a professional mourner materializes from the building's innards, adding her broken, runny-nosed lament to the density of sound: "Ohhh, Jeees-us! Ohhh, Jeees-us! Have mercy! Have mercy, Jeees-us!" The mercy at hand is to move beyond this and into the wake of the slowly toiling hearse that seems almost to sweat beneath the hundreds of hands that caress its passage amidst them.

As always on such occasions there is a plethora of recording devices, these growing in number and sophistication with the advances of time as the jazz eminences die out and the whole funeral tradition becomes progressively divorced from its authentic cultural roots that reach back to West Africa. There, as in the Yoruba or Ibo cultures, a family would reduce itself to bones in order to assure the deceased relative the proper and necessary send-off. Reduced possibilities of that here since conditions are already generally impoverished, and so the white photographers and sound men must pick their ways through an unfamiliar terrain of glittering glass, burned mattresses, wasted clumps of cement in weed-grown lots. Walking backwards in the peculiar occupational gait their technology has forced them to learn, they stumble over the features of another way of life, and our route to the church is accompanied by the sounds and images that are the barely suspected inside of the jazz sound as they are also those of Jim Robinson's life and leave-taking.

This part of the journey ends on the strains of a second rendering of "Oh, What a Friend We Have in Jesus," one of several religious songs associated with Jim Robinson. Inside the church most of the space has already been assumed by the photographers, tourists, and others out for the holiday this provides. And while the coffin is brought in and set up and its lid opened one more time, the accompaniment most obvious is the measured whirring and meshing of camera gears, the bold and confident faces behind them taking this little field as an open one.

Against a wall at the front three ministerial presences confront

and counterpoise all this with black-capped severity and vestments
that seem out of another, more coherent time. In support of them and
of the disposition of the coffin the organist plunges heavily into
"Amazing Grace." The majority whites do not know the words so that
articulation is slow and confused, but surging, inevitable as a tide,
and as the last notes are rolled one of the three dark presences ap-
proaches his bulwark; mounted behind it, he takes up his incanta-
tions where the sung cadences leave off. As his high tenor voice
settles into the rhythm it has risen to achieve a cameraman below
switches on the glare of his big machine and turns Jim Robinson's
face a counterfeit green. Somewhere farther back a walkie-talkie
erupts in incomprehensible squawking and just as abruptly quits.

The minister, asking mercy for Jim Robinson, gives way to the
one whose words had ushered the coffin out into the streets, and as
this exchange takes place the ancillary sounds rush in to fill the
space: people pushing to get in at the doors, muttered altercations,
and the unawed talk of spectators at a public event. But once the
smallish, skull-capped man has attained his stride this babble is
drowned in the menace of his tones.

Sweeping the back of his hand outward and downward towards
the coffin, he warns us that he will not bother to repeat the eulogies
of last night's wake with its useless talk of "Robason and what a
good man he was. All that"—again the downward, dismissive wave—
"can't do Robason any good now." And here his voice drops down a
bit:

"Last Sunday I had the privilege of attending Brother Robason at
Touro Hospital. He wanted to tell me something, but the voice was
too weak. The voice was too weak. I baptized him in the name of
the Lord."

Sensing the moment, a temporary vulnerability in even this audi-
ence pondering the existential crisis he has raised into view, he shoots
home his bolt: "*Don't* make the mistake Robason made!" he thun-
ders, dropping the "Brother" now. "*Don't* wait! God won't be played
with!" And then again, and finally: "All this won't help him now.
He can't hear it."

On this he turns to the last of the ministers, a spectral figure who
has patiently endured the shots of the cameras, impervious to their
flickering nuisance. He is the church's pastor, the Reverend Arthur
James Alexander, and as he rises and stares a long moment at the
crowd there is a momentary hush. He looks like God's judgment in
rusty cerement.

This hush—awe, amazement, and curiosity—lasts into his opening
words which are borne on a voice as dry and raspy as sifted cinders,
and then the lower noises rise again, obscuring all but the barest
outline of the old man's message: ". . . raised together . . . ." ". . . Jim

Crow . . . ." ". . . a promise made more than fifty years ago. If he died first, I would bury him. If I died first, he would see to my burial." Then, signifying that he was here fulfilling that promise, he looks in the direction of the coffin and seems to speak of Jim Robinson's late redemption and its efficacy, his voice rising and filling out on his last words, ". . . because He has never failed, and never will fail!" On which affirmation the other two ministers escort him back to his chair from which he sits looking hard and sightless beyond the buzzing room.

Jim Robinson's harsh assessor now for the third time assumes command and introduces the final speaker with the preliminary admonition that his speech will be "about two and a half minutes." In fact, the address of the hip young minister goes considerably beyond that, and though it runs to cliches, as all such addresses must, considering the repetitiveness of the occasion, still it is heartfelt and knowing, and his voice breaks as he remembers Jim's singing of "Bye and Bye." Here once again the master of the ceremony is on his feet, guiding the audience into this song which begins to lilt a little, as if in involuntary tribute to the man who once so joyously sang it accompanying himself with a waving white handkerchief.

The respite is brief: the minister insists again on the grim necessities, and where perhaps the service might have degenerated into a group sing, instead he commands those who would view the body once more to assemble and file past. Whipped by the scorn of his voice and its terrific judgment, we follow one another meekly under his eyes. There is nothing more or less to see than before, and I take this opportunity to escape the remainder of the service.

This proves short enough since I have barely wedged my way out through the crowd on the low wooden steps before a pallbearer emerges behind me, crying out at the crowd, "Won't you let the body out? Please! Make way for the body!" Murmurs among us, "Make way," "Make way." "The family . . . ." "The family . . . ." ". . . family . . . ." A path opens and teen-aged Tammy, tearful and uncertain on high platform shoes, and Joe, his hand on her back, pass down it and into one of the limousines. Then the coffin again, borne atop the crowd and then lowered amidst umbrellas, heads, and shoulders, out of sight until an obscured flash of metal tells us the hearse door has been closed. The bands, already hushed twice by the grand marshal, now strike up once more, "Just a Closer Walk with Thee," and Jim Robinson has passed on to the last stage.

Once more the cortege takes up its way, inching through the crowd and the tumult, both considerably augmented since the funeral home. Lost in this and unwillingly carried along by it, I cannot even touch the hearse with its dark cargo behind drapes. I am one of those the limousine-drawn mourners glance out at, somber-eyed now and perhaps justly offended by this motley show of strangers who in their turn stare in at them, curious, vacant, suppositious. I see the car with Tammy and Joe pass by me, and in another few minutes the one with Jim's cousin George, riding behind sunglasses in the passenger's seat. I cannot see his eyes.

The procession now moves through the last edge of the old Downtown area with its ranked frame houses adorned with scroll-worked eaves, the bars and barbecue shacks, the glass-seeded streets; dogs bark our intrusion and the emptied cans roll into the gutters, kicked aside by a thousand scuffed, shuffling shoes. Our goal is the entrance to a freeway. There the cortege will break loose of its shambling retinue, scoop up one of the bands for the graveside service, and hurtle through asphalt isolation five miles out to a newer cemetery on the Airlines Highway where Jim Robinson will lie next to Pearl. In the old days the entire procession would have gone all the way to the graveside and then returned together with the hot, purgative notes of "Didn't He Ramble" and "South Rampart Street Parade" washing through them. But in the old days there weren't cemeteries five miles out from the center of town, nor were there automobiles.

We follow as far as we can, but as the entrance looms and the long cars swing heavily up its ramp, the crowd breaks and eddies, uncertain now that the feature attraction is being whisked from them. But there is yet another band and a "second line" to be formed, and in a few minutes resolution begins to overtake bafflement, and the parade generates its own power. The crowd with umbrellas waving turns back into old Downtown.

Breasting the last buildings before the arid expanse of the freeway, I see the cortege ahead, balked, stalled, still within reach: one of the limousines has broken down—vapor lock, perhaps. Its hood yawns upward like a patient with a toothache, and I can see that the hearse too has stopped and opened its doors for ventilation. Hot delta sunlight invests the butt of the coffin. Powerless as ever to efface this last misery, I turn back. In the darkness of the overpass the parade rages and swirls.

SOMEONE SWEET ANGEL CHILD

SHERLEY A. WILLIAMS

*"No, no. Bessie didn't smoke pot, not Bessie, nothing
like that—just regular reefers."*

Bessie on my wall: the thick triangular
                nose wedged
                in the deep brown
                face nostrils
                flared on a last
                long hummmmmmmmm.

                Bessie singing
                just behind the beat
                that sweet sweet
                voice throwing
                its light on me

fifteen: I looked in her face
and seed the woman
I'd become. A big
boned face already
lined and the first line
in her fo'head was
black and the next line
was sex cept I didn't
know to call it that
then and the brackets
round her mouth stood fo
the chi'ren she teared
from out her womb. And
yo name Bessie; huh.
she say. (Every one
call her Ma o' Ol
Lady) Bessie; well
le'me hear you sang.
She was looking in
my mouth and I knowed
no matter what words
come to my mind the
song'd be her'n jes as
well as it be mine.

port arthur: what he do you
nonya

(I seed the eye swolled shut)

how much he take
nonya

(I seed this in a dream)

Make yo hand in a fis'

They jes lay there open
in her lap short stump-
like fingers curved ova
the callused grey-white palms

his ass go when Time come

gir'—she can't talk plain 'count
of her lip—gir' I whip
any bitch that got two
legs won't think twice on it

Make yo hand in a fis'

She ain't heard and her hands
is meaty, deep veined wid
red brown lines a little
lighter than her skin her
nails bite down past the quick

Don't no man jes beat on
me but time I whip my
nigga ass don't care who
right who wrong that's the time
he stop bein my man

what he do you
nonya

(the lower lip puffed and black)

how much he take
nonya

(I seed this in a dream)

I Want Aretha to Set   I surprised girlhood
This to Music: in your face; I know
my own, have been a
prisoner of my own

dark skin and fleshy
lips, walked that same high
butty strut despite
all this; rejected
the mask my mother
wore so stolidly
through womanhood and
wear it now myself.

I see the mask, sense
the girl and the woman
you became, wonder
if mask and woman
are one, if pain is
the sum of all your
knowing, victim the
only game you learned.

Old and in pain and
bearing up, bearing up
and hurt and age
are the signs of our
womanhood but I'll
make book Bessie did
more than just endure

recollections: Man, first time she come to the
studio with Blue—that was
something. She was fine as fine
could be. A dark blue suit and
orange feather boa a
little cloche with a feather
that curved down around her cheek,
all woman—even after
she got heavy, which she wasn't
that day. Blue was tellin folks—
that's *every*one what to do.
I mean he'd say Miss Smith—last
time we'd recorded they'd said
Bessie, not Miss, not Ma'm—don't
like the piano so loud
Miss Smith want horns right here
lookin at the arrangements
sayin Mister sayin please
and steady pickin his teeth
It was years before I knowed
the man couldn't read no music
that's how strong his talk was.
The white mens didn't know how to

take it. They flash a look at
Bessie and she just sittin
there with them fine legs crossed, one
shoe danglin off the end of
her toe Aw, man, Bessie was
just natchally what her
song say: some sweet angel chile.

from a   the pearl caught
  picture   just so in
    taken at the long fingered
    start of her hands and the
    career   hands held close
                 to her heart

                 the strength to
                 break the strand
                 a smile to
                 break the heart

                 and the lines
                 that bracket
                 the long lips'
                 end.
                   this is
                 no yearbook
                 pose.
                   her pearls
                 were the last
                 jewels she sold

                 hear it? what's out there
                   knockin is what the
                     world don't get enough of
                       meanin love meanin love

fragments: This cold but it ain't
              no reflection on
              you: what you touch, babe,
              you make it yo own

              Bessie walk like water, yo'all
                hold the whole world in her smile
                  she touched me and I knowed her
                    saw love as her natchal style

              I play but ain't no
              player . . . call me a
              king with a castle
              call me . . . whateva

who gon live yo life
till you do? this ain't
Ma I'm talkin to. Let
Blue comm-mon in. Let

fragments: Aw just move toward me
          baby, like you did
          in the woods that day

          Aw move close to me
          honey; be the light
          that show me my way

          Ahhh come down on me
          baby; see me like
          you saw me that day

thirty-nine: It wa'n't all moanin and cuttin the fool
          Listen, I have glowed some in my time.
          My eyes can still sparkle carry
          that soft young girl shine.

The Old Lady Singing of Bessie: People will tell you a boy is yo heart
          and I know you git life wit a girl
from the   A boy may be yo heart
portrait   but a woman life tied up in a girl
finished   Tha's what make you scream make you holla
after her   say, Lawd, it only posed to be
death   one me in this worl'

fragments: when I think about
          ol Blue leavin me
          I think what he knew
          the hurts he coulda
          done me and didn't do

down torrey pines road: This could be that road
          in Mississippi
          though this one winds up
          the hill from the sea

          The way the moonlight washes
          out all colors and
          the high beams bounce shadows off
          the overhanging
          trees, the way cars come round the
          curves gathering speed
          for the climb up the road to

the canyon rim is
something like Mississippi
        that stretch of highway
outside Coahoma close by
        Clarksdale and the Jim
Crow ward in the hospital
        that used to be there.

I dare each curve to
        surprise me as I
round it show me the
        rear-end of some truck
before I can stop.

I beep the solitary
        biker, worry that
his leg mounted flash won't shine
        far enough, sweep on
to the traffic light at the
        summit. This is not
the road to Clarksdale. I say
        over and over
what my name is not.

            [*for Carlos and Iris Blanco*]

THE BLUES ROOTS OF CONTEMPORARY
AFRO-AMERICAN POETRY

SHERLEY A. WILLIAMS

ETHNOPOETICS IS FOR ME THE STUDY OF THE NEW FORMS OF POETRY
which develop as a result of the interfaces or confrontations between
different cultures. The spirituals, play and work songs, cakewalks
and hoe-downs, and the blues are the first recorded artifacts to grow
out of the complex relationship between Africans and Europeans
on the North American continent. Afro-American oral tradition, of
which these lyric forms are a part, combines with white American
literature whose traditions are rooted more in the literate cultures
of the West than in the oral traditions, either indigenous or trans-
planted, of the New World. Afro-American literature is thus created
within the framework of multiple relationships, and the tension
between the white literary and the black oral traditions informs
and influences the best contemporary Afro-American poetry at the
level of structure as well as theme. The themes of the poetry are
usually accessible to non-black audiences, but the poets' attempts
to own the traditions to which they are heir create technical trans-
formations which cannot be analyzed, much less evaluated, solely
within the context of their European roots. Most critics pay lip service
to the idea that Afro-American music, speech and life-styles influ-
ence the form and structure of Afro-American writing. Thus Stephen
Henderson's discussion, in *Understanding the New Black Poetry*
(1973), of some of the techniques of Afro-American speech and
singing which have been carried over virtually unchanged into Afro-
American poetry is rare in its concrete descriptions of these devices.
This paper builds on his work, concentrating on the transformations
which result when the blues of Afro-American oral tradition inter-
faces with the "poetry" of European literary tradition.

Blues is essentially an oral form meant to be heard rather than
read; and the techniques and structures used to such powerful pur-
pose in the songs cannot always be transferred directly to the literary
traditions within which, by definition, Afro-American poets write.
Blues is viewed here as a verbal—as distinct from musical—genre

which developed out of the statement (or call) and response patterns of collective work groups. Blues culminated in a "classic" form (heard most consistently in the early blues recordings of Bessie Smith, Ma Rainey and the other "classic blues" singers) which embodies the distinctive features of Afro-American song forms in a standardized structure. In some contemporary Afro-American poetry, the devices and structures of the classic blues form are transformed, thus allowing the poetry to function in much the same way as blues forms once functioned within the black communities across the country.

I. FUNCTION

Afro-American music still functions to some extent as a reflector of a wide range of values in the national black community and often serves as a catalyst for discussions, reviews and revisions of these values. The immediacy of this process has been diminished by the advent of huge impersonal concerts, but records and local "soul" stations keep alive this supra-entertainment function of the music. The professional songwriter had modified what used to be a very close and personal relationship among singer, song, and the group tradition on which all depended for the act of creation and which the act of creation affirms and extends. In an age where almost everyone is singing someone else's song, performance has to some extent taken the place of authorship. Thus Otis Redding's version of "Respect," while very popular, was never made into the metaphor of Black Man/Black Woman or, just as importantly, Black/White relationships that Aretha Franklin's version became. Of course, Aretha was right on time, but there was also something about the way Aretha characterized respect as something given with force and great effort and cost. And when she even went so far as to spell the word "respect," we just knew that this sister wasn't playing around about getting Respect and keeping it. Early blues singers and their growing repertoire of songs probably helped to solidify community values and heighten community morale in the late nineteenth and early twentieth centuries. The singers provided welcome entertainment and a necessary reminder that there had to be more to the lives of audience than the struggle for material subsistence—if they were ever to achieve and enjoy the day the sun would shine in their back door. Michael S. Harper, in his liner notes to the album *John Coltrane*, alludes to the communal nature of the relationship between blues singer and blues audience when he speaks of the audience which assumes "we" even though the blues singer sings "I." Blues singers have also been aware of this function of their art, for as Henry Townsend said in an interview with Samuel B. Charters (*The*

Poetry of the Blues, 1963):

> You know I'm going to put this a little blunt. I don't know if I
> should say it or not, because it might hurt the religious type of
> people, but when I sing the blues, I sing the truth. The religious
> type of people may not believe that it's good, because they
> think the blues is not the truth; but the blues, from a point of
> explaining yourself as facts, is the truth and I don't feel that
> the truth should be condemned. . . .

Unlike sacred music, the blues deals with a world where the in-
ability to solve a problem does not necessarily mean that one can,
or ought to, transcend it. The internal strategy of the blues is action,
rather than contemplation, for the song itself is the creation of
reflection. And while not all blues actions achieve the desired result,
the impulse to action is inherent in any blues which functions out
of a collective purpose. But while the gospels, for example, are
created for the purpose of preparing the congregation to receive
the Holy Spirit and become possessed by it, the blues singer strives
to create an atmosphere in which analysis can take place. This
necessary analytic distance is achieved through the use of verbal
and musical irony seldom found in the singing of the spirituals
or the gospels. Thus Billie Holiday, in "Fine and Mellow," con-
cludes the recital of the wrongs her man has done her with the mock-
ing observation that

> Love is like a faucet
>   it turns off and on
> Sometimes when you think it's on, baby
>   it have turned off and gone.

The persona pointedly reminds her man that her patience with his
trifling ways has its limits at the same time that she suggests that
she might be in her present difficulties because she wasn't alert to the
signs that her well was going dry. The self-mockery and irony of the
blues pull one away from a total surrender to the emotions generated
by the concreteness of the experiences and situations described in
the song. Even where the verbal content of the song is straightforward
and taken at face value, the singer has musical techniques which
create ironic effects.

The vocal techniques of Afro-American music—melisma, inten-
tional stutters and hesitations, repetitions of words and phrases, and
the interjection of exclamatory phrases and sounds—are used in the
spirituals and gospels to facilitate emotional involvement. In blues

singing, however, these same devices are often used in a deliberately random manner which emphasizes unimportant phrases or words as often as it does key ones. The devices themselves, especially melisma and changes in stress, have become standardized enough to have formed a substantial part of the artistry of Billie Holiday. At their worst, the devices become no more than meaningless vocal calisthenics, but at their best they disengage meaning from feeling. Put another way, the singer objectifies, almost symbolizes, the emotional content of the song through the use of melisma, stuttering and variations in stress, and, in so doing, places the situation in stark relief as an object for discussion. Thus, a member of the blues audience shouts "Tell it like it is" rather than "Amen" or "Yes, Jesus" as a response to a particularly pungent or witty truth, for the emphasis is on thinking, not tripping.

Charles Keil's analysis (*The Urban Blues*, 1966) of a Bobby Blue Bland performance illustrates how even the selection of songs in a blues performance underscores the relationship of singer and audience and the manner in which communal values are incorporated into the presentation of the blues performer's act. Many contemporary Afro-American poets consciously assume the role of people's voices— see, for example, Marvin X's second volume of poetry *The Son of Man*—and ask black people (rather than whites) to affirm their stance. That initial gesture may have grown out of the learned intellectual model provided by Marx and Herskovits; once having made it, however, it became real for many poets, at more than just the level of rhetoric and "kill the honkey" poems. We witness this realness in the increasing sureness with which Afro-American poets challenge the primacy of European forms.

II. STRUCTURE

A number of Afro-American poets have written poems based on the less structured blues forms; few, however, have attempted to utilize the deceptively simple classic blues structure. Langston Hughes is an exception. The sophistication of meaning and form which characterizes Hughes's poem "Young Gal's Blues" is, of course, characteristic of classic blues at its best and the literary sophistication is in fact made possible by the existence of such songs as "Backwater Blues" or the more contemporary variation on the classic form "Your Friends." "Young Gal's Blues," in which a young woman tries to fortify herself against the prospect of death (which can come at any time) and the loneliness of old age (which will certainly catch her if death don't do it first), is an example of an oral form moving unchanged into literary tradition:

> I'm gonna walk to the graveyard
> 'Hind ma friend, Miss Cora Lee
> Gonna walk to de graveyard
> 'Hind ma dear friend Cora Lee
>
> Cause when I'm dead some
> Body'll have to walk behind me.

Hughes worries the first line by dropping "I'm" in the repetition of the first half line and adding "dear" when he repeats the second half-line. Repetition in blues is seldom word for word and the definition of worrying the line includes changes in stress and pitch, the addition of exclamatory phrases, changes in word order, repetitions of phrases within the line itself, and the wordless blues cries which often punctuate the performance of the songs. The response to this opening statement repeats and broadens the idea of death even as it justifies and explains the blues persona's action. Ideally, each half line is a complete phrase or clause; but Hughes, even in breaking the line between "some" and "body" rather than after "dead," keeps within the convention of half lines on which the classic structure is based. The stanza is a closed unit without run-over lines or run-over thoughts; and the same pattern, response justifying the statement, is followed in the second stanza in which the persona tells of her determination to visit old Aunt Clew in "de po' house" because "When I'm old an' ugly/I'll want to see somebody, too." The "po' house" evokes the known social and political conditions rather than stating them directly.

In evoking rather than stating these conditions, Hughes makes the same assumption about his audience that a blues singer makes: both poet (singer) and audience share the same reality. The lives of the audience are bound by the same grim social reality in which one faces an old age characterized by the same grinding poverty which destroys youth before it can flower and makes the fact that while work is still necessary, one is no longer capable of doing it—this being the only distinction between middle and old age. The particularized, individual experience rooted in a common reality is the primary thematic characteristic of all blues songs no matter what their structure. The classic song form itself internalizes and echoes, through the statement/response pattern, the thematic relationship between individual and group experience which is implied in these evocations of social and political reality.

> De po' house is lonely
> an' de grave is cold.

O, de po' house is lonely
De grave is cold.
But I'd rather be dead than to
be ugly and old

The statement in this stanza is more general than the statement
in either of the first two stanzas and while the stanza is self-con-
tained, it places the personal reflection of the preceding stanza
within a larger context. The response returns to the first person, the
subjective testimony, as the persona says quite frankly that she would
rather die than be ugly. It is also Hughes's definition of what it is to be
young; to care more for the quality of one's life than the fact of life
itself. Thus the response in this stanza makes explicit the persona's
choices in life. But neither choice, death at an early age or an old
age endured in poverty and loneliness, is particularly happy and the
persona, recognizing that love is one of the few things which make
any life bearable, concludes the fourth stanza and the poem with the
plea "Keep on a-lovin me, daddy/Cause I don't want to be blue."
   The response can also be the antithesis of the statement as in the
opening stanza of "Billie's Blues,"

I love my man
I'm a lie if I say I don't
But I'll quit my man
I'm a lie if I say I won't.

where the paradox also provides the frame for the distinctions which
the persona later makes between being a slave, which she is quite
prepared to be for her man, and a "dog" which she refuses to be-
come, between mere good looks typified by white features ("I
ain't good looking and my hair ain't curled") and the confidence,
the affirmation of self necessary to get one through the world.
   The change in focus from individual to communal reality may be
done as in the Hughes poem or through simply worrying the line as
in the blues standard "The Things I Used to Do": "The things I used
to do/I won't do no more./Lawd the things I used to *I'm tryna tell
yo' all*/I won't do no more," where the singer appeals directly to the
audience to witness his situation and, in effect, to affirm his solution
to his problem. The abrupt change of subject or theme as in "Sweet
Sixteen" serves the same purpose. The persona describes his love for
a flighty, headstrong young girl who has run away from her home
and now wants to "run away from old me, too." The persona is now
desperate and the song is really a plea to the woman to do right, love
him as he loves her. The third stanza ends with the line, "Seems like
everything I do [to try and keep you with me] is in vain."
   Then, in a dramatic shift in subject and perspective:

My brother's in Korea
My sister's down in New Orleans
You know I'm having so much trouble, people
I wonder what in the world's gonna happen to me.

At the level of the love theme, the absence of family ties under-
scores the persona's loneliness; hence his dependence on this rela-
tionship. His scattered family exists within the framework of the
ruptured family relationships, caused by the oppressive and re-
pressive system of the country, which characterizes too much of the
Afro-American experience. The response to this statement of lone-
liness is one of complete despair, addressed to "people," the audience
whose private pains are set within the same kind of collective expe-
rience. The next stanza is again addressed to the woman and re-
iterates, at the level of their personal relationship, the persona's
realization that he has lost pride, dignity, and a necessary sense of
himself as a result of this relationship:

Treat me mean, baby,
    but I'll keep on loving you anyway
But one of these olds days, baby,
    you're gonna give a lot of money to hear someone call my name.

Billie Pierce's version of "Married Man Blues," recorded by
Samuel B. Charters in New Orleans in 1954, uses what had become
a traditional statement/response description of the problems of loving
a married man to place the song within a more universal context.
The persona has loved only one man, a married man, in her life. And
despite the fact that she "stole him from his wife" she is still in
trouble because she has stolen only his affection, not his continued
presence. The traditional verse is used to summarize her situation:

Girls it's awful hard
    to love another woman's man
Cause you can't get him when you wanna
    have to catch catch as catch's can.

The last half-line in the response is Billie's personal variation on the
standardized wording, "got to catch him when you can," and the
rhythmical variation plays nicely against the established rhythm of
the statement. The stanza, in addition, serves as a transition, tying
together the fictive first person experiences and the more "real"
first person admonitions of the last part of the song.
    The second portion of the song opens with an assertion of individ-

uality: "My first name is Billie/and my last name is Pierce." The assertion of individuality and the implied assertion—as action, not mere verbal statement—of self is an important dimension of the blues. Janhienz Jahn (*Neo-African Literature*, 1968) is essentially correct when he describes the blues in terms of this assertion of life-force rather than the usual ones of melancholy and pain. The assertion of self usually comes at the end of the blues song after the description/analysis of the situation or problem and is often the only solution to that problem or situation. In "Married Man Blues," Billie's assertive stance is underscored in successive stanzas which imply some of the values inherent in a good love relationship:

> Aw, you want me to do right there, Little Dee Dee
> And you ain't doing right yourself
> Well you get yourself another woman
> And I'll get me somebody else.
>
> Well, at my first time leaving you, baby
> Crying ain't gone make me stay
> Cause the more you cry Dee Dee, baby
> Well the more you gonna drive little Billie away.

The sting of the stanzas is balanced by the fact that they are part of the anonymous oral tradition, and Billie Pierce was a master at combining such traditional verses with written songs ("Saint Louis Woman," "Careless Love," for example) to create her own personal versions of these songs. Here, she also underscores the closeness of her musical relationship with her husband, Dee Dee Pierce, who accompanies her on trumpet, by the encouragements spoken throughout this portion of the song to, "Play it nice, play it the way I like it Dee Dee, baby."

This complex interweaving of general and specific, individual and group, finds no direct correspondence in Afro-American literature except in the literary blues. But the evocation of certain first person experiences and the extensive use of multiple voices in Afro-American poetry may be, at least in part, an outgrowth from this characteristic of the blues. Nikki Giovanni's "The Great Pax Whitey" which seems a rather pedestrian and undigested patchwork of folk and personal legend and black nationalist philosophy becomes, when viewed (or better yet, read) as a poem in which a congregation of voices speaks, a brilliant literary approximation of the kind of collective dialogue which has been going on underground in the black community at least since the nineteenth century and of which the blues in its various forms was an important part.

III. TRANSFORMATION

Blues songs are almost always literal, seldom metaphoric or symbolic except in sexual and physical terms. And, while similes are used extensively, much of the verbal strength of the blues resides in the directness with which the songs confront experience and in what Stephen Henderson identifies as "mascon images," Afro-American archetypes which represent "a *mas*sive *con*centration of black experiential energy." Often the mascons are not really images in the literary sense of the word, rather they are verbal expressions which evoke a powerful response in the listener because of their direct relationship to concepts and events in the collective experience. Thus the graveyard and the po'house in "Young Gal's Blues" might be described as universal archetypes or mascons, while the calling of the names in "Sweet Sixteen" is a specifically black one. The latter expression grows directly out of traditional people's belief in the strong relationship between name and personal essence and the corresponding Afro-American preoccupation with titles (Miss, Mr., Mrs. and, with great deliberation and care, Ms.), with the naming of children and the acquisition of nicknames and sobriquets—and who may use them. In such an atmosphere, to call someone out of their name, as the Monkey tells the Lion that the Elephant has done him in the "Signifying Monkey," is punishable, in children, by a beating. And the changing of one's names as most blacks did after emancipation and many more did during the sixties takes on an added significance.

Very often, the meanings of mascons cut across areas of experience usually thought of as separate but which in Afro-American experiences are not mutually exclusive. Thus the term "jelly roll," as Henderson illustrates, moves at a number of different levels, while the expressions centered in the concept of "home" move at both a spiritual and material level, and "The Streets," which has developed into a mascon as a result of the Afro-American urban experience, involves both pleasure and pain. Despite the fact that these expressions are used over and over again by blacks in everyday conversations as well as in more self-conscious verbal events, they escape being clichés because their meanings are deeply rooted in a constantly renewed and thus *living* reality. They are distinguished from the vernacular vocabulary of black speech in that the vernacular rests on the idea that the standard English version of a word, say "bad" or "dig," has one meaning and the standard black version has another, often contradictory, meaning: excellent and understand. Mascons, on the contrary, concentrate their massive force within the frame of the literal meaning of the standard English word. And it is this literal yet figuratively complex relationship which

makes the response in the final stanza of "Sweet Sixteen" such a
powerful climax to the song. But one of these old days, the persona
tells his woman, you would even get up off some money, just to have
back the man I was when I met you, the man that loving you de-
stroyed. Thus mascons are a compression, as well as a concentration,
whose power is released through the first person experience.

When Harriet Tubman, in Robert Hayden's "Runagate Runagate
Runagate" invites us to "ride my train," it is not merely the thought
of the Underground Railroad to which blacks respond. But Harriet's
"train" is also the train whose tracks throughout the South were
laid by black men who also worked on them as cooks, porters, and red
caps and which many blacks rode to the promised land of the North.
And despite the fact that trains are no longer a significant part of our
day to day reality, they live on in the metaphors of the "Gospel
Train" which many plan to ride to glory and the "Soul Trains" which
proclaim the black musical presence in the world. It is the stored
energy of this mascon which enables Afro-American poets to play so
lovingly and meaningfully with John Coltrane's name and they
capture something of his function as an artist in their use of his nick-
name, Trane.

Many Afro-American poets have used techniques which approxi-
mate or parallel various blues devices and Lucille Clifton, in her
first volume of poems, *Good Times*, uses these transformations con-
sistently and successfully. Like the blues, her poems are firmly
based in a living black reality which is more concerned with itself
than with direct confrontations with white society and its values.
There are several poems about whites in the volume, but even here,
the impression is of a black person, involved in a conversation with
other blacks, who occasionally tosses a comment to the white man
she knows is waiting in the wings. His presence does not cause her
to bite her tongue, however, and the opening poem "in the inner
city," is addressed as much to the white man in the wings as it is to the
black audience.

> in the inner city
> or
> like we call it
> home
> we think a lot about uptown
> and the silent nights
> and the houses straight as
> dead men
> and the pastel lights
> and we hang on to our no place

happy to be alive
and in the inner city
or
like we call it
home

Clifton's poems are created out of the collective experience which culminates in and is transformed by the inner city. Those experiences in their broader outlines are evoked rather than stated, through vignettes told in the first person; and the individual experience plays against the assumed knowledge of that collective history in much the same way that the communal pattern of statement and response plays against the individual experience expressed in the blues. The inner city of which Clifton speaks is neither that of the "deviants" who inhabit most sociological studies about blacks nor the statistics which politicians manipulate so skillfully for their own gains; it is the community, home. "Inner city" becomes both the literal ghetto and the metaphoric inner landscape of black hearts which has seldom been explored so sensitively and revealingly as in Clifton's *Good Times*.

The spareness of Clifton's poetry depends in part on mascon images. "Pushing," a mascon of enormous contemporary force, is used to climax "For deLawd," Clifton's tribute to the long "line/of black and going on women" from which she comes. Grief for murdered brothers, murdered husbands, murdered sons has kept on pushing them, kept them "for their still alive sons/for their sons coming/for their sons gone/just pushing." And pushing is both the will to struggle on toward a long sought goal, even in the face of enormous odds (as Curtis Mayfield and The Impressions exhort us to do in "Keep on Pushing") and the double consciousness which blacks have of this country and its institutions—a consciousness which many would rather not have for it often highlights the futility of trying to "make it" in America (the expression, "I'm so pushed" is used interchangeably with "I'm hipped"). And this reading of "pushing" complements the ironic use of "making it." For it is against the background of the collective experience of "making it through . . . sons" murdered literally and figuratively by the society and the individual prospect of what can happen to her sons that the persona knowingly goes on about her business. The ability to keep on pushing, to keep on keeping on, to go on about one's business is the life-force, the assertion of self amidst collective and individual destruction which comes directly out of the blues tradition. This is what the persona's mother in "Billie's Blues" passes on to her daughter and what makes the closing of that song so delightful:

Some men call me honey
Some think that I've got money
Some men like me cause I'm snappy
Some because I'm happy
Some men tell me, Billie
Baby, you're built for speed
Now when you put that all together
It makes me everything a good man need.

The loss of that sense of vitality makes the persona in "Sweet Six-
teen" a tragic figure. Clifton expresses this life force again and
again, and it provides a continuing frame for and necessary counter-
point to the often fatal despair which also stalks the inner city.

The power of first person experiences is balanced by distancing
techniques—shifts in diction, voice, and focus which parallel the ways
in which distance is achieved in the blues. After a series of first
person poems whose diction hovers marvelously between the stan-
dard and the black dialects (and thus embodies both), Clifton will
place a poem written from a third person perspective in precise
standard diction. The shift in viewpoint immediately makes the sub
ject of the poem its object.

Robert

was born obedient
without questions

did a dance called
picking grapes
sticking his butt out
for pennies

married a master
who whipped his mind
until he died

until he died
the color of his life
was nigger

"Robert" as both poem and person is such an object and comes after
a series of poems in which a female persona talks about members of
her immediate and extended family who have lost the battle for
psychic survival in the society. The focus within this series of four
poems (which begins with "My mamma moved among the days")

shifts from the destruction of these others to the survival of the persona, and the series ends with the lines, "I stand up/through your destruction/I stand up." The reference is not only to the destruction of Miss Rosie, who is the subject of this poem, but to the persona's mother, father, and sister who have each appeared in previous poems. Clifton implies that the only thing which makes the destruction of these others somewhat bearable is the persona's ability to stand up, to affirm herself because these others have died that she might live. Robert is an immediate contrast to the lives sketched in these mini-portraits for he begins his existence in defeat and "until he died/the color of his life/was nigger." This poem further enlarges the context in which each poem in the series exists and its impersonal, objective stance returns, at a more abstract level, to the general/collective tone of "in the inner city," the poem which serves as introduction to this sequence and to the volume as a whole. The shift from first to third person perspective provides both an inner and outer view of the inner city and creates an atmosphere which encourages one to enter into and understand the experiences presented in the poems at both an emotional and analytic level. Sequences of poems are used to develop themes beyond the limits of a single poem; and individual poems come, in fact, to function in much the same way that individual classic blues stanzas function within the classic song. The individual expression is always seen within the context of the collective experience.

Lucille Clifton and other poets who work or even attempt to work in a similar mode extend the verbal traditions of the blues in the same way that the Swing of Count Basie and the bebop of Charlie Parker extend the instrumental traditions of the blues, making those traditions "classic" in a recognizably Western sense while remaining true to the black experiences and black perceptions which are their most important sources. But unlike the oral lyrics which, of necessity, preserve their group traditions only in their forms or structures and need a separate history to preserve a concrete sense of the collective life styles, values, and experiences which they represent, poetry, as a written form, carried with it the possibility of functioning simultaneously on both levels. Thus while B. B. King in "Sweet Sixteen" can allude to, even symbolize, collective experiences or internalize the necessary and sustaining relationship between group and individual in the statement/response pattern and structures, Clifton, in her poetry incorporates elements of the older oral traditions, re-asserts the collective at concrete levels even as she deals, through subjective testimony, with individual experiences. And this is the beginning of a new tradition built on a synthesis of black oral traditions and Western literate forms.

PACKWOOD'S SERMON BY FIRELIGHT

LEON FORREST

. . . BUT WHAT WAS NOT TRULY SAID WAS WHAT WAS NOT RE-
corded, except in the heavens. The advent of Rachel, when she was
struck down dead to life in those Wanted Dead Or Alive terrible
woods (haunted by Wilks Jackson's lynched form, which still arose
and walked the forests, bloodthirsty, with the carving knife of his
castration, each midnight; haunted also by Bloodworth in lust-rape-
passion; jazz trumpet-drumming negroes; sheets of Klansmen;
voodoo dolls; blood of brother against brother; liquor-roasted In-
dians; Hollywood on location), yet bearing witness to the Light of
Thunder over Jordan, and testifying, accepting Church while "the
blood swam in her head," and streaking down her legs, Lord, in
the mud, and she was lifted up and long and away upon wings of fire
by the righteous timbre, by moon witnessing campground preacher,
Packwood. He was a chariot lifting up her quaking form, chasing the
evil spirit, imploring God for the victory over the Devil, his fire-
bellowing voice echoing through the haunted woods. She came up-
wards as if from the baptizing river, gasping for life in life. He hurled
her spirit like a dancer's body and flung the garment of her soul at
his feet. And then he (who was once upon a time a Blues-prince, with
a singing harp like a steel guitar, struck down in the woods himself,
ten years before, and dragged by the very hands of God Almighty for
three hundred yards, until he fell into K. C. Ford's arms) cried.

". . . For this daughter, Church, down here shaking upon her knees,
is yet wrestling herself loose and free from the serpent's lashes of
soul-driving pirate merchants, even unto the roots of Calvary—like
one at the scaffold-peak of a nightmare—NOW moving onto get free
of even him, Mister Lucifer's noose. But now I must surely tell you
her story culled from the depths of blood, earth and clay, upon this
night. And pray her back on homewards, totally, Church. She's been
a long ways from home.

"For even now I can see it, hear it, and remember, and you Church
ought be remembering how this soon-rising daughter (who sprang
up unclean, and out of the moldering womb of the earth itself, this

This is a section from Leon Forrest's most recent novel, *The Bloodworth Orphans*
(Random House, 1977).

night, in our midst) was sprung from the body of a royal mother; yes, and was sired out of the body of a blood-seed, who had once upon a time been wealthy of substance and rare of unscaled radiance but who had lost all of his estate, his fortunes, his domain, and was banished down into a poverty harness and maimed upon his knees, yoked and cursed into a bloody bondage of boils, famine, pestilence, disease and ruined crops; Lord, a man of nobility—upright, princely in every way once upon a long-gone time, installed in grief, stripped of his land, his heritage, and pruned of his name, who died, I am told, wondering what God he had defiled, in act or secret wish. Or was he brought low because of some deep Ancestral Agony?

"But before her birth didn't *They* scandalize in the market-place, and through the very streets of the world, her parents' marital union and her birth, Lord, through lies extending down the length of her days, even unto this very occasion! So that she was nameless in the councils of men, and terrorized in the books, and in the fields, merchandized in the cities, and I am told cursed down inside the empty mailbox, and in the very eyeteeth of the powerful, the rich and the Mighty. And Me——iiiiiIIIII alone——am called upon to return her name, her honor, her stride, her station, her soul, her crown, her patched-up riddled wings, her gospel shoes filled with holes, her ashy long white robe, back up unto this night so that the Almighty God can hear of her testimonial Dawn-Crying . . . For Lord God the spat-upon harvest of her terrorized Soul seemed to her as a dungeon of dregs before this night.

"But, Church, I'm gonna redress her in what we got left over—while her world-polluted rags are bathing for eternity's keepsake, upon the brooding Horizon. For she was sprung before us like pilgrim sack of Dry Bones, grieving for the nourishing blood of rare gospel meat.

"And I am told that this sister's name was plowed up in a scandal that was cast across the very seed of her conception, signifying that she was spawned by adulterous parents, and not only that but parents who were themselves brother and sister. I don't believe you see what I'm talking about this night, Church—"

 —AMEN, THEY CRIED . . . TEACH,
 REVEREND PACKWOOD, TEACH
 AND LEAD YOUR CHILDREN.

"Yes, and not only that, Lord. I am also told that her very paternal grandfather sought to have her aborted as she was forming in her mother's womb, even as the ripened majesty of her father was now reduced to cleaning rifles he could not use, nor, I am told, knew how to use either. A merciless grandsire, mad, rich and senile, who had drowned the land with his wild seed but who was ravaged now with the disease of the blood and believed that he had made his own

granddaughter, another one he had never owned up to, pregnant—
not that he cared, or cared to know the truth, but only cared about
the scandal, and about the insult to him, if it was not true. What
kind of man was he, Church?

"But didn't the Lord A'Mighty God strike her polluting plague of a
grandsire down with the lockjaw, even as he stood upon the apron of
an improvised stage, with a salt box in his hands? And then transact
with a shepherd over her life—a shepherd who lived along the side of
the mountain. Plucking her from the troubled arms of her cast-down
mother, who later went mad, and gave her to the shepherd upon the
condition that she would be his—or nothing—upon her thirteenth
birthday (whether she wanted to or not, or whether or not she had
started or not) if she proved unfit to look upon, not that it would
have come into the shepherd's merciless mind, but only as long as
she did not show her face back into the streets demanding the knowl-
edge of her parents or her birthright.

"And the grandsire commanded like the very voice of the moun-
tain: 'But let twelve birthdays fly by, before either you slay her or
lay her' . . . Lord, Church, I tell you this child was sold as a sacrifice—
marked down in the basement. It was a horse-trade, with the shep-
herd giving thirty pieces of silver. Her body bridled, yoked and har-
nessed upon a lease so that her eyes became swiftly acquainted with
the earth from whence she just this moment sprang like a newborn
flesh animal with the afterbirth still robing its body, and her eye-
vision parched like Dry Bones, AMEN!"

—AMEN, THEY CRIED . . . LEAD: TEACH:
NOURISH US—ALL NIGHT LONG.

"And it is truly said that her grandmother used to steal away into
the cave where the child dwelt with the shepherd and his enfeebled
wife, and nourished the babe through sickness and storms and bad
times, from the milk of the sheep and those old nanny goats of the
mountain, and that she grew up in the cave away from the lyelike
eyes of man, excepting One; yes, and that the grandmother nourished
her upon the lessons of survival and how to make food out of what
was left over, even unto the wild plant life surrounding the cave;
yes, and how to pronounce words, and how to write upon a slate, by
candlelight, and how to make offerings of words from those lessons
unto someone called the God Almighty; and how to hold on.

"Yes, by flickering light, and no light; by making threads bind
together, with straw for burning light to see forwards and back-
wards, when even the candles failed; and yet how to keep her lamps
trimmed and long glowing, when they were available, and not avail-
able. Yes, and the constant lining-out lesson, that this and this is put

together with this, was for that day, that time, when she could be truly free to renourish and improvise on what she had learned, and come out of that cave, as a harvest-bearing lesson of honor. Yes, the old lady, *see* her now, Church, crying and counseling, scolding and disciplining, schooling and chastising, mocking and deriding, loving and celebrating, but at a pitch so that the girl knew she lived in the jaws of imminent extinction, but also saying *ain't no grave and no man can hinder your body and hold your spirit down*, now that you getting onto this and especially this and linking up your star to a wagon to a chariot, and teaching about roads, and robes, bodies of water, the depths of rivers, and how to lay dead, and hold yourself upright, so that you can float on top of the water, and remain *weightless* . . . And I am told that it *all* kept her from sinking fast—even though she was sacked in a cave dungeon of stark desolation, that terrible passageway, a way out of no way—from sinking down into the boiling stream depths, below the surface of humanity, where dwells an afflicted river people, where life cannot behold itself, a river brooding with life that cannot roll without blood, yet upon which folk nourish and suckle. But she hardly spoke at all to this child about her parents, their royalty, and what had gone on before—that it was all too much to know, given the life the child had in front of her and before her . . . I don't believe you see what I am talking about—"

—TALK ABOUT IT, PACKWOOD, MAKE IT PLAIN.

"And I am told that she came to see that grandmother as her very own mother, the mother lode of the North Star. But she began to see less of that grandmother, who was elderly, as the Rock of Ages, and barely able to walk, yet Lord God still highly mo-bile, for the shepherd came to observe this girl more as a woman, and he barred the grandmother from the very apron of the cave.

"Now at this time our dear sister was waiting on the shepherd and his long-dying wife, hand and foot, using what she had learned from the withered grandmother. And the young girl of twelve came to see the shepherd as her Papa, for the grandmother had told this child only of the stripped, scaffolded radiance of her true father, and that he had fallen upon Bad Times and was now dying away down in the hole of an underground prison, but she also saw the shepherd's wife, a scrawny, dying woman, as her stepmother.

"Yet this child's true soul-condition was like a blind lamb in the pathway of a humming tractor, conducted by a gagged man who thought he was driving a chariot of damned souls. She was ransom in that stifling cave that swarmed like a drug den of spiritual lethargy . . . Yet, Church, captivity don't have to mean isolation! For in the beginning Satan'll hold you fast, and change your form, your name,

before he sheds his skin to make you seem, close up, as he was once
upon a time . . . But more than likely, if I know anything about you,
you'll change your name, in the very name of righteousness without
changing your claim, and call him tar-baby, before you'll call a spade
a spade. I don't believe you see what I'm getting at—"

    —RIDING HOME ON THE WINGS OF RIGHTEOUSNESS,
      REVEREND PACKWOOD . . .
    —LORD, A MOTHERLESS CHILD
      FLUNG IN THE EYETEETH OF THE STORM . . .
    —A MUSTARD SEED OF STIRRING . . .
      MAKE IT PLAIN AS SALT, MINISTER,
      PLAIN AS SALT . . .

And now sister Rachel seemed to go wild, hugging and clinging
to each in the front row, as if running to long-lost found brothers
and sisters. Then returning to Packwood's arms, her body flopping
and waving, as if a flood was about to overturn her soul like a canoe
caught up in the sweep of a hysterical rapids.

"Yes, and it is truly written— not upon parchment, either, but on
the Remembrance wings of morning—that upon a mountain top the
shepherd laid his wife's dying body, and sacrificed one of his sheep,
and let the burning Essence smoke to the nostrils of the Heavens, as
a witness and a sacrifice for divine light and the healing of the
woman. *But* with one eye, and one prayer; YEA, and the prayerful
hope that HE would deliver this child to the shepherd's arms just as
HE, the heavenly Father, took the old woman onto Glory! Can I get
a Witness over here now through my left hand, and Witness of Arising
recognition on my right-hand side?"

    —IN THE CARE OF YOUR TEACHING,
      GUIDE US HOMEWARD, PACKWOOD,
      THOUGH THE PATHWAY BE SOWN IN PITFALLS . . .
      'CAUSE WE AIN'T NOTHING BUT SKIN AND BONES.

"AMEN . . . And then the shepherd forced her to lay with him by
night, before she came to know herself, saying that she would be
Queen of Paradise, and thereby would be lifted the very curse of her
Origins . . . And despite what her grandmother had told her, and not
told her, she often wondered what Curse and what Origins . . . Mixing
it all up with his kindness, and god-fathering father, and loving him,
and despising him. For she served him body and soul, Church, and
nourished him like he was a natural man, even though he was as
polluted as her scandalous grandfather. Yet evidently, all the
while, she was humming something like that song of old, 'Singing
with a Sword in My Hand.'

"And Almighty God took pity upon her, whispered in her ears day and night the pure words of· freedom, echoing the grandmother. Now the girl saw that the shepherd's beguiling words of guidance lacked deliverance power. And then one night the Word of God came beautiful, flaming, and chariot-swinging sweet and low unto her ears, as she knelt upon the mud of the apron at the tip of the cave, where she had last seen her beloved grandmother knocking upon the rattling gate to get in, until her knuckles were like bruised ivory. The old man snored as if his soul had been taken off into the heavens for *overhauling.*

"And there in that kneeling moment the Lord God said unto her, 'Upon the morning say to your Master: "Yea, Shepherd and Master, let us now arise and go unto the mountain and lay up a sacrifice of a sheep upon the plateau." But when he then commences lifting the sacrifice unto the burning timbers, my child, as you are kneeling and yet praying, you will hear the spearlike voice of a trumpet upon the wind, birthing fire and smoke, and then the horn-blowing—but you and you alone will hear of it, and then you will know my Word and will know the hour and know what to do, and what to be, and not to be . . . But if I free you, you must pledge to be a witness, whatever the price, wreckage, ruin, or joy . . . Even though you may not know, or may know, in your lifetime, and then even *then* know it not: the great mystery of that Act, that set you free. . . . I will see you in the morning.'

"And upon the morning, Church, this child's swinging head, now at my fingertips, did utter unto the shepherd these things. And as they ascended the mountain, she cried, 'I'll be so glad, when that old evening sun goes down' (Lord, but she didn't know what the sun was doing inside the horizon, after that rainstorm—which is why she is here with us tonight). Now as they, man and woman, daughter and stepfather-shepherd stood upon the plateau of the mountain, the shepherd bade her sit down—for he was weary—and she said unto him: 'Master, my Soul's so happy that I can't sit down.'

"But as the sheep's body burned in sacrifice—she commenced to hear the spearlike voice of a trumpet—the animal lifted off from the bowels of the grave towards the heavens through its smoke, and she crept up upon the man, as he had always crept up upon her, and she heaved, and she pushed, as if he were the rock that stood in the way of her deliverance, sending him spinning with all of her built-up bitterness and strength, like he was a cart of defilement, with her shoulder into the action, you might say, and the shepherd went off, body and soul, into the flames of the pyre, like the one over there where our roasting lamb offering is filling the night and rising to God in sacrifice.

"Church, you ain't praying with me. You acting like your very soul is lined out in sleeves of diamonds and wine-head forgetfulness this night, you thinking you gonna die on your way towards Heaven—gonna float on in.

"And my God, and your God, that's where she's at this very night, still on that plateau, that old precipice, where she's been for a long time, and a long way from home, why-er this ransomed soul's in the recovery ward, Church . . . but we got to have another Operation, in order to truly Revivify and Re-ah-Suscitate this ravished cargo back onto the shores of the living out of the jaws of that whalelike extinction, Death and spiritual parching damnation. Lord: ALL NIGHT LONG, she's been praying and hoping for the next step home, out of chaos still a-grieving, and a-crying for her grandmother—mother, I oughta say—and especially freedom, upon that old plateau of the mountain, in that banished land of godlessness; not yet free, yet free of one Demon, anyhow, with the stench of his burning polluted body still in her nostrils, and swimming in her head . . .

"For Church, you may be throned in the clean robes of Tomorrow, but be sure to remember that your proud salvation-condition ain't washed the horizon of this land as clean."

And now Reverend Packwood, exorcising Rachel, chasing the evil spirit, imploring the God for the victory over Lucifer; his voice baying through the long woods, all down the long night, now grunting, then chanting, now whispering, then wailing, now humming, now crying, then singing; his head rocking; Sister Rachel's head wobbling in Packwood's long surgeon-like fingers; the church victory-calling, and stomping in the mud, shrieking and awe-struck.

". . . Come out of there, Satan, you lying wonder, and leave this Sister be. Give yourself up to God, Sister; accept; move; COME ON HOME; truly; WALK; DE-NOUNCE; RE-NOUNCE; BE-LIEVE; Help me, Church, pray with me, if you please. Sister, spit him out, down there upon that ground, back where you left part of that old mortgaged soul-garment. Child, I tell you he is de-filing the world; he's defiling your very insides. Sister, you need yet another Operation . . . my God, Satan's got this world wallowing in bloody-filth hoggishness: leave these woods; flee out of this weeping Sister's soul mister piggish swine. Spit him out, Dear Sister; LOOOOSE HER, LUCIFER, LET MY DAUGHTER GO; take your lying, filthy, polluting and scandalizing hands from her throat, her temple, her insides, her outsides, her backbone." (And Rachel's head bobbing, bopping in Reverend Packwood's cuplike palms and molding surgeon-like fingers, within the hallow motion-making.)

—OPERATE, PACKWOOD, OPERATE!

CLEAN HER UP AND OLD LUCIFER OUT.

"He's collecting his elect in this rainstorm; Lord, I can hear Him;
Church, can't you hear Him call a Witness to this willful, wayward,
wicked world? Calling to the Sister, Oh Babylon's falling. Church,
can't you hear His voice and them bricks collapsing? Flock, your
soul is motionless as if you haven't been anchored in the bloodstream
of the blood . . . But old folks say until your soul has hung over hell
like a spider's web you can't know salvation; so He's teaching *you*
through this fire-processed daughter that you got to keep dipping
your body in the icy waters of tragedy to make that old Jordan roll
and keep on rolling. Witness?"

And now humming, chanting and crying, as the church implored
and ignited within his huge voice their echoes, wounds and joys:

"Why-er can't you smell the mortar? Can't you hear the fire
crackling? CAN'T YOU SEE THE WORLD'S ON FIRE, CHURCH? Just as
plain as Babylon's sleeve laced up in America's straitjacket?
And this Dear Sister been knee-deep in sin, and sleep, now arising;
arise, Lord, ARISE; LOOOOOSE HER SATAN; dispossess Him,
Father; TAKE HER BACK, FATHER, to the Mansion. She's gonna find
that true father now. Hear Him, Church, upon the wind, taking them
filthy garments of hers upon the Horizon; she's been a polluted
sleepwalker defiling the flesh. For this child like you, Church, has
drunk at the basin of iniquity, as if it were the waters of Jordan; you
are a multitude of impudent, forgetful, confused people . . . But this
child-woman in my hands tonight is getting a New Condition . . . See
her filthy garments washing in the rainstorm; new way of walking;
new way of talking; BABYLON, you falling with Satan's spirit being
LOOOSED in the raging Soul of these woods, and then re-destroyed
by the smoke of that sheep purifying this forest, so Church can
breathe PURE RIGHTEOUSNESS. Witness?

"You, Mister Lusting Lucifer, the Wrathful Almighty making them
bricks to fall and setting your house on fire, but I'm going to throw
your clothes upon the fire and let the Church watch your abominable
fleshy existence go up in flames like timber and cotton and the
shepherd sacrifice, upon that mountain top, when this daughter be-
fore us heard her true Father's Command."

—BRING IT HOME . . .
    LEAD YOUR LOST-FOUND CHILDREN, PACKWOOD.

"Why-er she heard from Heaven that very day about a sacrifice
on the plateau looking on towards Glory—Arising, as she is finally
arising out of my very hands, now Oh LORD. Come onto Him, Sister,
you moving like a tot through a half-mad train of thieves, gamblers,
adulterers, liars, abodimators, for your victory, but God, my God
is the sterling CONDUCTOR; ain't no way-station for hitchhikers, this

here is a long-haul mission, yea, though it be meted out upon broken scales in a spiritual slaughterhouse. Child, you ain't alone; grave can't hold you, couldn't hold Jesus. Break on down, willful Church, as this New Sister is lifted upwards; healing process going on, and it's hard, perilous, precious time, in the sewing-up of the Victory; but are you as clean as she is be-coming in her new BEING-NESS? Lord, you plucked the sheets of destitution from a whore at a well; help me, Lord, I can feel her coming out of this last stage of the hoggish inferno of Lucifer's kingdom and the lacerating of soul waste. Motherless and looking for her grandmother—mother I should say—and behind that for her true father-royal, but Lord she didn't know how royal. Witness? LORD iiiii—IIIII can feel her rising through the fingertips burning like candles in my right hand, over here. And ah-I CAN FEEEL YOU, Father, streaking that Babylon Satan out of her in my left hand fingertips on fire over here . . .

"I ain't afraid of this rainstorm in these woods. For my Father is a Rainmaker. Didn't He arise in a Windstorm? And He's gonna return. Return in a Storm. Going to be royal and radiant with hair like lamb's wool; eyes like balls on fire. Gonna have a rainbow like a scarf about His shoulders. Gonna set upon a *Rock* and these here storms ain't gonna be able to move you, Church, if only you are celebrated in the Refuge-*Rock* of His Essence. If you have planted your soul in the blood of His crucified *Rock*-Divinity.

"Re-claiming Eden, this night. Let the lightning drive these woods so that no tree is left with leaves and disrobed to its essentials, carved and barren, and forced to learn to grow and thrive on what's left over. Lost-found floundering Angel of Darkness returning to the new witness, fruitifying garden of Eden upon the Eagle's bloody, storming wings, speaking out of Eden's four rivers in Tongues. Deep rivers quaking and fitful with cotton, gold, oil, whales, and the many thousands perished in the blood of our once-upon-a-time radiant genesis-essence. O He sent a Raven to the North and to the South and to the East and to the West—AHAHAHA . . . He'll set an alien Rock on fire, if you try to bury your face upon it, Church, trying to avoid the scandalous ways you've fixed the face of your barnstorming soul against His word, and He's gonna make the face of your soul as brimstone.

"But look now, Church, see how this fugitive child is climbing. See her outlawed spirit gathering up gospel wings. For this merchandized and scandalized daughter is gonna learn of the origins of her banished royal father and she's gonna learn of the radiance of my Kingly Father . . . For I tell you, Church, in my Father's house there are a multitude of mansions, where she will sing without scorn, and pirate abuse; where there are many sanctuaries, and she can wing from capital to prairie . . . Now that Lucifer's loose, her spirits off the scaffold; now that Satan's loose, she can know her Father; now that fang-eyed Satan's loose, she can possess the Wings of the Morning.

"Why-er heard you promise Hosea you would ransom them from the grave; heard you, Father, promise Moses you would stand by your people in the wages of their bondage; heard you reveal the meaning of the ladder to Jacob of a soul-collecting Nation; heard you stir the intelligence and faith to Ezekiel's tongue to know that Dry Bones can live . . . Why-er she gonna see her nourishing grandmother, yea though she was sacked in a dungeon of dregs and desolation, and left for blind, and dead and not wanted dead or alive this orphan is gonna take the wings of the morning, her soul is so happy she can't sit down, and now it is a Witness, and an eagle, yea, though it possess the gentleness of a dove."

And Now Rachel ran through the mud and the rain, back and forth, weeping and hugging the sisters, and falling and kissing the hem of the preacher's long garb—and crying and singing: "I'm Running on, I'm Running On/ I done left this world behind/ I done crossed the separating line/ I done left this world behind."

And Packwood putting his coat about her shoulders in the thunderstorm, and the church fell to its knees in the mud, exceedingly ecstatic.

"Oh Yonder come the chariot,/ and the horses are swept up in white like foam,/ and the front wheels are running by the goodness of God,/ and the back wheels are running by love," Sister Rachel sang as she pointed into the night.

And Reverend Packwood and Sister Rachel climbing into the tree—she upon his shoulders—as the rain poured and the lightning uprooted all life upwards into the storming night and they seemed to vanish into the night, seemed to explode into the very throes of the night.

And as the church stormed back against the night with hand-clapping and tambourines ablaze, crying and shouting and weeping and whispering, trembling, shuttering and wailing; they all heard her (Rachel) cry upon the wings of the storm, her body shuddering like leaves upon the tree:

"I'm done with rebukes and abuses . . . I'm gonna fly from mansion to mansion."

And behind that the voice of Packwood sounding like the voice of Jordan rolling from the depths:

"Church, He give me the word and He told me to go, way up in the Kingdom . . . CAN I GET A WITNESS?"

"IF HE CHANGED MY NAME"

AN INTERVIEW WITH LEON FORREST

[MARIA K. MOOTRY]: Your novel *There Is a Tree More Ancient Than Eden* is a highly experimental work. I see in it a montage of narrative styles: the reflexive language of poetry, the immediacy of dramatic monologue and the high rhetoric and eloquence of the Afro-American sermon tradition. Do you think style in itself is a message?

[LEON FORREST]: If a writer attempts to approach his materials in an imaginative manner, more than likely he's going to be inventive about the mode he casts them in . . . the manner in which he reshapes or structures those "story-laden," symbolic patterns of human essence, culled from the consciousness of the family, race, and nation. Certainly this is true with much of the great literature, and the author-models of technical power, whose works I found fascinating long before I attempted to write, and probably upon whose shoulders I have climbed, in order to attempt an entry into the ring of champions. All were master stylists to be sure: Joyce, Proust, Twain, Hawthorne, Melville, Faulkner, Dylan Thomas, and Mr. Ralph Ellison. These craftsmen were my principal literary mentors, and in the main, I am proud to say, authors who raised the moral questions and the spectre of moral hypocrisy.

[M]: Now you sound like Ellison protesting that the "greats" were his masters. Aren't there black roots in your work?

[F]: Yes, for behind all of this was the nourishing information and *intelligence* of the spirituals, jazz, and the blues, and their influence and ground-swelling shaping of my consciousness and my sense of the possibilities of form, black life, responsibility and challenge, and of course style in grand Negro manner, and finally the Afro-American ranges of eloquence, in the pulpit and on the platter. As a child I used to listen to my parents' fine record collection. My mother loved the vocalists, and understood what was happening,

Journalist, editor, scholar, writer, Leon Forrest published his first novel, *There Is a Tree More Ancient Than Eden*, with Random House in 1973. This interview with Mr. Forrest was conducted in his office at Northwestern University, Evanston, Illinois, in 1975. The interviewer is Maria K. Mootry.

for instance, in Holiday's art. Again, on my mother's side there is the New Orleans influence particularly about jazz, and my uncle George White, who was and still is a kind of walking legend about early jazz. My father was greatly interested in what the instrumentalists were doing. Also my father knew or had met many of the great musicians, like Cootie Williams, on the old Santa Fe Railroad, the Super Chief, where he served for many years as a bartender. And he brought that kind of information home, in terms of his own thinking and his selection of records. But also my dad used to sing in the choir of Pilgrim Baptist church, and he was interested in the spiritual singing. He possessed a fine singing voice, started writing lyrics in his late twenties, and even recorded some of his songs.

[M]: I see something of a concern for excellence here . . .

[F]: Yes, there was always this tradition of doing it right, whatever you were doing, a sense of perfection—which when you deal with it from the old time Negro perspective was not only obsessional, but linked to survival or death. . . . Added to all of this many-sided nourishment was an inordinate number of gifted story-tellers and liars on both sides of the family. . . . And always a sense of standards and style and substance, if you were scrubbing a floor, or lying, or generally attempting to stand tall and be counted in the world, and a sense that if your standards were up and elevated that of course you would be making a contribution. . . . Perhaps what I loved in Ray "Sugar" Robinson's athletic artistry was exactly this combination of excellence, style and artistry. Now I doubt if Mr. Robinson has read my novel (or will ever read any of my novels; I would be honored if he did, of course), but I always want it to embrace the traditions I learned from him and others: this will to win, to be the best, no matter what you attempted. . . .

[M]: Most of *Tree* is set in Chicago. Nathaniel's birthdate would, I gather, be approximately your own, and the dominating theme of the loss of a parent coincides with your personal experience. There seems to be an autobiographical element in the novel, but I'm wondering if you found achieving a proper distance a problem?

[F]: Well, since it all leapt out of my head, I guess it's all autobiographical; and I'll claim that child . . . [laughs] . . . Seriously, though, knowing or not knowing whether the writer (who is always a liar) considers the book highly autobiographical, or slightly so, doesn't help the critic one damn bit in solving the literary questions of the novel which is an imaginative act. Perhaps it is more important for the critic to know those well-springs of nourishment from whence the artist's materials derive than the biographical material. . . . And

I'm not a new writer. I'd been writing about fifteen years before
Tree was published. . . . *Wood-shedding,* you might say. The writer
can't be concerned about distance, only how to win the champion-
ship, the title (in fifteen rounds or less)—fifteen chapters or less and
how to marshal his killer instinct (a combination of the super-ego
and the ego) which he or she must possess, or be doomed to the
amateur ranks forever. What's more important than autobiography
is the continuity of the writer's kind of mind, which is universal. . . .
You are talking about a highly associative kind of memory-mind;
a highly reflective person, who does his work in isolation, and trains
his mind—his imagination—on books and folklore. He must have a
love and a fury for work, work, and re-working. He must love re-
writing the way an actor loves rehearsals. For finally literature is
about the projection of a vision of life, and as he re-writes endlessly
he comes to gain a control over the chaos of his materials which
floods up from his unconscious.

[M]: I'm wondering whether your experiences as a journalist helped
or hindered your work.

[F]: Well, as I suggested earlier, during much of the writing of
There Is a Tree, I was working in editorial positions, sometimes at
half the salary of a beginning journalist, with the daily papers—even
though I had been in the field for ten years. Even in the last years
my salary was only half that of a managing editor at a larger metro-
politan newspaper. But the freedom to go for broke on the hard
issues of the '60's and early '70's, in a field that is so corralling, was
quite attractive to me. I lived the semi-dormitory life of the appren-
tice writer, in the early years of that news career, which the young
writer must be willing to go through. I was unmarried, still rather
young; yet not so young either. But I could absorb the surface protest
of my firelight there at the newspapers, so that in the evenings I
was forced to seek out the soul of black folk, at a deeper level for the
soul-meat of my fictional vision. Then too, even in the early days
editors usually got me writing features, figuring I was either too
dumb or too imaginative to write straight news. But this worked in
my favor, in terms of the fiction, because it took me back to my love
of language—allowed me to play around with words in the features—
yet forced upon me a continual sense of the compactness of language
and structure. . . . The organizational possibilities in a brief space;
also, of course, quick character delineation. ("Give me a feature
story, Forrest, in three pages or less on this guy.")
      I was rarely in a position of putting out stuff in a soup-line or
mill-factory situation. Thus, I never was confronted with the perils

of becoming a hack, although if I had stayed around long enough, ultimately that might have happened. Still as you get older your energies wane, and I would hate to have come home from a day of writing to tackle a novel. . . . One of the hundreds of reasons why so much of the so-called black protest writing of the 1960's is a bore today, comes from the fact that much of it was not about coming consciousness at all, but rather emotional, narcissistic, one-dimensional heat, perhaps only simple letters-to-the-editor, in the form of limericks. Leaving aside the question of talent, some might have been saved, if they had been forced to empty out that surface outrage in some form, and then got down to that Body and Soul in their fiction, or poetry.

[M]: Have you experimented with other genres?

[F]: Well I started off wanting to write poetry, and I did for a time. I went through a longer period writing plays and thinking that I had found a home. I wanted to write verse-plays. But being a snob, I stupidly declined to work in the theatre. An absolute essential for the playwright.

[M]: Yes. And today more than ever black theatre is being projected as community theatre for a community audience. Do you write for any particular audience?

[F]: No. I only write for people who are interested in serious literature.

[M]: *Tree* is peopled by several striking personalities. There is, of course, the indomitable, yea-saying Auntie Breedlove; there are also several memorable lesser figures. What do you try to do in creating character?

[F]: Well I'm always trying to find their own true voice . . . not to dominate them or get in their way. They have a right to their own lives, and if that right is worthy to be presented before the reader, then it's my responsibility to get the hell out of their mouths and let them do the talking. I try not to push Forrest off on them, always to approach them with respect, and present them in their broadest possible dimensions.

[M]: Perhaps it was a personal predilection, but I noticed a bird/ angel/flight pattern of imagery permeating the novel. I was reminded of other writers who incorporated similar dichotomies in their fictions. In Ellison's much-anthologized short story, "Flying Home," for instance, the rather naive aspiring black pilot is forced into an ignominious landing. Once on the ground he is forced to deal with his rural, ancestral past. Or, in the case of Nigerian writer, Wole Soyinka, the protagonist of his novel *The Interpreters,* while aspiring to climb a social ladder, nearly "drowns" in an ancestral grove. There seems to be a multiple dialectic going on in which social, spiritual and metaphysical longings are countered by the awareness of the character's lowly social origins, his demanding flesh, and his "human" epistemology. Do you feel that this kind of imagery has special meaning in black history and culture?

[F]: I am always trying to bring into my work those images or motifs that seem to have sustained themselves longest in the culture, black and white. Some of this is quite conscious and some of it isn't at all. But I think the danger, always for me at least, is that the language and imagery come rather rapidly, and sometimes are highly personal, ergo, a peril, for I learned long ago never to trust anything that comes easy. In order to test the image, I must set that part of the writing aside for a while and go back again, lest my writing become victimized by what I guess must be my long suit, if I have a long suit. But those that you mentioned are out of the black experience, and I am always trying to see how many shapes and sides I can squeeze from the images; that's perhaps another long distance test of their life, and my skill or lack of skill.

[M]: You have cited Joyce and Faulkner, "mainstream" writers, as writers whose work you most admire. Do you feel that being in an African-American Department is somewhat problematical? Do you get an itch to teach a course, say on Hemingway or Joyce or Faulkner?

[F]: No. My basic itch about Hemingway, Joyce or Faulkner is to beat them. Write better works. I'm only completing my second year at Northwestern so I might do a great many things before I leave. Might even teach journalism. But I do teach Faulkner in a class entitled: The Oral Tradition and the Creative Process . . . I use his *Sound and the Fury*. I also use his work in my novel class—*Light in August*. I am still shaping the oral tradition class; and next year I'll be using some of Achebe, the Nigerian novelist, when we discuss the Oral Tradition in terms of the West African writers. In another course, I shall teach Joyce and Hemingway and Faulkner incorporated along with Baldwin, Ellison, Toomer and Forrest and Murray. This novel course will be about sensibility, initiation as manifested and revealed in language, as *the* motif shaper of coming wakefulness—regional, ethnic and personal. Actually, I am the only member in the department who teaches under introductory studies *and* English department aegis, and when I was hired the dean asked me what I wanted to teach. . . . And of course I will continue to teach what I want to teach. Just as I write what I want to write. But, on the other hand, I would not teach certain novels of Faulkner's, just as there are novels by black writers that I would not teach now, because I don't feel enough about them or because I am not knowledgeable enough about them. I only itch to teach those writers whose work will fit into the thrust of my class and will be helpful to my students.

[M]: It seems that many writers today are affiliated with some university. Do you see a positive relation between teaching and writing, or does your role as an academician conflict with your role as an artist?

[F]: I am not an academic. I talk literary techniques in classes as I have learned, and incorporated them in my own writings . . . I am an artist and for that kind of writer, life is never compartmentalized. The teaching techniques—literary craft knowledge in my case that I employ in the classroom are related to those techniques I employ on paper, at home before the typewriter. The university is, can be, a nourishing center for thought. This is the place where the Word is taught and standardized and sanctified in the libraries and in the classroom; I try to reshape, purify, standardize, and sanctify language in my own way. And you have been most generous in your responses to my failed attempts in this regard. But you see, Maria, one of my visions as a black artist is the sense of ancestral responsibility, of purifying the language to get our eloquence and rounded felt-life in the center of the arena. Now the more serious modern writers, the men who have gone before me, like Ellison and Bellow, are back in the university for the possible intellectual nourishment and development so necessary for the writer in the second and third stages of his development. The university supplies the place for us that newspapers once furnished for writers, in terms of intellectual content, writing excellence, the tension between the fierce street-life contests and how to re-order all of that at the typewriter. Many of these newsmen were really fiction writers, who had no other way to support themselves, and the newspaper-reading public benefited greatly from the material under their by-lines. The university doesn't have to be the entrapping monolith it was perhaps at one time. One can still get back out on the streets. It's entirely up to you.

[M]: You teach two of N. Scott Momaday's novels in your course on American Indian writing. Are the problems of Native American writing and writers similar to those of the black writing and writers? Is there a debate among American Indian *literati* similar to that among blacks?

[F]: Momaday is on the list for the same reasons Faulkner and Ellison are there: all three have broken out of the narrows of land, regionalism, or racial entrapment and have given us the broadest kind of vision of life. My students (I have never unfortunately had any Native Americans in my classes) enjoy Momaday because, while he celebrates the *Indianness* of his people, honoring their strengths and castigating their weaknesses, he offers a vision of modern man's terror-riddled complexities in the virtual no-man's land that is America. . . . Momaday is on the list because he celebrates much of the richness of Indian folklore. And of course there is some universality about all folklore at its richest. . . . Recently I have been doing some things in both my class work and my new novel with the Orpheus myth. There is a complete watershed cycle of materials on that Indian-variation of the Orpheus myth, which stretches from one end of the country to the other.

[M]: How do Native Americans respond to this universal-in-particular?

[F]: Now, Momaday is not so popular among certain Indians, just as Ralph Ellison is unpopular with some blacks. Because they think that the soul of the Race, the over-riding power, the anguish and the protest is lodged away in the narrows, in the provincial aspects of the group. I understand this. But, my job as an artist, and I imagine Mr. Momaday must feel this way, is to get the major projected vision into that literary arena, and compete with my peers working the modern novel, today. Momaday's Indian critics don't like the fact he has received all of this applause by whites. So Momaday is not universally loved. But many Jews don't like Bellow either, because they feel Bellow gives up too much of the ethnic thing as he reaches out to touch the condition of modern man (with the use of the wandering Jewish intellectual, with all of the old pratfalls of the Jewish monologue-spiel character, speeding along from one fool's errand to next) in the hellish wilderness of North America. They like Malamud much better. He's closer to their Jewishness. Yet in a name-dropping contest they would probably mention meeting Saul Bellow much more than Malamud.

[M]: Are there pressures on Native American writers to be more political?

[F]: I met a leading Native American intellectual at a conference recently who was quite critical of Momaday for going to Moscow University to teach for a period of time and not staying here for the war his people must fight for liberation. . . . Now where have you heard that before?

[M]: Yes, sounds familiar. Where are we in the development of Native American fiction?

[F]: There just have not been that many first-rate novels by Indian-Americans. First-rate in the way Momaday is first-rate. But a monumental body of folklore is there for the writer to develop and build from. Much of the most interesting writing too, like ours, has been autobiography, or biography, rather than fiction. But like the blacks, when the revolutionary talk of the '60's went down, volumes of misinformation tumbled down upon the scenes. Well, themes such as identity crisis, alienation and affirmation from the past and by the past, the role of the ancestral intelligence, the conflict over the quest for a personality center that's meaningful, the role of liberals in the struggle; these are some of the questions that are quite similar to the questions faced by black writers—in some ways all American writers. . . . But black writers have the especial duty to reveal how our people have been dominant carriers and reshapers in a very fundamental way in the cultural life of America . . . Then too, the blacks have a thriving and active middle and upper-middle class, from which much of our institutional leadership derives, and which is highly American and highly proud of its combined heritage. Indians don't have this.

[M]: Getting back to your position as a member of an African-American Department, how would you assess the impact of Black Studies on black and white students? And what would you predict for Black Studies?

[F]: Well in order to survive, departments will have to deal with the universities on a highly sophisticated level, demand that their staffs be culled from the best people available, and not the rhetorical bullshit artists. They'll have to get more and more involved in the general life of the campus—dominate it intellectually and in terms of inventive vitality. They'll have to make up their minds to intellectually dominate reality, the American reality. The administrations *knew* if they laid in the cut and waited, student apathy would save them from having to deal with the formidable question of the absence of black heritage in the intellectual life of the university. So that the departments can't depend on the students to fight battles with the university—not in today's atmosphere. Black students by and large simply aren't competitive enough. And when we suggest the literature of blacks is complicated, complicated in the way we are as a people, many don't want to hear. The white students are more competitive on the average and do better.

[M]: There is a continuing debate on the allegiances or non-allegiances of the artist. Do you think a writer should use his art to change society?

[F]: That presumes of course that he knows anything about anything other than writing sentences, creating lasting metaphors, and memorable characters. But we Americans assume because a man is good at one thing he is the man to answer the call of a discipline of highly developed techniques and skills, even if he is without training. Most writers work alone—even to some extent if you write musicals. Politics and social or societal changes must connect with day-in-and-day-out power, persuasion, struggle, and cunning, and have the capacity to deliver a rather constant set of immediate victories for a group of people. . . . Some writers perhaps can do all of that but most can't, even when they say they can. . . . Most times they don't have the craft, knowledge, the staying power, the constituency, the temperament, the mind-set.

[M]: In other words there is a fundamental difference between the artist and the activist?

[F]: Well, all we know for certain is that said writer has an interesting way of re-telling the old stories with new renditions. He's an imaginative editor with a projected vision of life that is so stunning we can't ever put down the book, at best . . . that he has reassembled a body of techniques over the chaos of materials abounding, and given us a new, haunting order and vision of our days upon this planet, even as he links our outrage, sense of tragedy and delight to the battle of our common ancestral search for Home, Freedom, Power, and Love. Well now, if he can do simply that, what a glory it would be.

[M]: In short, you would agree with the aestheticians that the artist's province is that of the mind and the imagination. . . .

[F]: That's the point. Now that same man might be a damn fool doing anything else, and don't you just know the political masters are going to laugh him off the floor of Congress. Also the question presumes of course that the writer can wield power in the immediate marketplace, jobs, crash welfare programs, political might, diplomatic grace, and that he knows something about technical grace and statecraft in a meaningful way, rather than a sophomoric way.

[M]: Then, where would a cultural essayist like James Baldwin enter into the picture? Is his type of intellectual barrage the best example of art as protest?

[F]: Now about Jimmy Baldwin . . . those essays of the fifties and early sixties worked so neatly in concert with the whole fashioning of a people's instrument towards political freedom, accommodations, voting rights, etc. And they were very significant in terms of re-enlightening rather enlightened, articulate white (and some black) readers in powerful, fairly stimulating journals, left of center (like *Esquire,* or *Harper's*), as the Movement itself called upon the conscience of the best in the freedom traditions of the country. Those essays worked well in terms of the total Freedom Movement gearshift, which came down hard, yet smoothly with grace (like Jimmy's essays), on the guilt of America—but those propaganda essays worked best upon the highly influential, radical chic of that day, people who had powerful political links. . . . They were one dimension of a many-sided sword. But, when Bull Connor let those dogs loose on black people, that touched the heart, albeit ever so fleetingly, of white people who had never read Baldwin. . . . Those essays were brilliant, immediate, but read today (after we got the rights, but not always the implementation) those essays, in the main, only stand up as good examples of the inventive construct of essay writing, in which Baldwin incorporated many of the techniques of the novelist. . . . Jimmy didn't know any deep history, or have any deep political thought, or any economic theories. . . . So, most of those essays now seem more like period pieces of the historical town-crier, addressed as Baldwin might say to a "grievously hypocritical Republic."

[M]: Well, most people think Baldwin's essays are superior to his fiction. Do you agree?

[F]: Not quite. Now, what was addressed to our long-haul story was a fine book, called *Go Tell It on the Mountain.* That book was never a part of the Civil Rights Freedom Movement's war-chest of immediacy, and frontal assaults, as were his essays. Yet *Go Tell It* apparently endures; it is literature. And it has within its resources the eloquence of literature, the imperishable hallmarks that a people might hold onto, and be uplifted by, and challenged through. That's a possible function of literature. A people can endure through it. *And,* with all of this talk about black survival nobody talks much about the possibilities of institutional inner strength in terms of what a great book can continually give a people, as they (generation after generation) read and re-read into its depths, and *their* depths. A book like *Invisible Man* keeps enriching the individual and informing him or her with each new reading about the human condition, the human predicament. . . .

[M]: Have any writers influenced you more than others?

[F]: I might think that one writer influenced me to an extent far greater than was actually the case. . . . Recently I've become quite interested in the minor influences of Hemingway upon Faulkner's work, particularly in certain sardonic understated dialogue scenes, for instance Max and Mame (and Bobbie) in *Light in August*—some of that dialogue. . . . Well, most people don't ever think of those writers together since they are so different; yet the influence is there. But, don't forget Hemingway was an all but universally acknowledged master of the short-story some time before Faulkner was to completely find himself, or shape his art.

But what's more important is the body of work, over the long haul, and the folklore which informs the intelligence of the people who nourish the author's art.

[M]: The multiplicity of black consciousnesses. . . .

[F]: Yes, you see the writer is a vulture in the sense that he'll feed on almost anything that can give him and his art nourishment—hopefully he'll have better taste than the vulture. I've said that he is a liar, and let me add that he is also a thief. . . . On the other hand, the whole nourishment from culture and form, from all the shapes he gets from other writers, from the weather, architecture, music, sculpture, is so implicit that only a critic, looking over an extended body of a writer's work, can point out, scientifically, the levels of influences. There you can take into account the body of literature which nourished a writer's earliest development; that's more important, since any first-rate writer reads a range of work that may basically touch his sense of form, or shape his language, but not affect his heart-core storehouse of character associations and the soul and guts of his own art. . . . For instance I couldn't see how Henry James has influenced me; but he strongly shaped Baldwin's essay/novel prose.

[M]: Today there is a wider range of black writing than ever before. Do you consider yourself part of a "school" in black writing?

[F]: Well, McPherson, Morrison, Murray, Ellison, Wideman and I are all club-members you might say.

[M]: What advice would you give to an aspiring black writer?

[F]: Well, clearly he must develop a writer's mind, which is highly associative—and deeply reflective—and constantly see story material possibilities in patterns, in symbolic connections, word transitions in the world about him, and within him. He must develop a fury for re-writing, for it is only via re-writing, endlessly, obsessively, that he can ever write into currents of energy, felt-knowledge memories. The writer's mind is possessed by a long and deep memory of the way things fit or are in paradox, but he must train his mind to find his form. He must be extremely ambitious—must possess a "killer-instinct," I believe—in that he is constantly thinking: well now, Joyce did it this way; or Faulkner did it this way. . . . Always testing himself against the masters, always thinking in terms of that—of the giants. How good I must be if I am going up against this champion. He must read constantly and nourish himself upon varied sources of reading. You're talking about an extremely stubborn intelligence—but because writing is the loneliest of the arts, the highest and the most demanding, and in our country the most spat-upon, and seriously regarded as an oddity, he had better be very stubborn. His writing must be nourished upon a storehouse of materials, which come from what he has read, what he has observed, and what he has experienced. But the life of the imagination is the most important, central complexity that he must develop.

[M]: Thank you very much.

THE ART OF ROMARE BEARDEN

RALPH ELLISON

I regard the weakening of the importance given to objects as the capital transformation of Western art. In painting, it is clear that a painting of Picasso's is less and less a "canvas," and more and more the mark of some discovery, a stake left to indicate the place through which a restless genius has passed . . .

THIS SERIES OF COLLAGES AND PROJECTIONS BY ROMARE BEARDEN represents a triumph of a special order. Springing from a dedicated painter's unending efforts to master the techniques of illusion and revelation which are so important to the craft of painting, they are also the result of Bearden's search for fresh methods to explore the plastic possibilities of Negro American experience. What is special about Bearden's achievement is, it seems to me, the manner in which he has made his dual explorations serve one another, the way in which his technique has been used to discover and transfigure its object. For in keeping with the special nature of his search and by the self-imposed "rules of the game," it was necessary that the methods arrived at be such as would allow him to express the tragic predicament of his people without violating his passionate dedication to art as a fundamental and transcendent agency for confronting and revealing the world.

To have done this successfully is not only to have added a dimension to the technical resourcefulness of art, but to have modified our way of experiencing reality. It is also to have had a most successful encounter with a troublesome social anachronism which, while finding its existence in areas lying beyond the special providence of the artist, has nevertheless caused great confusion among many painters of Bearden's social background. I say *social,* for although Bearden is by self-affirmation no less than by public identification a Negro American, the quality of his *artistic* culture can by no means

This essay is reprinted from the catalogue introduction to an exhibition of Paintings & Projections by Romare Bearden at the Art Gallery of the State University of New York at Albany, November 25 through December 22, 1968. © Copyright Ralph Ellison.

ROMARE BEARDEN
THE ODYSSEUS COLLAGES

Romare Bearden

The Odyssey—surely the greatest story ever told—is marred only by the tediousness of its gods. The same gods who dominate *The Iliad,* who ordain and usually carry out, under various disguises, all the major actions of the Trojan War, are strangely ineffectual when we come to the later saga. In *The Odyssey* it is men and women who control events, acting sometimes in contravention of divine will. The poem's great theme, the wanderings of the hero who longs for home, has been described by Julian Jaynes in his recent study as "an odyssey toward subjective identity and its triumphant acknowledgment out of the hallucinatory enslavements of the past."

Romare Bearden's Odyssey series is not literature but painting, of course, and his technique is that talismanic twentieth century one, collage. The placement and displacement of images in a chosen space. An act of necromancy, requiring cunning, grace, nerve, intelligence and luck (defined as the ability to take good advantage of chance—or the gods). The images that he chooses and the manner in which he places them create vibrations, waves that carry us into regions not visited but remembered, dimly or vividly, from previous experiences with the myth.

Odysseus was one of the original suitors for the hand of Helen. Despairing of success he married Penelope instead. We assume that he was in luck there, too, although the end of that story remains in doubt. One of the legends about him says that he met his death at the hands of Telegonia, his son by Circe, who had come to Ithaca to make himself known to his great father and slew him by mistake. It is difficult to escape the past, as Homer and Bearden so splendidly remind us.

Calvin Tomkins

BATTLE WITH CICONES 32" x 44"

CIRCE TURNS A COMPANION OF ODYSSEUS INTO A SWINE   32″ x 44″

ODYSSEUS LEAVES CIRCE   32″ x 44″

THE SEA NYMPH   44" x 32"

ODYSSEUS LEAVES NAUSICAA 32" x 44"

HOME TO ITHACA   14" x 22¾"

ROMARE BEARDEN was born in Charlotte, N.C. in 1914. He studied at
N.Y.U., the Art Student's League (with George Grosz), and at the Sorbonne.
He first exhibited in 1945. In 1971 he was honored with a major retro-
spective at the Museum of Modern Art in New York.

The collages reproduced here are with the permission and assistance
of Cordier & Ekstrom of 980 Madison Avenue, N.Y.C. The color separations
were provided through the courtesy of The Press of A. Colish of Mount
Vernon, New York. The portrait photograph of Romare Bearden is by Niki
Ekstrom. The foreword by Calvin Tomkins is from the Cordier & Ekstrom
catalogue of The Odysseus Collages by Romare Bearden.

THE MASSACHUSETTS REVIEW
WINTER 1977
MR

be conveyed by that term. Nor does it help to apply the designation "black" (even more amorphous for conveying a sense of cultural complexity) and since such terms tell us little about the unique individuality of the artist or anyone else, it is well to have them out in the open where they can cause the least confusion.

What, then, do I mean by anachronism? I refer to that imbalance in American society which leads to a distorted perception of social reality, to a stubborn blindness to the creative possibilities of cultural diversity, to the prevalence of negative myths, racial stereotypes and dangerous illusions about art, humanity and society. Arising from an initial failure of social justice, this anachronism divides social groups along lines that are no longer tenable while fostering hostility, anxiety and fear; and in the area to which we now address ourselves it has had the damaging effect of alienating many Negro artists from the traditions, techniques and theories indigenous to the arts through which they aspire to achieve themselves.

Thus in the field of culture, where their freedom of self-definition is at a maximum, and where the techniques of artistic self-expression are most abundantly available, they are so fascinated by the power of their anachronistic social imbalance as to limit their efforts to describing its manifold dimensions and its apparent invincibility against change. Indeed, they take it as a major theme and focus for their attention; they allow it to dominate their thinking about themselves, their people, their country and their art. And while many are convinced that simply to recognize social imbalance is enough to put it to riot, few achieve anything like artistic mastery, and most fail miserably through a single-minded effort to "tell it like it is."

Sadly however, the problem for the plastic artist is not one of "telling" at all, but of *revealing* that which has been concealed by time, by custom, and by our trained incapacity to perceive the truth. Thus it is a matter of destroying moribund images of reality and creating the new. Further, for the true artist, working from the top of his times and out of a conscious concern with the most challenging possibilities of his form, the unassimilated and anachronistic—whether in the shape of motif, technique or image—is abhorrent, an evidence of conceptual and/or technical failure, of challenges unmet. And although he may ignore the anachronistic through a preoccupation with other pressing details, he can never be satisfied simply by placing it within a frame. For once there, it becomes the symbol of all that is not art and a mockery of his powers of creation. So at best he struggles to banish the anachronistic element from his canvas by converting it into an element of style, a device of his personal vision.

For as Bearden demonstrated here so powerfully, it is of the true artist's nature and mode of action to dominate all the world and time through technique and vision. His mission is to bring a new visual order into the world, and through his art he seeks to reset society's clock by imposing upon it his own method of defining the times. The urge to do this determines the form and character of his social responsibility, it spurs his restless exploration for plastic possibilities, and it accounts to a large extent for his creative aggressiveness.

But it is here precisely that the aspiring Negro painter so often falters. Trained by the circumstances of his social predicament to a habit (no matter how reluctant) of accommodation, such an attitude toward the world seems quite quixotic. He is, he feels, only one man, and the conditions which thwart his freedom are of such enormous dimensions as to appear unconquerable by purely plastic means—even at the hands of the most highly trained, gifted and arrogant artist.

"Turn Picasso into a Negro and *then* let me see how far he can go," he will tell you, because he feels an irremediable conflict between his identity as a member of an embattled social minority and his freedom as an artist. He cannot avoid—nor should he wish to avoid—his group-identity, but he flounders before the question of how his group's experience might be given statement through the categories of a non-verbal form of art which has been consciously exploring its own unique possibilities for many decades before he appeared on the scene; a self-assertive and irreverent art which abandoned long ago the task of mere representation to photography and the role of story-telling to the masters of the comic strip and the cinema. Nor can he draw upon his folk tradition for a simple answer. For here, beginning with the Bible and proceeding all the way through the spirituals and blues, novel, poem and the dance, Negro Americans have depended upon the element of narrative for both entertainment and group identification. Further, it has been those who have offered an answer to the question—ever crucial in the lives of a repressed minority—of who and what they are in the most simplified and graphic terms who have won their highest praise and admiration. And unfortunately there seems to be (the African past notwithstanding) no specifically Negro American tradition of plastic design to offer him support.

How then, he asks himself, does even an artist steeped in the most advanced lore of his craft and most passionately concerned with solving the more advanced problems of painting as *painting* address himself to the perplexing question of bringing his art to bear upon the task (never so urgent as now) of defining Negro American identity, of pressing its claims for recognition and for justice? He feels, in brief, a near-unresolvable conflict between his urge to leave his mark upon the world through art and his ties to his group and its claims upon him.

Fortunately for them and for us, Romare Bearden has faced these questions for himself, and since he is an artist whose social consciousness is no less intense than his dedication to art, his example is of utmost importance for all who are concerned with grasping something of the complex interrelations between race, culture and the individual artist as they exist in the United States. Bearden is aware that for Negro Americans these are times of eloquent protest and intense struggle, times of rejection and redefinition—but he also knows that all this does little to make the question of the relation of the Negro artist to painting any less difficult. And if the cries in the street are to find effective statement on canvas they must undergo a metamorphosis. For in painting, Bearden has recently observed, there is little room for the lachrymose, for self-pity or raw complaint; and if they are to find a place in painting this can only be accomplished by infusing them with the freshest sensibility of the times as it finds existence in the elements of painting.

During the late Thirties when I first became aware of Bearden's work, he was painting scenes of the Depression in a style strongly influenced by the Mexican muralists. This work was powerful, the scenes grim and brooding, and through his depiction of unemployed workingmen in Harlem he was able, while evoking the Southern past, to move beyond the usual protest painting of that period to reveal something of the universal elements of an abiding human condition. By striving to depict the times, by reducing scene, character and atmosphere to a style, he caught both the universality of Harlem life and the "harlemness" of the national human predicament.

I recall that later, under the dual influences of Hemingway and the poetic tragedy of Federico Garcia Lorca, Bearden created a voluminous series of drawings and paintings inspired by Lorca's *Lament for Ignacion Sanchez Mejias*. He had become interested in myth and ritual as potent forms for ordering human experience, and it would seem that by stepping back from the immediacy of the Harlem experience—which he knew both from boyhood and as a social worker—he was freed to give expression to the essentially poetic side of his vision. The products of that period were marked by a palette which, in contrast with the somber colors of the earlier work and despite the tragic theme with its underlying allusions to Christian rite and mystery, was brightly sensual. And despite their having been consciously influenced by the compositional patterns of the Italian primitives, and the Dutch masters, these works were also resolutely abstract.

It was as though Bearden had decided that in order to possess his world *artistically* he had to confront it *not* through propaganda or sentimentality, but through the finest techniques and traditions of painting. He sought to re-create his Harlem in the light of his painter's vision, and thus he avoided the defeats suffered by many of the aspiring painters of that period, who seemed to have felt that they had only to reproduce out of a mood of protest and despair the scenes and surfaces of Harlem, in order to win artistic mastery and accomplish social transfiguration.

It would seem that for many Negro painters even the *possibility* of translating Negro American experience into the modes and conventions of modern painting went unrecognized. This was, in part, the result of an agonizing fixation upon the racial mysteries and social realities dramatized by color, facial structure, and the texture of Negro skin and hair. And again, many aspiring artists clung with protective compulsiveness to the myth of the Negro American's total alienation from the larger American culture—a culture which he helped to create in the areas of music and literature, and where in the area of painting he has appeared from the earliest days of the nation as a symbolic figure—and allowed the realities of their social and political situation to determine their conception of their role and freedom as artists.

To accept this form of the myth was to accept its twin variants, one of which holds that there is a pure mainstream of American culture which is "unpolluted" by any trace of Negro American style or idiom, and the other (propagated currently by the exponents of *Negritude*) which holds that Western art is basically racist and thus anything more than a cursory knowledge of its techniques and history is to the Negro artist irrelevant. In other words, the Negro American who aspired to the title "Artist" was too often restricted by sociological notions of racial separatism, and these appear not only to have restricted his use of artistic freedom, but to have limited his curiosity as to the abundant resources made available to him by those restless and assertive agencies of the artistic imagination which we call technique and conscious culture.

Indeed, it has been said that these disturbing works of Bearden's (which virtually erupted during a tranquil period of abstract painting) began quite innocently as a demonstration to a group of Negro painters. He was suggesting some of the possibilities through which commonplace materials could be forced to undergo a creative metamorphosis when manipulated by some of the non-representational techniques available to the resourceful craftsman. The step from collage to projection followed naturally since Bearden had used it during the early Forties as a means of studying the works of such early masters as Giotto and de Hooch. That he went on to become fascinated with the possibilities lying in such "found" materials is both an important illustrative instance for younger painters and a source for our delight and wonder.

Bearden knows that regardless of the individual painter's personal history, taste or point of view, he must, nevertheless, pay his materials the respect of approaching them through a highly conscious awareness of the resources and limitations of the form to which he has dedicated his creative energies. One suspects also that as an artist possessing a marked gift for pedagogy, he has sought here to reveal a world long hidden by the clichés of sociology and rendered cloudy by the distortions of newsprint and the false continuity imposed upon our conception of Negro life by television and much documentary photography. Therefore, as he delights us with the magic of design and teaches us the ambiguity of vision, Bearden insists that we *see* and that we see in depth and by the fresh light of the creative vision. Bearden knows that the true complexity of the slum dweller and the tenant farmer require a release from the prison of our media-dulled perception and a reassembling in forms which would convey something of the depth and wonder of the Negro American's stubborn humanity.

Being aware that the true artist destroys the accepted world by way of revealing the unseen, and creating that which is new and uniquely his own, Bearden has used cubist techniques to his own ingenious effect. His mask-faced Harlemites and tenant farmers set in their mysterious, familiar, but emphatically abstract, scenes are nevertheless resonant of artistic and social history. Without compromising their integrity as elements in plastic compositions, his figures are eloquent of a complex reality lying beyond their frames. While functioning as integral elements of design they serve simultaneously as signs and symbols of a humanity which has struggled to survive the decimating and fragmentizing effects of American social processes. Here faces which draw upon the abstract character of African sculpture for their composition are made to focus our attention upon the far from abstract reality of a people. Here abstract interiors are presented in which concrete life is acted out under repressive conditions. Here, too, the poetry of the blues is projected through synthetic forms which, visually, are in themselves tragi-comic and eloquently poetic. A harsh poetry this, but poetry nevertheless; with the nostalgic imagery of the blues conceived as visual form, image, pattern and symbol—including the familiar trains (evoking partings and reconciliations), and the conjure women (who appear in these works with the ubiquity of the witches who haunt the drawing of Goya) who evoke the abiding mystery of the enigmatic women who people the blues. And here, too, are renderings of those rituals of rebirth and dying, of baptism and sorcery which give ceremonial continuity to the Negro American community.

By imposing his vision upon scenes familiar to us all Bearden reveals much of the universally human which they conceal. Through his creative assemblage he makes complex comments upon history, upon society and upon the nature of art. Indeed, his Harlem becomes a place inhabited by people who have in fact been *resurrected,* re-created by art, a place composed of visual puns and artistic allusions and where the sacred and profane, reality and dream are ambiguously mingled. And resurrected with them in the guise of fragmented ancestral figures and forgotten gods (really masks of the instincts, hopes, emotions, aspirations and dreams) are those powers that now surge in our land with a potentially destructive force which springs from the very fact of their having for so long gone unrecognized, unseen.

Bearden doesn't impose these powers upon us by explicit comment, but his ability to make the unseen manifest allows us some insight into the forces which now clash and rage as Negro Americans seek self-definition in the slums of our cities. There is a beauty here, a harsh beauty which asserts itself out of the horrible fragmentation which Bearden's subjects and their environment have undergone. But, as I have said, there is no preaching; these forces have been brought to eye by formal art. These works take us from Harlem through the South of tenant farms and northward-bound trains to tribal Africa; our mode of conveyance consists of every device which has claimed Bearden's artistic attention, from the oversimplified and scanty images of Negroes that appear in our ads and photojournalism, to the discoveries of the School of Paris and the Bauhaus. He has used the discoveries of Giotto and Pieter de Hooch no less than those of Juan Gris, Picasso, Schwitters and Mondrian (who was no less fascinated by the visual possibilities of jazz than by the compositional rhythms of the early Dutch masters), and has discovered his own uses for the metaphysical richness of African sculptural forms. In brief, Bearden has used (and most playfully) all of his artistic knowledge and skill to create a curve of plastic vision which reveals to us something of the mysterious complexity of those who dwell in our urban slums. But his is the eye of a painter, not that of a sociologist, and here the elegant architectural details which exist in a setting of gracious but neglected streets and the buildings in which the hopeful and the hopeless live cheek by jowl, where failed human wrecks and the confidently expectant explorers of the frontiers of human possibility are crowded together as incongruously as the explosive details in a Bearden canvas—all this comes across plasticly and with a freshness of impact that is impossible for sociological cliché or raw protest.

Where any number of painters have tried to project the "prose" of Harlem—a task performed more successfully by photographers—Bearden has concentrated upon releasing its poetry, its abiding rituals and ceremonies of affirmation—creating a surreal poetry compounded of vitality and powerlessness, destructive impulse and the all-pervading and enduring faith in their own style of American humanity. Through his faith in the powers of art to reveal the unseen through the seen, his collages have transcended their immaculateness as plastic constructions.—Or to put it another way, Bearden's meaning is identical with his method. His combination of technique is in itself eloquent of the sharp breaks, leaps in consciousness, distortions, paradoxes, reversals, telescoping of time and surreal blending of styles, values, hopes and dreams which characterize much of Negro American history. Through an act of creative will, he has blended strange visual harmonies out of the shrill, indigenous dichotomies of American life and in doing so reflected the irrepressible thrust of a people to endure and keep its intimate sense of its own identity.

Bearden seems to have told himself that in order to possess the meaning of his Southern childhood and Northern upbringing, that in order to keep his memories, dreams and values whole, he would have to re-create them, humanize them by reducing them to artistic style. Thus in the poetic sense these works give plastic expression to a vision in which the socially grotesque conceals a tragic beauty, and they embody Bearden's interrogation of the empirical values of a society which mocks its own ideals through a blindness induced by its myth of race. All this, ironically, by a man who visually at least (he is light-skinned and perhaps more Russian than 'black' in appearance) need never have been restricted to the social limitations imposed upon easily identified Negroes. Bearden's art is thus not only an affirmation of his own freedom and responsibility as an individual and artist, it is an affirmation of the irrelevance of the notion of race as a limiting force in the arts. These are works of a man possessing a rare lucidity of vision.

THE SCHOONER *FLIGHT*

DEREK WALCOTT

I

RAPTURES OF THE DEEP

In summer doldrums, when the sea soft,
and all the Antilles drift to oblivion
like leaves on a lake, I switch off the light
of that star in my heart: Maria Concepcion,
and ship as a sailor on the Schooner *Flight*
Maria Concepcion, when the tired day puts on
its bright silk pyjamas, and night, like a bride,
sidles under the sea with your starry laugh,
I know with you there is no forgetting,
is like telling mourners 'round the grave-side
about resurrection. They want life as it is,
so I tell myself also is no use repeating
that the sea have more fish. I don't want her
dressed in the sexless light of a seraph,
I want those round, brown eyes of a marmoset, and
(may God forgive me for being a man)
those claws that tickle my back in the sweating
Sabbath afternoons, like a crab on wet sand.
As I ride watching these rotting waves come
from the bow that scissors the sea like silk,
I swear to you now, by my mother's milk,
by these stars whirling from the night's furnace,
that I loved you as the poets loved the poetry
that kills all of them, as drowned sailors the sea.

With you, I must answer for all our sins,
how you wreck my life on the Cape of Good Horn,
how, though you horn me, I had no other thought
walking early early round and round the port
when the right sides of dories, schooner and yacht
were being repainted by the light of the sun,

reading your name in each writhing reflection,
tired, tired of this life, and dying to be gone.
I seen the Antilles from Cedros to Nassau,
a rusty-head sailor with sea-green eyes
that they nickname Shabine, the patois name for
every peeling red-nigger, but, as I tell the sea:
I got Dutch, Bajan white, and nigger in me,
I had a sound colonial education,
so either I'm nobody, or I am a nation.
Lord, when I think how this whole thing begin.

II

Smuggled Scotch for O'Hara, big Government man,
between Cedros and the Main, so the Coast Guard couldn't touch us,
and the 'Pagnol pirogues always met us half way.
Well, a voice kept saying: "Shabine, see this business
of playing pirate? Watch out!" So said, so done!
That whole racket crash. I did it for a woman,
for her laces and silk, Maria Concepcion.
All that time I was sweating cold sweat in the sun,
you could guess what happen, she pick up with a man,
right, my whole life crash on the Cape of Good Horn.

Ay, ay! Next thing I hear, some Commission of Inquiry
was being organised to conduct a big quiz
with himself as Chairman investigating himself!
Well, I knew damned well who the suckers would be:
not that shark in shark's skin, but his pilot fish,
little khaki-pants nowherians like you and me.
All this time I quarrelling with Maria Concepcion,
so I swear: "Not me, in this business again!"
It was mashing up house and family;
I was so broke all I needed was shades and a cup,
or four shades and four cups, in four-cup Port of Spain,
I didn't have to play blind to see what justice was.

You saw their pictures in the morning papers
preaching faith to the poor, one hand at their back
for the pay-off, while police guarding their house,
and the Scotch pouring in, through the back door.
As for that minister-monster who smuggled the booze,

that half-Syrian saurian, I'd get so sick to see
that face thick with powder, the warts, the stone lids
like some dinosaur caked with primordial ooze
by the lightning of flashbulbs, knee-deep in wealth.
So I said, Shabine, this is shit, understand!
But he got somebody to kick my crutch out his office
like I was some artist. That bitch was so grand,
couldn't get off his high horse and kick me himself.
Man, I seen some things that would make a slave sick
in this place I christened The Limers' Republic.
I plead guilty okay, but what I was involved in
was not original sin, but official theft.
That's how niggers behave since the white man left,
fooling their own brothers, then doing them in.

I couldn't get the ocean out of my head,
any more than I could Maria Concepcion,
so I took up salvage-diving with a crazy red Mick
by the name of O'Shaughnessy, and a Limey called Head.
But this Caribbean Sea choked with the dead!
Even when I dived under bright coral water
whose ceiling climbed rippling like a silk green tent,
and I never tell this to nobody before,
I saw first the corals, brain, fire and sea-fans,
the dead men's fingers, and then the dead men,
man, I saw that all that white sand was bones
from the coast of Senegal to San Salvador.
Then I panicked third dive, and surfaced for a month
in the Seaman's Hostel. Fish-broth and sermons.
When I thought of the woe I had brought my wife,
when I saw my worries with that other woman,
I wept under water, salt seeking salt,
for her beauty had fallen on me like a sword,
cleaving me from my children, flesh of my flesh!

There was this barge from Saint Vincent, but she was too deep
to float her again. When we drank, the Limey
soon tired of my sobbing for Maria Concepcion,
he claimed he kept "getting the bends." Good for him!
The cramp in my side for Maria Concepcion
was worse than the bends, in the rapturous deep.
There was no cleft in the rock where my soul could hide
like the boobies at sunset, no sandbar of light

on some secret cay only pelicans know.
So I said I got raptures down there and saw God
as a harpooned grouper bubbling: "Shabine, leave her,
and I shall give you the morning star."
So, they let me go, and I tried other women,
but, once they stripped naked, their spiky cunts
bristled like sea-eggs, so I really couldn't dive.
The chaplain'd come round. I paid him no mind.
Where is my rest-place Jesus? Where is my harbour?
Where is the pillow I will not have to pay for,
and the window I can look from that frames my life?

III

SHABINE LEAVES THE REPUBLIC

i

I no longer believed in the Revolution.
I no longer believed in the love of my woman
I have seen the moment which Aleksandr Blok
immortalised in "The Twelve." It was between
The Police Marine Branch and The Hotel Venezuelana
on the wharf one Sunday: young men waving the flags
of their shirts, their bare bodies waiting for holes.
They went on marching into the mountains, and
they ceased shouting as foam fades into the sand.
They went into the hills like the bright rain, every one
with his own nimbus, leaving a shirt in the street
and a shout at the end of the street. The banana-leaf fan
revolves over the Senate, the Judge sweats in carmine,
and the Saturday street is choked with limers marching
by standing still. They say it's a matter of timing,
that we have had too much protest and too much grief,
till the Lime Republic turns over a new leaf.
In the 12:30 double-features the projectors had best
not break down, or you go see Revolution! Aleksandr Blok
enters and sits in the third row of Globe eating choc-
olate palette waiting for a spaghetti West-
ern starring Clint Eastwood and featuring Lee Van Cleef.

I have no nation but the imagination.
Neither the niggers nor the white man wanted me
when the power swung tó their side.
One bust my head with a stone and muttered, "Sorry, History,"
the next one said I wasn't black enough for their pride,
and that's why Shabine cast his vote for the sea.
The sea, and that sad happiness called poetry.
Sometimes in the stagnant afternoon,
I saw the Caribbean scaled with light
like a rotting whale crested with small islands,
stuck in the brain with history's harpoon,
the lice milling in her like a seaside town.

I saw History once, but he didn't recognize me;
an old man with a parchment skin as mottled with warts
as a barnacled sea-bottle, he crawled crab-wise through the shade
of the Creole Quarter, from Castries to Christiansted,
through holes in the net that was cast by the thread
of ironwork balconies, in cream linen and Leghorn hat,
with blue, rheumy eyes and a neck pink as a buzzard's,
and, making history, I shouted with affection:
"Ay, sir! Is me, Shabine, your unhistorical
grandson; you remember Grandma, your black cook at all?"
The deaf bitch spat. It's worth a thousand words.
That's all those bastards left us anyway. Words.

IV

THE FLIGHT PASSING MATELOT

Gulls wheel as from a gunshot, and
waves turn to amber that were white.
Lighthouse and star are making friends.
Down every bay, the long day ends.
Meanwhile on the last stretch of sand,
on beaches bare of all but light,
the sea is pushing up the night
as far as it can go inland.

SHABINE ENCOUNTERS MIDDLE PASSAGE

Night pass, and day rise out of the sea.
Well, boy, if I tell you the next thing I see
you go say, I mad. Thank God I could write,
cause I write it down. You could read it still:
From the log of *The Flight:* "Passed this sunrise, three
crazy looking schooners with the cross of Castille,
going the wrong way. Signalled by flag, then by obscenity,
then physically pelting everything we find
at them Carnival sailors: 'Back-back! Reverso!'
They look through us like ghosts, so
was no use saying the America-ca they'd find.
I suppose if I saw black fellers coming back
from where God sent me to discover, I'd feel unsound
not only in mind, but in my divine purpose.
So we bawl, cry, cuss, but they never turn round.
We pass slavers daily. Flags of all nations.
Our children on-board them too deep below deck
to hear us crying their names. Must stop. Growing dark.
Can't read my own writing. The sea brings patience.
Accepting the loss of Maria Concepcion.
I am slowly learning to write, I suppose.
Some day I will see. Tomorrow, at dawn,
our first landfall will be, The Barbados."

VI

THE SAILOR SINGS BACK TO THE CASUARINAS

You see them in marches on the low Barbados hills,
swaying like wind-breaks, needles for the hurricane.
Mast-high, they trail the cirrus like torn sails.
When I was green like them, I used to think:
"These cypress-like trees leaning on the sea,
that borrow the sea-noise into their branches,
are not real cypresses, but casuarinas."
I once lived by resemblance, not the thing,
which was nothing, except it first resembled
the original, by which I could be taught.

All fruits were imitations of the apple,
so the cypress-resembling casuarinas
were named by mimicry of their first cause,
even when their pliant bodies swayed like women
in classic pain, when some schooner came home
with news of one more sailor drowned again,
swaying like Cassandras in delirium
before Troy fell, or from the hurricane.
Cassandras, casuarinas, cypresses,
the wind itself was full of quotations,
remote Bermudas and the pearls of eyes,
that those trees shied away from us like lies,
deceiving us, as we deceived ourselves,
that we could ever be anything else
but what they named as the imagination's.
So the word "cypress" held more resonance
than the green one "casuarina," though the same
wind might have bent and blent them with one name
till all were trees, with the one will, to dance,
and metaphor might have made one green flame
of all trees' heavenward leaping, but you'd have
to be colonial to see the difference,
to have blest those trees with an inferior love,
to have known the pain of history words contain,
and to have thought: "Those casuarinas move
like cypresses, their hair hangs down in rain
like women, also." They are almost trees, and we,
if we move in those ways our namers please,
by such assiduous mimicry could be men.

VII

THE FLIGHT ANCHORS IN CASTRIES HARBOUR

When I was young under the stars of the Castries,
I loved you alone and I loved the whole world.
What does it matter that our lives are different?
Burdened with the loves of our different children?
When I think of your young face washed by the wind
and your voice that chuckles in the slap of the sea?
The lights are out on La Toc promontory
except for the hospital. Across at Vigie
the marina arcs keep vigil. I have kept one

promise, to leave you the one thing I own,
you whom I loved first and last, my poetry.
We are here for one night. Tomorrow, *The Flight* will be gone.

VIII

The bowsprit, the arrow, the longing, the lunging heart!
The search for that island which heals us with harbours
and a guiltless horizon! Where the leaf's shadow does not
injure the sand. There are so many islands anyway.
There were so many islands, all breeding from my hand.
There was a whole mythology of roiled waters
waiting for my hand, and the sea said: "Shabine,
take the salt from the rotting wharves, the fresh rancour
of quay-side quarrels between captains and vendors,
the rime-crusted cussing of Bridgetown's spider-men
jammed in dock-traffic, and the serene naming
when the man-o'-war passes like a scissors floating
"ciseau la mer," by a black Saint Lucian boy.
The Caribbean choked with the dead, boy, that's right.
For when I went diving under sunshot water,
whose ceiling came rippling like a green silk tent
(and I never told this to anybody before)
I saw first the corals, brain, fire, and dead men's fingers,
and then the dead men. That the white sand was bones
of dead niggers from Dakar to San Salvador.

But I was afraid of poetry and its penalties,
since school, those books packed thick with pain!
Madness, self-murder and drink, I saw that these
happened to greater, undeserving men.
But I dreamt that I entered Westminster Abbey
with proper immigrant awe, seeking half my ancestors
among the stone brows with their ponderous frowns
baffled by the immortal absence of a body,
but when I said, I think I'm a poet too, sirs,
not one of those mighty marbles would acknowledge me,
you'd think that they were the living, and I was
the dead. So the scale of what I had undertaken
tired and terrified me. I now had no home,
and no destination but the star-apple kingdom
of that branched sky from which meteors are shaken
like full fruit. If stars fall, so can cultures,

so will this world. That's how it always was,
on the one hand, Venus, and on the other, Mars.
So it was me alone. When I saw the frozen foam
of the Milky Way, and the horizon flame
like a catching comet, then I too was shaken
by something older than faith, by the black fear
of nothing. But nothing cannot be, and I grew calm,
when, out of nothing, the day-hidden stars,
unbidden, but abiding, came.

Editor's note: These poems appear in somewhat different form in Mr. Walcott's latest
book, *The Star-Apple Kingdom* (1979).

TOWARD A WORLD
BLACK LITERATURE & COMMUNITY

MELVIN DIXON

WRITERS OF THE AFRICAN DIASPORA CONTINUALLY EXPLORE THE IDEA
of racial community for theme, imagery, and heroic characterization.
Their works, brought to international attention through the French
and English languages, define man in relation to his particular ethnic,
regional and national identity, and examine the universal conflict
between the individual and society. Through the literature of the
Harlem Renaissance, the Negritude movement in Africa, the In-
digenist movement in Haiti and throughout the Caribbean, modern
black writers have identified the broad frontiers of human need and
racial progress. Their themes assess the role of the artist within
society and the contribution of black peoples to world culture. This
thematic concern rejects provincial colonial mentality, expands the
goals and dimensions of black life. The quest for community ex-
pressed in these New Negro movements offers a point of cultural
contact and comparison in the literature and contemporary issues
which shaped world black writing during the past fifty years.

In the United States, southern blacks migrated north hoping to
share in America's new industrial growth, national identity, and the
international success of Allied victory in World War I. North Ameri-
can blacks helped to forge one of the most energetic periods in their
cultural history. The Harlem Renaissance generated new racial
awareness and encomium as defenses against political disfranchise-
ment, lynchings, and early Jim Crow legislation.

Almost simultaneously, Caribbean populations, particularly in
Haiti, suffered similar discrimination under American occupation
which began in 1915. Haitian intellectuals, notably Emile Roumer,
Jean Price-Mars, Jacques Roumain, Daniel Heurtelou, found a
new strength in their identity as black Haitians face to face with a
common white intruder. Through their patriotism and spirit of
resistance, they became interested in folklore and native traditions,
"studied passionately the customs, beliefs, popular tales, and dis-
covered them intact and living well among the Haitian peasants."[1]
In 1927 these writers founded *La Revue Indigène*. Of the founders,

it was Jacques Roumain who became friends with Langston Hughes and studied at Columbia University in 1932. For years thereafter, even when the review ceased publication, Roumain was to play a "capital role as liaison between the Afro-American renaissance and the indigenist movement."[2]

The Harlem Renaissance was brought to a close by the Depression in 1930. But that year in Paris, a Dr. Sajons of Haiti and sisters Andrée and Paulette Nardal of Martinique founded *La Revue du Monde Noir*, which diffused the ideas of the Renaissance and the Indigenist movement to the black French-speaking world. Paulette Nardal, a student of English, translated many Renaissance poets for the magazine, and, encouraged by René Maran, began translating Alain Locke's *New Negro* into French. Traveling writers offered other means of mutual contact. In the salon of the Nardal sisters, black American writers "met with those who went on to found the negritude movement."[3] Maran himself became a close friend of Alain Locke and opened his Paris home to Countee Cullen, Claude McKay, James Weldon Johnson, Langston Hughes, and others.

La Revue du Monde Noir ceased publication after six issues. Then in 1932 Martiniquan students began *Légitime Défense,* which exposed West Indian middle-class assimilation, its corruption and prejudice, its "treason towards its own race." With one stroke the West Indian literary tradition, built upon conscious imitation of European writers, was discarded. The tiny brochure caused an enormous sensation and was prohibited almost immediately. Two years later *L'Etudiant Noir* was started by other university students grouped around Léopold Senghor of Senegal, Aimé Césaire of Martinique, and Léon Damas of French Guyana. The magazine attacked cultural assimilation and voiced the grievances of many blacks. The writers rejected France, indeed all of Europe, as a cultural model and encouraged black intellectuals to examine native cultures as well as the impact of the African presence throughout the world.

By 1935 black writers on all three continents were claiming their legitimate defense against cultural exclusion and isolation. They expressed the shared assumptions of racial progress which made ethnic and regional groups cohesive. They changed the course of modern literature by demanding that the African voice be heard. In the span of twenty-five years, 1920-1945, a world black literature was fashioned that cemented the identity of the New Negro and an international community as his audience. Moreover, these movements laid intellectual foundations for the struggles for African independence in our time.[4] My discussion of the theme of community in modern black fiction emphasizes three novels which examine parameters for this world black community and the moral value it sustains for the ultimate freedom of the individual *and* his race. The novels, broadly representative of the three literary movements, share themes and influences: *Batouala* (1921), by René Maran; *Banjo* (1929), by Claude McKay; *Masters of the Dew* (1945), by Jacques Roumain.[5] Each of these novels questions the black man's relationship to Western civilization, exposes the destruction of African and New World societies by imperial Europe or America, and posits some alternative whereby blacks may find themselves again in a community of free men.

One of the most controversial works of its time, *Batouala* received the Prix Goncourt in 1921. The recognition accorded Maran was mixed, yet it legitimized black literary expression on an international scale. The wide circulation of the book meant that a larger audience had access to Maran's work and that of other black writers in the future. It could also provide an arena for shared literary expression. *Batouala* initiated dialogue across cultural and linguistic lines.

The novel depicts tribal life during the colonial administration of French Equatorial Africa. Maran, a native of Martinique and reared in France, worked for the administration. He "learned the language of the country and often listened to the natives talk among themselves without their knowing. . . . He understood that the complaints of the natives weren't unfounded."[6] Maran gave voice to those complaints in his preface:

> Civilization, civilization, pride of the Europeans, and their burying-ground for innocents; . . .
> You build your kingdom on corpses. Whatever you may want, whatever you may do, you act with deceit. At your sight, gushing tears and screaming pain. You are the might which exceeds right. You aren't a torch, but an inferno. Everything you touch, you consume. . . . (pp. 8-9)

From 1921 until 1938, when Maran published the definitive edition of *Batouala*, and even thereafter, he incurred the wrath of many French critics and the admiration of younger African writers. The novel, itself, argues no polemic. The author comments: "It doesn't even try to explain; it states facts. It doesn't show indignation; it records" (pp. 7-8). But in its precise detail of everyday life in this African region, the novel contrasts the African world view to the European one. For the first time from a black perspective, as even Ernest Hemingway was quick to acknowledge, we "smell the smells of the village . . . eat its food . . . see the white man as the black man sees him."[7]

In the traditional society of Ubangui-Shari, Batouala, the chief, calls his villages together to celebrate the feast of Ga'nza, the ceremony of circumcision of the boys and excision of the girls. As the village prepares for the feast, Bissibi'ngui, a young warrior, tries to seduce Yassigui'ndja, Batouala's first and most prized wife. They consummate their affair publicly in the dance of love which draws the entire region into one carnal ritual. The celebration is suddenly broken by the white commandant who has forbidden the ceremony, the sudden death of Batouala's father during the uproar, and Batouala's fierce jealousy at finding himself cuckolded. Although perversions are permitted by custom in the Ga'nza celebration, Batouala is enraged by his wife's public infidelity. Enduring his grief alone, he then plots revenge against Bissibi'ngui, which results, ironically, in his own death.

"That is all there is to the story," Hemingway's review continued. "But when you have read it, you have been Batouala, and that means it is a great novel." Fortunately, there is more to this "véritable roman negre" than Batouala himself or the plot of an African love story. Although the novel is concerned with a fictional representation of tribal life and custom, it also examines what threatens to destroy that life: the younger Bissibi'ngui who deposes Batouala, and the colonial whites who contribute to the breakup of traditional society. According to Batouala, African life has its own subtle value: "To live from day to day without remembering yesterday, without worrying about tomorrow, not anticipating: that is excellence, that is perfection" (p. 17). The whites, Batouala argues, "have made the zest for living disappear in the places where they have taken up residence" (p. 72). The changes European colonization has made in this region are not described with the same haunting impact as in Chinua Achebe's more recent novel *Things Fall Apart*, but the threats to the stable, tradition-bound community are as severe.

Custom is the total experience of life in this community. And Batouala as chief is the guardian. "He remained faithful to the traditions which his ancestors had passed on to him, but didn't go deeply into anything outside of that. If anything were in opposition to custom, all reasoning was useless" (p. 23). By their intrusion, colonial whites defy tradition. The Africans grumble, "we should have massacred the first one who came to our land" (p. 70), and yearn for the times when they knew peace, not oppression:

> They used to be happy in other times, before the arrival of the "boundjous." Working a little, and only for oneself, eating, drinking and sleeping; at long intervals some bloody ceremonies when they took out the livers of the dead in order to eat their courage and to absorb it—those were the only tasks of the blacks in other times, before the arrival of the whites. (p. 76)

Intrusion upon these rituals and beliefs signals the probable end to traditional society. Also, the violation of tradition on the part of native Africans may suggest how obsolete those values have become in the modern era. The plight of Yassigui'ndja and Bissibi'ngui indicates this second level of conflict.

Yassigui'ndja defies tradition when she is blamed for the sudden death of Batouala's father and refuses to submit to trial by ritual. According to custom, man was born to live. "If one dies it must be because someone has made a 'yorro' or uttered incantations" (p. 98). Batouala's other wives, envious of her beauty and position, denounce Yassigui'ndja. She asks her lover Bissibi'ngui to leave the village with her. He would find work as a "tourougou," an agent of the commandant, and collect taxes from the other chiefs. Yassigui'ndja implores:

> Let's leave! I don't want to take poison. I don't want to plunge my hands into boiling water. I don't want my loins to shrivel under the bite of a hot iron. I don't want my eyes to die. I don't want to die. Young, healthy, robust, I can live for many more rainy seasons. (pp. 107-8)

Just as Yassigui'ndja is implicated in the death of Batouala's father, one expects that Bissibi'ngui will be similarly implicated when Batouala dies from the wounds of a panther during a hunt—a hunt which, according to custom, is the struggle between the two men over Yassigui'ndja. The adulterous lovers must atone for their infidelity and probable murder in a ritual determined by the community to uphold its morality. Colonization, however, undercuts the process through which a divisive tribe might heal itself by offering an alternative identity for the victims. Instead of subjecting themselves to a ritual which may cause their death or vindication, Yassigui'ndja and Bissibi'ngui opt to leave the community for jobs as agents of the colonizer. Thus at the moment of Batouala's death, which is the symbolic tragedy of traditional African civilization, the lovers discover individuality, a concept alien to traditional African thought: "Alone in the world and masters of their destiny, nothing could prevent them from belonging to each other from now on" (p. 148). As Batouala rises feebly from his deathbed in one last gesture of revenge, but falls finally to the ground "heavily, as a large tree falls," Yassigui'ndja and Bissibi'ngui have "already fled in the night" (p. 149).

More surprising than the decline of African society or the characters' search for individuality is that these individuals will carry out the destruction of African life which colonial whites have only initiated. Outcasts such as Bissibi'ngui serve colonial interests. He resolves:

> Let the hunts finish. Right after that, I shall go to Bangui to join the
> tourougou service, to become a militiaman as the whites say, with a
> rifle, cartridges, and a big knife hung on his left side by a leather belt.
> He wears a red tarboosh. He is paid every month. And every Sunday
> . . . he goes to enjoy a little leave in the villages, where women admire
> him.
> . . . instead of paying taxes, it is we who help collect them. We do
> that by ransacking both the taxable villages and those who have paid
> their due. We have the rubber worked and recruit the men . . .
> Such is the work of the militiaman. . . . Those little satisfactions
> make the tourougou's life sweet, pleasant, easy, indeed delightful,
> even more so because the commandants hardly know the language of
> the country they are administering, that is to say, our country and our
> language. (p. 108)

Having access to their village's language and customs and the
colonial regime as well, Bissibi'ngui and Yassigui'ndja become mas-
ters of their destiny, yet betray the communal values of their African
home.

Maran's exposé is tempered by his non-African background and
his rather full assimilation of European culture. But working for
the colonial administration for thirteen years, he was able to observe
both traditional society and the destructive influence of the French
regime. His characterization of Batouala and the young lovers is
ambivalent. The novel exposes the abuses of colonization, but
finally, not colonization itself; it appeals to the "equity and justice
of the French community" to correct those abuses.[8] In the novel's
intended objectivity, conflicts are presented without neat resolution
and neither character is more heroic than the other. Nevertheless,
the conflicts outlined (traditional Africa v. modern colonial civili-
zation, adulterous love v. tribal custom and fidelity) had a tremen-
dous impact on black writers everywhere, many of whom shared
Maran's ambivalence for both Africa and imperial Europe, such as
Countee Cullen in his poem, "Heritage." But there is little wonder
why younger African and Afro-American writers would rally around
Maran: "He was the first black, in France, to dare tell the truth
about certain methods of colonization, to reveal the true mentality of
blacks and what they thought of European occupation."[9]

The tensions of custom, community, and international politics in
the novel initiated a dialogue among black writers throughout the
world. W. E. B. Du Bois, writing in the landmark Renaissance an-
thology, *The New Negro*, stated that: "Maran's attack on France . . .
marks an era. Never before have Negroes criticized the work of the
French in Africa."[10] Charles Chesnutt commented that while Maran

"is not a U.S. Negro, I think his triumph is one of which all those who share the blood of his race . . . may well be proud."[11] And Léopold Senghor, one of the founding poets in the Negritude movement, wrote, "it is only with René Maran that the West Indian writers freed themselves from docile imitation of the Metropole."[12] Black writers could no longer escape conditions in Africa or the policies of Europe. Maran paved the way for writers of the diaspora to deal realistically with their past and racial heritage; he became a link "between the English and French speaking black universe between the two world wars."[13]

For the writers of the Harlem Renaissance, *Batouala* had special significance. Countee Cullen's poem, "The Dance of Love," included in his first collection, *Color* (1925), was subtitled in parentheses, "After reading Rene Maran's 'Batouala.' " The poem begins:

> All night we danced upon our windy hill,
> Your dress a cloud of tangled midnight hair,
> And love was much too much for me to wear
> My leaves; the killer roared above his kill,
> But you danced on, and when some star would spill
> Its red and white upon you whirling there,
> I sensed a hidden beauty in the air;
> Though you danced on, my heart and I stood still.

Cullen draws from the ritual described by Maran in order to voice his own sensuality mingled with an American puritan ethic. Through the dance the speaker is united with his love: "We flung ourselves upon our hill and slept."[14] Cullen had a thorough knowledge of French and most likely read the novel when it first appeared. Another Renaissance francophile, Jessie Fauset, praised the novel in two book reviews which appeared in the *Crisis* in 1922. Claude McKay, who spent most of the years attributed to the Renaissance abroad, frequented Maran's salon. The exchange there may have led McKay to comment, almost prophetically, in 1932 before the appearance of *L'Etudiant Noir* that: "Negroid Africa will produce in time its own modern poets and artists peculiar to its soil."[15] Maran's importance for McKay can also be seen in *Banjo*, published in 1929. The protagonist, Ray, a Haitian, meets a Martiniquan student with aristocratic pretensions. When Ray questions him about *Batouala* the student replies that its sale was banned in his country, yet hastens to add "it was a naughty book, very strong, very strong" in order to defend the censure. This incident further educates Ray about the differences among West Indians and helps him to overcome them in his own progress toward racial awareness.

Ray's racial and cultural education is the unifying thematic element in *Banjo*. The novel, subtitled "a story without a plot," centers around the picaresque adventures of beachcombing vagabonds in Marseilles. The leader, if there is in fact *one* leader, is Lincoln Agrippa Daily, otherwise known as Banjo because of the instrument he plays. The novel outlines a man's search for a community which will unite the exotic, spontaneous impulses of life with the more distanced, sober, intellectual reflections. The two main characters, Banjo and Ray, embody these qualities respectively. Through Banjo, Ray is initiated into a community composed of the poor black rejects from Europe, Africa and America. These are the men of the Quartier Revervé, affectionately known as the "Ditch." Through the unity established among them, a composite black hero emerges, who, like Ray, is able to define his relationship to an African cultural past and a New World future.

To understand the full extent of Ray's detachment from his race, we must go to McKay's first novel, *Home to Harlem* (1928). Here we first meet Ray, a Haitian student, working his way through school as a pullman car waiter. He befriends Jake Brown, army deserter, carefree lover of many women and the good life of Harlem speakeasies. Through the friendship between them, McKay sets up a dialectic between civilization and primitivism, and the two characters, as in *Banjo*, represent these aspects respectively. Within Ray, McKay treats the problem of cultural dualism. Ray feels attracted and repelled by the spontaneity of life that Jake enjoys so naturally. Ray's education distances him from the common lot of black Americans, and his race distances him from full participation in the mainstream culture. A night of drinking on a pullman run reveals the contrast between Jake and Ray and Ray's interior distress:

> Jake fell asleep as soon as his head touched the dirty pillow. Below him, Ray lay in his bunk, tormented by bugs and the snoring cooks. The low-burning gaslight flickered and flared upon the shadows. The young man lay under the untellable horror of a dead-tired man who wills to sleep and cannot. (p. 151)

The center of Ray's malaise is his inability to realize a source of kinship with blacks in America:

> Ray fixed his eyes on the offensive bug-bitten bulk of the chief. These men claimed kinship with him. They were black like him. Man and nature had put them in the same race. He ought to love them and feel them (if they felt anything). He ought to if he had a shred of social morality in him. They were all chained together and he was counted as one link. Yet he loathed every soul in that great barrack-room, except Jake. Race . . . why should he have and love a race?
>
> Race and nations were things like skunks whose smells poisoned

the air of life. Yet civilized mankind reposed its faith and future in their ancient, silted channels. Great races and big nations! There was something mighty inspiriting in being the citizen of a great strong nation . . . Something the black man could never feel nor quite understand. (p. 154)

Exiled from his native Haiti because of American occupation, Ray feels impotent. Part of his bitterness towards American blacks is the extent to which he identifies them with the occupation forces. But Ray must learn that black Americans are oppressed at home by the same power that justifies American imperialism: "He remembered when little Haiti was floundering uncontrolled, how proud he was to be the son of a free nation. He used to feel condescendingly sorry for those poor African natives; superior to ten millions of suppressed Yankee 'coons.' Now he was just one of them and he hated them for being one of them" (p. 155). Through Jake, Ray expands his New World identity.

Ray's dilemma is very close to McKay's. Although much of the novel's exposition comes through Ray's perception—and this is also the case in *Banjo*—he is not simply McKay's mouthpiece. Rather, through Ray, McKay comes to understand himself and other blacks similarly estranged: "My damned white education has robbed me of much of the primitive vitality, the pure stamina, the simple un-swaggering strength of the Jakes of the Negro race."[16]

Ray learns from Jake how to enjoy Harlem in its best and worst character. He must immerse himself in it, down to the bottommost rungs in order to connect with his fullest emotions, however contra-dictory they may be:

Going to Harlem . . . Harlem! How terribly Ray could hate it some-times. Its brutality, gang rowdyism, promiscuous thickness. Its hot desires. But, oh, the rich blood-red color of it! The warm accent of its composite voice, the fruitiness of its laughter, the trailing surprises of its jazz. He had known happiness, too, in Harlem, joy that glowed gloriously upon him like the high-noon sunlight of his tropic island home. (p. 267)

Ray's ambivalence about Harlem, about being black in a color-conscious Western civilization, helps him resolve to become a writer. By observing lives which reflect upon his own, and giving that pain a voice, perhaps Ray would realize a community to which he belonged. Unlike Jake, Ray "drank in more of life than he could distill into active animal living. Maybe that was why he felt he had to write" (p. 265). Ray's full identity as a writer emerges in *Banjo*. Jake is replaced by Banjo, "a great vagabond of lowly life," who helps Ray articulate his identity in a new black community.

Banjo is not merely a continuation of bawdy Harlem set in a foreign port town. Here the vagabonds come from all parts of the world, and rather than lean on national identity (as the partying blacks in New York do), these men rely on their basic survival instincts and the brotherhood which poverty and exile bring. In the Ditch, the men survive best in groups where they might be fed by the cook on a docked ship, discover a wine keg, play music, or share living quarters. Alone, they risk barroom brawls, venereal disease, tuberculosis, murder by an angry prostitute or her pimp. Man's search for community in his most extreme need binds the characters of the Ditch. In this "international beehive," Ray finds blacks not too different from himself, from the lowest vagabond to the most assimilated Martiniquan. The national identity as a Haitian which set him apart from Harlem blacks, Jake, Zeddy and Congo Rose, does not apply in the Ditch. And Ray discovers how all blacks are unfortunate waifs of Western civilization, but in their abandonment and poverty there is life, color, music, language. Ray touches all of these:

> In no other port had he ever seen congregated such a picturesque variety of Negroes. Negroes speaking civilized tongues, Negroes speaking all the African dialects, black Negroes, brown Negroes, yellow Negroes. It was as if every country of the world had sent representatives drifting into Marseilles. A great vagabond host of jungle-like Negroes trying to scrape a temporary existence from the macadamized surface of this great Provençal port. (p. 68)

In the Ditch of Marseilles, "Europe's best back door," that great port along the Mediterranean where the European and African worlds meet, Ray and Banjo, "a child of the Cotton belt," join up with Senegalese Dengel, West Indian Malty Avis, Ginger, and the Arab-Oriental mulatto Latnah. Banjo's love for music and his dream of forming an orchestra (itself symbolic of a unity of disparate instruments) provides order to the chaos of bumming and some semblance of plot. The love of wine, music, food, money and adventures bring the characters together in a common search for each of these. Just as dance and ceremony consolidated Batouala's chiefdom, barroom dancing and musical improvisation join the men and women of the Ditch:

> "Beguin," "jelly-roll," "burru," "bombé," no matter what the name may be, Negroes are never so beautiful as when they do that gorgeous sublimation of the primitive African sex feeling. In its thousand varied patterns, depending so much on individual rhythm, so little

on formal movement, this dance is the key to the African rhythm of life . . . (p. 105)

Ray looks to find in his writing the same binding rhythmic force of the dance. He discovers that story-telling, in its most folkloric manner, unites the men of the Ditch as much as music and dance when they gather to trade yarns. As Ray becomes quite fully the writer/artist of this composite ethnic community, he finds his literary voice:

> . . . . If I am a real story-teller, I won't worry about the complexion of those who listen and those who don't. I'll just identify myself with those who are really listening and tell my story . . . a good story, in spite of those who tell it and those who hear it, is like good ore that you might find in any soil—Europe, Asia, Africa, America. The world wants the ore and gets it by a thousand men scrambling and fighting, digging and dying for it. The world gets its story the same way. (p. 115)

Oral verbal communication, like music and dance, assumes a classic integrative value in this community. These cultural forms which unite the beach boys inform Ray, as well, of the false, unnecessary tension between what is civilized and what is primitive. For Ray, Banjo and the beach boys are primitive in that they follow their instinct and natural *joie de vivre*. The story within this continual celebration of life is Ray's initiation into the primitive side of himself which he has suppressed, in part, for intellectual achievement. Through Banjo, the dispossessed Africans and the West Indians, Ray learns how civilization will continually oppress and ostracize him. He saves himself by rediscovering his composite racial identity. From this confrontation, largely within himself, and his friendship with the beach boys, Ray can assert himself in the argument with the fully assimilated Martiniquan student towards the end of the novel:

> You must judge civilization by its general attitude toward primitive peoples, and not by the exceptional cases. You can't get away from the Senegalese and other black Africans any more than you can from the fact that our forefathers were slaves. . . . We educated Negroes are talking a lot about a racial renaissance. And I wonder how we're going to get it. On one side we're up against the world's arrogance—a mighty cold hard white stone thing. On the other the great sweating army—our race. It's the common people, you know, who furnish the bone and sinew and salt of any race or nation. In the modern race of life we're merely beginners. If this renaissance we're talking about is going to be more than a sporadic and scabby thing, we'll have to get down to our racial roots to create it. (p. 200)

And when the student refuses to go "back to savagery," Ray declares: "Getting down to our native roots and building up from our own people . . . is not savagery. It is culture." (p. 200)

What Ray discovers through the vagabonds, McKay himself discovered through years of wandering. But once in Marseilles, as it had been in North Africa, "it was a relief [for him] to live in among a great gang of black and brown humanity. . . . It was good to feel the strength and distinction of a group and the assurance of belonging to it."[17] But McKay never relinquished those traits which made him unique: his essential cultural dualism, which, favorably, is a peculiarity among people of all New World societies due to the cultural syncretism between African, Indian, and European civilizations out of which the New World was born. McKay wrote: "Whatever may be the criticism implied in my writing of Western Civilization, I do not regard myself as a stranger but as a child of it. . . . I am as conscious of my new-world birthright as of my African origin, being aware of the one and its significance in my development as much as I feel the other emotionally."[18]

Through the culture of the common people Ray distills from this great variety, he learns how to survive. He takes from the Ditch what will strengthen him and his art. He leaves with Banjo at the close of the novel for parts unknown. But an important change has taken place. Ray has found himself by recognizing his birthright:

> The Africans gave him a positive feeling of wholesome contact with racial roots. They made him feel that he was not merely an unfortunate accident of birth, but that he belonged to a race weighed, tested, and poised in the universal scheme. They inspired him with confidence in them. Short of extermination by the Europeans, they were a safe people, protected by their own indigenous culture [and] . . . defended by the richness of their fundamental racial values. (p. 320)

McKay has reversed our notion of the Ditch as the bottommost rung of society by imbuing it with worthy values of community, brotherhood, and regeneration. Ray personifies a composite hero drawn from Africa, America, and the Caribbean. We can well imagine him as a latter day Bissibi'ngui, who, having rebelled against the strictures of traditional African society and experiencing the negative results of colonization, finally rejects imperial Europe and its label of inferiority. Perhaps this broad theme in *Banjo* led Du Bois to find in it an "international philosophy of the Negro race."[19]
race."[19]

Continuing our thematic study of the community and its hero we shall view Manuel Jean-Joseph, the protagonist of Jacques Roumain's *Masters of the Dew*,[20] as an extension of Ray. The hero learns the values of community and racial progress abroad (Roumain was educated in Paris, Switzerland, Germany, and Spain; Manuel worked as a laborer in Cuba) and returns home. He engages in a spectacular mission of redemption for the individual and his community—a theme of exile and return that nourishes both man and nation.

Complex individual fate and the problem of human redemption are central to Roumain's novel. The author argues that man must fulfill the fate which both his religion and his community have revealed to him in order to become a master of his land, his people, and himself. Manuel Jean-Joseph's destiny leads him back to his native Haiti, after fifteen years in the cane fields of Cuba, to find a source of water to irrigate the desolate fields in his village. In fulfilling this mission, Manuel saves his community. And in his final martyrdom, he points the way to both an individual and collective salvation.

Roumain reveals this theme by presenting a compact synthesis of the political and the religious life in Haiti, and embodying it in the character and spirit of Manuel. The hero emerges as a spiritual agent of social change and moral redemption. He is both man and god, sufferer and redeemer. Manuel and his community undergo a symbolic *rite de passage* from an individual to a group consciousness for liberation. Moreover, Manuel is the medium through which this liberation is achieved.

Haitian writers have often used religious iconography to express the spirit of their people. There, Christianity and traditional African religions fuse into the national religion of Voudou, which remains basically African in its language and mythology. According to ethnologist Jean Price-Mars, one of the first Haitian scholars to study indigenous culture, Voudou borrows its sacred language from Dahomey, Nigeria and the Congo just as the Catholic religion borrows its canon from Rome.[21] Similarly, Haitian literature develops as a syncretistic neo-African literature. In the literal and figurative meaning of the work, we can identify African beliefs. The characters in Roumain's novel can be viewed in light of this symbolic frame in order to illuminate the spiritual meaning in the narrative. This method helps to identify *Masters of the Dew* as an allegory of Haitian folk religion, and as Roumain's greatest literary achievement. Manuel embodies the spirit and destiny of his people in order to reveal to them the path they must take to freedom from an otherworldly Christianity that enslaves and impoverishes them.

Turning to the novel itself, we find that Roumain's goal is not the familiar Marxist or Western dialectic common in religion and politics, but a synthesis. Although Roumain became a communist and leader of the Haitian Communist party following the withdrawal of American occupation forces in the mid-1930's, Roumain used his first contact with Haitian peasants through the indigenist movement as a way of adapting his leftist ideology to the culture he describes. Manuel, as both man and loa, peasant and politician, becomes representative of indigenous folk tradition and political self-consciousness. The fusion of these two ideologies is necessary for collective advancement.

Misery and boredom establish the opening scene in *Masters of the Dew*. Manuel's parents have resigned themselves to a life of extreme poverty and spiritual decline. The earth has dried up, money has become scarce, and rain will not come. Their prayers to a remote Christian God are useless for Bienaimé because "so many poor creatures call continually upon the Lord that it makes a big bothersome noise. When the Lord hears it, he yells, 'What the hell's all that?' and stops up his ears. Yes, he does, leaving man to shift for himself" (p. 23).

In the opinion of these peasants, God has not only abandoned man, but created suffering in the first place. The only hope that remains for the mother, Délira, is that Manuel will return home before she dies. Here her prayers are not to a Christian God, but to Papa Legba. She entreats: "O Master of the crossroads, open to him a road without danger" (p. 34). About the same time the village neighbor, Clairemise, has a dream which reveals "a black man, a very old man. He was standing on the road where it crosses the path of macaw trees, and he said to me, 'Go and find Délira.' . . . Maybe it was Papa Legba" (p. 46). Upon Roumain's suggestion of divine intervention, the manner in which African gods enter the lives of men through dreams, Manuel returns home.

He enters the village strolling "toward a mound crowned with macaw trees . . . he wanted to embrace the countryside from above, to see the plain spread out before him and glimpse, through the trees, the thatched roofs and irregular fields and gardens" (p. 35). At once, Manuel reaches the crossroad outside his village which is guarded spiritually by Legba. Symbolically, it is only at crossroads such as this where the human and the divine axes meet that contact with the divinities takes place. It is here, perhaps, that Manuel meets Legba. Manuel notices that he has forgotten nothing of his country as familiar odors greet him. All the barriers in nature appear to open. He is one with the land.

Legba, in Haitian mythology, is "the interpreter of the gods, who translates the requests and prayers of men into their language. In Haiti he has the function of opening the barriére that separates men from the loas."[22] This description of Legba as intermediary is perhaps our most important link between the literal character of

Manuel as a man, and the more symbolic representation of him as a god. As the novel develops, Manuel experiences an apotheosis. He interprets the will of the gods to his fellows, opens the barrier between the two feuding families in the village, and establishes a unity among men and a corresponding unity with the gods.

Manuel teaches his first important lesson to his family. He chastises his mother, Délira, for mistreating the land:

> . . . the earth is a battle day by day without truce, to clear the land, to plant, to weed and water it until the harvest comes. Then one morning you see your ripe fields spread out before you under the dew and you say—whoever you are—'*Me—I'm master of the dew!*' and your heart fills with pride. But the earth's just like a good woman: if you mistreat her, she revolts. I see that you have cleared the hills of trees. The soil is naked, without protection. It's the roots that make friends with the soil, and hold it. It's the mango tree, the oak, the mahogany that give it rainwater when it's thirsty and shade it from the noonday heat. That's how it is. . . . (p. 45)

Man has mistreated, indeed raped nature for material benefit. Now she revolts with soil erosion and dry spells. Manuel observes, "It's not God who betrays us. We betray the soil and receive his punishment: drought and poverty and desolation" (p. 45).

This revelation is one step in the spiritual possession of Manuel. It also sets the stage for the redemption of all the peasants through the important discovery of water. Water, in Haitian folklore, is the home of several gods; through it man communes with them. Water is also a symbol of rebirth. Manuel clarifies this message of nature for his community. He tells them it is their duty to respond to nature's warning. They must fulfill their human destiny by becoming masters in their own right. Otherwise they will wither like the weeds and die:

> You pray for rain, you pray for a harvest, you recite the prayers of the saints and the *loas*. But providence—take my word for it—is a man's determination not to accept misfortune, to overcome the earth's bad will every day, to bend the whims of the water to your needs. Then the earth will call you, 'Dear Master.' The water will call you 'Dear Master.' And there's no providence but hard work, no miracles but the fruit of your hands. (p. 54)

Thus directing his community to fulfill its responsibility as a group of workers, "masters," Manuel reaffirms his own commitment to the earth:

> Growing things, my growing things! To you I say 'Honor!' You must

answer, 'Respect,' so that I may enter. You're my house, you're my
country. Growing things, I say, vines of my woods. I am planted in
this soil, I am rooted in this earth. To all that grows, I say 'Honor.'
Answer 'Respect,' so that I may enter. (pp. 55-56)

Finding water to irrigate the village is a matter of life or death, sal-
vation or destruction. Manuel's mission is to lead his people not
only to a spring, but to a renewed communion with the earth that
will guarantee the community's survival.

On the religious level, the search for a spiritual community is
also important. It is described within the actual Voudou ceremony.
In the ritual of Thanksgiving for Manuel's safe arrival, the houngan
becomes possessed by Legba and says, "I see that your affairs are
going badly with this drought. But that will change, that will pass.
. . . I, Legba, I'm master of this crossroad. I'll help my Creole children
find the right road. They will leave behind this road of misery"
(p. 66). But this message only indicates the first level of struggle.
More is required. Another spirit, Ogoun, the fearful loa, "god of the
blacksmiths and god of killers" addresses Manuel directly:

> *Bolada Kimalada! O Kimalada!*
> *We'll dig the canal! Ago!*
> *We'll dig a canal, I say! Ago ye*
> *The vein is open, the blood flows.*
> *The vein is open, the blood flows! Ho!*
> *Bolada Kimalada! O Kimalada!* (p. 70)

Manuel's fate is sealed. He is the leader with a two-fold purpose.
He accomplishes the first by discovering an underground source
beneath a fig tree, but the second task is more costly. He must
reunite his village already split by a long and violent family feud in
order to get everyone's cooperation in digging the canal.

The success of Manuel's mission depends on each man doing his
part. Through his love for Annaise, Manuel joins the two feuding
families, but their union is a dangerous one. It costs Manuel his life
at the hands of Gervilen, who attacks him at night. Dying of his
wounds, Manuel learns the final painful lesson needed to unify his
people, to open the barriers among themselves and between them
and the gods: "You've offered sacrifices to the loas. The blood of
chickens and young goats you've offered to make the rain fall. That
hasn't done any good—because what counts is the sacrifice of a man,
the blood of a man" (p. 158). He admonishes his mother to tell the
village leader where water is, but he never tells her the name of his
assassin which would only continue the feud. Death is the last
barrier that Manuel breaks open; he secures reconciliation in his
secret so that "life can start all over again, so that day can break

on the dew" (p. 158). He tells his family to "sing my mourning with a song of *coumbite*," which is the system of cooperative labor that will bring prosperity to the village.

Manuel's martyr death gives the members of his community new responsibilities for maintaining unity. Délira delivers to the village leaders information on where the water is. Annaise's duty is to bear Manuel's child. "He loved me and I loved him," she tells Délira. "Our paths crossed." Through the unity of family and village, Manuel has secured his individual redemption and immortality. And each man's further fulfillment of his individual fate becomes the prerequisite for the redemption and liberation of the entire community. Manuel has opened the path. At the crossroad of life and death, Manuel, as loa, has achieved a unity between man and the gods. He now offers that same harmony, implicit in the continual pattern of life, death, and immortality to his countrymen. They, too, must be saved. The ending of *Masters of the Dew* is an important beginning for all New World societies.

The pattern of identity we find developing from Batouala and Bissibi'ngui, to Ray, Jake, and Banjo, and finally to Manuel, is indicative of the historical development of world African-American literature. *Batouala* did much to free francophonic African and Caribbean writers from a colonial mentality, as *Banjo* did by demanding a broader moral and cultural awareness from writers of the Harlem Renaissance. Similarly, Jacques Roumain related much of his European education and Marxist ideology to very specific problems in his native land as the artist/hero returns home.

In the character of Manuel, African man has reached a new synthesis—a spiritual harmony in the New World which is essential to sustaining the African-American way of life. He has achieved immortality through the collective advancement of his village community. He has achieved a unity with the divine forces so that the individual and the community together are redeemed.

Manuel's character, as it represents this synthesis, also represents the syncretistic nature of neo-African literature and philosophy—a fusion of African thought and New World cultural forms. For Jacques Roumain, the emphasis is on the more dominant African world view which the peasants guard in their religion and folklore where European influences tread very cautiously; or, for McKay, the lore of the low-life robust characters in Vieux Port, Marseilles.

Manuel Jean-Joseph is a new heroic figure—a revolutionary defined in a new language and symbolic structure beyond the immediate African tradition which identified Batouala or European colonization that attracted Bissibi'ngui and that rejected Ray. In the figure of Manuel, the hero has returned to the life and lore of the common people through which he saves himself and them.

The thematic development which encompasses these characters, their respective quests and initiations, leads us to an important assessment of the idea of community in world black literature. Out of the historical movements already cited, each writer has related literature as a cultural expression from incidents which have raised the level of consciousness of the victims: whether American occupation in the Caribbean, French imperialism in Africa, or the two world wars. Each event necessitated a global vision for the writers to assess change and respond to it in order for the black presence to become, in the words of Alain Locke, a "conscious contributor" to world culture. Writers of the African diaspora have defined their specific characteristics which distinguish the writer and his society. By also engaging readers most intensely on the tribal, familial, or regional plane of identity, they have touched universal concerns. And black writers continue to define particular national contributions to a world literature—be it African for Ousmane Sembene, Camara Laye, Chinua Achebe; Caribbean for René Depestre, Derek Walcott, George Lamming, Wilson Harris, Andrew Salkey; American for Ralph Ellison, James Baldwin, Ernest Gaines, Paule Marshall—through which the parameters of community, ethnicity and morality are further enriched, and men continue to be free.

NOTES

[1] Lilyan Kesteloot, *Les Ecrivains noirs de la langue française: naissance d'une littérature*, 4me ed. (1963; rpt. Bruxelles: Université Libre de Bruxelles, 1971), p. 35. This important study has recently been translated into English by Ellen Conroy Kennedy as *Black Writers in French: A Literary History of Negritude* (Philadelphia: Temple University Press, 1974). Quotations included in the present text are my own translations.

[2] Michel Fabre, unpublished article, "*La Revue Indigène* et le Mouvement Nouveau Noir," p. 11. I am indebted to Professor Fabre for allowing me to read and quote from this forthcoming article. See also Naomi Garret, *The Renaissance of Haitian Poetry* (Paris: Présence Africaine, 1963), pp. 106-117. Garret quotes at length an interview with Roumain by Antonio Vieux, "Entre Nous: Jacques Roumain," *La Revue Indigène*, September, 1927, p. 106, in which Roumain describes being a citizen of the world and sharing the reciprocal influences in literatures of the twentieth century. He mentions "une florissante poésie nègre. Et originale," in the United States. "Countree Cullins [sic] par exemple."

[3] Kesteloot, *Intellectual Origins of the African Revolution* (Washington, D.C.: Black Orpheus Press, 1972), p. 29.

[4] *Ibid.* Kesteloot noted previously that the writers of the Harlem Renaissance were the first to express themes of negritude and revolt. And more than the French authors, they were the true fathers of the black cultural renaissance in France. This point, made clear in her earlier work, *Les Ecrivains noirs*, bears upon her tracing the origins of ideas for independence: ". . . cette littérature américaine contient déjà en germes les principaux thèmes de la 'négritude' et, à ce titre, on peut affirmer que les véritables pères de la renaissance culturelle nègre en France ne furent ni les écrivains de la tradition antillaise, ni les poètes surréalistes ou les romanciers français d'entre les deux guerres, mais les auteurs noirs des Etats-Unis: Ils marquerent si vivement nos écrivains dans la mesure où ils prétendent représenter toute une race et lançaient un cri dans lequel tous les noirs se reconnurent, le premier cri de révolte" (p. 64).

[5] Rene Maran, *Batouala*, trans. Barbara Beck and Alexandre Mboukou (1921; rpt. London: Heinemann Educational Books, 1972); Claude McKay, *Banjo* (1929; rpt. New York: Harvest Books, 1957); Jacques Roumain, *Masters of the Dew*, trans. Langston Hughes and Mercer Cook (1947; New York: Collier Books, 1971). Subsequent page references refer to these editions.

[6] Kesteloot, *Les Ecrivains noirs*, p. 84.

[7] *Toronto Star Weekly*, March 25, 1922.

[8] Maryse Conde, rev. of *Batouala*, *Présence Africaine*, 87 (Third Quarter, 1973), pp. 212-213.

[9] Kesteloot, *Les Ecrivains noirs*, p. 84.

[10] William E. B. Du Bois, "The Negro Mind Reaches Out," in *The New Negro*, ed. Alain Locke (1925; rpt. New York: Atheneum, 1975), p. 392.

[11] Unpublished letter, Charles Chesnutt to Benjamin Brawley; March 22, 1922, Spingarn Collection, Howard University. Quoted in Michel Fabre, "René Maran: The New Negro and Negritude," *Phylon*, 36:3 (September, 1975), p. 341. This article details Maran's friendship with Alain Locke and other writers of the Renaissance.

[12] Léopold Sédar Senghor, et al., *Les plus beaux Ecrits de l'Union Française* (Paris, 1947), pp. 256-257.

[13] Fabre, "René Maran," p. 340. For a further discussion of Maran's influence on younger Caribbean, African and Afro-American writers see Fabre, "Autour de Maran," *Présence Africaine*, 86 (Second Quarter, 1973), pp. 165-172, and Kesteloot, *Les Ecrivains noirs*, pp. 83-87.

[14] *Color* (New York: Harper & Row, 1925), p. 19.

[15] McKay, "A Negro Writer to His Critics," in *The Passion of Claude McKay*, ed. Wayne Cooper (New York: Schocken Books, 1973), p. 137. This article appeared in the *New York Herald Tribune Books*, March 6, 1932.

[16] McKay, *A Long Way From Home* (1937; rpt. New York: Harvest Books, 1970), p. 229.

[17] *Ibid.*, p. 277.

[18] McKay, in *Passion*, ed. Cooper, p. 137.

[19] *The Crisis*; July, 1929, p. 234. I am indebted to Michel Fabre for allowing me to read his forthcoming article, "Aesthetics and Ideology in Banjo" in manuscript form, which makes use of Du Bois' and other reviewers' comments, as well as McKay's correspondence to his editor, to illuminate McKay's awareness of his audience when writing *Banjo*.

[20] *Gouverneurs de la rosée* was originally published posthumously in 1945. Langston Hughes' friendship with Roumain began many years earlier when he traveled to Haiti with a letter of introduction from Walter White. See Hughes, *I Wonder as I Wander* (1956; New York: Hill and Wang, 1964), pp. 29-32. Hughes later translated several of Roumain's poems, and Roumain wrote the poem "Langston Hughes" around their common experiences. In addition to translating Roumain's novel with Mercer Cook as *Masters of the Dew*, Hughes translated the poetry of Nicholas Guillen and other black Hispanic poets. He became one of the most salient links between black writing in French, English, and Spanish and their mutual influences.

[21] Jean Price-Mars, "Survivances africaines et dynamisme de la culture noire outre-Atlantique," *Présence Africaine*, 8:10 (1956), p. 277.

[22] Janheinz Jahn, *Muntu: The New African Culture*, trans. Marjorie Green (New York: Grove Press, 1961), p. 42.

I THOUGHT I KNEW THESE PEOPLE:

RICHARD WRIGHT & THE AFRO-AMERICAN LITERARY TRADITION

ROBERT B. STEPTO

ONE OF THE CURIOUS THINGS ABOUT RICHARD WRIGHT IS THAT while there is no question that his best works occupy a prominent place in the Afro-American canon, or that a survey of Afro-American literature would be incomplete without him, many, including myself, find it difficult to describe his place in the Afro-American literary tradition. Part of this feeling may be attributed to a growing concern over how often "canon," "survey," and "tradition" have been casually treated as synonymous terms and unthinkingly inter-changed. We all have distinctive, "working" definitions for these terms, but frequently in our teaching, if not so much in our writing, they are blurred and offered, perhaps in the same discussion or lecture, as three verbal lunges at a single vague but tacitly under-stood idea. When we try to clarify them and teach accordingly, teaching becomes infinitely more difficult, especially when one as-sumes the task of illuminating a tradition as opposed to following blindly dates of publication or of biography, or proceeding along the slightly more arduous path of identifying what are commonly held to be the "best" texts. An author's place in a tradition depends on how he reveals that tradition. It is not simply a matter of when his works were published but also of how they illuminate—and in some cases honor—what has come before and anticipate what will follow. In Afro-American literature particularly, the idea of a tradition in-volves certain questions about the author's posture not only among his fellow writers but also within a larger artistic continuum which, in its exquisite commingling of materials spoken, played, and written, is not the exclusive property or domain of the writer alone. Richard Wright is a fine writer, perhaps a great one; he has influenced, in one way or another, almost every important black writer who has followed

This essay is based on a paper of the same title delivered at the Fifth Biennial Meeting of the American Studies Association, San Antonio, Texas, November 8, 1975.

him. But Wright forces us to face a considerable problem: to what extent may we qualify his place in the artistic tradition and still submit that he is unquestionably a participant in it? I don't pretend to be able to solve this problem, but I can explore three of the questions involved: What was Wright's posture as an author, and how did it correspond with models provided by the tradition? How do his works illuminate or complement those Afro-American texts preceding them? And, what has been his effect on our contemporary literature and culture? In answering these we will be a little closer to understanding Wright's place—or lack of one—in the tradition.

I

Many passages in Wright's works illustrate the issues concerning his authorial posture, but the following one from "I Tried to Be a Communist" seems particularly appropriate, partly because it is autobiographical and partly because it raises all the familiar arguments regarding Wright's posture toward his audience. In the passage, Wright describes what happened when he spoke before a unit meeting of black communists in Chicago (*The God That Failed,* R. Crossman, ed., New York, 1965):

> The meeting started. About twenty Negroes were gathered. The time came for me to make my report and I took out my notes and told them how I had come to join the Party, what few stray items I had published, what my duties were in the John Reed Club. I finished and waited for comment. There was silence. I looked about. Most of the comrades sat with bowed heads. Then I was surprised to catch a twitching smile on the lips of a Negro woman. Minutes passed. The Negro woman lifted her head and looked at the organizer. The organizer smothered a smile (p. 113).

When the organizer finally breaks the silence, Wright recoils from his comments, significantly remarking, "His tone was more patronizing than that of a Southern white man. . . . I thought I knew these people, but evidently I did not" (p. 114). Then Wright informs us:

> During the following days I learned . . . that I . . . had been classified as an *intellectual* . . . that the black Communists in my unit had commented upon my shined shoes, my clean shirt, and the tie I had worn. Above all, my manner of speech had seemed an alien thing to them. . . . 'He talks like a book,' one of the Negro comrades had said. And that was enough to condemn me forever as bourgeois (p. 114).

Wright's ambivalent attitude toward his race and its rituals is amply revealed here, and, while it is not a matter which should enter into our evaluations of his art, it does haunt and becloud our feelings concerning his place in the tradition. Aware of the vivid scenes in *Black*

Boy, wherein racial bonds are shown to be either hypocritical or forms of submission, and recalling as well how he argues in "Blueprint for Negro Literature" (see *Amistad 2*, John Williams and Charles Harris, eds., New York, 1971) for Negro writers to transcend "the nationalist implications of their lives" (p. 9), we are able to comprehend his behavior at the unit meeting but not necessarily approve of it. What brands him an intellectual in this instance is not, strictly speaking, his clean clothes or his articulateness. If this were the case, then most of the black preachers in America—whom Wright termed "sainted devils" (*Ibid.*, p. 15)—would bear the same mark and be cast from church and pulpit. That Wright "talks like a book" is closer to the heart of the matter, for it is Wright's *mode* of articulation, and the related matter of how he did not (or could not) acknowledge kinship with his black brethren while articulating the Party line, which most troubled his black audience and, in turn, bothers us.

Wright's refusal to partake of the essential intra-racial rituals which the situation demanded suggests that he was either unaware of, or simply refused to participate in, those viable modes of speech represented in history by the preacher and orator and in letters by the articulate hero. The question of articulation does not rest exclusively with matters of verbal facility, but, on a higher plane, with the expression of a moral consciousness which is racially-based. And of course this involves a celebration of those honorable codes of conduct among one's kin.

Wright's dilemma reminds one of Du Bois' short story in *The Souls of Black Folk* entitled "Of the Coming of John," in which the "black" John, John Jones, comes home from college to teach school and "rescue" his black townspeople from their "backwardness." His chance to address neighbors and kin occurs at the black Baptist church, and despite his college-honed elocution he fails miserably in his purpose, partly, one imagines, because he attempts to assault those rituals of behavior which the humble building in which he speaks both represents and reinforces. Divorced from the community, condemning blindly all intra-racial codes as formulae for submission, speaking an oddly-cadenced tongue, John Jones fails because of his inarticulateness; and as the story unfolds, he becomes the prototype for Bigger Thomas when he finally expresses himself by bludgeoning the "white" John, John Henderson, kissing his momma, and running away. Jones would have done well to take Wright's advice in "Blueprint" that one only transcends what is "national" in their lives by first embracing it. But he did not, and it is questionable whether Wright did either.

In both the story of John Jones and Wright's "I Tried to Be a Communist," the failure to articulate is at once a matter of the voice assumed and of how that voice relates to the audience at hand. While

Jones did not speak to or of his audience, Wright compounded Jones's error by speaking beyond his immediate audience to another, which in this case was Big Brother. We might see our way to calling a truce and sounding a grace note if, when Wright states that the blacks condemned him as "bourgeois," we could be certain that he is employing both the Party-line and "black culture-based" senses of the term. This might have suggested his awareness, in retrospect, of the violation of intra-racial codes. But the evidence is, if not exactly to the contrary, at least unconvincing.

The "unit meeting" passage hints at many complaints laid at Wright's door, but none loom larger than Ellison's lament (*Shadow and Act*, New York, 1966) that Wright "could not for ideological reasons depict a Negro as intelligent, as creative or as dedicated as himself" (pp. 126-27). The charge pertains particularly to Bigger Thomas, but as we see in *Black Boy* and in "I Tried to Be a Communist," Wright's limited depiction of the Negro extends occasionally to self-portraits as well. It is hard to believe that the bumbling black writer alienating black folk and performing a poor job of propagandizing for the Party is supposed to be Wright himself, but for reasons neither wholly self-effacing nor wholly aesthetic it is, alas, poor Richard.

The issue is really Wright's idea of the hero, although I believe none of his critics put the matter quite this way. If we assume, as I do, that the primary voice in the tradition, whether in prose or verse or music, is a personal, heroic voice delineating the dimensions of heroism by either aspiring to a heroic posture, as do the voices of Douglass and Du Bois, or expressing an awareness of that which they *ought* to be, as we see Johnson's Ex-Colored Man and Ellison's Invisible Man doing, then the mystery of what is unsettling about Wright's voice (and protagonists) begins to unfold. Bigger Thomas is hardly the only maimed or stunted or confused figure in Afro-American literature; this is not what makes him different. What *does* is his unawareness of what he *ought* to be, especially as it is defined not by the vague dictates of the American Dream but by the rather specific mandates of a racial heritage. When Ellison complains (*Shadow and Act*, pp. 121-22):

> Wright could imagine Bigger, but Bigger could not possibly imagine Richard Wright. Wright saw to that.

his lament is really that Wright did not place Bigger in the tradition. Interestingly enough, placing *Wright* in the tradition was exactly what Ellison tried to do in 1945 (but later renounced in "The World and the Jug" in 1963) when he argued that *Black Boy* was a blues in prose (*Shadow and Act*, pp. 89-104).

All in all, Wright's authorial posture is much like that of Booker T. Washington. Both men are, to use George Kent's phrase, "exaggerated Westerners" (*Blackness and the Adventure of Western Culture,* Chicago, 1972, p. 82), especially with regard to the voice and posture each perfected in order to reach those whom they perceived to be their audience. Responding to what might be termed the literary offences of Washington, Du Bois argued in *The Souls* that part of what was wrong with the Tuskegee Spirit was the degree to which "the speech and thought of triumphant commercialism" was indeed *becoming* that spirit, or at least the *expression* of it. Ellison makes a similar point about Wright when he says, " . Wright found the facile answers of Marxism before he learned to use literature as a means for discovering the forms of American Negro humanity" (*Shadow and Act,* p. 126). In the case of both men, the speech and thought they espoused led to a necessary denial, at least in print, of certain Afro-American traditions. Hence, they were, in their authorial posture, exaggerated individuals alienated from their race and, to some degree, themselves. Even when they are about the task of creating themselves in autobiographies, their vision is shaped and possibly warped by this state of "exaggeratedness." Thus, in *Up from Slavery,* Washington models himself as the ideal fund-raiser and public speaker and defers to the facile portraits of himself by journalists, while Wright, in *Black Boy,* suppresses his own extraordinary human spirit by rendering himself a black "biological fact" (see Kent, *Blackness,* p. 78)

But as with most comparisons there are distinctions to be made. Beyond all questions of era and place rests the simple fact that Washington was in control of the implications of his authorial posture while Wright was not. When, for example, Washington rebukes the models and motifs of the slave narratives by casting *Up from Slavery* in the vein of the Franklinesque source book and, to some degree, the Horatio Alger tale, we sense that this was the price he willingly paid to exchange his full life story for funds for Tuskegee and other, sometimes clandestine, projects. He knew what he was about and the dollars most certainly came rolling in. When Wright, on the other hand, even in the writing of *Black Boy,* embraces the example of Dreiser, Lewis, and Mencken far more than that of Toomer, Johnson, Hughes, or Hurston, we want to know what was the tradeoff, what the exchange or sacrifice comparable to Washington's? In sum, Wright was more the victim of his posture than the master of it, and in this he is not alone in Afro-American letters. If he indeed occupies a prominent place in the tradition because of his views on author and audience, it is because the founders set aside a large space for confused men.

II

Turning to the question of how his books may confirm Wright's place in the tradition, we find ourselves on what seems to be surer ground but in the end is not. Despite Wright's apparent ignorance of Afro-American literature during his youth and rise to literary prominence, there are distinct links between certain preceding narrative types, the slave narrative and plantation tale in particular, and his own writings. But the question remains as to whether these links are mere repeated patterns or of the resilient stuff that establish author and text in an artistic continuum.

Native Son, for example, may be viewed as a plantation tale, not only because there are ties between it and the "revisionist" plantation tales of Charles W. Chesnutt, but also because certain features of setting, action, and character are recognizably those of a nineteenth-century American plantation society. The setting is roughly that of a plantation, with the slave quarters west of Cottage Grove Avenue, a respectful long block from the Big House of the Dalton's on Drexel Boulevard. Dalton may not be a slaveholding captain of early agri-business, but his immense profits do come from the land and from the hard toil of blacks in that, as president of the South Side Real Estate Company, he landlords over hundreds of over-priced rat-infested tenements, including that in which Bigger and his family lead their sorry lives. This provides the essential irony of the famous cell-block scene where Mrs. Thomas kneels before Mrs. Dalton and begs for her intervention, saying (*Native Son*, New York, 1940):

> 'Please, don't let 'em kill my boy! You know how a mother feels! Please,
> mam. . . . We live in your house. . . . They done asked us to move. . . .
> We ain't got nothing . . . I'll work for you for the rest of my life! . . .'
> (pp. 279-80).

Mrs. Thomas' plea is in part one for Mrs. Dalton to honor a sense of commitment initially established by the covenant between master and slave. Her offer to work for the Daltons the rest of her life is, under the circumstances, a gift she has already given and will continue to give as long as she is trapped in one or another tenement of Dalton's ghetto.

Besides the Daltons and Mrs. Thomas, there are other minor characters such as Britten, who in his functions as a private eye turns out to be more and more like an overseer. And of course there are the major characters, Bigger, Mary Dalton, and, I would argue, Attorney Max. When George Kent writes that "A major source of the power of *Native Son* derived from Wright's ability to articulate the relevant rituals of black and white cultures—and Bigger's response to them," he refers to those rituals emphasizing the presence or absence of "rational drive, curiosity, revolutionary will, individualism [and] self-consciousness" (see *Blackness*, p. 93). But he should have also mentioned those ritualized postures of the black male and white female which, one imagines, have prevailed in the mainstream of the culture since the races first came into contact. Despite her flirtation with communism, Mary Dalton is still the young, white, and (as her Christian name implies) virginal belle on the pedestal. She might at first sit alongside Bigger in the front seat of her father's car, but in the end, she removes to the rear with her boyfriend, Jan, only to reinforce the distance by reminding Bigger to cart her trunk to the station in the morning. And so the shuttle is set in motion, orders one moment, her drunken head on Bigger's shoulder the next. If Bigger is confused, the police and newspapers are not: Mary is the white beauty, Bigger the black brute.

These postures are, unfortunately in our world, timeless, and we would be wrong to suggest that they are in some way the exclusive property of the antebellum South. And because Mary and Bigger are in this sense conventional types, we must wonder whether the third major character, Attorney Max, is as well. Like Mary's boyfriend, Jan, Max resembles the sympathetic white found in the slave narratives who is somewhat removed from the system. But while Jan remains within the type—and is therefore as one-dimensional as are most of the novel's characters—Max's status is more problematic. While he never gains the intimacy with Bigger he so desperately seeks, Max does nevertheless, more than any other, spark Bigger's fleeting glimpse of the possibilities of life and of human communion. Moreover, as his courtroom speech implies, he sees, more than the rest, how America has made Bigger far more than Bigger has fashioned himself. Max's use of language is what allows him to break out of the plantation tale type. It contrasts not only with Bigger's verbal deficiencies and with the corruption of language by the State's Attorney and the press, but also, on a subtler scale, with Mary and Jan's insensitive verbal gropings across the racial chasm (" 'Isn't there a song like that, a song your people sing?' ") which only fill Bigger with "a dumb, cold, and inarticulate hate" (*Native Son*, pp. 66, 68).

Indeed, what most distinguishes *Native Son* from its antecedent plantation tale texts is not its bleak urban landscape but the fact that the traditional heroic modes of transcending travail in this world, such as the gift of uncommon insight and speech, have been given not to Bigger but apparently to Max instead. Thus, the issue of Bigger's sub-heroic posture is further confused by the question of whether Wright intends Max to be the novel's heroic voice and, by extension, Wright's voice as well.

All this brings us to Max's celebrated courtroom speech. If Max speaks for Wright, we must assume that he specifically does so in the courtroom episode where he is not only eloquent but forthright and compassionate. Yet this poses a considerable problem, for in implicitly espousing the classic liberal notion that truth will invariably foster justice, Max blunts the raw revolutionary fervor which Bigger generated and which first seduced the communists to come to his aid. In doing so, Max exchanges his credentials as a radical for a heroic posture which is very much in the American grain. Thus, while transcending the character type in the slave narratives which he first resembles, Max soon takes on the features of a familiar turn-of-the-century type, the "white moral voice," of whom Charles W. Chesnutt, in Afro-American letters, provides us with at least four examples.[1] Max is, then, a revolutionary manqué; a reformer possessing a grand but ineffectual idealism which leaves him horror-struck before the fact of Bigger's pending execution.

If Max is *not* Wright's voice, or at least not the heroic voice in the novel, then we would expect him to be sketched ironically, with the stress falling on what may be less than heroic in his words and character. But this is not the case. What we have instead is a confusion of political language and purpose, compounded by the troublesome fact that Wright seems to have bestowed the gift of eloquence on Max with no clearly discernible end in mind.

The problem with Max seems to be a fictive equivalent of Wright's own dilemma in "I Tried to Be a Communist." In each case, the speaker's articulateness does not meet the needs of the occasion and in that sense is a kind of illiteracy, especially of the sort that is enforced by America's rituals along the color line. If, in *Native Son,* Max is indeed Wright's voice, it is not because of the content of his speeches but rather because he shares with his author a misperception of audience, grounded in what we may term an extraordinary and almost myopic innocence. Thus, despite the novel's many and varied images of American slave society, the absence of an articulate hero whose posture and language tends to modulate the forces of a hostile environment renders *Native Son* a most problematic novel in Afro-American letters.

Black Boy, on the other hand, is more clearly conceived and is hence the better of Wright's two greatest published works. The dominant voice of the book seems to be finally that of its author precisely because it has a fair measure of human proportion. To be sure, we are almost overwhelmed by those relentless passages in *Black Boy* in which Wright fashions himself a black "biological fact." But countering these are the moments of marvelous self-assertion, the Whitmanesque catalogs of sensual remembrances, and overall, the presence of a questing human being seeking freedom and a voice. Here, a hostile environment *is* modulated by an emerging, extraordinary figure, and the resulting narrative establishes a place for itself in the continuum founded by the slave narrative.

One may list a number of motifs *Black Boy* shares with the slave narratives—the violence and gnawing hunger, the skeptical view of Christianity, the portrait of a black family valiantly attempting to maintain a degree of unity, the impregnable isolation, the longing and scheming to follow the North Star resolved by boarding the "freedom train"—but the most enduring link is the motif (and, one might argue, the narrative form) of the narrator's quest for literacy. Frederick Douglass provides the most compelling statement (*Narrative of the Life of Frederick Douglass, An American Slave*, New York: Signet, 1968) of how literacy and freedom are entwined goals when he relates:

> Very soon after I went to live with Mr. and Mrs. Auld, she very kindly commenced to teach me the A, B, C. After I had learned this, she assisted me in learning to spell words of three or four letters. Just at this point of my progress, Mr. Auld found out what was going on, and at once forbade Mrs. Auld to instruct me further, telling her, among other things, that it was unlawful, as well as unsafe, to teach a slave to read. To use his own words, further, he said, 'If you give a nigger an inch, he will take an ell. A nigger should know nothing but to obey his master—to do as he is told to do. Learning would *spoil* the best nigger in the world. Now,' said he, 'if you teach that nigger (speaking of myself) how to read, there would be no keeping of him. It would forever unfit him to be a slave. He would at once become unmanageable, and of no value to his master. As to himself, it would do him no good, but a great deal of harm. It would make him discontented and unhappy.' These words sank deep into my heart, stirred up sentiments within that lay slumbering, and called into existence an entirely new train of thought. It was a new and special revelation, explaining dark and mysterious things, with which my youthful understanding had struggled in vain. I now understood what had been to me a most perplexing difficulty—to wit, the white man's power to enslave the black man. It was a grand achievement, and I prized it highly. From that moment, I understood the pathway from slavery to freedom (p. 49).

While Wright's quest for literacy was hardly this arduous, it was nevertheless difficult and, especially by the time he was nineteen and in Memphis, fraught with danger. As he intimates in *Black Boy* (New York, 1945), there were white men who might have killed him had they known he was reading Mencken and Sinclair Lewis and absorbing their indictments of America. Unlike Douglass, Wright did not have to dupe white boys in the streets in order to learn how to cipher, but he did have to discover a sympathetic Irishman who

secretly lent him his library card before he could break the isolation
and read ". . . books that opened up new avenues of feeling and
seeing. . . ." (*Ibid.*, p. 221). And it was this reading, as well as the
writing of stories and even commencement addresses, which
prompted young Richard to follow the North Star and, in a supreme
act of self-assertion, free himself.

All in all, our comparison of *Black Boy* and *Native Son* provides us
with a number of strong, revealing contrasts, but none presses with
greater urgency and portent than that of the self-assertive, self-
aware narrator of *Black Boy* seeking literacy and a voice appositioned
against the image of Bigger and his inert cohorts assaulted by the
mindlessness of B-grade Hollywood films and the rhetoric of propa-
ganda emanating not only from the communists but also from the
Daltons, the government, and the press. Clearly, Wright could match
his model of the writer described in "Blueprint" who is "something of
a guide in [our] daily living," but it is remarkable that he did so only
in the writing of his autobiography.

III

Despite what we've previously said about Wright's distance from
the race and his problems concerning voice and audience, there is
considerable evidence of his influence on, and enshrinement by,
the contemporary black writer and critic. In 1964, while participating
in a symposium on Wright, Saunders Redding declared: "Certainly,
if we are in a renaissance, as it were, more or less similar, though
very, very different from the renaissance of the Twenties, it is be-
cause of Richard Wright."[2] Given the year in which Redding made
this statement, one may assume that he was referring to the ascend-
ing careers of several writers, of whom Baldwin and Ellison might
very well have topped the list. Their protests to the contrary, Baldwin
and Ellison *were* influenced by Wright; one might even argue that a
significant part of their drive to write derived from a desire to
"humanize" Bigger. A great deal of ink has been spilled on this
subject, and I won't contribute mine. Rather, I would like to explore
briefly Wright's influence on the critics and authors of Afro-American
literature of the last decade.

Perhaps the most obvious evidence of Wright's influence is pro-
vided by the titles of several widely disseminated studies of Afro-
American literature published in the 1950's and 1960's. In addition
to Baldwin's *Notes of a Native Son* (1955) and Cleaver's "Notes on
a Native Son" in *Soul on Ice* (1968), we have Edward Margolies'
*Native Sons: A Critical Study of Twentieth-Century Negro American
Authors* (Philadelphia, 1968). Yet another quasi-sociological survey
of Afro-American writing, and one which systematically excludes

black women writers (the title is no reasonable rationale for this), Margolies' book is hardly a ground-breaking performance. One imagines that it was rushed to print, as were many other titles, to meet the needs of the new market created by the rise of Afro-American Studies. But it is worth our attention because Margolies attempts, in a very modest way, to forge a critical approach to Afro-American literature based on the example and impact of *Native Son*. He writes in his introductory chapter:

> The example of *Native Son* enabled others to deal with a body of subject matter they had hitherto warily skirted. Wright opened up for Negro writers not only the bitterness of their lives, but other taboo matters as well —miscegenation, homosexuality, the white-Negro power structure, and even the singular freedom a Negro feels in a society that denies him any recognition of his humanity. The courage to 'tell it the way it is' is the prime requisite of artistic integrity. Human revelation is the business of the artist; he must write about what he *knows* to be true—imaginatively or otherwise—and the first truths he must know are about himself. *Native Son* provided many Negro authors with these precedents. In its way it liberated them as no other book has done since (pp. 19-20).

We are not entirely happy with this statement; one hopes, for example, that Margolies' list of "taboo matters" beginning with miscegenation and ending with the "singular freedom" of the Negro is not supposed to reflect the order of their importance. But the idea of treating *Native Son* as some sort of watershed in Afro-American literature is not altogether amiss, especially if one wishes to investigate the course of Afro-American literary *art*. However, Margolies is centrally concerned with "the Negro's evaluation of his historical and cultural experience in this century"; for him, *Native Son* is a point of departure more for social scientific evidence than for the discovery of an artistic tradition.

As the Black Aesthetic critics and writers surfaced in the late sixties, partly in response to the critical inadequacies of approaches like Margolies', they embraced Richard Wright as a novelist and also as an aesthetician. In some instances, however, it was not so much Wright but Bigger Thomas who, strangely enough, was promoted as the black artist's model. For example, Sarah Webster Fabio writes in her contribution to Addison Gayle's *The Black Aesthetic* (New York, 1972):

> No turning back, though. This is the day of Biggers and the ghosts of Biggers. Black writers—most of them poets plus—have always been barometers, even when America kept the bell jars on them. Have always been/still are/will be. Always traveling with ears to the ground; attuned to the drumbeats of the age (p. 181).

One assumes that Fabio, who usually makes better sense, is being rhetorical. Buried in here somewhere is the notion that black writers, armed with poems and novels for weapons, must "kill" as Bigger did in order to feel the pulse of time and, for the first time in their lives, feel free. As rhetoric this may be powerful and, for some, inspiring, but it hardly suggests a viable aesthetic ideal, nor does it pay proper credit to Richard Wright. Addison Gayle, however, offers a more fruitful line of inquiry when he correctly turns to the example of Wright, not Bigger, and argues:

> The task of pointing out northern duplicity was left to the black artist, and no writer was more effective in this undertaking than Richard Wright. When Wright placed Bigger Thomas and Mr. Dalton in a northern setting and pointed up the fact that Bigger's condition resulted from Dalton's hypocrisy, he opened up a Pandora's box of problems for white liberals and Negro leaders, neither of whom could bring themselves to share his vision. . . . The liberal ideology—both social and literary—of the northern Daltons has become the primary target of the Afro-American writer and critic (pp. xviii, xx).

Above and beyond the issue of how Gayle views contemporary black writers and critics pursuing their muse, this statement is questionable as a "political" reading of *Native Son*. The total picture of liberal thought in the novel includes, as we've indicated before, the words and deeds of Attorney Max, even though it is through him that the most explicit and vitriolic condemnation of the Daltons is expressed. If a critic values such features in literature and actually intends to build an aesthetic upon such foundations, as Gayle apparently does, then Wright's inability to portray Max as a "pure" radical should conceivably becloud his view of *Native Son* as a seminal book. But apparently this is not a problem for Mr. Gayle. Our point is, however, that here is another attempt to trace a pattern in Afro-American literature which has *Native Son* as its source. As Margolies emphasizes the socio-cultural, Gayle, albeit with greater attention to the Afro-American artist's posture in society, stresses the political, the literary war against an ideology. Since each of these patterns has a considerable history beginning well before the publication of *Native Son* in 1940, one might say that both Margolies and Gayle are trying, from what often seems like opposite corners of the earth, to move toward an articulation of a tradition. But patterns aren't traditions, and even a combination of the Margolies and Gayle approaches does not illuminate all we want to know about books like *Native Son* and *Black Boy*. If indeed, as some are saying, the black art-as-sociology and Black Aesthetic theories of the 1960's are outmoded, it may be because the latter is but an extension and political radicalization of the former, and neither approach is fully in tune with the heartbeat of the artist and his art.

By and large, the chief limitation to most of the criticism of *Native Son* is that the critics have dwelled on what we may loosely call the novel's content. Whether *Native Son* actually shocked the proverbial banker's daughter (who might identify, one supposes, with Mary Dalton) as Wright hoped it would remains unclear. What *is* clear, however, is that Wright's critics have been preoccupied by those very features to the novel which are presumably distressing to proper young ladies. Generally, most of the criticism of *Native Son* falls into one of two categories: predictable, journeyman-like studies of imagery (light and dark; animal references) and symbolism (the soaring airplane, various timepieces, the Christian crosses); or, responses to those features which, as Baldwin has written, "whet the notorious national taste for the sensational."[3] The problem, we discover, is that these approaches unduly isolate the text from the corpus of American and Afro-American literature and direct discussion of *Native Son* toward yet another ritualized, pseudo-scientific rehash of the Black Man's Plight.

As I have tried to indicate earlier in these pages, Wright's influence on the contemporary critic may lead to the pursuit of other types of questions. Our sense of an Afro-American literary tradition can be sharpened and enhanced, for example, by assaying Wright's departures from it. We need to develop what has already been ventured about Bigger and Wright's entanglement in the web of double-consciousness so that we may come to know them and the place of *Native Son* in the artistic continuum. We need to assess why, from the standpoint of artistic and even aesthetic considerations, Wright earnestly desired to become a jazz critic in the twilight of his career. Above all, we must not hesitate to discover the Americanness of Richard Wright. Such an activity is actually part of the legacy handed down by such pioneering Afro-American critics as William Stanley Braithwaite and Sterling A. Brown. Wright's departures from Afro-American traditions generally serve to confirm his place in the mainstream of American letters, and, for the moment, it seems like the knowledgeable Afro-Americanist critic is best suited to articulate Wright's stature in both literary worlds.

Turning to Wright's influence on the contemporary black writer, especially those writers first published during the last decade, we find a predictable array of responses ranging from celebrations of Bigger to what we can only deem more thoughtful considerations of Wright's work which frequently re-examine those rituals of black and white cultures of which we've already spoken. The celebrations of Bigger more often than not represent the exploitation of these cultural rituals, and seem to be generated by psychological needs sur-

facing as strategies for political power, or by unadulterated greed.
Writers are often found in the former camp (Eldridge Cleaver, for
example), while the would-be artists behind the spate of "blax-
ploitation" films may be designated to the latter. If indeed, as
Kichung Kim writes, "For many Black Americans . . . Bigger is
probably the one character they find most authentic in all of Ameri-
can literature . . . ,"[4] we need not wonder why these writers and
filmmakers have a considerable audience. None of this is Wright's
doing or intention. The man who split the atom did not drop the
bomb. However, like the scientist who foresaw the holocaust of
Hiroshima, Wright, in his portraits of Bigger fantasizing at the movies
and dreamily reading detective stories, seems to have prophesied
what is a lamentable feature to our present cultural state. What he
understandably could not foresee is that today not only is Bigger
still in the audience, but his fantasized self is on the screen.

A far more honorable and direct response to Wright may be dis-
covered in the recent fiction of black women authors. We have
alluded to the effort to "humanize" Bigger but the attempts to revise
and redeem Mrs. Thomas and both Bessies (the one in *Native Son*
and the one in *Black Boy*), launched mostly by black women writers,
must be mentioned as well. There is little written discussion of this;
but looking at the literature itself, we can find types of Mrs. Thomas
and both Bessies leading richer lives and having more going for
them than a false church, a whiskey bottle, and, as Wright says of the
Bessie in *Black Boy*, a peasant mentality.

Ann Petry's *The Street* (1946) and Toni Morrison's *The Bluest Eye*
(1970) are two novels from what may be termed the antipodes
of the contemporary period which support our point. Although Lutie
Johnson in *The Street* is ultimately defeated by the dimensions of
racism and sexism at work and at home in Harlem, she, unlike the
Bessie in *Native Son*, possesses a fair measure of pride, will, and
grace. The fact that near the end of the novel she kills her black
lover, not to silence him, but because of the continual sexual and
psychological assault he has made on her life, would suggest that
Petry was about the task not only of redeeming Bessie but of re-
vising Bigger as well.

In *The Bluest Eye*, virtually all of the black women, whether they
be prostitutes or keepers of the hearth, are far more compelling,
complex, and differentiated than Wright's. Mrs. Pauline Breedlove
and her daughter, Pecola, may be likened to Mrs. Thomas and her
daughter, Vera. Both sets of women are entrapped by the burdens of
being poor, black, and female. But for all their woes, or perhaps
because of them, Mrs. Breedlove and Pecola are the dreamers in
Morrison's novel. Their dreams may be false and irredeemably

warped—Mrs. Breedlove covets Jean Harlow's hair, Pecola desperately searches for blue eyes—but they dream just the same; they have an inner life. Most importantly, in terms of the tradition of the articulate hero, the arresting story of all the Breedloves (Pauline, Pecola, Sammy, and the father, Cholly) is told by a young woman, Claudia MacTeer, whose accumulation of the facts and rendering of the tale softens our horror while yielding her a special knowledge with which she can face and endure adulthood.

All in all, the black women novelists of our age seem to be agreeing with Alice Walker that "black women are the most fascinating creations in the world."[5] Thus, out of necessity, they are turning to Toomer, Hurston, Brooks, and Petry, and not to the majority of black male writers for their models and encouragement. In this light, the rise of a feminine and sometimes feminist voice in contemporary Afro-American fiction may be directly related to the narrow and confining portraits of black women in earlier modern fiction, including that of Wright.

Besides the revision of characters, we also find evidence of the contemporary writer treating the aforementioned cultural rituals as lore handed down; as essential metaphors to be combined with others such as the heroic black athlete and the veil. For example, in "Heartblow," Michael Harper's series of poems for Wright in *Debridement* (1973), we find this poem entitled "Afterward: A Film":

Erect in the movies
with a new job,
Trader Horn
and *The Gay Woman*
unfold in a twinbill:
drums, wild dancing,
naked men, the silver
veils on the South Side.
He imagines nothing:
it is all before him,
born in a dream:
a gorilla broke loose
from his zoo
in a tuxedo: baboon.
You pick your red bottom.
The Daltons are the movies.

On my wall are pictures:
Jack Johnson, Joe Louis,
Harlow and Rogers:
'see the white god and die.'

Underground I live in veils,
brick and cement,
the confession beaten out,
slung with hung carcasses,
a bloody cleaver grunting,
a dead baby in the sewer:
'all the people I saw were guilty.'

Marked black I was shot,
double-conscious brother in the veil—
without an image of act or thought
double-conscious brother in the veil—

The rape: 'Mrs. Dalton, it's me,
Bigger, I've brought Miss Dalton
home and she's drunk:'
to be the idea in these minds,
double-conscious brother in the veil—
father and leader where is my king,
veils of kingship will lead these folks
double-conscious brother in the veil—
'see the white gods and die'
double-conscious brother in the veil—

The opening stanzas take two of Wright's most effective images of Bigger the empty vessel being inundated and filled by the celluloid flotsam of popular culture, and integrate them into one flowing portrait of assault, first at the theatre and finally in his quarters at the Dalton home. All this is done with careful and loyal attention to the text. The gorilla reference is, for example, almost a quotation of Jack's playful response to Bigger's musings over what it would be like to attend a party like that in *The Gay Woman*, only now the self-debasing racial comment at the heart of Jack's joking is fully exposed and relentlessly pursued. Furthermore, in the second stanza, mention of the photos on Bigger's walls at the Dalton's serves to remind us of how, according to Wright's vision, Bigger and Mary will encounter each other in a dance designed by warped yet powerful cultural and historical forces; a dance of psycho-sexual and racial ritual along the color line. In short, stanzas one and two present those cultural forces affecting Bigger in Book I of the novel as much as stanza three captures Bigger's mood in Book II.

In the third stanza, the series of images transports us back to the scene of Mary's dismemberment and forward to Bigger's confession while immersing us in Bigger's flight underground in Dalton's ghetto. The primary image is that of a hellish landscape, peopled by the victimized and oppressed, which the poet places in a historical continuum, not so much as Wright did by means of economic and political reference, but rather by ancient metaphor, the veil. Through this metaphor, Harper can now expand upon his image of Bigger until it approximates the fullest dimensions of the artistic continuum. Thus, in the remaining stanzas, the line *"double-conscious brother in the veil"* becomes at once a musical refrain and, like a repeated color in African woven cloth, the agent and source for a compelling visual rhythm.

In poems such as these, Wright, I feel, is restored to his proper stature as a participant in Afro-American letters. Harper's mining of Wright's primary images and placement of them in the continuum, as well as his implied suggestion that Wright deserves a place in the pantheon where we find Du Bois, yields the kind of evidence which balances all we know of Wright's shortcomings. And it is this balanced view of Wright, as an author who could argue "Tradition is no longer a guide. . . . The world has grown huge and cold" while providing us with archetypes which generations of writers would in turn place *in* the tradition he rejected, that begins to define his stature in the Afro-American tradition.

NOTES

[1] See the sheriff in "The Sheriff's Children" in *The Wife of His Youth and Other Stories of the Color Line* (1899; rpt. Ridgewood, N.Y.: Gregg Press, 1967); Judge Straight in *The House Behind the Cedars* (1900; rpt. New York: Collier-Macmillan, 1969); Lee Ellis (a journalist) in *The Marrow of Tradition* (1901; rpt. Ann Arbor: University of Michigan Press, 1969); and Colonel French in *The Colonel's Dream* (1905; rpt. Upper Saddle River, N.J.: Gregg Press, 1968).

[2] J. Saunders Redding in "Reflections on Richard Wright: A Symposium on an Exiled Native Son," in *Anger, and Beyond: The Negro Writer in the United States,* Herbert Hill, ed. (New York: Harper Perennial Library, 1968), p. 204.

[3] James Baldwin, "Many Thousands Gone," in *Notes of a Native Son* (New York: Bantam Books, 1964), p. 28.

[4] Kichung Kim, "Wright, The Protest Novel, and Baldwin's Faith," *CLA Journal,* XVII (March, 1974), 390.

[5] Alice Walker, in *Interviews with Black Writers,* John O'Brien, ed. (New York: Liveright, 1973), p. 192.

FROM *SULA*

TONI MORRISON

A good white farmer promised freedom and a piece of bottom land to his slave if he would perform some very difficult chores. When the slave completed the work, he asked the farmer to keep his end of the bargain. Freedom was easy—the farmer had no objection to that. But he didn't want to give up any land. So he told the slave that he was very sorry that he had to give him valley land. He had hoped to give him a piece of the Bottom. The slave blinked and said he thought valley land was bottom land. The master said, "Oh, no! See those hills? That's bottom land, rich and fertile."

"But it's high up in the hills," said the slave.

"High up from us," said the master, "but when God looks down, it's the bottom. That's why we call it so. It's the bottom of heaven—best land there is."

So the slave pressed his master to try to get him some. He preferred it to the valley. And it was done. The nigger got the hilly land. . . .

From Toni Morrison's *Sula* (New York: Alfred A. Knopf, 1973), p. 5.

"INTIMATE THINGS IN PLACE"

A CONVERSATION WITH TONI MORRISON

[STEPTO]: I WANT TO START WITH SOMETHING WE'VE TALKED ABOUT before, and that is this extraordinary sense of place in your novels. By that I mean you create communities, the community that Pecola, Claudia and the rest live in, in *The Bluest Eye*, and of course, in *Sula*, the Bottom. The places are set in time; there are addresses— we know Sula's address, right down to the house number. Years are mentioned, seasons are mentioned, details are given, and I was struck by these features in two ways. First, by the extent to which you seem to be trying to create specific geographical landscapes, and second, by how landscape seems to perform different functions in the two novels.

[MORRISON]: I can't account for all aspects of it. I know that I never felt like an American or an Ohioan or even a Lorainite. I never felt like a citizen. But I felt very strongly—not much with the first book; more with the second; and very much with the one I'm working on now—I felt a very strong sense of place, not in terms of the country or the state, but in terms of the details, the feeling, the mood of the community, of the town. In the first book, I was clearly pulling straight out of what autobiographical information I had. I didn't create that town. It's clearer to me now in my memory of it than when I lived there—and I haven't really lived there since I was seventeen years old. Also, I think some of it is just a woman's strong sense of being in a room, a place, or in a house. Sometimes my relationship to things in a house would be a little different from, say my brother's or my father's or my sons'. I clean them and I move them and I do very intimate things "in place": I am sort of rooted in it, so that writing about being in a room looking out, or being in a world looking out, or living in a small definite place, is probably very common among most women anyway.

This interview was conducted in Ms. Morrison's office at Random House Publishers in New York City on May 19, 1976. The interviewer is Robert B. Stepto.

The other thing was that when I wrote *Sula* I was interested in making the town, the community, the neighborhood, as strong as a character as I could, without actually making it "The Town, they," because the most extraordinary thing about any group, and particularly our group, is the fantastic variety of people and things and behavior and so on. But nevertheless there was a cohesiveness there in my mind and it was true in my life. And though I live in New York, I don't relate easily to very, very large cities, because I have never lived in a huge city except this one. My tendency is to focus on neighborhoods and communities. And the community, the black community—I don't like to use that term because it came to mean something much different in the sixties and seventies, as though we had to forge one—but it had seemed to me that it was always there, only we called it the "neighborhood." And there was this life-giving, very, very strong sustenance that people got from the neighborhood. One lives, really, not so much in your house as you do outside of it, within the "compounds," within the village, or whatever it is. And legal responsibilities, all the responsibilities that agencies now have, were the responsibilities of the neighborhood. So that people were taken care of, or locked up or whatever. If they were sick, other people took care of them; if they needed something to eat, other people took care of them; if they were old, other people took care of them; if they were mad, other people provided a small space for them, or related to their madness or tried to find out the limits of their madness.

They also meddled in your lives a lot. They felt that you belonged to them. And every woman on the street could raise everybody's child, and tell you exactly what to do and you felt that connection with those people and they felt it with you. And when they punished us or hollered at us, it was, at the time, we thought, so inhibiting and so cruel, and it's only much later that you realize that they were interested in you. Interested in you—they cared about your behavior. And then I knew my mother as a Church woman, and a Club woman—and there was something special about when she said "Sister," and when all those other women said "Sister." They meant that in a very, very fundamental way. There were some interesting things going on inside people and they seemed to me the most extraordinary people in the world. But at the same time, there was this kind of circle around them—we lived within 23 blocks—which they could not break.

[s]: From what you're telling me, it would seem that creating Medallion in *Sula* might have been a more difficult task than creating the neighborhood in *The Bluest Eye.*

[m]: Oh, yes, Medallion was more difficult because it was wholly fabricated; but it was based on something my mother had said some

time ago. When she first got married, she and my father went to live in Pittsburgh. And I remember her telling me that in those days all the black people lived in the hills of Pittsburgh, but now they lived amid the smoke and dirt in the heart of that city. It's clear up in those hills, and so I used that idea, but in a small river town in Ohio. Ohio is right on the Kentucky border, so there's not much difference between it and the "South." It's an interesting state from the point of view of black people because it is right there by the Ohio River, in the south, and at its northern tip is Canada. And there were these fantastic abolitionists there, and also the Ku Klux Klan lived there. And there is only really one large city. There are hundreds of small towns and that's where most black people live. You know, in most books, they're always in New York or some exotic place, but most of our lives are spent in little towns, little towns all throughout this country. And that's where, you know, we live. And that's where the juices came from and that's where we *made it*, not made it in terms of success but made who we are. So I loved writing about that because it was so wide open.

Sula was hard, for me; very difficult to make up that kind of character. Not difficult to think it up, but difficult to describe a woman who could be used as a classic type of evil force. Other people could use her that way. And at the same time, I didn't want to make her freakish or repulsive or unattractive. I was interested at that time in doing a very old, worn-out idea, which was to do something with good and evil, but putting it in different terms. And I wanted Nel to be a warm, conventional woman, one of those people you know are going to pay the gas bill and take care of the children. You don't have to ask about them. And they are magnificent, because they take these small tasks and they do them. And they do them without the fire and without the drama and without all of that. They get the world's work done somehow.

[s]: How did Nel get to that point, given the background you provided her with? Why does her grandmother have those "questionable roots"? How does that lead to Nel?

[m]: It has to do with Nel's attraction for Sula. To go back, a black woman at that time who didn't want to do the conventional thing, had only one other kind of thing to do. If she had talent she went into the theater. And if she had a little voice, she could sing, or she could go to a big town and she could pretend she was dancing or whatever. That was the only outlet if you chose not to get married and have children. That was it. Or you could walk the streets; although you might get there sort of accidentally; you might not choose to do that. So that Nel's grandmother just means that there's that kind of life from which Nel comes; that's another woman who was a hustler.

that part is already in Nel and accounts for her attraction to Sula. And also those are the kinds of women there were. Here is this woman, Nel, whose mother is just busy, busy, busy, reacting against her own mother, and goes to the far extreme of having this rather neat, rather organized, rather pompous life, forcing all of the creativity out of Nel. But Nel wants it anyway, which is what makes it possible for her to have a very close friend who is so different from her, in the way she looks at life. And I wanted to make all of that sort of reasonable. Because what was the attraction of Nel for Sula? Sula for Nel? Why would they become friends in the first place? You see? And so I wanted to say, as much as I could say it without being overbearing, that there was a little bit of both in each of those two women, and that if they had been one person, I suppose they would have been a rather marvelous person. But each one lacked something that the other one had.

[s]: It's interesting you should mention this, because my students wanted to pursue the question of Sula and Nel being perhaps two sides of the same person, or two sides of one extraordinary character. But this character is nevertheless fractured into Sula and Nel.

[M]: Precisely. They're right on target because that was really in my mind. It didn't come to me quite that way. I started out by thinking that one can never really define good and evil. Sometimes good looks like evil; sometimes evil looks like good—you never really know what it is. It depends on what uses you put it to. Evil is as useful as good is, although good is generally more interesting; it's more complicated. I mean, living a good life is more complicated than living an evil life, I think. And also, it wasn't hard to talk about that because everyone has something in mind when they think about what a good life is. So I put that in conventional terms, for a woman: someone who takes care of children and so on and is responsible and goes to church and so on. For the opposite kind of character, which is a woman who's an adventurer, who breaks rules, she can either be a criminal—which I wasn't interested in—or lead a kind of cabaret life—which I also wasn't interested in. But what about the woman who doesn't do any of that but is nevertheless a rule-breaker, a kind of law-breaker, a lawless woman? Not a law-abiding woman. Nel knows and believes in all the laws of that community. She *is* the community. She believes in its values. Sula does not. She does not believe in any of those laws and breaks them all. Or ignores them. So that she becomes more interesting—I think, particularly to younger girls—because of that quality of abandon.

But there's a fatal flaw in all of that, you know, in both of those things. Nel does not make that "leap"—she doesn't know about herself. Even at the end, she doesn't know. She's just beginning. She just barely grabs on at the end in those last lines. So that living totally by the law and surrendering completely to it without questioning anything sometimes makes it impossible to know anything about yourself. Nel doesn't even know what questions she's asking. When they come to touch one another in the bedroom, when Sula's sick—Nel doesn't even know why she's there. Sula, on the other hand, knows all there is to know about herself because she examines herself, she is experimental with herself, she's perfectly willing to think the unthinkable thing and so on. But she has trouble making a connection with other people and just feeling that lovely sense of accomplishment of being close in a very strong way. She felt that in a way, of course, with Nel, but then obviously they lost one another in friendship. She was able to retrieve it rather nicely with a man, which is lovely, except that in so many instances, with men, the very thing that would attract a man to a woman in the first place might be the one thing she would give over once she learned Nel's lesson, which is love as possession. You own somebody and then you begin to want them there all the time, which is a community law. Marriage, faithfulness, fidelity; the beloved belongs to one person and can't be shared with other people—that's a community value which Sula learned when she fell in love with Ajax, which he wasn't interested in learning.

[s]: Richard Wright said in "How Bigger Was Born" that there were many Biggers that went into creating Bigger Thomas. Are there many Pecolas in Pecola? Or many Sulas in Sula?

[m]: Oh, yes! Well, I think what I did is what every writer does—once you have an idea, then you try to find a character who can manifest the idea for you. And then you have to spend a long time trying to get to know who those people are, who that character is. So you take what there is from whomever you know. Sula—I think this was really part of the difficulty—I didn't know anyone like her. I never knew a woman like that at any rate. But I knew women who looked like that, who looked like they *could be* like that. And then you remember women who were a little bit different in the town, you know; there's always a little bit of gossip and there's always a little bit of something. There's a woman in our town now who is an absolute riot. She can do anything she wants to do. And it occurred to me about twenty years ago how depleted that town would be if she ever left. Everybody wanted her out, and she was a crook and she was mean and she had about twenty husbands—and she was just, you know, a huge embarrassment. Nevertheless, she really and truly was one of the reasons that they called each other on the telephone. They sort of used her excitement, her flavor, her carelessness, her restlessness, and so on. And that quality is what I used in Sula.

[s]: What about Sula's mother and grandmother?

[M]: Oh, Hannah, the mother—I tell you, I think I feel more affection for her than for anybody else in that book. I just loved her. What I was trying to do was to be very provocative without using all of the traditional devices of provocation. And I think—that's why I wrote so slowly—I think I know how to do it by simply relying an awful lot on what I believe the reader already knows. I wanted Sula to be missed by the reader. That's why she dies early. There's a lot of book after she dies, you know. I wanted them to miss her presence in that book as that town missed her presence. I also wanted them to dislike her a lot, and to be fascinated, perhaps, but also to feel that thing that the town might feel—that this is something askew. And I wanted for them to realize at some point—and I don't know if anybody ever realizes it—that she never does anything as bad as her grandmother or her mother did. However, they're alike; her grandmother kills her son, plays god, names people and, you know, puts her hand on a child. You know, she's god-like, she manipulates—all in the best interest. And she is very, very possessive about other people, that is, as a king is. She decided that her son was living a life that was not worth his time. She meant it was too painful for her; you know, the way you kill a dog when he breaks his leg because he can't stand the pain. He may very well be able to stand it, but you can't, so that's why you get rid of him. The mother, of course, was slack. She had no concept of love and possession. She liked to be laid, she liked to be touched, but she didn't want any confusion of relationships and so on. She's very free and open about that. Her relationship to her daughter is almost one of uninterest. She would do things for her, but she's not particularly interested in her.

[S]: That conversation in the kitchen . . .

[M]: That's right: "I love her, but I don't like her," which is an honest statement at any rate. And she'd sleep with anybody, you know, husbands. She just does it. But interestingly enough, the point was that the women in the town who knew that—they didn't like the fact—but at the same time *that* was something they could understand. Lust, sexual lust, and so on. So that when she dies, they will come to her aid. Now Sula might take their husbands, but she was making judgments. You see what it was—it wasn't about love. It wasn't about even lust. Nobody knows what that was about. And also, Sula did the one terrible thing for black people which was to put her grandmother in an old folks' home, which was outrageous, you know. You take care of people! So *that* would be her terrible thing. But at the same time, she is more strange, more formidable than either of those other two women because they were first of all within the confines of the community and their sensibilities were informed by it. Essentially, they were pacific in the sense of what they did do. They wanted to make things come together; you know, bring it together. Hannah didn't want to disturb anything. She did her work and she took care of people and so on; and Eva was generous, wide-spirited, and made some great sacrifices.

[s]: I'm fascinated by all of the women in the two novels: your portraits are so rich. It's not just the main characters—you get that woman from Meridian, Geraldine, in *The Bluest Eye*, and of course Mrs. McTeer, who isn't always talked about, but she certainly is the kind of figure you were describing earlier as a mother to anybody and everybody who will take you in and knows how to raise everybody. With all of these various characters that you've created, certainly you must have some response to the feeling in certain literary circles that black women should be portrayed a certain way. I'm thinking now of the kinds of criticism that have been lodged against Gayl Jones.

[m]: Do you mean black women as victims, that they should not be portrayed as victims?

[s]: Either that or even—and I'm thinking more of Sula here—as emasculating.

[m]: Oh yes. Well, in *The Bluest Eye*, I try to show a little girl as a total and complete victim of whatever was around her. But black women have held, have been given, you know, the cross. They don't walk near it. They're often on it. And they've borne that, I think, extremely well. I think everybody knows, deep down, that black men were emasculated by white men, period. And that black women didn't take any part in that. However, black women have had some enormous responsibilities, which in these days people call freedoms—in those days, they were called responsibilities—they lived, you know, working in other people's, white people's, houses and taking care of that and working in their own houses and so on and they have been on the labor market. And nobody paid them that much attention in terms of threats, and so on, so they had a certain amount of "freedom." But they did a very extraordinary job of just taking on that kind of responsibility and in so doing, they tell people what to do. Now I have to admit, however, that it's a new idea to me—the emasculating black woman. It really is new—that is, in the last few years. I can only go by my own experience, my own family, the black men I knew—the men I knew called the shots, whether they were employed or unemployed. And even in our classic set of stereotypes—Sapphire and Kingfish?—he did anything he was big enough to do! Anything! Talk 'bout free! And she bitched—that she was going to work and so on. But there is an incredible amount of magic and feistiness in black men that nobody has been able to wipe out. But everybody has tried.

Now, Sula—I don't regard her as a typical black woman at all. And the fact that the community responds to her that way means that she's unusual. So she's not the run-of-the-mill average black woman.

[s]: If she weren't unusual, they'd know how to deal with her.

[M]: That's right. There wouldn't have been that confusion about her. They did not know how to deal with her. So she's very atypical and perhaps she would be, you know, a kind of ball-breaker, in that sense. However, the one man who talked to her, and thought she was worthy of conversation, and who let her be, was the one man she could relate to on that level that would make her want something she had never been interested in before, which was a permanent relationship. He was a man who was not intimidated by her; he was interested in her. He treated her as a whole person, not as an extension of himself, not as a vessel, not as a symbol. Their sex was not one person killing the other—that's why I pictured her on top of him, you know, like a tree. He was secure enough and free enough and bright enough —he wasn't terrorized by her because she was odd. He was interested. I think there was a line in the book—he hadn't met an interesting woman since his mother, who was sitting out in the woods "making roots." When a man is whole himself, when he's touched the borders of his own life, and he's not proving something to somebody else— white men or other men and so on—then the threats of emasculation, the threats of castration, the threats of somebody taking over disappear. Ajax is strong enough. He's a terribly unemployed dude, who has interests of his own, whose mother neglected him, but nevertheless assumed all sorts of things about him that he lived up to like he knew he was doing. So he had a different kind of upbringing. Now that, I think, is interesting; that part of it interested me a lot, so that when he would see a woman like Sula, who had been somewhere and had some rather different views about life and so on, he was not intimidated at all. Whereas a man like Jude, who was doing a rather routine, macho thing, would split—you know, he was too threatened by all of that. Just the requirements of staying in the house and having to apologize to his wife were too much for him.

[s]: Now you mention Jude, and that balance between Jude and Ajax is clear in the book. What about Ajax and Cholly Breedlove in *The Bluest Eye*?

[M]: Exactly alike, in that sense. I don't mean that their backgrounds were alike. But in a way, they sort of—through neglect of the fact that someone was not there—made up themselves. They allowed themselves to be whomever they were. Cholly, of course, lives a very tragic life, tragic in the sense that there was no reward, but he is the thing I keep calling a "free man," not free in the legal sense, but free in his head. You see, this was a free man who could do a lot of things;

and I think it's a way of talking about what some people call the "bad nigger." Not in the sense of one who is so carousing, but that adjective "bad" meaning, you know, bad and good. This is a man who is stretching, you know, he's stretching, he's going all the way within his own mind and within whatever his outline might be. Now that's the tremendous possibility for masculinity among black men. And you see it a lot. Sometimes you see it when they do art things, sometimes just in personality and so on. And it's very, very deep and very, very complex and such men as that are not very busy. They may end up in sort of twentieth-century, contemporary terms being also unemployed. They may be in prison. They may be doing all sorts of things. But they are adventuresome in that regard.

And then when you draw a woman who is like that, which is unusual and uncivilized, within our context, then a man like that is interested in her. No, he doesn't want to get married, he doesn't want to do all those things, for all sorts of reasons, some of which are purely sociological. The other kind of man who is more like the Nel syndrome would be very, very preoccupied with it, and his masculinity is threatened all the time. But then you see a man who has had certain achievements—and I don't mean social achievements—but he's been able to manipulate crap games or, you know, just do things—because Cholly has done *everything*—in his life. So that by the time he met Pauline, he was able to do whatever his whims suggested and it's that kind of absence of control that I wanted—you know, obviously, that I'm interested in characters who are lawless in that regard. They make up their lives, or they find out who they are. So in that regard Cholly Breedlove is very much like Ajax.

[s]: Is the progression from girlhood in *The Bluest Eye* to womanhood in *Sula* an intentional progression? Might we view the two novels in these terms?

[m]: Yes. I think I was certainly interested in talking about black girlhood in *The Bluest Eye* and not so interested in it in *Sula*. I wanted to move it into the other part of their life. That is, what do the Claudias and Friedas, those feisty little girls, grow up to be? Precisely. No question about that.

The book that I'm writing now is about a man, and a lot of the things that I learned by writing about Cholly and Ajax and Jude are at least points of departure, leaping-off places, for the work that I'm doing now. The focus is on two men. One is very much like Ajax and Cholly in his youth, so stylish and adventuresome and, I don't know, I think he's truly masculine in the sense of going out too far where you're not supposed to go and running toward confrontations rather than away from them. And risks—taking risks. That quality. One of the men is very much like that. The other will learn to be a complete person, or at least have a notion of it, if I ever get him to

the end of the book. When I wrote that section on Cholly in *The
Bluest Eye*, I thought it would be very hard for me because I didn't
know that as intimately as I knew Pauline. And I thought, well, let
me get started on this 'cause I'm going to have a tough time trying to
really feel that kind of thing. But it's the only time I've ever written
anything in my life when it all came at once. I wrote it straight
through. And it took me a long time, maybe eight or nine hours the
first time, not stopping at all.

When I got to Pauline, whom I knew so well, I could not do it. I
could not make it. I didn't know what to write or how. And I sort of
copped out anyway in the book because I used two voices, hers and
the author's. There were certain things she couldn't know and I had
to come in. And then there were certain things the author would say
that I wanted in her language—so that there were the two things, two
voices, which I had regarded, at any rate, as a way in which to do
something second-best. I couldn't do it straight out the way I did
every other section. That was such a fascinating experience for me
to perceive Cholly that way.

[s]: Will these two men in the new book balance as Nel and Sula do?

[m]: No. That is, they're friends and they're different from each
other, but they're not incomplete the way Nel and Sula are. They are
completely whoever they are and they don't need another man to give
them that. They love each other—I mean, men love the company of
other men—they're like that. And they enjoy the barber shop and the
pool room and so on, and there's a lot of that because they aren't
just interested in themselves. But their relationship is based on
something quite different. And I think in the friendship between men
there is, you know, something else operating. So the metaphors
changed. I couldn't use the same kind of language at all. And it took
a long time for the whole thing to fall together because men are
different and they are thinking about different things. The language
had to be different.

[s]: Will neighborhood or a sense of neighborhood be just as im-
portant in this book?

[m]: Yes. Well, I have one man who is a sort of middle-class black
dude, whose mother was the daughter of the only black doctor. His
father, who is a kind of self-taught man, owns a lot of shacks in the
black part of the town and he loves things, you know, he's accumulat-
ing property and money and so on. And his son is the main character
who makes friends with people in the kind of community that is
described in *Sula*. You know, it's a different social class, there is a
leap, but I don't think the class problems among black people are as
great as the class problems among white people. I mean, there's just
no real problems with that in terms of language and how men relate

to one another—black men relate to one another whatever class they come from.

[s]: Sort of like people living on the same block, going to the same barber shop . . .

[m]: Yes, because whatever it is, you know, the little community is by itself. You go to the same barber shop and there you are. So this one has a little bit of money and that one doesn't but it doesn't make any difference because you're thrown into the same and you get your "stuff" from one another.

[s]: Will there also be a character somewhat like Soaphead Church or Shadrack in this book? Tell me something about your two crazies.

[m]: Well, in the first place, with Shadrack, I just needed, wanted, a form of madness that was clear and compact to bounce off of Sula's strangeness. And you know, he likes her and she goes to his house and he remembers her and so on. So there's a connection between the two of them. And I wanted the town to respond to him in one way and to her in another. They're both eccentrics, outside the law, except that Shadrack's madness is very organized. He has organized the world. He just wants all this to be done on one day. It's orderly, as madness is—isolation, total isolation and order. You know, it's trying to get order in what is perceived by the madman as a disordered world. So the town understands his own way of organizing chaos, once they find out what he's doing—you know, National Suicide Day.

   With Soaphead, I wanted, needed someone to give the child her blue eyes. Now she was asking for something that was just awful—she wanted to have blue eyes and she wanted to be Shirley Temple, I mean, she wanted to do that white trip because of the society in which she lived and, very importantly, because of the black people who helped her want to be that. (The responsibilities are ours. It's our responsibility for helping her believe, helping her come to the point where she wanted that.) I had to have someone—her mother, of course, made her want it in the first place—who would give her the blue eyes. And there had to be somebody who *could*, who had the means; that kind of figure who dealt with fortune-telling, dream-telling and so on, who would also believe that she was right, that it was preferable for her to have blue eyes. And that would be a person like Soaphead. In other words, he would be wholly convinced that if black people were more like white people they would be better off. And I tried to explain that in terms of his own West Indian background—a kind of English, colonial, Victorian thing drilled into his head which he could not escape. I needed someone to distill all of that, to say, "Yeah, you're right, you need them. Here, I'll give them to you," and really believe that he had done her a favor. Someone who would never question the request in the first place. That kind of black. It was very important in the story that the miracle happen, and she does get them, although I had to make it fairly logical in that only she can see them and that she's really flipped by that time.

[s]: Does your job as an editor get in the way of your writing? I ask this partly because I remember so well having a creative writing teacher who told me once how his being an English major in college got in the way of his writing, so he became an anthropology major . . .

[m]: In order to free himself?

[s]: Yes. A number of things can get in the way of writing; lots of teachers of literature would like to write, but perhaps their teaching gets in the way of the writing. Now, you are a writer, and an editor, and a teacher—how do you do it?

[m]: Well, I suspect that full-time teaching would get in the way of writing for me because you have to think a certain way about the literature you're teaching, and I think that would spill over into the way in which one has to think when writing. The critical stance— which is what teaching is—sometimes makes me feel, if I move right into my writing, too self-conscious. You're so aware of the theory and the effort and so on, that you become very self-conscious and maybe a little too tight about it. For me, it has to be very private and very unrelated. When I write, I can't read other people that I like. I have to read detective stories or things like that. I have to feel as if it's being done almost in a very separate womb of my own construction. Wholly free. And because it's the only activity at all that I engage in wholly for myself, it's the one place that I can't have any other interference of that sort.

The editing is no problem, because that is such a different way of thinking about things. I don't have to exercise the same skills or talent. I don't create as an editor, I simply do more of what one does in teaching, but in terms of someone who is creating—you see, that is my work, so I don't feel anything strong or deeply personal about it at all. What I want to do with an author is to get him into the position to do the best work he can, and then to try to publish it so it will receive the widest amount of attention, and look elegant, and be well-received. That's quite different. It's sort of like fishing—you catch fish, which is different from cooking them. You don't have to know one in order to do the other, and you can do one well and not do the other well. So that I don't find a conflict there. The problem, of course, is time, trying to find enough time for all of those things. And I like it all, you know, but probably the only one that I couldn't live without is the writing. I think that if all the publishers disappeared, I would write anyway, because that is a compulsion with me. To write, to think that way.

[s]: How did the teaching go this term?

[M]: Oh, I enjoyed it. I really did. I had a good time in both classes and in the "Black Women and Their Fiction" class, it was nice because I was able to discuss contemporary women and maybe introduce students to some women that they had never read before. And also, it was nice going into almost untrammeled territory with them. There isn't a lot of first-rate criticism about black women writers, so that in their papers I insisted that they make reference to the text that we had read in class. And I had given them outlines and general questions which we dealt with in class to get around to a decent topic for term papers. But they knew that they were very free to introduce ideas—in other words, there were not a lot of secondary sources to which they could go. I told them to feel free to draw their own conclusions. A couple of them did really first-rate work.

[S]: You're quite right—there isn't very much good criticism of black literature and particularly of the literature by black women. What kinds of things do you feel, as a writer, a teacher, and as an editor, need to be pursued in this regard? Should criticism take a particular direction—do certain questions need to be asked more than others.

[M]: Certain questions occur to me when I try to think of the body of black literature that there is in general and the body of black literature that women have produced. In the course, for example, I was very interested in how contemporary black women looked at the stereotype of black women. Did they accept that role? Did the writers believe, in the works we studied, that that was pretty much the way we were? Were there characters representative of the mammy, whore, whatever? show-girl, whatever? And emasculation and so on? How political were they? Were the writings very, very directed by new political awarenesses or were they distant from that, were they outside the so-called realm of politics? What were their perceptions about their role? How did they really see themselves? And even—if we could get a little bit deeper, if you could think in terms of not just characters but plot and tone and the attitude of the woman writer toward the world in which she lives—does she really feel burdened and harassed? Frequently, what I found so lacking in most black writing by men that seems to be present in a lot of black women's writing is a sense of joy, in addition to oppression and being women or black or whatever. With some exceptions. Gayl Jones is an exception to that. She never writes about joy. I think that's because she's young. But with others, there is a sense of comfort in being who one is, there's an expression of good times, not in the sense of "going out somewhere." There's a scene in *Sula* where the women are just having some fun, talking to one another. They enjoy that. That kind of woman. In Lucille Clifton's *Generations,* there's that sense of fun and joy. In Toni Cade, there's that sense of high-spiritedness. I don't mean comedy, and I don't mean jokes or anything. But part of this business of living in the world and triumphing over it has to do with a sense that there's some pleasure. And where do they get that pleasure from: How do they look at what we would call beauty in the world? What do they think it is? What pleases them? Just to see what the black woman's sensibilities are when she writes. What is she preoccupied with? What does she think are the crucial sorts of questions about existence, life, man-woman relationships? Are they seen the same way as the way in which the men have seen them?

[s]: Most of the major male characters in black literature are in motion. They're frequently much more like Ajax—maybe not always as grand and high-spirited as Ajax—but mobile. I think of such books as *Invisible Man* and *Autobiography of an Ex-Colored Man*, where there's this movement and quite often, there's no name, in contrast to how women are named, how they are lovingly named. An exception to this might be Leon Forrest.

[M]: But even there, he has that marvelous man, James Fishbond, you know, who is just a traveling man. Both of these things are very interesting to me. The name thing is a very, very strong theme in the book that I'm writing, the absence of a name given at all, the odd names and the slave names, the whole business, the feeling of anonymity, the feeling of orphanage. That's very important and became immediately clear to me in this new book. But the first thing you said about being in motion is also true, because I think that one of the major differences between black men's work—the major black characters—and black women's work is precisely that. The big scene is the traveling Ulysses scene, for black men. They are moving. Trains— you hear those men talk about trains like they were their first lover— the names of the trains, the times of the trains! And, boy, you know, they spread their seed all over the world. They are really moving! Perhaps it's because they don't have a land, they don't have dominion. You can trace that historically, and one never knows what would have been the case if we'd never been tampered with at all. But that going from town to town or place to place or looking out and over and beyond and changing and so on—that, it seems to me, is one of the monumental themes in black literature about men. That's what they do. It is the Ulysses theme, the leaving home. And then there's no one place that one settles. I mean, one travels. And I don't mean this in the sense of the Joycean character or even in the sense of just going off to find one's fortune in the classic sort of fairy tale, going off to see where the money is. But something else. Curiosity, what's around the corner, what's across the hill, what's in the valley, what's down the track. Go find out what that is, you know! And in the process of finding, they are also making themselves. Although in

sociological terms that is described as a major failing of black men—
they do not stay home and take care of their children, they are
not there—that has always been to me one of the most attractive fea-
tures about black male life. I guess I'm not suppose to say that. But
the fact that they would split in a minute just delights me. It's part
of that whole business of breaking ground, doing the other thing.
They would leave, go someplace else. There was always that possi-
bility. They were never—I don't say they were never, obviously there
were exceptions to all of this—but they didn't just let it happen, just
let it happen. That's part of that interesting magic I was talking
about. And you know, the traveling musician, the theater group,
those people who just stayed on the road, lived a different life. It's
very beautiful, it's very interesting, and in that way, you know, they
lived in the country, they lived here, they went all over it.

[s]: It's interesting to compare that motif to what you did to Sula,
in that she is in motion in a sense . . .

[m]: Very much.

[s]: . . . at the same time that she is most stationary and in those
enclosures, like that bedroom where she dies.

[m]: She is a masculine character in that sense. She will do the
kinds of things that normally only men do, which is why she's so
strange. She really behaves like a man. She picks up a man, drops a
man, the same way a man picks up a woman, drops a woman. And
that's her thing. She's masculine in that sense. She's adventuresome,
she trusts herself, she's not scared, she really ain't scared. And she is
curious and will leave and try anything. So that quality of mascu-
linity—and I mean this in the pure sense—in a woman at that time is
outrage, total outrage. She can't get away with that—unless she were
in this sort of strange environment, this alien environment—for the
normal—which would be the theater world, in which you realize, the
people are living, even there, by laws. You know, somebody should
do something interesting on that kind of show business woman—Billie
Holiday, Bessie Smith—not just their art form, but their lives. It's
incredible, that sense of adventure that those women had. And I
think that's why they were there in the first place. They were outside
of that little community value thing. It's more normal among men,
but it's attractive, and with men, it seems to me to be one of the very
interesting things to talk about when one is doing any criticism of
black writing, rather than doing those books in which you do five
hundred people and you say a little bit about this one, a little bit
about that one. If somebody could get one or two of the really major
themes that are part and parcel of this canon. And there are some
traceable, identifiable themes, and that's the kind of criticism that
I would love to see. There may be some things that you could do

with both men and women. But certainly this seems to me one of the major themes. And then there's the black woman as parent, not as a mother or father, but as a parent, as a sort of umbrella figure, culture-bearer, in that community with not just her children but all children, her relationship in that sense, how that is handled and treated and understood by writers, what that particular role is. We talk about all these things in terms of what her huge responsibilities have been, but a really penetrating analysis might be very helpful.

[s]: You've just described, very well, some new directions for criticism. Can you say something about new directions in fiction?

[m]: What I think is happening?

[s]: Well, what you think is happening, what may happen in fiction by some of the writers we've been discussing, in this decade.

[m]: Oh, I went to some meeting recently and there was a great deal of despair, it seemed to me, about what was happening in publishing and black fiction, the suggestion being that there was not much being published but that now it's not so popular anymore and that white publishers have decided that our age is over and that we are no longer fashionable as we were in the late sixties or early seventies. I think part of that's right—that is, we're no longer fashionable in that sense—all of which I am so grateful for, absolutely relieved to find, because some brilliant writers, I think, can surface now. Once you get off of the television screen, you can go home and do your work, because your responsibilities are different. Now I don't mean that there's any lessening of political awareness or political work, but I do think that one can be more fastidious, more discriminating. And it's open, it's just freer, that's all, and there's room, there's lots of room. People tend to think that the whole literary thing is a kind of pyramid, that somebody is on top, which is total anathema to me. There is enormous space! I think of it in terms of the one other art form in which black people have always excelled and that is music, an art form that opens doors, rather than closes them, where there are more possibilities, not fewer. But to continue to write the way some-body believes is the prescribed way is death. And if I know anything about black artists, I know they don't pay any attention to any pre-scriptions that anybody gives them at all!

It's harder perhaps in literature, because it has to be purchased by somebody in a publishing house, so that you're always under the eye of some other person. Nevertheless, it's exciting and it's new and it's marvelous and it's as though somebody pulled out the plug and we were left again to our own devices, not somebody else's, not the television's devices, not the New York *Times'* version of what we were supposed to do, but our own devices, which are the ones which we have to be left to. White writers, you know, write about us all the time. There are major black characters in Updike, in *Ragtime*, in all of them. That's where all the life is. That's where the life is. And the future of American literature is in that direction. I don't mean that's the only group, but that certainly is one of the major groups. Obviously, lots of people are interested in it, not just for research purposes as you know, but in terms of the gem, the theme, the juice, of fiction. And we are certainly, obviously, interested; we have all sorts of philosophical attitudes about "the predicament." There's that incredible kind of movement which yields an artistic representation of something that one takes for granted in history. I think that accounts for the success of Gayl Jones's first book, where you have the weight of history working itself out in the life of one, two, three people; I mean a large idea, brought down small, and at home, which gives it a universality and a particularity which makes it extraordinary.

But there's so much that nobody ever, ever does. You know, I go sometimes and, just for sustenance, I read those slave narratives— there are sometimes three or four sentences or half a page, each one of which could be developed in an art form, marvelous. Just to figure out how to—you mean to tell me she beat the dogs and the man and pulled a stump out of the ground? Who is she, you know? Who is she? It's just incredible. And all of that will surface, it *will surface,* and my *huge* joy is thinking that I am in some way part of that when I sit here in this office and that somehow there must be those of us in white established publishers where a black author can feel that he's going to go and get some respect—he doesn't have to explain every- thing—somebody is going to understand what he's trying to do, in his terms, not in somebody else's, but in his. I'm not saying that only black editors can do it, but I'm certainly saying that it's important that we are here to participate, to contribute to "the shelf"—as Forrest likes to call it.

[s]: I have one last question. What's the name of the new novel?

[M]: At the moment, it's called *Milkman Dead.* [The novel was published as *Song of Solomon* in the fall of 1977.]

SIRAS BOWENS OF SUNBURY, GEORGIA
A TIDEWATER ARTIST IN THE AFRO-AMERICAN
VISUAL TRADITION

ROBERT FARRIS THOMPSON

> *Old Aunt Mackie, wizen-faced, walker-with-a-stick . . . given to dramatic trances and fiery flights. . . .*
> —RALPH ELLISON, "A Coupla Scalped Indians"

> *The women . . . put different colored bottles, broken glass and sea-shells all around the grave of Aunt Dicey. In that way they showed their love for her.*
> —WILLIAM J. FAULKNER, *The Days When the Animals Talked*

TO HONOR MEN AND WOMEN WITH SPIRITUALLY REASONED OBJECTS is a noble enterprise. In such a tradition emerged part of the burial ground of the Sunbury Baptist Church in Georgia, near the site of the old colonial port of Sunbury.[1] Well within this century, it seems, African-born blacks were still remembered in this portion of tidewater Georgia. A few kept alive their African speech: "Old man Dublin, he belong to the Andersons o' Sunbury, and every day or two Miss Bertha would send me over for him—to talk the old African talk."[2]

The persistence of African speech (Kimbundu? Ki-Kongo?) in Sunbury was a measure of resistance to demands implicit and not-so-subtle that blacks give up all heritage in favor of Western ways, suggesting the possibility of further cultural assertions. And, in fact, wood sculptures for the dead, shaped and sited in ways strongly suggesting Kongo and Angola influences, are found in the village cemetery. Here there are "bi-lingual" graves, with sea shells and glass bottles and porcelain containers (sometimes perforated and placed on the ground upside-down) sited on axis between the Western foot- and head-stones (Plate 1).[3]

Depositing—on hallowed ground—an upturned basin with single tiny perforation, "kills" the object and sends it to the other world with the departed owner; this device mirrors custom in Kongo (Plate

2).[4] To this day men and women in Bas-Zaïre associate the concept, *bikinda*, "spirit of a dead man in the ground," with its verbal root, *kindama*, "to be upside-down."[5] In other words, the belief that death turns things upside-down persists and provides background for the southern black custom of sometimes inverting flower-pots or porcelain bowls over a final resting-place.

Plate 1

The founding tradition is very much alive in 1976 in Bas-Zaïre and extends as far east as the Gwembe Valley in Zambia.[6] Like graves documented in Mayombe country, in Bas-Zaïre, and in Mwemba territory, Zambia, the Afro-Georgian custom of breaking or perforating, inverting, and depositing funereal objects on the surface of a grave or tomb is defined in its abbreviation, as distinguished from the large cluster of bottles on the graves of old Kongo chiefs of the last century.

But some objects are placed right-side-up upon the grave. These include bottles and pitchers, meant to incarnate the perpetual refreshment of the spirit as well as to manifest a mourner's love.[7]

Speaking to the dead with objects was the black paradigm out of which an Afro-American folk artist named Siras Bowens emerged in the first half of this century. An intense black man with burning eyes, he stood up one day in the middle of the Great Depression and, some say, heard voices tell him, tell him "make images in wood in honor of your family dead."

He began to roam the pine forests surrounding Sunbury, looking for unusual branches, twigs, and chunks of trees. Where others saw lumber, he discovered shadowed presences. He knew what he needed and where to find it. And the talent became a matter of common admiration: "he'd go in the woods, find him a tree, all kinds of different pine trees with crooks in them. I doubt if *I* could find stuff like that."[8]

Plate 2

The focus of his selectivity recalls certain Kongo icons of metaphysical power and discernment; for trees with crooks in them and twisted roots, so it is believed in Bas-Zaïre, are the very signs of Funza, the spirit who brought to mankind, ages ago, the sacred medicines (*minkisi*) of God.[9] In addition, consultation of the lore of the Chokwe of northern Angola reveals that the forked stick represents a witch, in the counters of indigenous divination, or, in the context of burials, the resting-place of chiefs.[10] This tells us that a forked stick in northern Angola is, and is not, a dangerous thing. There is further lore in point from this classical area of Central African civilization. Thus in North Kongo the noble medicine-bundle called *nkita* is imputed the power to create crooked shapes in nature and another strong charm, *ndembo*, takes shape in twisted roots and singular plant formations.[11] Thus, in terms of the iconology of Bas-Zaïre and Northern Angola, whose sons and daughters were illegally brought to the coast of Georgia as late as the 1850's, Siras Bowens was carrying terrible things into his Georgia graveyard, bad things, things resonating with power from the other world.

Documented Kongo influence in the making and naming of certain charms made for and by traditional black people in the South,[12] in addition to the concordance of the types of wood Bowens used with iconographies of Kongo and Angola healing, suggests one reason for his powers of discernment: he could go into the forest and find things an ordinary man could not because his eye had been sharpened by the lore of the local healers. The practice of indigenous healing

Plate 3

still goes on in tidewater Georgia and the Carolina low country; and the more famous of these "root men" and "root women" have begun to earn the respect of students of indigenous healing and parallel medicine. As the life of Bowens melts into legend, at least one person has suggested that here was a black man who really knew how to work with leaves and roots.

Although his role as an outright healer remains to be established, it is clear that Bowens meant to communicate inherent power in his standing monoliths of forked wood. Thus, in the 'thirties, he designed the entrance to the family portion of the cemetery so that visitors were caused to pass through flanking columns of crooked pine set before matching shafts of brick. These staffs indicate the way to the dead (Plate 3). Inside the family enclosure, Bowens erected four sculptures made of available pieces of forest wood and aligned them

carefully. They faced the entrance. There were four sculptures stand-
ing in 1939 (Plate 4). The right was guarded by a vital sculpture of a
snake, set upon a pedestal of forked wood. Shaping a curved length

Plate 4

of raw branch into the semblance of a snake added menace to strangeness of material and, at the same time, recalled the persistent theme of the reptile (snakes, alligators, turtles, and lizards) in the iconography of the black walking-sticks of the South, particularly those associated with healers, "root men," "root women," those "walkers-with-a-stick . . . given to dramatic trances," as Ralph Ellison characterizes one of them in an excerpt from his novel-in-progress. The snake-on-a-pedestal and a remarkable, soaring, serpentine structure flank an abstract figure of a standing human presence, essentially a sphere with eyes set upon a cylinder. The eyes of the figure (which alone of the four sculptures was still standing in 1975) were deeply hollowed, dramatically shadowed, spectral. The presence of a spirit, trapped in geometric reductiveness, was communicated here. The motif of the head at the summit of a column recalled the marking of many chiefly staffs in both Kongo and Afro-Georgian walking-sticks; the latter were carved at Darien, on the Georgia coast, as late as 1938. Almost unnoticed stands a small shaft of wood, set in the earth to the right of the column with hollowed eyes in shadow, like a junior spirit in relation to the major sculptured presences.

The most arresting of the standing sculptures is the soaring meander cut from the long branch of an unusual forest pine. Curving like a serpent and standing like a person or a tree, this work draws upon deep and primary sources of vitality. The branch makes one rapid, dramatic, single curve or loop; and Bowens seized upon this particularity, bringing into explicit focus the shaping of a circle, by adding a bar of wood. He placed within this circle a long horizontal small cylinder of wood. He set at right angles to the exact center of this line-within-the-circle a coffin-shaped piece of board. The motif does not exactly match the form of the ordinary Christian cemetery cross or even the Celtic styling of a cross-within-a-circle. But it overlaps completely the black folk healers' sign of "the four corners of the world"[13] [A], itself very probably derived from the sign of the cosmos and reincarnation in ancient Kongo [B] which also re-

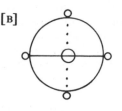

emerged,[14] among slaves from Bas-Zaïre, in Haiti and in Rio. This sign universalizes, in this case, concern with clan persistence. A full attestation of this symbol was collected by Harry Middleton Hyatt at nearby Waycross, Georgia, in a context of spiritual command:

> "draw you a circle on that clean sheet of paper and put a cross in there . . . that's the four corners of the earth . . . put that seal on the ground [the cross drawn within a circle] . . . put your right foot on it and you turn your face to the west . . . which is the sun going down . . . you can speak the words if you ain't got it wrote out, you say [a person's name], you come to me and do as I say to you. . . ."[15]

This soaring sculpture recalls the tall pointed staffs in North Kongo, *nsungwa*, which are sometimes decorated with the motif of the cross in the circle.[16] Seen as an expressive whole, the four staff-like presences may be taken as scepters for the dead or even as embodiments of the dead. They guard the departed members of the Bowens clan with expressions of ancestral power.

II

Siras Bowens was almost certainly influenced by streams of philosophical continuity from Kongo and Angola. If we compare his carefully staged enclosure with an enclosure of ancestor-trees in Northern Angola several formal similarities flash into immediate being. Let us consider, for example, a special compound built in this century to honor the ancestors of Chief Mwafima, head of a Chokwe village near the town of Dundo in the north of Angola.[17] This Chokwe spirit-enclosure is circular, the borders marked with a margin of forked stumps. Inside the circle, trees were planted as special embodiments. They became guardians in living wood. The designated spirits included the *Mutondo Mukumbi* tree, representing the protective spirits of the founding ancestors, together with termite mounds, symbolizing various families composing the village; a cylindrical shaft of wood with summit carved in the shape of a head—another ancestral presence; more termite earth; a tree believed to bring luck to men and hunters; and a wooden animal figure elevated on two stakes, believed propitious for hunting and the fecundity of women.[18]

Forked stumps to mark the margins of the dead certainly echo suggestively the deliberate positioning of similar shapes at the entrance to the Sunbury burials. In both memorial contexts a post surmounted by a head appears, as does a tree-form soaring in a curve of continuous growth. Moreover, the elevation of the Georgian snake in wood on a forked pedestal can be compared with the elevation of an animal figure on two stakes in Angola. Sunbury, of course, is not a Chokwe village and many discontinuities—ant heap symbolism, allusions to the hunt and women—criss-cross with continuing threads of custom. Manifestly, however, both programs of sculpture share concern with blurring together the image of the forest and the image of the grave the better to harness immortal powers.

We now consider the actual graves which these Afro-Georgian sculptures guard. The elaboration of their stylistic means most strongly recall Kongo and Angola. Bowens used, in four instances, a length of iron pipe to mark a line, in the air, from head- to foot-stone. These metal accents create a sense of armature and strength, like a brace for the persons in the earth. The great Mu-Kongo savant, Fu-Kiau Bunseki, maintains that pipes on Afro-American traditional burials relate to hollow stalks called *mwinga* in Ki-Kongo, used to symbolize a bridge between two worlds.[19]

Where pipe connects the markers, in two instances, an automobile headlight has been embedded in the headstone. This is reminiscent of Kongo visions of the flash of the spirit in shining motion. It also compares with the placement of lamp chimneys or small lamps with wicks on Carolina graves today and, in Yombe country in Bas-Zaïre in 1976, with the insertion of mirrors in headstones and the deposit of hurricane lamps over tombs. The headlight illumines the way to the other world. Its sparkle is a sign of spirit. Lengths of iron pipe possibly bridge the way in permanence. Porcelain pitchers, embedded right side up in the concrete surface of certain of the graves, indicate love and perpetual refreshment. This is one interpretation. Here is background for another, focused on the alleged relation between hollow iron pipe and hollow stalks in a context of the dead:

> The word, *mwinga,* is interesting and appears to embody a specific and appropriate symbolism. *Mwinga* is a hollow stalk, especially a cane that survives a fire. The perdurability of ghosts is commonly symbolized by grassland trees that survive the annual burning.[20]

This interpretation fits the parallel usage of stumps and forks to suggest the dead. There can be little doubt that the time-resistant quality of metal pipe on Afro-American traditional graves is an important element of its intrinsic meaning. Although a stone would have served equally as well, the grave of Rosa W. Allen, who died on

4 March 1960 at Mt. Nebo, South Carolina, has placed before her
stone, and upturned flower-pots, a section of iron pipe as an auton-
omous icon. In fact iron pipe appears all over the South in black
graveyards as an alternative to or companion with the headstones.
Pipe and headstone combinations mark one of these conscious con-
frontations of Western- and African-derived stylistic means which
add tension and grace to many forms of black American expressive
consciousness, comparable to the insertion of a field holler in the
flow of a three-line blues. Examples include burials at Algiers,
Louisiana; Snow Hill, Maryland; and the Carolina low country,
particularly between Charleston and the North Carolina border. For
a series of coincidences, these phenomena seem remarkably re-
dundant in time and space and may well represent an Afro-American
innovation fit within an ancient body of assumptions about time and
the persistence of clan and name.

To return to the important matter of embedding headlight glass in
tombstones, custom in Sunbury can be immediately compared to the
insertion of agate marbles or ball-bearings in tombstones of the south-
western quadrant of Mississippi. These traits probably reflect black
American rephrasings of the custom of inserting mirrors into the walls
or pillars of tombs in Bas-Zaïre, as well as the famous Kongo statues
of the last century, used for power and medicine, and displaying a
mirror embedded in the abdomen as a sign of mystic vision.

In sum, then, Siras Bowens of Sunbury, Georgia unified, in a
single program of cultural assertion, forked-branch standing pres-
ences, glass insertions for spiritual flash, a tree-form encapsulating
the sign of the cross-within-the-circle, a reptile on a forked support,
a spectral staff with hollowed eyes. And all of this was added to grave-
sites covered with sea shells, classic Kongo symbol of the spiral
journey from one world to the next and similarly reasoned on St.
Simons Island off the Georgia coast, plus iron pipe, plus pitchers,
plus perforated basins turned right side up. Because of the density of
these cultural expressions and their systematic connection with
Kongo and Angola metaphysics, it is permissible to characterize the
Sunbury burials of Siras Bowens as a monument in the transatlantic
tradition of black art history.

Bowens died at Sunbury on 19 February 1966. I visited the ruins of
his house in late December 1968. Already the structure was only
half-extant, roof removed by passing storms. Inside, the blue of
heaven was reflected in the dressing-table mirror of the departed
craftsman. His comb, hat, glasses—every object had been left in place.
No one dared disturb them. His broken house with its panoply of
possessions recalled the broken vessels on certain of the Bowens'

graves. A concrete slab lies hidden in the wild grass before the vanished steps and on its surface Siras Bowens had incised the legend "1940" and impressed, while the concrete still was wet, a shoe-print. At the very time his sculptures had begun to attract the attention of serious scholars and photographers, Siras Bowens had signed and dated the entrance to his house as another kind of monument. He remained to the end a guardian of black historical consciousness and responsibility.

NOTES

[1] Paul McIlvaine, *The Dead Towns of Sunbury and Dorchester* (Asheville: Grove Printing Co., 1971), second edition. At page 10 McIlvaine notes African-derived hoe cultivation and head portage among the blacks of old Sunbury.

[2] Lydia Parrish, *Slave Songs of the Georgia Sea Islands* (Hatboro: Folklore Associates, 1965), reprint edition, p. 45.

[3] The photograph, by the author, was taken at Sunbury in December 1968.

[4] I thank Ragnar Widman for making a copy of this photograph from the Stockholm archives of the Svensk Missionforbundet available to me. The photograph, taken not far from the modern Zairois city of Mbanza Ngungu, dates from last quarter of the nineteenth century.

[5] Professor Wyatt MacGaffey, personal communication, March 1976. In a forthcoming volume I fully discuss the historical matrix of this cultural phenomenon.

[6] Barrie Reynolds, *The Material Culture of the Peoples of the Gwembe Valley* (New York: Praeger, 1968), pp. 25-26. A field visit to Mayombe country in Bas-Zaire in May 1976 established the vibrant continuity of this custom among modern Bakongo, especially in the Tchela and Boma zones.

[7] Talk with Fu-Kiau Bunseki and Mbuta Wamba, both from the North Kongo region of Manianga, summer 1975, to whom I am grateful for many insights and patient response to my inquiries about tradition in Kongo.

[8] Aaron Bowens, in an interview taped by Robert Allardice at Sunbury, 5 August 1969, who has generously shared this research with me.

[9] Professor Wyatt MacGaffey, March 1976.

[10] Professor John Janzen, personal communications, April 1976.

[11] John H. Weeks, *Among the Primitive Bakongo* (London: Seeley, Service & Co., 1914), p. 159. Cf. Lydia Parrish, p. 31: "E. J. Glave . . . gives a picture of a distorted [Kongo] 'charm root' which explains the use of eccentric wood growths in the decoration of the Negro graveyard at Sunbury."

[12] For example, the Kongo charm for luck, *tobe,* compounded of grave earths and other substances, and moistened with palm wine, surely gave rise to the New Orleans black charm of the same name, similar ingredients (whiskey is used in lieu of palm wine) and function—i.e., to bring good luck. For details, cf. K. E. Laman, *Dictionnaire KiKongo-Français,* II (Brussels, 1936), 978, and Harry M. Hyatt, *Hoodoo—Conjuration—Witchcraft—Rootwork* (Hannibal, Missouri: Western Publishing Co., 1970), I, 655. The latter version of the *tobe,* moistened with oil of clover when activated, was documented at Algiers, Louisiana.

[13] Hyatt, II, 1266.

[14] Fu-Kiau Bunseki, *N'-ongo Ye Nza Yakun'zungidila: Nza-Kongo* (Kinshasa: Office National de la Recherche et de Developpement, 1969), Illustrations T-20 and T-23.

[15] Hyatt, II, 1173.

[16] Source: Fu-Kiau, interviews, August 1975. This custom may be restricted to the Manianga region; I did not find any trace of it in northern Mayombe.

[17] Marie-Louise Bastin, *Art Decoratif Tshokwe* (Lisbon: Compania de Diamantes de Angola, 1961), I, 184. See also Mesquitela Lima, *Fonctions sociologiques des figurines de culte hamba dans la société et dans la culture tshokwe* (Luanda, 1971). Professor Janzen suggests that Bowens, in bringing natural objects into the human realm, in erecting a tall forked stick with coil at the bottom, plus carving an allusion to the serpent, strikingly recalls details of the Chokwe *nzaji*, or lightning cult.

[18] Bastin, p. 184.

[19] Personal communication, February 1975.

[20] Wyatt MacGaffey, personal communication, February 1975.

AFRICA, SLAVERY, & THE ROOTS OF CONTEMPORARY BLACK CULTURE

MARY F. BERRY &
JOHN W. BLASSINGAME

THE AMERICAS BECAME AN OUTPOST OF WEST AFRICAN CULTURE between the sixteenth and the middle of the nineteenth century. Traces of that culture are still found in the United States in the last decades of the twentieth century in music, folktales, proverbs, dress, dance, medicine, language, food, architecture, art and religion. African cultural patterns also influenced American slavery as an institution.

From a contemporary perspective, the importance of slavery lies in two areas. First, it has been the major determinant of American race relations. The legacy of slavery led in the nineteenth century to the institution of Jim Crow laws designed to separate blacks and whites, to segregated housing and schools, to discrimination in the dispensation of justice, to the myths about interracial sex, and to economic and political oppression. Second, slavery played a crucial role in the creation of contemporary black culture and the preservation of African cultural elements in the Americas.

At the same time that the African slave contributed much to American culture, he stood as America's metaphor. As long as the black man labored in chains, the Declaration of Independence and the Constitution symbolized the American white man's ability to lie to himself. Having lived so long with this lie, American whites found it increasingly difficult to resolve the contradiction between equality and discrimination once they had ended the conflict between slavery and freedom. Although some form of involuntary servitude had existed in practically all societies before the creation of the United States, in none of them did the fundamental documents and philos-

This article is an excerpt from a forthcoming book, *Long Memory: The Black Experience in America.* (Copyright © Prentice-Hall, Inc.)

ophies so unequivocally assert that slavery was a violation of divine and natural law. Because of the glaring contradiction between their belief in freedom and equality and their practice of enslaving and discriminating against blacks, antebellum American whites suffered from a massive guilt complex.

To escape the residue of this guilt in the twentieth century, white historians have tried to prove that the slaves received better treatment than white workers, that the blacks were content as slaves, that none of the social problems afflicting Afro-Americans in the twentieth century have their roots in the peculiar institution, and that slaves were so assimilated that their culture should be stamped, "Made in America." All of these arguments are mythological and have little relationship to the realities of bondage.

The greatest crime committed by slavery scholars in the first half of the twentieth century was their attempt to prove that blacks were inferior. The long-suffering Christ-like Uncle Tom, the unbelievably loyal child-man Sambo, and the Mammy who loved her master more than her own family are unfounded stereotypes of incredible longevity. So many whites accepted these stereotypes and similar ones about Africans that many blacks rejected the study of slavery and Africa. They both were part of a dismal past best forgotten. But just as American whites cannot assuage their guilt by turning to myths, blacks cannot live in a present without roots in the past.

The assertion by some scholars and Afro-Americans in the 1960's that "black history began in 1865" has been productive of much evil. First, it enabled white scholars to ignore the contributions blacks made to more than 250 years of American history. Second, such views discouraged blacks from investigating their own history. Although the ancestors of practically all white Americans were at one time slaves, twentieth-century blacks were led to believe that they were the *only* Americans who were descendants of bondsmen. One significant result of the guilt feelings blacks felt over this was that they had less interest in genealogy than any other group of Americans.

A third result of the denial of the slave past was the virtual destruction of many unique and functional aspects of Afro-American culture as twentieth-century blacks rushed to adopt the values of American whites. It was only in the 1960's that masses of blacks discovered that many of the values and customs of whites were less functional for the survival of an oppressed minority than those of their slave ancestors.

"It is of consequence," America's premier folklorist, William Wells Newell, declared in 1894, "for the American Negro to retain the recollection of his African origin, and of his American servitude." This was necessary, Newell said, because "for the sake of the honor of his race, he should have a clear picture of the mental condition out of which he has emerged: this picture is not now complete, nor will be made so without a record of song, tales, beliefs, which belong to the stage of culture through which he has passed." The collection of the data noted by Newell had reached a point by the middle of the twentieth century that scholars could begin to answer the question of the origin of black culture. There is, however, no unanimity. The debate on origins has centered on the folktale.

Richard M. Dorson, in his *Negro Folktales in Michigan* (1956) argued that an overwhelming majority of Afro-American folktales came originally from Europe. Since Dorson compiled his tales in the 1950's, his theory may be correct for the latter half of the twentieth century. Obviously, the spread of literacy, radio and television sets in the twentieth century led to the diffusion of European folklore in the black community. Just as obvious, however, is the fact that the widespread illiteracy of slaves and the absence of mass communications media in the nineteenth century severely limited the diffusion of the folklore of European immigrants in the slave community.

Given the degree of isolation between antebellum whites and blacks and differences in languages and roles, it is inconceivable that European sailors—when transporting Africans to the Americas—or that white plantation owners and overseers—while the slaves were at work or rest—regaled the blacks with European folktales, proverbs, and riddles. Most of the diffusion of folklore in the nineteenth century involved whites borrowing from blacks: slaves customarily entertained their master's children with tales, white folklorists regularly visited the quarters and recorded them, and large segments of the white community read the stories compiled by Joel Chandler Harris, Charles C. Jones, Jr., Alcée Fortier, and others.

Whatever the situation in the twentieth century, about 65% of the folktales of slaves in the American South in the nineteenth century came from Africa. The 200 slave tales recorded by Abigail Christensen in South Carolina, Joel Chandler Harris and Charles C. Jones, Jr. in Georgia, Alcée Fortier in Louisiana, and Hampton Institute's black folklorists all over the South between 1872 and 1900 were generally identical in structure, detail, function, motif, attitudes, and thought patterns to African ones. Rarely did the slave's tales show any trace of the sentimentality and romanticism characteristic of European folklore.

The African origin of nineteenth-century black folktales has long been recognized by the collectors of African folklore. In 1892, A. Gerber compared Afro-American and African folklore and asserted that "not only the plots of the majority of the stories, but even the principal actors, are of African origin." African scholars found striking parallels between the Uncle Remus stories collected by Harris and West African folktales. According to Alta Jablow, the traditional West African animal stories "served as the prototype of the well-known Uncle Remus stories." And in 1966, H. A. S. Johnston, after studying more than 1,000 traditional Hausa and Fulani folktales in Nigeria, asserted: "Brer Rabbit is undoubtedly the direct descendant of the hare of African folktales. Not only are his characteristics exactly the same as those of the Hausa Zomo but the plots in at least thirteen of the Uncle Remus stories are parallels of those in Hausa stories."

A number of the nineteenth-century collectors of slave folktales also recognized their African origin. William Owen, in one of the first analyses of black folklore, wrote in 1877 that the slave's tales were "as purely African as are their faces or their own plaintive melodies . . . the same wild stories of Buh Rabbit, Buh Wolf, and other *Buhs* . . . are to be heard to this day in Africa, differing only in the drapery necessary to the change of scene." Although Joel Chandler Harris knew very little about African folklore, one of the scholars (Herbert H. Smith) he contacted about the origin of his first series of Uncle Remus stories wrote: "One thing is certain. The animal stories told by the negroes in our Southern States and in Brazil were brought by them from Africa." Christensen pointed out that the ancestors of her South Carolina informants had "brought parts of the legends from African forests." In fact, one of her informants, Prince Baskins, told Christensen that he had first heard the tales from his grandfather, a native African. Many of the tales collected by Christensen, Joel Chandler Harris, and Fortier even contained African words in them.

The folktale served some of the same functions in the slave quarters as it had in Africa. It was a means of entertainment, inculcating morality in the young, teaching the value of cooperation, and explaining animal behavior. Like the Africans, the slaves were preoccupied with "pourquoi" stories, or why animals got to be the way they were. The why stories constituted 29.5% of the tales recorded by Hampton Institute collectors and 23.5% of those collected by Christensen in the nineteenth century.

Among the slaves the folktale was also a means of training young blacks to cope with bondage. By modelling their behavior on that of the rabbit or tortoise, the slaves learned to use their cunning to overcome the strength of the master, to hide their anger behind a mask of humility, to laugh in the face of adversity, to retain hope in spite of almost insuperable odds, to create their own heroes, and to violate plantation rules while escaping punishment. In many of the tales a slave used his wits to escape from work and punishment or to trick his master into emancipating him. They also reveal the slave's sense of humor:

Once an old slave used to make it his practice to steal hogs. The way he would be sure of the animal was he would tie one end of a rope around his prey and the other around himself. The old Negro had been successful for many years in his occupation, but one time when he caught one of his master's hogs he met his equal in strength. He was fixing to have a big time on the next day, which was Sunday. He was thinking about it and had the old hog going along nicely, but at last as he was coming up on the top of a very high hill the hog got unmanageable and broke loose from the old fellow's arms. Still the old man made sure it was all right because of the rope which tied them together, so he puffed and pulled and scuffed, till the hog got the best of him and started him to going down the steep hill. The hog carried him clear to his master's house, and the master and his family were sitting on the porch. All the Negro could say, as the hog carried him around and around the house by his master, was "Master, I come to bring your pig home!"

Until the end of the eighteenth century the black slaves retained their African names. Most of what scholars know about this phenomenon comes from ads placed in colonial newspapers by masters trying to recapture fugitive slaves. In attempting to anglicize the names the masters distorted many of them. As they had done in Africa, the slaves continued to name their children according to the day of the week on which they were born:

Male	Female	Day
Cudjoe	Juba	Monday
Cubbenah	Beneba	Tuesday
Quaco	Cuba	Wednesday
Quao	Abba	Thursday
Cuffee	Phibba	Friday
Quamin	Mimba	Saturday
Quashee	Quasheba	Sunday

While these and their variants were the most common cognomens, 92 different African names appeared in South Carolina runaway ads alone. African names, indicating a connection to the ancestral home, continued to be marks of status in the free black community throughout the nineteenth century. Significantly, many of them appeared in Carter G. Woodson's list of free blacks included in the census of 1830.

Between five and ten percent of the names of free blacks were African derivatives, with Juba, Cuffy, Abba, Cudjo, Tinah, Quashee, Chloe, Selah, Mingo, Sawney, Ferriba, Garoh, Wan, and Bena being the most popular. Occasionally the free blacks had such African derived surnames as the following:

Quashy Baham	Wilson Africa	Edward Affricaine	Kedar Africa
Elikaim Bardor	Byer Affrica	Wright Africa	Gadock Coffe
Pyror Biba	Alford Bim	Cuff Cawon	Ally Africa

African appellations disappeared from the lists of slaves in the nine-
teenth century because masters frequently chose the cognomens
applied to their bondsmen. On the South Carolina Sea Islands, how-
ever, the blacks clung tenaciously to their African names. Even as
late as 1940, the Sea Islanders used an anglicized name in their
dealings with whites and an African name in their conversations with
other blacks.

"A proverb," say the Yoruba, "is the horse of conversation."
Before the arrival of European invaders, West Africans relied on
proverbs more than any other people. They were used as greetings,
played on drums, included in songs, provided the ending for folk-
tales, and applied as nicknames. Until the last decades of the twen-
tieth century, proverbs served as precedents in reaching judicial
decisions. The scholar George Herzog, writing in the 1930's, said that
in Liberian "legal proceedings it may happen that at a certain stage
most of the discussion narrows down to quoting proverbs." Among
the Ashanti, when a master called his slave's name, the bondsman
always answered with a proverb. As a revelation of the philosophy
of a people and as a way of utilizing the past to cope with a new
situation, the West African proverb differed little from those found
among Europeans. But West African proverbs had greater flexibility
of imagery and application, symmetrical balance, poetic structure,
and rhythmic quality than European ones. The correct use of prov-
erbs in African society often involved an intricate and artistic por-
trayal of abstract ideas.

The primary objective of the proverb was to teach modes of
conduct, religious beliefs, hospitality, respect for elders, caution,
bravery, humility, and cooperation by drawing on the lessons learned
from history, mythology, and the observation of flora, fauna, and
human behavior. The proverb survived the coming of the Europeans.
One of the major reasons for this was that the moral of a tale was
stated as a proverb; often the proverb remained when the tale was
forgotten. Through the fables of Aesop, the slave trade, and the
writings of travellers, many African proverbs were incorporated
into the sayings of Europeans, Arabs, and Asians. It is not surprising,
therefore, to find that many of them appeared in the language of
nineteenth-century slaves in the southern United States.

Largely banned from acquiring literacy, the slaves remained, like
their African ancestors, an oral people. They resorted to proverbs to
teach morality and behavioral skills to their children. A compari-

son of the 382 proverbs contained in the folklore collections of J. Mason Brewer and Hampton Institute with 7,000 proverbs from West Africa shows that 122 or 31% of them were brought by the blacks directly from Africa. Many of the proverbs are identical in form and meaning to West African ones, but often reflect the impact of slavery and the American environment.

About 50% of the proverbs the slaves used reflected the plantation experience. They borrowed less than 20% of them from their white masters. These plantation proverbs contained advice about how much labor the slave should perform, how to avoid punishment, and frequently referred to such activities as ploughing and harvesting cotton, corn, and wheat, religious meetings, corn shuckings and singing. They included such sayings as the following: "The overseer regulates the daybreak. Don't fling all your power into a small job. Don't say more with your mouth than your back can stand (be cautious in talking to the master). You got eyes to see and wisdom not to see (don't tell master everything). Tomorrow may be the carriage-driver's day for ploughing (fortune changes). Tired cutter in the wheat field gets sassy at the end of the row."

It is a testament to the wisdom of the slaves that many of their proverbs (or variants) were still being used by Americans, black and white, in the last decades of the twentieth century. They included: "The sun shines in every man's door once (fortune changes). If you can't stand the hot grease, get out of the kitchen. To wall-eye (show anger). His tongue knows no Sunday (he's too talkative). Mr. Hawkins is coming (cold weather—'the Hawk'—is coming)."

The place the witch, ghost, and medicine man had in traditional African society was occupied by hags, hants, and conjurors in the slave quarters. They shared many identical characteristics. Although similar in many ways to its European counterpart, the traditional African witch was a more malevolent and frightful reality. Possessing the ability to turn people into animals, ride, kill, and eat them, the witch caused sores, incurable diseases, sterility, impotence, adultery, stillbirths, and robbed a person of his money or food. Since witches were persons inhabited by demons, they could change into any animal form or become invisible and enter a dwelling through the smallest opening. The African detected witches by spreading pepper around or through dreams. Amulets, rings, chains, and bags of powder worn on the body or placed in dwellings offered some protection, as did objects placed under pillows, the blood of fowls, effigies, and shrines. Persons proven to be witches were killed.

Ghosts play a prominent role in African religions and cosmology. Viewed as the indwelling spirit or soul of a man which departs his body on his death, the ghosts retain an interest in the affairs of the living and punish or frighten them for misdeeds, aid descendants, remain in the vicinity of their graves, and sometimes inhabit the body of newly born infants. The African's belief in ghosts is part of the process of honoring ancestors and functions to preserve social order.

The African medicine man or priest was a mediator between the living and the dead, a discoverer of witchcraft, and a physician. He could prepare poisons to be placed in the food of or on a path frequented by an intended victim. He sold powders and charms to insure success in love, war, planting, hunting and other activities.

There were some inversions and combinations of roles in the transfer of witches, ghosts, and medicine men from Africa to America. The witch, or hag, for example, lost some of its malevolence. Even so, the slaves continued to believe that witches met as a group, took the shape of animals, and rode a person at night. They were invisible, entered a dwelling through a keyhole, and sometimes caused death. If one cut off the limb of a hag while in the shape of an animal, that limb would be missing when the witch returned to its human form. Protection against hags included sticks, sifters, horseshoes, and bottles of salt over the door, or Bibles, forks, and needles under the pillow. Salt and pepper burned the skin of the witch.

Many features of African cosmology regarding ghosts were retained in the Americas. The slaves believed that a person's soul remained on earth three days after death, visiting friends and enemies, and that ghosts remained near graveyards, communicated with and could harm or help the living, and might return to claim property which had belonged to them. The main function of the ghost in the quarters was, as in Africa, to engender respect for the dead. The slaves universally believed, according to many nineteenth-century observers, that if "the living neglect in any way their duty to the dead, they may be haunted by them."

The conjurer, claiming to have received his power from God and believed by many to be in league with the devil, combined the malevolence of the witch with the benevolence of the African medicine man and priest. In the slave's world the conjurer was the medium for redressing wrongs committed by his master or fellows and served as his druggist, physician, faith healer, psychologist, and fortune teller. Bondsmen believed the conjurer could prevent floggings, guarantee successful rebellions or flights for freedom, cast and remove spells, and cause and cure illness. He was the source of love potions, poisons, and "trick bags." Spells resulted from the ingestion of his potions or simply from walking over ground containing a trick bag. Like the Africans, slaves believed that the conjurer used items of personal property or hair and nail clippings to cast spells. In removing spells and curing illnesses he used what was tantamount to autosuggestion or hypnotism and his knowledge of herbs. Mixing teas made from boiling sassafrass, nutmeg, asafoetida, or wild cherry, oak, dogwood, and poplar bark with vinegar, cider, whiskey, turpentine, quinine, calomel, molasses, and honey, the conjurer was remarkably successful in curing the slaves of colds, fevers, chills, etc.

It would take several volumes to describe all of the cultural elements the slaves brought with them from Africa. Some indication of the extent of the African survivals in Afro-American culture appears in a study of Georgia blacks in the 1930's, *Drums and Shadows* (1940). The Georgia investigators found 70 elements of African culture in the region. In addition to the things noted above, they included funeral rites, spirit possession, decoration of graves, taboos, woodcarving, and weaving. Other scholars have noted that the rhythmic complexity and call and response pattern of black music, children's games, religious practices and some dances of American blacks have their origin in Africa.

According to most scholars, the most obvious African retentions in black American culture have been in music and dance. The melody, harmony, rhythm, form, emphasis on percussion, and aesthetics of slave music were all African. In West Africa and among blacks in the antebellum South music was an intimate part of life, of play, religion, and work. Harold Courlander in *Negro Folk Music, USA* (1963) wrote that the black work song "particularly the kind sung by railroad gangs, roustabouts (stevedores), woodcutters, fishermen, and prison road gangs, is an old and deeply rooted tradition. Few Negro musical activities come closer than gang singing does to what we think of as an African style . . . the overall effect instantly calls to mind the group labor songs of Jamaica, Haiti, and West Africa."

The ring games and songs of slave children also originated in Africa. A Nigerian scholar, Lazarus Ekwueme, concluded from his study of African and Afro-American forms: "A black Louisiana housewife sings to her crying baby not too differently from the way a Jamaican mother does or an Ewe woman in Ghana. The children's games, 'Ring around the Rosie' or 'Bob a needle,' each with its accompanying song, have counterparts in Africa, such as the 'Akpakolo' of Igbo children in West Africa or the funny game-song of the Kikuyu of Kenya called 'R-r-r-r-r-na ngubiro,' which is a special East African follow-your-leader version of 'Ring around the Rosie.' "

In contrast to the music and games, few of the slaves' omens and signs appear to have come from Africa. The major reason for this was that there was such a difference in the flora, fauna, and weather in Africa and America. The correct interpretation of signs and omens was extremely important in the slave quarters. By carefully observing the habits of animals, the slaves developed (as did most rural people) skill in predicting changes in the weather. Although this was the primary function of signs, the slaves used them for many other reasons. First, they utilized them as taboos in an effort to teach good manners to children. Young slaves were taught that bad luck followed when they stepped over grown-ups, washed in water used by someone else, tore their clothes, beat cats and dogs, swore, kept their hats on when entering the cabin, or made fun of a cross-eyed person. Second, the slaves insisted that slovenly housekeeping habits (sweeping the floor or cleaning the table after dark) lead to bad luck and death in the family. Third, they used taboos to promote good work habits: "Don't skip a row in planting or someone in your family will die." A fourth function of the signs, omens, and taboos was to inculcate morality in the young. In an effort to prevent girls from being promiscuous, for example, the slaves said: "If you kiss a boy before you marry, you'll never care much for him."

One of the major functions of signs was to enable the slave to deal with the ever present and always unpredictable specter of death. The actions of owls, killdeer, roosters, dogs, cats, hogs, and rabbits were the most frequent signs of an impending death. Every sign called for a corresponding action to prevent death. Typical ways for stopping the screeching of an owl, for instance, were to put an iron poker, horseshoe, or salt in the fire, or to turn your pockets wrong side out.

Seeking control over a harsh world where masters and overseers were capricious and irrational, the slaves developed an unshakable belief in the infallibility of dreams and signs as predictors of future events on the plantation. Primarily an effort to determine when whippings and separations were going to occur, these signs reflect the major fears of the slaves: "If your left eye twitches, you will soon receive a whipping. If you dream of your owner counting money, some slave is going to be sold. If you mock an owl, you'll get a whipping. Kildee hollering, patrollers coming. To mock a whip-poor-will is a sure sign of a whipping. To dream about dollars is a sure sign of a whipping. If you mark the back of a chimney, your back will be marked the same way by a whipping. If you have rice, peas, and hominy on New Year's day, you will have plenty to eat all year. If a rabbit crosses your path at night, you'll soon get a whipping. If you burn poplar, just as the wood pops, so will the master pop his whip on your back."

The slaves transmitted many elements of their culture to twentieth-century blacks. The clearest example of this, of course, is the spiritual; many of those religious songs of the slaves could still be heard in black churches in the last decades of the twentieth century. What is less obvious is the slave's contribution to another distinctive genre of American music—the blues. Practically all of the motifs and patterns of the blues were present in the non-religious or secular songs of the slaves. Like the twentieth-century blues singers, the slaves often sang about their work:

> Old cotton, old corn, see you every morn,
> Old cotton, old corn, see you since I's born.
> Old cotton, old corn, hoe you till dawn,
> Old cotton, old corn, what for you born?

The oppression of whites, bouts with patrollers, floggings, and conflicts with masters and overseers represented major themes in the slaves' secular songs. In their ironic and humorous twists these songs became the prototypes for similar characteristics in the blues. The slaves approached artistry when they commented on the hypocrisy of their owners:

> My old missus promise me
> When she die she set me free
> She live so long her head git bald
> She give up de idea of dyin' a-tall.

When the slaves sang of love and courting, they probably came closest to the blues. References to unfaithful partners were frequent in both types. According to the slave, "When I'se here you call me honey, when I'se gone, you honies everybody." Metaphoric references to sexual intercourse were often identical in the slave songs and in the blues. For example, the blues singer often uses the word "rocking" to refer to sexual intercourse. In one blues song a woman sang in the 1920's:

> Looked at the clock, clock struck one,
> Come on daddy, lets have some fun.
> Looked at the clock, clock struck two,
> Believe to my soul you aint half through.
> Looked at the clock, clock struck three,
> Believe to my soul, you gonna kill poor me.
> Looked at the clock, clock struck four,
> If the bed breaks down we'll finish on the floor.
> My daddy rocks me with one steady roll,
> Dere ain't no slippin' when he once takes hold.

While revealing little of the rhythmic complexity of this song, the slaves obviously referred to sexual intercourse when they sang:

> Down in Mobile, down in Mobile,
> How I love that pretty yellow gal,
> She rock to suit me—
> Down in Mobile, down in Mobile.

The slaves also resorted to the double meanings and veiled mes-

sages of the blues in other sexual references: "cake" and "chicken"
meant a woman and "shake" and "pushing" signified sexual inter-
course in both types.

One characteristic of the blues frequently noted by musicologists is
boasting. The slave singers boasted of their ability to trick their
masters:

> I fooled old Mastah seven years
> Fooled the overseer three;
> Hand me down my banjo
> And I'll tickle you bellee (belly).

They emphasized their ability to fight, "to get drunk agin," and their
sexual conquests: "When I was young and in my prime, I'se a
courtin' them gals, most all de time."

Like the blues men, the slaves were always looking for a "do right"
woman. They asked "what make de young girls so deceivin? so de-
ceivin, so deceivin"; warned other men "don't steal my sugar";
lamented "When I got back my chicken was gone"; made the query,
"Whose been here since I been gone?"; scorned former lovers who'd
gotten pregnant by another man ("her apron strings wouldn't tie,")
or observed that "Many a man is rocking another man's son when he
thinks he's rocking his own."

The women boasted of their ability to steal someone else's lover:
"You steal my partner, and I steal yours." They enjoined their mates
to treat them "good" or suffer the consequences: "If you treat me
good, I'll stay till de Judgement Day. But if you treat me bad, I'll
sho' to run away." Another distinctive feature of the blues is a pre-
occupation with getting revenge on a lover who has "done you
wrong." This theme also appeared in the slave songs.

> I'm going to poison you, I'm going to poison you,
> I'm just sick and tired of the way you do,
> I'm going to sprinkle spider legs around your bed,
> An' you gonna wake up in the morning and find yourself dead.
> You beat me and kick me and you black my eyes,
> I'm gonna take this butcher knife and hew you down to my size,
> You mark my words, my name is Lou,
> You mind out what I say. I'm going to poison you.

Twentieth-century blacks obviously inherited what folklorists call
"skill in the verbal arts" from the slaves. Precursors of those most
distinctive features of twentieth-century black culture—the dozens,
toasts, prayers, sermons, slang, and signifying—appear in collections

of slave folklore. The slave was the quintessential folk poet. In his courtship rituals, toasts, and greetings he demonstrated those rhythmical patterns characteristic of twentieth-century black speech. The sources permit, however, only slight glimpses of some of these forms in the quarters. The practice of playing the dozens and signifying, for example, involves the use of so much profanity and so many explicit references to copulation that Victorian nineteenth-century folklorists refused to record them. Even so, some elements of signifying and the dozens (parody, taunts, verbal dueling by indirection, allusion and innuendo, and metaphoric references) can be found in slave speech.

In Harlem in the 1940's, the typical answer to the greeting "whatcha know ole man?" was "I'm like the bear, just ain't getting nowhere." The formalized greetings of the slaves were similar; they would answer the question "How do you do" or such variants as "How is all?" or "How do you shine?" in one of the following ways: "I'm kicking, but not high. I'm barking, but I won't bite. White folks calculating to keep me behind, but I have to keep on gwine (going). I'm fat, but don't show it. When you are half dead and running, I'll be up and coming. I'm hanging and dragging like an old shoe. I'm fat and fine."

The verbal "put down" of a protagonist characteristic of the dozens also appeared in slave responses to verbal boasts and threats: "You can saddle me, but you can't ride me. I was never run out of a pond by a tadpole yet. No use clouding up, you can't rain."

Similarities in the verbal art of the bondsmen and twentieth-century blacks are clearly apparent in their courtship practices. According to the folklorist William Ferris, twentieth-century blacks in the rural South have a highly formalized courtship ritual involving the propounding of a series of questions to determine one's availability as a sexual partner. Called "high pro" by the blacks, the practice is a verbal duel.

The prototype of "high pro" was created in the slave quarters where old men taught the young the art of courtship. In order to win a mate, a young man or woman had to "know how to talk." The courtship ritual consisted of riddles, poetic boasting, innuendos, put downs, figurative speech, repartee, circumlocution, and a test of wit. In an effort to determine whether a young lady was free to go courting a young man would typically ask: "Are you a rag on the bush or a rag off the bush? (Answer—If a rag on the bush, free, if off, engaged)." If the lady were not married or engaged, the young man then tried to discover if she accepted him as a suitor: "Dear lady, suppose you an' I was sittin' at de table wid but one dish of soup an' but one spoon, would you be willin' to eat out ob de dish an' spoon wid me?" If this question went unanswered, he might assert:

> If you was passin' by
> And seed me hangin' high
> Would you cut me down and lie
> Or would you let me hang there an die?

To show that she accepted her suitor, the young girl had to frame a suitably clever response: "I hears dat you is a dove flyin' from lim' to lim' wid no where to res' your weary wings. I's in de same condition an' hopes you kin fin' a place to res' your heart."

Having found someone to "eat out of the dish" with him, the young man would begin boasting of his prowess and proclaiming, through poetic allusions, his love for her: "Dear miss, ef I was starving and had jes one ginger-cake, I would give you half, an' dat would be the bigges' half." Success at this point might move the man to declare:

> Dear me, kin' Miss, you is de damsel of my eye,
> Where my whole joy and pleasure lie.
> If I has some money I'll give you a part,
> If I has no money I'll give you my heart.

According to the former slave Frank D. Banks, "on the plantation the ability to understand and answer the figurative speeches of her lover was the test of wit and culture by which the slave girl was judged in the society of the quarters." The blacks interviewed by Ferris in the 1970's felt that through a courtship formula remarkably similar to that of the slaves, "you can test a lady out to see what she is and what she stands for and who she really arc."

The more religious slaves displayed their verbal skills in church. The chief medium for this was the prayer. Reduced to formulas, taught to young converts, the prayers were intoned in a musical rhythmic chant with frequent pauses for audience responses (usually moans). The power of the prayers came from their method of delivery and the vivid word pictures, fervid imagery, metaphors, and imaginative flights. The bondsman began his prayer by expressing his humility and then called on God to "come sin-killing, soul-reviving" to "the low grounds of sorrow and sin" and confront sinners and "Hammer hard on their hard rock hearts with the hammer of Jeremiah and break their hearts in ten thousand pieces." God had to come and revive his flock because

> We believe that love is growing old and sin is growing bold and Zion wheel is clogged and can't roll, neither can she put on her beautiful

garments, but we ask you to come this way, seal her with love, type her with blood and send her around the hill sides clucking to her broods and bringing live sons and daughters to the marvelous light of thy glorious gospel as the bees to the honey comb and the little doves to the window of Noah's ark, I pray thee.   (Moan)

The slave's religious beliefs differed from those of his master in a number of ways. First, most black Christians believed in conjurers, and according to one observer, they talked "freely at their religious gatherings of 'tricking' and 'conjuring' and tell marvelous tales of the power of those endowed with supernatural gifts." Second, many of the death and burial customs differed from those of whites, with funerals held long after burials and graves being decorated with articles belonging to the deceased. Third, music was more important in black than white churches and had a more complicated rhythmical structure. The conversion experience was a long one and had to end with a definite sign that one had been saved. Blacks considered dreams as messages from God, signs of conversion or of being called to preach.

Among other unique features of the theology of the slave was his belief that it was no sin to steal from masters, that "no white people went to Heaven," and that faith, not acts, was all-important. In contrast to the staid services in most *white* churches, the slave's service was a blur of motion with constant shouting, clapping of hands, and stamping of feet.

Although the first slaves learned of Christianity from white missionaries, they quickly fused it with West African beliefs to create their own religion. The "frenzied shouting" frequently noted by white observers was, for example, a variant of African spirit possession. So was the ring shout, the call-and-response pattern of sermons, prayers and songs, the unrestrained joy, and predilection for total immersion. Ekwueme asserted that religion was an "area in which Africans share a common heritage with their brothers in the New World, as evidenced in the similarity of modes of worship . . . The music, dances, and occult rites associated with Voodoo have equivalents in most parts of Africa. The concomitant ecstasy and quasi-psychical entranced upliftment capturing the minds and physique of participants, achieved more through the medium of music than by any other means, have been adopted by black Christian churches in the United States to the point that they are now a *sine qua non* in religious worship for all black people."

The interpreter of black theology was the slave preacher. Since white ministers were always calling upon the slaves to obey their masters, the bondsmen naturally turned to those men who could discover a promise of their salvation and freedom in the Bible. Possessing a memory bordering on the photographic, the black preacher created his sermon from a few details of white church services, verses read to him by whites, or, when literate, his own reading of the Bible, and a close attention to the troubles and dreams of his congregation. Delivered in a musical recitation with pauses for audience response, the antebellum sermon was a model of folk poetry unmatched in its metaphors, figures of speech, and vivid word pictures. The black preacher told his flock that as with the Israelites, God was on the side of the blacks. The historian Eugene Genovese declared that the slaves "guided by their preachers, resisted slavery's psychological assault manfully; they learned to love each other and have faith in their deliverance." In uplifting and guiding the bondsmen, the slave preacher created a style which would later be imitated in evangelical white churches and remained unchanged in its essential ingredients in most black churches in the twentieth century.

In religion, as in other aspects of their lives, the slaves left a legacy to Americans, black and white, which is still evident. However much debate there is regarding the extent of African survivals, many scholars accept the veracity of the Ashanti proverb, "Ancient things remain in the ears." Although fewer of the ancient African practices and beliefs remained in the ears of American blacks than in the ears of those in Latin America, it was the African memory which made the Afro-Americans a distinctive people. Without Africa and slavery, American folklore, speech, music, literature, cooking, and religion would be unimpressive replicas of European ones, barren and somewhat sterile. Without Africa and slavery, America would not have created spirituals, blues, jazz, or rock and roll. Nor would European immigrants in the Americas ever have escaped from the constricting tentacles of the sexual repression they inherited from the Middle Ages. In short, Africa and the slave experience are central to an understanding of the American past and present.

SHADOWS IN THE MOONLIGHT

JOHN STEWART

The moonlight came down bright like a cool yellow sun, except for up high where the night was still blue and secret. From her doorway Olga looked out on the fields of shiny cane stalks, their arrows glistening smooth as white gold for as far as she could see across the way to Golconda. The moonlight was brighter than she had seen it in a long time, yet in a funny way that hid things where they should have been most plain. The black pitch road that separated her lot from the fields passed no more than a rod or so from where she sat, and two or three times when she had caught movement along it out of the corner of her eye she had turned to stare, waited for the dog, manicou, or mongoose to come plain, but there had been nothing there. Once she even thought she had seen the shape of a man in the distance coming towards her house, and she waited for him to come plain too. But neither man nor animal ever came clear enough for her to be certain of what she had seen, and she had to laugh at herself for thinking she was seeing spirits.

The night wore an eleventh-hour stillness, and she heard her laugh carry for a long time over the fields. She was alone. Her house stood apart from the rest of the village by almost a quarter-mile, and the houses she could see before the road took a bend were already dark. She laughed again, a little louder, more self-consciously, to see if her voice would carry as it had before in the stillness. It carried. Then Olga was quiet, and resumed waiting for her child to come home.

It was a good thing that she was mistaken about seeing a man coming down the road, because tonight she did not want to be touched. Not that she had anything against being sweet with a man on a night like this, she having had her share of that. In fact, it made her a little sad to realize the number of times she had undressed under the moon, when there was so little now to show for all that giving and taking on the damp dew grass. But that wasn't what tonight was about and Olga pushed away the sad feelings. She had to put her thoughts together before Gracie came home. She had to get them together soon, because church must have been over at least an hour ago, and the child was already late. She had to be sharp and ready in her thoughts, even though in the back of her mind a voice kept asking "What for?," keeping high the suspicion that she herself was too late with what she planned to do. But to that suspicion she would not submit, because, even if at that very moment the child was already bedded down under the shadow of the American traveller, there would still be time enough when she came home for Olga to say what she had to say, and be free. And this time there would be no slapping, no hot-bloodedness, nothing but her telling the child truthfully what she knew about getting started. If questions came up, she would have to answer them straight. Olga had to put her thoughts together, but with the moonlight playing tricks on her nerves, it wasn't easy getting much of anything to make sense.

She never knew her Mammy to be anything but a sweet woman, and although she had promised since childhood that no such thing would ever happen to her it had happened anyway, and now she wasn't sure how. She was one of the few girls of her time to stay in school until fourteen, and she was bright enough for the headmaster to recommend her to the high school in town fifteen miles away, but she never did go there. Her Mammy couldn't raise the money for clothes and books.

Olga had cried for a week over seeing that chance pass by, and Bertie, the reverend's son, himself already a student at the high school, used to come to their house to comfort her. She was a lead soprano in the church choir then, and very much in love with Bertie. He loved her too, just like a reverend's son should—cleanly, truly, and with high understanding. His touch was the most painful sweetness in those days. And when on Sunday afternoons after Sunday school he took her hand in his and led her on their long walks along the country road from the village, he usually kept her out of breath not from the walking, but from the steady leaping and settling of her heart—like a frog with saltwater on its back.

Henry used to dog them then, alone, or with friends of his, and the many times they chased him "Shoo black nigger" made no difference. Just the sight of him used to get her blood up, though at times she would feel sorry for him too, and if he wasn't so black would have asked Bertie to stop chucking stones at him. But Henry or no Henry, the first hour of darkness when they had to come back to the church for evening service was usually the tenderest of all, because then Bertie's arm would come around her waist and it would be like she walked without touching the ground, until they came to the lighted churchyard where he had to let her go.

That was in 1940 when the Germans were bombing England, and the newspaper was full of photos about it every day.

The next year Bertie went into uniform. He was just seventeen. And everybody in the village said he had to go because his family was from England, but that couldn't have been true because the other village boys who went into uniform were all black and their families had never seen England. She was never quite sure why Bertie went in, but he looked good in his pressed khakis the day he left with Henry and four others, riding in the back of a government truck. Henry was black and full of grins as ever, but he didn't look half as decent as Bertie.

The boys were taken to a camp in the North, past Port of Spain, and she did not see Bertie for a long time after that—although he did write once a week for twelve weeks, then once a month for nine months.

And all that time she was still staying in the two-room house with Mammy, sleeping on the other side of a cloth blind from where Mammy made some money every night. Sometimes the men used to ask her to take a drink with them, but she never paid any attention. Usually she would read until her eyes grew tired, then go to sleep. There were two men, Samuel and Marcus, who used to leave her money. Sometimes a dollar, sometimes just a shilling or two. There was another man, Berry, who used to promise her plenty of money if she would let him sleep on her side of the blind sometime, but she never even spoke a word to him. Mammy used to think that was funny.

"What kind of daughter is that you have here Mammy?" Berry used to shout, and Mammy would just chuckle. "That girl sure acts like a miss somebody," Berry would go on. "She walk in here, and don't say a word when she's spoken to . . . I have a good mind to take my belt off and give her a licking."

And Mammy would really break out laughing then. "You make child to give licking?" And after laughing at Berry used to say, "That girl too much of a lady for you Berry. She my great little lady, sometime I think she more of a lady than I know what to do with."

"She don't act like she's your daughter at all Mammy."

"I believe sometimes she too much of a lady for me in truth. She act more like her father every day," Mammy would end it.

And that would make Olga think of her father—though not in the same way she used to when she was just a little girl. Start her thinking about her father, where was he, and what was he doing, and who was he, really. Because all she had ever been told about him was that he was a white man, "Bakra Johnny" Mammy used to say, just barely holding back from spitting, and that would be the end of all Mammy said about her father. Of course, everybody could see she was the child of a white man because Mammy was black, big-lipped, had knappy hair; while she was high-brown herself, and her hair came down past her shoulders in soft smooth waves. Where Mammy was loose, overflowing in front and behind, she was slender and tight.

But it never did any good thinking about her father. He remained unknown, except in her imagination. At first she used to tell herself one day he would come, and although there could be no question of his living with them, at least he would bring money enough to make his daughter and Mammy well off. While she still believed he would come, she used to be very excited each time the English staff changed at the sugar factory, and would spend hours matching features with the new arrivals. She wasn't sure why, but she knew her father had to be English. Not French, or Spanish, or Dutch, or Portuguese, although he could have been any of these. She was certain he was English. Yet her imagination did no good because no father ever showed up. None of the English factory bosses ever came near Mammy, and by 1941 she had finally come to forget about having a father except when Mammy said, "She acting more like her father every day." And even then, "Wherever he is, he might at least send something" used to be the only thought to cross her mind about him.

In the meantime, the village men on whom Mammy depended were already saying things when Olga passed; and even when they said nothing you could see it in their eyes, like greedy boys watching the tree for the next sapodilla to turn ripe. But not one of them could shift her mind off Bertie. She had a lot of time to long for him, too, and answer his letters. She was not in school; she was not about to go to work in the cane fields or in any overseer's kitchen; nor was she even considering going to the town to look for work. Seemed like every village girl who ever went there ended up the same way—turning tricks on the street, or scrubbing somebody's floors. She was going to wait. And in her waiting, her longing for Bertie, she dreamed and imagined him coming home a hero to marry her and do whatever he wanted with her after that.

In 1942 the Yankees came to Trinidad. There wasn't any war in Trinidad, but they came anyway. They were very rich, and very wild with their money. The newspaper was full of stories about the Yankees and their money. Some people were scared then that the Germans would come for sure to drop their bombs and wipe out Trinidad, but that did not prevent them from going to work for the Yankees.

The Joes wanted some army base built, they wanted it in a hurry. They were paying more money a week than many a Trinidadian had ever seen in a lifetime.

Men, women, and children left their homes, trekked North to find jobs with the Yankees, and she thought of going North too, to work as an office girl, maybe, and make a lot of money, but Mammy said, "Not a foot. Them Yankees ain't good for nothing but killing people."

And the paper was full of that too, how the Joes ran over people with their jeeps and army trucks, then stopped only long enough to pin hundred-dollar bills to the corpses. They bought all the whores in Port of Spain, and it was nothing to find on a Sunday morning two or three of the mopsies or their black boyfriends dead in the gutter. Sometimes an American would be dead there too; then a lot of people went to jail. And although the Yankees paid good money, they make every man, woman, and child sweat for it. Work up to twelve, fifteen, eighteen hours a day, and if you couldn't do that they literally kicked you off the job.

When Mammy said, "Not a foot. Them Yankees ain't nothing but murderers," Olga did not talk back too hard, because Mammy didn't mind if she just sat around waiting, and that was what she really wanted to do more than anything else. She read over her last schoolbooks about Joan of Arc, and the children of the new forest, and King Arthur. She read them over more than once because her other old books were about buccaneers fighting and burying gold, and she didn't like those stories. They were for boys.

Sometimes the village men who managed to get home from the Yankee base for a day or so brought Mammy picture magazines from America, and Olga liked these more than anything else she had to read. They had the best love stories. The photographs showed clean, rich, healthy, good-looking men, all heroes; and beautiful girls who never went without a thing they could wish for. She used to wish she was one of those girls, but that did not stop her dreaming of Bertie coming home a hero to marry her. Sometimes when she pictured him in her mind it was with a different head, one not so English as Bertie's, more American. And other times when his head came the body was not so bony and narrow as his but taller, more husky and bronze. Yet it was Bertie every time.

She dreamed about him even after she started learning how to sew at Aunt Sylvie's. She would walk down the village road to the far end, and get to Aunt Sylvie's at eight o'clock in the morning, then come back home at four in the afternoon. In both going and coming she would have young men following, riding slowly beside her on their bicycles. They had the same look in their eyes as Mammy's men, only less dangerous, and she seldom listened to a thing they said, but they helped time to pass less noticeably. Sometimes they would say things that were really funny, then she would have to laugh. But she didn't listen to a thing they said all up to the time Mammy died, and even for a long time after she had the two-room house to herself.

She couldn't keep them from hanging around, though. They followed on the street, and came right up to the house. A few of the older men who had belonged to Mammy came by the house too, but not Samuel. He died before Mammy. Berry and Marcus still came, though with Mammy gone Marcus turned just like Berry, to offering money to let him sleep in her bed. All of them, grown men and young, would come to her house, sit in her yard and talk most of the night; and it was no secret they were making bets to see who would get into her first. That only made her long harder for Bertie to come home and take her away, but her longing didn't do a thing to the war, and Bertie remained in his camp or wherever he was training or gone to the war. After twelve months she got no more letters, but never once lost faith that Bertie would return to her. It was only the war holding them apart for the moment.

Then she woke up one morning, and before she moved, knew it had happened. She wasn't sure how, or who. She remembered going to bed alone and having dreams about Bertie, or someone like him, come home to marry her, but that was all. She tried hard, but could remember nothing past talking with two of the young men during the night, turning them off when they wanted to put their hands on her, then closing her door behind them. Not locking it, because she had never seen Mammy lock their door once, and there was nothing in the village to keep her afraid even when she was alone. Turning them off, and then sleep with her regular dreaming. But somebody must have really come in, and she had no remembrance of who. She lay in the bed and cried. Then after she heard the bread man pass by, she got up and went to Aunt Sylvie's as usual.

She did not try to run when the boys followed her on the way home that evening, but at night she locked the door, or rather, put a chair behind it, because there was no lock.

Then things came back to being usual for a long time, until another night when she did not put the chair behind the door just to test what would happen. Somebody came in. She wasn't asleep. She lay quietly, trying to figure out who he was in the darkness. He crept straight to the bed and climbed over her. And after she had managed to stop herself from screaming, it was all right. He never said a word, but finally lifted himself off her and left, she still not knowing who he was for sure, but in a dim way thinking it was Berry. In the morning she had the same idea because there was some money on the table. Yet Berry was too old and rough to have been as nice and strong as the one who had slipped in on her in the dark.

She wasn't afraid, but she went back to putting the chair behind the door again, until she had saved enough money from what Aunt Sylvie paid her to get away. She knew she had to go, and did not stop to wonder why, except it seemed the things she had dreamed Bertie would come back and do didn't much matter anymore, and she had to find something else to do besides wait for him. She had to look after herself. And when she was ready, she got dressed one morning, packed her clothes in a bag, and, while a few villagers watched, boarded the bus that ran into town.

There it was noisy and crowded. Strange men looked her up and down everywhere she turned—but that did not start anything. That did not start her being a whore. Didn't seem like anything started her, really.

It was hard to remember.

And how would she answer the first thing Gracie was bound to ask, "What I do to make you say I getting to be a whore?" Gracie had much more fire than she had when she was young, and she could see her now, nostrils flaring, the blood pounding at her temples, demanding what right anybody had to accuse her of getting to be a whore. Perhaps it would be better to think of a different word. Only Olga had nothing to say against whoring. Her only concern was that Gracie should know what to do for her own protection. She had nothing against whoring, the word or the deed, although in the town she had done none of it herself.

She had taken a job at a textile shop, but didn't stay there long because the work required her to be on her feet ten hours every day except Sundays, and after paying five dollars each week for her room rent, and buying food, she could hardly save any more than a two-dollars from her pay. Besides, the other salesgirls were heavy competitors, and more than once they ganged up and prevented her making any of the big sales that gave good commissions. As one of them said, she was lucky she had a pretty face, or else she might never have made a wage in that store at all. And finally, although she had never forgotten Mammy saying that Yankees were murderers, after three months away from the village she left town, and found herself at the American army base.

Never before in her life had she seen so many white men working just as hard as niggers. Stripped to the waist, burnt brown, sweat streaming off their backs, they were out there digging and driving piles, running tractors, hammering nails, laying bricks, just like anybody else. They didn't look the way she expected they would at all. She didn't like them. Not one of their heads would have fitted on Bertie's body, not one of their bodies could have taken Bertie's head. They were coarse, loud, and rough. They swore steadily, so you couldn't tell when they were doing it because they were vexed, from when they were doing it because it sounded good in their ears. She didn't like them. Their eyes looked the same all the time. Not lurking like the men's in the village, or plain hungry like the boys', but naked and flat, as though they had no secrets, and deliberately cared nothing for privacy. And she could believe what Mammy said about them then, because that's exactly how they looked, like they would think nothing of killing somebody or something if it suited their feelings. They gave her a job, though, marking time cards and inventory cards twelve hours a day, every day in the week, and they paid her enough.

There was nothing but cocoa forest all around the base, and Arima, the nearest town where civilians could live, was eight miles away. She rented a bed there, in a room with five other women, and at first she used to be so tired when she got home, she would just take her shoes off and flop down until it was time to start back to the base in the morning. But gradually her body got accustomed to sitting in the rigid straight-backed chair for twelve hours straight, and she grew so she didn't mind being confined all that time to one half of a bungalow room with three other workers, the tin roof no more than an arm's length above her head, the bare electric bulbs lower than that. Eventually she got so she could do the job without thinking how tired it made her back and neck, and although she never stopped being tired when she got to her room at night, she started feeling restless too. The women with whom she shared went out every night, but they weren't friendly. She never went out of her way to be friendly either, because that gave people a chance to take advantage of you. Suckers were a new and growing breed, the newspaper said.

One evening when she came in two of her roommates were changing their clothes, talking about some dance they were going to. A hot one, they said, and asked her if she didn't like to dance. She never particularly liked dancing, but she didn't say that. They said she should go with them. She didn't feel like hurrying, and they were so well near ready, they went off and told her she could meet them there. The dance was at a schoolhouse less than a mile from where she roomed, and after she had rested a while, she got up, put on her black satin dress trimmed with white, because Mammy's year wasn't up yet, and walked over.

The school hall was crowded and hot. She couldn't find the other girls. Everyone was sweating. She saw quite a few Americans, and one or two other white boys who didn't look like Americans at all, and for a few minutes her legs trembled with the sudden remembrance of Bertie, the expectancy of perhaps coming upon him in the crowd. There were some black boys from Port of Spain in zoot suits and Cab Calloway hats. Some of them looked nice. The brown-skinned boys from Arima wore less flashy clothes but were better looking.

She said no to about six men who asked her to dance, half-hoping all the time to see Bertie materialize in one of the white faces. He never did, and finally she started hearing the music and wishing one of the brown-skinned boys would ask her again. It was one of the rough, loud Yankees though who came up and said, "Hi baby! Whatcha got hot?" She didn't know what to answer because she didn't have anything hot. She was hearing the music, and smelling the rum and sweat and body powder going around in the room, and she wanted to dance.

"Any poozle on the market tonight?" he asked. And she just smiled again, trying not to look too straight into his face because she had no idea what poozle was. He danced with her and tried to press his sweating body close; and while she couldn't help being stiff, she didn't want to hold him off too far, because everybody knew any American could make you lose your job in the morning if he felt like it.

"Blood on the moon tonight, huh?" he asked another stupid question. "Jordan flowing 'round the bend?" She wasn't even interested in catching his meaning, and so she just nodded her head and smiled. When the music stopped, he left her and walked away.

Then a fight started between the brown boys from Arima and the black boys from Port of Spain. The Arima boys were jumping around, trying to swear like Yankees, but the black boys were doing a better job at that, and besides they held knives. There was a lot of pushing and screaming and police whistles. The music played louder. And as she was trying to get out of the way, a brown boy rushed up and, grabbing her around the throat from behind, started pushing her in front of him right through the fight. She didn't even have time to scream. Before she knew what was happening he had pushed through to the edge of the floor, whirled, and had her dragging backwards out the door. At the bottom of the steps he let go her throat but grabbed her wrist, then started off running in the dark, dragging her behind him. They went for about a quarter-mile down the road, then he dashed into an empty yard and flopped down under a tree. "Those bitches going to pay," he said. "They ain't getting out of this town alive tonight."

She remained quiet. She was afraid, but only because it was so dark, she couldn't see what he might do before he tried. The boy sounded tired.

"You think I'm afraid, eh?" he said. "Think that's why I run, eh? You want to know something? Feel that." He put something in her hand, but she couldn't tell what it was right away. "That razor can cut your head off zap! Only one stroke." He let go her wrist, and she remained sitting on the ground beside him. "Only thing," he went on, "it's my uncle's razor, and I don't really want to fight with it." Then suddenly he stopped breathing hard and said, "You're a pretty girl," groping for her wrist again. She let him take back the razor, and moved away a little so he couldn't find her hand in the dark. "You're a real pretty girl," he said, trying to sound like a Yankee. Then he asked her to be his girl and she smiled to herself because when he asked he reminded her of a yard dog ready at the same time to bite or run. She said no, she just wanted to go home. She was tired and had to work the next day. He walked her to her room too, muttering all the way about what he and his pals would do to the Port of Spain boys when the dance was over.

She said no the night of the dance, but she said yes three nights later, and they returned to the same spot in the dark under the tree, where he pulled his pants down, and she lifted her dress, and he did what she said she would let him do. There was no reasoning behind her saying yes, either. She didn't want anything from him, he never brought her anything, and even if meeting him on the grass beneath the tree did make her body feel good, she didn't find it half so great as he claimed he did.

Yet she went back time after time, until it became nothing but a regular way to spend the night, and she stopped going.

Then after Lloyd it was another brown-skinned boy from Arima who didn't take her out under the dew; he had a room in a house two doors from where she stayed. Regularly every night, sometimes as soon as she came in from the base, she would go over to stay with him. He never gave her anything either. In fact, he was bold enough to ask her to buy him some shirts, and that was when she stopped going to his room.

Who was next, she wasn't sure; but there were two or three others before Lou. She remembered them dimly—the way one might have felt, the way another might have smelled—but they weren't important. They were never too important because all the time she spent with them was time spent in waiting. Not dreaming about Bertie anymore, but waiting, hanging on to the promise of a husband and house of her own. A promise never made her by anyone, to be sure; a promise which, though she had no reason to hold, she held anyway, because that was what she wanted and she didn't see how anything else could be of much importance. Then Lou seemed like he was the one to bring that promise true.

He was one of the few Americans whom she did not find coarse. He came during her second year, when she had mastered the job well enough to do it with one eye, and carry on conversations with the other girls. In fact, she was one of the senior girls at the office then, because few workers lasted long and all the girls whom she had met there, but one, were gone. She was a senior girl, and when Lou came, pink and smooth off one of the airplanes that were landing just outside the office window twenty times a day now, it fell to her to show him the routine. Lou was so openly nervous, so pink skinned and smooth, he talked so softly and with such kind words, that immediately she felt he needed her to protect him. The American staff was shifting all the time too, and when Lou was put fully in charge of the payroll and inventory department she used to stop over late whenever it was necessary to help make sure the pay sheets were done on time, because somehow she felt it had fallen to her to make this pink-faced boy's life as easy as she could.

In his turn Lou promised great things. He was a Methodist farm boy from Iowa, and when he talked she saw the little white church at the foot of his town, the town itself mostly white, except for a red school-building, big rough oak trees, a blue stream passing through; and peaked roofs red or gray, making the houses little spots of color in the wide-open countryside, until winter when everything was really white for sure, everything that is except the people bundled, pink, and cheerful, clean and smiling whether they were slopping hogs or coming from church. Whenever Lou talked about his town she saw a little nest lodged between miles and miles of corn, a nest where she really could settle; and she heard in Lou's voice the promise that their settling together was not only possible, but very strongly in the offing, if only he could make up his mind to it finally.

She helped him. She couldn't recall exactly how, but it was managed, and he did finally ask her to stay with him one night, though not at all in the way of the other American who had started talking about poozle— she had later found out what that meant—but asked like a gentleman who was lonely and shy. Yet once they were naked and hot together his tongue was set so free that all the quarter-promises she had heard only at the back of his voice came from his lips clearly. And she herself, a little dizzy, a little wild, was saying inside and outside a deep yes; and even all the while that first night was being multiplied into all the nights they could cram into six months, she kept saying yes, yes, to his pleading, his tasting, his promising. So that the day he left she felt no pain.

She watched him climb aboard one of the gray-colored airplanes headed for the east, that was true, but his orders said within eighteen months he would be home again, safe in the heart of his Iowa homeland, and he had taught her they should have faith in his orders. Besides, the promise that they should spend the rest of their lives together once the war was won had been made over and over so many times she didn't see how things could be any different. So the day of parting was no day to be sad. She had his faithful promise that once home he would send for her, and she was so full of visions of a house in the midst of the little white town, her children running home from the red school-building, herself being a wife to Lou, forever tantalizing him with her sweetness, that she saw the plane heading east as the first preliminary to her journey west.

She was full of visions to fill the waiting; but she never saw Lou again, or heard from him either, except once—a postcard from Spain saying he was learning how to eat bread and onions, and learning how to drink wine from a skin. That was when she returned home to the village—one of the times in her life when she actually thought out what to do before doing. For this reason she was always proud of her coming back, even though she had done so in disgrace—with a seven-month belly. She wasn't the first village girl to come home like that, nor was she the last, and with her own house, money enough saved from the job so she had to depend on no one, she was in a better position than most who had come back carrying unborn bastards. And thank God for Grandma Thompson.

All the same Olga hoped that Gracie would have no bastards. If the American traveller was telling the child anything about little pretty white towns, Olga hoped she would know enough to put him off until he made a more sensible promise. Not that that might make much difference with this one. He was very different from Lou. With his long hair and beard, his guitar and old clothes, he seemed like the sort that had a lot of practice saying anything that was for saying at the moment. A body couldn't tell what to expect, but if she happened to pass suddenly there was no Grandma Thompson to take her place and care for Gracie.

Grandma Thompson, who couldn't bear the thought of a child being born in the village without her horny hands delivering it, started coming around soon after Olga came home from the base, and it was comforting to have the old lady there sitting with her blousy skirts drawn tight in her lap the way Mammy sometimes used to sit, smelling strongly of tobacco and stale herbs, telling what to expect and what to do for the least suffering.

During the last month before Gracie came Grandma moved right in, started sleeping in Mammy's old bed, and the little two-room house had a deeper feeling of comfort about it than ever before. Instead of the rumble of Mammy's and some man's voices coming from the other side of the curtain, it was she and Grandma talking through the blind, Grandma repeating what to do once the baby started fighting its way out, she remembering to the old lady what a sweet father Lou would have made if the war hadn't sent him away.

Then one day just before the baby was born Bertie came home. Only it wasn't home for him anymore, inasmuch as his father, the reverend, had been transferred to a church in St. Lucia and had already gone there. Olga was never sure whether Bertie came through wanting to see her. When Henry and another soldier in his camp were coming home to Palmyra on weekend leave, Bertie came along too. That was all he said. He didn't stay. The few hours he spent in the village were passed mostly sitting in her chair, watching her laid back in the bed under her big stomach.

"Is it hurting you much?" he asked.

"It's not hurting at all. Not yet."

"What are you going to name it?"

"I don't know. The father's name is Lou."

"Sounds American. Is it?"

"It is."

"Is that what you are going to call him?"

"I guess so."

"And if it's a girl?"

"I don't know. I will have to leave that to the godparents."

The army had made Bertie into a strong man. He was burnt browner than he had been before leaving the village, his hair was lighter and cropped short, his shoulders were wide and heavy and even his eyes had become less gleaming and steadier. He wasn't the same person that she knew before he went away, and she found herself wondering how many whores had he paid, because everyone knew all the boys in the army did that. And she was ready, if he mentioned having missed her, to tell him she knew what men in the army were up to, but he never got around to saying he had. Instead, "Do you really feel all right?" for the second time.

"Yes. I feel all right."

"What're you going to do after the baby comes?"

"Stay here, I guess."

"You won't be going to America?"

"That's up to Lou."

"Oh. I see."

She didn't know what he meant by that, because he wasn't even looking at her. He was gazing off with his newly flat eyes away past her head, away out of the room it seemed.

"You're going back to the army?" She tried to call his attention.

"Oh yes. I have another nine months. I do wish I get sent to the front before it's all over. We drill every day, you know, and keep sentry duty at night, but that's not being in the real thing."

"Maybe the Germans will bomb Trinidad," she said.

"Not a chance. They're on their last legs right now. I do wish I get sent before they give in."

"Don't you want to go to St. Lucia and live with your family?"

"No. I'll probably settle in England once the war is over."

"And you won't come back to Trinidad at all?"

"Oh yes. I'll come back."

"To Palmyra?"

"Of course. Don't forget, my cord's buried here," he said. "But I won't stay. I'll visit, but I couldn't stay. Not here." He stood suddenly to lean above her, and his movement startled her. All he did was take her hand and squeeze it, and for a moment tried being sweet little Bertie again with his eyes, but the feeling didn't come close to what it was like on those old Sunday walks. Her heart did not lunge; she did not float an inch above the bed. In fact, she felt no feelings at all, and if Bertie was disappointed he did not show it. When he sat down again he seemed really quite cheerful. "What's the new reverend like?" he asked. "I hear he comes from Barbados."

"He's a nice man," she said. "Grandma Thompson says he visits all the sick people regularly."

"Did he ever come to see you?"

"He came to say the church would accept the child. Wanted me to give him sufficient notice for the baptism, but I haven't seen him since. He was nice, though."

"My father would have given you a lecture."

"I know. But this Bajan's pretty good for himself. I hear he's in with a few of the girls around here already. Besides, he has a young boy, but nobody's ever seen the boy's mother."

"That was my father's main weakness," Bertie said. "He never was nice enough to the village women . . ."

And some other nonsense they talked, until Grandma Thompson came in saying the boy Henry was drunk, talking out of his head at the rumshop, looking for a fight, and Bertie hurried off saying soldiers had to take care of one another.

That was the last she saw of Bertie. But in the weeks that followed she saw all she wanted to of Henry, because when it came time for them to return to the camp he wouldn't go. He hid from the army jeep that came and picked up the other two and remained in Palmyra. What difference did that make, really? He always used to find other places to go when he was a boy supposed to be in school, and now he was just a runaway soldier.

Like her, Henry became a disgrace to the village. He sold his uniform buttons to buy rum, and after they got tired of his uproarious drinking and constant fights his family put him out. Unlike with her, however, there was nothing independent about Henry. And after his family kicked him out, and he'd had enough of sleeping on the open gallery of the rumshop, he came to her, begging a place to sleep, even if it had to be on the floor.

Grandma Thompson didn't like the idea, but Olga allowed Henry to rest on her floor. He never stopped drinking, and it didn't take long for him to lose his strength for fighting and become just another tame village drunk who accepted his picong good-naturedly. He even added to it sometimes by marking time in the shop, lifting his knees high the way they did in the army, slapping his arms and shoulders meantime in something he called quartermaster drill.

When the baby came, Henry was there on her floor deep in a drunken sleep, and it didn't disturb him once, her groaning, or Grandma Thompson's talking her through then bustling back and forth with hot water and towels, or the baby crying. Yet when he woke up the first thing he wanted to do was hold the child, and Grandma said no. Because he was too dirty. Henry went off and washed himself, then came back in a clean pair of pants, a shirt he had borrowed from his brother, and lifted up the child to his face. He put a dollar inside the baby's clothes and asked, "Does she have a name already?"

"No. Nobody's named her yet."

"Good. I name her Grace."

That was how Grace got her name, how she got a second father too, because Henry loved the baby so much he went off to find a job so he could help take care of her.

Henry became a fisherman on the sea from Sunday to Friday, but that couldn't be helped. The Englishmen at the sugar factory would never have hired him. On the weekends when he came in from the sea he brought the child clothes and toys, and brought things for Olga too. Gracie grew, and Henry grew more fond of her. It used to be nice, seeing him with her when he was home on Saturdays. He played with her all morning before going to the rumshop, and when at night he returned, he would have two pockets full of sweets, fruits, and other little things the child might like.

Of course, by then Henry didn't sleep on the floor anymore. He was still black, that's true, but he was a kind man, and when one night after coming home from the sea he got into her bed, it seemed natural as anything that she should please him.

Saturdays were nice, then, and Sundays too; until one in the afternoon, when Henry had to leave to go back to the sea.

Then Gracie was old enough to be away at Sunday school when it was time for Henry to leave, and he didn't like that. He missed her kissing goodbyes, he claimed; missed her eyes telling him to bring her nice things when he came home next Friday night. Olga herself never once asked Henry for anything. She took what he brought, and let him sleep in her bed, but she never asked for anything. Henry liked to behave as though he really was a father. He liked Gracie wrapping her arms around his leg and reminding him to bring her back something next Friday. And so he missed her when she had to be away at Sunday school.

In the meantime Olga was looking her best as a woman. She was no longer thin. After the child her breasts remained high and round, her hips spread a little, and her legs took on flesh. And just as the men used to flock to her house in the days before she went to work for the Yankees, so they started coming back. One or two of the older ones had died, but there were young ones to take their places—fresh boys just starting work at the factory. These and the middling ones who used to follow her in the old days on their bicycles, they were always around, hanging about her doorstep, her yard, eager to do her errands, always bringing her gossip, bringing her yams or chickens, whatever they could lay hands on, even though she never asked them for anything. Henry was no bother to them either. They came just the same when he was home, and sometimes he would bring a bottle and finish it with the grown men in the yard. He never quarrelled with them and they never minded him. If he came home drunk and staggering, two or three would always be there to help him in. Other times they just shifted their bottoms on the steps so he could get by.

After the child, and having Henry, it turned out that Olga wasn't bothered by the eyes anymore. And she couldn't tell really how it happened, but one day she had it suddenly clear in her mind that it was her special blessing to have men look at her that way. And with this in mind, she could sit in her open doorway whenever the men were around and turn every eye up under her dress, then shut her legs and turn them out again, watching all the time how the men would lose control of their thoughts, even those who tried to appear cool and indifferent. She could make them shift from thinking about rain, or sickness, or the government. She would bend their minds on the sly, pretending her moves were all accidental, and after they were gone would feel a great pleasure deep inside that brought laughter, and the child sometimes asked, "What you laughing at, mama?" And that was mostly the only fun she had, because she never went to dances, or church, or anywhere else anymore, except to the town sometimes when she had to buy clothes or pay taxes. But that was only for a time.

One Sunday, with Henry gone, Gracie away at Sunday school, Olga listened to the men talking about a dance which had passed the night before, and their talk brought back memories of the dance at which she had met Lloyd in Arima. She told them the story. The men made a racket about it. "You could've been killed," Reggie said, and she had to admit that that was true. "Those Yankees and those town boys, they don't play. They could have killed you, and we'd never have heard about you again." That was true. And the memories helped make her feel safe and cradled in the attention of the village men. She was at home all safe and knew she would be taken care of the rest of her life by these men for whom she was an adventuress, a mystery all rolled into one.

Olga let them continue their racket, and while she was waiting for sundown to bring Gracie home from her Sunday walk she went on letting them catch a glimpse under her dress every now and then, smiling to see the way it made the veins at their temples tick faster. When early darkness came, and the men started going off to supper, Reginald did not go. He remained seated on the step beneath her knees and when she rose to go in said, "You know Olga, you really could've been killed up there in Arima." She stopped but didn't say anything.

Then he got up too and said, "Let me come tonight."

And she said, "All right. After Gracie's gone to evening service."

Maybe it was recalling times with Lloyd and Lou made her agree, she thought, as close to eight o'clock that same night she lay watching Reginald put on his clothes, pondering whether Henry would quarrel with her when he found out. It didn't seem that he should.

On Monday night after the men went away, and Gracie was asleep behind the curtain, she let Reginald come again, but on Tuesday night she would not let him, because he seemed wanting to make a habit of it. On Wednesday night she would not let him again, and he quarrelled. On Thursday night, just to show Reginald that he shouldn't be stupid, she let Dudley stay. He had been asking with his eyes for a long time. On Friday Henry came home, and everything went as usual. But

Sunday it was Reginald again, then Dudley, and Reginald again, and Dudley, and when they quarrelled with one another she let Winston come.

Olga couldn't remember how it first started, but somebody gave her—left her—five dollars once, which she took and hid in the sweatband of a church hat she didn't wear anymore. And the next one who came brought five dollars too, which she took. And the next one brought ten which she didn't mean to take, but he left it beneath her pillow, and she was later glad because Henry didn't come home that weekend. Or any other weekend. He just never came back to the village.

And on. Three, four, five, six, soon more than ten or twelve men who came each brought a little offering which she took; and though she never knew of any agreement they made among themselves, they stopped quarrelling with one another. That made everything easy. She simply left the door unlatched, and after it was time for Gracie to be asleep someone would come in softly to her bed, and leave what he could when it came daybreak and time for him to go. The women of the village began wandering past her home more frequently than usual, and twice she found blue bottles of asafoetida and scorched calabashes beneath the steps, but that didn't worry her.

Olga and her daughter never wanted for anything. The child grew up smoothly, with shoes to wear to school, and a new dress for confirmation. She had her own schoolbooks, and a shilling every day to buy little things she wanted. As for prettiness, the child had no competition, and besides, who else in the village could boast a true Yankee American father? Gracie had days brighter than any Olga herself had had. Olga never tied her down. She let her go into town Saturday mornings to see theater, or buy *Seventeen* magazines at the bookstore. The girl was singing in the choir, always had a nice dress to wear for church functions, and took her walks on Sundays with the reverend's boy who was just two or three years older than she and not from an English family but a high-class Bajan home, which was not too far different, but different enough to make a future marriage less troublesome.

In an unspoken way Olga was taken by the sweetness and beauty of her daughter, and secretly hoped the child was on her way to becoming the lady she herself might have been if the war hadn't come along to take Bertie. And she wasn't prepared when the child said no, she didn't want any high school, no more education, she just wanted to go to America . . . "I don't want to go to no high school. I old enough to go to America, and I want to go live there with my father. I hate this village . . ."

Olga wasn't prepared, and it seemed that the child was betraying her. To grow out of the village, yes. But to say you hate it and only want to go to America? "And how about the reverend's boy?" Olga had asked. "What're you going to do about him?"

"He's just a friend." It was clear to see Gracie had no intention of spending her years with him, in a nice home with flower gardens and servants, and good-looking, clean, respectable children. And Olga didn't know how to take it, except to feel hurt for days, and outraged, because the child really had no true feelings for her father. Had never once shown an interest in the meaning of Lou's attentions for Olga. Had, in fact, been hostile to Olga reminiscing with the village men about Lou's warmth and his weaknesses. And now, as though deserving of some special privilege in daughterhood, calling upon him as ticket or passport to some dreamed-about life in America. It was while Olga was in this hurt and confused state with her child that the traveller showed up in the village.

He kept saying he was from Hollywood, but nobody was stupid enough to believe that. Any fool knew from the movies that Hollywood had the best-looking, cleanest, healthiest people in the world, and this boy looked more like a long-haired stray dog than anything else. He came to the village nobody knew how, and started calling everybody "brother," but he was neither black, nor brown, nor white, and with his sickly color like a parboiled baby nobody in the village wanted to be his brother. And spending as much time in the rumshop as the Chinese owner himself but not drinking, the men said, he was just there playing on his guitar, singing what he called folksongs, and buying the men drinks to get them to sing him some kind of worksongs he said belonged to the Island. Nobody was fool enough to believe he was American. Nobody, that is, except Gracie.

The child was taken with this stranger right away, and had more than the time of day to give him Grandma Thompson said, whenever she went to the shop, or passed him on the road. Swinging her little bottom, and looking at him as though he were some sort of prize. "You ought to talk to that girl," Grandma said. "You know she think she too high-class to listen to nobody else. You better talk to her."

And Olga had said, "Not to worry Grandma. Gracie won't do nothing stupid, you know. She just trying out herself to learn what she can do."

"But it don't look good," Grandma said. "The other Sunday she carried on right in front the reverend's boy while they taking their walk and pass this Yankee on the road. Even stop to talk with the Yankee while the poor boy stand up like a fool waiting in the grass."

"Well he better learn something quick," Olga had said. "And his father is a lady's man? He better ask his daddy what to do when his girl start making sweet-eyes at another man."

"You taking this like a joke," Grandma had said then, in a bitter and tired voice. "But you know Gracie don't listen to nobody else in this village. And mark my word . . . if you don't talk to her soon you going to be sorry. Too late, too late, shall be the cry: Jesus of Nazareth will have already passed by . . ."

Olga promised she would talk to Gracie, but didn't; even after she heard they had been seen in the town together, and when she asked Gracie the girl said no. Intuitively Olga knew Gracie was lying, but didn't feel she should cut off the child's chance to grow.

And later Grandma asked again, "You talk to Gracie yet? She not going to choir practice any more. You know."

That made Olga feel lonely. Something like that she should have been told already. Unless people had washed their hands of this case with her daughter. "She's not?"

"No, she's not. You can pass down by Terrell's Bridge any time you like and see where she really is while she's supposed to be in choir practice." Grandma wasn't even bitter anymore. Her voice just had the tiredness now. "All you young people, you're too harden. All you laughing at that boy with his nasty clothes and dirty hair, say he can't be a Yankee. But he is. Watch his eyes. He no different from the madmen who passed through here in the war. Mark my word . . ."

Which made Olga try to recall what it was like holding hands with Lou in the moonlight. Had he really been different? Had she missed something about him? If he came now to ask her to go away to Iowa, would she go? Olga searched her feelings for answers, but got nowhere. In the end she said yes to Grandma, meaning it this time. She would have a talk with Gracie. But instead, Gracie had a talk with her that day after school, saying, as though the fifteen years she had put in on the child had just dropped away, "I going to America next week."

Olga felt like she'd received a heavy blow to the stomach that knocked her breath away. But she kept herself calm and finally said, "Is so?"

"Mickey wrote to his friends and they answered they ready to accept me as one of their family and see I get to be an actress in Hollywood."

"Is so?"

"Mmmm hmmm."

"And how you know you're leaving next week? You have passage already?"

"Mickey's going to pay my passage and I'll pay him after I start making money."

"And how about your other papers and such?"

"He's fixing all that."

"What day next week?"

"Either Tuesday or Wednesday. He didn't fix that yet."

"So then, you're leaving this house . . .?"

The child won't even let her finish, but lashed out, "What you want me to do? Let myself rotten in this place? I told you to find my father, but you didn't do it. What you want me to do . . .?"

And before Olga knew what her hand was doing she had twisted Gracie's face. The child backed off with the slap still ringing in the house between them, and not another word was said until the darkness came and Gracie mumbled, "I going to choir practice," and walked out the door.

The moon was getting low. It was already time for one of her men friends to be trying her door, but nobody came. At the window Olga grew tired of leaning over the sill, and stood up. Her eyes were tired from straining themselves on the road. Her whole body, in fact, felt like she had put in a long day laboring. And she stretched to ease the tiredness in her muscles. It was already late, but no matter what time the child got home Olga would be there to have that talk with her.

Gracie had never seen a real Yankee, nor heard them curse, nor heard the way they talked about poozle. Nor had she seen them wipe their feet on the mopsies of Port of Spain. She was too young to remember days when Yankees drove their jeeps up and down the wrong side of the road, killing whoever stood in their way, and throwing money on the bodies as though that was all a man or a woman was worth anyway. Lou, of course, was different. And if it should be that he was back in his little white town it would be nice for Gracie to go there, even if her mother couldn't, and send pictures of herself wearing sweaters with school letters printed in front and behind. They would have to go to the American consul to find out how to get in touch with Lou, and that might be a better service to the child than any advice about whoring.

Olga was a little disgusted with herself for having taken so long to see, but a little relieved as well, and she went into the trunk and brought out the dresses they would wear to Port of Spain in the morning. She set out tea things too, so they wouldn't have to turn around too long before setting out, because they would have to catch the first bus to reach the consulate before the morning crowd. Then she returned to the doorstep, and continued waiting.

The moon got low down enough to send her house shadow pointing towards the cane; still Olga sat in the doorway waiting. Once or twice it seemed laughter came back to her from across the fields, but she couldn't be sure. Everything was quiet; the night was dead still. Once she thought she saw a man and woman pass swiftly along the road, but that couldn't be, because it was too late for anybody to be heading out the lonely stretch into the country. Besides, the man and woman she thought she saw didn't look familiar, and she didn't even hear them make footsteps against the pitch road as they glanced by. Olga closed her eyes to rest them a little while, so she would stop seeing things.

PHILOME OBIN, MASTER PAINTER

PHOTOGRAPHS BY
LAWRENCE SYKES

MORNING LIGHT

OLD MAN OF LA BOUDET

CONJURGRAPH 7

CONJURGRAPH 2

CONJURGRAPH 4

PROCESSIONAL VARIATION I

LAWRENCE F. SYKES

was born in Decatur, Alabama in 1931. He has degrees from Morgan State College and Pratt Institute. He has taught in the New York public schools and was the Director of the Carl Murphy Fine Arts Center at Morgan. He is presently Associate Professor of Art at Rhode Island College in Providence—teaching photography and film making. Since 1970 he has concentrated on the African Continuum —traveling to the Caribbean, Africa, South America, and Alabama to develop his "diaspora themes." His prints are in the collection of the American Museum of Natural History, the Embassy of Ghana, Washington, D.C., West Virginia State University, the College of Art, U.S.T., Kumasi, and others.

THE STAR-APPLE KINGDOM

DEREK WALCOTT

There were still shards of an ancient pastoral
in those shires of the Custos where the Herefords drank
from their pools of shadow from an older sky,
surviving from when the landscape copied such subjects as
"Herefords at Sunset in the Valley of the Wye."
The mountain water that fell white from the millwheel
sprinkling like petals from the star-apple trees
and all of the windmills and sugar mills moved by mules
on the treadmill of Monday to Monday would repeat
in tongues of water and wind and fire, in tongues
of Mission School pickaninnies, like rivers remembering
their source, Parish Trelawny, Parish St. David, Parish
St. Andrew, the names afflicting the pastures
the lime groves and fences of marl-stone and the cattle
with a docile longing, an epochal content.
And there were, like old wedding lace in an attic,
among the boas and parasols and the tea-coloured
daguerreotypes, hints of an epochal happiness
as ordered and infinite to the child
as the great house road to the Great House
down a perspective of casuarinas plunging green manes
in time to the horses, an orderly life
reduced by lorgnettes day and night, one disc the sun,
the other the moon, reduced by a pier glass:
nannies diminished to dolls, mahogany stairways
no larger than those in an album in which
the flash of cutlery yellows, as gamboge as
the piled cakes of teatime on that latticed
bougainvillea verandah that looked down towards
a prospect of Cuyp-like Herefords under a sky
lurid as a porcelain souvenir with these words:
"Herefords at Sunset in the Valley of the Wye."

Strange, that the rancour of hatred hid in that dream
of slow rivers and lily-like parasols, in snaps
of fine old colonial families, curled at the edge
not from age or from fire or the chemicals, no, not at all,
but because, off at its edges, innocently excluded
stood the groom, the cattle boy, the housemaid, the gardeners,
the tenants, the good Negroes down in the village,
their mouths opening together in a silent scream.
A scream which opened the doors to swing wildly
all night, that was bringing in heavier clouds
more black smoke than cloud, frightening the cattle
in whose bulging eyes the Great House diminished
as in a pier-glass; a scorching wind of a scream
that began to extinguish the fireflies,
that dried the water mill creaking to a stop
as it was about to pronounce Parish Trelawny
all over, in the ancient pastoral voice,
a wind that blew all without bending anything
neither the leaves of the album or the lime groves:
blew Nanny floating back in white from a feather
to a chimerical, chemical pin-speck, that shrank
the drinking Herefords to brown porcelain cows
on a mantelpiece, Trelawny trembling with dusk,
the scorched pastures of the old benign Custos, blew
far the decent servants and the life-long cook,
and shrivelled to a shard that ancient pastoral
of dusk in a gilt-edged frame now catching the evening sun
in Jamaica, making both epochs one.

He looked out from the Great House windows on
the sunset which he had inherited:
He saw the Botanical Gardens officially drown
in a formal dusk, where governors had strolled
and black gardeners had smiled over glinting shears
at the lilies of parasols on the floating lawns,
the flame trees obeyed his will and lowered their wicks,
the flowers tightened their fists in the name of thrift,
the porcelain lamps of ripe cocoa, the magnolia's jet
dimmed on the one circuit with the ginger-lilies,
and left a lonely light on the verandah,
and had his mandate extended to that ceiling
of star-apple candelabra, he would have ordered
the country to sleep, saying, I'm tired,
save the starlight for victories, we can't afford it,

leave the moon on for one more hour, and that's it.
But though his power, the given mandate, extended
from tangerine daybreaks to star-apple dusks,
his hand could not dam that ceaseless torrent of dust
that carried the shacks of the poor, to their root-
                    rock music,
down the gullies of Yallahs and August Town
to lodge them on thorns of macca, with their rags
crucified by cactus, tins, old tyres, cartons,
from the black Warieka Hills the sky glowed fierce as
the dials of a million radios,
a throbbing sunset that glowed like a grid
where the dread beat rose from the jukebox of Kingston.
He saw the fountains dried of quadrilles, the water music
of the country dancers, the fiddlers like fifes
put aside. He had to heal
this malarial island in its bath of bay leaves,
its forests tossing with fever, the dry cattle
groaning like winches, the grass that kept shaking
its head to remember its name. No vowels left
in the mill wheel, the river. Rock stone. Rock stone.

The mountains moved like whales through phosphorous stars,
as he swayed like a stone down fathoms into sleep,
drawn by that magnet that pulls down half the world
between a star and a star, by that black power
that has the assassin dreaming of snow,
that pole-axes the tyrant to a sleeping child.
The house is rocking at anchor, but as he falls
his mind is a mill wheel in moonlight,
and he hears, in the sleep of his moonlight, the drowned
bell of Port Royal's cathedral, sees the copper pennies
of bubbles rising from the empty eye-pockets
of green buccaneers, the parrot fish floating
from the frayed shoulders of pirates, sea horses
drawing gowned ladies in their liquid promenade
across the moss-green meadows of the sea,
he heard the drowned choirs under Palisadoes
a hymn ascending to earth from a heaven inverted
by water, a crab climbing the steeple,
and he climbed from that submarine kingdom
as the evening lights came on in the Institute,
the scholars lamplit in their own aquarium,
he saw them mouthing like parrot fish as he passed

upward from that baptism, their history lessons,
the bubbles like ideas which he could not break:
Jamaica was captured by Penn and Venables,
Port Royal perished in a cataclysmic earthquake.

Before the coruscating facades of cathedrals
from Santiago to Caracas, where penitential archbishops
washed the feet of paupers (a parenthetical moment
that made the Caribbean a baptismal font,
turned butterflies to stone, and whitened like doves
the buzzards circling municipal garbage),
the Caribbean was borne like an elliptical basin
in the hands of acolytes, and a people were absolved
of a history which they did not commit;
the slave pardoned his whip, and the dispossessed
said the rosary of islands for three hundred years,
a hymn that resounded like the hum of the sea
inside a sea cave, as their knees turned to stone,
while the bodies of patriots were melting down walls
still crusted with mute outcries of La Revolucion!
"San Salvador, pray for us, Saint Thomas, San Domingo,
ora pro nobis, intercede for us Sancta Lucia
of no eyes," and when the circular chaplet
reached the last black bead of Sancta Trinidad
they began again, their knees drilled into stone,
where Colon had begun, with San Salvador's bead,
beads of black colonies round the necks of Indians.
And while they prayed for an economic miracle,
ulcers formed on the municipal portraits,
the hotels went up, and the casinos and brothels,
and the empires of tobacco, sugar and bananas,
until a black woman, shawled like a buzzard,
climbed up the stairs and knocked at the door
of his dream, whispering in the ear of the keyhole:
"Let me in, I'm finished with praying, I'm the Revolution.
I am the darker, the older America."

She was as beautiful as a stone in the sunrise,
her voice had the gutturals of machine guns
across khaki deserts where the cactus flowers
detonate like grenades, her sex was the slit throat
of an Indian, her hair had the blue-black sheen of the crow.
She was a black umbrella blown inside out
by the wind of revolution, La Madre Dolorosa

a black rose of sorrow, a black mine of silence,
raped wife, empty mother, Aztec virgin
transfixed by the arrows of a thousand guitars,
a stone full of silence, which, if it gave tongue
to the tortures done in the name of truth,
would curdle the blood of the marauding wolf,
a fountain of generals, poets and cripples
who danced without moving over their graves
with each Revolution; her birth scar was stitched
by the teeth of machine guns, and, every sunset,
she had carried the Caribbean's elliptical basin
as she had once carried the penitential napkins
to be the footbath of dictators, Trujillo, Machado,
and those whose faces had yellowed like posters
on municipal walls. Now she stroked his hair
until it turned white, but she would not understand
that he wanted no other power but peace,
that he wanted a revolution without any bloodshed,
he wanted a history without any memory,
streets without statues,
and a geography without myth. He wanted no armies
but those regiments of bananas, thick lances of cane,
and he sobbed, "I am powerless, except for love."
She faded from him, because he could not kill,
she shrank to a bat that hung day and night
in the back of his brain. He rose in his dream.

The soul, which was his body made as thin
as its reflection and invulnerable
without its clock, was losing track of time,
it walked the mountain tracks of the Maroons,
it swung with Gordon from the creaking gibbet,
it bought a pack of peppermints and cashews
from one of the bandanna'ed mammies outside the Ward,
it heard his breath pitched to the decibels
of the peanut-vendors' carts, it entered a municipal wall
stirring the slogans that shrieked his name: SAVIOR!
and others LACKEY! he melted like a spoon
through the alphabet soup of CIA, PNP, OPEC,
that resettled once he passed through with this thought:
I should have foreseen those seraphs with barbed-wire hair,
beards like burst mattresses and wild eyes of garnet
who nestled the Coptic Bible to their ribs, would
call me Joshua, expecting him to bring down Babylon

by Wednesday, after the fall of Jericho, yes, yes,
I should have seen the cunning bitterness of the rich
who left me no money but these mandates:

His aerial mandate, which
contained the crows whose circuit
was this wedding band that married him to his island.
His marine mandate, which
was the fishing limits
which the shark scissored like silk with its teeth
between Key West and Havana,
his terrestrial:
the bled hills rusted with bauxite,
paradisal:
the chimneys like angels sheathed in aluminum.

In shape like a cloud
he saw the face of his father,
the hair like white cirrus blown back
in a photographic wind,
the mouth of mahogany winced shut
the eyes lidded, resigned
to the first compromise
the last ultimatum
the first and last referendum.

One morning the Caribbean was cut up
by seven prime ministers who bought the sea in bolts,
five thousand miles of aquamarine with lace trimmings,
one million yards of lime-coloured silk,
one bolt of violet, leagues of cerulean satin,
who sold it at a mark-up to the conglomerates
the same conglomerates who had rented the water spouts
for ninety-nine years in exchange for fifty ships,
who retailed it in turn to the ministers
with only one bank account, who then resold it
in ads for the Caribbean Economic Community,
till everyone owned a little piece of the sea
from which some made saris, some made bandannas
the rest was offered on trays to white cruise ships
taller than the Post Office, then the dogfights
began in the Cabinets as to who had first sold
the archipelago for this chain store of islands.

Now a tree of grenades was his star-apple kingdom,
over fallow pastures his crows patrolled,
he felt his fist involuntarily tighten
into a talon that was strangling five doves
the mountains loomed leaden under martial law,
the suburban gardens flowered with white paranoia
next to the bougainvilleas of astonishing April,
the rumours were a rain that would not fall,
that enemy intelligence had altered the roaches'
quivering antennae, that bats were flying like couriers
who piped their secrets between the embassies,
over dials in the War Rooms, the agents waited
for a rifle-crack from Havana, down shuttered avenues
roared a phalanx of Yamahas. They left
a hole in the sky that closed on silence.

He didn't hear the roar of the motorcycles
diminish in circles like those of the water mill
in a far childhood; he was drowned in sleep,
he slept, without dreaming, the sleep after love
in the mineral oblivion of night
whose flesh smells of cocoa, whose teeth are white
as coconut meat, whose breath smells of ginger,
whose braids are scented like sweet potato vines
in furrows still pungent with the sun.
He slept the sleep that wipes out history
he slept like the islands on the breast of the sea,
like a child again in her star-apple kingdom.

Tomorrow the sea would gleam like nails
under a zinc sky where the barren frangipani
is nailed, a horizon without liners,
tomorrow the heavy caravels of clouds would wreck
and dissolve in their own foam on the reefs
of the mountains, tomorrow a donkey's yawn
would saw the sky in half, and at dawn
would come the noise of a government groaning uphill.
But now she held him, as she holds us all
her history-orphaned islands, she to whom
we came late as our muse, our mother,
who suckled the islands, who, when she grows old
with her breasts wrinkled like eggplants
is the head-tie mother, the bleached-sheets-on-the-river-
                                    rocks mother,

the gospel mother, the t'ank-you-parson mother
who turns into mahogany, the lignum-vitae mother,
her sons like thorns
her daughters dry gullies that give birth to stones,
who was, in our childhood, the housemaid and the cook,
the young grand' who polished the plaster figure
of Clio, Muse of History, in her seashell grotto
in the Great House parlour, Anadyomene washed
in the deep Atlantic heave of her housemaid's hymn.

In the indigo dawn the palms unclenched their fists,
his eyes opened the flowers, and he lay as still
as the waterless mill wheel. The sun's fuse caught,
it hissed on the edge of the skyline and day exploded
its remorseless avalanche of dray carts and curses,
the roaring oven of Kingston, its sky as fierce
as the tin box of a patties cart. Down the docks
between the Levantine smells of the warehouses
nosed the sea wind with its odour of a dog's damp fur.
He lathered in anger and refreshed his love.
He was lathered like a horse, but the instant
the shower drenched him and he closed his eyes,
he was a bride under lace, marrying his country,
a child drawn by the roars of the mill wheel's electorate,
those vows reaffirmed, he dressed, came down to breakfast,
and sitting again at the mahogany surface
of the breakfast table, its dark hide as polished
as the sheen of mares, saw his father's face
and his own face blent there, and looked out
to the drying gardens and its seeping pond.

What was the Caribbean? A green pond mantling
behind the Great House columns of Whitehall
behind the Greek facades of Washington,
with bloated frogs squatting on lily pads
like islands, islands that coupled as sadly as turtles
engendering islets, as the turtle of Cuba
mounting Jamaica engendered the Caymans, as, behind
the hammerhead turtle of Haiti-San Domingo
trailed the little turtles from Tortuga to Tobago,
he followed the melancholy trek of the turtles
leaving America for Africa, for the open Atlantic,
felt his own flesh loaded like the pregnant beaches
with their moon-guarded eggs, they yearned for Africa,

they were lemmings drawn by magnetic memory
to an older death, to broader beaches
where the coughing of lions was dumbed by breakers.
Yes, he could understand their natural direction
but they would drown, sea eagles circling them,
and the languor of frigates that do not beat wings,
and he closed his eyes, and felt his jaw drop
again with the weight of that silent scream.

He cried out at the turtles as one screams at children
with the anger of love, it was the same scream
which, in his childhood, had reversed an epoch
that had bent back the leaves of his star-apple kingdom,
made streams race uphill, pulled the water wheel backwards
like the wheels in a film, and at that outcry,
from the tight ropes and tendons of his throat,
the sea buzzards receded and receded into specks,
and the osprey vanished.
                          On the foot-hollowed steps   .
of the crusted cathedral, there was a woman in black,
the black of moonless nights, within whose eyes
shone seas in starlight like the glint of knives
the one who had whispered to the keyhole of his ear,
washing the steps, and she heard it first.
She was one of a flowing black river of women
who bore elliptical basins to the feet of paupers
on the Day of Thorns, who bore milk pails to cows
in a pastoral sunrise, who bore baskets on their heads
down the hemophilic red mornes of Haiti,
now with the squeezed rag dripping from her hard hands
the way that vinegar once dropped from a sponge,
she heard as a dog hears, as all the underdogs
of the world hear the pitched shriek of silence.
Star-apples rained to the ground in that silence,
the silence was the green of cities undersea,
and the silence lasted for half an hour
in that single second, a seashell silence, resounding
with silence, and the men with barbed-wire beards saw
in that chasm of light that was made between
the noises of the world that was equally divided
between rich and poor, between North and South,
between white and black, between two Americas,
the fields of silent Zion in Parish Trelawny,
in Parish St. David, in Parish St. Andrew,

leaves dancing like children without any sound,
in the valley of Tryall, and the white, silent roar
of the old water wheel in the star-apple kingdom;
and the woman's face, had a smile been decipherable
in that map of parchment so rivered with wrinkles,
would have worn the same smile with which he now
cracked the day open and began his egg.

Editor's note: This poem appears in somewhat different form in Mr. Walcott's latest book, *The Star-Apple Kingdom* (1979).

REFLECTIONS
BEFORE AND AFTER CARNIVAL:
AN INTERVIEW WITH DEREK WALCOTT

[SHARON CICCARELLI]: Mr. Walcott, critics have stated that the tradi-
tional conception of poetry as primarily dramatic narrative is nearly de-
funct. Your work, especially the drama, seems to challenge this state-
ment. Does the folk content of your plays necessitate the various devices
you employ—chorus, masks, chants, drumming—or are such devices a
deliberate attempt to re-create an older form of dramatic narrative?

[DEREK WALCOTT]: The rapid development of the novel has reduced the
necessity of poetry as narrative, although a great deal of narrative po-
etry was written during earlier periods (for example, during the Victo-
rian age) of the novel's development. Poetry has been backed against a
wall by the existence of numerous narratives in the media, on film, tele-
vision, etc. The concept of leisure has affected the concept of the poem
as story-telling, since so many narrative forms are either immediately or
ultimately visual. The only recent narrative poets who come to mind are
Frost and Edward Robinson. It has to do with the decline of the epic
and the deterioration of tribal sense because of industrialization.

The point I am coming to is this: a lot of novelists who begin as poets
think that the novel, because of its simultaneity, can serve them just as
well as an epic poem. The greatest example of this is Joyce's *Ulysses*. It
seems that a lot of modern poets ultimately turn to narrative forms,
principally the novel, and sometimes theatre.

The modern reader is an individual. The whole custom of reading to
the family (which continued until the Victorian period), whether from a
poem or from a novel, has been replaced by television and the cinema.
Today, the visual narrative entails an individual spectator who is not
read to. No one is told a story by a living voice.

The narrator as performer does not exist any more except in primal
societies. And by primal society I mean any tight, familial, tribal society
in which the reader or poet has a function. This society could be the soci-
ety of Homer or the society of a Swahili tribesman.

This interview was conducted in January and March 1977. The first session occurred in
Port of Spain, Trinidad; the second, in New Haven, Connecticut. The interviewer is
Sharon L. Ciccarelli.

Literature developed from the ear first, then the eye. That is, from an oral to a written tradition. So the society that existed before printing was invented, e.g., Homer's society, and the one that still exists without printed literature become the same in terms of oral narrative. West Indian society is within an oral tradition. This is a question of literacy rather than intelligence, and the reasons for such a society are many: poverty, poor access to written materials, isolation . . .

Story-telling, singing, and other forms of tribal entertainment continue with such phenomena as the calypso tents. That tradition is also African. The union of voice and drum, the drum being the most natural accompaniment of the human voice, is still very strong, and is the basis of our music.

If one begins to develop a theatre in which the drum provides the basic sound, other things will develop around it, such as the use of choral responses and dance. If we add to this the fact that the story-teller dominates all of these, then one is getting nearer to the origins of possibly oral theatre, but certainly African theatre. Oral theatre may be Greek, or Japanese, or West Indian, depending upon the shape percussion takes.

I don't think that in any of my plays there is innovation or discovery in terms of theatre. Rather, I attempt to use all the still viable, vital elements in a play.

The mask, for instance, is not, as it is in metropolitan theatre, a device: it is a totem. In my own experience, I have always been aware of the power of the mask, or mask-like make-up. In contemporary Carnival, masks have been forbidden, but they used to be an essential part of Carnival. The words "play masks" really mean "to play with a mask." It is a pity that the mask has been removed from Carnival, as it affects the power of the costume. If the face is bare, the rest is only rigid and artificial design. When one puts on the mask, one is creating theatre.

Modern playwrights who use masks (Genet and Brecht, for example) are not avant-garde, but are returning to the primal formalities of Chinese, Japanese, and African theatre.

[c]: In *Ti Jean and His Brothers* the events of the tale occur over several days, yet the dramatic action emphasizes the compactness of time and event. In particular, the use of characters to recount action that has already occurred, or will occur, and the choral refrains that separate scenes concentrate the effect of the fable and heighten the anticipation of conflict between Ti Jean and the Devil. What is your conscious manipulation of time as it relates to the narrated action of various characters, and how does this affect the way the plays are produced on stage?

[w]: Once you have a strong or accepted narrator, and once the audience gets into the rhythm of a piece, time ceases to be a problem. If the

rhythm is strong, there is no need to show an interval as progressing chronologically.

In legend, a narrator manipulates his audience into the state of a child impatient with details of time. Such audiences are thus reduced to the credibility of children. Keats's phrase about "suspension of disbelief" is applicable to this phenomenon, but is not always true of naturalistic fiction. To get back to *Ulysses*, which is the supreme work of naturalistic fiction, Joyce set himself twenty-four hours as a frame, not merely in order to retain any Aristotelian "unity," but because the accretion of detail and the creation of infinite sequences of epiphanies (making any object radiate its "whatness") could not extend beyond that time. The next day would demand another book of equal length.

I am strongly influenced by Japanese Noh theatre in which essentials are important, so that a piece of cloth becomes a stream, or a movement of the hand a fountain. In the final analysis, every play of that kind moves closer to a poem.

I attempted in *Dream* to let the action come out of successive detonations of images not dominated by a narrative logic, as occurs in the creative process of a poem, or in the integrity without logic of a dream.

When *Ti Jean* was produced in the park, the lighting man said he would have problems with the many switches from day to night. Yet the play was written for conditions without technology, sets, or lighting. If the narrator is strong enough to say "is now night"—it is night; there is no need for technology. This may be what Brecht is after: getting rid of the restraints, the chiaroscuro of metropolitan theatre.

The people in the forefront of twentieth-century theatre keep fighting technology. Brecht, Genet, Brook, they are all simply getting back to the true needs of theatre—to the human body alone, not gilded by equipment or effects. Too many plays (and I myself have been guilty of this) require the imitation of reality; whereas Aristotle's first principle still holds: drama depends not on the imitation of reality, but on the imitation of action. Real action in theatre doesn't require any furniture or machinery.

What the actor ultimately aims at is for his audience to contemplate his body as the only true instrument of theatre. The greater the actor, the less he needs around him.

The strongest theatre will always be the theatre of a primal society, one that goes directly to the elementals of art: ritualistic tragedy, satire, and comedy. Because the audience shares in, rather than being instructed by, the experience.

[c]: The tension between dream and reality in *Dream* becomes a vehicle that forces the ritualistic resolution. The relationship between dream, prophetic vision, and madness seems to be comparable to the relation-

ship of image, metaphor, and symbol within the play. Was there a conscious linking of these psychological and literary terms? You refer to both Fanon and Sartre in epigraphs. Did your readings of their works influence the form of *Dream?*

[w]: I spent ten years, working on and off, creating this play. I worked on it in the same way I approach a poem, where the lines survive until the poem, ultimately, is finished. The impulse of creating scenes one out of another reflects the same process. It is essentially one metaphor with many components. Metaphor is basically a contradiction, though apparent, since two textures are fused. The comparison of a moon to a half-sucked sweet illustrates this; we know the contradiction inherent in this. But the moment of metaphor is not a moment of contradiction, even if the two elements are apparently opposite. My example is bad, because one can always ask ordinary questions. True, unshakable metaphor is one that causes the astonishment of truth. This process is not *shown* in poetry, but rather on stage where the metaphor cannot be simply heraldic. It becomes evident because theatre is action. Therefore the metaphor of a play is the full progression, even through contradiction of a final heraldic image. The great figures of theatre are metaphors, and in contemporary theatre, even if a figure lacks the support of legend, the greatest come closest to this.

In theatre we see this metaphor as a human being. The metaphor of *Dream* was, for me, an old man who looked like an ape, and above his shoulder, a round white full moon. And the journey of that moon which drew the man/ape through the cycle of one night multiplied (like all metaphors) into questions of human evolution, racial evolution, the search for self-respect and pride, and the reality which comes with the morning. Once a gong has been struck, the visible resonances of figure, sound, and image will all be concentric and will be subject to all kinds of true and perhaps contradictory interpretations. If one looks hard at any bright object it will multiply itself, will send out dimmer images around it. In *Dream*, the process of writing with that image in mind—the man, the moon, and the mountaintop—made the writing of the play equivalent to the poetic experience where the dominant metaphor creates others.

[c]: Do you feel that there is any connection between West Indian narrative forms and dionysian ritual?

[w]: The Greeks had so many gods they were godless in a way. In *Dream*, the frenzy comes out of a man's relationship to his dream. If this had been realized more heraldically, its power would have been akin to the power of Shango. Yet this might have been impossible, for if the play becomes that powerful, it becomes the ceremony it is imitating. The play is probably a little overwritten.

But to get back to your question . . . Carnival, which happens throughout the Caribbean, is a godless festival. Based on a Catholic conception of the last days before Lent, it is also related to crop-over (the burning of the cane). It is very African except for the fact that there is no god. It is interesting that *bacchanal* is the Trinidadian word for Carnival. The total surrender to the senses is what Carnival is about. But in Shango, one surrenders to the god. Carnival became more decorative as faith diminished, and now there is no one figure that represents the festival. And in dionysian ritual, the surrender to the senses is a means of surrendering to the god Dionysus. Yet in Carnival, we have a ritualistic mass form in which the high priest is the poet, the calypsonian, but there is no god. Or perhaps the only deity existing in Carnival is art, because in all of the song, orchestration, and costumes there is competition for recognition as an artist. Art substitutes for the god. There is nothing wrong in this, no inherent blasphemy, and when Carnival is over, the deification will not continue; there is no use trying to interest a Trinidadian in Carnival after the fact.

I suppose this is all a long way of saying "no," the West Indian narrative is not a dionysian ritual. All over the Caribbean one discovers repressed creativity: the steel bands, wire sculpture, the huge body of music produced within the folk culture. This is a society whose highest ritual is art, and that is pretty good.

[c]: In your essay "Twilight" you wrote: "In that simple schizophrenic boyhood one could lead two lives: the interior life of poetry, the outward life of action and dialect." Could you elaborate on this with regard to the development of a dramatic style? How does involvement with a particular acting company affect your writing?

[w]: The longer one remains in the Caribbean, the more certain things become evident. One cannot make a living as an artist, yet one is aware of a vitality that comes from living in certain root areas. Since a man does not choose to reduce himself to poverty, the exile of the West Indian artist has become a reality.

This society is still patterned on the stratification between rich and poor black. He who has acquired education finds himself on the thin line of the split in society. The artist instinctively moves towards his people on that root level, and yet, at the same time, he must survive. This split is equivalent to a state of schizophrenia.

Much deeper is the historic racial split resulting in two kinds of bloods, almost two kinds of people. Language and the experience of illiteracy among the poor is a profound problem that divides the West Indian writer. The more sophisticated he becomes, the more alienated is his mental state. It is not his business to lower his standards to insult the poor. When one is confronted with this problem of language, two situations occur: wanting to reach one's people; and realizing the harsh realities of the society, the depression and the economic exploitation. At the same time that one's intellect becomes refined, and one learns more about the society, there is a movement away from that society.

[c]: Black writers in the sixties formed a literal conception of language, approaching the essay; Ted Joans, for instance, influenced by this kind of writing, talks about "hand grenade poems." Do you think this was a necessary if futile theoretical exercise?

[w]: I think that, in the pressure of the physical revolution that was taking place, the poetry and the anger were synonymous. There are certain periods where a poet may consider the language of revolution more important than the poem itself. And if the poet knows that what he is doing is using the form of poetry as a weapon, without concerning himself too much with the poem, then I don't consider it to be futile. In a way, it *is* necessary, because any group of men marching or going in a common direction moves to a rhythm, whether it is an army in step or whether it is a bunch of people who are united by a song, or a slogan, or a shout. At that point a poet can provide the equivalent of a slogan or a shout through his poems, as if he were at once a drummer and a poet, someone beating the rhythm. The poem's development would depend, I think, on the urgency with which the poem is surrounded, on the pressure of events surrounding the revolt. Now I have never been close to such a situation, but I would imagine that, like any other poet, one could articulate in a poem the expression of a common group in a rhythmic, defiant sort of sense. The only thing I would say here is that one may be convinced of the right in something that may be consciously ephemeral—just as a revolution between one goal and the next is a moment, however long that moment lasts—and it may then become expedient to write that kind of poem. I haven't had this kind of experience, but I can understand why, I can understand the necessity in fact, of poets expressing the feelings or beliefs of a revolution in their poetry. All great revolutionary movements have had hymns and poems which united them in their beliefs.

I couldn't have been influenced by their poetry because I wasn't in the presence of that revolution, but I can understand Ted Joans's use of the phrase "hand grenade poems." If a poem is thrown at an enemy, it detonates some response on the part of people who are afraid, or who understand that there is a likelihood of intense violence. I *understand* the use of the phrase, as I said, but (however conservative this may seem) there is another conception of poetry—a kind of universal reasoning—that may be more effective than abrupt, abusive, or hostile poems. Somebody, Auden I think, said that poetry makes nothing happen. Poetry itself may not make anything happen, but it has incited people to make things happen. The danger for a poet—for there is excitement in the passion of what he is believing—is to confuse what he thinks a poem can do with poetry itself. One must choose a language, or a tone. There is a tendency to oversimplify and also, of course, to take sides; and in one sense it is a kind of reduced poetry. But, as I said earlier, I think that if the poet knows that this is poetry used for a particular perhaps didactic function, and that it may not last beyond his time, he can justify this kind of writing.

[c]: What is the role of the artist in a political struggle?

[w]: If the struggle is intense, the role of an artist is to pick up a gun like everyone else. It depends on how physical the struggle is. One can write poems *and* carry guns, you know. So I think that if there is an active struggle, the role of the artist is to involve himself physically in the struggle.

[c]: T. S. Eliot postulated that all works of Western art, starting with Homer and extending in what he called an "unbroken arc" to the present, comprise a simultaneous existence and order. Do you think that the black arts comprise a similar, or the same, unbroken arc? And could this concept be expanded into a Pan-African movement? Or do political, cultural, and economic differences between Africa and Afro-America preclude such a notion?

[w]: I don't know . . . You've got to think a long, long time about that thing from Eliot . . . I suppose what Eliot is saying is that you can see Western civilization as a whole, as one immense sensibility starting with Greek moral and aesthetic traditions, that includes anyone who considers himself within the tradition of Western civilization. But I don't think that this general statement would necessarily be true of every Western culture; I can't say that this applies to the Americas. The whole of Western civilization *does not* share one sensibility. If one postulates that, then one would have to overlook racial or religious differences that exist in the very context of Western civilization. The statement is, for me, too general, and would bear a heavy amount of particular examination. It is contradictory, in a sense. Take Spain, for example. One has to talk about the Moorish influence and how this compares with Homeric ideals. Or take the Afro-American situation: is it contained within an unbroken arc, reaching from Africa to the Americas? What we have, obviously, is a *broken* arc; we only know half the arc, and anything beyond that half arc has been torn from our memory. I don't think that there is anything "pure" on this side of the world; the whole feel of it is multitudinous, several races with various ancestral ties. Does not America—and I mean the land from Greenland right down to Tierra del Fuego—argue against this unbroken arc, particularly in light of the

African experience, in light of the conditions in which he was brought to the New World? The more time accelerates, the less we remember—collectively—and it becomes impossible, artificial even, to try to find this unbroken arc. When one considers the education of the black in the Western world, and his being taught ideas such as Eliot was talking about, the image of one unbroken arc seems even ironic. A sensibility that has been broken and re-created is, I think, a more accurate description of our present situation.

[c]: Earlier you mentioned that the folk form is a major part of your mythic system. Do you think that the power of the folk idiom is effectively portrayed in your drama?

[w]: No, I would say that a lot of it has had to be diluted theatrically, for clarification. For instance, I can't create in pure Creole, French, or English, for all sorts of reasons. You might be in a situation where accents differ within a small area, among people who all speak French Creole. The same applies to English Creole in the Caribbean. It is very difficult, in one sense, for a Trinidadian to understand a Jamaican, or for a Jamaican to understand a Barbadian, but since one considers the Caribbean—the English-speaking Caribbean—as a whole, as sharing one language with various contributory sources, one must try to find, using syntaxes from various dialects if necessary, one form that would be comprehensible not only to all the people in the region that speak in that tone of voice, but to people everywhere. It is like making an amalgam, a fusion, of all the dialects into something that will work on stage. For instance, I've done a play, a Rasta play, that was not written in pure Jamaican; it was conceived and performed in Trinidad, it was played by Trinidadian actors, and I had forgotten a lot of the complexities of Jamaican construction. If I do it in Jamaica, I'll allow rephrasing of the wording, but I believe that the tone itself is accurate. Even if, for instance, it is spoken with a Trinidadian accent. In one of the best productions of my work I have seen—a production of *Dream*—the actors settled on a common accent for the entire company. The play thus had a harmony that grew out of their decision to speak in the same way. You have such a number of dialects in the West Indies, you have to decide that you are going to use a general sound, even if you draw from more than one dialect.

[c]: What about the Calypso play you just finished? Do you think that it successfully rendered the folk accent?

[w]: Well, another thing about dialect is that since it is the jargon of the people, of the street, it changes rapidly. You may have written something two years ago, and now find a phrase already outdated. The same is true, I think, of American black speech. But if the sound of the work is

right, usually all that is needed is to change an expression or two, within what is being said.

[c]: Your characters are often highly typed, sometimes mythical; their names and roles are not only symbolic of biblical or African traditional figures, but it seems that, at times, they are even allegorical. What relation does this kind of characterization have to the reduction of the play's elements to an essential form, the kind of process you mentioned earlier? Were the characters in *Dream* conceived as archetypes?

[w]: No, I think that the strength of the characterization does not come from me, it comes from the imagination of my people. When, like in a fable, a character is given an animal's name, like Tigre, or Souris, or Makak, he becomes akin to the mythical figure. An animal becomes a man, a man becomes an animal. So that what I am doing is broadening, or clarifying, the kind of common folk imagination that ascribes an animal's characteristics to a person. That happens in all cultures, of course. In terms of reducing the play, I think it gives the play a kind of form, the form of a fable. As soon as you do that, then you are utilizing a very hierarchical, ritualistic, accepted form of story-telling; the narrator says "once upon a time there was . . ." and the "once upon a time" acts upon the structure of the play, making it into a fable structure with a beginning, a middle, and an end. Whatever happens within the play must support the cycle. To me that kind of conception is more powerful than the individual attempt of avant-garde writers to restructure the idea of theatre. I think it is inescapable that once you open your mouth, you'll want to tell a story. If you don't open your mouth, if you work your device around the direct narration, there still remains an elemental progression from action to action. A man walks across the stage, you *know* something is going to happen; everything on stage is done for a reason, everything contributes to the general outline of the play. There is just no time for superfluities in drama. Think of how the ancients were weighed line for line . . .

What appears to be the most old-fashioned aspect of Third World writing, or to West Indian writing in particular, is really its most powerful aspect: the tribe is being told a story that comes from the memory of that tribe. I have had one volume of plays published, and those plays are all set in elemental situations. The elemental is the background, and people move within that element. These elements are as much forces within the plays as are the characters themselves; at times they are more important to the play's development than the characters that exist inside them. The sea is the major force in *Sea at Dauphin*; the forest—with its superstitions, its religion—dominates *Ti Jean*; the rain is the cleansing force in *Malcochon*, etc. But I have written a lot of other plays which are set within an urban or a naturalistic situation, and where a man moves through a non-elemental setting. *Sea at Dauphin* was an attempt to do the same kind of thing that Synge did. I made the figure of Afa larger than the average fisherman, and he may even be archetypical. I guess you could say my plays are like the flip sides of a coin; the one side naturalistic, the other ritualistic or elemental. And I do find that a lot of my principal characters are heightened by the fact that they come out of the depth of a folk consciousness.

[C]: How would you relate this to the idea of myth? Does the folk consciousness have a mythic structure?

[W]: I don't think one starts out consciously to create myth. The poet encounters many dangers when his work evolves from myth. He might just relate the story in a very one-dimensional manner. Most storytelling exists on this level; it is all incident, really, without any development of character. Or he might lean too heavily on the figures given in the fable, figures that have no psychology. These kinds of figures cannot be successfully played by actors. But in the Greek theatre, for instance, there is a psychology that motivates the characters. It is not only ritualistic; it is psychological as well. Oedipus and Creon are men, but the structure and mode of the play are ritualistic. This is a delicate point for Third World or West Indian theatre, which is only beginning to absorb the concept of psychology, of creating a character within a myth and of making the figure a man. But the very fact that these societies remain close to the mythical origins of story-telling can be turned into a creative advantage. Because we live in a society in which myth, superstition, and the folk memory are very strong, where ritual celebration abounds, there is the possibility that the character may become more than just a psychological figure. This character, because of the vitality of the story-telling tradition, may move towards the largeness of the mythical figure and still retain the essential quality of manhood.

[C]: Do you think that black writers should write in the language of their ex-colonizers; for instance, Césaire writing in French, or Soyinka writing in English? Should they attempt to master a traditional language—Swahili, Yoruba? Or should they work towards a fusion, say the way McKay used the Jamaican *patois* in his first volume of poetry, *Songs of Jamaica*?

[W]: I think the writer writing in English or in Spanish is lucky in the sense that he can master the original language, or the language of the master himself, and yet have it fertilized by the language of dialect. Someone who knows what he is doing, a good poet, recognizes the language's essential duality. The excitement is in joining the two parts. I don't think that one should attempt to destroy the syntax of one's own conversation. A Marquez or a Fuentes should follow the syntac-

tical progression of someone speaking in Spanish. He may know the
dialects of the country people, or of the ghetto people of his own coun-
try, and if so, he should capture their tone. It is like having two hands;
one hand knows the language of the master, the other hand knows the
language of dialect, and a fusion of both limbs takes place in the ex-
pression that you write down. I think it is a futile, stupid and political
exercise to insist on "creating" language. One works within a language.
Look at Ishmael Reed, who to me is one of the most exciting writers
in the States, much more so than a lot of the celebrated Jewish novelists,
for instance. To the extent that one can judge a writer and what he
invents, the exercise must reflect the excitement one gets in reading
him. And every time I re-read Reed, his work is as fresh to me, and as
exhilarating and as funny as it was at the first reading. There is a delight
in it—the same kind of delight I get when I read Joyce. I'm not com-
paring them in stature, but to me Reed's is a most fertile kind of writing.
     What we should do, and there is so much to do, as African, or as
African-sourced people, is not just learn Swahili—I don't have the
time to go and learn Swahili, it would be more useful for me to learn
Spanish—but one should be completely aware of the epic origins of
one's literature, and of one's own race. If there is a great Swahili epic
poem, then I should find it, and enjoy it, and I would perhaps find
things there that would relate to me, to my writing. The fantastic thing
about Trinidad—and it has been ignored to an amazing extent—is
the diversity of culture: Chinese, Hindu, African. All of these races
have their epics, and there is a kind of Hindu epic drama still performed
on the island. If there could be even the most concentrated or minimal
means of access to all of this racial knowledge, to the collective mem-
ory, one could enrich one's writing to a great extent. If I am a West
Indian living in Trinidad, and if the Chinese, and the Indians, and the
Africans all live there, and if I share my life with them, then, ideally, I
should know the origins of all and yet still be *of* my race. That, I think,
would be complete fulfillment for a West Indian. I'm not speaking
about genealogy, I don't need so much to know *who* was my great-
great-grandfather, but *what* was my great-great-grandfather, how did
he live? One would know not Chinese, but the Chinese . . .

[c]: Could you elaborate a little on your comment about how learning
Spanish would be useful to you?

[w]: Well, I live in a part of the world where a dominant culture influ-
ence is Spanish, Spanish-sourced anyway. I have found more of an
affinity in Spanish-American poets than I have found in poets writing
in England, or in America. We have a similar historical origin, similar
problems of self-resolution, and I can recognize a sensibility as being
very close to mine. So not only is there a possibility for geographical
or political exchange, there is the possibility of real cultural and cre-

ative exchange. Yet I cannot really know how an African thinks; I don't think in the African mode. And I'm not saying that knowing Swahili would make me an African. The person over on this part of the world is an American, whether he be a Latin American, an Afro-American, or a West Indian American. Even the white American had the same problem of identification. In fact, I think this—identity—has been the obsession of any race in this part of the world. Americans themselves have been made to feel inferior to England in terms of literature, painting, etc. They used to be considered an inferior culture in general when compared to the richness of European culture. White, black, any color, it has been a problem for the American in this part of the world. So that if I understand Spanish, if I can read Marquez in *his* language, then I understand him through my immediate inquiry: what do we have in common? Whereas I know that (and I say this without any desire to give offense) I have a way of thinking that may be totally alien to the African. I probably am a total stranger to the African, whereas I am not a stranger to Marquez, or Fuentes, or Paz.

[C]: Who do you read?

[W]: Well, mostly I have been reading the poetry, and I have read a couple of the novels in translation. The usual people . . . But I haven't had access to enough Spanish-American novels, and of those I have read, I find some too long, too unwieldy; they are often poorly modeled on the European epic, and frankly I find many boring. I'm more interested in writers like Marquez who have an instinctive way of handling the natural and the legendary in close proximity. This is very understandable to me in my part of the world; something not quite fantasy, and so much more compelling than the stilted naturalism of much metropolitan literature. He creates more than a mere replica of what happened during the day, more than a record of who said what.

[C]: Do you think it is a mistake for black writers to turn to white writers?

[W]: I don't think there is any such thing as a black writer or a white writer. Ultimately, there is someone whom one reads. Yet there is no man that can, or should wish to escape his race; he should accept and then begin to worry about being a good writer. If you think of the greatest prose innovator of our time, Joyce, you might ask: who is Joyce? You know that Joyce is an Irishman, that he has written about Ireland, very particularly about Ireland; but is that Joyce? An Irish novelist? One can't approach literature that way. And this has been said many times before. Say a black man comes along and writes a *Ulysses*, something of that stature. You know that it is *by* a black man, that it might be *about* his own race; but ultimately one must go beyond these simple statements. If a writer learns from anyone he must learn from a great writer. What black writer can I learn from? I can't think of a black writer who I would call a master very simply because black writers have really evolved at the same time as I have—they are my contemporaries. And that writer I choose as a master would have to be someone of enormous and proven stature within the language, within the imagination of blackness, for me to learn from him. Generally, one learns from the great dead. Do you think of Shakespeare as a white writer? Or Tolstoy? Or Aeschylus? I would not like to be called a black writer, I would not like to be told that a white writer or a white reader would not read me because I am black. It doesn't make any sense.

[C]: What about Soyinka as a master?

[W]: I'm not saying that there aren't emerging black writers who could not be great, that there are not masterpieces among the emerging literature. I consider *The Road* a masterpiece. But the man is a contemporary of mine; we have gone through the same evolution in terms of writing in countries where, previously, there had not been a large body of recorded literature. So this masterpiece, any masterpiece created by a contemporary, is *his*. There is no one among my contemporaries whom I wish to apprentice myself to. If I were aware of some epic, some ancestral masterpiece, then I would perhaps regard that as a masterwork. But the fact remains, the masterpieces of the language in which I work are from a white literary history. That must not prevent me from mastering the language; it is not a matter of subservience, it is a matter of dominating. One becomes a master, one doesn't become a slave.

[C]: Do you see any valid place for "relevance" or political commitment in black aesthetic and critical values, or do you think that the way a poet uses language should be the critic's foremost concern?

[W]: I don't think you can separate the two things. A man, for instance, might say: "All this fuss the niggers are making (to make the statement crude and succinct) is a pain, and I'm withdrawing from it, and that's my attitude, and I'm going to live in my black ivory tower and not involve myself in any revolution." All right, that's his stance. As a matter of fact there is a terrific West Indian writer, V. S. Naipaul, who is very cynical of Caribbean political and racial endeavors. That has been his consistent position, and yet one is able to admire him as a writer, and to respect his stance because he *writes* out of it, and even to admit that he is a very good writer. I don't think any critic can point out to him that his argument, that his cynicism, is wrong and thus ignore his achievements as a writer. Reed speaks to this problem. Every year a new bunch of people tell you to join this group, to do this and that, they point out the people who are more politically involved than you are, more revolutionary. A writer could go crazy trying to keep up with the changes . . . He's got to find his own pivot, his own stance—to know what he believes in—and this has to be, for him, a respectable truth. This is what enables him to write, and that is the important thing. It is not the business of any critic to tell any writer what his position should be, certainly not from the point of view of criticism. From the politician's point of view, possibly. But it is not the critic's duty to say, "You write terrific poetry, but you should be more relevant."

THE MILITANCE OF A PHOTOGRAPH
IN THE PASSBOOK OF A BANTU
UNDER DETENTION

MICHAEL S. HARPER

The wrinkles on the brown face
of the carrying case
conform to the buttocks,
on which the streaks of water
from a five-gallon can
dribble on the tailfront
of the borrowed shirt
he would wear if he could
drain the pus from his swaddling
bandages, striations of skin
tunneling into the photograph.

This is no simple mugshot
of a runaway boy in a training
film, Soweto's pummeled wire,
though the turrets of light
glisten in smoke, the soft
coal hooding his platform
entrance, dull and quiet.

His father's miner's shoes
stand in puddles of polish,
the black soot baked
into images of brittle torso,
an inferno of bullets laid
out in a letter-bomb,
the frontispiece of one sergeant-
major blackening his mustache.

On the drive to Evaton
a blank pass away from Sharpeville
where the freehold morgans
were bought by a black bishop

from Ontario, Canada, on a trek
northward from the Cape in 1908,
I speak to myself as the woman
riding in the back seat talks
of this day, her husband's
death, twenty-three years ago,
run over by an Afrikaner in the wrong
passing lane; the passbook on the shoulder
of the road leading to Evaton
is not the one I have in my hand,
and the photograph is not of my great-
grandfather, who set sail for Philadelphia
in the war year of 1916.
He did not want a reception, his letters
embarking on a platform at Queenstown
where his eloquence struck two Zulu warriors
pledged to die in the homelands
because they could not spin their own gold.

These threaded beads weigh down the ears
in design of the warrior, Shaka,
indifferent to the ruthless offerings
over the dead bodies of his wives,
childless in his campaigns with the British,
who sit on the ships of the Indian Ocean
each kraal shuddering near the borders;

her lips turn in profile
to the dust rising over a road
where his house once stood;
one could think of the women
carrying firewood as an etching
in remembrance to the silence,
commencing at Sharpeville,
but this is Evaton, where he would come
from across the galleyship of spears
turning in his robes to a bookmark;

it is a good book, the picture of words
in the gloss of a photograph,
the burned image of the man who wears
this image on the tongue of a child,

who might hold my hand
as we walk in late afternoon
into the predestined sun.

The press of wrinkles on the blanketed
voice of the man who took the train
from Johannesburg,
is flattened in Cape Town,
and the history of this book
is on a trestle where Gandhi
worshipped in Natal,
and the Zulu lullaby
I cannot sing in Bantu
is this song in the body
of a passbook
and the book passes
into a shirt
and the back that wears it.

AN IMAGE OF AFRICA

CHINUA ACHEBE

IT WAS A FINE AUTUMN MORNING AT THE BEGINNING OF THIS academic year such as encouraged friendliness to passing strangers. Brisk youngsters were hurrying in all directions, many of them obviously freshmen in their first flush of enthusiasm. An older man, going the same way as I, turned and remarked to me how very young they came these days. I agreed. Then he asked me if I was a student too. I said no, I was a teacher. What did I teach? African literature. Now that was funny, he said, because he never had thought of Africa as having that kind of stuff, you know. By this time I was walking much faster. "Oh well," I heard him say finally, behind me, "I guess I have to take your course to find out."

A few weeks later I received two very touching letters from high school children in Yonkers, New York, who—bless their teacher—had just read *Things Fall Apart*. One of them was particularly happy to learn about the customs and superstitions of an African tribe.

I propose to draw from these rather trivial encounters rather heavy conclusions which at first sight might seem somewhat out of proportion to them: But only at first sight.

The young fellow from Yonkers, perhaps partly on account of his age but I believe also for much deeper and more serious reasons, is obviously unaware that the life of his own tribesmen in Yonkers, New York, is full of odd customs and superstitions and, like everybody else in his culture, imagines that he needs a trip to Africa to encounter those things.

The other person being fully my own age could not be excused on the grounds of his years. Ignorance might be a more likely reason; but here again I believe that something more willful than a mere lack of information was at work. For did not that erudite British historian and Regius Professor at Oxford, Hugh Trevor Roper, pronounce a few years ago that African history did not exist?

If there is something in these utterances more than youthful ex-

---

This paper was given as a Chancellor's Lecture at the University of Massachusetts, Amherst, February 18, 1975.

perience, more than a lack of factual knowledge, what is it? Quite simply it is the desire—one might indeed say the need—in Western psychology to set up Africa as a foil to Europe, a place of negations at once remote and vaguely familiar in comparison with which Europe's own state of spiritual grace will be manifest.

This need is not new: which should relieve us of considerable responsibility and perhaps make us even willing to look at this phenomenon dispassionately. I have neither the desire nor, indeed, the competence to do so with the tools of the social and biological sciences. But, I can respond, as a novelist, to one famous book of European fiction, Joseph Conrad's *Heart of Darkness*, which better than any other work I know displays that Western desire and need which I have just spoken about. Of course, there are whole libraries of books devoted to the same purpose, but most of them are so obvious and so crude that few people worry about them today. Conrad, on the other hand, is undoubtedly one of the great stylists of modern fiction and a good storyteller into the bargain. His contribution therefore falls automatically into a different class—permanent literature—read and taught and constantly evaluated by serious academics. *Heart of Darkness* is indeed so secure today that a leading Conrad scholar has numbered it "among the half-dozen greatest short novels in the English language."[1] I will return to this critical opinion in due course because it may seriously modify my earlier suppositions about who may or may not be guilty in the things of which I will now speak.

Heart of Darkness projects the image of Africa as "the other world," the antithesis of Europe and therefore of civilization, a place where a man's vaunted intelligence and refinement are finally mocked by triumphant bestiality. The book opens on the River Thames, tranquil, resting peacefully "at the decline of day after ages of good service done to the race that peopled its banks." But the actual story takes place on the River Congo, the very antithesis of the Thames. The River Congo is quite decidedly not a River Emeritus. It has rendered no service and enjoys no old-age pension. We are told that "going up that river was like travelling back to the earliest beginning of the world."

Is Conrad saying then that these two rivers are very different, one good, the other bad? Yes, but that is not the real point. What actually worries Conrad is the lurking hint of kinship, of common ancestry. For the Thames, too, "has been one of the dark places of the earth." It conquered its darkness, of course, and is now at peace. But if it were to visit its primordial relative, the Congo, it would run the terrible risk of hearing grotesque, suggestive echoes of its own forgotten darkness, and of falling victim to an avenging recrudescence of the mindless frenzy of the first beginnings.

I am not going to waste your time with examples of Conrad's famed evocation of the African atmosphere. In the final consideration it amounts to no more than a steady, ponderous, fake-ritualistic repetition of two sentences, one about silence and the other about frenzy. An example of the former is "It was the stillness of an implacable force brooding over an inscrutable intention" and of the latter, "The steamer toiled along slowly on the edge of a black and incomprehensible frenzy." Of course, there is a judicious change of adjective from time to time so that instead of "inscrutable," for example, you might have "unspeakable," etc., etc.

The eagle-eyed English critic, F. R. Leavis, drew attention nearly thirty years ago to Conrad's "adjectival insistence upon inexpressible and incomprehensible mystery." That insistence must not be dismissed lightly, as many Conrad critics have tended to do, as a mere stylistic flaw. For it raises serious questions of artistic good faith. When a writer, while pretending to record scenes, incidents and their impact, is in reality engaged in inducing hypnotic stupor in his readers through a bombardment of emotive words and other forms of trickery, much more has to be at stake than stylistic felicity. Generally, normal readers are well armed to detect and resist such underhand activity. But Conrad chose his subject well—one which was guaranteed not to put him in conflict with the psychological predisposition of his readers or raise the need for him to contend with their resistance. He chose the role of purveyor of comforting myths.

The most interesting and revealing passages in *Heart of Darkness* are, however, about people. I must quote a long passage from the middle of the story in which representatives of Europe in a steamer going down the Congo encounter the denizens of Africa:

> We were wanderers on a prehistoric earth, on an earth that wore the aspect of an unknown planet. We could have fancied ourselves the first of men taking possession of an accursed inheritance, to be subdued at the cost of profound anguish and of excessive toil. But suddenly, as we struggled round a bend, there would be a glimpse of rush walls, of peaked grass-roofs, a burst of yells, a whirl of black limbs, a mass of hands clapping, of feet stamping, of bodies swaying, of eyes rolling, under the droop of heavy and motionless foliage. The steamer toiled along slowly on the edge of a black and incomprehensible frenzy. The prehistoric man was cursing us, praying to us, welcoming us—who could tell? We were cut off from the comprehension of our surroundings; we glided past like phantoms, wondering and secretly appalled, as sane men would be before an enthusiastic outbreak in a madhouse. We could not remember because we were travelling in the night of first ages, of those ages that are

gone, leaving hardly a sign—and no memories.

The earth seemed unearthly. We are accustomed to look upon the shackled form of a conquered monster, but there—there you could look at a thing monstrous and free. It was unearthly, and the men were—No, they were not inhuman. Well, you know, that was the worst of it—this suspicion of their not being inhuman. It would come slowly to one. They howled and leaped, and spun, and made horrid faces; but what thrilled you was just the thought of your remote kinship with this wild and passionate uproar. Ugly. Yes, it was ugly enough; but if you were man enough you would admit to yourself that there was in you just the faintest trace of a response to the terrible frankness of that noise, a dim suspicion of there being a meaning in it which you— you so remote from the night of first ages—could comprehend.

Herein lies the meaning of *Heart of Darkness* and the fascination it holds over the Western mind: "What thrilled you was just the thought of their humanity—like yours. . . . Ugly."

Having shown us Africa in the mass, Conrad then zeros in on a specific example, giving us one of his rare descriptions of an African who is not just limbs or rolling eyes:

And between whiles I had to look after the savage who was fireman. He was an improved specimen; he could fire up a vertical boiler. He was there below me, and, upon my word, to look at him was as edifying as seeing a dog in a parody of breeches and a feather hat, walking on his hind legs. A few months of training had done for that really fine chap. He squinted at the steam gauge and at the water gauge with an evident effort of intrepidity—and he had filed his teeth, too, the poor devil, and the wool of his pate shaved into queer patterns, and three ornamental scars on each of his cheeks. He ought to have been clapping his hands and stamping his feet on the bank, instead of which he was hard at work, a thrall to strange witchcraft, full of improving knowledge.

As everybody knows, Conrad is a romantic on the side. He might not exactly admire savages clapping their hands and stamping their feet but they have at least the merit of being in their place, unlike this dog in a parody of breeches. For Conrad, things (and persons) being in their place is of the utmost importance.

Towards the end of the story, Conrad lavishes great attention quite unexpectedly on an African woman who has obviously been some kind of mistress to Mr. Kurtz and now presides (if I may be permitted a little imitation of Conrad) like a formidable mystery over the inexorable imminence of his departure:

She was savage and superb, wild-eyed and magnificent . . . She stood looking at us without a stir and like the wilderness itself, with an air of brooding over an inscrutable purpose.

This Amazon is drawn in considerable detail, albeit of a predictable nature, for two reasons. First, she is in her place and so can win Conrad's special brand of approval; and second, she fulfills a structural requirement of the story; she is a savage counterpart to the refined, European woman with whom the story will end:

> She came forward, all in black with a pale head, floating towards me in the dusk. She was in mourning. . . . She took both my hands in hers and murmured, "I had heard you were coming" . . . She had a mature capacity for fidelity, for belief, for suffering.

The difference in the attitude of the novelist to these two women is conveyed in too many direct and subtle ways to need elaboration. But perhaps the most significant difference is the one implied in the author's bestowal of human expression to the one and the withholding of it from the other. It is clearly not part of Conrad's purpose to confer language on the "rudimentary souls" of Africa. They only "exchanged short grunting phrases" even among themselves but mostly they were too busy with their frenzy. There are two occasions in the book, however, when Conrad departs somewhat from his practice and confers speech, even English speech, on the savages. The first occurs when cannibalism gets the better of them:

> "Catch 'im," he snapped, with a bloodshot widening of his eyes and a flash of sharp white teeth—"catch 'im. Give 'im to us." "To you, eh?" I asked; "what would you do with them?" "Eat 'im!" he said curtly . . .

The other occasion is the famous announcement:

> Mistah Kurtz—he dead.

At first sight, these instances might be mistaken for unexpected acts of generosity from Conrad. In reality, they constitute some of his best assaults. In the case of the cannibals, the incomprehensible grunts that had thus far served them for speech suddenly proved inadequate for Conrad's purpose of letting the European glimpse the unspeakable craving in their hearts. Weighing the necessity for consistency in the portrayal of the dumb brutes against the sensational advantages of securing their conviction by clear, unambiguous evidence issuing out of their own mouth, Conrad chose the latter. As for the announcement of Mr. Kurtz's death by the "insolent black head in the doorway," what better or more appropriate *finis* could be written to the horror story of that wayward child of civilization who willfully had given his soul to the powers of darkness and "taken a high seat amongst the devils of the land" than the proclamation of his physical death by the forces he had joined?

It might be contended, of course, that the attitude to the African in *Heart of Darkness* is not Conrad's but that of his fictional narrator, Marlow, and that far from endorsing it Conrad might indeed be holding it up to irony and criticism. Certainly, Conrad appears to go to considerable pains to set up layers of insulation between himself and the moral universe of his story. He has, for example, a narrator behind a narrator. The primary narrator is Marlow but his account is given to us through the filter of a second, shadowy person. But if Conrad's intention is to draw a *cordon sanitaire* between himself and the moral and psychological malaise of his narrator, his care seems to me totally wasted because he neglects to hint however subtly or tentatively at an alternative frame of reference by which we may judge the actions and opinions of his characters. It would not have been beyond Conrad's power to make that provision if he had thought it necessary. Marlow seems to me to enjoy Conrad's complete confidence—a feeling reinforced by the close similarities between their careers.

Marlow comes through to us not only as a witness of truth, but one holding those advanced and humane views appropriate to the English liberal tradition which required all Englishmen of decency to be deeply shocked by atrocities in Bulgaria or the Congo of King Leopold of the Belgians or wherever. Thus Marlow is able to toss out such bleeding-heart sentiments as these:

> They were all dying slowly—it was very clear. They were not enemies, they were not criminals, they were nothing earthly now—nothing but black shadows of disease and starvation, lying confusedly in the greenish gloom. Brought from all the recesses of the coast in all the legality of time contracts, lost in uncongenial surroundings, fed on unfamiliar food, they sickened, became inefficient, and were then allowed to crawl away and rest.

The kind of liberalism espoused here by Marlow/Conrad touched all the best minds of the age in England, Europe, and America. It took different forms in the minds of different people but almost always managed to sidestep the ultimate question of equality between white people and black people. That extraordinary missionary, Albert Schweitzer, who sacrificed brilliant careers in music and theology in Europe for a life of service to Africans in much the same area as Conrad writes about, epitomizes the ambivalence. In a comment which I have often quoted but must quote one last time Schweitzer says: "The African is indeed my brother but my junior brother." And so he proceeded to build a hospital appropriate to the needs of junior brothers with standards of hygiene reminiscent of medical practice in the days before the germ theory of disease came into being. Naturally, he became a sensation in Europe and America. Pilgrims flocked, and I believe still flock even after he has passed on, to witness the prodigious miracle in Lamberene, on the edge of the primeval forest.

Conrad's liberalism would not take him quite as far as Schweitzer's, though. He would not use the word "brother" however qualified; the farthest he would go was "kinship." When Marlow's African helmsman falls down with a spear in his heart he gives his white master one final disquieting look.

> And the intimate profundity of that look he gave me when he received his hurt remains to this day in my memory—like a claim of distant kinship affirmed in a supreme moment.

It is important to note that Conrad, careful as ever with his words, is not talking so much about *distant kinship* as about someone *laying a claim* on it. The black man lays a claim on the white man which is well-nigh intolerable. It is the laying of this claim which frightens and at the same time fascinates Conrad, ". . . the thought of their humanity—like yours . . . Ugly."

The point of my observations should be quite clear by now, namely, that Conrad was a bloody racist. That this simple truth is glossed over in criticism of his work is due to the fact that white racism against Africa is such a normal way of thinking that its manifestations go completely undetected. Students of *Heart of Darkness* will often tell you that Conrad is concerned not so much with Africa as with the deterioration of one European mind caused by solitude and sickness. They will point out to you that Conrad is, if anything, less charitable to the Europeans in the story than he is to the natives. A Conrad student told me in Scotland last year that Africa is merely a setting for the disintegration of the mind of Mr. Kurtz.

Which is partly the point: Africa as setting and backdrop which eliminates the African as human factor. Africa as a metaphysical battlefield devoid of all recognizable humanity, into which the wandering European enters at his peril. Of course, there is a preposterous and perverse kind of arrogance in thus reducing Africa to the role of props for the breakup of one petty European mind. But that is not even the point. The real question is the dehumanization of Africa and Africans which this age-long attitude has fostered and continues to foster in the world. And the question is whether a novel which celebrates this dehumanization, which depersonalizes a portion of the human race, can be called a great work of art. My answer is: No, it cannot. I would not call that man an artist, for example, who composes an eloquent instigation to one people to fall upon another and destroy them. No matter how striking his imagery or how beautifully his cadences fall, such a man is no more a great artist than another may be called a priest who reads the mass backwards or a physician who poisons his patients. All those men in Nazi Germany who lent their talent to the service of virulent racism whether in science, philosophy or the arts have generally and rightly been condemned for their perversions. The time is long overdue for taking a hard look at the work of creative artists who apply their talents, alas often considerable as in the case of Conrad, to set people against people. This, I take it, is what Yevtushenko is after when he tells us that a poet cannot be a slave trader at the same time, and gives the striking examples of Arthur Rimbaud, who was fortunately honest enough to give up any pretenses to poetry when he opted for slave trading. For poetry surely can only be on the side of man's deliverance and not his enslavement; for the brotherhood and unity of all mankind and against the doctrines of Hitler's master races or Conrad's "rudimentary souls."

Last year was the 50th anniversary of Conrad's death. He was born in 1857, the very year in which the first Anglican missionaries were arriving among my own people in Nigeria. It was certainly not his fault that he lived his life at a time when the reputation of the black man was at a particularly low level. But even after due allowances have been made for all the influences of contemporary prejudice on his sensibility, there remains still in Conrad's attitude a residue of antipathy to black people which his peculiar psychology alone can explain. His own account of his first encounter with a black man is very revealing:

A certain enormous buck nigger encountered in Haiti fixed my conception of blind, furious, unreasoning rage, as manifested in the human animal to the end of my days. Of the nigger I used to dream for years afterwards.

Certainly, Conrad had a problem with niggers. His inordinate love of that word itself should be of interest to psychoanalysts. Sometimes his fixation on blackness is equally interesting as when he gives us this brief description:

A black figure stood up, strode on long black legs, waving long black arms.[2]

as though we might expect a black figure striding along on black legs to wave *white* arms! But so unrelenting is Conrad's obsession.

As a matter of interest Conrad gives us in *A Personal Record* what amounts to a companion piece to the buck nigger of Haiti. At the age of sixteen Conrad encountered his first Englishman in Europe. He calls him "my unforgettable Englishman" and describes him in the following manner:

> [his] calves exposed to the public gaze . . . dazzled the beholder by the splendor of their marble-like condition and their rich tone of young ivory . . . The light of a headlong, exalted satisfaction with the world of men . . . illumined his face . . . and triumphant eyes. In passing he cast a glance of kindly curiosity and a friendly gleam of big, sound, shiny teeth . . . his white calves twinkled sturdily.[3]

Irrational love and irrational hate jostling together in the heart of that tormented man. But whereas irrational love may at worst engender foolish acts of indiscretion, irrational hate can endanger the life of the community. Naturally, Conrad is a dream for psychoanalytic critics. Perhaps the most detailed study of him in this direction is by Bernard C. Meyer, M.D. In this lengthy book, Dr. Meyer follows every conceivable lead (and sometimes inconceivable ones) to explain Conrad. As an example, he gives us long disquisitions on the significance of hair and hair-cutting in Conrad. And yet not even one word is spared for his attitude to black people. Not even the discussion of Conrad's anti-Semitism was enough to spark off in Dr. Meyer's mind those other dark and explosive thoughts. Which only leads one to surmise that Western psychoanalysts must regard the kind of racism displayed by Conrad as absolutely normal despite the profoundly important work done by Frantz Fanon in the psychiatric hospitals of French Algeria.

Whatever Conrad's problems were, you might say he is now safely dead. Quite true. Unfortunately, his heart of darkness plagues us still. Which is why an offensive and totally deplorable book can be described by a serious scholar as "among the half dozen greatest short novels in the English language," and why it is today perhaps the most commonly prescribed novel in the twentieth-century literature courses in our own English Department here. Indeed the time is long overdue for a hard look at things.

There are two probable grounds on which what I have said so far may be contested. The first is that it is no concern of fiction to please people about whom it is written. I will go along with that. But I am not talking about pleasing people. I am talking about a book which parades in the most vulgar fashion prejudices and insults from which a section of mankind has suffered untold agonies and atrocities in the past and continues to do so in many ways and many places today. I am talking about a story in which the very humanity of black people is called in question. It seems to me totally inconceivable that great art or even good art could possibly reside in such unwholesome surroundings.

Secondly, I may be challenged on the grounds of actuality. Conrad, after all, sailed down the Congo in 1890 when my own father was still a babe in arms, and recorded what he saw. How could I stand up in 1975, fifty years after his death and purport to contradict him? My answer is that as a sensible man I will not accept just any traveller's tales solely on the grounds that I have not made the journey myself. I will not trust the evidence even of a man's very eyes when I suspect them to be as jaundiced as Conrad's. And we also happen to know that Conrad was, in the words of his biographer, Bernard C. Meyer, "notoriously inaccurate in the rendering of his own history."[4]

But more important by far is the abundant testimony about Conrad's savages which we could gather if we were so inclined from other sources and which might lead us to think that these people must have had other occupations besides merging into the evil forest or materializing out of it simply to plague Marlow and his dispirited band. For as it happened, soon after Conrad had written his book an event of far greater consequence was taking place in the art world of Europe. This is how Frank Willett, a British art historian, describes it:

> Gauguin had gone to Tahiti, the most extravagant individual act of turning to a non-European culture in the decades immediately before and after 1900, when European artists were avid for new artistic experiences, but it was only about 1904-5 that African art began to make its distinctive impact. One piece is still identifiable; it is a mask that had been given to Maurice Vlaminck in 1905. He records that Derain was "speechless" and "stunned" when he saw it, bought it from Vlaminck and in turn showed it to Picasso and Matisse, who were also greatly affected by it. Ambroise Vollard then borrowed it and had it cast in bronze . . . The revolution of twentieth century art was under way![5]

The mask in question was made by other savages living just north of Conrad's River Congo. They have a name, the Fang people, and are without a doubt among the world's greatest masters of the sculptured form. As you might have guessed, the event to which Frank Willett refers marked the beginning of cubism and the infusion of new life into European art that had run completely out of strength.

The point of all this is to suggest that Conrad's picture of the people of the Congo seems grossly inadequate even at the height of their subjection to the ravages of King Leopold's International Association for the Civilization of Central Africa. Travellers with closed minds can tell us little except about themselves. But even those not blinkered, like Conrad, with xenophobia, can be astonishingly blind.

Let me digress a little here. One of the greatest and most intrepid travellers of all time, Marco Polo, journeyed to the Far East from the Mediterranean in the thirteenth century and spent twenty years in the court of Kublai Khan in China. On his return to Venice he set down in his book entitled *Description of the World* his impressions of the peoples and places and customs he had seen. There are at least two extraordinary omissions in his account. He says nothing about the art of printing unknown as yet in Europe but in full flower in China. He either did not notice it at all or if he did, failed to see what use Europe could possibly have for it. Whatever reason, Europe had to wait another hundred years for Gutenberg. But even more spectacular was Marco Polo's omission of any reference to the Great Wall of China nearly 4000 miles long and already more than 1000 years old at the time of his visit. Again, he may not have seen it; but the Great Wall of China is the only structure built by man which is visible from the moon![6] Indeed, travellers can be blind.

As I said earlier, Conrad did not originate the image of Africa which we find in his book. It was and is the dominant image of Africa in the Western imagination and Conrad merely brought the peculiar gifts of his own mind to bear on it. For reasons which can certainly use close psychological inquiry, the West seems to suffer deep anxieties about the precariousness of its civilization and to have a need for constant reassurance by comparing itself to Africa. If Europe, advancing in civilization, could cast a backward glance periodically at Africa trapped in primordial barbarity, it could say with faith and feeling: There, but for the grace of God, go I. Africa is to Europe as the picture is to Dorian Gray—a carrier onto whom the master unloads his physical and moral deformities so that he may go forward, erect and immaculate. Consequently, Africa is something to be avoided just as the picture has to be hidden away to safeguard the man's jeopardous integrity. Keep away from Africa, or else! Mr. Kurtz of *Heart of Darkness* should have heeded that warning and the prowling horror in his heart would have kept its place, chained to its lair. But he foolishly exposed himself to the wild irresistible allure of the jungle and lo! the darkness found him out.

In my original conception of this talk I had thought to conclude it nicely on an appropriately positive note in which I would suggest from my privileged position in African and Western culture some advantages the West might derive from Africa once it rid its mind of old prejudices and began to look at Africa not through a haze of distortions and cheap mystification but quite simply as a continent of people—not angels, but not rudimentary souls either—just people, often highly gifted people and often strikingly successful in their enterprise with life and society. But as I thought more about the

stereotype image, about its grip and pervasiveness, about the will-
ful tenacity with which the West holds it to its heart; when I thought
of your television and the cinema and newspapers, about books read
in schools and out of school, of churches preaching to empty pews
about the need to send help to the heathen in Africa, I realized that
no easy optimism was possible. And there is something totally wrong
in offering bribes to the West in return for its good opinion of Africa.
Ultimately, the abandonment of unwholesome thoughts must be
its own and only reward. Although I have used the word *willful* a
few times in this talk to characterize the West's view of Africa it
may well be that what is happening at this stage is more akin to
reflex action than calculated malice. Which does not make the situa-
tion more, but less, hopeful. Let me give you one last and really minor
example of what I mean.

Last November the *Christian Science Monitor* carried an inter-
esting article written by its education editor on the serious psycho-
logical and learning problems faced by little children who speak one
language at home and then go to school where something else is
spoken. It was a wide-ranging article taking in Spanish-speaking
children in this country, the children of migrant Italian workers in
Germany, the quadrilingual phenomenon in Malaysia and so on.
And all this while the article speaks unequivocally about *language*.
But then out of the blue sky comes this:

> In London there is an enormous immigration of children who speak
> Indian or Nigerian dialects, or some other native language.[7]

I believe that the introduction of *dialects*, which is technically erro-
neous in the context, is almost a reflex action caused by an instinc-
tive desire of the writer to downgrade the discussion to the level of
Africa and India. And this is quite comparable to Conrad's with-
holding of language from his rudimentary souls. Language is too
grand for these chaps; let's give them dialects. In all this business a
lot of violence is inevitably done to words and their meaning. Look
at the phrase "native language" in the above excerpt. Surely the
only native language possible in London is Cockney English. But
our writer obviously means something else—something Indians and
Africans speak.

Perhaps a change will come. Perhaps this is the time when it can
begin, when the high optimism engendered by the breathtaking
achievements of Western science and industry is giving way to doubt
and even confusion. There is just the possibility that Western man
may begin to look seriously at the achievements of other people. I
read in the papers the other day a suggestion that what America
needs at this time is somehow to bring back the extended family.

And I saw in my mind's eye future African Peace Corps Volunteers coming to help you set up the system.

Seriously, although the work which needs to be done may appear too daunting, I believe that it is not one day too soon to begin. And where better than at a University?

NOTES

[1] Albert J. Guerard, Introduction to *Heart of Darkness* (New York: New American Library, 1950), p. 9.

[2] Jonah Raskin, *The Mythology of Imperialism* (New York: Random House, 1971), p. 143.

[3] Bernard C. Meyer, M.D., *Joseph Conrad: A Psychoanalytic Biography* (Princeton, N.J.: Princeton University Press, 1967), p. 30.

[4] *Ibid.*, p. 30.

[5] Frank Willett, *African Art* (New York: Praeger, 1971), pp. 35-36.

[6] About the omission of the Great Wall of China I am indebted to *The Journey of Marco Polo* as recreated by artist Michael Foreman, published by *Pegasus* Magazine, 1974.

[7] *Christian Science Monitor,* Nov. 25, 1974, p. 11.

POEMS

ROBERT HAYDEN

NAMES

Once they were sticks and stones
I feared would break my bones.
Four Eyes. And worse.
Old Four Eyes fled
to safety in the danger zones
Tom Swift and Kubla Khan traversed.

When my fourth decade came,
I learned my name was not my name.
I felt deserted, mocked.
Why had the Haydens lied?
No matter. They were dead.

And the name on the books was dead,
like the life my mother fled,
like the life I might have known.
You don't exist—at least
not legally, the lawyer said.
As ghost, double, alter ego then?

ASTRONAUTS

Armored in oxygen,
   faceless in visors—
mirrormasks reflecting

the mineral glare and
shadow of moonscape—
    they walk slowmotion
floating
    the lifeless
dust of Taurus
    Littrow. And Wow, they
exclaim, oh boy, this is it.

    And sing, exulting
(though trained to be wary
    of "emotion and
philosophy"), breaking
    the calcined stillness
of once Absolute Otherwhere.

Risking edges, earthlings
    to whom only
their machines are friendly
    (and God's radar-
watching eye?), they
    labor at gathering
proof of hypothesis;
    in snowshine of sunlight
dangerous as radium
    probe detritus for clues.

    What is it we wish them
to find for us, as
    we watch them on our
screens? They loom there
    heroic antiheroes,
smaller than myth and
    poignantly human.
Why are we troubled?
    What do we want of these men?
What do we want of ourselves?

ZINNIAS

(for Mildred Harter)

Gala, holding on
    to their harvest and wine
      colors
with what seems
    bravura
      persistence:

    We would
    scarcely present
bouquets of them
    to Nureyev
      or Leontyne Price:

Yet isn't
    their hardy élan one way
    of exclaiming
More More More
    as a gala
      performance ends?

A LETTER FROM PHILLIS WHEATLEY
(London, 1773)

Dear Obour
    Our crossing was without
event. I could not help, at times,
reflecting on that first—my Destined—
voyage long ago (I yet
have some remembrance of its Horrors)
and marvelling at God's Ways.
    Last evening, her Ladyship presented me
to her illustrious Friends.
I scarce could tell them anything
of Africa, though much of Boston
and my hope of Heaven. I read

my latest Elegies to them.
"O Sable Muse!" the Countess cried,
embracing me, when I had done.
I held back tears, as is my wont,
and there were tears in Dear
Nathaniel's eyes.

    At supper—I dined apart
like captive Royalty—
the Countess and her Guests promised
signatures affirming me
True Poetess, albeit once a slave.
Indeed, they were most kind, and spoke,
moreover, of presenting me
at Court (I thought of Pocahontas)—
an Honor, to be sure, but one,
I should, no doubt, as Patriot decline.

    My health is much improved;
I feel I may, if God so Wills,
entirely recover here.
Idyllic England! Alas, there is
no Eden without its Serpent. Beneath
chiming Complaisance I hear him hiss;
I see his flickering tongue
when foppish would-be Wits
murmur of the Yankee Pedlar
and his Cannibal Mockingbird.

    Sister, forgive th'intrusion of
my Sombreness—Nocturnal Mood
I would not share with any save
your trusted Self. Let me disperse,
in closing, such unseemly Gloom
by mention of an Incident
you may, as I, consider Droll:
Today, a little Chimney Sweep,
his face and hands with soot quite Black,
staring hard at me, politely asked:
"Does you, M'lady, sweep chimneys too?"
I was amused, but Dear Nathaniel
(ever Solicitous) was not.

    I pray the Blessings of Our Lord

and Saviour Jesus Christ
will Abundantly be yours.

Phillis

from THE SNOW LAMP

it is beginning oh
it begins now
breathes into me
becomes my breath

out of the dark
like seal to harpoon
at breathinghole
out of the dark

where I have wait-
ed in stillness that
prays for truth-
ful dancing words

ay-ee it breathes
into me becomes
my breath spiritsong
of Miypaluk

he who returned to us
bringing festive speech
Miypaluk hunter of seal
and walrus and bear

and who more skilled
at building sledge
and igloo ay-ee
the handler of dogs

Miypaluk was the name the Eskimos (Innuits) gave Matthew A. Henson, co-discoverer, with Admiral Robert E. Peary, of the North Pole. He became a legend among these people.

the pleaser of girls
Miypaluk who came
from the strange-
ness beyond the ice

he who was Inouk
not knowing one of us
Inouk returned
to his people ay-ee

Miypaluk Miypaluk
Across lunar wastes of wind and snow
Yeti's tract
               chimera's land
horizonless
               as outer space
through ice-rock sea
and valley
               (palm tree
fossils locked
in paleocrystic ice)

through darkness dire
as though God slept
in clutch of nightmare

through crystal and copper light
welcome as the smoking blood
of caribou
               desolate
as the soul's appalling night
toward Furthest North
                    where all
meridians end
               toward

(cairn)

No sun these months. Ice-dark and cold.

Blind howling. Demonic dark that storms the soul
with visions none visionless can bear. We are down
to the last of the pemmican. Soon must kill and eat
ɔur dogs.

The Angakok chants magic words against
evil spirits, wrestles them. Prepares for his
descent into the sea, there to comb maggots from
Queen Nerrivik's hair that she send forth her fish
and seals lest we starve.

We strive against the wish to die. We use
the Innuit women to satiety. By this act alone
knowing ourselves still men, not ghosts. We have
cabin (igloo) fever. We quarrel with one another
—over the women, grow vicious (as the Innuits
do not). We are verminous. We stink like the
Innuits. We fight the wish to die.

FOUR POEMS

MICHAEL S. HARPER

BRISTOL:
BICENTENARY REMEMBRANCES OF TRADE

Shuttles in the rocking loom of history,
the dark ships move, the dark ships move,
their bright ironical names
like jest of kindness on a murderer's mouth;
. . .
Voyage through death,
        voyage whose chartings are unlove.
                —ROBERT HAYDEN: Middle Passage

I wish to be a Member of Parliament to have
my share of doing good or resisting evil.
        —EDMUND BURKE: Speech at Bristol, 1780.

I

Though I stand before these words
I don't remember your real aims
of evil or good, my ancestors
don't know either, though I read
at local libraries about your Bristol,
the great fleets skiffing along wave-
tops, cries of kinsmen below,
great schools of sharks forming a crescent
in caravans of corpses buffered in chains.

I buy a handbook for the great events
of this city, post six postcards
to friends, prepare to read of:

"Jesus, Estrella, Esperanza, Mercy"
Desire, Adventure, Tartar, Ann:"
the great testimonial to complicity in voices
of excuse for the triangular trade.

II

I visit a center called "Ink Works,"
where two black Jamaicans paint the day-
nursery, go up to the rec hall for orange
crush, the converted factory of ink
blossoming under grants from agencies
of self-help and annoyance
for the numbers of St. Paul are small.

In the hotel, in a heatwave that goes on
a second week of air-stagnation
and *mooing* trains, the talk is of drought,
crops burning in the midlands, the Avon
buoying the crafts in convergence with sea;
one could tour the 18th century mansions
or sip some Bordeaux wine in the air-conditioned
bar, or put on a tie for some roastbeef and pie;

on a corner near the exiting uniforms of soldiers
taking shots of "head on the nail,"
the corn riots billow up on screens
of sails on returning ships,
their holds half-empty, the efficient ship-
owners in Liverpool where the moon lifts
and two uniformed Africans carry banners
announcing a ball. The train to Paddington
is quick, hot-shades cover the windows
from a setting sun; newspapers gleam
in smeared headlines of Soweto, my black
baggage hangs on the rack above my head
as I rock to waystation in London
and the transport home to old shores
in Rhode Island.

MADE CONNECTIONS

the wages of dying is love, GALWAY KINNELL

Rich with gifts on your return to Edinburgh
your voice quakes in sayable poems chiming
images of your ancestors, the kite in the eye
drawn off into highland village of first
offerings, the misspelt bookmarker for *Alex
Kinell, 1843,* given by his beloved; your grandfather's
snuffbox made from horn into an animal
full of snuff, the gift-bible of the pastor
to your father on his first trip to this city:
all these caretaken by a yawning ninety year old
aunt, your relatives rolling in the omphalos
dreams of castles, high manors of war in words.

We sit awhile in first-class bypassing derailment,
the sea suggesting your father's ship, crestfallen
with his leaving homelands for the Boer War;
I open the paper to a photo of a black man bleeding
at the feet of a South African policeman, his boots
caked in "riots"; one schoolboy locked in a room
littered with corpses, babies and old grannies
moaning on litters, chants his lessons in Afrikaaner
begging to get out; the train lumbers on thick with uniformed
cadets in fatigues on their way to maneuvers.

Locked in trenches of France and Belgium,
or jumping ship in West Virginia with a friend,
your father makes cabinets as his son makes
testimony in stone, images scribbled on a rocking
train, the image of kite being drawn off into the Hebrides,
or the village where a young girl gave the gift of passing
hours, her tongue forcing books to give up light
knowing he would come back to read to an old
woman, of war and travel, the comfort of a sleepy
child, in the moon-arms of her father, made in America.

CROSSING LAKE MICHIGAN

The amp light on the station
wagon has just gone off;
we climb up the hatch-stairs
to the deck, the clouds mildewed
as storms move east, bucketing
the interstate with torrential rain.
The ferry bucks my daughter's soft
forehead into my neck, dreaming,
of strawberry patches,
she investigates from bright
spots ripening as she skips
the white; late one August evening,
she appeared lost for hours
as storm clouds rocked
in rowboats moving in swirls
of leaves under lakeside elms,
when she was discovered, her rear-
end skyward, bent, we foraged for pure
red signals of strawberry.

I brush her hair back from her face
so similar to my sister's at the same age,
smile, though I overhear two Michigan
tourists, returning home, talk of menace
of cities, how King asked for glory
of newsprint and ate the balcony railing
in conspiracy of his lost appetite;

I think of amp lights that will ignite
our three darkened hours to Ann Arbor,
a call made to an all-night self-service
garage where you can buy parts.

She wakes with songs learned from her teacher,
her mother trailing a lawnmower of seeds
on the furrowed lawn, catching the tune
of a great thrush lock-stepped in imitation.
His one song of politics, the power of the ferry
climbing swells to a future of hungry birds
lost in Michigan, where a strike wavers near a highway
I will go by: she will ask for the strawberry's whiteness,
and why men will not eat at her table of red,
and what song to sing to vacationers returning to Michigan.

SMOKE

Smoke is my name for you,
gray crystalline hammocks
of smoke in your scowls
wavering over linoleum
of flowers making bread
to kill the starter
yeast in a cold oven,
your thoughts on film,
prints of my daughter
in the playhouse quick
of fire in framed song
memorized as a puzzle,
in the making of bread
in nine unbasted tins.

In a new crafted darkroom,
your hands swimming
in the six-foot sink
fiberglassed over planks
of wood as the coffin
of your father, whose heart
turns in the suturing fingers
of a medical student
learning of thrombosis,
your hands throb the images
with old chemicals that won't
work their magic
of bringing back his face,
his top shelf of broken
teeth caving in,
his thick fingers poised
at his beltbuckle,
your last sigh
like his, slightly bloody
on the top lip,
sink where the heart
leaps in the dusty manure
of horses, his loose boots,
the lunch eaten in chatter
churning no more.

A new batch of dough

rises in tins to such comfort
of the heated oven;
an image bakes in the body
of the six foot sink,
and when he stands up
in your enlarger
he will ask for butter,
cut you the heel,
look for the jam
as if to light a match
in the name of smoke,
demanding his spot
in your photo album.

IN MY FATHER'S HOUSE

ERNEST J. GAINES

IT WAS RAINING THAT DAY HE GOT OFF THE BUS IN ST. ADRIENNE. Not a heavy rain, but a cold, steady, unrelenting rain—one that could go on for days and days. It might stop an hour in the morning, maybe another hour or two in the afternoon, then start all over again.

Two people got off the bus before Robert did. A white man hurried to a car parked under a willow tree on the riverbank side of the road. A white woman went inside the station. Robert started to follow her, but changed his mind when he saw another black man standing in the garage door left of the station watching him.

Parlane Henderson was a mechanic, and he also loaded and unloaded the buses that came in. There was nothing to put on the bus today, and the driver had already signaled to him that there was nothing to take off, so he stood just inside the garage door out of the rain watching the passengers. Now he saw Robert coming toward him. Robert wore an old mackinaw Army overcoat that was too big and seemed much too heavy for his frail slender body. An Army field cap was pulled all the way down to his ears. He had a navy blue laundry bag, about half full of clothes, slung over his right shoulder. He carried no other luggage.

"You can tell me where colored live round here?" he asked Parlane.

Parlane made a half-circular motion with his head. "All over the place," he said. "Anybody particular?"

"Looking for a place to stay," Robert said.

Parlane took a dirty gray rag out of the back pocket of his blue overalls and wiped his hands. At the same time he was looking Robert over to see if he knew him. Robert was tall, thin, brown-skinned, in his late twenties. His eyes were weak and bloodshot from a lack of sleep. His scraggly little beard grew fairly well on his chin, but hardly at all on the sides of his face. After looking him over a moment Parlane knew that he had never seen him before.

Parlane started to point up the street, when he noticed Fletcher Zeno coming toward him. Fletcher was the only black cabdriver in St. Adrienne, and he was lucky to get more than three fares on any weekday. If he got more than a half dozen on weekends, counting

Saturday and Sunday, he considered himself more than lucky. Parlane knew this, and he thought he would let Fletcher get the seventy-five cents that he charged to take someone back of town.

"Taxi here, taxi here," Fletcher said.

Fletcher was a small jet-black man with quick motions. Not only did he walk fast or turn fast, but he talked fast, laughed quickly, and stopped abruptly.

"Back of town?" he said. "Up the river? Down the river? The Island? This way. This way."

He grabbed at the blue laundry bag that Robert had slung over his shoulder, but Robert didn't release it. Instead, he asked Fletcher how far was back of town.

"Too far to walk on a day like this," Fletcher said. "You agree there, Parlane?"

Parlane nodded his head. "You'll get wet 'fore you get halfway back there," he said.

"I don't mind getting wet," Robert said. "How far is it?"

"Cost no more than seventy-five cents," Parlane said.

"How far is it?" Robert asked again.

"Mile. Maybe little more," Parlane said. "Mile and a quarter, I reckon."

"Which way?" Robert asked him.

Parlane looked at Fletcher who had started shaking his head. Fletcher shook his head with the same quick motion that he did everything else.

Robert saw what was going on between them, and went inside the station. The bus station was a small office, and four or five people could fill it easily. John LeDoux, the big Cajun from Pointe Coupee who ran the garage and the bus station, was sitting behind his desk talking to the woman who had just come in there. Neither one paid any attention to Robert. But after a while the woman did glance back over her shoulder at him, but said nothing. LeDoux went on talking as if no one else had come in. LeDoux sold you tickets through a window. If the weather was bad he would let some white people he knew come inside and stand by the heater. Since it was his office, and not a waiting room, he didn't have to let blacks in there, and he never did. The blacks could go into the garage where Parlane worked and stand by the heater there if they wished.

After Robert had been in the office about ten minutes the woman looked back at him again and asked him if he wanted to see Mr. LeDoux about anything. Robert told her he only wanted to know where he could find a place to stay. The woman turned and pointed up the street. She told him to walk three blocks, then turn left. After going a quarter of a mile he would see a hardware store, then a lumberyard. Then after crossing the railroad tracks he would see a big gray house on the left that advertised rooms. Robert thanked her and went out.

"I wonder why they didn't tell him that out there," she said to LeDoux. "It seemed such a simple—"

But she never finished. Because LeDoux had just hollered for Parlane to get in there. It was so loud and abrupt the woman jumped back from the desk patting at her breast. Parlane came inside the office with his cap in his hand. LeDoux had started talking to the woman again, and he went on talking to her another couple of minutes before looking at Parlane.

"I want that car ready tonight," he said.

"Mr. LeDoux, you said I could finish it tomorrow," Parlane said. "I mentioned I had that little business I had to 'tend to tonight."

"That was before I was interrupted," LeDoux said. "Now I want that car ready before you go home tonight."

"I couldn't come in early in the morning—"

LeDoux was talking to the woman again. Parlane turned slowly and went back out. He was not angry with LeDoux, he was not even angry with Robert; he was looking for Fletcher, because it was Fletcher who had brought on this trouble for him. But as usual, Fletcher had quickly disappeared.

II

Virginia Colar was standing in the kitchen looking out of the window when she heard the knocking at the front door. She could see how the wind was blowing the limbs in the pecan tree, and she thought the knocking was no more than a limb brushing against the side of the house. She turned from the window to check the pot of soup cooking on the stove. After tasting it to see if it was seasoned well enough she nodded with satisfaction and lowered the flames.

She heard the knocking again, this time louder than before. She was sure there was somebody out there now, and she went to the front to let him in. When she opened the door she saw Robert standing in front of her soaking wet. Water ran from the cap down his face, leaving crystal drops hanging from the scraggly beard on his chin.

"They told me you have rooms," he said.

"I got—" But she stopped.

She didn't like him from the beginning. He was too thin, too hungry-looking. She didn't like the little knots of hair on his face that he called a beard. She knew he was sick. His jaws were too

sunken-in for a young man. His eyes looked at you but didn't see you.
He could have just been released from Angola penitentiary. He
definitely looked like someone who had been locked in. They prob-
ably had let him go because they figured they had punished him
enough already, and they knew he would die soon.

Something in the back of her mind told her to tell him that she
had made a mistake about having rooms. She had just rented the
last one to a—to an insurance man this very morning. But she asked
herself where else could he go. Uptown to one of those back rooms of
the white motel? Would they let him in? By law they were supposed
to, but couldn't they say they didn't have any vacancy either?

She stepped to the side to let him come in, then she looked outside
again. She was looking for Fletcher's cab, but she knew it wouldn't
be out there. Because Robert's clothes and the laundry bag wouldn't
have been so wet if Fletcher had brought him to the house.

"That's a dollar a day," Virginia said, still holding the door open.
She wished he would say a dollar was too much for a room, then she
would have a good excuse to send him back out there.

"I want it for a week," he said.

"That'll be seven dollars," she said. "And I 'preciates my money
in advance."

She waited until he had reached into his pocket before she
closed the door and told him to follow her to her office. Her office was
a small desk and a chair that she had setting in one corner of her
living room. At the door she told him to stay out there in the hall
while she went into the room to get his key and the receipt book.

"Where you from?" she called, from inside the room.

He didn't answer her.

She came back out.

"I asked where you was from," she demanded this time.

"Chicago," he told her.

She looked at him, and at the laundry bag he still had slung over
his shoulder. She didn't believe he was from Chicago.

"The money," she said.

He gave her a wrinkled five-dollar bill and some change. The
change money was black with corrosion, as if it had not been used
in a long time.

"Your name?" Virginia said.

"Robert."

"Last name?"

"X," he said.

She was holding the receipt book against the wall while she wrote
down the information. When he told her to put X she drew down one
line and stopped. She wasn't looking at him yet, she was still looking
at the receipt book, trying to recall what group called themselves X.

She couldn't remember now whether it was the Black Panthers or the Black Muslims.

Something in the back of her mind told her to give him back his money. But something else asked, where else would he go? Uptown? The whites would not let him in there either. They had turned down fatter ones and dryer ones than he; and she was sure no X had ever slept in any one of those beds.

She looked at him now. "I don't want no trouble in here," she told him. "I run a nice orderly place here. I don't bother the law, the law don't bother me. You hear me, don't you?"

He didn't answer her, he wasn't even looking at her, he was looking at the receipt book she held against the wall. She had drawn half of his last name, and he might have been looking at that. Virginia couldn't tell from his gaze where his mind was. She slashed the other line cross the first, and told him to follow her upstairs.

"You must'a' walked from the station?" she asked.

He didn't answer her this time either, and after climbing another step, she stopped and looked back at him. He was standing two steps below her, beads of water still in his beard, and that blue laundry bag slung over his shoulder as if he was leaving instead of coming in.

"I'm 'customed to people answering me," Virginia said. "Besides that it show breeding."

"I walked," he said.

"Wasn't Fletcher there? A little ugly black man with red beady—"

"He was," he said.

"He was?" she said. She wanted to say: "And he didn't stick a gun in your back?" or "And he didn't drag you to his cab?" But she didn't say it, because he wasn't looking at her, he was looking past her as though she wasn't even there. Something in the back of her mind told her again to give him back his seven dollars. But something else said, where else would he go?

She led him up to his room and lit the little gas heater, then she went to the bathroom down the hall to get a bucket of water to set on top of the heater. The water would keep moisture in the room. All the time that she was in the room with him, he stood at the window looking out at the rain. He had not taken the laundry bag from his shoulder, or taken off the cap or unbuttoned the coat.

"The toilet and the shower down the far end of the hall," she said to his back. "I change sheets and pillowcase once a week— Saturday. They already clean, so I won't change them tomorrow. When you get hungry, the best place round here is Thelma's cafe— three blocks farther back of town. Her husband, Wrigley, runs the nightclub next to it—place called the Congo Room."

He didn't seem interested in what she was saying, and she went back downstairs to the kitchen. She dished up a bowl of soup and sat down at the table to eat. But she hadn't eaten more than a couple of spoonsful when she thought about Fletcher, and she went up the hall to her office to telephone him. Fletcher's cabstand was at Thelma's cafe, and Fletcher must have been sitting at the counter or standing nearby, because soon as Thelma answered the telephone, Virginia heard her say: "It's for you."

"Fletcher," he said.

"You rich?" Virginia asked him.

"I see," Fletcher said. "He found his way."

"So y'all did talk?" Virginia said. "And you didn't stick a gun in his back to make him get in that cab?"

"I had Parlane beg for me," Fletcher said. "That don't work neither."

Virginia heard him drink something quickly. It could have been a cocktail or a cup of hot coffee. He did everything quickly.

"You got your money?" Fletcher asked. "He wasn't exactly throwing it away round that bus station."

"I got a week in advance," Virginia said.

"Cold rain do that," Fletcher said. "Make you change your outlook on life." Then he laughed. It sounded like "hee-hee," and stopped.

"Look like any people you know?" Virginia asked.

"Nobody I know, nobody I care to know," Fletcher said. "Say where he come from?"

"Chicago," Virginia said.

"Where?" Fletcher asked.

"That's what he told me," she said.

"And nothing but that blue laundry bag?"

"He calls himself Robert X," Virginia said.

"One of them, hunh?" Fletcher said. "Well, you got something on your hand now."

"What you mean?" Virginia asked.

"You'll find out," Fletcher said, and laughed again.

Virginia hung up the telephone and went back into the kitchen. From the table she could see the rain touching lightly against the window. She could see the soft swaying of the limbs in the pecan tree beside the house. There was not a pecan on the tree, not a leaf, not one bird sat on any of the limbs. The tree was bare and gray—the low-hanging sky above it was the same ashy gray color. The kitchen was warm and comfortable, but Virginia felt sad and cold just by looking out of the window at the rain.

Virginia thought about her tenant upstairs in number four. She wondered if he was hungry. She did not serve food at the house, but she had cooked much more than she could ever eat. If she ate soup every day for a week, there would still be some left over.

It was her conscience bothering her again, she told herself. It was not satisfied that it had made her let him into the house, but now it was trying to make her feed him, too.

When Virginia got through eating she dished up another bowl of soup, and put some crackers on a plate, and took it up to his room. After knocking twice, and still not getting an answer, she pushed the door open and went in. She would set the plate on the bucket of water, and the food would still be warm when he woke up. She noticed that he had taken off his hat and coat and had hung them on the closet door. But halfway cross the room she suddenly felt strange, as if she was being watched, and she jerked around to look back at the bed. He lay there wide awake, not watching her, but looking out of the window. Virginia had turned so suddenly that she had spilled some of the hot soup out of the bowl onto the plate and some even on her hand. She was so angry now that she couldn't do anything for a while but stand there and look at him. She didn't know whether she ought to curse him and leave the food there, or curse him and take the food back down to the kitchen.

"I didn't know I was disturbing your honor," she said. "I just thought your honor could be hungry. Your honor look like he been starving to death."

Robert sat up slowly, and reached into his pocket to get her some money.

"It's free," she said. "I don't serve no food here. I just try to be a good Christian."

She set the plate on the lamp table at the head of the bed and backed away. She was at the door when she heard him asking: "Any churches back here?"

Virginia was a short, plump, very black, very emotional woman. But nothing could change her attitude about a person quicker than hearing him mention the church or the name of God. She stopped at the door to look back at Robert, who had picked up his plate and started eating.

"Churches?" she said. "We got three—if you said churches. You said churches?"

He nodded his head, without looking at her. He was eating, and looking out at the rain against the window.

"You need to go to church?" she asked him.

"No," he said.

"Just want know where they at, huh?"

He nodded again, but so slightly that if she hadn't been watching him closely she never would have seen it.

"We have two Baptist and a Catholic," she said. "But we don't have none for the Mus—" she stopped.

"Baptist," she heard him say.

"We got one just up the street there," she said. "Solid Rock Baptist Church. My church. Reverend Phillip J. Martin, pastor. I suppose you done heard of Reverend Martin up there in Chicago?"

She thought she heard him say no.

"No?" she said. "He's been in all the newspapers. On TV. He's the civil rights leader here in these parts. He's our Martin Luther King. Everybody proud of him—black and white. Thinking 'bout sending him to Washington. Would be the first one from round here, you know."

"Must be a good man," she heard him say.

"The people think so. Course there's some 'gainst him—black and white—you find that everywhere; but most of them all for him. He'll be a good man in Washington. He's done some wondrous here."

"What's he done?"

"What's he done?" Virginia said. "What's he done?" she said again. "He's done everything. Everything. Done changed just about everything round here, 'cept for old Chenal up there. It won't be long 'fore Chenal fall, too. He'll fall like all the rest. Old white man uptown, don't want pay the colored nothing for working. Own the biggest store up there, everybody go in his store, still don't want pay his colored help nothing for working. He'll change his mind when Phillip get through with him—mark my word."

"Phillip Martin?" she heard Robert saying.

"He's the man round here. The man we count on."

Virginia saw him nod his head. But he never did look back at her.

That evening just after dark he came downstairs and left the house. Virginia stayed up watching television late that night, but she didn't hear him come back in. The next morning around six o'clock, even before she had gotten out of bed, Fletcher Zeno called her on the telephone.

"Want hear something good?" he asked her.

"No," she said, and hung up.

He called back.

"What you want, Fletcher?" she said. "You know what time it is."

"Five to six, 'cording to my watch," he said. Virginia heard him drink something quickly. She figured he was at home and drinking hot coffee. "Seen your boy sitting behind Reverend Martin's church door last night," he said. "Midnight—on my way home. First, I thought I was seeing a ghost. But I said to myself, 'Man, come on, you know you don't believe in no such thing.' Then I thought maybe it was a dog. But what dog in his right mind would lay behind that door in all that rain when he could go under the church and stay dry." Virginia heard him take a quick sip from the hot coffee again. "I turned around at Brick O'linde store and came on back to get another look. I got out this time. I thought it might be Dago Jack or Unc Matty sick there and couldn't get home. Halfway up the walk I seen who it was—your boy there. Slumped back 'gainst that door with his hands jobbed down in his pockets. Could have been sleeping for all I know. I turned around and went on home. Well?" Another sip from his coffee. "What you think? Think he's crazy—or just like cold rain?"

"I don't think he's crazy, I don't think he like rain, neither," Virginia said. "I think you making all that up 'cause you didn't get them seventy-five cents yistidy."

All day long Fletcher told the same story to other people, but like Virginia, no one wanted to believe him. Two days later everyone did.

Monday, at Thelma's cafe, Abe Matthews told the people how he had seen Robert standing under one of the big oak trees in the cemetery. He said it was a little dark, just after sundown, so he was not ready to swear on a stack of Bibles that it was definitely Robert. But if it was not, then it was a ghost wearing a long Army overcoat that was much too big for him and an Army cap pulled all the way down to his ears—exactly like the clothes that the Muslim wore. Evalena Battley, on her way to work at the St. Adrienne Laundry, saw him at six o'clock in the morning on the bank of the St. Charles River. The rain had fallen steadily the past two weeks, and the river was high and rough, flowing swiftly southward toward New Orleans. Robert stood on the bank among the hanging branches of the weeping willows, staring down at the water, oblivious to Evalena, to everything else round him, except the river. And that same evening, Dago Jack, on his way home from Brick O'linde's grocery store where he had spent the day sitting and talking, saw him standing across the street in front of Phillip Martin's house. Dago mentioned it to the people at the store the next day, but since they had seen him practically everywhere else already they thought nothing of it.

He had two meals at Thelma's cafe. On Saturday, the day after he arrived in St. Adrienne, he came into the cafe around noon and sat down at a table in the corner. When Thelma told him what was on the menu for the day, he told her to bring him a plate of red beans and rice, mustard greens, and a piece of corn bread. The next day he came back about the same time and he ordered giblets, rice, greens, and corn bread. He sat at the same table as before, a little red-and-white-checkered oilcloth-covered table in the corner. Neither time did he take off his cap or his coat. Both times he paid for his meals with change money. The money, quarters, nickels, dimes, was black with corrosion.

Monday, he started buying his food at Brick O'linde's grocery store. Abe Matthews, Tall White, Unc Matty, Dago Jack, and Fletcher Zeno sat or stood round the heater. They had been talking about him just before he came in, but now they were quiet, one, then another, glancing at him at the counter. He bought sausage, cheese, bread, and a bottle of cheap muscatel wine. After he had paid for his groceries he left the store without saying a word to anyone, and went back to his room to eat.

"More that black money?" Fletcher asked Brick.

Brick O'linde looked at the money that he still held in his hand, and nodded his head.

"Hunh," Dago Jack said.

"Mostly peculiar," Unc Matty said.

"You said something, Unc Matty?" Tall White asked.

"Peculiar, peculiar," Unc Matty said.

Later that evening they saw him walking again. He never spoke to them, he never asked about anyone, he never visited anybody that they knew of. But day and night, whether it was raining or not, they would meet him or pass him walking the street. Several people had seen him on St. Anne Street watching the house where the minister and civil rights leader Phillip Martin lived.

ALMEYDA

GAYL JONES

"It is indeed true that the force and stronghold of the Negroes
of Palmares located in the famous Barriga range is conquered . . .
and that their king was killed (by a party of men from the
regiment of the petitioner, which came upon the said King
Zumbi on the twentieth of November, 1695) and the survivors
scattered. Yet one should not therefore think that this war is
ended. No doubt it is close to being terminated if we continue
to hunt these survivors through the great depths of these forests,
and if the regiment of the petitioners is kept along the frontier.
If not, another stronghold will suddenly appear either here in
Barriga or in any other equally suitable place. . . ."

Petition presented to His Magesty
BY DOMINGOS JORGE VELHO, "field master"
in the campaign against Palmares, 1694

I REMEMBER WHEN WE CAME TO EACH OTHER, AND WE BOTH HAD
heavy smiles, Anninho, because this was not the time or place for
a man and woman, and so we bore heavy smiles, it was no time
for an easy smile, and we came together without speaking, because
there were no words for such a time, and we would not have known
each other's voices even if we had spoken. It was a time when a
man and woman could not recognize each other's voices. Recogni-
tion came only with a way of touching, a smell, and even that was
heavy and full of sweat. But we recognized each other and we were
somehow smiling. We tightened our lips together and our blood
became one, our sweat became one.

Always wear your hair that way.

Do you like it?

Hand on my waist.

Speak to me so close with a kiss. I will make all my laughter a
love song, but it can only be a heavy laughter, a laughter that takes
up the sounds of the things I am not telling you, it can only be that
kind of laughter. And all those things, Anninho, all those things my
mouth wouldn't form.

This episode is from *Almeyda*, a new work-in-progress.

Watch out here.
He takes my arm.
Are you frightened?
No.
Be careful. Don't fall.
No.
You're okay.
Yes.
Oh, our smiles were so heavy and we could both feel that thing
weighing our insides. We could both feel it.
He made her naked.
Yes, I saw him undress her and she held her hands out like flowers.
Now I must have a double vision, Anninho, I must be alone here
and still see us doing those beautiful things.
A man wants to be able to take a woman someplace anyplace and
not just a place inside a dream either but a place hard with reality
and desire.
My ankles are paining.
We'll stop here.
No.
I said we'll stop.
There is a cool wind near this river. You have your hands on my
wrists and my wrists are throbbing.
There was something we forgot back there.
What?
I don't remember.
I don't remember either.
And it is a time when you can't go back for the things, you must
remember everything with your blood because you can't go back
for them.
Your forehead is full of ditches, Anninho. There is grass sticking
to your hair.
I stand near the river, the place where the mud is soft. I walk
without any shoes.
Come on.
He is watching me.
I'm coming.
You're a woman now, Almeyda.
Yes. I'm still riding beneath your shoulders.
Come and dance.
This is no time. The mud here is too soft.
No place you mean.
No. No time.
We'll have to go farther in this way. Your eyes are sad, woman.

There was only one time I saw them light up and your dreams were as large as life.

Our life now?

Any life.

My smile then is as heavy as life. And you kept putting seeds and shells in my hands, telling me to put them in a safe place and you would string them later.

It has been years since I knew what a man was like.

What?

I said it's been years since the flesh of a man flowed into me. And since that river of blood stopped and the big wound closed.

What?

Never mind.

From where?

Can't you see without my telling?

I wanted my womb to grow deep for you, Anninho, even in a time like this one, in spite of the time. I wanted my womb to grow deeper than the earth. I wanted my womb to grow deeper than the earth. But my womb was angry. Maybe time made my womb. Maybe the times. And then that bitterness sucked my womb dry. I opened my legs and you touched me, not saying anything. I felt the heaviness of bread soaked in water.

There is a cool wind blowing near this river. You hold my breasts and my breasts are throbbing.

Did you feel the wind? There's a cool wind now.

Yes.

It's a good feeling.

GAYL JONES: AN INTERVIEW

[HARPER]: DO YOU HAVE ANY MODELS FOR ARTISTIC CONCEPTION, literary, historical, or autobiographical?

[JONES]: I used to say that I learned to write by listening to people talk. I still feel that the best of my writing comes from having *heard* rather than having read. This isn't to say that reading doesn't enrich or that reading isn't important, but I'm talking about foundations. I think my language/word foundations were oral rather than written. But I was also learning how to read and write at the same time I was listening to people talk. In the beginning, *all* of the richness came from people rather than books because in those days you were reading some really unfortunate kinds of books in school. I'm talking about the books children learned to read out of when I was coming up. But my first stories were heard stories—from grown-up people talking. I think it's important that we—my brother and I—were never sent out of the room when grown-up people were talking. So we heard their stories. So I've always heard stories of people generations older than me. I think that's important. I think that's the important thing.

Also, my mother would write stories for us and read them to us. She would read other stories too, but my favorite ones were the ones she wrote herself and read to us. My favorite one of those was a story called "Esapher and the Wizard." So I first knew stories as things that were heard. That you listened to. That someone spoke. The stories we had to read in school—I didn't really make connections with them as stories. I just remember us sitting around in the circle and different people being called on to read a sentence. But my mother's reading the stories—I connected with that. And I connected with the stories people were telling about things that happened back before I was born.

When I was in the fifth grade, I had a teacher who would have us listen to music and then write stories. We had to write the stories that came to us while we were listening and then we would have to read the stories aloud to the whole class. I had started writing stories when I was in the second or third grade, when I was seven or eight,

---

This interview was conducted at Brown University in the spring of 1975, just after publication of Jones's first novel, *Corregidora*. The interviewer is Michael S. Harper.

but didn't show them to anybody until her. Of course, my mother knew I was writing. Of course, I showed things to her. But my fifth-grade teacher was the first teacher I showed any work to. Her name was Mrs. Hodges. I remember I used to make stories and put the names of people in the class in them so that everybody would laugh. So then there was the music and the heard stories. It was an all-black school. I went to an all-black school until the tenth grade when there was integration. I say that because I think it's important. I think it's important about the music and the words, too.

A lot of connections I made with tradition—with historical and literary things—I started making later. I was writing stories in first-person before I made connections with the slave narrative tradition or the tradition of black autobiography, before "oral storytelling" became something you talked about. At first, I just felt that the first-person narrative was the most authentic way of telling a story, and I felt that I was using my own voice—telling a story the way I would talk it. I liked the way the words came out better than the way they came out in third-person. And I liked writing dialogue in stories, because I was "hearing" people talk. But I hadn't made any of the kinds of connections you make with your traditions other than the connections you make in living them and being a part of them. I didn't really begin to make the other kinds of connections till graduate school. I still don't like to stand away from the traditions, talking about them. You ought to be able to talk about them standing right inside of them.

In storytelling, you can do that—that's why I like storytelling. When you tell a story, you automatically talk about traditions, but they're never separate from the people, the human implications. You're talking about language, you're talking about politics and morality and economics and culture, and you never have to come out and say you're talking about these things—you don't have to isolate them and therefore freeze them—but you're still talking about them. You're talking about all your connections as a human being. You're talking about many dimensions instead of just one. You don't start with the answers. Someone asked me what answers did I have for such and such a thing. I said that I didn't have any answers. She said that when she read my book she could see answers. She could see I had answers. But you don't start with the answers, I don't start with the answers, I start with the telling, and sometimes the answers come out of the telling.

[H]: Can you distinguish between oral and literary or written influences?

[J]: Yes. When I'm working even. I know I can reconnect them if I read over something. There are a lot of sounds, though. A lot of times, literary (written) things also become oral influences for me, because of the way I read. I have to hear the words in my head—almost in my ears, too—all the sounds have to be there when I read—and when I'm writing too. I don't necessarily have to re-read things out loud because I hear the words while I'm writing them. In the process of writing them I have to hear them. My mouth isn't moving, but the vocal connections are being made, the sound connections—the same kind of speech energy is being used. When I write I can also hear other people talking. A lot of times if I'm having a person say something, other connections are being made with people I've already heard. Of course, sometimes I'll have people say things that I've heard said in another context. But other times, I'll just remember the patterns of the way things were said. The people will be saying entirely different things, but they'll be saying it with the patterns, the rhythms, that I've heard before. So a lot of times one's own speech rhythms and the speech rhythms of other people go into making a story. All the "heard" things go there.

I have a tendency to trust a lot of my oral influences more than my literary ones, with some exceptions. Those have to do with personal contacts and trusting the people's writing whose "voice" I can trust and who I feel can "hear." I usually trust writers who I feel I can hear. A lot of European and Euro-American writers—because of the way their traditions work—have lost the ability to hear. Now Joyce could hear and Chaucer could hear. A lot of Southern American writers can hear. Chaucer had to hear because he was writing in the "vernacular" at a time when "writers" wrote in Latin. The ballads were in the vernacular but they were oral. The "people" made them, not "writers." So Chaucer had to hear. Joyce had to hear because of the whole historical-linguistic situation in Ireland—the Irish spoke a different kind of "English," and of course they were forced to speak English by the invaders, and of course language has its obvious political implications. But *Finnegans Wake* is an oral book. You can't sight-read *Finnegans Wake* with any kind of truth. And they say only a Dubliner can really understand the book, can really "hear" it.

Of course, black writers—it goes without saying why we've always had to hear. And Native American writers, and Latin American writers. It's all tied in with linguistic relationships, and with the whole socio-psychological-political-historical manifestations of these linguistic relationships. I could keep giving reasons why different people have to hear and others don't. If you don't have to hear, if your humanity isn't somehow involved in hearing, you don't. Hearing has to be essential. You have to be able to hear other people's voices and you have to be able to hear your own voice. You say, in one of your poems, a man is another man's face. Maybe a man is another man's voice too. Most of my influences are essentially oral because even the written ones have to be "translated" into the oral before I can understand them. "Understand" really isn't the word, because "understand" is one-dimensional and it's a multi-dimensional thing. Maybe I should say: "I have to bring the written things into the oral *mode* before I can *deal with* them."

I guess language as heard fascinates me more than language as written—but I like to see words, too. I really do. I guess I wouldn't write if I didn't also like to see them. To hear them and to see them while I'm hearing them. But I don't always have to see them while I'm hearing them. But I always have to hear them while I'm seeing them. So many things in writing, though, are simultaneous. It's a simultaneous process. Many things occupy the same space and time.

[H]: Do you depend on any preconception of fiction or storytelling when you sit down to tell a story?

[J]: Well, for me fiction and storytelling are different. I say I'm a fiction writer if I'm asked, but I really think of myself as a story-teller. When I say "fiction," it evokes a lot of different kinds of ab-stractions, but when I say "storyteller," it always has its human connections. First, the connection to the listener, the hearer; but there's also the connection between the teller and the hearer. "Story-telling" is a dynamic word, a process word. "Fiction" sounds static. "Storytelling" for me suggests possibilities, many possibilities. I'm really talking now about feeling response to words. I have a feeling response to the two words, as well as to the fact that they mean two different things to me.

But I have no preconceptions of either one, really. When I sit down to tell a story I have to have the people there, and the voices, and they have to be in a relationship to each other. I don't think I've ever written a story with just one person. There are always at least two people, and there's always dialogue. I've never written a story without dialogue. I always have to have people talking. Speech has to be there. I guess you could say my method is improvisational. When I tell a story, the process of telling determines the way of telling.

I see myself as a storyteller also because of the connection between the spoken and the written. A lot of times things are imposed upon the storyteller from the outside—other people's preconceptions—but I won't go into this. There are a lot of things you have to work in, through, and around. But the important thing for me is always to keep the human connections. The bad thing for me is when the writer loses the human—or humanistic—connection; when the writer is irresponsible with language. Writing is a very responsible thing. It documents human experience, and when it documents it wrongly —that's the really bad thing. Black people and Native Americans in this country can attest to that. That's why it's necessary to make the connections between the oral traditions and written documentation, unless you're in an environment that maintains the integrity of the oral traditions. When you're not, it's necessary to document the traditions—to counteract the effects of the false documentations.

[H]: Is there a particular method you follow in writing a novel? You said recently that you began with situation. Could you develop this in terms of plot, or its absence, mode of speech, character quality, the building of climax, what is revealed and concealed in your treatment of situation?

[J]: I start with story—people—speech—relationships—situation. Story for me isn't "action" or "plot sequence" or theories about how things should be/are. It's people doing/being certain things *in relationship* to other people—mainly men and women. I'm mainly concerned about relationships between men and women. But it's also interesting to see how two men relate to each other, how two women relate. In *Corregidora*, I explore women-women relationships but not really men-men. The only men-men relationships are in the context of their response to women. But it's probably because I only know about men-men relationships in the context of their being with women—I don't know. But it's important for me to clarify relationships in the book—relationships in *situation*, rather than to have some theory of the way men are with women and vice-versa, or the way a daughter and mother are with each other.

The way Ursa is with her mother grew out of the situation of storytelling and my own living and seeing, and the same thing with the men and women. I didn't know how they would be with each other until they were being that way. When I was first writing the book, I really did think Ursa would stay with Tadpole. I really didn't expect him to do what he did. But after he did it, there wasn't anything else Ursa could do. Some things you start with. Other things are worked out in the process of creating and clarifying the relationships. It's like what Ursa said at the end of the book: "I didn't know yet what I would do." She didn't know what she was going to do until after she did it or right while she was doing it; she didn't know she was going to go back to Mutt until she was doing it. She didn't know until it happened in *situation* in *relationship*.

In a way, this is also a comment on how I write. Things have to happen *in process*. There's a question I ask—which one of the women asks—near the end of *Corregidora*: "What is it a woman can do to a man that makes him hate her so bad he wants to kill her one minute and can't get her out of his mind the next?" I didn't know the answer to that when I wrote the question. I didn't know the answer to that till the end of the book. I didn't know what the end of the book was going to be. I didn't know the answer till I had Mutt and Ursa being in relationship to each other at the end of the book. Then I made the connection between that and what it was that the Great Grandmother had done to Corregidora. Ursa only made the connection then. I only made the connection then. I only made the connection then, in the process of writing. Because, you see, I didn't know what it was that Great Gram had done to Corregidora, not in the beginning.

So I don't have any one method. For me, the idea of things happening *in process* is important because it strengthens my own feeling of connection with the oral storytelling and black music continuum. Modes of speech, character quality, all work themselves out in process. Maybe it's like what you mean when you talk about a musician creating an "environment." I don't know. But everything has to happen for me in the process of doing it. Sometimes I know how a story will end. And I know certain things that I want in a story, certain scenes, certain relationships, etc. But there are still all those "in process" things. I remember you said poetry is about process. Storytelling is about process, too. But I have no particular method. I always like everything to be different. I have always liked everything to work itself out differently. If I've done something, I don't like to do it again. Why do something again when you've already done it? Why say something the same way again? Why sing something the same way twice? I'm thinking about Billie Holiday here, of course. That's the tradition. I like to change a tune.

[H]: Did *Corregidora* go through any other conceptions than the novel? What forms were you experimenting with?

[J]: I never did type or show the very first version of *Corregidora* to anyone. The whole thing was sort of a song. The narrative wasn't storytelling—it was a kind of ritual. And there was dialogue, but it wasn't the same kind of dialogue. The transitions were ritualistic. It was written in second-person, the "you" narrative. Ursa was the one being addressed. No, actually it moves between the second and third and first—it starts off with "you." There are no real sequences of events. It doesn't have "scenes." I think I like Ursa telling the story better. I'd like to read over this very first version, though, to see what kinds of movements I make, or if I write a sequel to *Corregidora*, I could write it as a "song" rather than a "story." I could make it a ritualistic novel.

Some parts of *Corregidora* fit the description of this version. When

I look over the first version I can see the "story" there, but it wouldn't have worked in the same way. The first version had everything in it except it didn't clarify enough relationships. My editor, Toni Morrison, felt that I should clarify the relationships between Ursa and her mother and between Ursa and Mutt. I added the scene where Ursa goes back and talks to her mother and also that one about Ursa and Mutt before the incident of the fall down the stairs. Now, that's very essential to the book. Both of those scenes are essential to the book. It became very important for me to clarify the relationship between Ursa and Mutt because I'd never done any really up-close scenes between a man and woman before. I don't just mean sexual things—I mean the way they were "being" with each other. That became very important to me to be able to do that. The "scene" when Ursa first meets Mutt and the way they talk to each other is very important to me. So, the final version combines the "ritualistic" and "dream" sequences of the very first version with many layers of storytelling. The first version could not have been called a novel. It might have been called a prose poem or a song. In the final version, I was able to put everything together, the storytelling and the other. I like a mixture of forms and kinds of language. I like that kind of movement. The thing about "storytelling" is it's the kind of "form" that can bring in everything—that can make movements between kinds of language and kinds of reality—dreams and memory also being kinds of reality. I'm very much concerned with "forms" that can bring in everything. I found out that storytelling can bring in a lot more than just "story."

I was also experimenting with something other than language. I was also looking for a perspective that was "up-close," where there was no separation between the storyteller and the hearer. That was important to me too. I used to think that experimentation had to do with just language—but people can experiment with a lot of different kinds of elements of "story"—perspective, point of view, ways of presenting characters, kinds of characters—a lot of different things that involve language, but in a different way. Perspective, for instance. You could say I was experimenting with oral storytelling, using things you can learn from oral storytelling. In oral storytelling, the perspective is always up-close, because of the kind of relationship you have between the storyteller and the hearer. But not only that, there's also the direct identification of the storyteller with the story. Toni Morrison said she didn't feel there was an "author" getting in the way. That's what happens in the oral story—the storyteller identifies so closely with the story.

Actually, in oral storytelling there are three kinds of identification—the identification of the storyteller with the story, the identi-

fication of the storyteller with the hearer, and the identification of
the hearer with the story. I was experimenting mainly with the
"form" of oral storytelling. You don't have to beat around the bush
to make a transition in oral storytelling. You just go on and make it.
You can be talking about 1929 and then go right on ahead and talk
about 1969, almost in the same breath, in the same space. Or like a
preacher, he can be talking about something that happened last
night in one kind of language and then start talking about Gabriel
in another kind. The sermon, for me, also suggests that kind of
"form" that can bring in all kinds of language, that can bring in just
everything. So I experiment with a lot of oral traditional forms be-
cause of the things they can do.

And there's also a special relationship between narrative and
dialogue in the oral story that helps to get the up-close perspective.
The narrative in the oral story has the same essential speech tradi-
tion as the dialogue, and you don't have the sense of distancing. And
so there is a freer movement, maybe a more natural movement be-
tween the two. I guess all experimenting involves language, but
language with a lot of different connections, not just changing
words and the syntax of sentencing in an obvious way. Many times it
has to do with the relationship between the words and the people
hearing the words, and not just the relationship between the words
themselves.

I said some of the dialogue in *Corregidora* is ritualistic and some
is naturalistic. I think most of the italicized dialogue between Ursa
and Mutt is ritualistic. I should explain that. What I mean by "ritual-
ized dialogue" is that either the language isn't the same that we
would use ordinarily, or the movement between the people talking
isn't the same. No, there are really three things: the language, the
rhythm of the people talking, and the rhythm *between* the people
talking. In those technical books, they might call it "inaction
rhythm." The forms I know just bring in everything. But there's
a certain kind of rhythm that people create when they talk, when
they start talking, a pattern of talk and response. So in ritualized
dialogue, sometimes you create a rhythm that people wouldn't
ordinarily use, that they probably wouldn't use in real talk, although
they are saying the words they might ordinarily use. But you change
the rhythm of the talk and response and you change the rhythm
between the talk and response. So in ritualized dialogue, you do
something to the rhythm or you do something to the words. You
change the kind of words they would use or the rhythm of those
words. But both things take the dialogue out of the naturalistic
realm—change its quality.

I want to go back and study that very first version, though, and see what I can learn from it. I like to make those kinds of connections, too.

[H]: Is there any connection between "Deep Song" and your general view of women singers—blues songs, the emblems of love and trouble between men and women?

[J]: The relationships between the men and women I'm dealing with are blues relationships. So they're out of a tradition of "love and trouble"—but I don't really have any general view of any of those things. I don't have any general view of women blues singers or of the relationships between men and women. But there is a relationship between "Deep Song," which is a blues poem, and *Corregidora*, which is a blues novel. Blues talks about the simultaneity of good and bad, as feeling, as something felt. In the poem, "Deep Song," how do people react to the words "good" and "bad"? I think people have just as much attraction to the line "Sometimes he is a bad dark man" as they do to the line "Sometimes he is a good dark man." It has to do with meanings and things having a lot of different meanings at once. The last line is "I love him." It isn't "But I love him." I think that's important because it has to do with being, and it doesn't set up any territories. It doesn't set some feelings off into a corner. "Sometimes he is a good dark man. Sometimes he is a bad dark man. I love him." It acknowledges both things. Blues acknowledges all different kinds of feelings at once. How do we know, for instance, "Sometimes he is a bad dark man" isn't really a repetition of "Sometimes he is a good dark man"? That's what interests me. Ambiguity.

Somebody said *Corregidora* was ambiguous. I think I wanted it to be. I always like it when there are a lot of different possibilities. I think that poem has a lot of different possibilities. Like, it's important to me that the man says something so softly that the woman can't even hear him. That's important to me, but I don't know why. I was listening to Billie Holiday when I wrote the poem—while I was writing it, I mean. I was writing it and listening at the same time. There was the record that had "Deep Song" on it and "Crazy He Calls Me." I think that's the title of the second one. It has that in it. The poem uses repetition, but I don't know why it came out the way it did. When I finished it, I knew it was different from my other poems.

[H]: Would you comment on your next novel, *Eva's Man,* in terms of situation, character, the elements of storytelling as the context changed for you, and the additions you made in the telling?

[J]: It's hard for me to talk about *Eva's Man* because of the way I wrote it—it went through so many forms, so many changes. It went from a novella to a short story to a novel, which is a strange sequence. If I try to describe the novella it will be much like describing the first version of *Corregidora*. It didn't progress by scenes. The woman was addressing the man, so the "you" narrative was used, and there were metaphors for a lot of things that had happened. Things were told as having happened, but they were metaphors for the things. And there was dialogue out of context of place and situation. It's really very different from the final version. The short story clarified "scenes"—the things that happened in the story—and it is told in the first-person. The woman tells the story, and only a little bit of her past is seen. (Actually, there are two short story versions. One keeps the "you" narrative and it moves between scenes and the essential form of the novella, and the other uses first-person and more scenes. Rather than saying "scenes," I should say it clarifies situations more.) The novel sort of reclaims the woman's whole past, and we see all the things that lead up to the later events—her relationship to the man at the end of the story—because we've seen other relationships that make a connection with that relationship.

Described that way, without saying what the events are, it sounds a lot like *Corregidora*, but it's not. The woman of the story isn't the same kind of woman either. There are stylistic differences in that I make a lot of different kinds of transitions between past and present and sometimes simultaneous showings of past and present events. Rather than have the woman thinking something, it becomes a scene without transition. It takes place at the same time in the narrative as the things that evoke the memory. Also, fantasy happens at the same narrative level as the "real" things. The movement is different. The way of telling is different. There aren't layers of story-telling, but there are many different dimensions to the woman's telling. I'm sort of dealing with memory and fantasy as well as storytelling but I want everything to be on the same plane of reality. I want one thing to move into the other without the feeling that they are essentially different. It's hard for me to put all the elements of storytelling together. But I did start with situation and character—the relationship between that particular man and that particular woman. In many ways, *Eva's Man* is a horror story. It really is. And I'm sure people will ask me if that's the way I see the essential relationship between men and women. But that man and woman don't stand for men and women—they stand for themselves, really. But I don't have any definition for the kind of man-woman relationship that *Eva's Man* describes. Their ritual isn't a blues ritual. I don't know what it is.

[H]: Would you comment on Zora Neale Hurston, her conception of fiction and how the study of anthropology might have affected her production and output as a writer and particularly as a black woman writer? Would you characterize her as a pre-feminist or feminist? What might her work teach upcoming women writers, and writers in general?

[J]: I think the problem of Zora Neale Hurston is a problem of perspective—and it has to do with the relationship between narrative and dialogue, and it has to do with where the storyteller is when he's telling the story. (They'll get on me about using "he.") I think storytelling and anthropology are two different poles in terms of perspective. In storytelling, you're inside the living experience; in anthropology, you have to step outside of it. I'm sure Zora Neale Hurston told stories differently before she had anthropological training than afterwards—I'm sure she did. When you're telling a story, you're looking at situations inside of them—in process. The anthropological perspective pulls you outside of the process, the situations. You have to make them static in order to talk about them. For me, *Their Eyes Were Watching God* is beautiful. It's one of my favorite stories. But there is a tension in the novel between the narrative and the dialogue; there is a problem of perspective—the world view in the narrative seems different from the world view in the dialogue. The narrative seems written out of a different tradition—one that separates the storyteller from the story and the people in the story, even though both Janie and Teacake come through for me as real and strong people. I feel as if the storyteller has been for some reason distanced from them, even though she knows them so well. But you know that she knows them. You know that she "lived" there.

And there is a separation between the hearer and the storyteller—something that comes between the storyteller and the story. In oral storytelling, the storyteller identifies not only with the story but also with the people in the story. The storyteller is standing in there with them—I don't mean that he has to be a character in the story, but he's in there. And there isn't a tension between the narrative and dialogue—both are out of the same linguistic and humanistic tradition. For me, Ernest Gaines solved the problem of perspective and narrative/dialogue relationship: the storyteller being a part of the same speech community, the same essential world view, and telling the story to those people who also identify with that language and world view and with those human values.

In her anthropology books, I don't feel that Zora Hurston stood outside of the community, talking about it; I feel that she addressed herself to people outside of that community of human values rather than that she herself was standing outside of it. All writers address themselves to their essential speech community, but when there have been historical breaks in the speech continuum, the writer has to mend those breaks—that is, if he is to write about the people in that speech community. I always feel it's important to write what you've heard rather than what you've read when you're dealing with how anybody talks. Certainly I feel the study of anthropology took Hurston away from the amount of "stories" she could tell. (The way anthropology looks at language should also be studied. The way it looks at language as well as people.) I would have liked to have seen her use what she'd learned in her "field trips" in stories that "coordinated" learning and living in a form that wouldn't have caused tensions between the two, because the form would have grown out of them. I mean here using a form and language that grows out of a certain community to express that community and at the same time that energy being directed back to that community, out of which the language came. It has to do with "energy relationships." The storyteller being energized and the people being energized. Storytelling is holistic—it brings in everything—and anthropology isn't. Anthropology is one-dimensional; it can't coordinate. It can't coordinate all the different kinds of forces that come at a person, that come at a storyteller. And the community Zora Neale Hurston came out of was about synthesis and coordinating all those different forces, all those different "energy relationships," and her storytelling would have stayed about that too, I think, if it hadn't been for anthropology. As I said, I have a lot of personal fears about those kinds of things—things that pull you outside of the synthesis, the coordination, how you handle in "story" all those forces, all those "energy relationships."

I don't want to characterize her as a pre-feminist or a feminist. I will say that she saw women as strong. And she has a sense of their wholeness. And this isn't necessarily at the expense of men. It doesn't diminish the men. In her autobiography, we have a sense of the kinds of tensions that can come from her feeling about herself as a woman, and what she could do and what she was as a woman. The Janie-Teacake relationship isn't one of authority-submission. The man and woman are both strong. And even though the woman in *Seraph on the Suwanee* feels the idea of "serving"—it doesn't diminish her strength. I kept thinking certain feminists might have got on Zora for that. But the man and woman are both strong in that book. Then, one also has to make a distinction between how a woman is in her own life and how she makes the characters in the book. Zipporah in *Moses, Man of the Mountain* isn't a whole woman. You have a sense that she could have been if it were her story. But the feminists would have probably gotten on Zora for that, too. But one can't really be consistent about a lot of different kinds of things in "story" because there are a lot of different possibilities, as in life. But I never like to categorize. I don't know what a pre-feminist is. I'm not really sure I know what a feminist is. I always write about independent women because that's important to me, and when you see *particular* women in certain ways, people have a tendency to say that's how you think. Right now, anyone who writes about independent women and/or from the point of view of a woman that shows the wholeness of that woman can easily be called a feminist. But the storyteller's vision as I see it shouldn't sacrifice the wholeness of anyone, man or woman. One might be able to call Zora Neale Hurston a feminist from her own living—or I should say feminists can identify with her, which is very different—and from the attitudes she expresses in her autobiography and her anthropological writings and the way you have the sense of her relating to men. She keeps her "wholeness."

I can't answer your question about what might her work teach upcoming black women writers and writers in general. Maybe her work might teach upcoming black women writers in terms of subjects and in terms of those things that it is necessary for the black woman writer to document—and I feel that there are things that only the black woman writer can document. (And there are things that a black man writer can document that a black woman writer couldn't, of course.) But I feel that *Their Eyes Were Watching God* is revolutionary because it does speak about the love relationship between a black man and woman—because it does speak about various relationships—and because Zora didn't have to go outside of the community. She could talk about the relationship of the man and woman to each other, and she could see that relationship as whole. She could see it in a whole way. I think about the Bigger-Bessie relationship here. You can't really see them because of those "other things" Bigger has to contend with. But in real life we see each other. And it's important that we see each other in fiction, in storytelling. I think that's an important contribution of Zora Neale Hurston—that she didn't have to see them before she could see us; or that she didn't have to see them and never fully see us. I mean our wholeness wasn't sacrificed because of them.

I think there are a lot of up-close man-woman relationship type things that the black woman as writer is able to document. June Jordan, in an article on Zora Neale Hurston and Richard Wright, was talking about that: how "love" as a subject is overlooked; how it's not considered important; and how this is a reason why *Their Eyes Were Watching God*, for instance, isn't considered as important as *Native Son*. But it is. She was saying that one thing

doesn't cancel out the other, but black women writers are being in-
fluenced that way in terms of the things we have to deal with. But
I also feel that we have to take the things we learn from Zora Neale
Hurston further. Because it has to do with legacy. We have to
solve the problems that she couldn't solve. We have to do something
about the tensions that she had. And we have to keep her, you
know. I feel good about Alice Walker that way. I feel that she is
doing that. You know, keeping and taking things further. That's
what legacy is.

You notice I haven't answered your question about writers in
general, because I don't know. I think there's that idea of "human-
ization"—the relationship of language to human relationship, the
human connections of language. All writers could learn about that.
But I don't know. I don't know about writers in general. Depending
upon how a person comes to Zora Neale and from where, they might
overlook things that I would see, that Alice Walker would see, or
that June Jordan would see, that would be important to us. And each
of us would see different things too, you know.

But I don't know what people will see and not see in Zora Neale
Hurston, or what they will refuse to see. I can only say what I feel
should be seen, and a lot of it has to do with human relationship and
language. What I mean is, Hurston is working out of a humanistic
tradition of writing. And she got a lot of the subjects together that
I think we will continue to deal with—the relationships between
men and women, the role of women, the use of folklore, folk-saying—
that kind of thing. She has a lot of insight in terms of the relation-
ships between men and women and the roles of women. And you
don't have the feeling that she had to go off somewhere to get sub-
jects for writing. The important things can be right in front of you
and very close to you: in the people and language that you know.

[H]: Have the Spanish novelists influenced your notions of fiction?
And would you comment here on Chaucer also?

[J]: When you say Spanish novelists, I have to clarify and say
Spanish American or Latin American novelists. (There's one Spanish
novelist I like very much—that's Cervantes—but I haven't read
many other Spanish novelists.) But the Latin American novelists—
they're the ones. How have they influenced my notions of fiction?
Well, the two that I think of right off are Carlos Fuentes and Gabriel
Garcia Marquez.

Influences: Image, myth, history, language, metaphor, move-
ment between different kinds of language and levels of reality,
different kinds of reality. Their influence has to do with the use of
language, the kinds of imagery, the relationship between past and
present with landscape. Because of the kinds of historical things that

have gone down—that continue to go down—the "revolutions," the
kinds of perpetual change—political things (Chile, Mexico, Brazil)—
you don't come across many morally and socially irresponsible
Latin American writers. They're technically innovative, but the
technical innovation isn't devoid of its human implications. In this
country and in Western Europe, you have writings where the human-
ity is lost, where the relationship of the word to the human being
and the relationship between the word and the social/moral implica-
tions is either lost or ignored. But among Latin American writers
as well as among black writers and native American writers—
because of the historical and contemporary things that are going
down—the "nightmares," the particular historical and contemporary
nightmares—these writers are always responsible. The human impli-
cations, the moral/social implications are always there. So I feel a
kinship with Latin American writers. I find them energizing.

And then there's also the language thing. For them, too, there's
the linguistic thing. The *European* Spanish, the *European* Por-
tuguese. There's the linguistic thing for them, too. There are all the
things that the language they have to use can't express for them
either, not if you're taking in the Indian (Amerindian) and African—
the *American* heritage. And so there's the *making* it express things.
For me, that's why all the kinds of images are there—in Marquez,
the movement from one kind of reality to another—because it gives
dimension to the language. The language is no longer flat and one-
dimensional. You have the sense that they're trying to make the
language do things. And it's not just to be playing with words,
either; they have a stake in it; it has to do with their being; it has to
do with what N. Scott Momaday calls "whole and consummate
being"; it has to do with their sense of their humanity. I don't think
I have to make the connections here. I think they go without saying.
We have one-dimensional words to try to express multi-dimen-
sional things. Some languages are multi-dimensional in that they can
account for more things than this one can. There are a lot of things
that this language won't account for, that are outside its perspective,
you could say, that it doesn't have either the words or the forms
for. That's what we're all looking for—the words and the forms to
account for certain things that we feel need to be accounted for.
Black people in this country have given the language more dimen-
sions than it formerly had. American English has more dimensions
than British English because of all the people who've gone into
making it—black people and Indian people and Chinese people, you
know, have forced the language to see more than it would have
on its own. It has to do with seeing. It has to do with seeing and
hearing.

The Latin Americans have helped me in making movements between different kinds of language and different kinds of reality. They've helped to reinforce my own traditions. And I trust them. When I read them I feel I can read them with trust. The same way with Native American writers—I feel I can read them with trust. That's very important to me. To be able to read with trust. It's like listening to someone. There are people you can listen to with trust. Others you have to be careful about. I've probably done a bad thing the past two years—depending on the way you look at it—with the exception of Chaucer and Cervantes, I've only read Latin American, native American, and black writers.

Chaucer. I like Chaucer because he's a storyteller. Nowadays, when they teach Chaucer, it's not so important for the students to learn how to read him aloud—that's put in the background. What's important is criticizing the work—sight-recognition of the words, even if you can't say them—reading for meaning, for what's going on in the story. So nowadays you have a lot of people who criticize Chaucer but don't know how to read him, don't know very much about the language. But what a lot of people don't realize is that during Chaucer's time things were written to be read aloud or recited. When you write like that a lot of things happen structurally that wouldn't happen otherwise. I mean, you do a lot of things that you wouldn't do if people weren't going to "hear" this. That's why I studied and learned how to read Chaucer out loud. For me, he is one of the real storytellers of their tradition. A lot of real story-tellers in English literature were back in the fifteenth century—the fourteenth—because they were good listeners. I mainly like to read Chaucer when I read him aloud. I can't really sit down and read Chaucer without starting to say things. He's also one of the few writers in the English literary tradition whose words can lift off the page. They're always talking about "winged." His words are "winged." The other storyteller of a later period that I like is Thomas Hardy. They—the critics, I mean—get on him, but that's because he's a storyteller. When you're a storyteller, you don't always follow all the structural patterns they tell you to. When the critics talk about a lot of the writers back in the fourteenth and fifteenth centuries, they talk about how English prose wasn't really "developed" then. They say that's the reason why Sir Thomas Malory, for instance, wrote the way he did. That's the reason his sentences were "simple" sentences, and why he did a lot of connecting with "and" rather than other words and used a lot of repetition. But Thomas Malory could *hear*, and speech is always developed. What happened later was that writers (and critics) stopped listening. They stopped listening, and how things "read" became more important than how they sounded. Even with dialogue, as long as dialogue read well, it was all right. It didn't really matter if it had any connection with how people really talked.

[H]: When you came to my class at Brown, before *Corregidora* came out, you read from the novel with specific reference to the read materials of the course. Would you comment on Afro-American tradition, as seen through Gaines, Toomer, Ellison, Hurston, Walker, Forrest, Wright, Hughes, Brown, Hayden, et al.?

[J]: I can't talk about it the way you've asked it. I can only talk about what I feel to be those writers' relationship to the Afro-American tradition. But I can't really do that. I can't deal with so many writers in the space of one answer and even begin to make all the connections. I'm not jiving my way out. I'm going on. I will try to point out *some* things.

You know, I say the names over in my mind, and I think about those people—who will speak of black writing as a "limited category," the implication being that it's something you have to transcend. And it surprised me, because I thought critics had outgrown that kind of posture. When I say the names over, every one of the people suggests and reflects all the possibility of human value. They're so very different, they do many different things stylistically— but in none of their writings are the human connections lost—the connections between words and human being.

In all the writers you mentioned, one can talk about the relationship between technique and social morality, conceptions of human value, the Afro-American world view. That's what I remember speaking about in your class. All of the writers are "saying" the Afro-American tradition. You know, I begin to say something and then I say, "But that doesn't say all of it. If you say this about Gaines, you have to say this and this and this. And if you say this about Toomer it's also true about Gaines and Walker." That kind of thing.

For me, Gaines maintains his connections through oral storytelling and his special relationship to the speech community he comes from. When I think of Gaines, I think of voice and story. I think of a perspective that's up-close and "inside." I think of ways of talking that I am unfamiliar with. I think of a form and language that can deal with horror as well as beauty—some forms and some language can't. I think of a person talking to me. I think of men and women talking to me. I think of voices that carry through time. I think of history and personal life memory.

Toomer—pain and beauty. A form that can take in pain and beauty. Poetry. Continual movement. The social reality of migration and displacement, human displacement. Language as magic and transcendent. Lyrical movement. Realistic view of reality. Women. Essences. Men and women.

Ellison—a long form. Prologue. Spaces. A long form that moves. Forms that move into other forms that move into many different conceptions and visions of reality. Jazz movement. Episode. Patterns. Identity. Shifts in identity in persons as well as the way of presenting situations. *Invisible Man* goes through many forms. For me, each chapter is a change of identity, of pattern, of ways of looking at self, reality. Picaresque. Slave narrative tradition. Storytelling. Other qualities of reality.

Hurston—close-up relationships between men and women. Concern with love, with folk-saying. Tension. A sense of separation in narrative and dialogue, between storyteller and speech community. Speech. Documentation of ways of talking. Folklore. Sense of community as integral.

Walker—concern with relationships. Tension in relationships. Men and women. Lyrical movement and moments. Relationships of tension. View of reality-experience—realistic. Caring. Pain and beauty. Like *Cane*, aesthetics and moral implications so interwoven that they cannot be separated. The word as magic, again. I also think of Jean Toomer and Zora Hurston. Acknowledgment.

Forrest—speech and music continuum. Jazz. Sermon. Incantation. Words as voice heard and music. Whole range of black speech and music. Ritual. A constant movement and flowing into. Magic song and sound and voice. Constant movement between different kinds of language. Social reality in whole form—history, language, sermon oratory and blues/jazz traditions, ceremonial, metaphorical legend, history and myth—the full range of verbal traditions.

Wright—blues storytelling, blues vision. Where is Bigger's history? Only a hint at his family life relationships and the way things are/ were with Bessie. No sense of fullness. And maybe that's all part of the theme. Everything integrated into the forward movement of the book—the book never stops. Are there any flashbacks, even personal recollections? Is there any memory? Movement—how does the form reflect a social reality? a vision of reality?—continual movement. Does Bigger ever know who he is? Who Bessie was?

Hughes—if a white writer had done the things he did to poetic structure he would have been called an innovator. Hughes takes the overall form from the folk tradition rather than incorporating folk material and folk-saying in the traditional Western poetic forms. So there isn't any tension between the forms, the overall structure of the poems, and the material, the subject matter of the poems. He, too, in many ways—in his poetry—solved the problem of

Zora Neale Hurston, by taking the overall structure of his poems from the speech and music continuum and traditions. Jazz, blues, folk-telling, etc. Forms that can bring in personal recollection and history and things happening around him. Montage. Improvisational.

Brown—storyteller. The rhythms, metaphors of black folk speaking from the poems take over the whole form. Storytelling talking—the whole form. To hear his voice saying the poem—the whole rhythm of his voice telling the poem. The poem is his voice telling. And the whole poem is the rhythm of that telling. Poet-storyteller. And the humor from that tradition, the humor that is hard reality speaking, that makes one see what is real. The humor that does not camouflage the reality. What is real and hard. The human connections. The poem is the man's voice telling. The man's voice goes way back, the man's voice goes way back, broad and deep—the deep well of experience and being. Storytelling magic and the voices always there.

Hayden—ritual. History and experience as transcendent and human. The forms. Cosmic affirmation. The social and moral and historical realities cannot be separated from the aesthetic realities. You cannot refuse to see what is there. The poetry is "beautiful," but at the same time it "sees." Its aesthetics take in the human realities, the beauty and cruelties. The human realities cannot be separated. The sense of permanence. The sense of magic. The sense that no human word in the poem is where it should not be. The sense of transcendence always. The spiritual and the human. Spiritual/human. The whole sphere. History, metaphor—spoken, told, written. Poetry is something cared for. Its human consequences.

[H]: Is any of your work autobiographical?

[J]: A lot of my earlier work—when I was in college—was autobiographical. I remember when I was in junior high school, that teacher, Mrs. Hodges, used to ask me to write plays for the elementary schoolchildren. I don't remember the plays, but I remember in them there were little rhymed things for the children to say. I remember they did two of them. I didn't keep copies of anything I wrote back then. And I remember even throwing things away that I'd written back in elementary school. So I don't have anything from way back then. Particularly now when I'd like to see the things.

I remember a couple of high school stories; one of them was a projection of the kind of life I thought I wanted. The woman character was a sort of anticipation of the kind of women I still write about—her independence, I mean. But in those days, when I was sixteen and seventeen, I had a romantic conception of what a writer was, and that story made use of that romantic conception. I used to write stories about writers, you know. Women who were writers. And the story would always take place somewhere far away. I remember a story called "The Guitar." The woman was a writer and all her friends were writers and they were someplace like Spain, sitting around at tables in one of those outdoor cafés and none of them ever had any money. That kind of thing. One of the things in the story was a real detail, though. Where the woman discovers a man sick in a hotel room and nobody will go take care of him, so she goes and takes care of him. I re-use this in a story called "The Roundhouse"—but the characters in "The Roundhouse" are more for real, in terms of me.

I didn't start writing about Kentucky until after I left Kentucky. Before, I would write about places far away that I didn't even know about. And I used to have an image of myself when I grew up—I didn't think it would really happen—but I was this independent woman, I never saw myself as being married or having children or anything like that, and I was always traveling, particularly to Spanish-speaking places, and I was a writer. It's funny to me about the traveling bit because I really don't have that desire now. I see myself back in Kentucky somewhere, still a single woman. A few friends, a few people I care about very much. But my whole conception is different. It wasn't until I was sixteen or seventeen though that I had all those romantic notions of what a writer was. Before that it was just something I was doing, and after that it became just something I was doing—but I think from about sixteen to nineteen was that very romantic time for me. Except at nineteen, I wrote my first Kentucky-oriented story, though it doesn't take place in Kentucky; it's about something in my grandmother's life, though not strictly biographical; it doesn't follow the events exactly. The working at the "roundhouse" during the First World War polishing engines, the taking care of the man—she hadn't met him at the roundhouse, he'd been staying at the same boardinghouse—the marrying him, the details from her life I knew from my mother's telling me. Sometimes I'll use real life "details" and imagine so many things around them that they're not really the same thing anymore.

Most of my autobiographical writing is out of my system now. I can't say that any of my stories have ever been strictly autobiographical, though. "The Return" certainly isn't. "The Welfare Check" is only in terms of the woman's being like me. The only strictly autobiographical writing was in poetry—poetic journals.

When I was in undergraduate school, I used to write poetic journals about real things that had happened. So all my poems were journals—real happenings—with dialogue in them, because I remembered. Now, sometimes I write storytelling poems, using the things I learned from those journals, the style, the use of the first-person manner of telling. So whenever I write storytelling poems they sound like they really happened, and I have to tell people they didn't really happen. Now, I like to write things that sound like they really happened, when I tell a first-person story. It has to be like it really happened. I have to identify so closely with it—like in the oral storytelling tradition—that it really happened and the woman telling the story (or the man telling it—I have two short stories with a man narrator—but they are usually women) is really telling the story. I'm not telling the story—the person telling the story is telling it. And the same goes for when I'm reading a story—out loud to people, I mean—it's that person that's telling it. It's like what Toni Morrison saw when she read *Corregidora*—the author isn't there anywhere. For that reason, a lot of people think the things I do are autobiographical; because when I'm telling the story or reading it out loud, I don't want to say "I" am those women, but those women are telling the story.

Then there was another stage after the poetic journals—where the woman narrator, even though the details of her life were different, was me in the sense that I needed her to explain myself. There was no way I could explain who I was to myself or anybody else except that way. Particularly my silence. I had to say something about it some way. In the short story, "The Welfare Check," although I never worked in a welfare office or knew a man like the one in the story, the woman not knowing what to say and that kind of thing was a self-portrait, I guess. (About the man—I should say that, rather than not knowing a man like the one in the story, he wasn't a *particular* man.) And I felt that if people read the story or if I read it to them, they would feel less badly about my not talking and it usually worked that way. So I needed the women to be me at that time. And there were always these things about people who didn't talk and didn't know what to say.

Actually, that's still there. In *Corregidora*, it's still there in the character of the mother who doesn't know what to say to the man, Martin—"It was just like my mouth was there, but I just couldn't say nothing." That kind of thing. But in Ursa—she knows what to say. She talks to people, you know. So Ursa isn't at all a self-portrait. Maybe there are some things, some points. But I think that "talk thing" somewhere will always enter, you know—in one or another of the characters. So there are those kinds of autobiographical usings. Things that have been the causes of tension in my own life might be re-directed in the lives of certain characters. The man in "The Roundhouse" works but doesn't say anything and people think he can't talk—that kind of thing.

But as for the details of my own life, I'm not an autobiographical writer at all. I "re-contextualize" a lot of the things in my own life. There might be things people say in stories that I've heard said—certain "scenes" that really happened—but the whole thing could never be autobiographical or even strictly biographical—I mean, in terms of the details of another person's life. Sometimes I put a few things from the lives of people I've been told about, for instance. But the details of my writing now wouldn't correspond with any details in my own life. But I do make certain connections in terms of my own experience and relationships. Relationships that are important to me in real life become important in fiction. Someone asked me, for instance, if I had a theory about generations as matrilinear or something. I said no. But in terms of my own living—the women I'm descended from have a special significance for me, have always had a special significance for me. So, although the women aren't the same kind of women and the details are different, that aspect is there and the generations of women are there because of something I needed to clarify in my own life, certain relationships between men and women, between mother and daughter, other relationships in the book.

You heard me mention how I always used to picture myself. Making generations. That can be "translated" into something in my own life. Ever since I was a kid I never really wanted or thought of myself as having children. At first, I thought, of course, that that was the natural thing that happened, that women naturally grew up and got married and had children. So I thought since that was what "naturally" happened, it would happen to me, too. I decided that I wouldn't get married till I was in my late twenties, though—which was unusual for the kind of community I grew up in. But then, when I was twelve, for some reason, I learned that you didn't just naturally grow up and get married and have children. So since I was twelve I decided that I wasn't going to ever get married or have children. And then something happened. I was going along—feeling that way—not feeling guilty about it or anything—not even thinking that other people might care about that kind of a decision—that whatever I chose to do was okay. I didn't think about how parents might feel. In fact, I thought as long as it was something that I'd decided, it was okay. But then I realized that when you make that kind of a decision, you're not just making it for yourself, you're making it for your mother and your grandmother—I speak of the women here for another personal reason—and your great-grandmother; that it's not just you making that decision for yourself but you're making it for all the generations that came before you.

What made me realize this was talking to my mother. I really didn't think it mattered, you know. I'd never even thought about it—how she might feel. Because I didn't see it that way. And we were talking and I said I wasn't going to have any children or didn't want to have any children and then she asked me, "What about the generations?" And then I realized that it wasn't just me. And ever since then I've had this tremendous feeling of guilt, you know. I don't know if I should call it guilt, but . . . ambivalence. Right now, I'm not doing anything about generations. But when she said that it just went clear through me, because I'd never really thought about it. All the connections, you know. And I can't explain my feelings—maybe changes in feelings—about children, I mean. But that's the reason I think that there's the generations and the command to make generations in *Corregidora*. I mean the metaphor for something personal. The historical parallels are already there. The reason Ursa can't have children—that's another thing, that's another matter. It has to do with my life, but it has to do with another woman's life, too—so I can't talk about that. But what I'm trying to say is that Ursa's relationships could be "translated" into details in my own life, but *Corregidora* is really a metaphor for things in my own experience rather than being a direct statement.

[H]: What do you think can be taught—or not taught—in writing classes? What was most valuable to you as a student, in terms of examples, persons, how you acquired techniques as well as ideas about writing and what you wanted to write about? What was useful, and useless, in your experience in and out of writing classes and programs?

[J]: Well, I see writing classes mainly as guidelines, you know. You can point out things to people, make them aware of the possibilities and that kind of thing, but the responsibility of "doing" is always theirs, the responsibility is finally always theirs. I also feel that it's important that a writer, storyteller, has a hearer. Some people need the sanction of many hearers before they feel sustained, others need very few, some need only one—that kind of thing. For me, as I said, I need that contact with one trusted person. And I guess there also has to be that feeling that *they* trust, that they trust the voice in my stories. So I've said what's been most valuable to me as a student. But I feel all writers, all storytellers, need the example of persons, the presence of persons, as reinforcement. Otherwise I don't feel you can really maintain that human relationship and connection in what you're doing. I think a storyteller can go only so long talking to himself, you know, or to no one. But I keep getting back to what you say about a man is another man's face. Because there is always that kind of relationship between a storyteller and a hearer—the seeing of each other. The hearer has to see/hear the storyteller, but the storyteller also has to see/hear the hearer, which the written tradition doesn't usually acknowledge. But writing is finally a "doing." It isn't something that you talk about. I don't think the actual "doing" can be taught. I don't think writing "process" can be taught.

I don't know how I've acquired techniques. I think I've acquired them from reading and listening. But for me, technique has to be finally something that you don't think about—that's internalized—and that, for each work, the way of telling should grow out of that particular work in the process of telling. Even when I revise, I don't think of technique as technique. I think about how something can be told better. Ideas about writing have come to me, too, through personal contact, reading, listening. What I want to write about is something that grows as I grow. Right now, there are things there for me to write about. I have them. I have them because of the kind of "continuum" way I've been writing. So right now for me there isn't the trying to find the things to write about but the having the time to write about the things that are already in my mind. There are also things that I can't deal with now that I might be able to deal with years from now. I mean certain relationships that I might speak about with a different vision or that I might be able to handle more fully than I can right now. I also have a sense of place in my writing. A lot of my earlier stories—either they went far away, or, like "The Return," they never located the people in time or place. Sometimes that is good, but like I was saying, one should have a storytelling center in terms of voice—which doesn't mean one can't go off here and there in terms of voice and language—it just means there's that deep well that one can trust, that center. I think it's the same with place and time—the sense of a location so that the storyteller doesn't lose a certain moral and human perspective—which doesn't mean the storyteller can't go off anywhere in place and time that he pleases—but that there's always that deep part that he knows, that human center.

DEEP SONG

FOR B. H.

GAYL JONES

The blues calling my name.
She is singing a deep song.
She is singing a deep song.
I am human.
He calls me crazy.
He says, "You must be
crazy."
I say, "Yes, I'm crazy."
He sits with his knees apart.
His fly is broken.
She is singing a deep song.
He smiles.
She is singing a deep song.
"Yes, I'm crazy."
I care about you.
I care.
I care about you.
I care.
He lifts his eyebrows.
The blues is calling my name.
I tell him he'd better
do something about his fly.
He says something softly.
He says something so softly
that I can't even hear him.
He is a dark man.
Sometimes he is a good dark man.
Sometimes he is a bad dark man.
I love him.

LOOKING FOR ZORA

ALICE WALKER

On January 16, 1959, Zora Neale Hurston, suffering from the effects of a stroke and writing painfully in longhand, composed a letter to the "editorial department" of Harper & Brothers inquiring if they would be interested in seeing "the book I am laboring upon at present—a life of Herod the Great." One year and twelve days later, Zora Neale Hurston died without funds to provide for her burial, a resident of the St. Lucie County, Florida, Welfare Home. She lies today in an unmarked grave in a segregated cemetery in Fort Pierce, Florida, a resting place generally symbolic of the black writer's fate in America.

Zora Neale Hurston is one of the most significant unread authors in America, the author of two minor classics and four other major books.

—ROBERT HEMENWAY, "Zora Hurston and the Eatonville Anthropology," from *The Harlem Renaissance Remembered,* ed. Arna Bontemps

On August 15, 1973, I wake up just as the plane is lowering over Sanford, Florida, which means I am also looking down on Eatonville, Zora Neale Hurston's birthplace. I recognize it from Zora's description in *Mules and Men:* "the city of five lakes, three croquet courts, three hundred brown skins, three hundred good swimmers, plenty guavas, two schools, and no jailhouse." Of course I cannot see the guavas, but the five lakes are still there, and it is the lakes I count as the plane prepares to land in Orlando.

From the air, Florida looks completely flat, and as we near the ground this impression does not change. This is the first time I have seen the interior of the state, which Zora wrote about so well, but there are the acres of orange groves, the sand, mangrove trees, and scrub pine that I know from her books. Getting off the plane I walk through the hot moist air of midday into the tacky but air-conditioned airport. I search for Charlotte Hunt, my companion on the Zora Hurston expedition. She lives in Winter Park, Florida, very near Eatonville, and is writing her graduate dissertation on Zora. I see her waving—a large pleasant-faced white woman in dark glasses. We have written to each other for several weeks, swapping our latest finds (mostly hers) on Zora, and trying to make sense out of the mass of information obtained (often erroneous or simply confusing) from Zora herself—through her stories and autobiography—and from people who wrote about her.

Eatonville has lived for such a long time in my imagination that I can hardly believe it will be found existing in its own right. But after twenty minutes on the expressway, Charlotte turns off and I see a small settlement of houses and stores set with no particular pattern in the sandy soil off the road. We stop in front of a neat gray building that has two fascinating signs: Eatonville Post Office and Eatonville City Hall.

Inside the Eatonville City Hall half of the building, a slender, dark brown-skinned woman sits looking through letters on a desk. When she hears we are searching for anyone who might have known Zora Neale Hurston, she leans back in thought. Because I don't wish to inspire foot-dragging in people who might know something about Zora they're not sure they should tell, I have decided on a simple, but I feel profoundly *useful,* lie.

"I am Miss Hurston's niece," I prompt the young woman, who brings her head down with a smile.

"I think Mrs. Moseley is about the only one still living who might remember her," she says.

"Do you mean *Mathilda* Moseley, the woman who tells those 'woman-is-smarter-than-man' lies in Zora's book?"

"Yes," says the young woman. "Mrs. Moseley is real old now, of course. But this time of day, she should be at home."

I stand at the counter looking down on her, the first Eatonville resident I have spoken to. Because of Zora's books, I feel I know something about her; at least I know what the town she grew up in was like years before she was born.

"Tell me something," I say, "do the schools teach Zora's books here?"

"No," she says, "they don't. I don't think most people know anything about Zora Neale Hurston, or know about any of the great things she did. She was a fine lady. I've read all of her books myself, but I don't think many other folks in Eatonville have."

"Many of the church people around here, as I understand it," says Charlotte in a murmured aside, "thought Zora was pretty loose. I don't think they appreciated her writing about them."

"Well," I say to the young woman, "thank you for your help." She clarifies her directions to Mrs. Moseley's house and smiles as Charlotte and I turn to go.

The letter to *Harper's* does not expose a publisher's rejection of an unknown masterpiece, but it does reveal how the bright promise of the Harlem Renaissance deteriorated for many of the writers who shared in its exuberance. It also indicates the personal tragedy of Zora Neale Hurston: Barnard graduate, author of four novels, two books of folklore, one volume of autobiography, the most important collector of Afro-American folklore in America, reduced by poverty and circumstance to seek a publisher by unsolicited mail.

—ROBERT HEMENWAY

Zora Hurston was born in 1901, 1902, or 1903—depending on how old she felt herself to be at the time someone asked.

—LIBRARIAN, BEINECKE LIBRARY, YALE UNIVERSITY

The Moseley house is small and white and snug, its tiny yard nearly swallowed up by oleanders and hibiscus bushes. Charlotte and I knock on the door. I call out. But there is no answer. This strikes us as peculiar. We have had time to figure out an age for Mrs. Moseley—not dates or a number, just old. I am thinking of a quivery, bedridden invalid when we hear the car. We look behind us to see an old black-and-white Buick—paint peeling and grillwork rusty—pulling into the drive. A neat old lady in a purple dress and white hair is straining at the wheel. She is frowning because Charlotte's car is in the way.

Mrs. Moseley looks at us suspiciously. "Yes, I knew Zora Neale," she says, unsmilingly and with a rather cold stare at Charlotte (who I imagine feels very *white* at that moment), "but that was a long time ago, and I don't want to talk about it."

"Yes ma'am," I murmur, bringing all my sympathy to bear on the situation.

"Not only that," Mrs. Moseley continues, "I've been sick. Been in the hospital for an operation. Ruptured artery. The doctors didn't believe I was going to live, but you see me alive, don't you?"

"Looking well, too," I comment.

Mrs. Moseley is out of her car. A thin, sprightly woman with nice gold-studded false teeth, uppers and lowers. I like her because she stands there *straight* beside her car, with a hand on her hip and her straw pocketbook on her arm. She wears white T-strap shoes with heels that show off her well-shaped legs.

"I'm eighty-two years old, you know," she says. "And I just can't remember things the way I used to. Anyhow, Zora Neale left here to go to school and she never really came back to live. She'd come here for material for her books, but that was all. She spent most of her time down in South Florida."

"You know, Mrs. Moseley, I saw your name in one of Zora's books."

"You did?" She looks at me with only slightly more interest. "I read some of her books a long time ago, but then people got to borrowing and borrowing and they borrowed them all away."

"I could send you a copy of everything that's been reprinted," I offer. "Would you like me to do that?"

"No," says Mrs. Moseley promptly. "I don't read much any more. Besides, all of that was *so* long ago . . ."

Charlotte and I settle back against the car in the sun. Mrs. Moseley tells us at length and with exact recall every step in her recent operation, ending with: "What those doctors didn't know—when they were expecting me to die (and they didn't even think I'd live long enough for them to have to take out my stitches!)—is that Jesus is the best doctor, and if *He* says for you to get well, that's all that counts."

With this philosophy, Charlotte and I murmur quick assent: being Southerners and church bred, we have heard that belief before. But what we learn from Mrs. Moseley is that she does not remember much beyond the year 1938. She shows us a picture of her father and mother and says that her father was Joe Clarke's brother. Joe Clarke, as every Zora Hurston reader knows, was the first mayor of Eatonville; his fictional counterpart is Jody Starks of *Their Eyes Were Watching God*. We also get directions to where Joe Clarke's store *was*—where Club Eaton is now. Club Eaton, a long orange-beige nightspot we had seen on the main road, is apparently famous for the good times in it regularly had by all. It is, perhaps, the modern equivalent of the store porch, where all the men of Zora's childhood came to tell "lies," that is, black folktales, that were "made and used on the spot," to take a line from Zora. As for Zora's exact birthplace, Mrs. Moseley has no idea.

After I have commented on the healthy growth of her hibiscus bushes, she becomes more talkative. She mentions how much she *loved* to dance, when she was a young woman, and talks about how good her husband was. When he was alive, she says, she was completely happy because he allowed her to be completely free. "I was so free I had to pinch myself sometimes to tell if I was a married woman."

Relaxed now, she tells us about going to school with Zora. "Zora and I went to the same school. It's called Hungerford High now. It *was* only to the eighth grade. But our teachers were so good that by the time you left you knew college subjects. When I went to Morris Brown in Atlanta, the teachers there were just teaching me the same things I had already learned right in Eatonville. I wrote Mama and told her I was going to come home and help her with her babies. I wasn't learning anything new."

"Tell me something, Mrs. Moseley," I ask, "why do you suppose Zora was against integration? I read somewhere that she was against school desegregation because she felt it was an insult to black teachers."

"Oh, one of them [white people] came around asking me about integration. One day I was doing my shopping. I heard 'em over there talking about it in the store, about the schools. And I got on out of the way because I knew if they asked me, they wouldn't like what I was going to tell 'em. But they came up and asked me anyhow. 'What do you think about this integration?' one of them said. I acted like I thought I had heard wrong. 'You're asking *me* what *I* think about integration?' I said. 'Well, as you can see I'm just an old colored woman'—I was seventy-five or seventy-six then—'and this is the first time anybody ever asked me about integration. And nobody asked my grandmother what she thought, either, but her daddy was one of you all.'" Mrs. Moseley seems satisfied with this memory of her rejoinder. She looks at Charlotte. "I have the blood of three races in my veins," she says belligerently, "white, black, and Indian, and nobody asked me *anything* before."

"Do you think living in Eatonville made integration less appealing to you?"

"Well, I can tell you this: I have lived in Eatonville all my life, and I've been in the governing of this town. I've been everything but Mayor and I've been *assistant* Mayor. Eatonville was and is an all-black town. We have our own police department, post office, and town hall. Our own school and good teachers. Do I need integration?

"They took over Goldsboro, because the black people who lived there never incorporated, like we did. And now I don't even know if any black folks live there. They built big houses up there around the lakes. But we didn't let that happen in Eatonville, and we don't sell land to just anybody. And you see, we're still here."

When we leave, Mrs. Moseley is standing by her car, waving. I think of the letter Roy Wilkins wrote to a black newspaper blasting Zora Neale for her lack of enthusiasm about the integration of schools. I wonder if he knew the experience of Eatonville she was coming from. Not many black people in America have come from a self-contained, all-black community where loyalty and unity are taken for granted. A place where black pride is nothing new.

There is, however, one thing Mrs. Moseley said that bothered me.

"Tell me, Mrs. Moseley," I had asked, "why is it that thirteen years after Zora's death, no marker has been put on her grave?"

And Mrs. Moseley answered: "The reason she doesn't have a stone is because she wasn't buried here. She was buried down in South Florida somewhere. I don't think anybody really knew where she was."

Only to reach a wider audience, need she ever write books—because she is a perfect book of entertainment in herself. In her youth she was always getting scholarships and things from wealthy white people, some of whom simply paid her just to sit around and represent the Negro race for them, she did it in such a racy fashion. She was full of sidesplitting anecdotes, humorous tales, and tragicomic stories, remembered out of her life in the South as a daughter of a traveling minister of God. She could make you laugh one minute and cry the next. To many of her white friends, no doubt, she was a perfect "darkie," in the nice meaning they give the term—that is, a naive, childlike, sweet, humorous, and highly colored Negro.

But Miss Hurston was clever, too—a student who didn't let college give her a broad "a" and who had great scorn for all pretensions, academic or otherwise. That is why she was such a fine folklore collector, able to go among the people and never act as if she had been to school at all. Almost nobody else could stop the average Harlemite on Lenox Avenue and measure his head with a strange-looking, anthropological device and not get bawled out for the attempt, except Zora, who used to stop anyone whose head looked interesting, and measure it.   —LANGSTON HUGHES, *The Big Sea*

What does it matter what white folks must have thought about her?
—STUDENT, "BLACK WOMEN WRITERS" CLASS, WELLESLEY COLLEGE

Mrs. Sarah Peek Patterson is a handsome, red-haired woman in her late forties, wearing orange slacks and gold earrings. She is the director of Lee-Peek Mortuary in Fort Pierce, the establishment that handled Zora's burial. Unlike most black funeral homes in southern towns that sit like palaces among the general poverty, Lee-Peek has a rundown, *small* look. Perhaps this is because it is painted purple and white, as are its Cadillac chariots. These colors do not age well. The rooms are cluttered and grimy, and the bathroom is a tiny, stale-smelling prison, with a bottle of black hair dye (apparently used to touch up the hair of the corpses) dripping into the face bowl. Two pine burial boxes are resting in the bathtub.

Mrs. Patterson herself is pleasant and helpful.

"As I told you over the phone, Mrs. Patterson," I begin, shaking her hand and looking into her penny-brown eyes, "I am Zora Neale Hurston's niece, and I would like to have a marker put on her grave. You said, when I called you last week, that you could tell me where the grave is."

By this time I am, of course, completely into being Zora's niece, and the lie comes with perfect naturalness to my lips. Besides, as far as I'm concerned, she *is* my aunt—and that of all black people as well.

"She was buried in 1960," exclaims Mrs. Patterson. "That was when my father was running this funeral home. He's sick now or I'd let you talk to him. But I know where she's buried. She's in the old cemetery, the Garden of the Heavenly Rest, on Seventeenth Street. Just when you go in the gate there's a circle, and she's buried right in the middle of it. Hers is the only grave in that circle—because people don't bury in that cemetery any more."

She turns to a stocky, black-skinned woman in her thirties, wearing a green polo shirt and white jeans cut off at the knee. "This lady will show you where it is," she says.

"I can't tell you how much I appreciate this," I say to Mrs. Patterson, as I rise to go. "And could you tell me something else? You see, I never met my aunt. When she died, I was still a junior in high school. But could you tell me what she died of, and what kind of funeral she had?"

"I don't know exactly what she died of," Mrs. Patterson says. "I know she didn't have any money. Folks took up a collection to bury her. . . . I believe she died of malnutrition."

"Malnutrition?"

Outside, in the blistering sun, I lean my head against Charlotte's even more blistering cartop. The sting of the hot metal only intensifies my anger. *"Malnutrition,"* I manage to mutter. "Hell, our condition hasn't changed *any* since Phillis Wheatley's time. *She* died of malnutrition!"

"Really?" says Charlotte, "I didn't know that."

> One cannot overemphasize the extent of her commitment. It was so great that her marriage in the spring of 1927 to Herbert Sheen was short lived. Although divorce did not come officially until 1931, the two separated amicably after only a few months, Hurston to continue her collecting, Sheen to attend medical school. Hurston never married again. —ROBERT HEMENWAY

"What is your name?" I ask the woman who has climbed into the back seat.

"Rosalee," she says. She has a rough, pleasant voice, as if she is a singer who also smokes a lot. She is homely, and has an air of ready indifference.

"Another woman came by here wanting to see the grave," she says, lighting up a cigarette. "She was a little short, dumpy white lady from one of these Florida schools. Orlando or Daytona. But let me tell you something before we gets started. All I know is where the cemetery is. I don't know one thing about the grave. You better go back in and ask her to draw you a map."

A few moments later, with Mrs. Patterson's diagram of where the grave is, we head for the cemetery.

We drive past blocks of small, pastel-colored houses and turn right onto 17th Street. At the very end, we reach a tall curving gate, with the words "Garden of the Heavenly Rest" fading into the stone. I expected, from Mrs. Patterson's small drawing, to find a small circle —which would have placed Zora's grave five or ten paces from the road. But the "circle" is over an acre large and looks more like an abandoned field. Tall weeds choke the dirt road and scrape against the sides of the car. It doesn't help either that I step out into an active anthill.

"I don't know about y'all," I say, "but I don't even believe this." I am used to the haphazard cemetery-keeping that is traditional in most southern black communities, but this neglect is staggering. As far as I can see there is nothing but bushes and weeds, some as tall as my waist. One grave is near the road, and Charlotte elects to investigate it. It is fairly clean, and belongs to someone who died in 1963.

Rosalee and I plunge into the weeds; I pull my long dress up to my hips. The weeds scratch my knees, and the insects have a feast. Looking back, I see Charlotte standing resolutely near the road.

"Aren't you coming?" I call.

"No," she calls back. "I'm from these parts and I know what's out there." She means snakes.

"Shit," I say, my whole life and the people I love flashing melodramatically before my eyes. Rosalee is a few yards to my right.

"How're you going to find anything out here?" she asks. And I stand still a few seconds, looking at the weeds. Some of them are quite pretty, with tiny yellow flowers. They are thick and healthy, but dead weeds under them have formed a thick gray carpet on the ground. A snake could be lying six inches from my big toe and I wouldn't see it. We move slowly, very slowly, our eyes alert, our legs trembly. It is hard to tell where the center of the circle is since the circle is not really round, but more like half of something round. There are things crackling and hissing in the grass. Sandspurs are sticking to the inside of my skirt. Sand and ants cover my feet. I look toward the road and notice that there are indeed *two* large curving stones, making an entrance and exit to the cemetery. I take my bearings from them and try to navigate to exact center. But the center of anything can be very large, and a grave is not a pinpoint. Finding the grave seems positively hopeless. There is only one thing to do:

"Zora!" I yell, as loud as I can (causing Rosalee to jump), "are you out here?"

"If she is, I sho hope she don't answer you. If she do, I'm gone."

"Zora!" I call again. "I'm here. Are you?"

"If she is," grumbles Rosalee, "I hope she'll keep it to herself."

"Zora!" Then I start fussing with her. "I hope you don't think I'm going to stand out here all day, with these snakes watching me and these ants having a field day. In fact, I'm going to call you just one or two more times." On a clump of dried grass, near a small bushy tree, my eye falls on one of the largest bugs I have ever seen. It is on its back, and is as large as three of my fingers. I walk toward it, and yell "Zo-ra!" and my foot sinks into a hole. I look down. I am standing in a sunken rectangle that is about six feet long and about three or four feet wide. I look up to see where the two gates are.

"Well," I say, "this is the center, or approximately anyhow. It's also the only sunken spot we've found. Doesn't this look like a grave to you?"

"For the sake of not going no farther through these bushes," Rosalee growls, "yes, it do."

"Wait a minute," I say, "I have to look around some more to be sure this is the only spot that resembles a grave. But you don't have to come."

Rosalee smiles—a grin, really—beautiful and tough.

"Naw," she says, "I feel sorry for you. If one of these snakes got ahold of you out here by yourself I'd feel *real* bad." She laughs. "I done come this far, I'll go on with you."

"Thank you, Rosalee," I say. "Zora thanks you too."

"Just as long as she don't try to tell me in person," she says, and together we walk down the field.

> The gusto and flavor of Zora Neal[e] Hurston's storytelling, for example, long before the yarns were published in *Mules and Men* and other books, became a local legend which might . . . have spread further under different conditions. A tiny shift in the center of gravity could have made them best-sellers.   —ARNA BONTEMPS, *Personals*

> Bitter over the rejection of her folklore's value, especially in the black community, frustrated by what she felt was her failure to convert the Afro-American world view into the forms of prose fiction, Hurston finally gave up.   —ROBERT HEMENWAY

When Charlotte and I drive up to the Merritt Monument Company, I immediately see the headstone I want.

"How much is this one?" I ask the young woman in charge, pointing to a tall black stone. It looks as majestic as Zora herself must have been when she was learning voodoo from those root doctors down in New Orleans.

"Oh, *that* one," she says, "that's our finest. That's Ebony Mist."

"Well, how much is it?"

"I don't know. But wait," she says, looking around in relief, "here comes somebody who'll know."

A small, sunburned man with squinty green eyes comes up. He must be the engraver, I think, because his eyes are contracted into slits, as if he has been keeping stone dust out of them for years.

"That's Ebony Mist," he says. "That's our best."

"How much is it?" I ask, beginning to realize I probably *can't* afford it.

He gives me a price that would feed a dozen Sahelian drought victims for three years. I realize I must honor the dead, but between the dead great and the living starving, there is no choice.

"I have a lot of letters to be engraved," I say, standing by the plain gray marker I have chosen. It is pale and ordinary, not at all like Zora, and makes me momentarily angry that I am not rich.

We go into his office and I hand him a sheet of paper that has:

ZORA NEALE HURSTON
"A GENIUS OF THE SOUTH"
1901   1960
NOVELIST   FOLKLORIST
ANTHROPOLOGIST

"A genius of the South" is from one of Jean Toomer's poems.

"Where is this grave?" the monument man asks. "If it's in a new cemetery, the stone has to be flat."

"Well, it's not a new cemetery and Zora—my aunt—doesn't need anything flat because with the weeds out there, you'd never be able to see it. You'll have to go out there with me."

He grunts.

"And take a long pole and 'sound' the spot," I add. "Because there's no way of telling it's a grave, except that it's sunken."

"Well," he says, after taking my money and writing up a receipt, in the full awareness that he's the only monument dealer for miles, "you take this flag" (he hands me a four-foot-long pole with a red-metal marker on top) "and take it out to the cemetery and put it where you think the grave is. It'll take us about three weeks to get the stone out there."

I wonder if he knows he is sending me to another confrontation with the snakes. He probably does. Charlotte has told me she will cut my leg and suck out the blood, if I am bit.

"At least send me a photograph when it's done, won't you?"

He says he will.

Hurston's return to her folklore-collecting in December of 1927 was made possible by Mrs. R. Osgood Mason, an elderly white patron of the arts, who at various times also helped Langston Hughes, Alain Locke, Richmond Barthe, and Miguel Covarrubias. Hurston apparently came to her attention through the intercession of Locke, who frequently served as a kind of liaison between the young black talent and Mrs. Mason. The entire relationship between this woman and the Harlem Renaissance deserves extended study, for it represents much of the ambiguity involved in white patronage of black artists. All her artists were instructed to call her "Godmother"; there was a decided emphasis on the "primitive" aspects of black culture, apparently a holdover from Mrs. Mason's interest in the Plains Indians. In Hurston's case there were special restrictions imposed by her patron: although she was to be paid a handsome salary for her folklore collecting, she was to limit her correspondence and publish nothing of her research without prior approval.   —ROBERT HEMENWAY

You have to read the chapters Zora *left out* of her autobiography.
—STUDENT, SPECIAL COLLECTIONS ROOM,
BEINECKE LIBRARY, YALE UNIVERSITY

Dr. Benton, a friend of Zora's and a practicing M.D. in Fort Pierce, is one of those old, good-looking men whom I always have trouble not liking. (It no longer bothers me that I may be constantly searching for father figures; by this time, I have found several and dearly enjoyed knowing them all.) He is shrewd, with steady brown eyes under hair that is almost white. He is probably in his seventies, but doesn't look it. He carries himself with dignity, and has cause to be proud of the new clinic where he now practices medicine. His nurse looks at us with suspicion, but Dr. Benton's eyes have the penetration of a scalpel cutting through skin. I guess right away that if he knows anything at all about Zora Hurston, he will not believe I am her niece. "Eatonville?" Dr. Benton says, leaning forward in his chair, looking first at me, then at Charlotte. "Yes, I know Eatonville, I grew up not far from there. I knew the whole bunch of Zora's family." (He looks at the shape of my cheekbones, the size of my eyes, and the nappiness of my hair.) "I knew her daddy. The old man. He was a hardworking, Christian man. Did the best he could for his family. He was the mayor of Eatonville for a while, you know.

"My father was the mayor of Goldsboro. You probably never heard of it. It never incorporated like Eatonville did, and has just about disappeared. But Eatonville is still all-black."

He pauses and looks at me. "And you're Zora's niece," he says wonderingly.

"Well," I say with shy dignity, yet with some tinge, I hope, of a

nineteenth-century blush, "I'm illegitimate. That's why I never knew
Aunt Zora."

I love him for the way he comes to my rescue. "You're *not* illegiti-
mate!" he cries, his eyes resting on me fondly. "All of us are God's
children! Don't you even *think* such a thing!"

And I hate myself for lying to him. Still, I ask my self, would I have
gotten this far toward getting the headstone and finding out
about Zora Hurston's last days without telling my lie? Actually, I
probably would have. But I don't like taking chances that could get
me stranded in central Florida.

"Zora didn't get along with her family. I don't know why. Did you
read her autobiography, *Dust Tracks on a Road?*"

"Yes, I did," I say. "It pained me to see Zora pretending to be
naive and grateful about the old white 'Godmother' who helped
finance her research, but I loved the part where she ran off from
home after falling out with her brother's wife."

Dr. Benton nodded. "When she got sick, I tried to get her to go
back to her family, but she refused. There wasn't any real hatred;
they just never had gotten along and Zora wouldn't go to them. She
didn't want to go to the county home, either, but she had to, because
she couldn't do a thing for herself."

"I was surprised to learn she died of malnutrition."

Dr. Benton seems startled. "Zora *didn't* die of malnutrition," he
says indignantly. "Where did you get that story from? She had a
stroke and she died in the welfare home." He seems peculiarly up-
set, distressed, but sits back reflectively in his chair: "She was an
incredible woman," he muses. "Sometimes when I closed my office,
I'd go by her house and just talk to her for an hour or two. She was a
well-read, well-traveled woman and always had her own ideas about
what was going on . . ."

"I never knew her, you know. Only some of Carl Van Vechten's
photographs and some newspaper photographs. . . . What did she
look like?"

"When I knew her, in the fifties, she was a big woman, *erect*. Not
quite as light as I am [Dr. Benton is dark beige], and about five foot,
seven inches, and she weighed about two hundred pounds. Probably
more. She . . ."

"What! Zora was *fat!* She wasn't, in Van Vechten's pictures!"

"Zora loved to eat," Dr. Benton says complacently. "She could sit
down with a mound of ice cream and just eat and talk till it was all
gone."

While Dr. Benton is talking, I recall that the Van Vechten pictures
were taken when Zora was still a young woman. In them she appears

tall, tan, and healthy. In later newspaper photographs—when she was in her forties—I remembered that she seemed heavier and several shades lighter. I reasoned that the earlier photographs were taken while she was busy collecting folklore materials in the hot Florida sun.

"She had high blood pressure. Her health wasn't good. . . . She used to live in one of my houses—on School Court Street. It's a block house . . . I don't recall the number. But my wife and I used to invite her over to the house for dinner. *She always ate well,*" he says emphatically.

"That's comforting to know," I say, wondering where Zora ate when she wasn't with the Bentons.

"Sometimes she would run out of groceries—after she got sick—and she'd call me. 'Come over here and see 'bout me,' she'd say. And I'd take her shopping and buy her groceries.

"She was always studying. Her mind—before the stroke—just worked all the time. She was always going somewhere, too. She once went to Honduras to study something. And when she died, she was working on that book about Herod the Great. She was so intelligent! And really had perfect expressions. Her English was beautiful." (I suspect this is a clever way to let me know Zora herself didn't speak in the "black English" her characters used.)

"I used to read all of her books," Dr. Benton continues, "but it was a long time ago. I remember one about . . . it was called, I think, 'The Children of God' [*Their Eyes Were Watching God*], and I remember Janie and Teapot [Teacake] and the mad dog riding on the cow in that hurricane and bit old Teapot on the cheek . . ."

I am delighted that he remembers even this much of the story, even if the names are wrong, but seeing his affection for Zora I feel I must ask him about her burial. "Did she *really* have a pauper's funeral?"

"She *didn't* have a pauper's funeral!" he says with great heat. "Everybody around here *loved* Zora."

"We just came back from ordering a headstone," I say quietly, because he *is* an old man and the color is coming and going on his face, "but to tell the truth, I can't be positive what I found is the grave. All I know is the spot I found was the only grave-size hole in the area."

"I remember it wasn't near the road," says Dr. Benton, more calmly. "Some other lady came by here and we went out looking for the grave and I took a long iron stick and poked all over that part of the cemetery but we didn't find anything. She took some pictures of the general area. Do the weeds still come up to your knees?"

"And beyond," I murmur. This time there isn't any doubt. Dr. Benton feels ashamed.

As he walks us to our car, he continues to talk about Zora. "She couldn't really write much near the end. She had the stroke and it left her weak; her mind was affected. She couldn't think about anything for long.

"She came here from Daytona, I think. She owned a houseboat over there. When she came here, she sold it. She lived on that money, then she worked as a maid—for an article on maids she was writing —and she worked for the *Chronicle* writing the horoscope column.

"I think black people here in Florida got mad at her because she was for some politician they were against. She said this politician *built* schools for blacks while the one they wanted just talked about it. And although Zora wasn't egotistical, what she thought, she thought; and generally what she thought, she said."

When we leave Dr. Benton's office, I realize I have missed my plane back home to Jackson, Mississippi. That being so, Charlotte and I decide to find the house Zora lived in before she was taken to the county welfare home to die. From among her many notes, Charlotte locates a letter of Zora's she has copied that carries the address: 1734 School Court Street. We ask several people for directions. Finally, two old gentlemen in a dusty gray Plymouth offer to lead us there. School Court Street is not paved, and the road is full of mud puddles. It is dismal and squalid, redeemed only by the brightness of the late afternoon sun. Now I can understand what a "block" house is. It is a house shaped like a block, for one thing, surrounded by others just like it. Some houses are blue and some are green or yellow. Zora's is light green. They are tiny—about 15 by 15 feet, squatty with flat roofs. The house Zora lived in looks worse than the others, but that is its only distinction. It also has three ragged and dirty children sitting on the steps.

"Is this where y'all live?" I ask, aiming my camera.

"No, ma'am," they say in unison, looking at me earnestly. "We live over yonder. This Miss So-and-So's house; but she in the horspital."

We chatter inconsequentially while I take more pictures. A car drives up with a young black couple in it. They scowl fiercely at Charlotte and don't look at me with friendliness, either. They get out and stand in their doorway across the street. I go up to them to explain. "Did you know Zora Hurston used to live right across from you?" I ask.

"Who?" They stare at me blankly, then become curiously attentive, as if they think I made the name up. They are both Afro-ed and he is somberly dashiki-ed.

I suddenly feel frail and exhausted. "It's too long a story," I say, "but tell me something, is there anybody on this street who's lived here for more than thirteen years?"

"That old man down there," the young man says, pointing. Sure enough, there is a man sitting on his steps three houses down. He has graying hair and is very neat, but there is a weakness about him. He reminds me of Mrs. Turner's husband in *Their Eyes Were Watching God.* He's rather "vanishing"-looking, as if his features have been sanded down. In the old days, before black was beautiful, he was probably considered attractive, because he has wavy hair and light-brown skin; but now, well, light skin has ceased to be its own reward.

After the preliminaries, there is only one thing I want to know: "Tell me something," I begin, looking down at Zora's house, "did Zora like flowers?"

He looks at me queerly. "As a matter of fact," he says, looking regretfully at the bare, rough yard that surrounds her former house, "she was crazy about them. And she was a great gardener. She loved azaleas, and that running and blooming vine [morning glories], and she really loved that night-smelling flower [gardenia]. She kept a vegetable garden year-round, too. She raised collards and tomatoes and things like that.

"Everyone in this community thought well of Miss Hurston. When she died, people all up and down this street took up a collection for her burial. We put her away nice."

"Why didn't somebody put up a headstone?"

"Well, you know, one was never requested. Her and her family didn't get along. They didn't even come to the funeral."

"And did she live down there by herself?"

"Yes, until they took her away. She lived with—just her and her companion, Sport."

My ears perk up. "Who?"

"Sport, you know, her dog. He was her only companion. He was a big brown-and-white dog."

When I walk back to the car, Charlotte is talking to the young couple on their porch. They are relaxed and smiling.

"I told them about the famous lady who used to live across the street from them," says Charlotte as we drive off. "Of course they had no idea Zora ever lived, let alone that she lived across the street. I think I'll send some of her books to them."

"That's real kind of you," I say.

I am not tragically colored. There is no great sorrow dammed up in my soul, nor lurking behind my eyes. I do not mind at all. I do not belong to the sobbing school of Negrohood who hold that nature somehow has given them a lowdown dirty deal and whose feelings are all hurt about it. . . . No, I do not weep at the world—I am too busy sharpening my oyster knife.   —ZORA NEALE HURSTON, "How It Feels to Be Colored Me," *World Tomorrow* (1928)

There are times—and finding Zora Hurston's grave was one of them —when normal responses of grief, horror, and so on, do not make sense because they bear no real relation to the depth of the emotion one feels. It was impossible for me to cry when I saw the field full of weeds where Zora is. Partly this is because I have come to know Zora through her books and she was not a teary sort of person herself; but partly, too, it is because there is a point at which even grief feels absurd. And at this point, laughter gushes up to retrieve sanity.

It is only later, when the pain is not so direct a threat to one's own existence, that what was learned in that moment of comical lunacy is understood. Such moments rob us of both youth and vanity. But perhaps they are also times when greater disciplines are born.

LOVE'S DOZEN

JAY WRIGHT

THE RITUAL TUNING

Now I will enter the house of affliction.

King carry me above myself in death.
Awake to the king of all,
I come, regal in my purpose,
out of the heated darkness.
Tune me only now;
I tune myself to your love
and your many-eyed longings,
to your deepest look into your life.

I am the contradictions that you make me.
Scaled, I climb your trees.
I lay my eggs, one by one,
and suckle them.
And in my sign I raise
the bright seed of my spirit.

I am two heads in one,
two lives in one.
I end my life in a double vision.
When I am eaten, you pass
this double deed among yourselves.

Love is to enter another's house
a creature coined from vision's deepest pain.

Here, creature of heaven,
I surround you with my sign,
and look upon your marriage bed,
and look upon your death.

LOVE IN THE WATER, LOVE IN THE STONE

Faithful bean lady of the plantain,
your tubular beads surround my voice.
You bring me a berry song so old
I hug the silences. You
embrace the silence and the clear light
on the track of your quest, to here.
I see now in that light myself
into the tangle of the river's bottom.

Knee-deep in another's bliss,
I wake and find myself a stone
                            at your lover's feet.
Then stone upon stone,
I rise into another's fire.
I touch your palm oil flesh
to light me from my cave.
And, if I rise, under your thunder,
into rain, I praise your touch.

Now, life-long a laterite,
a rain of beads, palm kernel oil
stipulate my clipped time.
The earth weaves eight gold bridal veils
to cast into the sea. The moon
is up at noon to catch me naked,
drunk and dancing with a ram.
I use the loom of seasons so;
I abuse myself.
And, even if I leave you,
I marry your worship in my wife's voice.

I begin the decline of having you
                            close;
your memories feed me.
These are my intolerable survivals.
And so I take my love's journey
from the language of your needs.
I mount my woman's earth smell

in the shadows of your ageless eyes.
I crawl to the altar of your thunderstones
and bleed for the bride whose blood
will fill my name.

LOVE IN THE IRON AND LOOM

Double the earth in northern light;
double the west in water.
Twin me in iron and weaving.
Binu, Lébé, my male hand
knows my woman's hardness.
I am the twin of my head, the twin of my hand.
Woven into cloth,
I slither from the dance a mask.
I am a dance in mask.
Who will answer the figure of the dance?
Who will unmask the twin at my heart?
My water shape in stone has a grip
                    upon the earth.
My river has a line around the star.
Shuttle and hammer, my life coheres.
My axe is the altar stone,
the loom of your love.
I know you as my cold light,
and as my dying light,
and as the barking star I ride
through love's light.
My lord's light is the deep pit
                    of my marriage bed,
the song of my sign within the dance.
Weep, weep, weep.
Brother mask, you leap
to double me from myself.
I am broken.
I am finished.
I weep for the twist of my craft
in the green river of my god's love.

LOVE AS HEAVEN'S NOSTALGIA

Rhine moonstone, light
of the devastated world,
I could name your nobleness
in minerals and stars,
or in the light's courage.
Yet in my ear the ages linger.
I know your passion for a melody,
your nostalgia for heaven.
I wait, under your touch,
for the vision of your governing.
Sisters, I will awaken in myself
your melodic temper.
Strange how my life runs down to reason
in the memory of a bright daughter;
I am at the gate of a lost life;
I am at the door of my own harmony.
And you, delivered from this world,
summon my purified soul to sit
in its nature with the stars.

ANAGNORISIS

Through blood
and into blood
my spirit calls.
You sit at my head
and weave my power.
Queen, I do not do as you
and deal in deaths.
I have no power to make
that male power crawl to my knees.
Yet I speak and am your seer,
chaste lover and your bridge
                    from the dead one's
blackened space
to the white sun of your prayer,

the red demon of your mother love.

You took the crescent moon and named me.
You bought my axe and sent me
through the desert of my southern dreams.
Clearly, in my sign,
I love
your overburdened body.
I love you
as the black chapel
                    of my penitence.
I love your forest's touch
in winter's memory.
Now, I grapple your deeds to my tongue.
And out of your woman's common eye,
. I take my son's pursuit
of the days he must live
                    to recall.

TRANSCENDENT NIGHT

Your feather hands
are love's nest in winter,
and yet I fly,
or do I dream I fly.
And I would fly
to nestle near your child's lake,
to press my needs upon your feather hands.
There at the lake,
in the shadow of the celt
I find there,
I dance in your spine's darkness;
I clothe you in your spirit's darkness
and in your body's darkness.
I awake to the light of your total darkness.
I keep, for my constant spring,
your feather hands upon my eyes.
My eyes will always take
the dark path to your heart.

My heart will drink its light
from the only heavy hands
                              you offer me.
Death of the dark. Death of the light.
I live in my spirit's web of love's
                         transcendent night.

LOVE IN THE WEATHER'S BELLS

Snow hurries
the strawberries
from the bush.
Star-wet water rides
you into summer,
into my autumn.
Your cactus hands
are at my heart again.
Lady, I court
my dream of you
in lilies and in rain.
I vest myself
in your oldest memory
and in my oldest need.
And in my passion
you are the deepest blue
of the oldest rose.
Star circle me an axe.
I cannot cut myself
from any of your emblems.
It will soon be cold here,
and dark here;
the grass will lie flat
to search for its spring head.
I will bow again
in the winter of your eyes.
If there is music,
it will be the weather's bells
to call me to the abandoned chapel
of your simple body.

THE CROSSES MEET

Patiently, I set your seat
in cedar and a bit of god,
and by its arms
I cross our lives.
And then I turn your body
toward the wind,
my path from worship
to certainty.
Now, may I house
my woman's meaning
in angels and in stone.
I hold this pagan three-in-one
under your lips
and under your last sign.
Could, now, I trade
your daemons for her body,
I would cut the hardwood
of your seat to peace.
But can you hear me
when I press my preservation
at her knees,
and leap from the tangle
of your seated cross
to the bell of my own voice
at her worship?
You hear me
as I walk from dark
                      to dawn
to save you.
And so I do save you
when my voice
is at her service.
I serve and preserve myself
in her grace.
I sit her on the tangled
stool of grace.
I take her voice alone
to rule in my politic body.

At last your crosses meet
in the love above love,
in the word that spells itself
                    in silence,
and I am the carpenter
of your new spirit
that speaks to hear itself
                    in stone.

LOVE PLUMBS TO THE CENTER OF THE EARTH

I will live with winter
and its sorrows.
Here, the earth folds its blanket
                    at noon.
The eastern crown appears,
disappears,
appears
to lie in pine
on the west ridge.
Some light has been lost;
a stillness has been betrayed.

I seem to feel your body
shake that stillness through the deep
water which separates us now.
Your husband, my father,
plumb of the earth
from our air to his,
lies in the silence of water
we gave to him.

You say you sit at night afraid,
and count the gifts you carried
                    to his bed.
I know that they contain
this fear of the winter's sorrows,
this offense of being left above
the deep water
to pluck this plumb string

for a tremor of love.
But it isn't the melody of loss
you have in your moon bucket,
nor the certainty of a line
                    to your own pain.
The clamor that rides this line
unhinges sorrow,
unburdens its beatific companions.
This single string,
a heart's flow,
is a music of possession.
And so you twin me
in the plain song of survival,
in the deep chant of winter
and its own sun.
Our balance is that body
and the sun extended
                    from our grief.

2
Today,
nine days
after the hunters have gone,
a buck walks from the forest,
and nuzzles at my snow-heavy trees.
I crown him king of the noon,
and watch the light drip from his coat.
In these woods,
his light is a darkness,
an accommodation with winter
and its mid-day shroud.
And, if at night, the moon
holds down its spoon cup,
he will be fed by light
that holds the darkness in it.
His body is the plumb line
the stars shake upon our earth.
Now, will I dare to follow
and to name his steps

through every darkness of our earth,
or shall I turn from that light
to my own winter's light?

3

Left. Right.
Turn. And counterturn.
I would have my foundation stone.
And so I carefully turn my words
about your longing.
Soil, water, root and seed,
the pin of light on which your love
will ride to air finds and turns
in the heart of each of its possessions.
You own me in the grief
                           you will not bear,
and in the act you will not name.
You crown my darkness in your silence,
and you crown me king of my engendered light.
If I possess a seat to rule,
I rule love's coming and the taut
sound of my father's voice in you.
Voices of that deep water stretch
into heaven on a thin line filled
with all we do not possess.

THE UNWEDDING OF THE MAGDALENE OF THE VINE

Down, on your bare feet,
with a wicker basket of tomatoes,
you come to the courtyard of blue roses,
rare garden on a rare day,
and you are pinioned in the waterfall
from which the day would seem to rise.
I rise on the curl of your hair into ecstasy;
my love boat knocks from shore to dark green shore.
The birds go braying where I hide
                           my intaglio of you.
This is my Mary lock and locket,

my chalice and the box I will not open.
Clearly, you have pruned me from your vines.
I know you through the earth's rising
and through the candles which you light
at your grandmother's grave.
Your red fruit defines a day you took from her bones,
sets my limits, calls my wedding bells.
Magdalene of the vine,
I would be free of the wicker of your day's duty,
your barter bays from dawn to twilight.
But in the waterfall's night, I hear you
call your familiar faces against me.
A Jesus of my continent veils your voices.
I am at rest as a shaker of serpents.
I once had a dervish depth to dapple you.
I once had my love's sorrow
                                        to draw you near me.
Now, I follow you down the sunshine,
and know the blood of the earth in the fruit,
the white pull of your bones upon the earth.
Now, here, I take the waterfall to wash
this stain of marriages from me.
I will not have you as my duty to the earth,
nor take the white pull of your bones
to reason with my days.
I have pitted your bare feet and wicker basket
against the jealous redness of my stripped love.
Unwed, I accept your turning of this our earth.

LOVE'S COLDNESS TURNS TO THE WARMTH OF PATIENCE

My blanket smells of burnt apples.
My hair is tangled in smoky birch.
I sleep. I wake to watch the snow
ease itself around the shivering hills,
the same ice tick off in islands on the lake.
In all these silent postures,
I burrow into the memory of winter,

and fall, past your warmth,
into the high air of your heart.
Now, I am with you when the birds
circle and redeem their own air
and press the sun to hide their losses
in rainbows and serpent skins,
and, while you read their Zeno's flight,
I read your stillness.
                              I see now
in your eye the birds are bronzed
to be set near our temples in the wood.
Water and bronze, the birds curled on a staff
lead me to the purity of my own coldness,
down where what is lit is still unseen
and the blind light is the token
                              of your only star.
For who hopes for what he sees?
But if we hope for what we do not see,
we wait for it in patience.
I wait for the turning to teach me
what can be seen and what,
as I sit near my north star,
my lost green wood reveals.
I take the clothing of my memory's winter
as a sign that you are patient still.
Surely, I am my own flight into stillness
and into the cadence of a necessary cold.
I comfort you in the bed of charity,
my soul redeemed in your body's expected fire.

NEW ADAM'S CROSS

Dove, I offer you my hand,
and, from my shadows,
try to contain your sacred flight.
If I can name you or your flight,
I contain you. Berry lady,
I say love is your succulence.

Or are you my moonfall at the waterfall?
I know you are the blue bead
and the chicken kick, the diamond
or the gold stuck upon my stool.
At noon, I hear your frothy roll
bleat upon my grove's shores.
You come in the rain, you come in the wind,
you come in the eastern star; rose and redhead,
lily of the desert, my balm and blackness,
you surround me with your signs
and with your perfect body.
If now I am Adam,
you are my Eve of morning
and yet you cannot take your form
from my desire or from the gods' design.
I know my lure is useless.
I know I lie in shadows
because I cannot see your true light.
I say all light appears in darkness,
and every body rises against emptiness.
I say I know you through your mother
and my uncertain knowledge of her body
and her spirit. I know you as the web of my
father's spirit's weave and caress you
as the infinite water sign you weave.
Is love the name you weave?
And do I stand in the white milk of dawn
with only a red star for a sign
and watch my only horse split the air
and watch you wave your benediction at our backs?
And through your transparent body
can I see old palm leaves become
my first dwelling,
my first altar stone,
my first bride's first bed,
my fire,
my first grave?
Do I see you as the first example of my being,
or as the oldest road I take into my being?
You are the cross my body hangs
upon its spirit, the light my eyes will take

to read these oldest questions.
I am not all of you, you draw away from me.
I break my unillumined bones.

LOVE AS THE LIMIT AND GOAL

What in me is best
I lead to the hard stone
under the sun,
or to the dark habitation
of the blessed dead
where love's music
will be cut from my ear,
my body laid to serve
a constant light.
The subject of my own desire,
I am egg and synapse,
the body's pulsing measure,
the gold and purple of the light
about my days.
And so I invest myself,
invest you, with all
by which I dispossess you.
Now, when I beat my temple drum
and shake my bell
and praise my love in you,
I see the altar lock its heart
against your ecstasy.
The burden of the key,
under the rainbow,
rides you still.
You take the corn
for the thread of your skirt.
Love is the limit and the goal
by which that death is measured.
This love is the kinship of the saints
we bleed to make us worthy.
I turn from the order

of this constant dispossession
to awaken my body to the spirit's
historical sign, the logic of my soul
enlightened by your grounded eye.
I turn from possession of your oneness
to the vision of your twin acts,
the breaking of the ground from which I rise,
invested with the light my grave reveals.

THREE POEMS

MICHAEL S. HARPER

PEACE ON EARTH

Tunes come to me at morning
prayer, after flax sunflower
seeds jammed in a coffee can;

when we went to Japan
I prayed at the shrine
for the war-dead broken
at Nagasaki;

the tears on the lip of my soprano
glistened in the sun.

In interviews
I talked about my music's
voice of praise to our oneness,

them getting caught up in techniques
of the electronic school

lifting us into assault;

in live sessions, without an audience
I see faces on the flues of the piano,

cymbals driving me into ecstacies on my knees,

the demonic angel, Elvin,

answering my prayers on African drum,

on *Spiritual*

and on *Reverend King*

we chanted his words
on the mountain, where the golden chalice
came in our darkness.

I pursued the songless sound
of embrochures on *parisian thoroughfares,*

the coins spilling across the arched
ballustrade against my feet;

no high as intense as possessions
given up in practice

where the scales came to my fingers

without deliverance,
the light always coming at 4 A.M.

Syeeda's "Song Flute" charts
my playing for the ancestors;

how could I do otherwise,

passing so quickly in this galaxy

there is no time for *being*

to be paid in *acknowledgment;*

all praise to the phrase brought to me:

salaams of becoming:

A LOVE SUPREME:

A NARRATIVE OF THE LIFE AND TIMES
OF JOHN COLTRANE: PLAYED BY HIMSELF
Hamlet, North Carolina

I don't remember train whistles,
or corroding trestles of ice
seeping from the hangband,
vaulting northward in shining triplets,
but the feel of the reed on my tongue
haunts me even now, my incisors
pulled so the pain wouldn't lurk
on "Cousin Mary";

in High Point I stared
at the bus which took us to band
practice on Memorial Day;
I could hardly make out, in the mud,
placemarks, separations of skin
sketched in plates above the rear bumper.

Mama asked "what's the difference
'tween North and South Carolina,"
a capella notes of our church choir
doping me into arpeggios,
into *sheets of sound* labeling me
into dissonance.

I never liked the photo taken with
Bird, Miles without sunglasses,
me in profile almost out of exposure:
these were my images of movement;
when I hear the sacred songs,
auras of my mother at the stove,
I play the blues:

what good does it do to complain:
one night I was playing with Bostic,
blacking out, coming alive only to melodies
where I could play my parts:

And then, on a train to Philly,
I sang "Naima" locking the door
without exit no matter what song
I sang; with remonstrations on the ceiling
of that same room I practiced in
on my back when too tired to stand,
I broke loose from crystaline habits
I thought would bring me that sound.

DRIVING THE BIG CHRYSLER
ACROSS THE COUNTRY OF MY BIRTH

I would wait for the tunnels
to glide into overdrive,
the shanked curves glittering with
truck tires, the last four bars
of Clifford's solo on "Round Midnight"
somehow embossed on my memo stand.

Coming up the hill from Harrisburg,
I heard Elvin's magical voice
on the tynes of a bus going to Lexington;
McCoy my *spiritual anchor*—
his tonics bristling in solemn
gyrations of the left hand.

At a bus terminal waiting to be taken
to the cemetery, I thought of Lester
Young's chinese face on a Christmas
card mailed to my house in Queens: Prez!
I saw him cry in joy as the recordings
Bird memorized in Missouri breaks
floated on Bessie's floodless hill:
Backwater Blues; I could never play
such sweetness again: Lady said Prez
was the closest she ever got to real
escort, him worrying who was behind
him in arcades memorizing his tunes.

Driving into this Wyoming sunset,
rehearsing my perfect foursome,
ordering our lives on off-days,
it's reported I'd gone out like Bird
recovering at Camarillo,
in an off-stage concert in L.A.

I never hear playbacks of that chorus
of plaints, Dolphy's lovefilled echoings,
perhaps my mother's hands
calling me to breakfast, the Heath
Brothers, in triplicate, asking me to stand
in; when Miles smacked me for being *smacked
out* on "Woodn't You," I thought how many
tunes I'd forgotten in my suspension
on the pentatonic scale; my solos
shortened, when I joined Monk he drilled
black keys into registers of pain, joy
rekindled in McCoy's solo of "The Promise."

What does Detroit have to give my music
as elk-miles distance into shoal-lights,
dashes at sunrise over Oakland:
Elvin from Pontiac, McCoy from Philly,
Chambers from Detroit waltzing his bass.
I can never write a bar of this music
in this life chanting towards paradise
in this sunship from Motown.

LATE COLTRANE

A RE-MEMBERING OF ORPHEUS

KIMBERLY W. BENSTON

*The power of music . . . to unfix and as it were clap wings
to solid nature, interprets the riddle of Orpheus*

—EMERSON, "History"

LATE COLTRANE. THOSE ECSTATIC EBULLITIONS, ATTACKS ON EXPECTA-
tion and consciousness, furied emotiveness: all this we yet hear,
possess as records of a fierce and visionary *askesis*, of a quest for
cosmic knowledge and salvation. Through a passion of innovation,
John Coltrane perfected his own calculus of musical impossibility
—for him, the world became regenerated inwardly by the musical
afflatus.

The power of Trane was apparent from his first sessions with
Miles Davis in 1955 (*vide* "Ah-Leu-Cha"). But those awesome mani-
festations of the Coltrane genius—the late (post-1962) compositions—
come after many often tortuous dissolutions, reformations, and re-
crystallizations of approach as the "heaviest spirit" (Imamu
Baraka's encomium) traveled the road from apprentice to rebel
to creative master.

Ultimately, passages in Trane's music became so bright and so
piercing that the sounds seemed to be words, or cries deeper than
words. He discerned or discovered for Afro-American music what
Rilke called "the language where languages end." Music became
the externalization of the *telos* within; it reflected Trane's attempt
to respond with fidelity to the incognito name and nature of our
universe. In turn, as he carried his horn in search of what he termed
"Selflessness," Trane himself became the sun and the node, the
zero point of the universe, and all things (incarnated by a variety of
rhythmic/percussional accompaniments) swirled in dynamic flux
around him. He knew the sense in which music could conceive the
very possibility of the future and then furnished that future in
joyous and terrified anticipation, thus preparing all of us (tech-
nically as musicians, spiritually as kinsmen) to inhabit it. For in the

last works of Coltrane, as in the late quartets of Beethoven, we witness genius challenging hitherto unglimpsed realms of imagination and expression and, in the same effort, somehow conquering them. We witness, in short, the mystery of the Orphic dismemberment and restitution: the destructive-creative threat to and recovery of Expression itself.

The effort of this essay is to touch upon the salient and haunting aspects of Coltrane's last phase. Only one dimension of Trane's final achievement is strictly musical: the stylistic, structural development which is carried by the actual notes. Equally important, however, are the cultural, aesthetic, and spiritual ideas which the music evokes: the links to contemporary Afro-American revolts, to the modern "black aesthetic," to the blues root of jazz impulses.

At every stage of this exploration we will discern a lineament of Orpheus who, above all for us, represents mastery of life through the power to create harmony amid the stillness of primordial silence or the ferocity of discord. For Orpheus, the savage beasts and Furies stand mute and listen. Yet a dark future awaits the vates, a violent destiny concealed (though perhaps also provoked) by the lyre's sound. The frenzied Maenads tear him to pieces, severing head from body. The voice of Orpheus seems to offend life in some hidden and primal way. Whatever that sin may be, expression, as signal of an emergent consciousness, is complicit in it. The mad jealousy of nature (the uncontrollable women) spends itself against a competing voice of fury, the Orphic hunger to order existence.

Trane partook of this Orphic fury, a metaphysical revolt without metaphysical surrender, a dialectic of violence in which the very being of man is put on trial. For if the Orphic voice is a response to Nature's chaos, it is also an appeal to man's own inner being, to the "perfection" and "deep peace" Trane sought for us all. It invokes a reordering of life by an alteration of consciousness; it summons apocalypse in its original sense of revelation by penetrating the moment's perplexities to the heart of awareness. Fury and Apocalypse: these are the obsessions of the Afro-American's Orphic imagination, the vital and dangerous necessities of its existence.

For the modern black art of which Trane was a prime mover, fury envisions apocalypse as the artist engages Euro-American culture in an agonistic relationship. This apocalypse is something more than the destruction conceived by the oppressed as retribution against their enemies. Implied in it is a nearly total rejection of Western history and civilization. The revolt of the Afro-American artist against specific literary or social conventions is, at bottom, a rebellion against authority and the memory of imposed systems. As trumpeter Clifford Thornton (alumnus of the fabulous Sun Ra cabal) declared, true revolution of consciousness begins by a radical "un-learning" of existent modes. It is not an improvement or modification of available techniques that the black artist requests; rather, his call is for an entirely new grammar, a "post-Western form" (Baraka et al.). Divorced from the enveloping society, he sets out on a fresh journey into the uncharted spaces of the self. He courts the dismembering anger of the herd by undertaking the liberating psychic descent.

Modern black culture wants to remake, to reconceive, that fundamental activity of mind we call art. It has come to realize, however, that all real transformations in the form of expression, all fruitful adventures in that domain, can only take place within a transformation of the idea of expression itself. Thus, while the new "black aesthetic" turns inside-out all the pieties of life and art, speaking outlandishly in no language we ordinarily hear, it still speaks for the life and increase presumably afforded by a new syntax of desire. That it has dared to do so in such assertive tones is certainly attributable to the startling discoveries of contemporary jazz musicians.

The sounds of John Coltrane, Ornette Coleman, Sonny Rollins, Sun Ra, Cecil Taylor, Albert Ayler, Archie Shepp, Pharaoh Sanders, and their fellow travelers unfolded before the black poet a new kingdom, a world which has little in common with the systematized reality around him, and in which he leaves behind all concrete feelings in order to discover within himself an ineffable longing. The "new wave" jazz—having extended and mastered the contribution of bebop—opened the floodgates of passion, anger, pain, and love, and aroused that fury for liberty which is the essence of the new black art. It joined itself to earlier, major epochs of black music by reaffirming the creative union between the improvising soloist and the total musical collective. But it also forged a new role for music in the hierarchy of black expressions—that of guide rather than mere analogue to other communicative modes.

The root of the black writers' elevation of music to a position of supremacy among the arts lies in the music's aversion for fixed thoughts and forms. By the very fact of its "otherworldliness," of its independence of values derived from empirical and alien experiences, it enters the Afro-American's consciousness on its own, necessarily general, terms. And because of their independence from familiar, "Western" idioms, these terms represent for the new artists the ethos of black nature with an absoluteness and an intensity denied to other creative media.

The thought of giving to words and prosody values equivalent to music is an ancient one, in African and Afro-American as well as Western culture. But with modern black literature, it assumes the force of a specific idea: the notion that black language leads *toward* music, that it passes into music when it attains the maximal pitch of its being. This belief contains the powerful suggestion that music is the ultimate lexicon, that language, when truly apprehended, aspires to the condition of music and is brought, by the poet's articulation of black vocality, to the threshold of that condition. Thus, in the verse of Baraka, Larry Neal, Alice Walker, Etheridge Knight, Michael Harper, and countless others, the poem, by a gradual transcendence of its own forms, strives to escape from the linear, logically determined bonds of denotative speech into what the poet imagines as the spontaneities and freedoms of musical form. Black poetry now unabashedly seeks the unfettered lyricism of "actual music" (Haki Madhubuti) for it is in music that the poet hopes to achieve both the individual creation—the *call* bearing the shape of his own spirit—and communal solidarity—the *response* of infinite renewal.

From Henry Dumas's Probe ("Will the Circle Be Unbroken?") to Ishmael Reed's Loop Garoo Kid (*Yellow Back Radio Broke-Down*), the artist in modern black fiction is, archetypically, a musician (especially a horn player); for it is only in music that aesthetic conventions can touch upon both the pure energy and improvisational wit necessary for survival in the black diaspora. This faith in the dominion of music leads the black poet to experiment in the use of words for their musical effect, inducing a mood proper to the experience, not of the static text, but of the jam session performance. The fullest statements of this hope, of this merging of the word with the musical ideal, can be found in the myriad poems directly inspired by Coltrane. The "Coltrane poem" has, in fact, become an unmistakable genre of black poetry and it is in such works—by Ebon, Madhubuti, Sonia Sanchez, Carolyn Rodgers, A. B. Spellman, and Harper, to list but a few—that the notion of music as the quintessential idiom, and of the word as its prelude and annunciator, is carried to an apex of technical and philosophic implication. Harper's "Dear John, Dear Coltrane," for example, in the brooding intensity of its incantatory lyricism, turns upon a metaphor of cosmic, and searing, musicality. It images the black man's spirit, Trane's essence, as a resolve to play the elemental notes despite the Orphic rending:

> there is no substitute for pain:
> genitals gone or going . . .
>   You pick up the horn
> with some will and blow
> into the freezing night:
> *a love supreme, a love supreme.*

All the poets, like Harper, felt in Trane's music the self-commitment to an exalted state, the "will" to pass beyond apparent limits of material (including political) existence or of mere method. Listening to Trane, they sensed that formal entities no longer derived from the dicta of an inherited tradition but from the spiritual unity of the artist's vision. Since this vision was inimical to existing structures, the traditional artistic forms would be incapable of containing them, and new forms, expressing the new attitudes and offering new stimuli, would necessarily arise. They did arise. And Trane's was the most magical of formal revolutions.

II

> ... The poet's limbs lay scattered
> Where they were flung in cruelty or madness,
> But Hebrus River took the head and lyre
> And as they floated down the gentle current
> The lyre made mournful sounds, and the tongue murmured
> In mournful harmony.

—OVID, *Metamorphoses,* Book Eleven

Whether the Maenads dismembered Orpheus at the behest of Dionysus or, as Ovid suggested, in a fit of sexual pique, one thing is clear: this supreme creator was the victim of an inexorable clash between the Dionysian principle, represented by the Maenad's ungovernable zeal, and the Apollonian ideal which he, as maker of songs, venerated. The power of Dionysus—which civilization inevitably tends to suppress—erupts with a vengeance. In the process, energy may overwhelm order, expression may burst into scream or dissolve into silence. The deformation of Orpheus is thus an attack on form itself. Yet, as Orphic bearer of new black culture, the Afro-American rebel-artist needs and celebrates his ancestrally privileged energy, and so must always risk the annihilation. On the other hand, should he fall too far back into the Dionysian sources of fervor, should he avoid all abstraction and structure, he will have expunged the motive for his being: the healing of the fractured communal will.

This complex tension is strongly felt behind the technical ingenuities of Coltrane's music. Its assault on form has, in all probability, no exact parallel in the history of Afro-American music. It is at once more various, destructive, and self-conscious than its precedents; it challenges the idea of form itself and resolves that challenge by forcing new demands on every aspect of the medium. No category of space or time, order or chaos, arrangement or improvisation, solo or ensemble, tone or mode remains quite intact after this upheaval of the imagination. Yet it is worth remarking, particularly in view of the misleading impression left by Trane's critics and admirers alike, that the supersession of established formal principles did not lead to formlessness, to an irreparable splintering of the Orphic lyre. The dynamic power that Trane and his "new wave" brethren unleashed seemed to shatter the very possibility of clarity and form—such was the force of the new content that was being freshly conceived. But there is a rigorous inner logic at the root of those works which, upon scrutiny, makes it hard to believe they were "amorphous," "random," or simply "shucking," as critics claim.

The late pieces present the greatest task for a structural explanation of Trane's career—they are in every way the summit. But, even in such a brief exposition of Trane's style as this will be, there is a path to be traced before one reaches that summit, before one can breathe its rarefied air. Trane came on the scene during the late flowering of bebop, establishing his presence under the tutelage of bop masters Dizzy Gillespie, Thelonious Monk, and Miles Davis. Until its first crucial turn in the early sixties, his style was a meticulous, intense development of Charlie Parker's vertical (harmonic) experimentation with melody and the chord. Trane's challenge to harmonic patterns, like Bird's, was principally rhythmic and, though seemingly anti-lyrical, was an attempt to liberate melody as well as tempo from the harmonic prison. The exploratory harmonic changes, coupled with sharp juxtapositions of asymmetric rhythmic shards, produced the "driving" momentum that remained a hallmark of Trane's method. In this era of "apprenticeship" (beautifully exemplified by the 1958 Miles Davis recordings), Trane mastered his impulse toward (chordal) progression, moving through arpeggios and three- or four-note scale fragments with remarkable alacrity and dexterity.

As Ornette Coleman undertook his revolution against bebop by discarding vertical for horizontal (melodic, thematic) improvisation, Trane began to undermine the chordal approach from within, by a systematic dissection and scattering of the individual chord. Rather than employing the intervals within or around the chord, Trane began to utilize the chromatic scale implied by the chord. Bird had a very advanced sense of the vertical sequence of intervals that make up the chord but it took Trane to liberate harmony, the relation of chords, from rigid tonal and stepwise progressions. His new chromatic relation to the chord, the playing of many chords upon or within a single implied chord, led to the famous *glissando* of his "sheets of sound." By the time of such Coltrane standards as "My Favorite Things" (first recorded in 1960), "Africa" (1961), and "Afro-Blue" (1963), Trane's rapid and free movement through various tones left him fairly bursting at the chord barrier. "I found," he remarked, "that there were a certain number of chord progressions to play in a given time, and sometimes what I played didn't work out in eighth notes, sixteenth notes, or triplets. I had to put the notes in uneven groups like fives and sevens in order to fit them all in." As a result, melody was achieved through polyrhythmic attack, 4/4 being explored increasingly over 3/4 for its greater flexibility. Trane was discovering that "these implied rhythms give variety" and that emancipation from chords provided vast room for improvisation. The near-frantic, yet ever-controlled flights through the register, from the growling lower to the screeching upper regions, were the exultant shouts of this new-found freedom.

In the late works, the redirection of Trane's characteristic swing from vertical progression to a multi-directional unfurling of diverse tempos and tonalities allowed him to "get in" all his new visions. What he was fighting for, as do all Afro-American artists, was an expanse sufficient to contain natural expressiveness, "living space" (to borrow the title of one of Trane's most intrepid late explorations) for a new race of men, yet unborn. The turbulence of this struggle is felt so awesomely in Trane partly because bare particles of musical form were made the crucibles of his explosive experimentation. Indeed, in the works of 1963 and after, form—as static or pure structure—feels content—as intensity of statement—straining its contours. Trane's music performed the grand, simple gesture of opening the infinity of form that makes content understandable, believable. His sharp melodic and rhythmic phrases took on their own multiforms, thereby creating an unexampled shape scarcely describable.

This quest for uninhibited musical freedom took several directions. Trane mastered a new instrument—the soprano saxophone—bringing that medium out of oblivion and to heights of lyric beauty comparable, perhaps, only to those achieved by Trane's avowed model, Sidney Bechet. He worked with a plethora of groupings (especially after the marvelous quartet of Trane, McCoy Tyner—piano—Jimmy Garrison—bass—and Elvin Jones—drums—disbanded), adding some instruments (including those of Africa and the East), doubling others, and consequently creating the first meaningful large ensemble works since Ellington. But the major acquisitions of space were made within the realm of the notes themselves. Influenced partly by nondiatonic aspects of Indian and African music, Trane moved completely away from both fixed tonality and strict verticality toward pan-modal, chromatic articulation. Chords, whether singular or multi-layered, were simply cut loose from any tonal center of gravity. In the music of *Interstellar Space* (a suite composed of "Mars," "Venus," "Jupiter," and "Saturn"), for example, each piece appears at first to rest upon a pentatonic scale but becomes ultimately a virtual cyclone of tonal assertion, moving in and out of the original scale's values. As complex as Rashied Ali's rhythmic ground becomes, Trane never stammers, tempo itself having been liberated from the "plot" of strictly vertical, strictly diatonic playing. As in all the late works, particularly those of the final period initiated by "Ascension" (1965), Trane here separates himself from the inner sphere of tones and becomes master of them. There ensues an electrifying vibration back and forth between one motif and another, producing a coruscating surface of shimmering timbre and pitch in which all things are continuously transformed in the tonal flux. In this manner, Trane achieved, like Bird and Louis Armstrong before him, the consummate act of generalization, of translating a private, obviously intolerable hurt into a code of public statement.

It is worth noting that, for all their apparent affinities, Coltrane's revolution in jazz improvisation and contemporary experiments in Euro-American avant-garde music are essentially dissimilar. The music of the white avant-garde, in its revolt from the "purposeful," teleological art of Western culture, is anti-tonal in order to be directionless, unkinetic, goalless. Its systematic use of chance as a technique of composition is designed to create sounds without syntactical-grammatical relationships, sounds as individual, discrete, objective sensations. The movement's foremost composer, John Cage, signals this phenomenological urge with his injunction to "let sounds be themselves rather than vehicles for man-made theories or expressions of human sentiments" (*Silence*). Hence the Euro-American modernists want tones without specific implications, not to create more space for the mind's free-play, but to drain the will from the act and arena of creation. In their work, as Ihab Hassan (the Gabriel of modern Euro-American Orphism) points out, "forms define themselves by their absence, their felt omissions." For them, mutilation is self-inflicted.

Trane and his followers' music is, as Frank Kofsky has observed, *not* atonal. They find themselves exhilarated, not exhausted, in the face of formal possibility. But the distinction between them and their Euro-American contemporaries runs deeper than the mechanics or even philosophy of form. For, to the Afro-American artist in search of his nation's potential, what could be more horrid than the denial of human will? As Harper saw, Trane's spirit was always Faustian in the Goethean sense, always striving for greater "manifestations" (Trane's word) of excellence. "There is never any end," Trane declared. "There are always new sounds to imagine, new feelings to get at. And always, there is the need to keep purifying these feelings and sounds so that we can really see what we've discovered in its pure state." Or, as Alice Coltrane, speaking for us as well as Trane, marvels: "He never stopped surprising himself."

III

He [Orpheus] has to vanish, so you'll understand:
Even though himself he fears this evanescence.
For while his word surpasses this existence,

He's gone alone already in the distance.
The lyre's grating does not curb his hands.
He is obedient, even when he transgresses.

—RILKE, "Sonnets to Orpheus"

If, in his capacity for surprise, Trane knew the scope and holiness of sound, he also divined the plenum of silence. Pauses and silences are often the climaxes of his late works, the still centers of the prophetic storm, the nuclei of tension around which the whole movement is structured. The more one listens the more those silences seem to be among the first causes of the overall effect. This is, again, partly a technical consideration. From pieces as early as the Miles Davis/hard-bop works, Trane was leaving large rests within lines, delicately spacing bursts of triplets, in the effort to achieve rhythmic variation within given harmonic limits. When his playing became liberated from the centripetal force of tonality, time became *his* prisoner and silence a consequent choice *against* time—a choice that facilitated expansion within the ultimately temporal musical order. The authority of the silences is a direct consequence of the late pieces' density of texture: each note and each rest is part of an integrated design of utmost economy and vigor. The mystical effect, to paraphrase Nathalie Sarraute's account of the new, "nontonal" novel, is that of a time that is no longer the time of our intended life, but of a hugely amplified present.

But this dialectic of sound and silence betokens more than just a technical imperial expansion over wide, new territories. Trane's is the silence of Orphic utterance momentarily stilled, of the voice that temporarily ceases singing in the face of mystery, only to embrace a new strain that will henceforward echo this silence, but *in song.* This silence presupposes the possibility of song and the relevance of expression to the life of the individual soul and the community. Trane, like his African forebears, was delving for the primal Sound that lends music its magical quality. The very possibility of such discovery, he intuited, begins in the silence of the quest, what Kenneth Burke termed the hunter's "silence of purposiveness."

Again, let us pause to distinguish this mystic silence of Trane from that of the Euro-American innovators. John Cage, once more, is the avant-garde's spokesman: "What we re-quire is silence. . . . Inherent silence is equivalent to denial of the will" (*Silence*). This is the

silence of discontinuity and indeterminacy, the dumbness of a
fatigued will alienated from its aimless universe. It desires a mute
surrender of memory, a gradual and inevitable dissolution of human
possibility itself. It is, simply, silence that indicates retreat from
the hunt.

But if the hushed moments of Trane's late pieces indicate a hidden
abundance, they still seem to issue out of the struggle and terror
preludial to ecstatic fullness. In "Out of This World" (*Live in Seattle,*
1965), for example, one senses the occasional need to draw back
completely from the horns' aching crescendo lest the vision be
destroyed at the border of a new mode. In such passages Trane
accelerates, sometimes lyrically, sometimes painfully, toward an
intimation of that which lies beyond eloquence. And, in works such
as "Evolution," "Cosmos" (both on *Live in Seattle*), "Expression"
(1967), as well as in "Out of This World," one feels a refusal to
transgress the bounds of known (even though recently discovered)
discourse, and the furious quest is taken up again on the other side
of the pause. There, silence is deceptive repose, like the stillness as
one enters the eye of the hurricane.

Yet in other works—e.g., "Welcome," "Vigil," "Kulu Se Mama"
(all on *Kulu Se Mama,* 1965), and "Ogunde" (*Expression,* 1967)—
Trane relentlessly pursues the numenous, converging on the ineffa-
ble root of expression. On "Ogunde," the polyrhythms and mixed
tempos gradually condense ballad-like lines into a single moment.
Trane's fading tenor, so lyrical and playful and yet reverent until the
final epiphany, plays cat-and-mouse with Alice Coltrane's piano,
sculpting a deep and wide space in the line. As the notes grow
fainter, in wider intervals, the silence aspires to an impossible
concreteness and luminosity, as though resurrection could emanate
from the quiet of the void. The piece ignores the expectation of
closure aroused by the underlying ballad structure. Instead, as horn
gives way to piano, which in turn strikes, in stillness, a tentative
note in unresolved tonality, we are left with a chilling, thrilling
whisper of the Orphic dream—the quest that leads, endlessly, to a
music without notes.

IV

His head is
at the window. The only
part
　　　that sings.

—BARAKA, "A Poem for Willie Best," Part 8

The silences of Trane's last works ask a haunting question: must not the head of the vates be severed so that he may continue to sing? Must not the self be destroyed before a new being can be born? The exquisitely poised moments of these pieces are the loci at which this negation and affirmation coalesce. More than anything, they prepared the ground for Baraka's stunning appraisal of the Coltrane-led movement: "New Black Music is this: Find the self, then kill it."

Baraka, Coltrane's most sublime critic, was trying to express what anyone of artistic awareness sensed in the presence of a music more powerful, more anguished and celebratory than any in recent memory. But there is a source to this power, despite the blinding sparks of Trane's titanic assault on tradition (which I have, admittedly, stressed somewhat tendentiously). What he actually did was to obey an obscure but profound impulse to revolt against established conventions in order to rediscover convention on a deeper level. Specifically, Trane recalled, for himself and for his generation, the old cry and shout of the *blues*. This impulse can be felt throughout his career; in his construction of melody, he always maintained a hint of the blues' folk scales. When, in the later works, the tonal centers were mixed and shifted in rapid succession, the blues did not disappear. On the contrary, they were asserted more energetically, more *primally* in the sheer outpouring of shout, screech, wail and cry, in the uninhibited pitch and movement within the register. Listen to "Manifestation" (1966), to "The Father and the Son and the Holy Ghost" (1965), to "Transition" (1965). There are long patches there which are virtual encyclopedias of oral tradition, with grunt, scream, joke, and soothing speech all intended as confessions and calls to the people.

One feels the blues as naked vocality especially in recordings of Trane's *live* performances. Trane always sought to pull his audience into the force-field of his long, explosive solos. His ideal, like that of the earliest jazz masters, was one of *collective improvisation*. "When you know that somebody is maybe moved the same way you are," he once said, "it's just like having another member in the group." Again, the contrast with the white avant-garde is revealing. To the latter, demands for communication and participation are not only irrelevant but disruptive of the fundamental rage for disorder. It seeks the dismemberment and abhors any interruption of its own destruction. For Trane, as for all black artists, the community's involvement in a *ritual of restitution* is paramount. It is they who must ultimately—and continuously—re-member his total Orphic being.

Trane submitted his spirit ceaselessly to the dangerous complexities of Orphic existence. His art was never content to rest in any single phase of that existence; it was a struggle for integrity and survival whose dialectical character was insured by Trane's insistence that each new discovery implied a new problem and hence a new stage of awareness. The aim of such constant "purifying," Trane ever insisted, was "to see more clearly what we are."

To envision clearly what he and his people could be was Trane's life mission. He said: "My goal in meditating on the unity in life through music remains always the same. And that is to uplift people, as much as I can. To inspire them to realize more and more of their capacities for living meaningful lives." These are revolutionary words; his music was revolutionary action. It did not argue, it did not ridicule. It made manifest and what it manifested were the two parts of one fact, split apart, with an ominous and powerful silence between them. In the silence lies the answer, barely stated. The mind is forced to act. His music forced the mind into union with the will, which is the condition of revolutionary action. Music, like all art in quest of the self, can be revolutionary by teaching us to walk past old idols, smiling at some, kicking others to hear the hollow sound. And if, instead, as Shaw said, music is the brandy of the damned, then the Orphic spirit of John Coltrane surely lies, funky drunk, in the deepest part of hell.

FROM EXPERIENCE TO ELOQUENCE:
RICHARD WRIGHT'S *BLACK BOY* AS ART

CHARLES T. DAVIS

Native Son[1] is the work for which Richard Wright is best known, but *Black Boy,*[2] an autobiography more or less, may be the achievement that offers the best demonstration of his art as a writer. This idea is not so startling given Wright's special talents—the eye of a skilled reporter, the sensibility of a revolutionary poet, alert to varied forms of injustice, and the sense of symbolic meaning carried by the rituals of ordinary life. The problem up to the present time is not the lack of attention the work has received. Like *Native Son, Black Boy* was selected by the Book-of-the-Month Club and was thus assured a wide distribution and a serious if somewhat skewed reading from many critics. In 1970 Stanley Hyman, in reviewing Wright's entire career, assigned *Black Boy* to a period in which Wright's "important writing" occurred—according to his definition, Wright's last years as a resident in America, from 1940 to 1945.[3] But *Black Boy* by itself failed to acquire as an original work of art the reputation it deserves.

It appears now, from the perspective of a generation, that a measure of distortion was unavoidable, given the political temper of the time. The history of the publication of the manuscript entitled *American Hunger,*[4] of which *Black Boy* was a part, encouraged a violent political response. It was well known that "I Tried to Be a Communist," which appeared in the August and September issues of the *Atlantic Monthly* in 1944,[5] were chapters of an autobiographical record to be published the following year, even though they were excluded finally with the rest of the matter dealing with the years in Chicago and New York. When *Black Boy* did appear, knowing critics read the book in light of the much-publicized account of Wright's difficulties with the Communist party. Baldly put, the situation for the critic encouraged a form of outside intrusion, a case of knowing too much, of supplying a frame of reference which a reading of the basic text does not support. The board of the Book-of-the-Month Club or Edward Aswell or both,[6] in suggesting a restriction of autobiographical matter to the period before migration to Chicago, exercised a judgment that displayed something more than the good sense of successful editors; indeed, that judgment pointed up the artistic integrity of the work. Someone concluded accurately that the intensity of *Black Boy* came from a concentration upon one metaphor of oppression, the South, and prevented the diffusion of power that would be the consequence of the introduction of a second, the Communist party.

If the political reaction created one kind of distortion in the eye of the examiner, more normal literary expectations created another. *Black Boy* baffled W. E. B. Du Bois, the most impressive black intellectual of his time. His review in the New York *Herald Tribune* states his dilemma: ". . . if the book is meant to be a creative picture and a warning, even then, it misses its possible effectiveness because it is as a work of art so patently and terribly overdrawn." [7] By 1945 Du Bois had published three major works with outstanding autobiographical elements, one of which, *Dusk of Dawn,* was a fully developed autobiography of considerable intellectual distinction,[8] and he could not be accused of responding merely to a sense of affront to his middle-class sensibilities. Du Bois was not prepared to accept Wright's bleak Mississippi; he was appalled not so much by the condition of terror there as by a state of mind that denied the possibility of humanity for blacks and frustrated all black efforts to achieve satisfaction beyond the minimal requirements for life. After all, Du Bois had vivid memories of his experience as a young teacher in rural Tennessee, where he encountered aspiring, sensitive pupils who, though often defeated or betrayed by their environment, were not totally crushed by Southern oppression.[9] Moreover, Du Bois joined, no doubt, a group of critics of *Black Boy* best defined by Ralph Ellison as consisting of readers who complained that Wright had "omitted the development of his own sensibility." [10] But this is to define sensibility in a way generally understood by the nineteenth century, which is to hold that sensibility is an orderly accretion of the mind and heart within an environment recognizably human, and not to accept Wright's radical equation of the existence of sensibility with survival.

Du Bois did not doubt that autobiography could be art, though more naive critics might. He could not accept the principles of an art as austere as Wright's was, one in which many of the facts of Southern life, so familiar to him, were excluded and in which generalization had been carried to such extreme lengths. After all, the book's title was *Black Boy,* not "A Black Boy," [11] with an appropriately limiting modifier. Viewed superficially, Richard's odyssey was unique primarily because it had a happy ending—the escape from the hell of the South, where, apparently, all of his black associates (he had no friends in the narrative) were destined to spend the rest of their days. Wright's generalizations about the dehumanizing relationships between whites and blacks and the almost equally unsatisfying connections between blacks and blacks shaped his South, and these assumptions Du Bois thought to be distorted. One sweeping statement by young Wright in Memphis, where he lived from his seventeenth to his nineteenth year and where he committed himself formally to becoming a writer,[12] would certainly extract from Du Bois an expression of disbelief, if not annoyance: "I knew of no Negroes who read the books I liked and I wondered if any Negroes ever thought of them. I knew that there were Negro doctors, lawyers, newspapermen, but I never saw any of them. When I read a Negro newspaper I never caught the faintest echo of my preoccupation in its pages."[13]

Not only Du Bois, but also other blacks, even those lacking the knowledge of black life in America which Du Bois had acquired from his surveys and research projects at Atlanta University,[14] would be appalled at Richard's confession of his cultural isolation. This is a moment when generalization approaches fiction, when we must say that a statement may be acceptable within its context, but that it is questionable as a fact standing on its own, as something that might be supported by the confessions of other black boys, especially those emerging from families with middle-class aspirations and pretensions like Wright's.

Editing the raw matter of life is necessary, of course, to write an autobiography with any claim to art. No one has described this activity better than Ellison has in his critical examination of *Black Boy:* "The function, the psychology, of artistic selectivity is to eliminate from an art form all those elements of experience which contain no compelling significance. Life is as the sea, art a ship in which man conquers life's crushing formlessness. . . ."[15] What Ellison did not say is that such editing requires the use of controlling principles that are invariably fictional. This is to say that the organizing ideas are assumptions that are not strictly true according to the most objective criteria. Operating from a strict conception of the truth, we have every right to question the emotional basis for *The Education of Henry Adams,* an especially intense form of self-pity coming from the most widely cultivated American of his time, who, nonetheless, constantly reminds us of his lack of preparation for the nineteenth century, not to mention the twentieth. And in *Black Boy* we are asked to accept Richard's cultural isolation as well as his vulnerability to all forms of deprivation—physical, emotional, social, and intellectual.

Some critics, carried off by the impact of *Black Boy,* tend to treat the autobiography as if it were fiction. They are influenced by the fact that much great modern fiction, Joyce's *Portrait of the Artist as a Young Man,* for example, is very close to life. And the tendency here is reinforced by the fact that the author himself, Wright, is a creator of fictions. Yielding so is a mistake because many of the incidents in *Black Boy* retain the sharp angularity of life, rather than fitting into the dramatic or symbolic patterns of fiction. Richard's setting fire to the "fluffy white curtains" (p. 4), and incidentally the house, is not the announcement of the birth of a pyromaniac or a revolutionary, but testimony primarily to the ingenuity of a small black boy in overcoming mundane tedium. We must say "primarily" because this irresponsible act suggests the profound distress and confusion an older Richard would bring to a family that relied heavily upon rigid attitudes toward religion, expected behavior, and an appropriate adjustment to Southern life. Richard's fire is not Bigger's rat at the beginning of *Native Son,* when the act of killing brings out pent-up violence in the young black man and foreshadows, perhaps, the events of Book Two, "Flight," when Bigger's position becomes that of the cornered rat.[16] Nor does Richard's immodest invitation to his grandmother during his bath (p. 49) offer disturbing witness of the emergence of a pornographer or a connoisseur of the erotic; rather, it points to something more general, the singular perversity in Richard that makes him resist family and the South. In *Black Boy* we exist in a world of limited probability that is not life exactly, because there is an order to be demonstrated, and it does not display the perfect design of a serious fiction. We occupy a gray area in between. The patterns are here on several levels. Though they may not be so clear and tight as to permit the critic to predict, they do govern the selection of materials, the rendering of special emphases, distortions, and the style.

We seldom raise questions about what is omitted from an autobiography, yet if we wish to discover pattern, we must begin with what we do not find. The seasonal metaphor in *Walden* (we move from spring to spring) becomes all the more important once we realize that Henry Thoreau lived on the shore of Walden Pond more than two years.[17] Franklin's few "errata" [18] point up the strong aridity of an autobiography that touches so little on the traumas of the heart. Franklin's education, his achievements in business and science, and his proposals for the benefit of society seem at times supported by an emotional sub-structure far too frail. But the purposes of both autobiographies—in *Walden,* to offer the model of a renewed life; in the *Autobiography of Benjamin Franklin,* to sketch a convincing design of a successful life in the new world, one that emphasizes the practical values that most Americans admired and many Europeans envied—were achieved in part because of the shrewdness in excluding truthful, though extraneous matter. So, too, *Black Boy* profits from rigorous and inspired editing.

One function of the omissions is to strengthen the impression in our minds of Richard's intense isolation. This is no mean achievement given the fact that Wright was born into a large family (on his mother's side, at least) which, despite differences in personality, cooperated in times of need. The father, because of his desertion of his mother, was early in Richard's mind, perhaps in the sentiments of other family members, too, an object of hate and scorn. There are no names in the early pages of *Black Boy*, not even that of Richard's brother, Leon Allan, just a little more than two years younger than Richard. When the names begin to appear in *Black Boy*, they tend to define the objects of adversary, often violently hostile relationships—Grandmother Wilson, Aunt Addie, Uncle Thomas. Two notable exceptions are Grandfather Wilson, an ineffectual man capable only of reliving his past as a soldier in the Civil War, and Richard's mother, Ella, a pathetically vulnerable woman of some original strength who, because of continuing illness, slipped gradually into a state of helplessness that became for Richard symbolic of his whole life as a black boy in the South.[19]

The admirable biography of Wright by Michel Fabre suggests another dimension for Richard's opponents in his embattled household. The climax of the violence in the family occurred with the confrontation with Uncle Tom, portrayed as a retired and defeated schoolteacher reduced at the time to earning a living by performing odd jobs as a carpenter. Richard resented the fact that he was the victim of Uncle Tom's frustrations, and he responded to orders from the older man by threatening him with razors in both hands and by spitting out hysterically, "You are not an example to me; you could never be. . . . You're a *warning*. Your life isn't so hot that you can tell me what to do. . . . Do you think that I want to grow up and weave the bottoms of chairs for people to sit in?" (p. 140). A footnote from Fabre adds more information about the humiliated uncle:

The portrait of Uncle Thomas in *Black Boy* is exaggerated. After living with the Wilsons, he moved next door and became a real-estate broker. In 1938, he was a member of the Executive Committee of the Citizen's Civic League in Jackson and wrote a book on the word *Negro*, discussing the superiority complex of the Whites and its effects on the Blacks. At this time Richard put him in contact with Doubleday publishers and the uncle and the nephew were completely reconciled.[20]

Wright includes in *Black Boy* a touching description of meeting his father again after a quarter-century. As the newly successful author looked at a strange black sharecropper in ragged overalls holding a muddy hoe, the old resentment for past neglect faded: "I forgave him and pitied him as my eyes looked past him to the unpainted wooden shack" (p. 30). But *Black Boy* contains no softening reconsiderations of Uncle Tom, or of Aunt Addie, who, like her brother, seems to have possessed some redeeming qualities,[21] or of Granny Wilson for that matter. Their stark portraits dominate the family and define a living space too narrow, too mean, and too filled with frustration and poverty for an imaginative youngster like Richard.

A growing boy, when denied the satisfactions of a loving home, looks for emotional support at school or at play, and if he is lucky, he finds something that moderates domestic discontent. But there is little compensation of this sort in *Black Boy*. The reality of the life away from the family seems to be less bleak than Wright represents it, though his schooling was retarded by early irregularity because of the family's frequent moves, and his play restricted, perhaps, because of the family's desperate need for money and Granny's Seventh Day Adventist scruples. Once again we are struck by the absence of names—of teachers like Lucy McCranie and Alice Burnett, who taught Richard at the Jim Hill School in Jackson and recognized his lively intelligence,[22] or Mary L. Morrison or the Reverend Otto B. Cobbins, Richard's instructors in the eighth and ninth grades of the Smith-Robinson School,[23] to whose dedication and competence, despite personal limitations, Wright paid tribute elsewhere.[24] There was no question about his marginal status in these institutions, since Richard stood regularly at the head of his class.

Black Boy is singularly devoid of references to rewarding peer associations. There is no mention of Dick Jordan, Joe Brown, Perry Booker, or Essie Lee Ward, friends of this period and so valued that Wright was in touch with several of them ten years later when he was living in Chicago.[25] The fact that a few of Wright's childhood associates did succeed in making their way to Chicago has an amount of interest in itself, serving, as well, to break the isolation that Wright has fabricated so well. Among the childhood activities that went unrecorded were the exploits of the Dick Wright clan, made up of a group of neighborhood boys who honored in the name of their society, no doubt, their most imaginative member. The clan included Dick Jordan, Perry Booker, Joe Brown, and also Frank Sims, a descendant of a black senator during the Reconstruction period, Blanche K. Bruce.[26] What is amply clear, then, is that Wright had a childhood more than a little touched by the usual rituals and preoccupations of middle-class boys growing up in America, but what is also apparent is that reference to them would modify our sense of Richard's deprived and disturbed emotional life, a necessity for the art of the autobiography, rather more important than any concern for absolute accuracy.

Wright has little to say directly about sex. Richard's most serious temptation for sexual adventure comes toward the end of *Black Boy* in Memphis, when he is taken in by the Moss family. Richard succeeds in resisting the opportunity to take advantage of a cozy arrangement with Bess, the daughter whom Mrs. Moss seeks to thrust upon him, with marriage as her ultimate objective (p. 185). There are some indirect references to frustrated, sublimated, or distorted forms of sexual energy—in Miss Simon, certainly, the tall, gaunt, mulatto woman who ran the orphan home where Richard was deposited for a period (pp. 25-28). And there were exposures to white women, all calculated to teach Richard the strength of the taboo prohibiting the thought (not to mention the fact) of black-white sexual relations in the South. But Richard never takes an aggressive interest in sex; the adventures that he stumbles into create traumas when they are serious and unavoidable, or are embarrassing when he can resist participation and control his reactions. Wright, indeed, seems to be even more discreet than Franklin was; by comparison, Claude Brown is a raving sensualist in *Manchild in the Promised Land*, though roughly the same period of growth is involved. It is strange that so little space is given to sexual episodes and fantasies in the record of the gradual maturing of an adolescent—unbelievable, given the preoccupations of the twentieth century. We face the problem of omission again. Wright deliberately seeks to deprive his hero, his younger self, of any substantial basis for sensual gratification located outside his developing imagination. The world that *Black Boy* presents is uniformly bleak, always ascetic, and potentially violent, and the posture of the isolated hero, cut off from family, peer, or community support, is rigidly defiant, without the softening effects of interludes of sexual indulgence.

Richard's immediate world, not that foreign country controlled by whites, is overwhelmingly feminine. Male contacts are gone, except for occasional encounters with uncles. The father has deserted his home, and the grandfather is lost in the memories of "The War." The uncles tend to make brief entrances and exits, following the pattern of Hoskins, quickly killed off by envious whites in Arkansas, or the unnamed new uncle, forced to flee because of unstated crimes against whites (pp. 48-49, 57-60). Thomas is the

uncle who stays around somewhat longer than the others do, long
enough to serve as the convenient object for Richard's mounting
rebellion. The encounter with Uncle Tom is the culminating episode
marking a defiance expressed earlier against a number of authority
figures, all women—Richard's mother, Miss Simon, Grandmother
Wilson, Aunt Addie. Women dominate in Richard's world, with the
ultimate authority vested in Granny—near-white, uncompromising,
unloving, and fanatical, daring Richard to desecrate her Seventh
Day Adventist Sabbath. The only relief from feminine piety is the
pathetic schoolteacher who, in a happy moment, tells an enraptured
Richard about Bluebeard and his wives (p. 34). But even this
delight, moved in part, no doubt, by Bluebeard's relentless war
against females, is short-lived. Granny puts a stop to such sinning,
not recognizing, of course, the working out of the law of com-
pensation.

Richard's odyssey takes him from the black world to the white—
from the problems of home and family to new and even more
formidable difficulties. The movement is outward into the world,
to confront an environment that is not controlled by Granny, though
it provides much that contributes to an explanation of Granny's
behavior. Richard's life among blacks emphasizes two kinds of
struggle. One is simply the battle for physical existence, the
need for food, clothing, shelter, and protection that is the over-
whelming concern of the early pages of *Black Boy*. The second grows
out of Richard's deeply felt desire to acquire his own male identity,
a sense of self apart from a family that exerts increasing pressure
upon this growing black boy to behave properly, to experience
Christian conversion, and to accept guidance from his (mostly
female) elders. Survival in two senses, then, is the dominant theme,
one which does not change when he leaves the black community.
The terms are the same though the landscape is new. Richard
desperately seeks employment in white neighborhoods and in the
downtown business districts in order to contribute to the support
of his family. He discovers, when he does so, that the demand to
accommodate becomes even more insistent and less flexible than
that exerted by his own family.

The difference is that the stakes are higher. Richard thinks he
must find a job, any job, to earn a living. This awareness represents
a step beyond the simple dependence that moves a small boy to
complain, "Mama, I'm hungry" (p. 13). If he does not find work,
Richard feels that he has failed his family in an essential way and
made its survival precarious. Though his independence in the black
world leads to harsh sanctions—threats, bed without supper, whip-
pings—he is not prepared for the infinitely greater severity of the

white world. It is cruel, calculating, and sadistic. Richard never doubts that he will survive the lashings received from his mother, Granny, and assorted aunts and uncles, but he does question his ability to endure exposure to whites. The ways of white folks are capricious and almost uniformly malignant. Richard understands that the penalty for non-conformity, down to the way a black boy walks or holds his head, is not simply a sore body, but death. When Richard gives up a good job with an optical company, with a chance, according to his boss, to become something more than a menial worker, he does so because of the opposition exhibited by whites who think he aspires to do "*white* man's work." Richard confides to his boss when he leaves the factory: "I'm scared. . . .They would kill me" (p. 168).

From the woman who inquires of Richard, looking for yet another job, "Boy, do you steal?" (p. 128) to the two young men who attempt to arrange for Richard to fight another black boy for the amusement of an assembly of whites (pp. 209-10), we witness an unrelieved set of abuses. Certainly omission of some mitigating circumstances and artful distortion are involved in this bitter report. Richard is gradually introduced to a white world that grows progressively more dominant, divisive, and corrupting concerning the black life that serves it. Richard understands fully what is expected of him:

> I began to marvel at how smoothly the black boys acted out the roles that the white race had mapped out for them. Most of them were not conscious of living a special, separate, stunted way of life. Yet I know that in some period of their growing up—a period that they had no doubt forgotten—there had been developed in them a delicate, sensitive controlling mechanism that shut off their minds and emotions from all that the white race had said was taboo. (p. 172)

In Wright's South it was unthinkable for a black boy to aspire to become a lens-grinder, much less to harbor the ambition to become a writer. When Richard is thoughtless enough to reveal his true aim in life to one of his white employers, the response is predictable: "You'll never be a writer. . . . Who on earth put such ideas into your nigger head?" (p. 129). Given his difficulties in adjusting to an oppressive Southern system, Richard sustains his interest in writing through a monumental act of will. We are led to the inevitable conclusion that Richard must flee the South if he is to remain alive, and the desire to achieve an artistic career seems less important in light of the more basic concern for life itself.

We have every reason to suspect that the treatment of whites gains a certain strength from artistic deletion, too. Michael Fabre points out that Wright's relationship with a white family named Wall does not fit the pattern of abuse and brutal exploitation that emerges from the autobiography: "Although *Black Boy* was designed to describe the effects of racism on a black child, which meant omitting incidents tending to exonerate white persons in any way, there is no doubt that the Walls were liberal and generous employers. For almost two years Richard worked before and after class, earning three dollars a week bringing in firewood and doing the heavy cleaning." [27] Fabre adds, with reference especially to Mrs. Wall and her mother, "Since they respected his qualities as an individual, he sometimes submitted his problems and plans to them and soon considered their house a second home where he met with more understanding than from his own family." [28] This is not matter that reinforces a design displaying increasing difficulty for Richard as he moves outward and into contact with white society. Nor does it support Richard's growing conviction that his survival depends upon his escape from the South. The design of *Black Boy* offers an accelerating pattern of confrontations, taking into account both an increase in danger for Richard and a mounting seriousness in terms of society's estimate of his deviations. Like Big Boy, Richard must flee or die.

The narrator of *Black Boy* has three voices. The simplest records recollected events with clarity and a show of objectivity. We may be troubled by an insufficient context surrounding or an inadequate connection linking these episodes until we become aware of the suggestion of a psychological dimension for them. The incidents illustrate basic emotions: the discovery of fear and guilt, first, when fire destroys Richard's house; the experience of hate, directed this time toward the father, in killing the kitten; the satisfactions of violence, in defeating the teenage gang; the dangers of curiosity about the adult world, in Richard's early addiction to alcohol. The psyche of a child takes shape through exposure to a set of unusual traumas, and the child goes forth, as we have seen, into a world that becomes progressively more brutal and violent. Style in this way reinforces the first theme of the autobiography, survival.

It is in hearing the more complicated and lyrical second voice of the narrator that we sense for the first time another theme in the autobiography. This is the making of the artist. The world, we have been told, is cold, harsh, and cruel, a fact which makes all the more miraculous the emergence of a literary imagination destined to confront it. The bleak South, by some strange necessity, is forced to permit the blooming of a single rose. Wright expends upon the nourishment of this tender plant the care that he has given to describing the sterile soil from which it springs.

A third, didactic voice offers occasional explanations of the matter recorded by the other two. It comments at times upon the lack of love among blacks in the South, the distortions in human relationships involving blacks and whites, and corruption in the social and economic systems. At other times it advises us of the necessity for secrecy when a black boy harbors the ambition to write, and explains the difficulties which he confronts when he seeks to serve an apprenticeship to his art. Despite formidable opposition and the danger of complete isolation, this ambition lives and forces the growth of Richard's imaginative powers.

We do not begin simply with the statement of the intention to become an artist. We start, rather, as Joyce does in *A Portrait of the Artist,* with the sense experience that rests behind the word. Richard's memory offers rich testimony of the capacity to feel objects of nature, small and large. Not only these. We note that accompanying the record of sensations is the tendency to translate sensation into an appropriate emotion—melancholy, nostalgia, astonishment, disdain. All of the senses achieve recognition in Richard's memory, and all combine to emphasize memories of violent experiences: the killing of the chicken; the shocking movement of the snake; the awesome golden glow on a silent night (pp. 7-8).

Apart from this basic repository of sensation and image, we sense early in Richard two other qualities just as essential to the budding artist. One is detachment, the feeling of being different from others. In two worlds to which he is exposed, that of the family and then the more muddled arena of affairs, he rejects all efforts to moderate his apartness. Though conversion and subsequent baptism apparently point to joining the company of the saved, viewed in the conventional way, damnation is assured by the refusal to deliver the right kind of valedictory at the graduation exercises of his grammar school (p. 153). Barely passing one ritual, he flunks another. He maintains under pressure his status as an alien, so ultimately he will be free to exercise the imagination that faces the cold world.

The second quality is curiosity. His mother tells Richard that he asks too many questions. Our young hero is apparently undaunted by the fact that his insistent prying has led to one of the earliest addictions to alcohol recorded in literature. But another addiction is more serious, to the truth in the appearances about him. "Will you stop asking silly questions!" his mother commands (p. 42). About names, about color, about the relationship between the two. Curiosity constantly leads Richard to forbidden areas more menacing than the saloon, to the mysterious privileged province

of whites in Mississippi and the equally mysterious restriction of
the blacks.

A neat form of inversion is involved in the development of
Richard's artistic talent. We note that the qualities supporting
and sustaining the growing boy's imagination are just those pre-
venting a successful adjustment to life in the South. To achieve
a tolerable existence, not even a comfortable one, Richard must
have firm relationships with the members of his family and with
his neighbors and peers; to survive in the larger, white-dominated
society he must accept without questioning the inflexible system of
Southern mores and customs. Richard, rejecting these imperatives,
responds to the demands of his own imagination.

Richard's sensations in nature anticipate a discovery just as
valuable and far reaching. This is literature itself. Of the encounter
with *Bluebeard* Richard says, "My sense of life deepened. . . ."
He recalls, further, a total emotional response, emphasized, no
doubt, by the background of an unresponding family, and he
realizes that he stands on the threshold of a "gateway to a for-
bidden and enchanting land" (p. 36). So, early, the opposition is
clear. On the one hand is the bleak environment frowning upon
any activity of the imagination, whether passive or active, and on
the other a determined Richard who will not be turned aside. His
reading would be done in secret, a clandestine activity abetted by
delivering racist newspapers and borrowing the library card of a
compliant white man. There is no evidence that he discussed his
reading with anyone, black or white. In Memphis, when he was able
to patronize second-hand bookstores and to buy magazines like
Harper's, Atlantic Monthly, and *American Mercury,* his tastes re-
flected the shape of his early conditioning (p. 198). He admired
the great liberators, the destroyers of provincial and private worlds
like the one that oppressed him; Mencken in a *Book of Prefaces
and Prejudices;* Sinclair Lewis in *Main Street* and *Babbitt;*
Theodore Dreiser in *Sister Carrie* and *Jennie Gerhardt* (pp. 217-19).

It might be said that Richard has the loneliness of a natural-
istic hero, of McTeague or of Carrie Meeber. Theirs are worlds in
which no one talks to anyone else, worlds entirely given over to
the expression of power. One person's drive pitted against that of
another, and the consequence of the struggle has more to do with
heredity or chemistry than with persuasion. Richard's behavior,
much like that of a character created by Norris or Dreiser, though
it is not governed by the tight probability of fiction, carries con-
stantly the solemn and overwhelming weight of the universe. He
cannot say "sir" without acquiescing to the ever-present power
of the white man, and he cannot read Mencken without the satis-

faction that he has triumphed over a hostile white South through subterfuge and trickery.

Richard's commitment to write precipitates confrontations. As we have seen, his honest admission of this aspiration to one white lady employer results in bitter ridicule, and Richard feels, despite the pressures of his situation, that his ego has been assaulted. His first publication, "The Voodoo of Hell's Half-Acre," is little more than the crude rendering of the stuff of *Flynn's Detective Weekly,* but Richard discovers that printing it is an act of defiance, further separating him from the world that surrounds him, both black and white (p. 146).

Richard does not intend to restrict his range to any half-acre, though his first is identified as "Hell." His province would be the real world around him. True, it is sometimes not to be distinguished from the subject area defined by his first literary effort. At a very young age Richard sees "elephants" moving across the land—not real "elephants," but convicts in a chain gang, and the child's awe is prompted by the unfortunate confusion of elephant and zebra (p. 52). An inauspicious beginning, perhaps, but the pattern of applying his imagination to his immediate surrounding is firmly set. Later, Richard says more soberly that he rejects religion because it ignores immediate reality. His faith, predictably, must be wedded to "common realities of life" (p. 100), anchored in the sensations of his body and in what his mind could grasp. This is, we see, an excellent credo for an artist, but a worthless one for a black boy growing to maturity in Mississippi.

Another piece of evidence announcing Richard's talent is the compulsion to make symbols of the details of his everyday experience. This faculty is early demonstrated in his tendency to generalize from sensational experience, to define an appropriate emotion to associate with his feelings. A more highly developed example is Richard's reaction to his mother's illness and sufferings, representative for him in later years of the poverty, the ignorance, the helplessness of black life in Mississippi. And it is based on the generalizing process that Richard is a black boy, any black boy experiencing childhood, adolescence, and early manhood in the South.

Richard leaves the South. He must, to survive as a man and to develop as an artist. By the time we reach the end of the narrative, these two drives have merged. We know, as well, that the South will never leave Richard, never depart from the rich imagination that developed despite monumental opposition. We have only the final promise that Richard will someday understand the region that has indelibly marked him.

Richard's ultimate liberation, and his ultimate triumph, will be the ability to face the dreadful experience in the South and to record it. At the end of *A Portrait of the Artist as a Young Man,* the facts of experience have become journal items for the artist.[29] At the conclusion of *Invisible Man,* Ellison's unnamed narrator can record the blues of his black life, with the accompaniment of extraordinary psychedelic effects. Stephen Dedalus is on his way to becoming an artist; Ellison's hero promises to climb out of his hole, half-prepared, at least, to return to mundane life.[30] The conclusion of *Black Boy* is less positive and more tentative. True, Richard has made it; he has whipped the devils of the South, black and white. But he has left us with a feeling that is less than happy. He has yet to become an artist. Then we realize with a start what we have read is not simply the statement of a promise, its background and its development, but its fulfillment. Wright has succeeded in reconstructing the reality that was for a long time perhaps too painful to order, and that reconstruction may be Wright's supreme artistic achievement, *Black Boy.*

NOTES

[1] (New York: Harper, 1940.) Dorothy Canfield Fisher in the introduction writes that the "novel plumbs blacker depths of human experience than American literature has yet had, comparable only to Dostoievski's revelation of human misery in wrongdoing" (p. x).

[2] The full title is *Black Boy: A Record of Childhood and Youth* (New York: Harper, 1945). Dorothy Fisher in the introductory note calls Wright's work "the honest, dreadful, heartbreaking story of a Negro childhood and youth . . ." (p. vii), without referring to its art or even its place in an American literary tradition.

[3] "Life and Letters: Richard Wright Reappraised," *Atlantic Monthly,* 225 (March, 1970), 127-32.

[4] *American Hunger* (New York: Harper & Row, Publishers) was published in 1977. It is not the whole autobiography but the second part, the continuation of *Black Boy.* Michel Fabre in the afterword provides an accurate brief history of the decision to publish only the first section in 1945. See pp. 143-44.

[5] *Atlantic Monthly,* 174 (August, 1944), 61-70; (September, 1944), 48-56.

[6] Fabre, "Afterword," *American Hunger,* pp. 143-44.

[7] W. E. B. Du Bois, "Richard Wright Looks Back," *New York Herald Tribune,* March 4, 1945, sec. 5, p. 2.

[8] The three are *The Souls of Black Folk: Essays and Sketches* (Chicago: A. C. McClurg, 1903), *Darkwater: Voices from Within the Veil* (New York: Harcourt, Brace, 1920), and *Dusk of Dawn: An Essay toward an Autobiography of a Race Concept* (New York: Harcourt, Brace, 1940).

[9] Chapter IV, "Of the Meaning of Progress," in Du Bois, *The Souls of Black Folk,* pp. 60-74.

[10] "Richard Wright's Blues," *Antioch Review,* 5 (June, 1945), 202. Reprinted in *Shadow and Act* (New York: Random House, 1964).

11 Wright wrote Edward Aswell, his editor at Harper's, on August 10, 1944, suggesting *Black Boy* as a title for the book. He added, for emphasis, that *Black Boy* was "not only a title but also a kind of heading to the whole general theme" (Fabre, "Afterword," *American Hunger,* p. 144).

12 Wright comments on this commitment in *Black Boy:* "I had once tried to write, had once reveled in feeling, had let my crude imagination roam, but the impulse to dream had been slowly beaten out of me by experience. Now it surged up again and I hungered for books, new ways of looking and seeing" (p. 218).

13 *Ibid.,* p. 220.

14 Between 1897 and 1915 Du Bois edited fifteen studies on the condition and status of blacks in America. These volumes represented the Proceedings of the Annual Conference on the Negro Problem, organized by Du Bois and held at Atlanta University.

15 Ellison, "Richard Wright's Blues."

16 *Native Son,* pp. 4-5.

17 Thoreau is precise about the length of his actual stay, despite the fact that the events of *Walden* fall within the design of a single year: "The present was my next experiment . . . for convenience, putting the experience of two years into one." Henry David Thoreau, *Walden,* ed. Sherman Paul (Boston: Houghton Mifflin, 1957), p. 58.

18 Franklin refers in this way to his neglect of Miss Read, to whom he was engaged, during a period spent in London: "This was another of the great errata of my life. . . ." "Autobiography" in Benjamin Franklin, *Autobiography and Other Writings,* ed. R. B. Nye (Boston: Houghton Mifflin, 1958), p. 38.

19 See Michel Fabre, *The Unfinished Quest of Richard Wright* (New York: William Morrow, 1973), pp. 1-17.

20 Fabre, *Unfinished Quest,* p. 533.

21 Another footnote by Fabre in *Unfinished Quest* suggests an additional dimension for Addie, who, "too, was not, spared in *Black Boy.* She reacted rather well to reading the book—she stated that if Richard wrote in that way, it was to support his family . . ." (p. 533).

22 *Ibid.,* p. 39.

23 *Ibid.,* p. 48.

24 E. R. Embree describes, in *Thirteen Against the Odds* (New York: Viking, 1944), Wright's attitude toward his education in Jackson: "He [Wright] remembers the Smith-Robinson school with some gratitude. The teachers tried their best to pump learning into the pupils" (p. 27).

25 Fabre, *Unfinished Quest,* p. 39.

26 *Ibid.,* p. 43.

27 *Ibid.,* pp. 46-47.

28 *Ibid.,* p. 47.

29 See James Joyce, *A Portrait of the Artist as a Young Man* (New York: New American Library, 1955), pp. 195-96.

30 Ellison's narrator states his final position with some care: "Thus, having tried to give pattern to the chaos which lives within the pattern of your certainties, I must come out, I must emerge." *Invisible Man* (New York: New American Library, 1952), p. 502.

DUKE ELLINGTON VAMPS 'TIL READY

ALBERT MURRAY

The personal recollections and reflections that Duke Ellington has left in *Music Is My Mistress* were programmed or routined into acts, rather than orchestrated into a literary equivalent of, say, his "Reminiscin' in Tempo." So the overall effect is somewhat like that of an all-star variety show, including special guest appearances. But formal structure aside, time and again the actual narration as such becomes so suggestive of Ellington's unique speaking voice and conversational mannerisms that you find yourself all but literally backstage looking on and listening in as he recalls people, places, time, circumstances, and events somewhat as if nudged into nostalgia by old friends or some very lucky interviewer.

Not that backstage is ever altogether offstage. But then Duke Ellington himself was never very far from the footlights for very long either. Nor did he ever show or express any overwhelming need to be. What he always needed was listeners, even at rehearsals, and audiences were as essential to his recording sessions as was the acoustical excellence of the studio equipment. After all, for him, in whom the instrumentalist, composer, and conductor were so totally and inextricably interrelated, performing music was absolutely indispensable to writing it. Not only was there almost always a keyboard instrument of some kind in his dressing room whenever space permitted; such was also the case with his hotel suites and even his hospital rooms. And he was forever noodling and doodling and jotting and dotting no matter who else was there or what else was going on.

In any case, among the anecdotes, vignettes, plugs, takeoffs, put-ons, whatnots, and what-if-nots in *Music Is My Mistress* there are also some that even seem not so much written as jive-riffed into the microphone onstage between numbers. Nor are they thereby any less representative than the rest. Ellington was mostly himself no matter where he was. Indeed, as the interviews published several years ago by Stanley Dance in *The World of Duke Ellington* bear out, the man behind the legend was, if anything, even more of a legendary figure to his closest associates than to his millions of worshipful admirers all over the world. As for his mike spiel, what with the orchestra there in the background, he was quite possibly as much at home on the job as he was ever likely to be lounging in an armchair by a fireside on a rainy night.

Which is not to say that he was ever given to making public such private (but by no means secret) personal involvements as his schedule permitted. References in *Music Is My Mistress* to his adult family life, for instance, are oblique at best: "I took him [arranger Billy Strayhorn] to 381 Edgecombe Avenue and said, 'This is my home, and this is your home, I'm leaving for Europe in a few days, but you stay here with my son Mercer and my sister Ruth. They will take good care of you.'" Mention of previous and subsequent adult addresses is less than oblique. And while there indeed was, as he says he discovered very early, always a pretty girl standing down at the bass clef end of the piano, the only "love interest" discussed concerns music. No kissing and telling for him. Or perhaps too much kissing for telling. But then the title of his book may have been intended as a statement of precisely the delimitation he wanted.

But even so, *Music Is My Mistress* is an authentic autobiographical document that is strong at precisely those points where so many other books by and about so-called black Americans are often exasperatingly weak. Seldom are such books concerned with making anything more than a political statement of some kind or other, mostly polemical. Rarely do they reflect very much personal involvement with the textures of everyday actuality as such. On the contrary, most often they are likely to leave the impression that every dimension of black experience is directly restricted, if not inevitably crippled, by all-pervading (and always sinister) political forces.

More often than not it is as if all of the downright conspicuous orientation to style in general and stylish clothes in particular, all of the manifest love of good cooking and festive music and dancing and communal good times (both secular and sacred), all of the notorious linguistic exuberance, humor, and outrageous nonsense, not to mention all of the preoccupation with love and lovemaking (that blues lyrics are so full of)—it is as if none of these things, otherwise considered to be so characteristic of the so-called black American's life-style, is of any basic significance whatever, once a so-called black American becomes the subject of biographical contemplation.

Actually most biographies and autobiographies of U.S. Negroes tend to read like case histories or monographs written to illustrate some very special (and often very narrow) political theory, or ideology of blackness, or to promote some special political program. Such writing serves a very useful purpose, to be sure. But the approach does tend to oversimplify character, situation, and motive in the interest of social and political issues as such, and in the process human beings at best become sociopolitical abstractions. At worst they are reduced to clichés.

The Narrative of the Life of Frederick Douglass, an American Slave, Written by Himself is as much a classic of nineteenth-century

American prose as are the works of Emerson, Longfellow, Hawthorne, Thoreau, Lowell, Holmes, and the rest, but still it is more of an auto-biographical *political* essay than a full-scale comprehensive autobiography. Booker T. Washington's *Up from Slavery* is an autobiographical essay on post-Reconstruction education, rather than the story of Booker T. Washington himself. In the "Apology" for *Dusk of Dawn,* which he called an essay toward an autobiography of a race concept, W. E. B. Du Bois flatly states: "My life had its significance and its only deep significance because it was part of a problem. . . ." As if people involved with problems have not always been as great a preoccupation of biography as of fiction and drama.

But all told, perhaps the most noteworthy exception to the general run of one-dimensional biographical writing by so-called black Americans is James Weldon Johnson's *Along This Way.* Johnson, who not only wrote the lyrics to "The Negro National Anthem" but also was the first executive secretary of the NAACP, was actively involved with problems of civil rights as few have been. But *Along This Way* is not political propaganda. It is a full-scale personal record of a marvelous American who was, among other things, also a professional music hall entertainer, poet, lawyer, diplomat, editor of anthologies of poetry and spirituals, and novelist. Indeed, for historical perspective, comprehensive grasp of circumstance, and sensitivity to the texture of life as such, it may well be the very best autobiography of a U.S. Negro to date.

None of which is to imply that *Music Is My Mistress* is comparable in overall literary merit to *Along This Way.* The two, however, do share basic virtues so often absent from so many autobiographical monographs geared primarily to political statement. To begin with, Ellington, like Johnson, always regarded himself not as a political theory but as a flesh-and-blood human being, a person of capability with many possibilities. Like Johnson, he remembers his parents, for instance, not as if they were mostly social problems, in urgent need of white liberal compassion, but as good-looking, affectionate, prideful, and authoritative adults who expected one to grow up and amount to something. Nor did his black elders treat him as if he were born under a curse. He was always somebody special. "Edward you are blessed," his mother, who certainly knew the facts of life, told him. "You don't have anything to worry about." And he believed her. And storybook Duke-designate that he already was, he went out and forged a magnificent sword and conquered the world.

In other words, as is entirely consistent for one whose all-pervading commitment is to an art form, the frame of reference of Ellington's most basic functional conceptions and definitions of himself and his purposes is not political but metaphorical. For all its concrete details, including such specifics as employment and budgets, his is the fairy-tale world of heroic encounters and endeavors, where obstacles are regarded not as occasions for welfare-oriented protest but as challenges to one's creativity. Thus the eight *acts* of *Music Is My Mistress* consist mostly of a recounting of the initiation rituals of the apprentice, the trials and contests of the journeyman, the offerings of the full-fledged practitioner. Then come some modest (and some tongue-in-cheek) words of wisdom and advice from the long since venerable Old Pro, followed by a listing of ceremonial honors and awards, and finally a catalog of his good works or exploits.

Such were day-to-day actualities no less than they were the symbolic terms of Ellington's existence. And to be sure, all of the key *felidae* (as he calls them) in his cast of characters were blue steel fables in the flesh. Which is also why, the dynamics of aesthetic feedback being what they are, references no matter how offhand to James P. Johnson and Willie the Lion Smith, Will Marion Cook and Will Vodery, Sidney Bechet and Louis Armstrong and Fletcher Henderson are absolutely indispensable sources of insight. Even the sketches of the personalities of the musicians in his orchestra over the years—even what he includes about Irving Mills, the agent who promoted him into the big time—provide more understanding of the structure as well as the content of Ellington's music than is ever likely to be derived from any examination of deep-seated anxieties resulting from political oppression, or ever likely to be revealed by even the most exhaustive confession of long-hidden personal hang-ups.

Moreover, although far too many students of history seem far too oversubscribed to the methodology of psychiatric case survey to realize it these days, in making references to people who struck him as being literally *fabulous,* Ellington is also addressing himself to precisely those basic rituals and myths that all truly serious scholars must discover in order to come to comprehensive terms with the definitive forces that motivate the effort and achievement (or cause the failures) and shape the life-style of the person who is the subject of any biographical study. After all, what the comprehensive, valid, and reliable biography or history must always add up to, for all its entirely proper preoccupation with specific facts, is fiction: the subject's vital statistics are such and such, and his doings and accomplishments are already a matter of public record and widespread acclaim. But what is his story? What, in other words, is his functional mythology, his personal frame of reference?

That Duke Ellington had no intention whatsoever of writing a conventional autobiography on the scale of James Weldon Johnson's *Along This Way* (or even on the lesser scale of W. C. Handy's useful but somewhat stilted *Father of the Blues*) need hardly be argued.

Nevertheless, in *Music Is My Mistress,* along with all the first-hand information and expert but seldom pontifical observations, he has left future biographers and historians the literary equivalent of some of the piano vamps he used to sit riffing until the ensembles and soloists were ready for the downbeat. He has, that is to say, improvised a prelude, an overture, an introduction that establishes the key, the tempo, the treatment, and overall mood and direction for those who wish to come to terms with what he was really about, rather than what they think he should have been about.

As for the autobiographical social science monograph, its short-comings are inherent not in its methodology as such (aside, of course, from the fact that it cannot be scientific enough) but in the all too obvious assumption that generalizations and conclusions drawn from measurable fact are not fiction. But aren't all formulations necessarily fabrications? In all events, what finally matters most about both formula and metaphor is extent of their functional immediacy or comprehensive applicability. As for those historical research specialists who set out to replace the legendary, the fabulous, or the mythical with scientific fact, what they end up with are all too often only stereotypes derived from social science—which, of course, is to say social science fiction.

BACKWACKING, A PLEA TO THE SENATOR

RALPH ELLISON

Braxas, Alabama
April 4th, 1953

To the Right Honorable
Senator Sunraider
Washington, D.C.

Dear Senator Sunraider:

*This evening I take my pen in hand to write you our deep apprecia-
tion for all the good things you have been doing for this pore beat
down country of ours. That Cadillac speech you gave us was straight
forward and to the point and much needed saying. So I thank you
and my wife Marthy wants to thank you. In fact we both thank you for
looking out for folks like us who firmly believe that all this* WELFARE
*the Guv. is shoveling out to the lazy nogooders and freeloaders is
something that stinks in the nostril of Heaven worse than a batch of
rotten catfish that some unGodly thief has stole and scattered all
over Courthouse Square at high noon on the 4th day of July. We are
with you Senator because you are a good man. You have done great
things for the God-fearing folks of this country and we respect you
for it. And as you are one of the very few men in Guv. who we can
depend on when the going gets real* TOUGH *I now take the liberty of
calling something to your kind attention that is taking place down
here in these parts.*

*I refer to this new type of sinful activity that has cropped up
amongst the niggers. It is known as "*BACKWACKING," *which I am
prepared to say under oath is probably one of the most* UNGODLY *and
also* UNATURAL *activity that anybody has ever yet invented! Senator,
it is no less than* RADICAL! *And so naturally the nigger has been
going at it so* HARD *that he is fast getting out of hand and out of
control. Here is what he is doing.* HE *and his woman have taken to
getting undressed and standing back to back and heel to heel,
shoulderblade to shoulderblade, and tale to tale with his against her's
and her's against his, and then after they have horsed around and
manuvered like cats in heat and worked as tight together as a tick to*

a cow's tit, HE *ups and starts in to* HAVING AFTER HER BACKWARDS!

*Now I know, Senator, that this sounds like he is taking a very
roundabout and also mullet-headed path to Robin Hood's barn, but
I have it on the most reliable authority that this is exactly how he is
going about it. Yessir! The facts have been well established even
though I have to admit that on account of he is not only defying
common decency but also* NATURE, *I cannot explain in full detail
just* <u>how</u> *the nigger is proceeding in this tradition busting business.
Because naturally he thinks that he has him a good thing going and is
trying to keep the* WHITE MAN *in the* DARK. *Even so, I want you to
know that ever since it was brought to my attention I been putting a
great deal of effort into trying to untangle what he is doing. I have
figgered* HARD *and I have figgered* LONG *but to date nothing I have
come up with seems to fit* WHAT *he is doing with* HOW *he is going
about it. Neither, I am sad to report, has anybody else. So it appears
that once again and after all the trouble we have seen we are being
VICTIMIZED by yet another so-called "nigger mystery." It is a crying
sin and a dirty shame but once again the nigger has tossed the re-
sponsible citizenry of these parts a terrible tough nut to crack. Once
again it appears that like the time he came back from Cuba at the end
of the Spanish American War and then again when he came back
from Paris France after World War I, he is* HELLBENT *on taking ad-
vantage of our good nature. But be that as it may, I hasten to assure
you that we down here are not taking it laying down. We are going
after him not only with might and main but with foresight and hind-
sight. And as for me personal, I am doing my level best to bring him
to heel and can be counted on to* KEEP ON *doing it! Senator, you have
my word on that. I have known niggers all my life and am well
acquainted with smart ones as well as dumb ones, but while hereto-
fore this has been an advantage in many a tight place in my dealings
with him, in this particular situation I am forced to admit that I have
yet to come across any as backwards-acting as my most reliable
information makes these here out to be. Evidently these are of a
different breed, because considering that I am a* GODFEARING *white
man in my 80th year if* <u>I</u> *have not heard of this "*BACKWACKING"
until now it has got to be something NEW! *So in my considered
opinion it is something that some black rascal has brought in here
from somewheres else, probably from up* NORTH.

*But Senator, wherever this "*BACKWACKING" *comes from it calls
for some ruthless* INVESTIGATING *and drastic* CONTROL! *Because
not only is the nigger conducting himself in this* UNGODLY *jiggsawing
fashion I have described to you, but there is* OVERPOWERING *evidence
that he is doing it too much for his own or anybody elses good, and I
say so for the following reasons. I am informed that when he and his
woman reach the climax of this radical new way of sinning they get*

*blasted by one of the <u>darndest</u> feelings that has ever been known to hit the likes of Man! My friend says it is like watching somebody being struck down by greased lightening, and he says that when it hits the nigger it is like seeing somebody being knocked down and dragged by an L & N freight train that has been doing a high-ball on a down-hill grade with its brakeshoes busted and with no red light ahead! Yes, sir! It is a mind graveler and a viscious back breaker. He says that watching it work on the black rascal is like seeing somebody get blasted to as close to dying as any normal human being can possibly come and still not die. Like he says this "*BACKWACKING*" is a real humdinging ripsnorter and a danger to life, limb and social order—only you wouldn't think so if you could see how some who are practicing it are around here strutting and grinning.*

*Yes, sir, Senator, they are out trying to make some slick nigger propaganda to the point that they had all at once jumped way ahead of the *WHITE* man! But of course and as we both well know, they are badly mistaken in this regard. Because if the truth be known, all they are doing is setting back their own *RACE*. There is no doubt about it, because it is a "well established fact" and as I have always held No race can pull itself up by their bootstraps and bring home the bacon that dedicates itself to indulging in such *UNATURAL* activity as the one these here are messing with. But yet and still and as niggers will, they are going at it like old fashioned common sense has gone plum out of style! Senator, the situation he is creating is no less than critical! And it is right here that we come face to face with the most confounding detail of this "*BACKWACKING*."*

*Now you would expect that all this powerful feeling he generates would knock the nigger out, and as I have stated it trully staggers him. It knocks the rascal as limber as a bacon rine that has been boiled in a mess of collards and turns his bones to rubber. Yes, sir! But then an absolutely *CONFUSING* thing takes place. Like I say, when this feeling strikes the nigger it blasts him so hard that it seems that it has knocked all such nasty notions out of his ignorant head. He goes out like a lantern in a wind storm and you would swear that he was already at the gates of hell, which is shorely where he is headed, yessir! But then it jacks him up, and the next thing you know he comes up with a quick second wind! That is the unGodly truth, Senator, and I'll swear to it. Instead of keeling over and breathing his last or at least taking him a nap, the nigger just lets out a big ole hoop-and-a-holler and leaps back to his position and commences to practicing this "*BACKWACKING*" again! So when you think about that and all the raw naked *POWER* he lets loose it is my firm opinion that this "*BACKWACKING*" must do no less than throw him into some new kind of *TRANCE*. Something about this new way of sinning he is practicing simply takes the rascal *OVER*. Otherwise I ask you how is* *it that as soon as he uses up his second-wind—which takes him a full five minutes longer by a good stop-watch—according to my friend he right away "BACKWACKS" his way into a third and then into a fourth and fifth wind? So it stands to reason that nothing less than a TRANCE can explain it, therefore I must stand on that. It simply has to be what happens, especially since he has been known to keep on going in this fashion until he is vibrating like a sheet-tin roof in a wind storm and his petered-out woman is wore plumb down to a slam-banging frazzel!*

Senator, after observing this disgraceful business on several occasions, my friend holds that it is a crying pity and a down-right shame that it don't just knock the nigger out of commission the first shot out of the box, and I wholeheartedly agree. Because if this "BACK-WACKING" was to kill off a few of the ornery ones who is practicing it this thing would be brought to a quick and abrupt conclusion. After that the rest of the niggers would sober up to the firmly grounded truth of the proposition which states that "No Race can prosper or long endure" that devotes itself to going against NATURE like these down here have been doing. Therefore they would go back and devote themselves to conducting their business in the old fashion way they was taught by the WHITE man back there in slavery.

Now mind you Senator, I say that that is the proposition the nigger OUGHT to be living by, but this being a new day and age, and one in which he has lost all sense of direction, he is NOT. Instead he is coming up daily with all KINDS of new minds and new notions, most of them nasty, radical and UNGODLY. So with the nigger continuing on his "BACKWACKING" rampage it is most unfortunate that some of the most responsible citizens in these parts are dying off while some of the rest have given up the struggle and grown discouraged. Some are even thinking about migrating to Australia! And only the other day a friend of mine was even talking about moving to South Africa, just to get away from some of the outrages taking place down here. He's ready to cut bait and run! "Let the nigger take over, and get out while the getting is good," he says "That's what I'm thinking, Just let him have it, lock, stock, barrel and gatepost, because that's exactly what he's out to do. One way or another, either by hook, or by crook or sinning, he means to seize control. So I'm going somewhere a WHITE man still has a chance to live in peace." That is what he says and he's from one of the finest old families in these parts. Yessir, that's just how pessimistic some folks have come to feel. But fortunately folks like my friend are in the minority and I hasten to assure you Senator that all is not lost, no, sir! Not by a long shot. Because while a few have let themselves become discouraged and intimidated by this recent rash of nigger outrages a determined

VANGUARD *remains on the firing line and is putting up a firm resistance. And for this I say "Praise the* LORD*!" as there is a growing concern that if the nigger ain't soon checked and returned to his proper balance—and I mean by any means* NECESSARY*—or if he don't just naturally run out of gas on his own accord, he will keep on plunging down this unatural path he is on until he is out on the street grabbing and "*BACKWACKING*" each and every female woman he can lay his corrupted eyes on. Such is the terrible prospect we face in a nutshell.*

*So it is my considered opinion that we are confronted by a crisis the likes of which we haven't had to face since back in 1918 when the nigger come home trying to talk and act like French men. Therefore I have tried to the best of my ability to give you a clear and accurate picture of our situation. What we actually have down here is not only a serious threat to our orderly society but we are in the middle of something that can best be described as a "clear and present danger"! I insist on that, Senator, and it is a danger that threatens everybody, including the nigger, who seems bent on no less than downright self-annihilation! And what makes our predicament so untenable is the fact that the nigger is so sly and devious. He knows we're watching him so he's coming up with all kinds of "diversionary tactics." But while we have yet to discover what he is sneaking around eating and drinking in order to do what he is doing and while he is keeping his hand well hid, down here in Alabama his offenses to common decency is causing a terrible stir. Senator, our backs are against the wall and our nerves are on edge and our patience is running thin. And it is doing it so fast that I tell you confidential that all this "*BACKWACKING*" he is doing has got our* STORM WARNINGS *up. By which I mean to say that this latest of many aggravating "nigger mysteries," grievous offenses, and attacks on moral integrity and clean living has got folks so flustered and upset that they are beginning to cry out loud for some* RELIEF*! So Senator it is in their name as well as my own that I am calling upon you to hurry down here with a committee of your best people and* INVESTIGATE*! We are calling upon you because from your Cadillac speech the other day we are firmly convinced that you are the* ONE *for the role. You have the "intestinal fortitude" to do what needs to be done and you have the authority to* SEE *that it is done. So please heed our plea. Because even if what the nigger is up to wasn't against* NATURE*, which it simply has to be, there is no question but that he is going both against the* BIBLE *and against our most hallowed tradition and therefore what he is doing calls for the firm and unyielding hand of the* LAW*!*

Senator, the above constitutes our unhappy bill of particulars, and as I appreciate that you are a busy man I beg pardon for taking up so much of your precious time. But *please understand that our situation is* DESPERATE *and we call upon your aid because you are one of the few that trully stands for* LAW AND ORDER *and really looks out for the welfare of the good* WHITE *people, who as I have tried to make crystal clear, are once again being sorely tried and tested. So in closing both me and Marthy thank you in advance for your kind consideration and look forward to the time when we will once again be safe and at peace with our fine and honorable tradition and our straightforward way of doing things. We wish you a long life and the best of everything, and we hope and pray that you will soon find time to lay the firm hand of the law on this* "BACKWACKING" *and bring it to a teeth-rattling* HALT! *Just look into the nigger is all we ask, and* GOD BLESS.

Respectfully Yrs.

Norm A. Mauler

A CONCERN CITIZEN

STUDY & EXPERIENCE

AN INTERVIEW WITH RALPH ELLISON

[STEPTO]: BOTH YOU AND WRIGHT STROVE TO READ, AND STROVE to write, but I think the situations were quite different. What we see sometimes is that people have the theory, an ancient one, of sons wanting to slay the fathers. . . .

[ELLISON]: Well, Wright and I were of different backgrounds, different ages, and from different regions. What united us was our mutual interest in ideas and the craft of fiction, not some fanciful notion of father and son. I've heard the metaphor used in justification of actions taken after the disruption of friendships between younger and older writers, and inevitably it is the younger who uses it in his own defense. I don't buy it because it misnames a complicated relationship.

[S]: What do you mean?

[E]: For one thing, I mean that writers as artists are sons of many fathers, or at least the sons of many writers' *styles*. This was true even of Dostoevsky and Henry James, and no matter what the personal relationship between two writers happens to be, unless the younger writer is a mere imitator his style will diverge from, and often negate in certain aspects, the style of his older friend. That's where the important conflict takes place and it's more or less inevitable and it only obscures matters when we drag in the father-son metaphor. Rather than a case of the son slaying the father, such rows are more like those instances wherein an unwedded mother gives her unwanted baby over for adoption. And then, after the child has been brought through the precarious period of infancy, toilet-training and whooping cough, she discovers that she has safely weathered the terrors of shame and uncertainty of her maternity and proceeds to demand the return of the child. In doing so she makes noble noises about the sacredness of motherhood and the imperiousness of the maternal instinct, and has nasty things to say about the manners,

---

This interview took place at Mr. Ellison's home in New York City on March 8, 1976. The interviewers were Robert B. Stepto and Michael S. Harper.

morals, and low human quality of those into whose hands she has
thrust her squirming infant. Neither metaphor is really adequate, but
sometimes a young writer seeks to place his infant talent in the care
of an older writer whom he hopes will nurture, instruct and protect
it and himself against the uncertainties that are a necessary phase of
his development. But then, after he has gained confidence and
achieved a sense of his own identity as a writer, he seeks to reclaim
his psychological independence. Thus it seems to me that instead of
seeking for a father principle, the writer, as *writer*, is seeking ways to
give birth to books. And what if during his formative period a male
writer is given support by a writer who is female? When he asserts
values that are in conflict with hers shall we say that the son must
slay the mother and thus brand him a "Mother"? Or if both writers
are women do we say that the younger mother of books is slaying
another mother? Seriously, a writer learns (and quite early, if he's
lucky) to depend upon the authority of his own experience and in-
tuition. He must learn to dominate them, but these are his capital and
his guide, his compass and crud-detector, his sword and his cross;
and he defers to the authority of others at the peril of his artistic
individuality. His drive is to achieve his own artistic possibilities
by whatever artistic means necessary. Of course a young writer may
have feelings of dependency that have their source in areas of his
personality that are not necessarily linked to his drive toward ex-
pression and would be present even if he were without artistic talent.
But in the writer, in the artist, such feelings of dependency find
relief in the act of creation.

[s]: So how do you view the relationship between a younger and
older writer where one is established and the other just beginning.

[e]: If we stick to the father-son metaphor I'd say that, given a
reasonable degree of psychological independence on the part of the
younger man, it would be difficult to decide who at any given moment
is in the position of "father," who of "son." Such relationships are
dramatic; it is a matter of give and take. Insight is determined less
by chronological age than by the density of one's felt experience and
by one's consciousness of implication. A younger man whose ado-
lescence was spent in a big city might well possess insights of which
an older man whose formative period was spent in a small town may
be innocent. I speak of possibilities, and of course the reverse is often
true, with the small town providing experiences and insights difficult
to come by in densely structured cities. Anyway, I would think that
when a younger man designates an older writer as his symbolic
father he would keep his projection subjective, miming it rather than
giving it utterance.

Because to name his attitude would be to concede far more to another than most assertive young men (and writers are very assertive types, at least psychologically) would wish to admit. What Kenneth Burke terms "courtship" is implicit in friendship, which is a relationship between, shall we say, two consenting adults who "woo" one another. In such relationships there are risks for both participants. For while the older writer might consider it flattering to be elected the "father" of a gifted symbolic "son," there is also the possibility that he might be repelled by the responsibility of that role. Remember that both Hawthorne and Henry James regarded the imposition of one's will upon the freedom of another as a sin against democratic individuality and gave considerable attention to the theme in their fiction. The lessons of his own experience, his own apprenticeship, might lead the older writer to feel that his young friend should undergo the risks that are part of the task of achieving an artistic identity. These risks are a part of his extended initiation. And if he is in fact psychologically mature enough to act out the "father" role he will have learned that artists are self-creating types—or at least that they tend to *pretend* that they are—and thus in their efforts in this direction they're apt to savage those into whose hands they've delivered themselves. Then there is a wavery line between the pieties of friendship and the subjective compulsion which writers feel to project their individual visions. Each writer interprets life as he sees it, and in the conflict of passion and insight which occurs when writers strive to project their individual visions the son-slaying-the-father metaphor becomes a source of needless confusion. Writers of different backgrounds and generations often disagree because they seek to make unique works of art out of the subjectivity of diverse experiences which are connected objectively by duration and by issues arising from within the social scene in which they find themselves. If friendships between writers are not strong enough to overcome these built-in sources of conflict and competition, they fail, but if the relationship has been fruitful it finds continuity in the works of art that came into being during the quiet moments of antagonistic cooperation which marked the relationship.

[s]: Still the father/son metaphor persists . . .

[e]: Yes, but let's not forget that often it isn't the self-justifying younger writer who drags it in, it is done by outsiders; this, perhaps, because it seems to simplify the relationship between an older and younger artist. It allows for a facile sense of continuity between the generations of artists and does away with the mystery surrounding the nature of artistic influence. This is especially true of those who look at culture in strictly racial terms; people, let us say, who don't know what to make of Richard Wright's early apprentice relationship

with James T. Farrell. Here I'm reminded of an incident that oc-
curred back when I still thought of myself as a musician.

Shortly after arriving in New York from Tuskegee I wrote one of
my teachers, that among other exciting developments, I had made
the acquaintance of a famous artist. In return I received an enthu-
siastic letter in which my teacher said in effect, "Isn't it wonderful
to be sitting at the feet of such an artist and to have the privilege of
breathing in the intellectual atmosphere which he exudes." Oh,
Lord! My reaction was to hit the ceiling. I wasn't particularly overt
in my youthful arrogance, but my teacher's well-meaning interpre-
tation of that relationship outraged me. For while I realized that the
man had much to teach me about art (far more, in fact, than most
of the older writers whom I found incapable of discussing writing
techniques with any precision) I also realized that he was far from
being an intellectual. Not only was he innocent of a serious interest
in ideas, but he hadn't *begun* to read the books that I had read, even
before entering college.

And yet in the romantic imagination of my delighted teacher this
man had been cast in the role of my intellectual "father"—simply
because he had achieved a fairly broad reputation and was some
years my senior. So given such misinterpretations the objective
complexity of such relationships can get lost and can happen
whether the younger individual is *looking* for a "father" or not.

But then again, most friendships have their vague areas of mystery
and the older member of a relationship between writers might him-
self project the younger in a role which obscures the extent of his
intellectual maturity or the extent and variety of his experience. One
of my early experiences with Dick Wright involved such an under-
estimation, with him assuming that I hadn't read many books with
which I was, in fact, quite familiar.

[s]: What sorts of things did he assume you hadn't read?

[E]: Well, among others, he assumed that I hadn't read any of
Marx . . . Conrad . . . Dostoevsky . . . Hemingway—and so on. I was
somewhat chagrined by his apparent condescension, but instead of
casting him in the role of misunderstanding "father," I swallowed
my pride and told myself, "Forget it, you know what you know; so
now learn what he thinks of in terms of his Marxism and the insights
he's gained as a developed writer of fiction." And that was the way
it went. At the time he was already working on *Native Son* and
possessed a conscious world-view, while I had only begun to write,
had no consciously formulated philosophy or way of structuring what
I had read and experienced. So I listened and learned even when I
disagreed. Speaking of fathers: I lost my own at the age of three, lost
a step-father when I was about ten, and had another at the time I met

Wright. I was quite touchy about those who'd inherited my father's position as head of my family and I had no desire, or need, to cast Wright or anyone else, even symbolically, in such a role.

However, his underestimation did make for a certain irony in our relationship; because sometimes, thanks to my own reading and quite different experience, I was in a position to have made suggestions for solving problems from which he might have benefited. But since I recognized that his subjective image of me did not encourage the acceptance of certain levels of advice I usually kept my opinions to myself.

[s]: To what extent does Wright's essay, "Blueprint for Negro Literature," represent his thinking when you were seeing him in New York in the late thirties and early forties?

[e]: That essay was written rather early. Wright had come to New York in June, 1937 and I met him the day after. He was preparing it for the first issue of *New Challenge*, of which he was an editor. Yes, I think it was a projection of his current thinking. It was polemical in relationship to the current line of the Communist Party, and his emphasis on nationalism, on how to deal with "Negro nationalism" (or "black chauvinism" as it was termed) was influenced by Joseph Stalin's pamphlet on the *National Question*. Wright was attempting to square the official communist "line" with certain resentments entertained by black communists as a result of their experience of American racism, some of which they found within the party. And as a writer he was struggling to work out an orientation for himself as one whose background lay in certain areas of Afro-American culture.

[s]: One thing that has troubled me about that essay, and I wonder if it troubled you, is the extent to which "folk materials" fall under the rubric of nationalism for him. That seems to me to be a rather limiting term for our various cultural traditions.

[e]: Actually, he was trying to work within the definitions of the Communist Party, which viewed Afro-Americans officially as a "nation" with geographical roots in the Black Belt of the South; a line which led some critics to hold that ultimately the white communists planned to segregate the blacks by herding them into the South and isolating them. I think that Wright was actually trying to deal with the confusion between race and culture within the limitations of communist theory. He held that "nationalism" was not the "black chauvinism" for which it was taken by white communists, and defined it as an "emotional expression of group feeling." However, I can't be too certain, since it's been years since I was familiar with the essay. I do know that Wright's attitude toward our Afro-American background was mixed. As a communist intellectual he appeared to consider Afro-American culture "naive" and "humble."

But then, in *Twelve Million Black Voices*, he makes lyrical use of certain folk materials. It isn't an easy question because at the time Wright was so embattled; fighting the official line of the Communist Party, defending himself against the anti-intellectual attacks of certain black communist leaders, attacking in turn those writers and intellectuals whom he considered "bourgeois Negroes." On a more objective level, however, his *Blueprint* was a projection of his own plan for action and, I would suggest, a manifesto through which he was announcing his authoritative assumption of literary and intellectual leadership. He was utterly serious in this independent assertion of leadership, but just as serious in his effort to maintain party discipline while remaining loyal to his racial experience.

Perhaps the last was why he was so embattled with those he considered bourgeois Negroes. He had little tact in dealing with them and I don't think that he was aware that his failure to communicate was often his own fault. He told me of an incident in which he went to a party at one of the colleges near Chicago where he was outraged to see that the black students were attired in tuxedos and evening dresses. As far as Wright was concerned, this alone marked them as "bourgeois" and I'm sure that his attitude made for the poor communication which resulted. His sartorial distrust of the group was reinforced by his communist ideology. However, Bill Attaway, the novelist, was present and although Attaway was not the intellectual that Wright was, he was certainly close to our Afro-American folk tradition—perhaps even closer than Wright—and a rather marvelous teller of folk tales and a serious writer in his own right. I suppose it was a matter of Wright's having seen the clothing and missed the people, a matter of an ideology-grounded, "trained-incapacity" to respect or communicate with Negroes who were formally educated. Perhaps it is one of the purposes of ideology to render it unnecessary to deal with human complexity. At any rate, you've raised questions that require scholarly investigation. In his essay on T. E. Lawrence, Malraux has stated that in revolutionary histories what runs counter to revolutionary convention (here let us say "ideology") is suppressed more imperiously than embarrassing episodes in private memoirs. I've always been struck by the fact that in the account which Wright gives in *Black Boy* of his running away from Mississippi he fails to reveal that the boys who helped him steal the canned goods and other articles with which he made his escape were, in fact, Zack and Wilson Hubert, the sons of the late President Hubert of Jackson College. This was a rather interesting detail to omit, I thought, from the account of one who was usually so sensitive to the class divisions within the Afro-American group. I happened to have known Zack and Wilson at the time their father was president of Langston University out in Oklahoma and found them rather lively and attractive young men. But perhaps it was a matter of conscious selectivity, of Wright's keeping his class views neat by filtering out certain contradictions that might have embarrassed his ideologically structured projection of experience. Perhaps their having been, or become, in his estimation "middle class" was inconvenient to the larger point he was making.

[s]: I guess one reason I have been thinking more and more about Wright is because we seem to be in a period of renewed interest in him. Why do you think this is so? Is this merely something cyclical, or is it something akin to the temper of the times?

[E]: Basically it's because he was a powerful writer and even though many of the solutions he offered were obviously inadequate, the issues which he explored haven't gone away. But I think much of it was stirred up by the Black Aesthetic people, who are *badly* in need of a hero, and an answer to James Baldwin's criticism of Wright. Now with Wright safely out of the way they can shape him and his work to their own convenience. Some of them would make him an outright cultural racist by way of giving authority to their own biases and confusions. But I think there is another reason: By now several generations of young people have been taught *Native Son* and *Black Boy* in high schools and colleges. After all, given a decade of emphasis upon "blackness" and "militancy" how many writers of Wright's stature are there to conjure with? It doesn't matter to the "Black Aesthetic" crowd that in tailoring him to suit their own threadbare arguments they are forced to overlook the fact that he was more concerned—at least during the period when his most powerful books were written—with Marxist-Leninist-Stalinist ideology than with even his own version of "black nationalism." He wasn't, as they say, in their "bag" at all; yet that's where they've sought to cram him, no matter that his head and limbs refuse to accommodate their efforts.

It would seem that these black "Black Aestheticians" are so hung up on race and color that they tend to imitate that species of worm which maintains its ranks by following a scent laid down by the leader. Introduce them to the rim of a swill barrel, let the leader negotiate one circle of the rim and even though you remove him the rest will continue to circle the swill indefinitely! It doesn't matter that the leader might have been taken off and gone on to become metamorphosed into a butterfly and flown away, they keep on circling. Frequently it appears that somebody or some thing has staked off a certain area of thought and endeavor and said, "Here, this is yours; this is where you're able to stay and we've marked it 'Black' so that you can be safe and comfortable. Therefore you stay right there and everything will be O.K.—You hear?" And oh, how so many Afro-American would-be intellectuals agree! They can't seem to imagine that books or authors that fail to mention "Black" explicitly might be of crucial importance in dealing with their own racial, cultural, and individual dilemmas. Thus it's ironic to see these people embracing Wright, because his was anything but such an attitude. In his effort to make some sort of intellectual *Gestalt* for himself, he read all kinds of books, entertained all kinds of ideas. And during the days when I knew him well he certainly didn't allow racial considerations to limit the free play of his intellect. After all, most of his friends, like both of his wives, were white.

[s]: Well, you mention the Black Aesthetic crowd: On the one hand, we have their interest in Wright, yet on the other we have very little fiction produced by these writers, these writer-critics. Why, in your opinion, don't they write fiction? Is it because of conventional notions of the novel being a bourgeois art form, or is it because a novel is so damn hard to write. [Laughter]

[E]: I can tell you this: they're damn hard for me! As for the others, I have no idea. I don't know most of those people, even though many seem to feel that we have a personal quarrel. But to put it into the vernacular, I would think that there's a heap of shucking going on and none of it stacks. They find it easier to issue militant slogans while remaining safely in the straitjacket of racist ideology—the ideology that has been made of what they call "Blackness"—than to deal with either the beautiful and confounding complexities of Afro-American culture or the difficulties that must be faced by those who would convert experience into the forms of the novel. If they can't grasp the meaning of what they live and read because their obsession with the mysticism of race and color has incapacitated their ability to see, then they certainly can't subject themselves to the discipline demanded by the novel. Which, after all, is a product of the *integrative* and *analytical* play of the imagination as it seeks to convert experience into forms of symbolic action. How can one abstract Afro-American experience from that of the larger culture of which it is so important a part without reducing it, in the name of "Blackness," to as vapid a collection of stereotypes as those created in the name of whiteness? As I say, imagination itself is *integrative*, a matter of making symbolic wholes out of parts. Afro-American culture is itself a product of that process carried on under the most difficult social and political conditions. Thus it would seem to me that any objective approach to its dynamics would lead to the basic conclusion that, here in the U.S. at least, culture has successfully confounded all concepts of race. American culture would not exist without its Afro-American component, or if it did, it would be quite different. Yet, certain people who are fixed on the concept of race at the expense of culture would claim Alexandre Dumas as a true blue "Boot," "Race Man," or what not, but this is to ignore his achievement, the language in which he thought and wrote, and the image which he held of himself. All this by way of elevating a part of his blood line to a position of total (really totalitarian) importance.

But not only was Dumas culturally a Frenchman, he was a Frenchman who worked and achieved himself in the novel, a literary form which in itself was influenced by developments taking place in England, in Germany and in Russia. Such people also claim Pushkin as their own, and not because of the fact that he was the father of modern Russian literature, but because there was an African or Ethiopian in his background. The relationship between biology and culture is mysterious; perhaps General Hannibal's sperm was precisely what was needed to release the greatness of Russian literature. But although he was a distinguished military man and engineer in his own right, we know of him mainly because of his great-grandson's *literary* achievements, not for his influence upon the Russian racial mixture. I suppose what I'm saying is that an over-emphasis on our own racial origins in Africa (an origin which is only partial) at the expense of the way in which our cultural expression has transcended race, our present social status and our previous condition of servitude, is to ignore much of what is most intriguing and admirable in Afro-American experience. Worse, it is to miss the fact that American culture owes much of its distinctiveness to idioms which achieved their initial formulation through the cultural creativity of Afro-Americans. White Americans have put tremendous energy into keeping the black American below the threshold of social mobility but they still had to descend to see what Negroes were making of the new democratic experience, in order to know what to make of their own. This was especially true of the vernacular idiom in the arts, where lessons were to be learned in everything from power to elegance.

[S]: So what are we to make of people who say, in echo of a certain black poet, that the black masses are uninterested in elegance?

[E]: To accept that notion you've got to have a tin ear and absolutely no eye for style. Elegance turns up in every aspect of Afro-American culture, from sermons to struts, pimp-walks and dance steps. Listen to a sermon by Howard Thurman or the Reverend Franklin, father of the famous singer. Listen to Jimmy Rushing sing the "How Long Blues." Listen to Basie, listen to Ellington; watch O. J. Simpson slice through an opposing line with a dancer's slithering grace. And doesn't all that Afro-American adoration of the Cadillac speak of elegance? Look at the elegance with which the dedicated worshiper of the Cadillac sits at the steering wheel of his chariot. If Bill Robinson and Honi Coles weren't elegant tap dancers, I don't know the meaning of the term. And if Louis Armstrong's meditations on the "Potato Head Blues" aren't marked by elegance, then the term is too inelegant to name the fastidious refinement, the mastery of nuance, the tasteful domination of melody, rhythm, sounding brass and tinkling cymbal which marked his style. Aesthetically speaking, when form is blended successfully with function, elegance results. Black Americans expect elegance even from prizefighters and basketball players and much of the appeal of Jack Johnson and Joe Louis sprang from the fact that each was as elegant as the finest of ballet dancers.

Such statements are products of ideological foolishness and are efforts to palm off sloganeering doggerel as poetry. Surprisingly, the verse of some of these people gives the lie to their assertions, for it reveals as much of the influence of E. E. Cummings and Emily Dickinson as of Langston Hughes or Sterling Brown. Blacks alone didn't invent poetics any more than they invented the American language; and the necessary mixture of cultural influences that goes into creating an individual poetic style defies the neat over-simplifications of racist ideologies. Some of the "Black Aesthetic" people say that nothing written before 1967 is of any value, but I'm pretty sure that those who do would *not* say that nothing done in surgery or law before that date was valueless; but then such people don't chatter about law or surgery because they recognize that they are too difficult to be reduced to empty verbalizing. An unserious familiarity with literature breeds contempt, so they feel that they can get away with any kind of irresponsible statement. Perhaps they'd feel less secure if our people were as interested in literature as they are in music. The Kansas City physician who accidently severed the jugular of band leader Benny Moten while performing a tonsillectomy was almost lynched by his own people in their outrage over the discovery that inept medical technique could end the life of a musician whom they revered for his musical excellence. I quote an extreme instance, but sometimes Afro-Americans have been known to call their own irresponsibles to account.

[s]: What did you think of the *Black World* issue on your work?

[e]: Hell, man, what would you expect? It was obvious that I couldn't have a fair exchange of opinion with those who used the issue to tee off on me, so there was nothing to do but treat them as I had bad dogs and bigoted whites down south: Mentally, I walked away from it. Long before that issue was published they had been banging away at a hateful straw man whom they'd labeled "Ellison" and were using it as a scapegoat for their discontents and disappointments, and it appeared that the more I refused to be provoked the more strident they became. I was amused by the time they wasted attacking me when it was really a couple of *books* that were making them mad, and the only way to win a fight with a book is to write a better book.

I could have respected them had they done that but I saw little evidence that this was going to happen. However, I did appreciate the essays by those who used the issue to express serious disagreement with my work and my position on social issues. I hoped that younger writers would read them as antidotes to the rantings of those who tried to reduce literary discussion to the level of the dirty dozens. I was also amused by the extent of the bad-mouthing because the editor of *Black World* was so persistent in his attempt at scapegoating, while I continued to function very much as I had always done. Even having a bit of influence. His conception of the cultural reality of the U.S. was puzzling because he appeared to have no idea of how books can reach beyond the boundaries of the black community. He seemed to think that he could kill the influence of a novel by attacking its author. That struck me as strange, since his organ reached but a few thousand readers while my books were being read by *many* thousands.

Then there was the other contributor to the issue who gave the impression of being as eager to burn books as any Nazi Gauleiter—which was rather obscene, considering that the man is an old communist and has spent a good part of his life working in a library. His example and that of a like-minded fellow contributor demonstrated that they could be just as vehement, provincial, and totalitarian in the name of "Black Militancy" and "Black Aesthetics" as they had been in the name of "Soviet Communism" and "Socialist Realism." I guess it's a case of Reds infiltrating Blacks, running into a stubborn Negro and turning blue in the face. But I can say this for them: Safe behind the fence provided by a black capitalist, they had one big "barking-at-the-big-gate" go at me. They even managed to convince a few students that I was the worst disaster that had ever hit Afro-American writing. But for all their attacks I'm still here trying—while if I'm asked where is *Black World* today my answer is: Gone with the snows of yester-year/down the pissoir—Da-daa, Da-daaa—and good riddance!

[S]: Our talk about groups reminds me of something Leon Forrest once said. He was asked if he belonged to a group or crowd, and I believe his response was, "I guess you might say that McPherson, Toni Morrison, Albert Murray, Ralph Ellison and I might constitute a crowd." Now what is your response to that?

[E]: It's an interesting grouping of writers whom I respect; still I am by instinct (and experience) a loner. There is no question, however, but that we share what Malraux has termed a "collectivity of sensibilities" and a high regard for the artistic potential of Afro-American experience. And certainly we're all more concerned with art than with ideology or propaganda. But as to our constituting a school, that kind of thing—no. I don't think it desirable even though it offers some relief from the loneliness of the trade. For when writers associate too

closely there is a tendency to control one another's ideas. I'm not
implying that association is itself necessarily a negative matter, but
I suspect that the loneliness of writing causes us to seek for a kind of
certainty among our peers—when very often it's the *uncertainty* of the
creative process which leads to new insights and to unanticipated
formulation. Nevertheless, I share ideas and certain goals with such
people as Forrest and McPherson, just as I do with a number of white
writers, and certainly with Al Murray, whom I've known since our
days at Tuskegee; but they do their own thinking and I do mine. (I
don't know Miss Morrison personally.) Perhaps Forrest was really
describing a collectivity of outsiders who are united by a common
attitude toward the craft.

[s]: He is also describing a group of *fiction* writers, and I can't help
but continue to link this issue to genre . . .

[e]: I agree, because a writer's point of view is determined to a large
extent by the form in which he works. The form shapes his sensibility,
it structures his emotions, and guides his imagination and vision.
That's most important: The novel is a complex agency for the sym-
bolic depiction of experience, and it demands that the writer be will-
ing to look at both sides of characters and issues—at least while he's
working. You might say that the form of the novel imposes its moral-
ity upon the novelist by demanding a complexity of vision and an
openness to the variety and depth of experience.
    Kenneth Burke says that language "moralizes" both mankind and
nature, thus the novel "moralizes" the novelist. Dostoevsky could be
pretty rabid in some of his ideological concerns, pretty bigoted in his
attitudes toward the members of certain groups, but when he chose
to depict characters identified with such groups he gave them all
the human complexity that the form and action of the novel de-
manded. I don't think that you can do this if your mind is made up
beforehand. You end up creating stereotypes, writing propaganda.

[HARPER]: Is there any sort of organization that you now see in the
fiction you've published over the years since *Invisible Man*? I've
put together the fiction I've seen in various places and it seems to
me that it is all of one piece—that is, I see certain kinds of relation-
ships. For example, could one go out and collect "Song of Innocence"
and "Juneteenth" and make a case for works-in-progress being
sections of the same novel?

[e]: Yes, they *are* parts of the same novel, but whether they will
remain in that relationship I don't know, because, you know, I lost a
good part of the novel in a fire. It's a long manuscript, and it just
might be two books.

[H]: I remember talking with some students at Harvard and two of
them were offended by "Juneteenth" where Hickman says that

Africans were heathens who didn't have any souls. They said this is a terrible thing! You got to get him up here!

[E]: They went on to say other things, didn't they? Did they read what was *there*?

[H]: Yes, but they were bothered by "heathen." Again, this is the old question of ideology. I think the source of their agitation was that they thought you were making a statement to the effect that when Africans came to this country they were soulless.

[E]: Oh, for God's sake! I didn't make that statement, *Hickman* did. He was preaching about transcendence; about the recovery from fragmentation; about the slave's refusal, with the help of God, to be decimated by slavery. He was speaking as a Christian minister of the role his religion had played in providing a sense of unity and hope to a people that had been deliberately deprived of a functional continuity with their religions and traditions. Hickman didn't attend college but, hell, he knew that all of our African ancestors didn't belong to the same tribe, speak the same tongue, or worship the same gods . . .

[H]: If they had proposed the argument that either Bliss or Hickman was the persona of Ralph Ellison *that* might have been debatable—it probably wasn't *right*, but it might have been debatable. The one-dimensional character, the way they view literary creation, is what bothered me. We got in a similar row over "Song of Innocence." In the minds of some students who are not familiar with literary convention and the whole business of creation, anything you write is autobiographical, it's about you.

[S]: This reminds me of students who write papers for me about *The Autobiography of an Ex-Colored Man*, and begin, "When *Johnson* gets off the train in Atlanta . . . ." [Laughter]

[H]: Do you get many inquiries about the chapter deleted from *Invisible Man* that appears in *Soon, One Morning*? Did you willingly cut it out?

[E]: Well, the book was long and they wanted cuts, and I found a better way than just cutting was to restructure. So, instead of that particular handling of the narrative sequence I just took it out. I think it would have probably worked better in.

[H]: Why isn't "Society, Morality and the Novel" in *Shadow and Act*? It came before.

[E]: I wanted to put it in but my editor said no. I think it was because we already had enough material.

[S]: Can you tell us about your teaching experiences? I'm especially interested in experiences resulting from attempts to teach certain texts side by side. For example, in 1970, I once began a course on the

Harlem Renaissance by assigning *The Great Gatsby*. I still think it was a great idea, but the students couldn't get with it—even on the level of establishing a milieu, or "counter-milieu."

[E]: I have had the same trouble getting that across with *Gatsby*. For instance, I find it significant that the character who saw who was driving the "death car" was a Negro; and yet, some students resist when I tie that in with Tom Buchanan's concern over the rise of the colored races, the scene in which blacks are being driven by a white chauffeur, and the characterization of the Jewish gangster. They miss the broader context of the novel that is revealed in the understated themes of race, class, and social mobility. The novel is set in what was called the Jazz Age, but what is the difference between Fitzgerald's Jazz Age and that of Duke Ellington and Louis Armstrong? I point out that Fitzgerald was familiar with Brick Top's nightclub and was often at the Harlem Cotton Club, and I suggest that after reading what Fitzgerald made of the experience the student should take a look at what Langston Hughes and other writers of the Harlem Renaissance made of it. It's ironic that some of the white writers were more open to knowledge relating to the Harlem of that period than are the black kids who refuse to study it seriously because they feel that they know it through their genes. They think affirmations of "Blackness" resolves all mysteries of time and place, circumstance and personality. But for a writer like Fitzgerald Harlem was one of the places where the action was, so, being a good novelist, with an interest in people and an eye for exciting new developments in the culture, he went where the action was unfolding. Now we don't have to like what white writers, musicians, and dancers made of what went on, but I do think we should recognize that across the division of race they were attempting to absorb and project some of the cultural complexity of the total American scene. They were responding in their individual ways to the vitality of the Afro-American cultural idiom. The "Black Aesthetic" crowd buys the idea of total cultural separation between blacks and whites, suggesting that we've been left out of the mainstream. But when we examine American music and literature in terms of its themes, symbolism, rhythms, tonalities, idioms and images it is obvious that those rejected "Neegroes" have been a vital part of the mainstream and were from the beginning. Thus, if a student is to grasp the complex sources of American cultural tradition he should assume that a major part of that tradition springs from Afro-America; because one of the few ways the slaves and their descendants had of expressing their inner sense of identity was by imposing their own aesthetic will upon those who assumed that they would have nothing to do with defining American experience. Today sociologists, many of them the first members of immigrant families to attend college, and who now teach at universities and advise politicians, are telling us that the American melting-pot didn't melt. But despite discrimination and other inequities in the society, its various cultural idioms did, indeed, melt and are continuing to do so.

[H]: Don't you teach a course in the vernacular?

[E]: Yes, from a base in American lit. I teach a course which allows me to touch many areas of American culture. American literature grew out of the development of American vernacular speech as it asserted its modes against European tradition and proper English usage. As the young nation achieved coherence the very pressures of Nature, of the New World "scene," forced Americans to create a flood of new terminologies: for naming the newly created social forms, the nuances of the individualism that was spreading throughout the young society, and the relationships between diverse groups. Out of the democratic principles set down on paper in the Constitution and the Bill of Rights they were improvising themselves into a nation, scraping together a conscious culture out of the various dialects, idioms, lingos, and methodologies of America's diverse peoples and regions. In this effort the English language and traditional cultural forms served both as guides and as restraints, anchoring Americans in the wisdom and processes of the past, while making it difficult for them to perceive with any clarity the nuances of their new identity. Given the reality of slavery and the denial of social mobility to blacks, it is ironic that they were placed by that very circumstance in the position of having the greatest freedom to create specifically *American* cultural idioms. Thus the slaves had the unnoticed opportunity to be culturally daring and innovative because the strictures of "good taste" and "thou shall-nots" of tradition were not imposed upon them. And so, having no past in the art of Europe, they could use its elements and their inherited sense of style to improvise forms through which they could express their own unique sense of American experience. They did so in dance, in music, in cuisine and so on, and white American artists often found the slaves' improvisations a clue for their *own* improvisations. From the very beginnings of the nation Afro-Americans were contributing to the evolution of a specifically *American* culture.

[H]: Are you happy with your students at N.Y.U.?

[E]: With some of them; you know, the quality varies from class to class. I am unhappy with the numbers who can't write. I consider myself as having had a fairly incomplete education, but as I look back I realize that even in high school there were a number of us who could write rings around some of my graduate students. Most of my students are white. I haven't had many black students, but when I work with those who are having difficulty I say to them, "All right, you are here now, so recognize that you have certain disabilities which I can't ignore. So let's not kid ourselves but face the fact that there's some catching up to be done. There's nothing wrong with your mind but there *is* a lot wrong with the kind of training you've had, if not then with the kind of attention you've given to learning. Face that fact and allow your experience to feed your study and you'll be surprised at how fast you can come up to par." Fortunately, a few understand that this isn't a put-down, but the truth.

The other day I had to tell a black student who wants to substitute militancy for study and who came up with an easy criticism of George Washington Carver that I didn't like Dr. Carver either, but for a specific and personal reason: At Tuskegee he was always chasing me out of Rockefeller Hall where I'd go to work out my harmonic exercises on the piano. My investigations into the mysteries of harmony interfered with his investigations of the peanut, and to me harmony was more important. But today I realize that not only did a large industry draw upon his experiments but by manipulating strains of peanuts he was growing himself an American President! Dr. Carver has been called an "Uncle Tom," but I keep looking at the announcement of prizes given in such fields as science and architecture, in biology and electronics and I'm chagrined over the fact that few of our students are getting them. Sheer militancy isn't enough, and when used as an excuse to avoid study it is disastrous. Today we're in a better way to learn and participate in the intellectual life of this country than ever before, but apparently we're taking fewer advantages of our opportunities than when we were limited to carrying bags and waiting tables. The availability of ideas and culture means little if we don't take advantage, participate, and compete with the best in our elected fields.

[H]: Bob and I know a folklorist who thinks you are one of the few people who really understand what folklore is and how it ought to be used. Would you care to comment on that?

[E]: Folklore has been such a vital part of American literature that it is amazing that more people (and especially writers) aren't aware of it. Constance Rourke points out that there are folk motives even in the work of Henry James. I guess one of the difficulties here is that people think of folklore as "quaint," as something that is projected in dialect, when in fact it is its style and wisdom that count. The same problem arises when you speak of *American* folklore in the general sense and overlook the complex influence of vernacular idioms, the mixture of vernacular styles, that operate in American culture. Considering the social condition of the slaves, what is to be made of their singing a comic song which refers to a black girl's dancing "Taglioni" in the street? Or what are you going to do with fairly illiterate jazz musicians who interpolate phrases from the likes of Bach, Verdi, or Puccini in their improvisations on the blues or popular melodies? In this country it is necessary to redefine what we mean by folklore, because, culturally, Americans are heirs to the culture of all the ages, and it is through the vernacular process that we blend folk and classical modes into an art that is uniquely American. Thus I believe it a mistake to think of the slaves as having been separate from the eclectic processes, the general culture, when in fact they were participating in it in many unexamined ways. Art was an inseparable part of their African forebears' lives, and they did, after all, do most of the building of Monticello! They made the bricks and did the carpentry and cabinetry. Recently *The Crisis* published an article calling attention to the manner in which historians tend to omit the slave craftsmen when describing the "cultural activities" of Thomas Jefferson, but my God, somebody was there doing the work and receiving the instructions necessary for carrying it to completion. If there are doubts as to this, all one has to do is observe the demonstrations down at Colonial Williamsburg. Slaves were craftsmen and artists as well as field hands and as such they absorbed and mastered the styles and techniques around them. That's how I see it and I can't imagine a human situation that would *not* be like that.

Perhaps we have too damn much of a wound-worshiping investment in the notion that the slaves were brutalized beyond the point of exercising their human will to survive. Which reminds me of an aspect of the uproar centering around *Time on the Cross*. Whatever the viability of their methods, the authors were saying that slavery wasn't as brutalizing as the usual view would have it. They held that the slaves were *not* reduced to a gas-oven state of docility, a view that would see each and every slave master as a Hitler and American slavery as a preview of the Holocaust. I'm no historian, but their view seems to offer a more adequate accounting for the character of the ex-slaves whom I knew in Oklahoma and Alabama. After all, I did see my grandaddy and he was no beaten-down "Sambo." Rather he was a courageous, ingenious old guy who owned property, engaged in the Reconstruction politics of South Carolina, and who stood up to a mob after they had lynched his best friend. When ordered to leave town, he told the lynchers, "If you're gonna kill me, you're gonna kill me here where I've got my family, and my property and my friends." He died there years later, in his own bed, and at the age of 76. I also knew one of his friends who, after years of operating a printing business for a white man, came north and set up his own printing shop in Harlem.

The other argument that I find interesting in *Time on the Cross*

is the authors' statement that, while the slaves in the Caribbean and
Brazil died off every ten years and had to be replaced from Africa,
those in the United States managed to reproduce themselves. And
of course they did! There were times when native-born blacks out-
numbered native-born whites. Unlike the slaves of the other Amer-
icas, they had a good injection of white European chromosomes which
made them immune to many European diseases. [Laughter] They
also became "Indianized," and certainly these biological facts show
in our faces. Still, many historians and sociologists act as though
these factors are irrelevant, and by ignoring them they contribute
to the divisive mystification of race.

[s]: I pointed that out to a historian the other day, and I could tell by the
look on his face that I was embarrassing him! [Laughter]

[E]: Then Fern Brodie published a biographical account of Jefferson's
long affair with his black mistress. Why don't the historians allow
these people their human complexity?

[H]: Well, we did!

[E]: That's right! [Laughter] It's amusing the way this thing works. In
my class I get raised eyebrows by pointing out that race is always at
the center of our uneasy preoccupation with American identity. It is
as abiding as our concern with the principles of freedom and equality.
Thus, when you read American literature and fail to see the words
"Black" or "Negro" or "Afro-American" in a given work, it doesn't
mean that they are not operating there symbolically. The old phrase
"There's a nigger in the woodpile" was more fact than fantasy. Just
examine the logic of a work's symbolism and you'll discover that there
are surrogates for blacks and the hierarchal motives they symbolize;
just as Negroes are often surrogates for the American Indian. Once
we were discussing the tragedy of the Indian, and someone said,
"Yeah, the Indian, he stood up to the white man; he didn't take that
crap." This went on until someone got serious and said, "Yeah, but
look here man, what *happened* to them damn Indians?" And I said,
"Well, don't you know? *You* became the damn Indians!" They
laughed but I don't think that it really got across. As a child watching
cowboy and Indian movies I frequently pulled for the Indians to win,
but as you know, they seldom did.

[H]: What would you like to see people researching and writing that
would begin to correct things?

[E]: Well, I would really like to see more studies that deal with the
actual pre-Emancipation scene; works that would place people. Who
was doing what jobs? And what happened to them after Emancipa-
tion, and later after the betrayal of Reconstruction? Where did people
go? I'd like to see more done on the role of geography in American
Negro history. Many black cowboys were slaves who, after their

owners moved west, were taken out of the cotton patch and put on horses. Many Afro-American characteristics that are assumed to spring from the brutality of slavery are partially the results of geography, of the localities in which they were enslaved. Some of this is suggested by the phrase "sold down the river." The Mississippi was as tremendous a force in Afro-American history as it was in the vision of Mark Twain. The geographical division of the country into political districts and regions with complementary agricultural and economic systems underlies much of Afro-American poetic symbolism. That the star points north is not important because of some abstract, mystical or religious conception, but because it brought into conjunction biblical references, concrete social conditions and the human will to survive—including the fact that if you got safely across certain socio-geographical boundaries you were in freedom. Writers have made much of the North Star but they forget that a hell of a lot of slaves were running away to the West, "going to the nation, going to the territory," because as Mark Twain knew, that too was an area of Negro freedom. When people get to telling stories based on their cooperate experience, quite naturally such patterns turn up. Because as significant scenes in which human will is asserted, they help organize and focus narrative. They become more poetic the further we are removed from the actual experience, and their symbolic force is extended through repetition.

I'd also like to see someone write about jazz in such a way that they cover those people who are the intermediaries, the mentors, the teachers, the transmitters of classical tradition. All around the country there were musicians, bandmasters, etc. who disapproved of the jazz life but who, nevertheless, were training people to read music and to perform on instruments. People who taught voice and staged operettas, and so on. You still have them in the colleges, you have them in the towns, giving piano lessons, teaching harmony. These are the links between the classical and folk traditions and jazz.

[H]: Thanks for letting us visit with you this afternoon.

[E]: It's been my pleasure. I enjoyed it.

AFTER MODERNISM, AFTER HIBERNATION: MICHAEL HARPER, ROBERT HAYDEN, AND JAY WRIGHT

ROBERT B. STEPTO

To become aware of our history is to become aware of our singularity. It is a moment of reflective repose before we devote ourselves to action again.
—OCTAVIO PAZ

Please, a definition: A hibernation is a covert preparation for a more overt action.
—RALPH ELLISON

Anochecí enfermo   Amanecí bueno
(I went to bed sick. I woke up well.)
—JAY WRIGHT

"After modernism"—what does it mean, to what does it refer? As Paul de Man has written,

> The term "modernity" . . . designates more generally the problematical possibility of all literature's existing in the present, of being considered, or read, from a point of view that claims to share with it its own sense of a temporal present. In theory, the question of modernity could therefore be asked of any literature at any time, contemporaneous or not. In practice, however, the question has to be put somewhat more pragmatically. . . .[1]

With de Man's "pragmatically" in mind, I would suggest that "after modernism" may yet have its day in the hermeneutical sweepstakes, provided that it is properly groomed and well ridden. Literary modernism may never end, but there exist in modern literature certain aesthetic as well as historical moments when the modern writer appears to call for a new order. Because it is his call, and because the new set of images demanded is to be in some sense a natural outgrowth of his own figurative language, we may say that the modern writer is prefiguring his epilogue, or at the very least inaugurating a rather specific type of post-modernist expression even though, as we know, modernism has not run its course. "After modernism" may therefore be discussed as a series of incidents in recent literary history wherein a literary exchange (call and response?) between modern writers and would-be post-modern writers yields epilogues (or epilogues to epilogues, as we will soon see) to the modernist's work. This is only a "working" definition of the phrase, but at least it works—and for the right reasons: it makes no effort to predict the death of one era and the genesis of a new one, or to plump up certain artists before others as avant-garde, and its goal is the correct one of trying to tell us something about literary history and literary process.

In Afro-American literature, the modernist/post-modernist exchanges that interest me most are those which evolve from the post-textual "call" of Ralph Ellison's novel, *Invisible Man*. Readers of the novel will remember that at the end (which is, of course, the beginning), Ellison's protagonist is marked by two extraordinary features: one, that he has lived through a series of hair-raising experiences and yet has come to control that personal history through the act of art-making; and two, despite his control of his history (symbolized rhetorically by the frame created in the novel's prologue and epilogue), he lives in a hole—a "clean, well-lighted place" to be sure, but a hole nonetheless. The Invisible Man is, as he says, "in a state of hibernation," and later he defines a hibernation as "a covert preparation for a more overt action."

In the prologue and epilogue, we are given many fascinating and often bizarre details about the hero's self-confinement, but those which further develop the idea of hibernation as a metaphor for an artist's apprenticeship—the "covert preparation" that the novel is really all about—demand our greatest attention. *Invisible Man*'s call, its prefiguration of epilogues to its epilogue (and prologue), is a clarion cry for multiple images and voicings of the Afro-American articulate hero's post-apprenticeship/post-hibernation condition. Recent literary texts which offer such images and voicings, and attempt as well to resolve the primary dilemmas of artistic apprenticeship which the novel identifies, are texts which create, in response to a specific modern text, a post-modern art.

In the following pages I take the liberty of discussing several recent poems by Michael Harper, Robert Hayden, and Jay Wright as responses to the prefiguring call of Mr. Ellison's novel and hence, in light of my definition, as post-modernist expressions. Each poem or sequence of poems displays a "post-apprenticeship" voice, and each situates that voice upon a rather specific "post-hibernation" terrain. The order of my presentation of the poems is almost chronological, but chronology is not the organizing principle of the discussion. My purpose is rather to begin with images of smaller physical landscapes and to end with depictions of larger ones, and in that way to impose a modest narrative order on the articulate hero's "overt activities" upon the landscape—and within the reader.

Michael Harper's "Photographs/*Negatives*," section IV of his third book of poems, *Song: I Want a Witness* (1972), is a sequence of nine poems that intersplice two variations upon the same basic photographic metaphor. One variation, stated and restated in five poems, "The Negatives," "Photographs," "Utility Room," "The Borning Room," and "Trays: A Portfolio," studies the process of printmaking—of negative becoming photograph—and in so doing orders a husband and wife's nightmare of child loss by presenting their activities in a cellar darkroom as a ritualistic search for the presence and images of children "torn away." In each of the five poems, printmaking initiates image-making of a different order:

> A simple enlarger
> a bulb with a shade,
> images born through her lens
> packed on the contact sheet;
> fatted negatives under thick
> condenser glass,
> prints from her uterus,
> cramps from her developing tank. . . .[2]

"Negative," above and beyond its obvious literal meaning, is both a referent to the children who might have lived and a description of an indelible yet skewed image of child loss repeated mercilessly upon the proof sheet of memory:

> The hypo fix
> fastens the images
> hardening against light
> on her film and papers.
> I imagine her movement
> at night as her teeth grind:
> I know she dreams the negatives. (*S*, 45)

The other metaphoric variation, generated within the lines of the four remaining poems, "The Night of Frost," "At the Cemetery," "The Families Album," and "History as Apple Tree," also studies the process of image-making, but in different terms. In these poems, the narrative situation to be invested with metaphorical properties is always that of the solitary poet, as articulate or self-conscious (as opposed to "double-conscious") hero, traversing what Octavio Paz would term a labyrinth of solitude. This labyrinth is simultaneously a literal landscape rich in lore and history (here, a south-of-Boston terrain including both Massachusetts and Rhode Island

land) and a figurative landscape of racial memory. In each poem, the landscapes link and appear as concentrated images of a grave-yard; and it is upon this land, this ritual ground as negative plate, that the poet as a potential human image—

> I walk as negative
> image over white crusted
> gravestones as my dark feet
> stamp their footprints . . . (*S*, 47)

—searches for the process by which he will "imagine" himself.

While we may identify certain poems in the series as "darkroom" poems or "cemetery" poems, we mustn't lose sight of how each type of poem feeds on the other and thus contributes to the series as a whole. The cemeteries, graves, and apple tree in one sub-series are of a piece with the darkroom, developing pans, and blossoming images of the dead in the other. Furthermore, the im-plicit fear pervading the entire sequence, that "human photographs" may remain "negative images" if process is not found and enacted, is conveyed both by the poet's quest—in all its racial involvements— upon the "white crusted" land, and by the parents' search for lost children who will only "develop" in "black and white eyes." Of course, the poet himself also binds the exterior and interior land-scapes of the series: he is a negative image to be imagined, a shadow to be cast on ritual ground, as well as a seeker for images in negatives of

> *two sons stoppered*
> *from isolette*
> *to incinerator. . . . (S*, 55)

But the unity of the sequence is perhaps best demonstrated by the manner in which the "cemetery" and "darkroom" poems share the burden of response to *Invisible Man*'s call. Whereas the former poems—especially "The Night of Frost" and "History as Apple Tree"—return the articulate hero to an above-ground labyrinth in which he must unravel the mysteries of personal history bound to public history, the latter sub-series, especially in lines like these from "Trays: A Portfolio":

> *contact: print:*
> *blacken our negatives with light . . . (S*, 56)

provides a photographic metaphor through which we may compre-

hend what the Invisible Man sought through his underground writing
(and lighting!). They also explain why he must end his hibernation
and return, while at least self-imagined (or self-"developed"), to a world
where, as an outwardly Invisible Man, he is, in varying degrees of ex-
posure, a negative.

These many figurative threads come together in the sequence's
concluding poem, "History as Apple Tree." The landscape of the
poem is a historical field, a culture's magic circle—

>   Cocumscussoc is my village,
>   the western arm of Narragansett
>   Bay; Canonicus chief sachem;
>   black men escape into his tribe . . . (S, 58)

—upon which the poet, aware of the private as well as public
dimensions of this ritual ground, may complete his self-willed
metamorphosis from "negative image" to "human photograph."
Historically, the landscape has been assaulted by certain European
preoccupations:

>   How does patent not breed heresy?
>   Williams came to my chief
>   for his tract of land,
>   hunted by mad Puritans,
>   founded Providence Plantation . . . (S, 58)

Yet to some degree the effects of assault have been assuaged by the
powerful workings of nature in its course:

>   In your apple orchard
>   legend conjures Williams' name;
>   he was an apple tree.
>   Buried on his own lot
>   off Benefit Street
>   a giant apple tree grew;
>   two hundred years later,
>   when the grave was opened,
>   dust and root grew
>   in his human skeleton;
>   bones became apple tree. (S, 59)

In the poem's final stanza, the poet's immersion and positioning
within this landscape, for which we are partially prepared by such
earlier lines as "black men escape into the tribe" and "Williams

came to my chief," unfolds as he becomes history—an orchestrated image of past and present—instead of remaining outside of it:

As black man I steal away
in the night to the apple tree,
place my arm in the rich grave,
black sachem on a family plot,
take up a chunk of apple root,
let it become my skeleton,
become my own myth:
my arm the historical branch,
my name the bruised fruit,
black human photograph: apple tree. (*S*, 59)

This portrait of a primal image-in-process is rich and exquisitely layered, but I admire even more its subtle humor. The joke, like those which keep the Invisible Man in stitches, depends for its effect upon the inability of people to *see* one another. Therefore, by employing a phrase from the spirituals ("steal away"), a phrase which plays wonderfully upon the theory that slaves had no rights to self-initiated mobility, Harper suggests that his poet's ritual act of claiming a place in history, a piece of the ground, is a self-configuration of his humanity. Clearly, just as the line "black sachem on a family plot" sustains the essential serio-comic quality of the poet's actions ("essential" because it is rooted in a culture's traditional modes of expression), the poem's final line, "black human photograph: apple tree," restates what is, in effect, a culture's right to be imagined.

Still, we must ask, especially since we are interested in how "History as Apple Tree" responds to the prefiguring call of *Invisible Man,* whether it is a "hibernation" or "post-hibernation" poem. I would argue that it is a "post-hibernation" (or "post-apprentice-ship") poem, partly because, as the final line tells us, it is a "tree" poem and not a "root" poem, and because the poet's achieved state is, in the language of Harper's conceit, not so much print as image. "Black human photograph" and "apple tree" as printed image and emblem emblaze each other through the lens which is at least one configuration of the line's colon; but this is only a fleeting parity, since the phrases are most certainly not interchangeable. As the emblematic manifestation of public and private history as well as racial memory converging upon ritual ground, the "apple tree," not the "black human photograph," is the poet's final destination; and yet it is, of course, through the photo or print that we *gain* the emblem. This passage through printed image to emblem transports the poet to a post-hibernation/post-apprenticeship state: in hibernation, the human photograph is processed or imagined; after hibernation, it is contextualized within a culture's figurative landscape and thereby made an initial manifestation of grander trope.

Once the articulate voice returns to the upper landscape or historical field, we are interested not only in his movements as a solitary seeker but also in how he reassumes the posture of kinsman. Of course, Harper's "Photographs/*Negatives*" poems study this matter: the "black human photograph" in organic relation to the "apple tree" is the "stoppered" children, as well as the poet blood-bound to the private *and* public family that might have been. Kinship is, in short, another term for the process envisioned and hopefully gained through immersion in the sequence's photographic metaphor. But kinsmen also have ties (Harper would say "responsibilities") to their extended tree. After hibernation, what is our voice's posture toward bloodline kin? Will he speak to adopted family? In what ways will the upper landscape be re-peopled once it assumes the proportions of a historical field larger, if not always more accoutred, than the Invisible Man's hole or Harper's poet's burial and birthing ground? Where are—in the language of Ellison's signbook—Supercargo and Tod Clifton? Where are Mary Rambo, Louis Armstrong, Buckeye the Rabbit, and the Lenox Avenue Yam Man? These questions are expressions of the prefiguring call of Ellison's text; and while Robert Hayden's recent series of poems, "Elegies for Paradise Valley," [3] does not answer all of these questions directly, it does provide a splendid example of a mature (that is, post-hibernation) voice re-embracing both bloodline and adopted kin, and in that way re-ordering a landscape experienced previously before hibernation.

The "Elegies for Paradise Valley" are presently eight in number, and while each poem may be said to be "set" in Paradise Valley—Hayden's name for his boyhood neighborhood in Detroit—the "Elegies" do not limn a place as much as they illuminate the ties between kinfolk who are bound as well to place. In this way, Hayden's "Paradise Valley" is a historical field—a culture's magic circle—much like the one established in Harper's "Photographs/*Negatives.*" And, just as Harper (like Ellison, in some measure) deliberately orchestrates his images so that both birth and burial are contextual properties of photograph and negative, darkroom and graveyard, human image and apple tree, the antipodes of Hayden's field are similarly conjoined and disparate because "Paradise Valley" is also a birthing and burial zone, a vision of the Garden as well as of the Pit of the Fall.

Indeed, it is with images of the Pit that the series of Elegies begins, forcing us to wonder if the series' narrative vector will chart upward and, if so, in what form the incremental stops will appear. The first poem is short and taut, a window on a wasteland infested with race rituals including those cultural carcinogens which, as Ellison's Invisible Man observed, promote certain phases of blindness:

> My shared bedroom's window
> opened on alley stench.
> A junkie died in maggots there.
> I saw his body shoved into a van.
> I saw the hatred for our kind
> glistening like tears
> in the policeman's eyes.

The second elegy, shorter still and possibly even more taut, offers through its negative definitions and images of time, place, and shelter (and hence, of historical field) another portrait of the pit:

> No place for Pestalozzi's
> fiorelli. No time of starched
> and ironed innocence. Godfearing
> elders, even Godless grifters, tried
> as best they could to shelter
> us. Rats gnawing in their walls.

It is in the third poem, however, that Hayden's landscape is peopled not just with neighbors and other adopted kin but most especially with the voices that inhabit the poet's memory. The poem opens with spare images of life (floral pieces, Christmas tree, Chinese lantern, freesias) stippled in such a way that they both veil and center the beautiful wooden coffin in which "Waxwork Uncle Henry / (murdered Uncle Crip)" lies. As it closes, however, the chill is (in memory) upon the poet as he learns amid Uncle Crip's warm laughter of a "wicked" song and dance of which they will partake together:

> Mahogany—I'd heard
> the victrola voice of
>
> dead Bert Williams
> talk-sing that word as macabre
> music played, chilling

me. Uncle Crip
had laughed and laughed.

The fourth poem introduces Madam Artelia, the fortune-teller
who attempts to "find" Crip's voice-in-death and is, with Aunt
Jemina of the Ocean Waves among others, one of the great women
in Hayden's canon. But it is in the lyrical fifth elegy that Paradise
Valley is transformed into a busy place full of the miscellaneous
visages so conspicuously absent from the Invisible Man's under-
ground hole. In that poem, in two chiseled yet plaintive ten-line
catalogs of questions answered by a single declarative refraining
line (based on Villon's *ballade*), the poet does not merely list his
adopted kin, he *calls* their names:

> And Belle the classy dresser, where is she,
> who changed her frocks three times a day?
>   Where's Nora, with her laugh, her comic flair,
>   stagestruck Nora waiting for her chance?
> Where's fast Iola, who so loved to dance
> she left her sickbed one last time to whirl
> in silver at The Palace till she fell?
>   Where's mad Miss Alice, who ate from garbage cans?
>   Where's snuffdipping Lucy, who played us 'chunes'
> on her guitar? Where's Hattie? Where's Melissabelle?
> Let vanished rooms, let dead streets tell.

In this catalog, so full of melody, and in the one following it
calling the names of menfolk including "Jim, Watusi prince and
Good Old Boy," "Tump the defeated artist," "Les the Huntsman,"
"Tough Kid Chocolate," and "dapper Jess," we receive—in language
Hayden may share with Harper—an orchestration of "negative
images" becoming "human photographs." Hayden's fifth elegy
very nearly completes the family album which is one of the se-
quence's responses to the prefiguring call of Ellison's novel.

Another response—quite possibly *the* other response—is stated
through the poet's resolution of his relationship with his Uncle
Crip. In the first few elegies we sense that Crip was both a boon
and a bane to his young nephew because he generated complex
situations and hence emotional confusion by mischievously pitting
and even blending the sacred and the profane. Crip, in brief, was
one of the ones—probably *the* one—who taught Hayden's artist-as-a-
young-man by gesture, word, and deed that the world in all its
complexity is as much "both/and" as it is "either/or." The artist's

search for Crip within a reincarnated Paradise Valley is, then, an effort not only to rediscover those singular moments when Crip's teachings took hold, but also to explore how Crip offered his knowledge (and himself) to his nephew—and how his gifts were received and embraced.

Knowledge and pedagogy, dilemma and resolution, elder and youth are fused in the poetic sequence by a simple, marvelous image and metaphor of dance. In the sixth elegy, for example, are the lines:

> I scrounged for crumbs:
> I yearned to touch
> the choirlady's hair,
> I wanted Uncle Crip
>
> to kiss me, but he danced
> with me instead;
> we Balled-the-Jack
> to Jellyroll
>
> Morton's brimstone
> piano on the phonograph,
> laughing, shaking the gasolier
> a later stillness dimmed.

And in the eighth elegy, after opening lines which speak both of inner tuggings to be resolved ("Of death, of loving, / of sin and hellfire too . . .") and of Crip's death (" . . . pitched / from the gamblingtable / Lord have mercy on / his wicked soul— / face foremost into hell . . ."), we witness the poet's dance with mentor and kin which comes when inherited gifts yield self-knowledge:

> We'd dance there, Uncle
> Crip and I,
> for though I spoke
> my pieces well in Sunday School,
>
> I knew myself (precocious
> in the ways of guilt
> and secret pain)
> the devil's own rag babydoll.

We appreciate the expression of affection that warms these final lines, as well as the manner in which youthful confusions are finally resolved. Crip is a devil, and the artist his rag babydoll, but like their richly peopled landscape they are self-defined and, as their dance suggests, triumphantly mobile. Hayden's revision of Paradise Valley is an answer to *Invisible Man*'s prefiguring call, not only because it re-peoples an exterior landscape and fashions an artist who "calls the names," but also because Paradise Valley is a landscape outside those definitions of history—and, hence, of historical fields—created by others. In his epilogue the Invisible Man declares, "Step outside the narrow borders of what men call reality and you step into chaos . . . or imagination." Paradise Valley, like the Harlem vibrating above Ellison's hero's head, is unreal because it is for the most part unseen. After hibernation, as Ellison and Hayden tell us, the unseen must be not only seen but also imagined.

But let's pursue these matters on yet a larger scale: after hibernation—after apprenticeship—how does the articulate figure view the universe (which I will define quite simply as *all he can see*)? What happens when his culture's magic circle of myth, rite, and landscape—its literal and figurative birthing and burial ground—*becomes* the world? What ordering of the universe—and fashioning of poetic voice—is prefigured by the Invisible Man's final question, "Who knows but that, on the lower frequencies, I speak for you?" Clearly, these questions constitute a call for field and voice of fantastic scale, and among Afro-American poets Jay Wright has made the most ambitious attempt to respond with images of macrocosmic proportions. His poet is a dyēli, another namer of the names,

> . . . a dark and dutiful dyēli,
> searching for the understanding of his deeds . . .[4]

whose song, "The Second Eye of the World," is part three of the first part of Wright's long poem, *Dimensions of History*. In Mande culture, a dyēli is, like the dyāru and gyeserē in Soninke and Songhay cultures, a professional archivist, a member of the caste responsible for the family histories of nobles. Thus, even though the kinship he studies binds the rites and fields of the world far more than it re-peoples a given field, Wright's dyēli is kin to Harper's and Hayden's questing artists. Like the passage from negative to print to emblem, and the circumchange of epilogue as prologue, the dyēli's journey upon and within a world as large as vision is a return to a primal world (Apple Tree, Paradise Valley) occasioned by the exhaustion of an increasingly sophisticated, and hence temporal, world's domain. Through Wright's dyēli, even more than through Harper's printed voice becoming metaphor, we hear a response to what may be the most baffling yet essential command of Ellison's text—the call for images of the return to hibernation (even Jack-the-Bear would admit to life's endless cycle) or at very least of hibernation's pulsing, clouded presence as a precursor rite birthing those other rites and fields which are the stuff of history, art, and vocation in this world.

"The Second Eye of the World" begins with selections from texts which, as incantatory rites, are fragments of the "one sentence" to be realized through vocation and the art that is the poem. "Anocheci enfermo / Amaneci bueno" is sung at the beginning to suggest, as Wright informs us, not simply the Arabic influence on the Spanish but also the essential oneness of the world and the one, the voice, who experiences it. The lines sketch the moral as well as linguistic geography of the poetic unit while providing a concentrated image of hibernation and its aftermath: "I went to bed sick. I woke up well." All of these energies are sustained by the second fragment, which is from *The Egyptian Book of the Dead:*

> 'I am the bennu bird in annu,
> I am the keeper of the book of things which are
> and things which shall be.
> Who then is this . . . ?
> The things which are the things which shall be
> are his dead body.' (*D*, 31)

To this is appended:

> My breath leaves my body in dreams.
>
> Who is mounted here?
> Who returned? (*D*, 31)

Like the artists in the Harper and Hayden poems, Wright's dyēli seeks images of personal history; but the dyēli pursues these images through a new kind of question, suggesting both the mobility and the stasis that accompany "the understanding of his deeds." "Who is mounted here?"—the kinetic image of the dyēli upon his mount initiated by "My breath leaves my body in dreams" is reversed soon thereafter in the lines:

> Under the white moon
> The gods will straddle you.
> Santiago on a white horse,
> twin bolts, or a lance,
> brother of Christ,
> give us a nation. (*D*, 31)

The ambiguity of "mounted" prepares us to see that the "nation"
is—for the dyēli as much as for the voices of Ellison, Harper, and
Hayden—a false capital, a center that cannot hold. "Nation"
initiates fragments:

> 'We must MAKE an ISSUE, CREATE an EVENT,
> and ESTABLISH a NATIONAL POSITION FOR OURSELVES . . .' (D, 31)

But since it does not circumscribe a spirited center, its verbal mani-
festations must be glossed:

> Muhammad to Mecca again
> for the weavers of souls,
> clothiers of a body gone fat with stillness. (D, 32)

What must be understood here is the fundamental incongruence
between the idea of nation and that of historical field (and, hence, the
distinction between static and perpetually evolving centers of spirit)
which informs the dyēli's song of self-discovery much as it in-
fluences the Harper and Hayden poems. *Invisible Man* calls for
certain very particular universal, as opposed to national, images
("Whence all this passion toward conformity anyway? . . . Life is
to be lived, not controlled. . . . Our fate is to become one, and yet
many—This is not prophecy, but description"), images which live
and enliven the living principally because they are not constrained
by national or generic boundaries. Harper's emblem of the apple
tree (blossom *and* root) and Hayden's portrait of kin (in death
and dance) are such images; they are evolving centers of spirit.
In "The Second Eye of the World," there is a greater sense of
dual, errant energy; both knight and grail are set in motion, both
center and circumference seek an understanding of their deeds:

>   Who chooses me?
> In Cuba,
> Black Melchior caresses the cobra.
> Dahomey dance   Havana Boa
> This Python, sacred serpent of Delphi,
> this Pythia, stretching the dark corners,
> dark herself, caught in darkness,
> sees the fat sin burned on the island.
>
> Upon a Day of Kings,
> these women dressed in white
> group themselves and pirouette,

and become my dawn,
 my sun,
 my earth,
 my lamb,
 my buzzard,
 my butterfly.
I live this day through them,
counting no clock time
but the blood's time,
the gentle rise and fall
 of a donu bird's wings.
I assert that I am twinned to your light within.
Will we get these symbols right?

In Lima,
Thirsting for the waters of worship,
the lost tribes keep our Lady of the Rosary
in the Monastery of Santo Domingo.
There in our brotherhood,
we awake with breath in place.
So many waters crossed,
yet crossing is no journey.

And will we get these symbols right?

Gold of Guinea, gold of Gao,
Morocco rides Gao under Judar Pasha.
Under the flat flags,
there is left a cannon
 with the arms of Portugal,
a statue of the Holy Virgin,
 a crucifix,
all these powers lying dead,
with no one to transform them.
Still, anochecimos enfermo   amanccimos bueno,
learning the dwelling-place of the act,
the spirit holding the understanding
of one life among ourselves. (*D*, 32, 33)

The map is full of symbol, dance, rite, and the melodic exchange of names; the persistent questions—pauses, signposts, catapults announcing pulsing energy—express both the stasis and mobility characterizing the dyēli's act of self-discovery. That act of self-discovery upon the map of rites and acts forces transgeographic compressions (South American Day of Kings rites restated, for

example, by "the gentle rise and fall" of an African riverbird's
wings) which pre-vision "the dwelling-place of the act" as much as
they delineate metaphorically the dyēli's deeds and hence sub-
stantiate the dyēli himself. This marvelous conjoining of voice and
place connotes a new space, a vital rhythm (". . . anochecimos
enfermo amanecimos bueno . . .") beyond stasis ("all these powers
lying dead, / with no one to transform them"), and we cannot help
but wonder whether this geography is to be understood as a vision of
hibernation or as a pre- or post-hibernation state. My feeling is that
it is a vision of all three, prefacing and epiloging each other, but that
the *return* to hibernation—the furthest reach of Ellison's circumference
and its contraction—is the phase imagined with greatest intensity and
attention to language.

In the lines just cited above are powerful images of the necessity
of regeneration and of hibernation as a precursor rite ("we awake
with breath in place . . ."). But as the dyēli's song continues, the
dominant images are of re-entry and descent—of the end which is
the beginning:

> Hawk-headed,
> with a disk upon my head,
>   and the ankh upon my knees,
> I sit in this sun bark.
> Your speech is the speech of hands upraised,
> your eyes give as much light as mine.
> I have heard the timid call
> The lord of the hidden world, great god,
> lord of the underworld.
> Shrine-clad,
> White feather crowned,
> he holds the emblems of dominion.
>
> Who is the greater teacher?
> What is the first act
> if not the body rising from itself,
> becoming itself again,
>   spirit, shadow, spirit,
> heart of its own bones,
> the name of the wise one?
>
> Can this be hidden from the hidden one? (*D*, 34, 35)

The glory of these lines is Wright's synthesis of process, vocation,
myth, and language. By and large, the other landscapes in "The
Second Eye" are horizontal—we travel *upon* circumference from Cuba
to Brazil (or Colombia) to African cities, from "Havana Boa" to

"lamb," "buzzard," "butterfly," "donu bird," and crucifix. But in this passage travel is vertical, circumference is crossed, the world is defined on high by the realm of Ra, the sun god, and in its nether regions by the domain of Osiris, "lord of the hidden world." One imagines, then, that the "X" formed by these two powerful vectors of symbolic geography denotes "the dwelling-place of the act" or, in the language of this essay, the site (sight) of hibernation, and that it is precisely this intense conjunction of seen and unseen as well as of exterior and interior language (". . . sun bark . . . speech of hands upraised . . . emblems of dominion . . . the body rising from itself, / becoming itself again . . .") which occasions the pattern of return to "the hidden one":

> I am always approaching my end,
> looking for the hidden one.
> Tongue-tied in time for my nani's deeds,
> I have done my trembling,
> but the soul must be an All in All,
> laid out in one sentence,
> over the Pool, over the absolute intention,
> Even the knowledge of death. (*D*, 35)

In his notes, Jay Wright reminds us that "Nommo of the Pool, among the Dogon, is sacrificed for the purification and reorganization of the universe"; this suggests that we are to understand the archivist's return to the hidden realm to be at the very least a rite of self-discovery through self-sacrifice. I would add the thought that the "one sentence" or "All in All" which the soul must become above and beyond the "speech" of the dyēli's trembling—and beyond the perpetuating circumferences of epilogues birthing prologues—is a fertile mantle *and* a lid: a supreme emblem beyond image of hibernation's dominion. Osiris—lord of hibernation, custodian of root, amanuensis of root tongue, alchemist of the nether side of the colon and, hence, of image before emblem—is both confined by the lid and renewed by the act of nurturing the fertile mantle. This is his distinction from Ra, the voyager within seen tongues whose "sun bark" is both vessel and tongue; this is why the dyēli seeks him out—Osiris knows the way out as well as the way in.

And so the song ends:

> We are born to trade upon and build
> the heads intent
>   in the river's seed,

the seed's irruption,
the milk of a lamb,
the star's sudden fall,
the rock's mountain breaking shape,
the saint bickering with the birds,
the sceptre, flail and crook,
the coffin at the neck of things,
the joker in the soul's bequest,
the eye,
the key,
the second eye.
This, before you,
is the life
of a dark and dutiful dyēli,
searching for the understanding of his deeds.

Let my words wound you
into the love of the emblems
of the soul's intent. (*D*, 35, 36)

With these lines, the "dwelling-place of the act" or site of hibernation is located upon yet another axis of language and ritual energy—that which fills the space between the intent of the head and that of the soul. Thus, the "X" created by the travels of speech and rite along and across geographies of circumference becomes a "*"—a star that is not so much the Southern Cross of our literal heavens, which the Dogon call "The Second Eye of the World," as it is the source of light in darkness which, for Wright's dyēli as well as for Ellison's Invisible Man, is the light by which one's form is finally seen.

NOTES

[1] Paul de Man, *Blindness and Insight: Essays in the Rhetoric of Contemporary Criticism* (New York: Oxford University Press, 1971), p. 166.

[2] Michael S. Harper, *Song: I Want a Witness* (Pittsburgh: University of Pittsburgh Press, 1972), p. 50. This volume will hereafter be cited as *S*.

[3] These poems appear elsewhere in this volume and in *American Journal* (Taunton, Mass.: Effendi, 1978).

[4] Jay Wright, *Dimensions of History* (Santa Cruz, Calif.: Kayak, 1976), p. 36. This volume will hereafter be cited as *D*.

[AMERICAN JOURNAL]

ROBERT HAYDEN

here among them   the americans   this baffling
multi people   extremes and variegations   their
noise   restlessness   their almost frightening
energy   how best describe these aliens in my
reports to The Counselors

disguise myself in order to study them unobserved
adapting their varied pigmentations   white black
red brown yellow   the imprecise and strangering
distinctions by which they live   by which they
justify their cruelties to one another

charming savages   enlightened primitives   brash
new comers lately sprung up in our galaxy   how
describe them   do they indeed know what or who
they are   do not seem to   yet no other beings
in the universe make more extravagant claims
for their importance and identity

like us they have created a veritable populace
of machines that serve and soothe and pamper
and entertain   we have seen their flags and
foot prints on the moon   also the intricate
rubbish left behind   a wastefully ingenious
people   many it appears worship the Unknowable
Essence   the same for them as for us   but are
more faithful to their machine-made gods
technologists their shamans

oceans deserts mountains grain fields canyons
forests   variousness of landscapes weathers
sun light moon light as at home   much here is
beautiful   dream like vistas reminding me of
home   item   have seen the rock place known
as garden of the gods and sacred to the first

indigenes   red monoliths of home   despite
the tensions i breathe in i am attracted to
the vigorous americans   disturbing sensuous
appeal of so many   never to be admitted

something they call the american dream   sure
we still believe in it i guess   an earth man
in the tavern said   irregardless of the some
times night mare facts we always try to double
talk our way around   and its okay the dreams
okay and means whats good could be a damn sight
better   means every body in the good old u s a
should have the chance to get ahead or at least
should have three squares a day   as for myself
i do okay   not crying hunger with a loaf of
bread tucked under my arm you understand   i
fear one does not clearly follow i replied
notice you got a funny accent pal   like where
you from he asked   far from here i mumbled
he stared hard   i left

must be more careful   item   learn to use okay
their pass word   okay

crowds gathering in the streets today for some
reason obscure to me   noise and violent motion
repulsive physical contact   sentinels   pigs
i heard them called   with flailing clubs   rage
and bleeding and frenzy and screaming   machines
wailing   unbearable decibels   i fled lest
vibrations of the brutal scene do further harm
to my metabolism already over taxed

The Counselors would never permit such barbarous
confusion   they know what is best for our sereni
ty   we are an ancient race and have outgrown
illusions cherished here   item   their vaunted
liberty   no body pushes me around i have heard
them say   land of the free they sing   what do
they fear mistrust betray more than the freedom
they boast of in their ignorant pride   have seen
the squalid ghettoes in their violent cities
paradox on paradox   how have the americans managed
to survive